Psychological Dynamics of Sport and Exercise

Fourth Edition

Diane L. Gill, PhD

University of North Carolina at Greensboro

Lavon Williams, PhD

Guilford College

Erin J. Reifsteck, PhD

University of North Carolina at Greensboro

HUMAN KINETICS

Library of Congress Cataloging-in-Publication Data

Names: Gill, Diane L., 1948- author. | Williams, Lavon, author. | Reifsteck,
  Erin J., author.
Title: Psychological dynamics of sport and exercise / Diane L. Gill, Lavon
  Williams, Erin J. Reifsteck.
Description: Fourth edition. | Champaign, IL : Human Kinetics, [2017] |
  Includes bibliographical references and index.
Identifiers: LCCN 2016044356 | ISBN 9781450484664 (print) | ISBN 9781492549949
  (e-book)
Subjects: | MESH: Sports--psychology | Exercise--psychology | Motivation |
  Psychological Theory
Classification: LCC GV706.4 | NLM QT 260 | DDC 796.01--dc23 LC record available at https://lccn.loc.gov/2016044356

ISBN: 978-1-4504-8466-4 (print)

The web addresses cited in this text were current as of January 2017, unless otherwise noted.

Acquisitions Editor: Bridget Melton; **Developmental Editor:** Ragen E. Sanner; **Managing Editor:** Stephanie M. Ebersohl; **Copyeditor:** Joyce Sexton; **Indexer:** Dan Connolly; **Permissions Manager:** Dalene Reeder; **Graphic Designer:** Denise Lowry; **Cover Designer:** Keith Blomberg; **Senior Art Manager:** Kelly Hendren; **Illustrations:** © Human Kinetics; **Printer:** Sheridan Books

Printed in the United States of America   10   9   8   7   6   5   4   3   2   1

Human Kinetics
Website: www.HumanKinetics.com

United States: Human Kinetics
P.O. Box 5076
Champaign, IL 61825-5076
800-747-4457
e-mail: info@hkusa.com

Canada: Human Kinetics
475 Devonshire Road Unit 100
Windsor, ON N8Y 2L5
800-465-7301 (in Canada only)
e-mail: info@hkcanada.com

Europe: Human Kinetics
107 Bradford Road
Stanningley
Leeds LS28 6AT, United Kingdom
+44 (0) 113 255 5665
e-mail: hk@hkeurope.com

For information about Human Kinetics' coverage in other areas of the world, please visit our website: www.HumanKinetics.com

E6252

Contents

PART IV   Emotions, Stress, and Coping   153

Preface

Sport and exercise psychology is an exciting and dynamic scholarly area with countless applications for professionals and participants in a wide range of settings. This book provides an overview of sport and exercise psychology—the scientific study of human behavior in sport and exercise and the practical application of that knowledge in physical activity settings. It cannot provide an in-depth review of all the literature; instead, we highlight key theoretical work and research studies, drawing from that scholarship to provide guidelines for using sport and exercise psychology in your professional practice or in your own physical activities.

This fourth edition reflects the continuing growth of sport and exercise psychology. In the first edition of this text (1986), I (D.G.) noted the growth in the field over 10 years of teaching sport psychology courses. By the second edition (2000), research and professional practice had expanded in many directions, and most of the chapters were greatly expanded with largely new material. With the third edition (2008), and now with this fourth edition, sport and exercise psychology has continued to grow, and this text incorporates newer material. However, we have not expanded the text but have selectively revised to emphasize content that is relevant to professional practice in kinesiology and physical activity settings.

Our goal is to present practical theory—guidelines based on the best available knowledge that can be used by teachers, trainers, consultants, and other kinesiology professionals to enhance sport and exercise experiences for all. Throughout this text, we have pulled together research findings, theories, and consistent themes to provide those guidelines. But a note of caution is in order. Human behavior is complex and dynamic—one size does not fit all, and you will not find any one correct answer for your many questions about physical activity behavior. This text will help you recognize the complexities and find practical theories that you can use.

The book is targeted to upper-level undergraduate and graduate courses in kinesiology, and the text is organized into five parts representing major areas that might be covered in such classes. Part I provides an orientation, with chapters dealing with the scope, historical development, and current approaches of sport and exercise psychology. Part II focuses on the individual, with chapters on personality, attention and cognitive skills, and self-perceptions. Part III covers the huge topic of motivation, addressing the "*why*" question of physical activity behavior. Part IV covers the broad area of emotion, as well as stress management. Part V, on social processes, contains chapters on social influence, social development, and group dynamics, as well as cultural diversity.

Introductions, chapter objectives, and key points are provided to guide your reading, and you can test your understanding with the review questions at the end of each chapter. Summaries appear at the end of each chapter, along with key references and recommended resources for readers who want to go beyond the text in their research or professional practice. An image bank with figures and tables from the book is available for instructors who adopt this book.

Application points are provided throughout each chapter to help you connect the content with real-world application. Also, each chapter concludes with a lab activity related to professional practice in kinesiology to illustrate the application of practical theory. Each application point is labeled with an icon representing one of the professional areas (teaching/coaching/consulting, exercise/fitness, or sports medicine/rehabilitation). We have tried to include application points and lab activities that reflect the wide range of professional settings. Several labs and application points overlap professional areas, and each one could be modified to apply to other areas. As you are reading the text, get some extra practice by changing each application point to fit a different professional area, or your own physical activity.

eBook available at HumanKinetics.com

We hope this book helps you understand and use sport and exercise psychology. The true test of your understanding is not answering the review questions or taking a course exam. The true test will come as you draw upon the knowledge and practical theories of sport and exercise psychology when you are teaching a middle school dance class, coaching a youth soccer team, consulting with an intercollegiate athlete, developing a program for a cardiac rehabilitation client, organizing a community physical activity program, or trying to maintain a healthy lifestyle in your hectic daily schedule. Perhaps you will think about intrinsic motivation as you consider the rewards in your soccer program or use your knowledge to help a client develop stress management skills. Perhaps you will find information that helps you become a more effective teacher or trainer, that guides your research, or that you can use to enhance your own physical activities. You will not find a prescription, but you will find practical theory—guidelines to use as you move through your sport and exercise psychology study into professional practice and throughout your life.

Acknowledgments

Diane Gill—Many people made important contributions to this text. Rainer Martens has been a continuing source of support throughout my career, and particularly with the first edition of this text over 30 years ago. Many people at Human Kinetics have helped with each revision. Special thanks go to division director Myles Schrag for his patient support through this long-overdue fourth edition, as well as with the previous edition. Special thanks also go to developmental editor Ragen Sanner, who persistently but patiently moved us through the editing to the final chapters. Again, as in all previous editions, I especially must acknowledge the contributions of my students, who have taught me much about sport and exercise psychology. Two of those outstanding former students and colleagues are coauthors on this fourth edition. Lavon Williams, who also coauthored the third edition, has made contributions beyond authorship as a valued colleague and friend who challenges me to think in new ways. Erin Reifsteck, one of the newest generation of sport and exercise psychology scholars, stepped into the coauthor role and kept us moving toward the finish line with invaluable contributions.

And, as always, I thank my family for being a consistent source of encouragement and support.

Lavon Williams—My appreciation is also extended to the people at Human Kinetics who have helped with this revision. I am grateful to my coauthors Diane Gill, who has been a valued and lasting source of support throughout my career, and Erin Reifsteck. Lastly, a million thank-yous to my family for all of their love and support—you are the greatest!

Erin Reifsteck—I would like to add my thanks to the Human Kinetics staff for their expert guidance throughout this revision process. I also want to express my gratitude to Lavon Williams and especially Diane Gill, who have provided invaluable mentorship to me over the years. I am humbled by the opportunity to join these two well-respected scholars in contributing to this fourth edition of the text. Finally, I want to thank my husband, Matt Shilling, and my entire family for always providing me with unconditional love and support.

Overview of Sport and Exercise Psychology

PART I

Part I of this text provides a framework for the psychological dynamics of sport and exercise. Chapter 1 introduces sport and exercise psychology as part of the multidisciplinary, applied field of kinesiology. Chapter 2 explores the roots of sport and exercise psychology and reviews its historical development from isolated studies to the diverse, multifaceted, global field of today.

Chapter 3 presents approaches to understanding sport and exercise psychology, as well as applications in professional practice. Physical activity participants and professionals are faced with sport and exercise psychology questions every day. Theory provides a guide; sound research provides evidence; and real-world questions are best answered by an educated, experienced professional who can integrate many sources of knowledge and apply practical theory in the real world.

Introduction to Sport and Exercise Psychology

Chapter Objectives

After studying this chapter, you should be able to

- describe the focus and scope of sport and exercise psychology,

- explain the relationship between sport and exercise psychology and other kinesiology subfields, and

- describe the role of the person and the environment in sport and exercise behavior.

In this chapter, we introduce sport and exercise psychology as a subarea within kinesiology that focuses on human behavior. Kinesiology is about physical activity and movement—how does psychology fit with kinesiology? Sport, exercise, and all physical activities involve human behavior. Teachers, trainers, coaches, fitness leaders, physical therapists, and consultants must answer questions about behavior every day. They seek accurate, reliable information about psychology, just as they seek information about physiology and biomechanics. Professionals use the best available information, along with experience and judgment, to enhance sport and exercise for all participants. Sport and exercise psychology is the branch of kinesiology that seeks to answer questions about human behavior in physical activity settings.

To become acquainted with some of the issues in sport and exercise psychology, consider the following questions:

- Should a coach help a junior tennis player psych up for a championship match?
- Will more middle school children participate in an after-school activity program if the physical education teacher sets up a point system with awards for the top students?
- Will the injured athlete stay focused and stick to rehab exercise better if the therapist keeps reminding her of her long-term goal to get back to the team?
- Will the participants in the Fit at Fifty-Plus program exercise longer in a group than alone?
- Should parents encourage their children to play aggressive sports in order to let off steam?
- Is there an "I" in team?

Check the responses to these warm-up question at the end of the chapter to see how your answers compare. For this warm-up, the answers given are as straightforward as possible, but they are not absolute. You will not find any one correct answer in this text or in the real world. Instead, you will find guidelines—information on how some characteristics affect some behaviors in some situations. Such information is never complete, but as our understanding of human behavior in sport and exercise advances, the guidelines become clearer. First, though, let's consider the scope of sport and exercise psychology, its place within kinesiology, and its relation to psychology.

Kinesiology: A Multidisciplinary, Applied Field

Sport and exercise psychology is part of kinesiology, which is the study of physical activity or human movement. As the definitions at the websites of the American Kinesiology Association and National Academy of Kinesiology suggest, kinesiology is a multidisciplinary and applied field. Kinesiology is multidisciplinary: It incorporates the entire range of sciences as well as scholarly areas from the humanities in the study of physical activity and movement. Kinesiology is also an applied or professional field.

Kinesiology is often defined as the discipline and science of the field, but kinesiology also includes professional programs (e.g., teacher education, fitness management, sports medicine). Kinesiologists apply selected theories, concepts, and methods from the basic disciplines (e.g., physics, sociology) and also develop theories, concepts, and methods to create unique knowledge about human movement.

Within kinesiology, the most prominent disciplinary subareas are as follows:

- Biomechanics, the subarea closest to the physical sciences, applies principles from physics to human movement.
- Exercise physiology, which is clearly aligned with biology, focuses on the anatomy and physiology of human movement and exercise activities.
- Sport and exercise psychology obviously applies psychology to human behavior in physical activity.
- Sociocultural sport studies draws from social sciences and humanities and includes the sociology, history, and philosophy of sport and physical activity.

Sport and exercise psychology borrows selected information from the associated discipline of psychology, and it also develops theoretical models and approaches unique to physical activity.

Key Point

A thorough understanding of sport and exercise behavior requires integrating information from all the kinesiology subareas: exercise physiology, biomechanics, sport and exercise psychology, and sociocultural sport studies.

Sport and exercise psychology, which is in the middle of the physical–to–social science continuum, overlaps with and draws from the other kinesiology subareas, as well as from psychology. Indeed, a thorough understanding of physical activity behavior requires information from all the kinesiology subareas. For example, you will understand the psychological effects of exercise more fully if you also consider the physiological effects. Biomechanical approaches may be particularly useful in the study of skilled movements, and sociocultural constructs are prominent in research on gender and group dynamics in sport and exercise.

Sport and Exercise Psychology as a Subdiscipline

Now let's look at sport and exercise psychology as a distinct subdiscipline. Sport and exercise psychology is the branch of kinesiology that incorporates theories and approaches of psychology.

Psychology: Science of Human Behavior

Psychology is about people and human behavior. The American Psychological Association (APA), in the glossary at its website, defines psychology as the scientific study of the behavior of individuals and their mental processes. Within psychology, the major topics fall into three large areas, which may be considered the ABCs of psychology: Affect (feelings), Behavior, and Cognition (thought). A, B, and C are interconnected and affect each other. Furthermore, people think, feel, and behave within specific situations and a larger social context—their environment (E). To fill in the alphabet, people and the ABCs are constantly changing—they are dynamic (D). Psychology seeks to understand people's thoughts, feelings, and behaviors within the dynamic context of their environment.

Psychology is a diverse field with many subareas. The American Psychological Association (APA), the primary professional organization in psychology, lists more than 50 divisions, including the larger divisions such as clinical, developmental, experimental, and personality and social psychology. It also includes such divergent specialties as military psychology and psychopharmacology, as well as exercise and sport psychology.

Sport and exercise psychology emphasizes certain aspects of psychology, particularly personality and social psychology. Some scholars take psychophysiological or developmental perspectives, and consultants often incorporate counseling and clinical psychology approaches. Other specialty areas within psychology, like sport and exercise psychology, integrate differing perspectives. Sport and exercise psychology is closely related to health psychology, an area that has grown tremendously in the last 15 years. Health psychology includes social, clinical, and psychophysiological perspectives, and health psychologists often work with colleagues from other disciplines in clinical and research settings.

Sport and Exercise Psychology and Motor Behavior

Given the wide scope of psychology, it is not surprising that sport and exercise psychology does not draw equally from all areas of psychology. The North American Society for the Psychology of Sport and Physical Activity (NASPSPA), one of the main professional organizations for sport and exercise psychology, includes two other psychology areas under the larger category of motor behavior:

- Motor learning and motor control align most closely with the areas of cognition and neuroscience. Motor learning specialists focus on cognitive processes involved in learning and performing motor skills, whereas motor control specialists emphasize the neuropsychological processes and biological mechanisms underlying controlled movements. (See Schmidt & Lee, 2014, for an overview of motor learning and control.)

- Motor development focuses on developmental psychology as it relates to physical activity and movement. Motor development overlaps with motor learning and motor control under the more general rubric of motor behavior, and motor development specialists might investigate the development of motor patterns and skilled performance across the life span. Haywood and Getchell (2014) provide an overview of motor development.

Using Motor Behavior Information in Coaching

Psychological kinesiology includes motor behavior as well as sport and exercise psychology. If you were coaching a soccer team of 10- to 12-year-olds, how could you use information from motor behavior to help you be a better coach? For example, you might consider cognitive and physical developmental stages, motor patterns, cognition, and attention, as well as motor skill learning. Give at least two specific ways you could use that information in coaching your young athletes.

The three areas within NASPSPA reflect the typical division of psychological kinesiology in North America, with sport and exercise psychology separate from motor learning, control, and development. Similarly, in this text we cover sport and exercise psychology but not motor behavior. Most sport psychology around the world includes cognition, perception, and other aspects of motor behavior. Moreover, international research on motor behavior is more applied and more directly related to sport and exercise than in North America. Indeed, the subareas within psychological kinesiology have much to offer each other. For example, the relationship between attention and performance is a prominent topic in both sport and exercise psychology and motor behavior, and educational programs for youth sport coaches draw upon knowledge from motor development and motor learning, as well as sport and exercise psychology.

Also, international sport psychology typically does not explicitly separate sport and exercise but considers "sport" to include the wide range of sport, exercise, and physical activities. That more inclusive understanding of sport psychology is in line with kinesiology. Indeed, "psychology of physical activity," or "psychological kinesiology," would be more accurate labels for our field and for this text. Because "sport and exercise psychology" is more common, at least at the present time and in North America, we use "sport and exercise psychology" in this text, but sport and exercise should be understood as one term encompassing the full range of physical activities.

Sport and Exercise Psychology: A Definition

As already suggested, the following are key aspects of our definition of sport and exercise psychology:

- Sport and exercise psychology is a branch of kinesiology. Those who have psychology backgrounds may consider sport and exercise psychology to be a branch of psychology, but in this text the scholarly base is in kinesiology and the applications are to physical activity settings. Also, sport and exercise is understood as one term encompassing a wide range of physical activities and settings.
- Sport and exercise psychology is about people and human behavior.
- Sport and exercise psychology involves scientific study to advance knowledge and understanding of human movement.
- Sport and exercise psychology is an applied field. This text emphasizes moving from research into practice—using sport and exercise psychology in the real world.

So, in this text, sport and exercise psychology is defined in the following way: Sport and exercise psychology is the branch of kinesiology that involves the scientific study of human behavior in sport and exercise as well as the practical application of that knowledge in physical activity settings.

Key Point

Sport and exercise psychology is the branch of kinesiology that involves the scientific study of human behavior in sport and exercise as well as the practical application of that knowledge in physical activity settings.

Using Sport and Exercise Psychology in Professional Practice

How can you use sport and exercise psychology? If you are (or plan to be) a kinesiology professional, think about that question. Or, think about your own physical activity. List three questions about people and human behavior that apply to your situation. Keep them in mind as you read through this text. The text does not give you absolute answers, but you will find relevant information and guidelines—and probably think of more questions. Apply that information to your situation and the people in it in order to use sport and exercise psychology to answer your questions.

Complexity of Sport and Exercise Behavior

In sport and exercise psychology, we try to understand meaningful or whole behavior as it occurs in the real world. This is no easy task—remember the ABCDEs. Human behavior in sport and exercise, as in any situation, is complex. Even when we think we understand a behavior (e.g., why an athlete choked in the big game), our explanation may not hold up a week later.

We're All Alike— We're All Different

Application Point

To illustrate two seemingly contrary "truths," try this group activity. Each group of four to six people has two tasks. First, find one thing that everyone in the group has in common. Second, find one unique thing for each person in the group. Groups can usually complete these tasks in a short time, and they always find something that everyone has in common, as well as something unique about each person in the group. This illustrates the two truths—everyone is alike, and everyone is different. These two truths apply to sport and exercise groups. Assume you are leading an exercise class at a fitness center. In what ways might all of the participants be alike? How might each one be unique?

To help understand the complexities of behavior, consider the following truths:

- Everyone is alike.
- Everyone is different.

To further illustrate the complexities, consider these insights from a sage observer of human behavior, William Shakespeare:

- I am that I am (Sonnet 121, line 9).
- Men are as the time is (*King Lear*, V, 3, 31).

These quotes illustrate two contrasting views of human behavior, and a modern update of these insights might read as follows:

- Genes and personality determine behavior.
- Environment and learning determine behavior.

Both views are correct. You are who you are (genes and your personality affect behavior), and you are as the time is (the situation and your experiences determine behavior). Recognizing that all of these statements are correct is a key to understanding and using sport and exercise psychology. All people are alike in some ways, but every person is unique. And, as Shakespeare recognized, both our individual characteristics and the environment determine our behavior. The last set of truths reflects a basic tenet of psychology set forth in a formal but simple way by Kurt Lewin (1935):

$$B = f(P, E)$$

That is, behavior is a function of the person and the environment. But, the "truth" is even more complex. In reality, we cannot separate the person and the environment so easily. As Lewin emphasized, individual and environmental factors do not operate independently; they interact. Personal characteristics influence behavior in some situations and not others; situational factors affect people differently; and perhaps most important, the person affects the situation just as the situation affects the person. Thus, the relationships among person (P), environment (E), and behavior (B) are complex and dynamic, changing over time.

Key Point

The relationships among the person (P), environment (E), and behavior (B) are complex and dynamic, changing over time. Kurt Lewin (1935) stated this tenet in the equation $B = f(P, E)$.

For example, a 10-year-old baseball player may make a costly error. A child who is anxious about competition (P) and then hears critical comments (E) likely will become even more anxious, which leads to more errors and changes the situation for future games. A child who is more confident and receives constructive feedback might be more prepared the next time and develop stronger skills and confidence.

The combined truths and complexities of behavior are captured in the biopsychosocial model, which is a widely used framework in health behaviors. In her APA presidential address, health psychologist Suzanne Bennett Johnson (2013) argued that the recent paradigm shift in medicine from the biomedical model to the biopsychosocial model is a welcome shift that should be embraced in psychology. As she noted, in contrast to the biomedical model, the biopsychosocial model rejects the separation of mind and body and incorporates

Person (P) and Environment (E) Affect Behavior

Behavior changes as the person and environment change. As a personal trainer working with a businessperson, you may find that one week he comes in energetic, confident, and eager to try everything, but the following week he is tense, is distracted, and doesn't respond to your suggestions. What personal or environmental factors might be influencing his behavior? Consider work (e.g., closing a major deal, conflicts with the boss) and personal life (e.g., health condition, family situations). In general, expect change and be ready to adapt.

environmental, social, and behavioral factors to understand health and well-being. In sport and exercise psychology, the biopsychosocial model has been applied to physical activity behavior, and as a framework for injury risk, response, and recovery.

Any behavior takes place within the context of many interacting personal and environmental factors, and everything changes over time. The dynamic complexity of sport and exercise behavior makes precise prediction nearly impossible. Still, greater understanding of the person, social processes, and the relationships of these factors with behavior leads to informed choices. We may not be able to predict how one child will react to a particular teacher's comments, but we can help the teacher relate to different people and enhance the physical activity experience for all participants. Sport and exercise psychology is a relatively young field that is just beginning to answer some of our many questions. As you read this text, use the information as a guide—not a prescription—to help answer your questions about sport and exercise behavior.

Sport and Exercise Psychology Warm-Up Questions

Should a coach help a junior tennis player psych up for a championship match?

No. Many of us believe that the best athletes prepare for competition by psyching up, and many precompetition coaching techniques aim to increase athletes' arousal levels. However, many athletes, especially those who are young, need to calm down. Exceptions exist; some top athletes do use psych-up strategies effectively to enhance performance. Still, emotional control methods should be used much more often, especially with younger, less experienced participants. See chapters 11 through 13 for more on emotion and performance, along with practical suggestions on stress management.

Will more middle school children participate in an after-school activity program if the physical education teacher sets up a point system with awards for the top students?

Yes. The chance to receive awards may act as an incentive to some children who would otherwise not participate. However, most children participate in physical activity for intrinsic reasons, such as fun and challenge. If most would participate anyway, using rewards accomplishes nothing and presents problems. Research indicates that when children see themselves as participating to get extrinsic rewards, they lose intrinsic interest. The more we emphasize extrinsic rewards, the more likely it becomes that many children (and adults) will participate only under those circumstances. Rewards and intrinsic motivation are discussed in chapter 8.

Will the injured athlete stay focused and stick to her rehab exercise better if the therapist keeps reminding her of her long-term goal to get back to the team?

No. It may seem that focusing on the long-term goal would be motivating, but in the rehab setting, you want the athlete focused on the task at hand—rehab exercises. Goal setting will be more effective if the therapist helps the athlete set specific, short-term goals for the exercise session. Effective goal-setting strategies are discussed in chapter 7.

Will the participants in the Fit at Fifty-Plus program exercise longer in a group than alone?

Yes. Research on social influence indicates that people usually exercise longer and work harder when others are present, and social support often helps people stay with an exercise program. However, the presence of others does not always help, and it may interfere with learning and performance. Chapter 14 presents additional discussion of social influence.

Should parents encourage their children to play aggressive sports in order to let off steam?

No. Some people argue that aggressive behavior is a natural response and that we should channel those impulses into nondestructive outlets, such as youth sport. However, the most accepted theories and research indicate that aggression is learned social behavior. Encouraging aggression in sport reinforces aggressive behavior, increasing the likelihood of aggression elsewhere. Aggression and moral behavior are reviewed in chapter 15.

Is there an "I" in team?

Yes. The standard locker room slogan, "There is no 'I' in team," provides a spelling lesson, but it is unwise psychologically. It implies that team members should forget about individual goals and focus only on the team; however, research indicates that we elicit the best performance from both individuals and groups when we explicitly recognize and reinforce individual contributions. Many coaches take steps to ensure that individual goals are set and individual achievements are reinforced. Chapter 16 includes more detailed explanations of group performance.

Putting It Into Practice

Summary

Sport and exercise psychology is the branch of kinesiology that involves the scientific study of human behavior in sport and exercise, as well as the practical application of that information in physical activity settings. Similar to the other disciplines within kinesiology, sport and exercise psychology can be applied to skilled movements, physical activities, health-related exercise programs, physical education, and competitive sport. Sport and exercise psychology draws upon many areas of psychology and connects with other kinesiology areas to focus on the complex relationships among the person, the environment, and behavior in physical activity settings.

Review Questions

1. Define sport and exercise psychology as the term is used in the text.
2. Discuss the relationship of sport and exercise psychology to motor control and learning, as well as to motor development.
3. Explain the dynamic relationships among the person, the environment, and behavior.

Recommended Reading

For those who really want to understand how to apply psychology to complex, real-world problems, I recommend reading the reissued version of Lewin's classics (Lewin, 1997) for new insights. If you're not ready to delve into Lewin, that's fine. Most people who have been in sport and exercise psychology for a long time are not at that point either.

To get more information about sport and exercise psychology—who's involved, what they do, the big questions in research and practice—go to the most current sources. Check recent issues of the major journals to get an overview of current topics. For a broader view of the field, and more practical information, check the websites of major organizations.

Journals

The original *International Journal of Sport Psychology* is still published, but the newer *International Journal of Sport and Exercise Psychology* is now the official journal of the International Society of Sport Psychology. It covers a range of sport and exercise psychology topics with an emphasis on international and cultural concerns. The *Journal of Sport and Exercise Psychology* emphasizes theory-based research, whereas *The Sport Psychologist* has a more applied focus and includes articles on professional activities as well as applied research. The *Journal of Applied Sport Psychology* is the journal of the Association for Applied Sport Psychology, and it emphasizes applied research. *Psychology of Sport and Exercise*, the official journal of the European Federation of Sport Psychology (FEPSAC), publishes high-quality research and reviews. The relatively new journal *Sport, Exercise and Performance Psychology* is the official journal of APA Division 47.

Websites of Sport and Exercise Psychology Organizations

Most of the major sport and exercise psychology organizations have websites that provide information not only on the organizations themselves but also on conferences, contact people, resources, and current issues. Check the following websites for more current information: Division 47 (Exercise and Sport) of the American Psychological Association (APA-47); the Association for Applied Sport Psychology (AASP); the International Society of Sport Psychology (ISSP); the North American Society for the Psychology of Sport and Physical Activity (NASPSPA); the Société Canadienne d'Apprentissage Psychomoteur et de Psychologie du Sport (SCAPPS); the European Federation of Sport Psychology (FEPSAC); and the Asian South Pacific Association of Sport Psychology (ASPASP). Following are the current websites:

- AASP: www.aaasponline.org
- APA: www.apa.org
- APA-47: www.apadivisions.org/division-47/
- ASPASP: www.aspasp.org
- FEPSAC: www.fepsac.com
- ISSP: www.issponline.org
- NASPSPA: www.naspspa.org
- SCAPPS: www.scapps.org

Applying the Model B = f(P, E) in Cardiac Rehabilitation

As the B = f(P, E) model suggests, behavior in sport and exercise depends on both the person and the environment. Assume you are an exercise instructor in a cardiac rehabilitation program. How could you apply that model as you work with the participants? First, remember that all people are alike, but every person is unique. Participants in the program are likely older with more established careers and home lives, and they are dealing with a life-threatening condition, which likely leads to uncertainty and anxiety. At the same time, everyone is different. Some will be new to exercise whereas others will be former athletes; some will be optimistic and confident whereas others will be apprehensive and withdrawn. They will all have different life stories and backgrounds, and they will have different views of the exercise program.

So, for this lab, consider the model, along with individual differences, to help you structure your program and tailor your instructions to encourage participants to stick with it and to develop healthy exercise behaviors. First, think about how your participants are alike and what you might do to meet the common needs, such as providing information about typical responses to exercise, or structuring the program to include a balance of different modes of exercise. Then, think about the "P" influence and how you could individualize your approach to clients. For example, one person might do better with encouragement and attention, whereas another might prefer to work on his or her own. To help you think more clearly, consider two specific participants. Participant 1, Arthur, is a 60-year-old business manager who is joining the program after recovering from bypass surgery. Before his heart attack and surgery he was healthy and an avid golfer, and this is his first time in an exercise program. Participant 2, Rita, is a 75-year-old retired teacher. She experienced angina several years ago and joined the cardiac rehab program at that time. She has not had any cardiac problems, but she has continued in the rehab program for over two years. First, expand on those brief descriptions and think about how these two people might differ in both person (P) and environmental (E) influences. How might those differences affect their behavior in your program? How might you vary your program or interact with each of them? Try to think of other ways in which you might consider the person and the environment in your program. Finally, remember that behavior is complex and dynamic—everything changes.

Chapter 2

History of Sport and Exercise Psychology

Chapter Objectives

After studying this chapter, you should be able to

- trace the roots of sport and exercise psychology, beginning over 100 years ago with psychology and physical education, and

- identify the key stages in the development of sport and exercise psychology as a subdiscipline.

This chapter traces the historical development of today's multifaceted, global sport and exercise psychology. Sport and exercise psychology is relatively young as an identifiable scholarly field, but there are traces of related research in psychology and kinesiology going back over 100 years. This chapter provides a brief review of that history; for more details, see Gill (1997) and Kornspan (2012).

Early Roots: 1890 to 1920

Psychology and kinesiology began to organize around the beginning of the 20th century, and that early work includes evidence of sport and exercise psychology. Several prominent psychologists are connected with sport and physical education. William James taught students in the physical training program (early kinesiology) at Harvard (Kornspan, 2012), and both Wiggins (1984) and Ryan (1981) cite the words of G. Stanley Hall (1908), founding president of the American Psychological Association:

> Physical education is for the sake of mental and moral culture and not an end in itself. It is to make the intellect, feelings and will more vigorous, sane, supple and resourceful. (pp. 1015-1016)

Early research includes E.W. Scripture's studies with athletes in the 1890s, which were conducted with early physical education leader W.G. Anderson, George W. Fitz's (1895) experiments on the speed and accuracy of motor responses, and a psychological study of American football by G.T.W. Patrick (1903). The most widely recognized early research is Norman Triplett's (1898) study of social influence and performance. Triplett observed that cyclists seemed motivated to perform better with social influence (pacing machine, competition), and he devised an experiment to test his ideas. As he predicted, performers did better on a lab task when in pairs than when performing alone. Other early scholars from both psychology and physical education espoused the psychological benefits of physical education and conducted isolated studies.

As well as the early research and writings of psychology and physical education scholars, Pierre de Courbertin, founder of the modern Olympic Games, developed an educational congress. Courbertin specifically called for psychology as well as physiology of sport, and part of the Congress held in France in 1897 focused on "psychology of exercise" (Kornspan, 2012).

Early Sport Psychology Labs: 1920 to 1940

Beginning around 1920, a few individuals developed sport psychology labs with more focused, systematic research programs. Coleman Griffith's work is most widely recognized, but similar sport psychology labs were also established in other countries.

Coleman R. Griffith began his systematic sport psychology work in 1918 as a doctoral student at the University of Illinois and soon caught the attention of George Huff, director of physical education for men, who established Griffith's athletics research laboratory. Griffith was a prolific researcher who developed research measures and procedures focused on psychomotor skills, learning, and personality. He taught sport psychology classes and published numerous articles, as well as two classic texts, *Psychology of Coaching* (1926) and *Psychology and Athletics* (1928).

Griffith also took his research onto the playing field. He used an interview with Red Grange after the 1924 Michigan–Illinois football game, in which Grange noted that he could not recall a single detail of his remarkable performance, to illustrate that top athletes perform skills automatically. In addition, he corresponded with legendary coach Knute Rockne on the psychology of coaching and motivation (see chapter 11 for details). When the lab closed in 1932, Griffith continued as a professor of educational psychology, and eventually provost, at Illinois, but he did not abandon sport psychology. In 1938 he was hired by Philip Wrigley as the sport psychologist for the Chicago Cubs.

Although sport and exercise psychologists most often cite Griffith's applied work with the Cubs, he actually was more concerned with developing the research and knowledge base. In the inaugural volume of the *Research Quarterly*, Griffith (1930) called for a more scientific and experimental approach to psychological topics such as skill acquisition and the effects of emotions on performance. He noted the abundance of anecdotal reports and lack of experimental approaches:

> Many of these popular articles tell interesting stories about psychological problems, but from the point of view of a science they do not get very far, either in the correct envisagement of the problem, or in its solution. (p. 35)

Griffith went on to discuss his studies of attention, mood, and reaction time with athletes and to outline 25 topics that might be investigated in his lab. The list included several topics that we continue to investigate with (perhaps) more sophisticated methods: the effect of exercise on length of life and resistance to disease, the nature of sleep among athletes, methods of teaching psychological skills in sport, photographic analysis of muscle coordination during fear, sex differences in motor skills tests, and the effects of nicotine and other toxins on learning—to name just a few.

Key Point

Coleman Griffith was the first person in North America to do systematic sport psychology research. He focused on psychomotor skills, learning, and personality. He developed a research lab, and he also took his sport psychology work outside of the lab and onto the playing fields.

Griffith maintained his scientific perspective while recognizing the expertise of coaches and athletes. His advice from 1925 still rings true today:

A great many people have the idea that the psychologist is a sort of magician who is ready, for a price, to sell his services to one individual or one group of men. Nothing could be further from the truth. Psychological facts are universal facts. They belong to whoever will read while he runs. There is another strange opinion about the psychologist. It is supposed that he is merely waiting until he can jump into an athletic field, tell the old-time successful coach that he is all wrong and begin, then, to expound his own magical and fanciful theories as to proper methods of coaching, the way to conquer overconfidence, the best forms of strategy, and so on. This, of course, is far from the truth, although certain things have appeared in the application of psychology to business and industry to lead to such an opinion. During the last few years and at the present time, there have been and are many men, short in psychological training and long in the use of the English language, who are doing psychology damage by advertising that

they are ready to answer any and every question that comes up in any and every field. No sane psychologist is deceived by these self-styled apostles of a new day. Coaches and athletes have a right to be wary of such stuff. (pp. 193-194)

Application Point

Advice for Coaches

As Griffith cautioned, coaches should be wary of stories that sound too good to be true. Useful sport and exercise psychology advice is based on evidence. Check out professional resources (e.g., coaching journals, newsletters, and websites) and find one or two sources of sport psychology advice a coach could use that are also supported by references to research or other evidence.

Griffith's research, publications, and thoughtful insights make him one of the most significant figures in the history of sport psychology, and he is widely characterized as the father of sport psychology in North America. However, as Kroll and Lewis (1970) note, Griffith was a prophet without disciples, and "father" is really a misnomer. That systematic sport psychology research did not continue in North America after Griffith's pioneering work.

During the same time period, parallel efforts in Germany by R.W. Schulte and in Russia by Peter Roudik established sport psychology labs and continuing research programs. R.W. Schulte was a student of Wilhelm Wundt, who is widely recognized as the father of experimental psychology and advisor to many prominent early psychologists. In 1920 Schulte became director of a sport psychology lab, and like Griffith, he conducted extensive research with athletes, lectured, and published books and articles. In the same year, Roudik developed the sport psychology department in Moscow at the Institute of Physical Culture. The labs and research programs in Germany and Russia continued to be led by psychologists and continued to focus on competitive athletes. A.C. Puni's sport psychology work in Russia in the 1950s and '60s is particularly notable (Ryba, Stambulova, & Wrisberg, 2005). In North America, psychologists did not pick up Griffith's work or devote attention to athletics, and physical education programs were more focused on biological sciences and teaching practices.

Isolated Sport and Exercise Psychology Studies: 1940 to 1965

From Griffith's time through the late 1960s, when an identifiable sport and exercise psychology specialization emerged, sport and exercise psychology research was sporadic and not sustained. C.H. McCloy (1930) of the University of Iowa examined character building through physical education, and Walter Miles (1928, 1931) of Stanford studied reaction time. After World War II, several scholars developed research programs in motor behavior that incorporated sport psychology topics, including Arthur Slater-Hammel at Indiana, Alfred (Fritz) Hubbard at the University of Illinois, John Lawther at Penn State, and Franklin Henry at Berkeley. Warren Johnson's (1949) study of precontest emotion in football is a notable contribution of this time and a precursor to later studies of competitive emotion.

In the 1960s, more texts that covered sport and exercise psychology began to appear, including Cratty's *Psychology and Physical Activity* in 1967 and Singer's *Motor Learning and Human Performance* in 1968. Bruce Ogilvie and Thomas Tutko published *Problem Athletes and How to Handle Them* in 1966. Their clinical approach and lack of a scientific framework and supporting evidence led to a cold reception from motor behavior and physical education scholars. However, Ogilvie and Tutko's work was popular in the coaching community and foreshadowed the influx of applied sport psychology works in the 1980s.

Emergence of Sport and Exercise Psychology as a Subdiscipline: 1965 to 1975

Despite the innovative work during the first half of the 20th century, sport and exercise psychology did not emerge as an identifiable field until the late 1960s, when several scholars in North America developed research programs, graduate courses, and eventually specialized organizations and publications. Simultaneously, at the international level, many people with psychology training became sport psychologists in other countries, particularly in Europe, and sport psychology became an established area.

International Organization

The International Society of Sport Psychology (ISSP) formed and held the first International Congress of Sport Psychology in Rome in 1965. Reflecting on the development of the ISSP, Miroslav Vanek (1993) cited the influence of the Sovietization of top-level sport in the 1950s. Thus, international sport psychology has a closer alignment with applied psychology and performance enhancement for elite athletes than in North America. Several sport psychologists from Europe and the Soviet Union, including Vanek, were instrumental in forming an international society, along with Ferruccio Antonelli, founding president of the ISSP and organizer of the first international congress.

The second international congress was held in Washington, DC, in 1968, and the proceedings of that congress (Kenyon & Grogg, 1970) provide a nice overview of sport psychology at that time. Antonelli remained ISSP president for several years, and in 1970 he founded the *International Journal of Sport Psychology*, the first sport psychology research journal.

Vanek (1985), who was president of the ISSP from 1973 to 1985, described the field as follows:

> The psychology of sport has become an institutionalized discipline within the sport sciences. . . . Our membership has grown, we have journals devoted to sport psychology, national and international societies, coursework and textbooks, specific courses for training in sport psychology, increasing research efforts, and so on. In fact, sport psychology has become a profession in many countries. (p. 1)

The ISSP has continued to expand, holds meetings every four years, and serves as the primary international forum for the field today.

North American and European Organization

As international sport psychology was organizing, North American scholars also began to organize, forming the North American Society for the Psychology of Sport and Physical Activity (NASPSPA). Loy (1974) reported that a small group began discussions at the 1965 AAHPER (American Association for Health, Physical Education and Recreation) conference, and that the first meeting of NASPSPA was held at the 1967 AAHPER conference; NASPSPA officially incorporated just after that meeting. The first independent meeting of NASPSPA was held at Allerton Park, Illinois, in 1973, and the proceedings of that conference (Wade & Martens, 1974) marked the start of Human Kinetics Publishers as well as a milestone for sport and exercise psychology.

The organization of the NASPSPA reflected the overlapping of sport and exercise psychology and motor behavior with subareas of motor learning, motor development, and social psychology of physical activity (now sport and exercise psychology). A separate Canadian organization, the Canadian Society for Psychomotor Learning and Sport Psychology (CSPLSP; now known as Société Canadienne d'Apprentissage Psychomoteur et Psychologie du Sport, or SCAPPS), was founded in 1969 and became an independent society in 1977.

Sport psychology organized in Europe in parallel with international and North American developments. The European Federation of Sport Psychology (FEPSAC) was established in 1968. The British and French Societies of Sport Psychology were both founded before FEPSAC in 1967, and the Association for Sport Psychology in Germany began soon after in 1969.

Publications

As sport and exercise psychology research, graduate programs, and organizations developed, scholarly publications emerged. Earlier studies appeared in psychology journals and in *Research Quarterly* (later renamed *Research Quarterly for Exercise and Sport*). As research expanded, sport and exercise psychologists developed specialized publications.

Key Point

The formation of sport psychology organizations, including the ISSP in 1965 and NASPSPA in 1967, marks the organization of sport and exercise psychology as a field of study.

The *International Journal of Sport Psychology* began publishing in 1970. For North American scholars, the most important publication during the 1970s was the NASPSPA proceedings, which were published from 1973 to 1980 as *Psychology of Motor Behavior and Sport*. With the 1979 appearance of *Journal of Sport Psychology*, NASPSPA stopped publishing full papers in proceedings. *Journal of Sport Psychology* (known as *Journal of Sport*

and Exercise Psychology since 1988) was immediately recognized, as it is today, as the leading publication outlet for research on sport and exercise psychology.

Development of the Subdiscipline: 1975 to 1999

From the 1970s through the 1990s, scholars of sport and exercise psychology in North America established research labs and graduate programs, held successful annual conferences, and developed a respected research journal. Rainer Martens' (1975) text, *Social Psychology and Physical Activity*, reflects the content and orientation of those early years. Major psychological theories (e.g., inverted-U hypothesis, achievement motivation theory) framed the content; most supporting research was from psychology, and the sport psychology work cited seldom involved sport but more likely involved laboratory experiments with motor tasks such as rotary pursuit and stabilometer tasks.

Key Point

In the mid-1980s, sport and exercise psychology moved to more applied issues and approaches, and it made a strong move to sport relevance with the development of sport-specific models and measures.

By the mid-1980s, sport and exercise psychology had grown in new directions. Martens' 1979 article in *Journal of Sport Psychology*, which he presented as "From Smocks to Jocks" at the 1978 CSPLSP conference, marked the beginning of a move toward more applied research and sport-specific concerns. Field research and applied issues moved to the forefront and captured the attention of students, psychologists who had previously ignored sport, and the public. In North America, before 1980, sport psychology was largely applied to physical education; but with the 1980s, sport psychology came to imply psychological skills training of elite competitive athletes, bringing it closer to the European model.

With more diverse students and researchers coming into sport psychology, the NASPSPA no longer fit all interests. John Silva initiated an organizational meeting at Nags Head, North Carolina, in October 1985, marking the beginning of the Association for the Advancement of Applied Sport Psychology (AAASP), which shortened its name to the Association for Applied Sport Psychology (AASP) in 2006. As summarized in the first issue of the *AAASP Newsletter* (1986), the AASP provides a forum for people interested in research, theory development, and application of psychological principles in sport and exercise. The first conference took place at Jekyll Island, Georgia, in 1986; annual conferences have been held since then, and AASP is a thriving sport psychology organization.

Martens' keynote address at that first AAASP conference challenged sport psychology to accept alternative approaches to science in order to develop truly useful knowledge. That widely cited paper (Martens, 1987b) was published in the inaugural issue of *The Sport Psychologist*, which focused on the emerging literature on applied sport psychology. With *The Sport Psychologist* emphasizing applied research and professional concerns, the *Journal of Sport Psychology* concentrated on strong research, and in 1988, during my editorial term, added "Exercise" to the title and more explicitly sought research on health-oriented exercise as well as sport. Also, the AAASP started its *Journal of Applied Sport Psychology* in 1989, which also publishes research articles.

Several people trained in traditional psychology programs moved into sport and exercise psychology in the 1980s. Bruce Ogilvie, whose earlier applied work had not been accepted in kinesiology in the 1960s, was recognized for those pioneering efforts when applied sport psychology organized in the 1980s. Richard Suinn, clinical psychologist and former president of the American Psychological Association (APA), and APA colleagues, including Steve Heyman and William Morgan, organized an interest group, and in 1986, Division 47—Exercise and Sport Psychology—became a formal division of APA.

The NASPSPA, AASP, and APA Division 47 are the primary organizations in the United States, and sport and exercise psychology also has a presence in other kinesiology organizations. AAHPERD (as of 2014 known as the Society for Health and Physical Education, or SHAPE America), the initial home of the NASPSPA, includes a Sport and Exercise Psychology Academy, and the American College of Sports Medicine (ACSM), a large organization traditionally dominated by exercise physiology and sports medicine, has expanded its psychology constituency in recent years. Suinn's

work with Olympic skiers in 1976 helped the U.S. Olympic Committee (USOC) recognize the role of sport psychology. In 1983, the USOC established an official sport psychology committee and a registry, and many sport psychologists have worked with athletes, coaches, and training programs through the organization since then. In 1987, the USOC hired Shane Murphy as its first full-time sport psychologist, and it continues to support sport psychology specialists.

Applied sport psychology caught the attention of students and the public, creating a market for more publications and resources. Few sport psychology texts existed when I wrote the first edition of this text (Gill, 1986), but the literature quickly expanded. Many applied sport psychology books appeared, including Robert Nideffer's *The Inner Athlete* (1976) and *Athlete's Guide to Mental Training* (1985); Dorothy Harris and Bette Harris' *The Athlete's Guide to Sports Psychology* (1984); Terry Orlick's *In Pursuit of Excellence* (1980); Rainer Martens' *Coaches Guide to Sport Psychology* (1987a); and Jean Williams' *Applied Sport Psychology* (1986; now in its seventh edition, 2014). The increased prominence of applied sport psychology soon led to more formal professional roles and standards.

Application Point

Psychology in Injury Rehabilitation

Sports medicine professionals recognize that injury and rehabilitation have psychological aspects, but they seldom have training in sport and exercise psychology. If you were a sports medicine professional, how might you learn more about sport and exercise psychology and how to use psychological skills and strategies in rehabilitation programs? Check the websites of sport and exercise psychology organizations to find resources and educational opportunities that a sports medicine professional might pursue. Look for specific courses, conference programs and workshops, and continuing learning and graduate programs that could provide information on useful sport and exercise psychology.

Professional Roles in Sport and Exercise Psychology

Sport and exercise psychology specialists work in three main professional areas—research, education, and consulting. Research and teaching are the primary roles for most specialists, who typically work in colleges and universities where they conduct research and teach sport and exercise psychology, usually in kinesiology departments. Many sport and exercise psychology specialists also engage in consulting. In addition, some counselors and clinical psychologists extend their practice to sport and exercise psychology consultation, and a few specialists devote their entire professional practice to consulting.

In the consulting role, the distinction between educational and clinical practice is important. Clinical psychologists have extensive graduate training and supervised experience, and they must be licensed by state boards in order to offer their services. Educational practice is just that—education. An educational sport and exercise psychology consultant might be considered a mental coach. Most often educational consultants provide psychological skills training to participants for performance enhancement or personal development.

Unlike clinical psychology, sport and exercise psychology is not a licensed specialty, and it is not immediately obvious where one could find information on qualified educational consultants. Competent sport and exercise psychology consultants will not profess to solve all problems or turn you into the next Olympic medalist. Instead, they might point out that psychological skills require just as much time and effort as physical skills.

Professional Standards and Certification in Sport and Exercise Psychology

Sport and exercise psychology organizations are concerned about maintaining standards and credibility amid the growing popularity of the specialty. Most notably, the AASP published certification guidelines in 1989. Members of AASP may apply for certification as consultants (CC-AASP); see the AASP website for details on the certification process and criteria. Generally, the guidelines require graduate work in both kinesiology and psychology, as well as supervised practical experience. Certification is not a license; rather, it indicates that the person has met certain competency standards.

The American Psychological Association (APA), the primary professional organization for psychology, certifies clinical and counseling psychology programs, and licensing as a clinical psychologist follows APA standards. The APA also

has long had ethical standards for all psychology training and professional practice. Although clinical psychology licensing is not required for educational sport and exercise psychology practice or AASP certification, the APA provides an established model that has been adopted for sport and exercise psychology training and professional practice. In 2003, APA's Council of Representatives approved a proficiency in sport psychology. The APA proficiency recognizes sport psychology as a postgraduate focus after a doctoral degree in one of the primary areas of psychology and licensure as a psychologist. This designation recognizes sport psychology as a particular aspect of psychology practice and provides guidelines for standards and practice in sport psychology. Go to the APA-47 website for more information on the proficiency.

Application Point

Finding a Sport Psychology Consultant

Many athletes seek professional help in developing psychological skills as well as physical skills. As a high school coach, you may have a young athlete who has the talent to move to the intercollegiate level and wants to work on the mental game. Review the resources at the AASP and APA websites and develop a list of guidelines that you could use to help the athlete find an appropriate sport psychology consultant. Consider the skills and credentials you would look for, as well as the services and outcomes you and the athlete would expect.

The AASP certification guidelines represent one step toward professionalization in that they establish criteria for designating qualified individuals. The AASP also adopted an ethical code, which is based on APA ethical standards, to accompany its certification guidelines. The introduction to the code begins this way:

> AASP is dedicated to the development and professionalization of the field of sport psychology. As we establish ourselves as a profession, we must attend to both the privileges and responsibilities of a profession.

The Ethical Principles and Standards of the AASP include an introduction and preamble, six general principles, and 25 standards that specify the boundaries of ethical conduct. The AASP website has the ethics code, and readers might also go to the APA website to check the more extensive and well-established APA ethics code, most recently updated in 2003.

The AASP certification guidelines provide a framework for identifying professional competencies, and the ethics code contains general guidelines for professional practice. These guidelines and the ethical codes were developed to meet the needs of professionals in consulting roles. However, the guidelines are applicable for all who practice sport and exercise psychology.

Sport and Exercise Psychology Today: 2000 to Present

In this new millennium, sport and exercise psychology has grown up and moved in many directions. Traces of its roots and development are evident—we still have theory-based experiments on social influence, and consultants do psychological skills training with Olympic athletes. However, sport and exercise psychology today is multifaceted and diverse in research and practice, and it is truly global.

During the 1980s and 1990s, attention shifted to sport and applied work with athletes. Attention has now shifted back to exercise in response to the public concern for health and fitness, with a strong move toward increased research and applied emphasis on physical activity and health. Indeed, some programs and publications intentionally separate exercise psychology from sport psychology, reflecting that newer emphasis. Research areas often considered "exercise psychology" include motivation and physical activity interventions, and more recently, expanding research on exercise and mental health and cognition. Current research that might be considered under a narrow "sport psychology" includes growing research on the psychology of injury risk and recovery. Research and applications related to the psychology of injury are just as applicable to physical therapy clients and exercisers as to athletes, and issues related to mental health and cognition are relevant in athletics. Again, as noted earlier, in this text, sport and exercise psychology is a single area—one that is large and diverse, to be sure.

At this point, it is appropriate to note that women have hardly been mentioned and, indeed, are often overlooked in reviews of sport and exercise psychology history. As I have argued elsewhere (Gill, 1995), women have indeed been present and influential throughout the history of sport and exercise psychology. Women were present, but often marginalized, in the earliest psychology and kinesiology programs. Women were active leaders in the organization of sport psychology. Dorothy Harris, who established her research and graduate program at Penn State, was active in ISSP and the first woman president of NASPSA. In 1974. Ema Geron of Bulgaria was one of ISSP's founding members and the first president of the European Federation of Sport Psychology from 1969 to 1973. Krane and Whaley (2010; Whaley & Krane, 2012) conducted life history interviews and described the influential contributions and challenges faced by several women in U.S. sport and exercise psychology.

Today's sport and exercise psychology is multifaceted, diverse, and global. Professionals include psychologists and kinesiologists in both academic research and in private practice who take varying scholarly approaches. Participants vary in gender, age, ability, and cultural background. Multiple organizations, publications, and Internet sites provide resources to participants, professionals, and the public. Settings are diverse. Sport and exercise psychology is found in training rooms, community youth programs, senior centers, and clinics, as well as on playing fields and in gymnasiums. Professional and personal goals include education, health promotion, life skills development, community development, and performance enhancement.

Sport and Exercise Psychology for a Senior Exercise Program

The popular perception of sport and exercise psychology is that it provides psychological skills for Olympic athletes, but it also is useful in health promotion and youth development programs. List at least two ways sport and exercise psychology could be used in an exercise program for older adults. (Check sport and exercise psychology or health promotion websites for ideas.)

Application Point

Most notably, sport and exercise psychology is global. The ISSP, which formed before any North American organization, has regained prominence. In addition to the ISSP, North American, and European organizations, there are established sport and exercise psychology organizations in Asia and Australia, with South American and African scholars developing sport and exercise psychology programs and joining the international sport and exercise psychology community.

Benchmarks in the History of Sport and Exercise Psychology

1898

Norman Triplett conducts the first social psychology experiment, confirming his observations that people perform tasks faster in the presence of others.

1925

The Board of Trustees at the University of Illinois establishes the Athletics Research Laboratory with Coleman R. Griffith as director.

1965

The International Society of Sport Psychology (ISSP) is formed and holds the first International Congress of Sport Psychology in Rome in 1965.

1967

The North American Society for the Psychology of Sport and Physical Activity (NASP-SPA) is officially incorporated on March 13, 1967.

1979

The first issue of *Journal of Sport Psychology* (*Journal of Sport and Exercise Psychology* since 1988) is published by Human Kinetics with Dan Landers as editor.

1985

The Association for the Advancement of Applied Sport Psychology (AAASP) is formed in 1985 with John Silva as president. (In 2006, the name is changed to the Association for Applied Sport Psychology, or AASP.)

1986

Division 47, Exercise and Sport Psychology, becomes a formal division of the American Psychological Association (APA) in 1986.

Putting It Into Practice

Summary

Although sport and exercise psychology is a relatively young field, we can trace its roots back over 100 years. We can identify isolated early studies, but apart from Coleman Griffith's still-enlightening work in the United States and similar work by Schulte in Germany and Roudik in Russia, sport and exercise psychology was not organized until the late 1960s, as marked by the official incorporation of the ISSP in 1965. Sport and exercise psychology expanded rapidly during the 1970s, creating a knowledge base and specialized publications. During the 1980s, sport and exercise psychology turned toward applied research and practice. Through the 1990s and into this century, sport and exercise psychology expanded in many directions, particularly addressing health-related exercise and physical activity. Today, sport and exercise psychology is multifaceted, diverse, and global.

Review Questions

1. Name the first person to do systematic sport psychology research in North America, and discuss his work.
2. Discuss the beginnings of sport and exercise psychology.
3. Discuss the development of applied sport psychology.
4. Describe the diverse topics, settings, and professionals in sport and exercise psychology today.

Recommended Reading

- Krane, V., & Whaley, D.E. (2010). Quiet competence: Writing women into the history of U.S. sport psychology. *The Sport Psychologist, 18,* 349-372. In this article, Krane and Whaley, taking a feminist perspective and using life history interviews, discuss the contributions of eight women who have influenced the development of sport and exercise psychology.

- McCullagh, P. (Ed.). (1995). Sport psychology: A historical perspective. *Sport Psychologist, 4.* This special issue contains several articles by scholars who know their history and want to communicate that historical knowledge to others. Read at least two articles and you will have a much better understanding of sport and exercise psychology. You might read Gould and Pick's (1995) article on the Griffith years (1920-1940) to learn more about Coleman Griffith's remarkable work, or read my article (Gill, 1995) for a reminder of women's place in sport and exercise psychology history. (Check Krane and Whaley's [2010] article for a more recent discussion of women's contributions.)

- Ryba, T.V., Stambulova, N.B., & Wrisberg, C.A. (2005). The Russian origins of sport psychology: A translation of an early work of A.C. Puni. *Journal of Applied Sport Psychology, 17,* 157-169. To help break out of a narrow North American perspective, read this article describing some of Puni's influential contributions. Puni was particularly active in sport psychology in the 1950s and '60s when North American sport psychology was largely dormant.

Psychology for Coaches: Lessons From the Past

Many years ago, before sport and exercise psychology was an established area of study, Coleman Griffith was doing research and consulting with athletes and coaches. As a high school coach who wants to use sport and exercise psychology today, what history lessons could you take from Coleman Griffith? As Griffith cautioned, be wary of advice that sounds like the magic key to success. Remember that Griffith started a lab, conducted research, and consulted with coaches and athletes before offering his services. Be sure that advice is supported by evidence. Keep those lessons (be wary; look for supporting evidence) in mind as you complete this lab.

Since Griffith did his pioneering work, sport and exercise psychology has developed organizations, publications, and websites. Today's coaches can look to organizations such as the AASP, APA, ISSP, and countless other resources for advice. Still, as we learned in chapter 1, behavior is complex and dynamic. Despite tremendous growth in the research base, sport and exercise psychology does not have the magic key to replace the insights and experience of the successful coach.

Keeping Griffith's advice in mind, go to some of those current resources. Find at least three current lessons that you could use as a high school coach. For example, those lessons could be on motivation, communicating with your athletes, organizing practices, or helping athletes (or yourself) develop concentration or stress management skills. Briefly explain how you could use each of the three lessons in a specific high school coaching situation.

Understanding and Using Sport and Exercise Psychology

Chapter Objectives

After studying this chapter, you should be able to

- discuss the relationships among theory, research, and practice,

- identify paradigms that have shaped the field of sport and exercise psychology,

- describe the scientific method and how it is used in sport and exercise psychology research, and

- describe the science and art of using sport and exercise psychology in professional practice.

To answer sport and exercise psychology questions such as those raised in chapter 1, professionals seek good information that they can use. For example, the tennis coach wants good information on anxiety and emotional control to help the junior tennis player prepare for competition. Good information is not only scientifically sound; it is also relevant and useful in professional practice. This chapter will help you understand and use sport and exercise psychology knowledge. First, we review theories, research methods, and paradigms that have shaped the knowledge base of sport and exercise psychology, and we emphasize practical theory as the key link between research and practice. We then focus on using sport and exercise psychology in professional roles.

Understanding Sport and Exercise Psychology

This chapter draws upon the work of other sport and exercise psychology scholars who have called for changes in our approaches to science and knowledge (e.g., Martens, 1987; Dzewaltowski, 1997) as well as Kurt Lewin's classic work, which becomes more insightful with each rereading, and more current but similar approaches to psychology research-into-practice. This blended approach frames the presentation of sport and exercise psychology knowledge in this text. We emphasize the person and behavior in context (as Lewin proposed), and we strive to communicate practical theory as guidelines to use within the ever-changing context of sport and exercise.

Theory, Research, and Practice

The first step toward understanding and using sport and exercise psychology is recognizing that theory and research are essential in professional practice. Theory, research, and practice are necessarily interconnected. Competent professionals in any area must understand the knowledge base, and familiarity with current research and theory is the hallmark of a professional. Evidence-based practice is the phrase commonly used to refer to effective professional practice, particularly in health-related professions. The American Psychological Association (APA) approved a policy statement on evidence-based practice in psychology, and that statement provides a clear, concise guide to professional practice in sport and exercise psychology. As the APA (2006, p. 273) policy states, "Evidence-based practice in psychology (EBPP)

is the integration of the best available research with clinical expertise in the context of patient characteristics, culture, and preferences."

All components of that definition are critical. First, professionals use the best available research. As the policy notes, the best research comes from a variety of methods and is both clinically relevant (practical) and internally valid (scientifically sound). Competent professionals use clinical (professional) expertise as well as research evidence. Professional knowledge comes from experience, training, and ongoing education, and expertise includes competencies in assessment, decision making, and interpersonal skills. Research and professional expertise must be integrated within the context of individual characteristics, preferences, and culture.

Clearly, research and practice are connected in evidence-based practice. The real world offers research ideas, and research results are ultimately tested for usefulness in the real world. To complete the picture, theory must be included. Theory is the critical link in the triad of theory, research, and practice.

Theory is both the guide to and goal of research. Theory, which is a systematic explanation of a phenomenon based on sound scientific evidence, is our goal because it explains behavior. For example, catastrophe theory, discussed in chapter 11, explains the relationship between anxiety and performance. And, as you will discover, catastrophe theory is a good example of how theories incorporate multiple constructs in a complex network of interrelationships. Theories are never final but are constantly revised or replaced with new information.

Key Point

Theory is the critical link in the triad of theory, research, and practice. It is both the guide to and goal of research—it serves as a source of questions to research and it explains behavior.

Thus, theory also serves as a source of questions and guide for research. As Forscher (1963) pointed out in "Chaos in the Brickyard," a classic gem of scientific wisdom, theory is the key to useful research. Research without theory as a guide gives us piles of bricks (facts) but no useful structures. Theory is also the key to effective practice. Too often practitioners look for a quick fix to a problem rather than searching for common themes and unifying principles that apply in varying contexts.

Setting the Direction: Identifying Research Questions

For a symposium and subsequent article (Gill, 1997), I was asked to identify measurement, statistics, and design issues in sport and exercise psychology—a formal way of asking, "How do we answer our questions?" But first we must ask, "What are our questions?" My main point then, and a central theme in this chapter, is that identifying our questions is the essential step. When research has a defined purpose and guiding framework, when constructs are clearly defined, and when clear, relevant questions are asked, we solve problems.

My favorite research advice was originally published in 1865 in *Alice's Adventures in Wonderland* (Carroll, 1865/1992). Alice (the searching researcher or student) asks the Cheshire Cat (the resident expert) for advice: "Would you tell me, please, which way I ought to walk from here?" The cat returns the question (as do all expert advisors): "That depends a good deal on where you want to get to." When Alice replies that she doesn't much care where, the sage responds, "Then, it doesn't matter which way you walk." If you don't know where you want to get to, no one can tell you how to get there.

In sport and exercise psychology, our questions are about behavior (e.g., Why does one athlete come through under pressure while a teammate chokes? How can I help my client stick to his exercise program?). Behavior is complex and answers are elusive, but we know where we want to go.

Paradigms and Sources of Knowledge

Just as there are many questions in sport and exercise psychology, there are many ways to answer those questions. Indeed, many questions are best answered with multiple approaches. For the best evidence, professionals look to science, and researchers use the scientific method (also known as normal science or positivistic methods) to answer questions. We will outline the scientific method, but first, let's consider some of the many ways professionals (e.g., teachers, exercise leaders) might answer their questions about behavior. If

you were an exercise instructor, how would you decide what to do to help a client who is having difficulty sticking to an exercise program? You are not likely to set up an experiment to answer your question; more likely you will use some of the nonscience methods listed next.

Nonscience Methods

Science is one way to answer questions, but we do not devise an experiment to answer all questions in life, or even in kinesiology. Nonscientific sources of knowledge include the following:

- **Tenacity**—Means clinging to beliefs, the way it's always been done, or superstitions
- **Intuition**—Includes commonsense or self-evident truths
- **Authority**—Refers to accepting the authority's truth (e.g., that of teachers, experts, rule books)
- **Rationalistic method**—Uses logic, such as the classic syllogism: All men are mortal; Socrates is a man; therefore, Socrates is mortal
- **Empirical method**—Includes experience, observation, and data gathering

Application Point

Using Nonscientific Sources of Knowledge in Rehab

Kinesiology professionals use many sources of knowledge every day. Assume you are an athletic trainer working with a client who is beginning a three-month rehab program after knee surgery. Give an example of how you might use each of the nonscientific sources (tenacity, intuition, and so on) in trying to help your client stick to the exercise rehab program.

We might use any of these sources to understand sport and exercise psychology. Even the most careful researcher is wise to rely on intuition in some cases, and professionals must rely on some authority in addition to their own judgment. Both the rationalistic (logic) and empirical methods are key parts of the scientific method; logic is critical in developing the problem and interpreting results, and gathering data is the empirical method. The scientific method incorporates logic and empirical methods in a systematic process as outlined in the following.

Scientific Method

Science is a process, and the scientific method is a systematic way to solve problems. Sport and exercise psychology developed as a discipline by following psychology and its reliance on traditional scientific methods. As described by Thomas, Nelson, and Silverman (2011), the scientific method is a series of steps.

1. **Developing the problem.** In the scientific method, the researcher must be specific, typically identifying independent and dependent variables. The independent variable is manipulated to determine its effect on the dependent variable. For example, we might compare the effects of two different incentives (independent variable) on exercise adherence (dependent variable).

2. **Formulating the hypothesis.** The hypothesis is the prediction or expected result. The hypothesis must be testable.

3. **Gathering the data.** The researcher must first plan the methods to maximize internal and external validity and then make observations to gather data. Internal validity means you are certain that the results can be attributed to the treatment. For example, if the choice group adhered to the exercise program more than the no-choice group, you are sure that choice was what increased adherence—you can rule out other alternatives. External validity refers to the generalizability of results. If choice increased adherence in the study, choice should increase adherence in other studies and settings.

4. **Analyzing and interpreting the results.** Most studies involve statistical analyses. The researcher must then interpret the results to support or refute the hypothesis and compare results with other research, theories, or other sources of information.

Key Point

The scientific method is a systematic way to solve problems. It includes the following four steps:

1. Developing the problem
2. Formulating the hypothesis
3. Gathering the data
4. Analyzing and interpreting the results

Multiple Research Methods and Knowledge Sources

The scientific method fits the assumptions of traditional science, but as the paradigms and approaches to knowledge have been challenged, alternative methods have become more widespread. Most researchers, and certainly most practicing professionals, realize that multiple sources of knowledge are useful. The scientific method is strong on internal validity—we can be confident that the results are reliable—but the results may not fit the real world. Other methods may provide less reliable but more relevant knowledge. Martens (1987) cited the DK continuum (see DK Continuum) to illustrate the degree of confidence we have in sources of knowledge. As the DK continuum suggests, when we use only intuition or our best guess, we don't know if we're correct. As we move up the continuum, perhaps by studying a single case, we are more confident. Finally, if we have information based on sound scientific research, we can be very confident in our knowledge.

Research methods courses and texts in psychology and kinesiology cover a range of methods along the DK continuum. Many researchers and publications focus on qualitative methodology, which includes a wide range of approaches such as ethnography and clinical case study. For example,

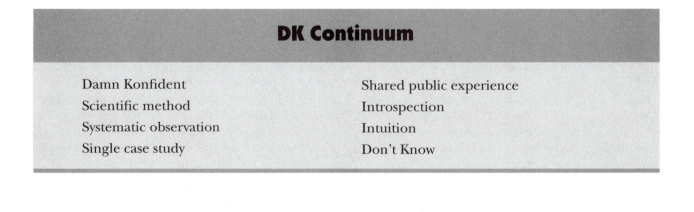

DK Continuum

Damn Konfident	Shared public experience
Scientific method	Introspection
Systematic observation	Intuition
Single case study	Don't Know

Thomas and colleagues' text (2011) lists the following major types of research:

- **Analytic research**—Includes historical and philosophical research as well as integrative reviews
- **Descriptive research**—Includes surveys, interviews, case studies, developmental research, correlational research, and epidemiological research
- **Experimental research**—The classic scientific method with experimental manipulation and control
- **Qualitative research**—Includes a variety of methods emphasizing narrative data and interpretive analyses rather than numerical data and statistics
- **Mixed methods**—Includes multiple methods, typically both quantitative and qualitative approaches

The scientific method has helped us develop a knowledge base and gain credibility, and it continues to dominate both psychology and kinesiology. However, several scholars argue for alternative methods and a wider acceptance of real-world knowledge. Those scholars challenge paradigms—the larger metatheories about knowledge and understanding.

Paradigm Challenges in Sport and Exercise Psychology

Martens' (1979, 1987) influential papers are often interpreted as methodological critiques, but they go beyond methods to challenge our paradigms. In his paper titled "Smocks and Jocks," Martens (1979) criticized sport psychology research for its lack of relevance to the real world and called for more research in the field. Although many interpreted that call as an excuse to abandon scientific rigor and theory, Landers (1983)—a strong advocate of theory testing—pointed out that Martens did not call for abandoning theory, but for using relevant theory, or theory that is relevant to the real world.

Martens' 1987 paper on science and knowledge in sport psychology was not simply methodological but a challenge to our assumptions about good research and what it means to know in sport and exercise psychology. Martens drew upon other criticisms of traditional science, which is objective, deterministic, and reductionistic. Science assumes there is an objective truth to be discovered. It is deterministic, assuming that we can discover causes or determinants and therefore predict behavior. And it is reductionistic in that scientists are constantly trying to find underlying mechanisms to explain behavior. Critics challenge all these assumptions, arguing that truth and knowledge are subjective.

Dewar and Horn (1992) and Brustad (2002) echoed many of Martens' concerns, but they extended the critical analysis with a stronger plea for contextualizing knowledge. Science is not neutral, and more to the point, sport and exercise psychology reflects the values and interpretations of the dominant culture. Dewar and Horn argued that we must interpret results in ways that are sensitive to social and political contexts in order to develop a more inclusive knowledge.

Dzewaltowski (1997) moved beyond critique to propose an alternative ecological metatheory. First, Dzewaltowski described the existing metatheories that guide our work:

- **Biological–dispositional**—These approaches emphasize person characteristics or physiological mechanisms as the source of behavior and regulation. They are closely tied to traditional science methods.
- **Cognitive–behavioral**—These approaches focus on the social and physical environment as a source of behavioral regulation and also rely on natural science, but they stress cognition (thought) rather than individual characteristics.
- **Cognitive–phenomenological**—These approaches are similar to the cognitive–behavioral, but they follow the Gestalt tradition to focus more on the whole than on isolated behaviors.
- **Social constructionist**—These approaches are the farthest removed from the scientific method and consider all knowledge as socially constructed and subjective.

Key Point

Dzewaltowski's ecological model stresses behavior and people in context, emphasizing the specific sport or exercise environment.

The key to Dzewaltowski's ecological model is the focus on the environment, specifically the person-in-environment. This approach focuses on the relationship between people and their environment and uses various descriptive, exploratory, and experimental methods. The environment is not static; the person transforms the environment just as the environment transforms the person. Dzewaltowski's model stresses behavior and people in context, emphasizing the specific environment. That emphasis seems critical if we are to answer questions about sport and exercise behavior in the real world.

Context Affects Behavior

The ecological model suggests that people's behaviors differ according to the context. Think about your own behavior and reactions (effort, aggression, emotional reactions, and so on) in various physical activity contexts. List some ways your behaviors and reactions might differ across the following three settings: a competitive volleyball match, recreational volleyball with friends, and a volleyball class.

Application Point

Research Into Practice

Although traditional research has dominated and established knowledge bases in psychology, kinesiology, and many other disciplines, recently many researchers in psychology and health-related areas have moved away from the traditional models to emphasize moving research into real-world settings. This involves both changing methods to move away from experimental lab-based research, and shifting paradigms away from behavioral and cognitive approaches toward more social–ecological models. And it also involves moving the research into the real world with all its complexities.

Oishi and Graham (2010) argued for a socio-ecological approach to psychology that investigates how mind and behavior are shaped in part by their natural and social habitats and how natural and social habitats are in turn shaped partly by mind and behavior. In their article, they bring Lewin's classic work and insights to modern psychology, highlighting the dynamic complexities of behavior and emphasizing the person-in-context. Other psychology works reflecting shifting paradigms focus on culture and neuroscience, and most interestingly cultural neuroscience. For example, Cacioppo and Cacioppo (2013), as part of a series on advances in psychological

science, describe the relatively new field of social neuroscience; Champagne and Mashoodh (2009) argue that the interactive influence of "genes in context" is critical in understanding individual differences; and Kitayama (2013) cites evidence from the rapidly growing field of cultural neuroscience to argue that genes, the environment, and brain all affect each other. All of these trends in psychology research reflect recognition of the dynamic, biopsychosocial complexities of behavior.

We can extend Dzewaltowki's (1997) ecological model by emphasizing the dynamic, biopsychosocial complexity of behavior in the sport and exercise environment. Some aspects of complexity models seem particularly relevant. First, complexity models are nondeterministic. We cannot specify all determinants of behavior, and we cannot predict behavior no matter how much we improve our measures. The best we can do is develop guidelines and descriptive patterns. Human behavior is far more complex than most of the phenomena that fit complexity models. We will not identify a pattern that fits all behavior or even all behavior in a very limited setting.

Not only is behavior complex, it is dynamic. Conditions constantly change, and seemingly trivial conditions can have tremendous impact later, as in the classic example of the butterfly flapping its wings and affecting distant storm patterns—or when an elementary physical education teacher makes one hurried comment to a child that affects the child's activity patterns as an adult. Moreover, that one comment is part of a limitless set of comments and events. Each combination is unique; and even under identical circumstances, people interact with their circumstances in unique ways.

One response might be to give up, to assume we cannot predict anything and therefore cannot use sport and exercise psychology. That is not at all the case. Instead of trying to find elusive answers to such questions as "How do I stick to an exercise program?" or "How can I help a soccer player control emotions?", look to the literature and other sources of knowledge to find guidelines and patterns. Research and theory provide those unifying principles that practitioners can adapt according to their experience and the immediate situation and thus move toward practical theory.

Practical Theory

"Practical theory" is not an oxymoron. Practical theory is theory—guidelines rather than facts, and it is practical—relevant to the real world. Lewin's (1951) statement, "There is nothing so practical as a good theory," reflects this view. Practitioners must look for theories rather than facts. Facts continually change in the real world; today's fact is tomorrow's outdated practice.

Lewin's line comes from a larger statement (1951) addressed to researchers:

> This can be accomplished . . . if the theorist does not look toward applied problems with highbrow aversion or with a fear of social problems, and if the applied psychologist realizes that there is nothing so practical as a good theory. (p. 169)

Boyer (1990) made the same point in noting that the scholarship of application is not a one-way street:

> It would be misleading to suggest knowledge is first discovered and then applied . . . the process is far more dynamic. . . . New understandings can arise out of the very act of application—whether in medical diagnosis, serving clients, shaping public policy or working with the public schools. In activities such as these, theory and practice vitally interact, and one renews the other. (p. 23)

Scholars must ask real-world questions with an eye on the person-in-context. Researchers as well as practitioners must stop searching for facts and aim for practical theory.

Key Point

Because facts continually change in the real world, practitioners must look for theories rather than facts. Scholars must ask real-world questions with an eye on the person-in-context.

RE-AIM Research for Practice

Many researchers in psychology, health, and kinesiology are taking up the challenge not only to address relevant practical issues but also to take the critical step of actually translating that research into the real-world setting. Translational research, which involves actually putting research into practice, is becoming more prominent in many areas, and particularly in health-related research. Translational research is not easy, and it involves much more than simply moving research into a real-world activity setting. Dzewaltowski, Estabrooks, and Glasgow (2004) adapted the Reach, Efficacy/Effectiveness, Adoption, Implementation, and Maintenance (RE-AIM) framework from public health research to bridge the gap between physical activity intervention research and the delivery of evidence-based programs in practice. The RE-AIM framework is as follows:

- **Reach**—The absolute number, proportion, and representativeness of individuals who participate in a given initiative compared to those who decline (or to the general population in that area).
- **Efficacy/Effectiveness**—Impact of an intervention on physical activity and other health outcomes, including potential negative effects, quality of life, and economic outcomes.
- **Adoption**—Absolute number, proportion, and representativeness of settings and intervention providers who are willing to initiate a physical activity promotion program.
- **Implementation**—The intervention providers' fidelity to the various elements of an intervention's protocol, including consistency of delivery as intended and the time and cost of the intervention.
- **Maintenance**—At the setting level, the extent to which a physical activity promotion program or policy becomes institutionalized or part of routine organizational practices and policies. At the individual level, the long-term effects of a physical activity promotion program on behavior after six or more months following the most recent intervention contact.

All aspects of the RE-AIM framework must be addressed to effectively translate research into practice. Most research in sport and exercise psychology does not get past efficacy, if it even goes that far. Sport and exercise psychology would be much more useful to professionals if more research followed the RE-AIM framework and intentionally translated research into real-world settings. Professionals in the field should keep in mind that most of our research findings and theories (even the practical ones) have not been fully translated into real-world settings. Thus, professionals need to consider the individual participants and unique environment in their particular context when using sport and exercise psychology in practice.

Using Sport and Exercise Psychology

Now that you understand approaches to knowledge and the key role of practical theory, we turn to using sport and exercise psychology in professional practice. Chapter 2 describes major professional roles for those who specialize in sport and exercise psychology; here we focus on the use of sport and exercise psychology by the wider range of kinesiology professionals.

Who Uses Sport and Exercise Psychology?

Obviously sport and exercise psychology specialists use sport and exercise psychology. Most specialists have doctoral training and may apply sport and exercise psychology in consulting with athletes or exercisers, conducting workshops for coaches or teachers, teaching future professionals in undergraduate and graduate kinesiology programs, and conducting research to contribute to the knowledge base. However, one does not need a PhD to use sport and exercise psychology. As noted in chapter 1, kinesiology professionals use sport and exercise psychology every day. Physical education teachers, exercise instructors, and sports medicine professionals all deal with people in physical activity settings. Understanding behavior in sport and exercise and using that knowledge to more effectively relate to people is the essence of evidence-based professional practice. Specialists have more training and likely are more familiar with the most current research. However, teachers, exercise instructors, and other kinesiology professionals have more experience and are more familiar with the specific context in which they practice. Understanding of the participants and the setting allows professionals to use practical theory more effectively.

Psychological Skills Training

Psychological skills training (PST), also known as mental skills training or mental coaching, involves putting sport and exercise psychology into practice in a training program. Psychological skills training is commonly used by sport and

exercise psychology professionals working directly with sport teams or individual clients. It is the systematic and consistent practice of mental or psychological skills for the purpose of enhancing the sport or physical activity experience. Psychological skills training is education or training, and as with physical skills, systematic practice over time is key to developing psychological skills and using them effectively. Psychological skills training programs may focus on one or two skills, or they may combine several skills in a more comprehensive training program. Whether training with just one skill or in a more comprehensive program, PST typically involves three phases: (a) education (increasing awareness and understanding, setting expectations), (b) acquisition (learning, practicing, and refining skills over time), and (c) practice–performance (using the skills in the actual activity). The ultimate goal in PST is self-regulation, which involves effectively monitoring and managing your thoughts, feelings, and behavior.

Psychological skills training is not just for elite athletes. Indeed, PST may be even more helpful in youth programs. And PST is not limited to sport and exercise psychology professionals. Many coaches do a great deal of mental coaching, and kinesiology professionals in many settings can put their sport and exercise psychology knowledge to use to help their students and clients. For example, you might have a client in therapy following knee surgery who is getting frustrated and ready to give up. Here's a simple PST routine you could suggest for your client. First, take a deep breath and relax. Then, focus on the exercise; you might use a cue word or phrase to help—"push through." Finish off with encouragement and support, and keep checking in with your client. Chapter 5 includes information and guidelines for using attentional skills and imagery; chapter 13 covers emotional control skills and stress management; and other chapters include psychological information and strategies that you can use in professional practice.

Professional Practice as Science Plus Art

Effective professional practice in sport and exercise psychology consulting, in physical education, in sports medicine, or in any profession, is both a science and an art. The science is emphasized in evidence-based practice. Professionals seek and use the best available evidence from the strongest, most reliable sources of knowledge. The art of professional practice involves adapting that evidence and applying practical theories with specific individuals in specific contexts. Individualizing (tailoring practice to the individual) and contextualizing (adapting practices to the setting and context) are essential to effective professional practice.

Adding the Art to Exercise Instruction

Theories and guidelines based on research can help professionals, but the best professionals also use their experience and insights. As an exercise instructor with a water aerobics class, what experiences and insights about the class and participants could help you use sport and exercise psychology theories so that participants gain optimal benefits from the class?

Application Point

Putting It Into Practice

Summary

Understanding the theory–research–practice triad and the key role of theory is critical to continuing progress. Sport and exercise psychology has advanced largely by using traditional science, but the scientific method has shortcomings. To advance sport and exercise psychology knowledge and provide practical theory to guide professional practice, we must continually reconsider the guiding paradigms and methods. The most promising routes to relevant, useful knowledge recognize the powerful influence of the social environment, focus on people in context, and stay mindful of the complex dynamics of sport and exercise behavior.

Both sport and exercise psychology specialists and kinesiology professionals use sport and exercise psychology. Using sport and exercise psychology effectively in professional practice is both a science and an art. That is, a professional must use the best available evidence (science) and also be ready to adapt to the individuals and the context.

Review Questions

1. Define theory and explain why it is the critical link in the theory–research–practice triad.
2. Explain what is meant by evidence-based practice and describe how it applies to kinesiology professionals.
3. Describe the scientific method and list its steps.
4. Explain the statement "There is nothing so practical as a good theory."
5. Explain what is meant by individualizing and contextualizing professional practice.

Recommended Reading

- APA Presidential Task Force on Evidence-Based Practice. (2006). Evidence-based practice in psychology. *American Psychologist, 61,* 271-285. The APA policy statement is a great resource describing how competent professionals integrate research and professional expertise in professional practice.

- Dzewaltowski, D.A., Estabrooks, P.A., & Glasgow, R.E. (2004). The future of physical activity behavior change research: What is needed to improve translation of research into health promotion practice? *Exercise and Sport Sciences Reviews, 32,* 57-63. This article describes the RE-AIM framework and how it might be applied to translate sport and exercise psychology research into practice.

- Forscher, B.K. (1963). Chaos in the brickyard. *Science, 142*(3590), 339. Forscher's short and entertaining article is a classic must-read for any graduate student. It reads like a fable, and like most fables, it has a clear message. Using the analogy of bricks and buildings, Forscher makes the point that theory (the blueprint) is the key difference between a useful building and a pile of bricks.

- Martens, R. (1987). Science, knowledge and sport psychology. *Sport Psychologist, 1,* 29-55. Martens' influential article urges changes in sport and exercise psychology to make research more relevant and to connect academic work to practicing sport psychology. The issues Martens raised 20 years ago remain; rereading the article and continual reconsideration of the issues will help you understand and use sport and exercise psychology knowledge.

LAB

Science and Art of Sport and Exercise Psychology

As an athletic trainer (AT), you may well want sport and exercise psychology information and strategies that you can use to help athletes with rehabilitation. But how do you find good information, and how do you use that information in practice? As discussed in this chapter, we can be confident in information that comes from sound scientific research. So, you could search research journals or publications aimed at professionals that draw from the research. Most practicing professionals do not have the time to go directly to research journals, but many professional journals, newsletters, and websites draw from research. Professionals who go to these sources should look for information that is indeed based on the best available evidence. So, for the first part of the lab, find at least two resources that are designed for professionals (e.g., websites, professional journals) with information the AT could use.

Another alternative for busy professionals who cannot read all the research or check all the resources is to look for a consultant who specializes in sport and exercise psychology. So, for part 2 of the lab, assume you are seeking advice from a consultant. First, what would you look for in a consultant (e.g., credentials and experience)? And second, what would you expect to get from the consultant (information, resources, and so on)?

Remember that science is not the only source of useful information. As an athletic trainer, you will often rely on advice from others, trial and error, and your experiential knowledge. You want to use the best evidence available (science), but professional practice is also an art. So, for the final part of the lab, list at least two ways that you could use your experience and insights to individualize and contextualize (add the art to) your AT practice.

The Person in Sport and Exercise Psychology

Sport and exercise psychology is about people and behavior in physical activity, and we begin by focusing on the person—individual characteristics. That is, we focus on the person in the classic formula defining behavior as a function of the person and the environment (see chapter 1). Chapter 4 covers personality and reviews personality research and application in sport and exercise settings. As the chapter reveals, general personality models and measures have been widely used, but they have not been very helpful in sport and exercise psychology. Sport-specific individual characteristics and approaches combining person and environmental factors have been more useful.

Chapter 5 addresses individual differences in attention and cognition, as well as related cognitive skills, such as imagery, that may be useful in sport and exercise. Chapter 6 covers self-perceptions, starting with self-concept and multidimensional models. Chapter 6 also covers physical self-perceptions and identity, as well as the extensive sport and exercise psychology work on self-efficacy.

Personality

Chapter 4

Chapter Objectives

After studying this chapter, you should be able to

- define personality,

- describe the major theoretical perspectives and models of personality,

- trace the sport and exercise psychology research on personality, and

- discuss the development and use of sport-specific personality and psychological skills measures.

As discussed in part I, psychology is about people and their behavior. Personality is about individual differences, or what makes each person unique. Personality plays a big role in sport and exercise behavior, and kinesiology professionals use personality information every day. Individual differences are obvious. One third-grader relishes performing on center stage during physical education whereas a classmate moves to the back of the line; one person goes on long, solo runs whereas a neighbor socializes at the fitness center; one gymnast rises to the challenge of competition, whereas another chokes and performs far below expectations.

Such individual differences reflect personality. Not only do we recognize these differences, but we assess personality when we size up opponents, consider how different students might react to feedback, or evaluate our own strengths and weaknesses. Those personality assessments in turn affect our behavior. Consider a diver awaiting the first dive of the competition. The diver who thinks, "Yes! I'm confident and ready to hit that first dive," will probably perform differently than one who is hesitant or worried about mistakes. We also use personality judgments when interacting with others. Instructors do not make the same comments to the student they consider fragile or sensitive as to the student they view as mentally tough.

Personality and Behavior

Professionals often evaluate personality and adjust their behavior when working with clients. As a personal trainer, list three ways in which two of your clients might differ in personality. Then, describe how your behavior and interactions with those clients might differ based on those differences.

The goal of personality research in sport and exercise psychology is to provide accurate, reliable information about individual differences and the relationship of personality to sport and exercise behaviors. This chapter first covers general personality psychology and then focuses on research and the role of personality information and measures in sport and exercise psychology.

Personality Defined

As you likely learned in Psychology 101, or perhaps read in Ahmetoglu and Chamorro-Premuzic's (2013) book, *Personality 101*, personality is your psy-chological profile, and personality helps explain why people behave differently. At the American Psychological Association (APA) website, you find personality defined as individual differences in characteristic patterns of thinking, feeling, and behaving. Thus, personality denotes characteristic or consistent differences in behavior. The personality characteristic of aggressiveness is attributed to a person who consistently displays aggressive behavior (e.g., often argues, easily angers, initiates fights). We commonly think of personality as including social characteristics, such as introversion or aggressiveness, but it also includes perceptual and cognitive characteristics, such as the ability to concentrate. Personality is the relatively stable, overall pattern of characteristics that make each person unique.

As well as thinking about the characteristics that make up personality, we can also think about personality on different levels. That is, some aspects of personality are "core" characteristics that are formed early, deeply ingrained, and not likely to change. Most personality characteristics that we recognize, such as conscientiousness or trait anxiety, are relatively stable dispositions that develop and change gradually over time. At the more superficial level we have more changeable characteristics and skills, such as attentional style, that may well change with the situation, over time, or with training. As we will discuss in a later section, these more superficial characteristics are more closely related to behaviors in sport and exercise settings and are often targeted in psychological skills training.

Although psychologists generally agree on what personality is, there is no clear consensus on why people have different personalities. No doubt individual differences have been obvious as long as people have interacted, and explanations can be found as far back as there are records. Personality theories range from simple, commonsense explanations to complex, sophisticated models and vary from the purely biological to purely environmental. In psychology, the major or "grand" theories to explain why we have personality are psychodynamic approaches, behaviorism, and social cognitive theories. In the next section we highlight early explanations and grand theories that have been used to explain personality. Then we turn to the models of personality, particularly the trait perspectives that dominate sport and exercise psychology research, and more recent work that incorporates multiple perspectives in more integrative models.

Key Point

Personality is the overall pattern of psychological characteristics that make each person unique.

Early Theories and Current Biological Perspectives

The ancient Greeks, who gave us the Hippocratic oath and early medicine, linked biology and behavior to explain individual differences. According to the Greeks, everyone had four basic body fluids or humors, and varying individual temperaments (personalities) were due to differing proportions of these humors. Blood was associated with a sanguine or cheerful temperament, yellow bile was associated with a choleric or irritable temperament, black bile was associated with a melancholic or sad temperament, and phlegm was associated with a phlegmatic or apathetic temperament.

Today's theorists do not refer to the four body fluids, but we can find biology in current personality research. Indeed, biological explanations for behavior are making a comeback, and with advances in genetics and neuropsychology, many biological explanations have considerable credibility. Current biological approaches are not as broad as the early Greek model, and even proponents of biological explanations do not claim a biological basis for all behaviors. For example, consider Jerome Kagan's work on the genetic aspects of temperament, specifically shyness versus outgoingness, which is widely respected and has considerable support.

Kagan titled his 1994 book, which summarizes much of that work, *Galen's Prophecy*, reflecting ties to Hippocrates and the later views of Galen, a second-century physician. Like Hippocrates and Galen, Kagan defines temperament as "any moderately stable, differentiating emotional or behavioral quality whose appearance in childhood is influenced by an inherited biology, including differences in brain neurochemistry" (p. xvii). Kagan has focused on the inhibited–uninhibited or shy–bold temperament and has amassed considerable evidence supporting a biological basis for this temperament. However, he also makes it clear that temperament cannot be reduced to biology but requires both biological and experiential conditions acting together over time.

In a more recent 2012 book, Kagan strongly called for psychologists to pay attention to the "missing contexts." He specifically suggested that psychologists replace the properties of an individual as the primary unit with the properties-in-a-context and award "equal power to genes and brains, on the one hand, and to culture, historical era, social class, and the local setting, on the other" (2012, p. 73). Kagan is explicitly calling for a biopsychosocial perspective, incorporating social context as well as biological and psychological components.

Key Point

Most personality theorists agree that personality is determined by multiple, interdependent factors, and we are not likely to identify simple biological or experiential factors.

Although few personality theorists explore biological factors, most would agree with Kagan. Personality is determined by multiple, interdependent factors, and we are not likely to identify simple biological or experiential sources. If we look for a biological or experiential base, we can find it, but we will understand personality and behavior better if we investigate their complexities and interdependent relationships.

Psychology Models of Personality

Much current personality research focuses on personality structure and identifying the dimensions that define one's personality. This work includes trait theories (personality is a collection of traits), as well as more current interactionist approaches. Before discussing these models, we briefly review those grand theories of personality psychology (see Ahmetoglu & Chamorro-Premuzic, 2013, for more detail).

Psychodynamic Approaches

Freud is the most widely known and cited psychologist, and his psychoanalytic theory has tremendous influence even though his methods have been criticized and his views have little influence on current personality research. In Freud's theory, the unconscious mind is a key driving force in personality and behavior. Typical self-report measures of personality would be useless for Freud because people do not really know their personalities. Freud also identifies three components of the mind. The id is linked to instinctual, unconscious drives, while the superego is the moral conscience. The ego is the conscious state that negotiates between the id and superego. Thus, the ego is in constant, dynamic (as in psychodynamic) struggle. According to Freud, personality reflects those struggles that begin in childhood and carry over into adult life. For example, if the superego "wins" a lot of the struggles, the person may become rigid and conservative. On the other hand, if the superego is weak, the person may be morally corrupt or even a psychopath.

Although Freud's work is widely known and has a place in clinical practice, psychodynamic approaches have little influence in current personality research, or any psychology research. Freud's psychoanalytic theory stemmed from clinical observations, focused on psychopathology, and offered few testable predictions, especially about healthy personalities. Humanistic approaches, such as self-actualization models, are related to psychodynamic approaches, but are more optimistic and posit self-change or growth. Sport and exercise psychologists who consult with clients may find the more holistic and optimistic approach useful in helping people develop healthy lifestyles, but these perspectives have little impact on research.

Behaviorism and Social Cognitive Theories

As Ahmetoglu and Chamorro-Premuzic (2013) point out, behaviorism became the dominant paradigm for psychology, including personality, in the mid-20th century. Behaviorism is nearly the opposite of psychodynamic approaches in that behaviorism focuses on observable behavior rather than the inner workings of the mind. An extreme view, such as B.F. Skinner's radical behaviorism, discounts personality altogether. According to Skinner, a soccer player exhibits aggressive behavior because the situation calls for it and because it has been reinforced in the past; any person in the same situation would display the same behavior. We discuss behavioral approaches in more detail in a later chapter. Behaviorism is about behavior and does not say much about personality per se.

More recent social cognitive theories departed from behavioral approaches by including mental processes and indeed emphasizing perceptions and cognitions. People do not just react to the environment but actively perceive, think, and decide how to behave. It should be noted that these mental processes are not typical personality traits. In fact, the inability of trait measures to predict behavior led many psychologists to renounce personality theories and adopt social cognitive approaches. In an often-cited critique, Mischel (1968) pointed out that even the most psychometrically sound trait measures predict only a small proportion of behavior. The aggressive soccer player does not display aggressive behavior in every situation and may even be quite nonaggressive in other settings. Bandura (1977), arguably the main social cognitive theorist, described a social learning perspective as follows: "Psychological functioning is explained in terms of a continuous reciprocal interaction of personal and environmental determinants" (pp. 11-12).

Social cognitive theories are prominent in psychology and in sport and exercise psychology. We discuss social cognitive theories in part III. As with behaviorism, social cognitive theories have little influence in personality psychology and might be considered anti-personality theories in terms of traditional personality psychology and the trait approaches that dominate. In the next section we focus on the trait approaches and structural models that dominate personality psychology.

Personality Traits or Dispositions

Most personality research and most common personality measures are based on trait or dispositional approaches. Traits are relatively stable, highly consistent attributes that exert generalized causal effects on behavior (Mischel, 1973). Trait theories imply consistency and generalizability of behavior; for instance, the person with a high level of shyness consistently displays shy behavior in varied situations, such as classes, team meetings, and activities. Trait approaches assume that once we identify traits, we can predict behavior. Thus, much of the work in personality psychology focuses on identifying traits and the structure of personality and on developing psychometrically sound personality measures.

Many psychologists cite Sir Francis Galton's (1883) attempts to categorize the many descriptive terms for people as one of the first dimensional models of personality. With the advantage of statistical analyses, Cattell (1943) used factor analysis to develop his model and the widely used Sixteen Personality Factor Questionnaire, commonly called the16PF. Eysenck (1970, 1991), one of the most influential personality psychologists, argued for fewer, more basic dimensions. He originally proposed two basic dimensions of personality, neuroticism and extraversion, and later added psychoticism in a three-factor model. Neuroticism reflects emotional stability, ranging from emotionally calm and stable to anxious and moody. Extraversion ranges from the very sociable and outgoing to the very shy introvert. Psychoticism ranges from responsible, caring individuals to impulsive sociopaths. Importantly, these are independent dimensions in Eysenck's model. Everyone can be located somewhere on each dimension, and everyone will have a unique place in the model.

Consider the two-dimensional model in figure 4.1 and decide where you might fall. For example, I would put myself very near the extreme introversion end of that dimension and very near the emotionally stable end of the other, falling in the lower left quadrant at point A. Person B is also relatively emotionally stable, but much more extraverted; B is more sociable, outgoing, and might be a leader. Person C, who is near the middle or average on extraversion, is more moody and really shows the thrill of victory and agony of defeat. Nearly all models of personality include neuroticism and extraversion, and they are the first two dimensions for the most widely accepted model today—the Big Five model.

Big Five Model of Personality

Psychologists continue to debate the structure of personality, but the literature suggests consensus on the Big Five model with its five major dimensions:

- Neuroticism—nervousness, anxiety, depression, anger versus emotional stability
- Extraversion—enthusiasm, sociability, assertiveness, high activity level versus introversion
- Openness to experience (culture or intellect in some versions)—originality, need for variety, curiosity, artistic sensitivity
- Agreeableness—amiability, altruism, modesty, trust versus egocentrism, narcissism, skepticism
- Conscientiousness—constraint, achievement striving, self-discipline

Neuroticism and extraversion are much the same as in Eysenck's model. Openness to experience reflects creativity, curiosity, and flexibility. Agreeableness is basically sociability. Conscientiousness is related to responsibility and self-discipline and is particularly relevant to performance and achievement. Most models of personality reflect some aspects of the Big Five. Although debate continues, the general five-factor structure is accepted, and corresponding measures have been developed. Specifically, the NEO (which originally stood for neuroticism, extraversion, and openness) Personality Inventory (NEO PI; Costa & McCrae, 1985) is widely used today. The NEO measure is lengthy, and shorter versions have been developed, including the Big Five Inventory (BFI; John, Donahue, & Kentle, 1991) and an even shorter 1-minute version, the BFI-10 (Rammstedt & John, 2007).

Assess Your Big Five Personality Profile

To determine your own Big Five personality profile, go to the Berkeley Personality Lab website and take the 1-minute version. Are your scores accurate?—do they reflect your personality? What do your scores suggest about your behavior?

Interactionist Approaches

Today, whether using the Big Five model or other measures, most personality psychologists prefer an interactionist approach that considers the interrelated roles of personality factors and situational factors as codeterminants of behavior. Certain personality characteristics predict behavior in some, but not all, situations. For instance, a tennis player

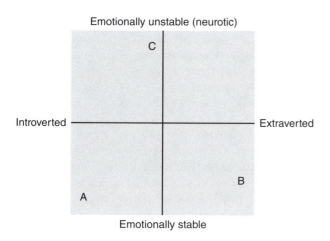

Figure 4.1 Eysenck's two-dimensional model of personality.

might consistently become anxious when facing competition but not when facing other challenges, such as academic tests or verbal presentations.

Key Point

Most personality psychologists prefer an interactionist approach. However, the approach does not provide simple predictions because any behavior is the function of a seemingly limitless number of personality and environmental factors.

B = f(P, E), the formula presented in chapter 1, is a simple representation of the interactionist approach, but the interactionist approach is not simple. Any behavior, such as aggressive behavior in ice hockey, is the function of a seemingly limitless number of personality and environmental factors. An opponent's insult may provoke an aggressive response from a player in one situation but not from another in the same situation, and perhaps not even in the same player in a slightly different situation (e.g., perhaps a lack of sleep or problems outside sport facilitated the aggressive response). The interactionist approach is more complex, but also more realistic, than the extreme trait and situational approaches. As noted in chapter 1, we should not expect simple answers to questions about human behavior.

Why Do Personalities Differ?

Application Point

Jason and Jack are brothers on the same soccer team. They have similar physical skills, but very different personalities. Jason is competitive and always up for a challenge, but he can get very down if things don't go well. Jack is more even-tempered and focuses on self-improvement in practices and games. Why are they so different? Answer that question and explain why they are different from each of the following perspectives: (a) psychodynamic, (b) social learning, (c) trait, and (d) interaction.

Integrative Models

Recent perspectives on personality go beyond the Big Five model and the interactionist approaches to take a more integrative, and often biopsycho-

social, approach to understanding the person. Mayer (2005) takes a systems approach, and defines personality as follows:

> Personality is the organized, developing system within the individual that represents the collective action of his or her motivational, emotional, cognitive, social planning, and other psychological subsystems. (p. 296)

Key Point

McAdams and Pals (2006) incorporate biological and social perspectives into an integrative model that emphasizes the complex, dynamic relationships among dispositional traits, characteristic adaptations, and integrative life narratives, as well as the continuing influence of cultural systems and practices within the social ecology of daily life.

Like Mayer, McAdams (2013; McAdams & Pals, 2006) incorporates biological and social perspectives into an integrative model. McAdams and Pals (2006) define personality in terms of a "new big 5"—five key principles that outline an integrative view of the whole person:

> Personality is conceived as (a) an individual's unique variation on the general evolutionary design for human nature, expressed as a developing pattern of (b) dispositional traits, (c) characteristic adaptation, and (d) self-defining life narratives, complexly and differentially situated (e) in culture and social context. (p. 204)

McAdams and Pals thus acknowledge basic human nature that exists in all people, but they emphasize the complex, dynamic relationships among dispositional traits (e.g., the Big Five), characteristic adaptations (e.g., goals, values, coping strategies), and integrative life narratives (i.e., stories that give life meaning, unity, and purpose), as well as the continuing influence of cultural systems and practices within the social ecology of daily life. This view is more complex, dynamic, and realistic in representing the person than the personality trait perspectives that have been used most often in sport and exercise psychology. Coulter, Mallett, Singer, and Gucciardi (2016) argue that McAdams' (2013) integrative personality framework, which emphasizes how individual differences in traits (actor), characteristic adaptations (agent), and life narratives (author) converge to provide a holistic understanding of people, can advance both scholarship and practice in sport and exercise psychology.

Personality Measures

Personality assessment can take many forms, including life histories, projective measures, in-depth interviews, case histories, and behavioral observations, but by far the most common are survey measures. Objective personality inventories involve structured responses (e.g., rating scales, multiple-choice or true–false items), are easily administered and scored, and can be compared with norms and other samples. Several of the most common personality measures, such as the Cattell 16PF, Eysenck Personality Inventory (EPI), and Big Five measures, as well as personality measures assessing single traits, such as Spielberger's (1966) State-Trait Anxiety Inventory (STAI), have been used with sport and exercise participants.

One of the most popular personality measures, the Myers-Briggs Type Indicator (MBTI), has seldom been used in research but is commonly found in training and educational settings. The MBTI reports preferences on four scales:

- Extraversion (E)–Introversion (I)
- Sensing (S)–Intuition (N)
- Thinking (T)–Feeling (F)
- Judging (J)–Perceiving (P)

With the MBTI, you can classify yourself on each scale (dichotomously as one or the other) to determine your overall personality type. The MBTI is popular and widely used, but most personality psychologists express reservations. The profile descriptions tend to be intuitively obvious, and the dichotomous classifications encourage stereotypes and labels. The MBTI may be a useful icebreaker, but it lacks theoretical base and evidence to support its use in sport and exercise psychology research or practice.

In line with the positive psychology approach, Seligman (2005) advocates assessing positive psychological characteristics and emphasizing strengths rather than focusing on problems. The Values in Action (VIA) Signature Strengths Survey parallels the *Diagnostic and Statistical Manual of Mental Disorders, Fourth Edition* (DSM IV), which is widely used to identify psychological problems and pathologies; but the VIA measure, available at the VIA Institute on Character website, assesses 24 positive strengths, including creativity, courage, intimacy, fairness, self-control, and spirituality.

Personality Research in Sport and Exercise Psychology

Personality has been a popular topic throughout the history of sport and exercise psychology. Perhaps the unique physical characteristics of athletes prompt a search for analogous psychological profiles. Most of the research involves questions such as these: Is there an athletic personality? Are runners more introverted than volleyball players? Can we predict success from personality information? Or, in reverse: How does physical activity affect personality? We might claim that sport fosters moral development, or that exercise improves mental health. Claims of general personality changes have not been supported, but research on specific physical activity effects on specific self-perceptions and emotions is promising (such work is discussed in later chapters).

Early Research on Personality Profiles of Athletes

As part of his pioneering sport psychology work, Coleman Griffith (1926, 1928) examined the personality profiles of successful athletes. Through observations and interviews, Griffith identified the following characteristics of great athletes: ruggedness, courage, intelligence, exuberance, buoyance, emotional adjustment, optimism, conscientiousness, alertness, loyalty, and respect for authority.

Many athletes have filled out many personality inventories since Griffith's time. In an early review, Ogilvie (1968) concluded that certain traits are associated with successful athletes. With colleagues, Ogilvie developed the Athletic Motivation Inventory (AMI) to measure those traits, which include drive, determination, leadership, aggressiveness, guilt proneness, emotional control, self-confidence, conscientiousness, mental toughness, trust, and coachability (Tutko, Lyon, & Ogilvie, 1969). You may notice the similarity between the AMI list and Griffith's list. As discussed in the following section, most scholars do not find such consistency in the sport personality research, and the AMI is no longer used.

Mental Health Model

Morgan's (1978, 1980) mental health model represents the most systematic earlier work on personality and sport. According to the model, positive mental health is directly related to athletic success, whereas psychopathology and success are inversely related. In studies with college and Olympic wrestlers, national-team rowers, and elite distance runners, Morgan demonstrated that successful athletes possessed more positive mental health characteristics and fewer negative mental health characteristics than the general population. That pattern, depicted in figure 4.2, has been termed the iceberg profile. On the Profile of Mood States (POMS; McNair, Lorr, & Droppleman, 1971), successful athletes typically score above the waterline (population norm) on vigor but below on the negative moods of tension, depression, anger, fatigue, and confusion.

Although Morgan's model is widely cited and the iceberg profile has been replicated with other samples, cautions are in order. It may seem that Morgan's model and research identify a personality profile for successful athletes, but that is not the case. First, the model is general. Not every successful athlete fits the iceberg profile, and many less than successful athletes do match the profile. It is not surprising that psychopathology is negatively related to success in athletics; it is negatively related to success in most endeavors. Furthermore, we cannot assume that the iceberg profiles of athletes necessarily imply that positive mental health (personality) leads to success—

success in sport may lead to more positive mood profiles and enhanced mental health.

Morgan's clearest results are with the POMS, a measure of moods, rather than with personality inventories. Rowley, Landers, Kyllo, and Etnier (1995) conducted a meta-analysis of POMS research and found that although athletes tended to show the iceberg profile, the effect size was a meager 0.15, accounting for less than 1 percent of the variance—raising questions about the usefulness of POMS in predicting athletic success. However, an offshoot of that POMS research offers more promise.

The POMS assesses mood, and unlike personality characteristics, mood varies over time and situations. Morgan and colleagues (e.g., Morgan, Brown, Raglin, O'Connor, & Ellickson, 1987) used POMS to track mood changes in athletes over a competitive season, and Raglin (1993) summarized that research. Generally, mood shifts away from the iceberg profile reflect overtraining: The profile of swimmers flattens in the midseason overtraining period, reflecting greater mood disturbance and tending to parallel physiological changes, but research has not pinpointed clear mechanisms, and many questions remain open.

Terry and colleagues (Terry, Lane, Lane, & Keohane, 1999; Terry, Lane, & Fogarty, 2003) developed a shorter version of POMS, the Brunel Mood Scale, to provide a quick assessment of mood states for adolescents and adults; see the In the Mood website.

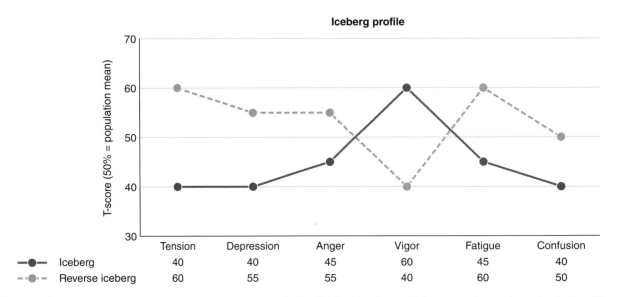

	Tension	Depression	Anger	Vigor	Fatigue	Confusion
Iceberg	40	40	45	60	45	40
Reverse iceberg	60	55	55	40	60	50

Figure 4.2 The iceberg profile. The ideal iceberg profile (solid line) is above 50th percentile on vigor, but below 50 on the negative mood states. The reverse iceberg (dotted line) is below 50 on vigor, but higher on the negative mood states.

As well as the research with athletes, several sport and exercise psychology researchers have used POMS or shorter adaptations to monitor mood with participants in varied physical activity programs. Such tracking of mood states may be especially useful for participants in varied health-related physical activity programs. For example, in activity programs for clinical populations, such as cancer survivors, mood changes may well be an important outcome measure. Relationships of mood with physical activity are certainly worthy of further research, but mood states and related research fall under emotions rather than personality.

Personality and Overtraining

Athletic trainers are in a good position to recognize overtraining. As an athletic trainer, how could you use personality information to identify overtraining and help athletes adjust training levels for optimal performance and health?

Problems With Sport Personality Research

Today, most scholars see little value in using global personality measures to profile athletes or predict behavior. Fisher, Ryan, and Martens (1976) concluded that global personality traits relate slightly, if at all, to sport participation or performance, and this skeptical view still holds today. The findings are as varied as the studies, and some findings are contradictory. For every study indicating that runners are more introverted than volleyball players, another shows no difference. Little evidence supports a general athletic personality type, a personality profile that separates elite athletes from everyone else, or specific personality profiles associated with specific activities.

More recently, Vanden Auweele, De Cuyper, Van Mele, and Rzewnicki (1993) reviewed the work on elite performance and personality and noted the limited information from earlier research. Their meta-analysis of 25 studies on introversion and extraversion of athletes showed an overall effect size of −0.10, indicating no difference between athletes and the norm. Vanden Auweele and colleagues suggested that sport personality research shift away from traditional personality measures and deterministic (predictive) models.

Key Point

Due to conceptual, methodological, and interpretive problems, the existing sport psychology research on personality tells us little about the role of individual differences in sport and exercise. Sound research must address meaningful questions, use appropriate samples and measures, and not overgeneralize results.

Individual differences play a crucial role in sport and exercise behavior, but the early research is plagued by conceptual, methodological, and interpretive problems and yields little helpful information. Unfortunately, many studies were undertaken because they were easy to conduct rather than to answer meaningful questions. The major conceptual problem in sport personality research is that many studies were done without a good reason. Nearly 50 years ago, Ryan (1968) stated,

The research in this area has largely been of the "shotgun" variety. By this I mean the investigators grabbed the nearest and most convenient personality test, and the closest sport group, and with little or no theoretical basis for their selection fired into the air to see what they could bring down. It isn't surprising that firing into the air at different times and at different places, and using different ammunition, should result in different findings. In fact, it would be surprising if the results weren't contradictory and somewhat contrary. (p. 71)

Without meaningful questions, research cannot provide meaningful answers. Once researchers identify meaningful questions, they must follow sound methodology, using appropriate samples (not a single basketball team to represent all basketball players) and appropriate, psychometrically sound measures (measures designed for clinical diagnoses are not appropriate for nonclinical samples). Even if research is conceptually and methodologically sound, we must be cautious in interpreting findings. The most common interpretive error is overgeneralization—trying to make too much of the findings. For example, suppose someone conducted a sound study and found that intercollegiate volleyball players were more independent than the norm. Should we assume that players scoring high on independence are better volleyball players? No! First, we cannot assume that independence makes a person a better volleyball player; the data are correlational. Correlations indicate a relationship, but not necessarily a cause–effect relationship. Perhaps the experience of playing volleyball leads to higher independence scores or some other factor influences both independence scores and volleyball participation. From a practical perspective, why would a coach want high independence scores? What does high independence mean in terms of actual performance or behavior in volleyball? Are high scores on independence (or any other personality factor) likely to override the influence of coaching, strategies, training, or team norms? Professionals should ask such questions and use their professional judgment when interpreting personality information.

Using Personality Measures to Screen Athletes

Despite the widely recognized issues with sport personality research, overgeneralization remains a problem. Unfortunately, some personality measures have been used to select participants, and one of the earliest sport personality measures, the AMI, is an especially notable—or notorious—example. Even if the AMI or another personality measure predicted certain behaviors, that would not justify dropping athletes. Height is related to success in volleyball; the relationship between height and volleyball success is certainly stronger and more reliable than that between any personality trait and success. Also, the relationship has a logical basis. But even given this strong, logical relationship, most coaches would not automatically select one starter over another because of a 1-inch (2.5-centimeter) height difference. Selection on the basis of personality measures is indefensible when reliable relationships are not established. Sport and exercise psychologists and all kinesiology professionals must be cautious about using and interpreting more current personality measures.

Key Point

Sport and exercise psychologists and all kinesiology professionals must be cautious in using and interpreting personality measures. Selection on the basis of personality measures is indefensible when reliable relationships are not established.

Current Personality Research in Sport and Exercise Psychology

Although global personality measures, such as the Big Five measures, are not useful for profiling athletes or predicting behavior, more recent sport and exercise psychology work helps clarify the role of those basic personality dimensions.

Several models and measures have proven particularly useful in research on health, and that work is often applied in sport and exercise psychology research and practice. Friedman and Kern (2014), in a review of personality and health, concluded that conscientiousness plays a significant role in health and well-being, and that striving and persistence are associated with health. In a related article, Hall and Fong (2013) also noted that conscientiousness is related to health behavior, including physical activity, but they also suggested that subfacets of conscientiousness, such as executive function, are better, more direct predictors of health behaviors.

Similarly, the related personality constructs of optimism, hardiness, and grit, have been linked to health outcomes and physical activity. Dispositional optimism measures, such as the Life Orientation Test (LOT; Scheier, Carver, & Bridges, 1994) and Trait Hope Scale (THS; Snyder et al., 1991), have been widely used in health psychology and behavioral medicine. See Carver, Scheier, Miller, and Fulford (2009) and Rand and Cheavens (2009) for updates on that work. Hardiness is a personality construct similar to resiliency in which people view stressful situations as challenges to overcome, remain committed, and feel in control of the situation (Kobasa, 1979). Grit is a similar personality construct that has been gaining attention in psychology and the public. Grit refers to perseverance and passion for long-term goals, characterized by strenuously working toward challenges and maintaining effort despite failure, adversity, and plateaus (Duckworth, Peterson, Matthews, & Kelly, 2007).

Optimism, hardiness, and grit, which all might fit under conscientiousness, are in line with the positive psychology movement, and related dispositional measures have been associated with positive health behavior, resiliency, and motivation. Within sport and exercise psychology, optimism and hardiness have been related to stress and coping, as well as to performance.

Rhodes (2006, 2014) has conducted the most relevant current work on personality in sport and exercise psychology, and he makes a good case for the relationship of personality (specifically the Big Five) with physical activity. Research suggests that neuroticism is negatively related to physical activity while extraversion and conscientiousness are positively related to physical activity. Extraversion includes preference for social and active settings, which is logically related to physical activity. Neuroticism reflects anxiety and depression, and the negative relationship to activity is logical. Conscientiousness, which reflects responsibility, determination, and self-discipline, logically relates to adherence to exercise and training.

Before jumping to the conclusion that highly conscientious people are more likely to stick to training and rehab programs, remember that traits are poor predictors of behavior. As Rhodes points out, the Big Five are broad, basic dimensions, and those basic dimensions are not direct predictors of behavior. The broad dimensions include several more specific facets that are more closely related to behaviors. Furthermore, Rhodes and others suggest that even those more specific facets are not direct predictors. Instead, personality dimensions or facets likely predict more specific motivational perceptions, which are the more direct predictors of physical activity behavior.

On a practical level, even if specific personality dimensions or facets were good predictors, that would not necessarily suggest interventions to match coaching or teaching styles to personalities, such as giving more direction to clients low in self-discipline. As Rhodes notes, little research on matching interventions exists, and that limited research doesn't demonstrate benefits. While targeted interventions based on personality merit investigation, at this time practicing professionals would be wise to target more direct predictors and mediators of behavior, such as perceived control or self-efficacy.

Relevant Personality Characteristics and Sport-Specific Psychological Skills

More valid and useful personality measures focus on specific, relevant characteristics and psychological skills and can be used within an interactionist perspective that considers the context of physical activity. Sport and exercise psychology consultants often assess personality to provide a guide for psychological skills training for performance enhancement and personal development. Like researchers, consultants seldom use global personality measures, but instead focus on characteristics and sport-specific skills relevant to the particular setting.

Specific Personality Constructs and Measures

As well as reexamining basic personality characteristics, such as the Big Five, researchers have used personality constructs and measures of perceived control, optimism, perfectionism, coping style, motivational orientation, and especially anxiety to help explain sport and exercise behavior. In most cases, these personality measures have been developed within conceptual frameworks that emphasize the interaction of personality with situational factors to influence behavior. Measures include both dispositional traits (e.g., trait anxiety) and more surface characteristic adaptations (e.g., values, coping strategies) from McAdams and Pals' (2006) personality model, and most have gone through considerable development and revision to be more useful in applied settings. Several sport and exercise psychology researchers have gone further to develop measures of relevant personality constructs specifically for sport and exercise settings, first and most notably in the area of anxiety.

Sport Competition Anxiety Test

Competition creates some anxiety in nearly everyone, and intense anxiety keeps people from performing well or enjoying themselves. Individual differences in competitive anxiety are obvious, and many consultants spend considerable time helping participants learn to control anxiety. Much of that work stems from Martens' (1977) competitive anxiety model and the Sport Competition Anxiety Test (SCAT), which set a model for sport-specific personality measures. Martens began with real-world observations and built upon existing psychological work following four guidelines:

• **Interaction approach**—Individual differences in competitive anxiety are easy to see, and situational factors also play a role. Close, important games create more anxiety than less important contests. Even the calmest athlete becomes anxious under some conditions. To understand competitive anxiety, we must consider the person, the situation, and the ongoing interactive process.

- **State–trait anxiety distinction**—Spielberger (1966) distinguished the relatively stable personality disposition of trait anxiety from the immediate, changeable feelings of state anxiety. Trait anxiety is the tendency to become anxious in stressful situations (a personality disposition). State anxiety is the actual state of apprehension and tension at any given moment (an emotional response). A high trait–anxious person might see an upcoming tennis match as a threat and respond with high state anxiety, whereas another might perceive it as a challenge and remain relatively calm.

- **General versus specific trait anxiety**—High trait–anxious people may not become equally anxious in all stressful situations. One person may become overly anxious in competitive sport but remain calm in academic exams. Another might never become anxious in competition but panic in social settings. Psychology researchers have demonstrated that situation-specific trait anxiety measures, such as test anxiety, predict state anxiety more accurately than more general anxiety measures in those specific settings. Following that line of thought, Martens proposed the personality construct of competitive trait anxiety, defined as "a tendency to perceive competitive situations as threatening and to respond to these situations with feelings of apprehension or tension" (1977, p. 23).

- **Competition process**—The final step places competitive anxiety within the context of the competition process. The primary situational source of anxiety in competition is evaluation. We want to do well and we worry about performing poorly. But people do not worry to the same extent. Competitive trait anxiety affects our perceptions and subsequent anxiety through the cognitive appraisal process that is central to all emotion.

Martens developed the SCAT to measure the sport-specific personality disposition of competitive trait anxiety. The SCAT has 10 items that ask people to indicate how they usually feel when competing in sport and games. On each item (e.g., "before I compete, I am nervous"), response choices are "hardly ever," "sometimes," or "often." People who score high (above the 75th percentile) tend to be quite nervous and tense in competition, whereas people with a low score probably control anxiety well and seldom choke in competition. The test items are simple and straightforward, but extensive psychometric testing indicates that those items best identify high- and low-anxious

competitors. Details on the development of the SCAT with reliability and validity data are published elsewhere (Martens, 1977; Martens, Vealey, & Burton, 1990). In brief, the SCAT meets all generally accepted standards for psychological tests, and considerable research demonstrates that it predicts state anxiety in sport competition.

Key Point

Although the SCAT meets all generally accepted standards for psychological tests, and considerable research demonstrates that it predicts state anxiety in sport competition, it remains a personality measure that should not be used without consideration of the situation and interactive processes.

The SCAT quickly became a useful personality measure in sport and exercise psychology, and Martens' extensive research set a model that others have followed in developing sport-specific measures. The SCAT, a valuable research tool, also has practical value in identifying competitors who might benefit from training in anxiety management. Still, the SCAT remains a personality measure that should not be used without considering the situation and interactive processes.

Sport Anxiety Scale

Research on competitive anxiety has progressed since Martens developed the SCAT. Multidimensional models, most often differentiating cognitive anxiety (worry) from somatic (bodily feelings) anxiety, dominate research today. Smith, Smoll, and Schutz (1990) used the multidimensional anxiety model to develop a sport-specific measure of cognitive and somatic trait anxiety, the Sport Anxiety Scale (SAS). The SAS includes two cognitive anxiety scales—worry and concentration disruption—as well as a somatic anxiety scale. In addition to providing good psychometric evidence for the SAS, Smith and colleagues (1990) reported that the concentration disruption scale was negatively related to college football players' performance. That finding suggests that multidimensional approaches may provide insights into the anxiety–performance relationship. The expanding literature that follows a multidimensional approach, discussed in later chapters on emotion, confirms the suggestion.

Perfectionism

Perfectionism has been of interest for some time, and the leading psychology researchers have extended their research to sport and exercise settings. Flett and Hewitt (2005), who developed one of the most widely used measures of perfectionism, the Multidimensional Perfectionism Scale (MPS; Hewitt & Flett, 1991), reviewed the literature on perfectionism in sport and exercise. They concluded that perfectionism is a maladaptive factor in sport and exercise that often undermines performance and fosters dissatisfaction. Although some scales and models refer to adaptive perfectionism and it seems that striving for perfection could be beneficial in sport, there is no evidence to support any benefits.

In a recent review, Hall, Jowett, and Hill (2014) suggest that perfectionism is multidimensional, encompassing achievement-related cognitions and behaviors associated with the compulsive pursuit of flawlessness. They further argue that the research demonstrates that perfectionism is not adaptive, and because of its debilitating features, professionals and participants should highlight strategies to manage perfectionism. Stoeber (2011, 2014) argues that perfectionism has a dual nature, with both negative and positive sides. Those two dimensions, perfectionistic concerns and perfectionistic strivings, have different relationships with athletes' emotion, motivation, and performance. Stoeber concurs with others that perfectionist concerns clearly are maladaptive. Perfectionistic strivings, on the other hand, may be healthy, but only when they are not accompanied by perfectionistic concerns.

Overall, the evidence provides little support for any perfectionism benefits, and in practice, the advice of Hall and colleagues (2014) to use strategies to manage perfectionism seems wise. Still, the literature leaves many questions unanswered. Further research, perhaps using sport-specific perfectionism measures (Araki & Gill, 2012; Dunn, Causgove Dunn, & Syrotuik, 2002), may help advance our understanding of perfectionism and its role in sport and exercise.

Mental Toughness

Mental toughness is prominent in early and current sport personality research, and several related measures have been developed. Unlike most other sport-specific personality constructs, mental toughness has been developed within sport and exercise psychology rather than by adapting broader constructs to sport and physical activity settings. Certainly mental toughness is related to general personality constructs, particularly to the positive constructs of optimism, hardiness, and grit. Unlike those constructs, as well as sport-specific personality constructs such as competitive trait anxiety, mental toughness is a broader construct and not clearly linked to specific behaviors. Mental toughness was discussed and assessed in early sport personality research, but we do not have a clear consensus on the construct. As Crust (2008) noted in a review, the concept of mental toughness is not new, but only recently do we find more rigorous, scientific approaches.

Mental toughness is generally viewed as a cluster of characteristics related to persistence, confidence, and performance excellence. Jones and colleagues (2002) described mental toughness as the natural or developed psychological edge that enables you to cope better than your opponents with the many demands that sport places on a performer, and specifically, to be more consistent and better than your opponents in remaining determined, focused, confident, and in control under pressure (Jones, Hanton, & Connaughton, 2002, p. 209). Some (e.g., Jones, Hanton, & Connaughton, 2007) describe mental toughness as multidimensional; others suggest that given the overlap in the constructs and related measures, mental toughness is best considered unidimensional.

The conceptualization of mental toughness as a cluster of characteristics related to confidence, consistency, perseverance, and resilience suggests links with optimism (confidence), hardiness (resilience), girt (perseverance), and the characteristics encompassed by conscientiousness. Given the breadth and overlap with more established personality constructs, Anderson (2011) suggests that mental toughness is old wine in new bottles, and questions its value for sport and exercise psychology. Still, even if not new, this cluster of characteristics seems particularly relevant to sport and exercise psychology, and several researchers have developed measures based on the literature that show good psychometric properties (Gucciardi, Gordon, & Dimmock, 2009; Madrigal, Hamill, & Gill, 2013). Studies have also found logical relationships of mental toughness with related constructs of optimism and hardiness, as well as relationships with stress and coping, and with performance (Nicholls, Polman, Levy, & Backhouse, 2008; Sheard & Golby, 2006).

Many other sport and exercise psychology researchers have developed sport-specific measures for use in research and practice. Several measures have been developed that relate to motivational orientation, and we cover those measures within the chapters on motivation.

Sport-Specific Psychological Skills Measures

In one of the first attempts to assess the psychological skills of elite athletes, Mahoney and Avener used interviews, surveys, and observations at the tryouts for the 1976 U.S. Olympic gymnastics team. Their study (1977) on Olympic qualifiers and nonqualifiers showed that qualifiers were more self-confident, were more likely to think and dream about gymnastics, were more likely to use self-talk and internal mental imagery, and were able to control worry and concentrate on the task at the time of performance.

Others replicated many of these findings, especially the higher confidence of more successful athletes (Gould, Weiss, & Weinberg, 1981; Highlen & Bennett, 1979; Meyers, Cooke, Cullen, & Liles, 1979); and, as the chapters on emotion relate, the ability to control anxiety seems to characterize successful performers. The work did not establish a personality profile for elite athletes; nevertheless, the initial findings encouraged similar investigations and set a direction for sport personality research.

Mahoney and colleagues continued their investigations of psychological skills and used the results to develop the Psychological Skills Inventory for Sports (PSIS; Mahoney, Gabriel, & Perkins, 1987). The PSIS parallels the skills identified in earlier work, with subscales for concentration, anxiety control, confidence, mental preparation,

motivation, and team emphasis. Mahoney and colleagues (1987) assessed several groups of athletes and also asked several sport psychologists to describe the ideal athlete on the PSIS measure. As expected, elite athletes reported stronger psychological skills than did the pre-elite and nonelite athletes, providing some validity evidence for the PSIS. Specifically, elite athletes

- experienced fewer problems with anxiety,
- were more successful at deploying their concentration,
- were more self-confident,
- relied more on internally referenced and kinesthetic mental preparation,
- were more focused on their own performance than that of the team, and
- were more highly motivated to do well in their sport.

Still, the elite athletes' self-reports were not quite up to the ideal athlete profiles provided by the sport psychologists; the ideal athlete was stronger on psychological skills, suggesting that even elite athletes have varying psychological strengths and can benefit from continued mental training.

Although the PSIS and initial comparisons among athletes provide information, caution is in order. The sample presented several confounds, and Mahoney and colleagues cautioned readers not to draw solid conclusions from preliminary results with measures lacking psychometric testing. Subsequent work by Chartrand, Jowdy, and Danish (1992) revealed problems with the PSIS and confirmed these cautions.

Other measures of psychological skills for sport fare better. Smith, Schutz, Smoll, and Ptacek (1995) developed and validated a multidimensional measure of sport-specific psychological skills, the Athletic Coping Skills Inventory (ACSI), as part of a project on coping with athletic injury. The ACSI assesses psychological skills similar to those assessed with the PSIS, but it has superior psychometric properties. The 28-item ACSI contains seven subscales:

- Coping with adversity
- Peaking under pressure
- Goal setting and mental preparation
- Concentration
- Freedom from worry
- Confidence and achievement motivation
- Coachability

Smith and colleagues (1995) demonstrated the factorial validity of the seven ACSI subscales, which can be summed to yield a score for personal coping resources. They also provided evidence for validity of the ACSI in measuring personal coping resources as a multifaceted construct with seven facets of underlying coping skills.

Thomas, Murphy, and Hardy (1999) developed the Test of Performance Strategies (TOPS), which, similar to the ACSI, is a self-report measure of psychological skills and strategies used by athletes. Thomas and colleagues provided evidence supporting the reliability and validity of eight subscales each for practice and competition. The subscales are similar, reflecting common underlying skills; but in competition, negative thinking replaced attention control as a factor, with attention control linked to emotional control. The TOPS subscales are as follows:

- Goal setting
- Relaxation
- Activation
- Imagery
- Self-talk
- Emotional control
- Automaticity
- Attention control (practice) and negative thinking (competition)

Both the ACSI and TOPS have been used in research and in applied mental training with athletes. As Woodcock, Duda, Cumming, Sharp, and Halland (2012) point out, when using measures such as TOPS to monitor skill development, it is important to consider not only the properties of the measure, but also the athlete or client cognitive processing and the demand characteristics of the setting to obtain valid results. That advice reflects the importance of individualizing (consider individual skills, needs, preferences) and contextualizing (consider the setting, culture) when consulting or engaging in any professional practice. Another technique often used to assess and monitor individual psychological skills in professional practice is performance profiling.

Performance profiling (Butler & Hardy, 1992) is a technique that can help individuals identify and assess psychological skills, such as those measured with the ACSI or TOPS. Performance profiling is not a personality measure with established psychological characteristics or skills. Rather than complete an inventory, an individual or a team, perhaps with the guidance of a consultant, first identifies relevant psychological skills and characteristics (physical skills could also be identified) for their sport or activity. Those skills are used as labels for segments on a circle (as in the example in figure 4.3). Individuals then rate themselves on each skill by filling in segments to create a profile or visual representation of their strengths and potential areas for improvement. We created the profile in figure 4.3, assuming that we were a quidditch team (as in the Harry Potter universe). We first identified six relevant psychological skills or characteristics (listed around the outside). Then, for the example, we rated the overall team (rather than individuals) on each skill. In this case, we rated our team high on teamwork and communication, about average on imagination, and lower on dedication and concentration. Performance profiling is one way to engage participants in the process of psychological skill development while also connecting the person and the situation in the given physical activity context. Gucciardi and Gordon (2009), in a review, note that profiling has been useful in increasing self-awareness and facilitating goal setting, communication, and interactions in coaching and consulting. They also suggest that profiling could be more effective by incorporating more of the personal construct psychology tenets that emphasize eliciting the athlete's personal views of the relevant constructs and their importance and use for that athlete.

Key Point

Performance profiling, which involves people identifying and rating themselves on relevant psychological skills, is one way to engage participants in the process of psychological skill development.

Sport psychology consultants continue to work on assessment, and many use the ACSI, TOPS, or alternative measures in applied work. Some personality comparisons have been confirmed in other research. Self-confidence, in particular, clearly relates to success in athletics and to successful performance of many sport and exercise behaviors. We explore self-confidence in greater detail in chapter 6. Similarly, concentration, emotional control, and mental preparation (e.g., imagery, goal setting) are consistently identified as important psychological skills for sport and exercise participants. When we cover those topics in later chapters, we highlight the critical role of individual differences.

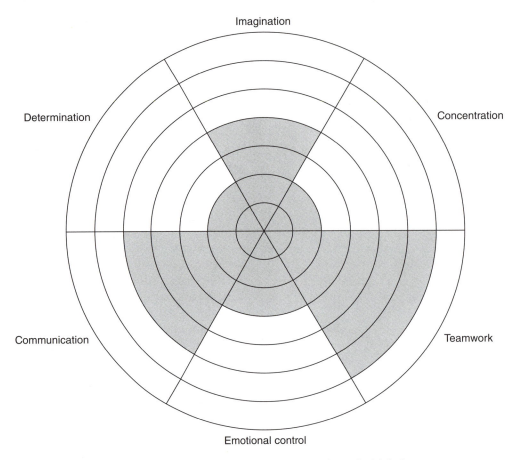

Figure 4.3   Performance profiling example. Team profile for a Quidditch team.

Putting It Into Practice

Summary

Personality is the overall pattern of psychological characteristics that make each person unique. Individual differences are obvious in physical activity settings, and personality plays a key role in nearly all sport and exercise behaviors. The vast research on personality, conducted throughout the history of sport and exercise psychology, has yielded little useful information; global personality measures are poor predictors of specific sport and exercise behaviors. This summary has changed little since the original 1986 edition of this text. However, sport and exercise psychology has advanced greatly in the understanding of individual differences. Those advances involve more specific characteristics and psychological skills, sport-specific measures, and more clearly delineated relationships among individual differences, situational factors, and specific behaviors. We continue to look at many of these specific personality–behavior relationships in later chapters.

Review Questions

1. What is personality?
2. Describe the Big Five model of personality and list the dimensions.
3. Describe Morgan's mental health model, as well as related sport and exercise psychology research.

4. Discuss the advantages of sport-specific personality measures for research and practice, using the SCAT as an example.

5. Describe performance profiling and discuss its use with sport and exercise participants.

Recommended Reading

- McAdams, D.P., & Pals, J.L. (2006). A new Big Five: Fundamental principles for an integrative science of personality. *American Psychologist, 61,* 204-217. McAdams and Pals' article gives an overview of their model, which goes beyond traditional personality perspectives to provide a comprehensive framework for understanding the whole person.

- Rhodes, R.E. (2006). The built-in environment: The role of personality in physical activity. *Exercise and Sport Sciences Reviews, 34,* 83-88. Rhodes provides a good review of the role of personality in physical activity. Although Rhodes cites research supporting relationships between the Big Five dimensions and physical activity, he also points out that these dimensions are not direct predictors, and it important to consider more specific motives and cognitions.

- Smith, R.E., Schutz, R.W, Smoll, F.L., & Ptacek, J.T. (1995). Development and validation of a multidimensional measure of sport-specific psychological skills: The Athletic Coping Skills Inventory-28. *Journal of Sport and Exercise Psychology, 17,* 379-398. Those who work directly with athletes find sport-specific measures much more helpful than global personality measures. Smith and colleagues have developed one of the stronger measures of sport-specific skills, the ACSI-28.

LAB

Performance Profile

For this lab you are to complete your performance profile for a specific activity and then answer the questions about your profile.

1. Identify psychological skills for your sport or activity. First, list the important psychological qualities or skills in your sport or activity (e.g., focus, goal setting, imagery, confidence). Brainstorm. There are no right or wrong answers, but you should try to list at least 10. Review the list, and select the six most important skills. List them in the table in the Performance Profile Worksheet in no specific order. Also write them around the outside of the blank performance profile. You should have one item or skill for each piece or segment of the profile.

2. Rate yourself on the six psychological skills. Use the scale of 1 (low) to 7 (high) and rate your ability on each of the six skills you listed in the table on the worksheet. Record your ratings in the table next to each skill.

3. Complete the profile by filling in your ratings on each segment of the profile. Use the blank performance profile (with your six skills listed around the circle). Starting from the inside of the circle and working outward, fill in each piece of the medal to match your rating. For example, if you rated yourself a 6 on self-confidence, fill in six lines within that piece of the profile. (See the example in figure 4.3.)

4. Answer the questions on your performance profile.

Performance Profile Worksheet

Name your chosen sport or activity: _____

Complete the Psychological Skills or Qualities Chart

List the six most important skills for your chosen activity in the table, then rate your ability from 1 (none or very low) to 7 (very high), with 4 meaning average, for each skill.

Psychological skills or qualities	Rating

Complete the Performance Profile

List the six most important skills around the outside of the circle, one for each segment; then fill in the segment to indicate your 1 to 7 rating for each.

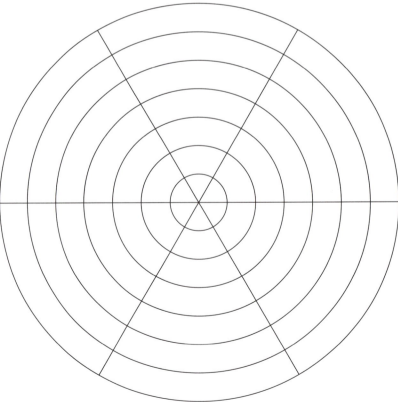

Questions on your Performance Profile

Answer the following questions after you have completed your profile.

1. What are your psychological strengths and weaknesses? Why do you rate yourself stronger or weaker in these areas?

2. How does your profile (strengths and weaknesses) affect your performance and behavior in your activity (e.g., how do you use your strengths or compensate for weaknesses)?

3. How could you use your profile to improve your psychological skills and performance in your activity (e.g., how could you use your strengths or develop stronger skills)?

From D.L. Gill, L. Williams, and E. Reifsteck, 2017, *Psychological Dynamics of Sport and Exercise,* 4th ed. (Champaign, IL: Human Kinetics).

Chapter 5

Attention and Cognitive Skills

Chapter Objectives

After studying this chapter, you should be able to

- define attention and describe individual differences in attentional style,

- discuss sport and exercise psychology research on attention and expertise,

- describe several attentional control and concentration techniques, and

- explain the use of imagery in psychological skills training.

Attention and cognitive skills are prominent in sport and exercise psychology research and practice. Most kinesiology professionals and sport psychology consultants devote considerable time to cognitive skills and strategies. You often hear professionals saying "Concentrate" and "Focus" in fitness clubs and physical education classes. Coaches tell 10-year-olds, "Keep your eye on the ball," and Olympic divers use imagery to mentally perform the dive while standing on the platform. Individual differences in attention and cognitive skills are obvious. Some 10-year-olds are better than others at keeping their eye on the ball. Diver Greg Louganis reported that imagery helped him perform, but other athletes find imagery to be more trouble than help.

Cognitive skills, such as the ability to focus, have clear implications for performance and behavior. To date, interest in and use of cognitive skills have outpaced the related research, but research is beginning to address many questions about the role of attention and cognition in sport and exercise behavior.

Attention Models and Perspectives

As many sport and exercise psychology scholars (Abernethy, Maxwell, Masters, van der Kamp, & Jackson, 2007; Boutcher, 2008; Essig, Janelle, Borgo, & Koester, 2014) have noted, interest in attention is at least as old as experimental psychology itself. In *The Principles of Psychology*, William James (1890) described attention as follows:

> Everyone knows what attention is. It is taking possession by the mind, in clear and vivid form, of one out of what seems several simultaneously possible objects or trains of thought. Focalization, concentration or consciousness are its essence. It implies withdrawal from some things in order to deal effectively with others. (pp. 403-404)

We still understand attention much as James described it, but today's cognitive psychologists have more to say about attention, learning, and memory for motor skills.

Boutcher (2008) categorized the literature on attention and performance into three perspectives—information processing, social psychological, and psychophysiological—but advocated a synthesis of the three perspectives for research and practice. Indeed, current research on atten-

Key Point

Attention is "taking possession by the mind, in clear and vivid form, of one out of what seems several simultaneously possible objects or trains of thought" (James, 1890, pp. 403-404).

tion incorporates multiple perspectives and is not so easily classified. In the next section, we cover Nideffer's attentional model and related research on attentional styles, which Boutcher considered social psychological. Nideffer's model promoted early research and application in sport psychology. As later sections reveal, research on attention and performance has advanced in many directions since then.

Nideffer's Attentional Model

Attentional style came to the attention of sport and exercise psychology largely through the work of Robert Nideffer (1976a), who proposed a two-dimensional model of attention. Width ranges from narrow to broad, focusing on a limited or wide range of cues. Direction may be internal, focused on one's own thoughts and feelings, or it may be external, focused on objects and events outside the body.

Combining width and direction gives us four types of attention: broad–internal, broad–external, narrow–external, and narrow–internal. Each of the four types is effective for particular situations or tasks, and using the appropriate attentional focus can enhance performance.

- A *broad–internal* focus is an analytical style useful for planning strategies or analyzing previous performances; coaches and teachers often need a broad–internal style.

- Many activities, especially highly interactive team sports and games, call for a *broad–external* attentional style, which involves taking in a great deal of information. A quarterback trying to pick out secondary receivers or a child trying to keep track of everyone in a game could use a broad–external focus.

- A *narrow–external* focus is useful for activities requiring concentration on a target, such as archery or bowling, or focusing on a spot to maintain balance in yoga.

- A *narrow–internal* focus is appropriate for mentally rehearsing a task, and focusing on internal body sensations may be helpful for distance running or weightlifting.

Although all attentional focuses are useful, problems arise when people rely too heavily on one style or use a style inappropriately. Most activities require shifting of attention. For example, a soccer goalie might use a broad–external focus in preparing for a shot, shift to a narrow–external focus to make the save, and use some broad–internal analysis to set up the shift to the offense.

Attentional style and the ability to use varying styles effectively are part of personality, although they are more "surface" and changeable than more basic personality traits. Nideffer (1976b) developed the Test of Attentional and Interpersonal Style (TAIS) in order to assess individual differences in attentional style. Nideffer provided preliminary information on the reliability and validity of the TAIS, and some initial work suggested that attentional styles relate to performance and behavior. However, continued research challenges the value of the TAIS.

Van Schoyck and Grasha (1981) developed a tennis-specific version (T-TAIS) that was more reliable and more consistently related to tennis scores than the TAIS. Dewey, Brawley, and Allard (1989) reported that TAIS subscores did not relate to behavioral tests of attention as expected, casting further doubt on the validity of the measure. These studies also raised questions about Nideffer's model. Van Schoyck and Grasha (1981) supported the width (narrow–broad) but not the direction (internal–external) dimension. Instead, they described a bandwidth dimension with two components, scanning and focusing. Landers (1981) concluded that the TAIS does not differentiate attentional direction, is a poor predictor of performance, and has limited value in sport.

Attentional Style and Performance

One of the most widely cited works on attentional style and performance is Morgan and Pollock's (1977) study of marathon runners. Many runners use a dissociative style, which means they focus on external objects or thoughts, perhaps replaying the day's events or playing songs in their minds—they focus on anything other than running and internal sensations. Surprisingly, elite marathoners did not use dissociation but instead reported using an associative strategy. They focused on their breathing, paid attention to the feelings in

their leg muscles, adopted an internal focus, and monitored their bodily sensations.

Morgan and Pollock's observations were widely cited to support the claim that an associative or narrow–internal focus is desirable for endurance events. However, Morgan and Pollock did not claim that association is advantageous for all runners at all times, and other evidence argues against such a blanket conclusion. In our study (Gill & Strom, 1985), female athletes performed an endurance task for as many repetitions as possible using either a narrow–internal focus on feelings in their legs or a narrow–external focus on a collage of pictures. Not only did the external focus lead to more repetitions, but nearly all participants preferred that style. Our study is not unique; Morgan's own research (Morgan, 1981; Morgan, Horstman, Cymerman, & Stokes, 1983) revealed that dissociation resulted in superior performance on a treadmill task, and that even elite marathoners sometimes use dissociation while running. Dissociation may reduce perceptions of pain or fatigue and help a performer keep going, as in jogging or training tasks. However, elite runners usually have goals (time or place) beyond simply maintaining performance. The runners in Morgan and Pollock's study apparently monitored bodily sensations to pace themselves and achieve performance goals.

Schomer (1987) had runners use two-way radios to report attentional focus during their runs. Content analysis confirmed that runners used both association and dissociation, with considerable variation during the run. Silva and Applebaum (1989) reported similar results based on retrospective reports of Olympic trial marathoners. Smith, Gill, Crews, Hopewell, and Morgan (1995) found that the most economical distance runners reported less use of dissociation and more use of relaxation than the least economical runners, but they did not differ in use of association. The results suggest that although relaxation strategies may benefit runners, association per se is not the source of the benefits.

More recently, Lind, Welch, and Ekkekakis (2009) found no consistent results, and Brick, MacIntyre, and Campbell (2014) stated that after more than 35 years, research on attentional focus in endurance activity is still mired in lack of consensus. They further argued that traditional approaches (such as the Nideffer model and association–dissociation classification) should be discarded for more dynamic cognitive frameworks. They cited Stevinson and Biddle's (1998) suggestion that both association (monitoring) and dissociation (distraction) can be internal or external and suggested further differentiations within those styles, such as between sensory monitoring and self-regulation and between pacing and cadence. Brick and coauthors also suggested using other models, such as the parallel processing model of pain advocated by Brewer and Buman (2006) and the mindfulness approach (Salmon, Hanneman, & Harwood, 2010) to gain insight into attention and endurance performance. Continuing investigations, with more flexible models and approaches, may help us understand how varying individual attentional styles interact with situational factors to influence sport performance and exercise behavior, as well as how more effective attentional styles might be developed through instructions, training, or experiences.

Boutcher (2008) advocated a multilevel, integrated model with the individual, environment, and behavior in continual, dynamic interaction, which reflects the general approach to sport and exercise behavior described in part I. Attentional processes are multidimensional and relationships with performance are complex. As Boutcher suggests, research that takes a multidimensional approach may be more relevant than focusing on simple models of attentional style. Fortunately, several scholars in sport and exercise psychology are incorporating more current cognitive psychology and psychophysiological approaches.

Mindfulness and Flow

Mindfulness, which is a form of attention, is increasingly popular in psychology and health research, as well as in professional practice. Mindfulness has also captured public attention; it was the cover story in the February 3, 2014 *Time* magazine. As Brick and colleagues (2014) suggested, a mindfulness perspective can add to our understanding of attention, and increasingly professionals are finding that including mindfulness training or mindful exercise, such as yoga or tai chi, can benefit participants. According to Kabat-Zinn (2005), who brought mindfulness to public and researchers' attention, mindfulness involves "an open-hearted, moment-to-moment, non-judgmental awareness" (p. 24). Thus, mindfulness is a type of attention, but mindfulness is not at all like the attentional styles in Nideffer's model, or attentional processing. With mindfulness, attention is not directed at anything and

there is no attentional processing. Instead, attention is passive, present, and nonjudgmental. Mindful attention is in the present, not thinking about past errors or what might happen in the future, which can be distracting and anxiety provoking and interfere with movements. Mindful, nonjudgmental, present attention is just as important for clients in exercise programs as for sport performers. For example, if your client who is recovering from anterior cruciate ligament surgery is thinking about how he got injured, or what he is going to do when he gets back to the team, he is not focused on doing the exercises to get through rehab successfully.

Mindfulness has many health benefits in addition to attentional control, and increasingly coaches, teachers, and exercise professionals are incorporating mindfulness and mindful exercise into their programs. Attention is the key aspect of mindfulness, and mindfulness also can be part of emotional control or stress management, as we discuss in the chapters on emotion and stress management. Not only does adding mindfulness to sport and exercise programs help with those programs, but the attentional and emotional control skills will also be useful for your clients and students in their everyday life.

Flow, a popular topic in sport and exercise psychology, is often described as being fully involved in the activity without conscious awareness. Thus, flow involves a type of attention that is much like mindfulness. As discussed in a later chapter on emotion, flow is of interest in sport and exercise psychology because it is associated with peak performance, optimal experience, and enjoyment. Much of the sport and exercise psychology research on flow (e.g., see Jackson & Kimiecik, 2008) emphasizes cognitive processes related to the flow state, and here we specifically consider the connection between mindful attention and flow. Ahearn, Moran, and Lonsdale (2011) cited the obvious conceptual similarity between mindfulness and flow (both constructs emphasize nonjudgmental focus on the present moment), and reasoned that mindfulness training might facilitate the flow state in athletes. They found that athletes who participated in mindfulness training increased in flow state experiences at follow-up whereas a control group of athletes did not change. Although this was a small study, their findings suggest that mindfulness training is a promising approach for helping athletes, or any participants in our physical activity programs, enhance their physical activity experience.

Research on Attentional Processes

As Boutcher noted, most of the research on attention in sport and exercise psychology has taken the information-processing perspective and draws heavily on cognitive psychology, although neuropsychology and psychophysiological perspectives are coming on strong. Much of the literature focuses on the main attentional processes of attentional selectivity, capacity, and alertness.

- Attentional selectivity is the ability to selectively attend to certain cues, events, or thoughts while disregarding others. James (1890) recognized the importance of selective attention, and attentional selectivity is a key skill in sport and exercise.

- Attentional capacity refers to limits in the amount of information that a person can process at one time. We can't attend to two things or think two thoughts at exactly the same time. Cognitive psychology theories differ on mechanisms and explanations, but all point to limited capacity. For example, listening for both the starter's gun and a coach's command could strain capacity and interfere with performance.

- Attentional alertness refers to the influence of emotion and arousal on information processing and attention. Increases in arousal tend to narrow attention and affect physiological as well as cognitive processes.

The three attentional processes are interrelated—because of attentional capacity, attention must be selective, and arousal or alertness affects processing. Attentional processes are especially important in learning and performance of motor skills, and considerable research in cognitive psychology, motor behavior, and sport psychology focuses on control and automatic processing.

Control and Automatic Processing

Control processing, or conscious thought (as when a golfer decides which club to use), is deliberate, slow, and effortful. Automatic processing, which typically occurs with well-learned skills, is fast, effortless, and not under conscious control. Although control processing requires great attention and effort, automatic processing does not and thus is not so limited by attentional capacity.

Skilled performers do complex tasks that would be impossible if they had to consciously process all information. As we learn and perfect skills, control processing gives way to automatic processing and effortless skilled performance. Professionals working with people who are learning and practicing skills must consider the implications of capacity limits to help them advance to more automatic skilled performance.

Key Point

Control processing is deliberate, slow, and effortful. Automatic processing, which typically occurs with well-learned skills, is fast, effortless, and not under conscious control. Although control processing requires great attention, effort, and awareness, automatic processing does not and thus is not so limited by attentional capacity.

As Coleman Griffith observed in his interview with football star Red Grange (see chapter 2), elite athletes often make skilled moves without thinking. More recently, Beilock and colleagues (Beilock & Carr, 2001; Beilock, Wierenga, & Carr, 2003) referred to expertise-induced amnesia to describe experts' tendency to remember less detail of a specific performance (episodic memory) due to automated processing. As Beilock and Carr (2001) confirmed, events that make the experts think about what they're doing can disrupt automatic processing and impair performance; this is popularly called "paralysis by analysis" and is one explanation for choking under pressure. Beilock and Gray (2007) are continuing to investigate the role of cognitive processes in performance and have extended the work in many directions. For a very readable and informative overview of Beilock's extensive work, read her 2010 book, *Choke*.

Beilock's work is in line with the work of several motor behavior scholars who have looked at the the role of attention and cognition in the learning and performance of motor tasks and sport skills. The work of Wulf and colleagues (Wulf, 2012, 2014) on attentional focus is particularly relevant. That research distinguishes an external attentional focus on the intended movement effect from an internal focus on body movements. Overall, findings from several studies confirm the superiority of an external focus of attention. Beilock and others suggest that experts use automatic processing, which is similar to the external focus. Wulf's work suggests that an external focus, which takes attention away from the processes of movement (control processing), is beneficial even when people are learning new skills and for people of different ages and skill levels. As Wulf suggests, focusing on the movement outcome promotes automaticity and facilitates learning.

Psychophysiological Approaches

Some motor behavior and sport psychology researchers have adopted a psychophysiological perspective to explore attention and performance. More specifically, researchers have used several psychophysiological and neuroscience techniques to look at the brain and cognitive processing in relation to performance and behavior. As Essig and colleagues (2014) noted, rapid advances in instrumentation have allowed researchers to identify underlying neural mechanisms of attention and provide a "window to the mind." Such techniques include heart rate, gaze, electroencephalogram (EEG) and functional magnetic resonance imaging (fMRI). These advances have led to the merging of psychophysiological perspectives with information processing and attentional focus research, and cognitive psychology is much more neuroscience today. Sport and exercise psychology researchers looking at attention have increasingly incorporated psychophysiological measures to gain greater understanding of attention and cognitive processing in sport and exercise.

Early research taking a psychophysiological approach looked at EEG and heart rate patterns in relation to performance. Hatfield, Landers, and Ray (1984) assessed right- and left-brain EEG activity of elite rifle shooters and found systematic patterns suggesting that these performers reduced unnecessary conscious mental activity of the left hemisphere at the time of the shot. Landers, Christina, Hatfield, Doyle, and Daniels (1980) found heart rate deceleration in elite shooters just before the shot, and subsequent studies showed similar deceleration on a golf putting task (Boutcher & Zinsser, 1990; Crews & Landers, 1991).

Hatfield and Kerick (2007) reviewed the increasingly sophisticated research showing that experienced performers allocate specific neural resources to the task and reduce irrelevant processing. They also cited newer research using fMRI that is providing greater insight into how anxiety and tension may affect neural processes that disrupt attention. Research findings with EEG readings and fMRI images may seem far removed from practical application, but Hatfield and Kerick make that connection. As they point out, research overwhelmingly confirms that high-level performance is marked by economy of brain activity that underlies mental processes. Given that, coaching and instruction should be clear and simple and should focus on correct movement skills. Focus on correct moves rather than reducing mistakes, and use reinforcement rather than punishment. As we discuss in the chapter on behavioral motivation, there are many reasons to emphasize reinforcement rather than punishment, and this research adds a neurophysiological rationale. Research continues to advance our understanding of brain–behavior links, and sophisticated measures have advanced our understanding of gaze behavior and expertise as discussed in the following section.

Attention and Expertise

Operating from an information-processing perspective and using a paradigm that originated with studies of chess experts (Chase & Simon, 1973), several sport and exercise psychology and motor behavior scholars have examined individual differences and cognitive processes in sport expertise and motor performance. For example, in one of the early studies, Allard, Graham, and Paarsalu (1980) found that basketball players were better than nonplayers at remembering slides from structured (basketball) situations but not unstructured situations, confirming Chase and Simon's findings that experts have better recall accuracy for specific game situations. Subsequent studies revealed similar perceptual and cognitive superiority for experts in field hockey, volleyball, and many other sports.

Studies using occlusion techniques with varied sport tasks (Abernethy et al., 2007; Abernethy & Russell, 1987) indicate that advance cues (e.g., racket position) can help predict ball flight, that experts are better at picking up this advance information, and that differences relate to selective attention. McPherson took a different approach and used verbal protocols to examine the role of knowledge and tactical decision making. McPherson's research with tennis players (McPherson, 2000; McPherson & Kernodle, 2003) indicates that experts have a greater declarative (knowing what to do) and procedural (doing it) knowledge base, and they have action plan profiles in memory to match current conditions, allowing them to make superior tactical decisions.

Janet Starkes and Anders Ericsson, who have each done much research on attention and expertise, compiled an excellent text with chapters by many leading researchers (Starkes & Ericsson, 2003); overall, that research confirms that experts demonstrate superior attentional skills and use more automatic processing. Abernethy and coauthors (2007) provide more detail on that research.

Quiet Eye

Joan Vickers has been conducting research related to attention and cognition in kinesiology for several years, and her work on the so-called quiet eye is particularly relevant. As discussed in her 2007 book, the quiet eye has four characteristics: It is directed to a critical location or object in the performance space, its onset occurs before the final movement of the skill, its duration tends to be longer for elite performers, and it is stable, confirming the need for an optimal focus before the final execution of the skill.

Vickers uses sophisticated eye-tracking technology in her research to monitor gaze and visual attention. She first identified the quiet eye with basketball free throw shooters (Vickers, 1996), and since then the quiet eye has been found in expert performers in several sports by several researchers. For a real-world sport example, read Vickers' January 2004 *Golf Digest* article, where she refers to lab research demonstrating that the quiet eye differentiates good and poor putters. Good putters fixate on the back of the ball where the putter will contact it. They use rapid shifts of gaze to connect the contact point to the spot on the golf hole and then maintain that quiet eye fixation for 2 or 3 seconds. Poorer putters are unable to maintain the quiet eye and have a more erratic gaze.

Considerable research has accumulated since Vickers began, and that research, using increasingly sophisticated measures and methods, supports the quiet eye findings. In a meta-analytic review of perceptual–cognitive skill in sport, Mann, Williams, Ward, and Janelle (2007) confirmed systematic differences in visual search behaviors, with experts using fewer fixations of longer duration, including prolonged quiet eye periods, compared with nonexperts. Not only have several researchers found the quiet eye associated with better performance, but studies have found that quiet eye training can improve performance. Both Vine and Wilson (2010) and Moore, Vine, Freeman, and Wilson (2013) found

that quiet eye training improved performance in novice golfers.

As Vickers suggests, attentional control and cognitive processing of the quiet eye are important not only for expert sport performance, but also in everyday skills like locomotion and in dealing with attentional disorders such as attention-deficit hyperactivity disorder (ADHD). See Vickers (2016) for an excellent review of the quiet eye research.

Development of Expertise

As well as examining differences between experts and nonexperts, sport and exercise psychology researchers have focused on the development of expertise. Several studies suggest that expertise and related cognitive skills are developed and that training may help. As Starkes and Ericsson (2003) and others report, and as popularized in Malcolm Gladwell's 2008 book *Outliers*, consistent research indicates that expertise is developed over 10 years or 10,000 hours of deliberate practice. The specific 10,000-hour criterion has been debated, and it may vary across activities and contexts, but scholars agree that deliberate practice, which is highly structured with increasing challenge and activities explicitly designed to improve performance, is the key to expertise. Research also suggests that with training, novices can become more like experts. Perceptual training is used successfully with many skilled professionals, such as pilots and surgeons, and some researchers have tested similar programs with sport performers. Williams, Ward, and Chapman (2003) found that novice field hockey goalkeepers who received perceptual training improved their decision time over those who did not receive such training.

Chambers and Vickers (2006) applied Vickers' decision-training model to investigate coaches' feedback and swimmers' times and technique. Decision training emphasizes bandwidth feedback; that is, rather than receiving precise feedback on every trial, performers receive feedback only when performance is outside a larger bandwidth. Bandwidth feedback is effective, particularly in transfer and retention. Based on related research, the combination of bandwidth feedback and questioning by instructors should promote active learning, problem solving, performance awareness, confidence, and control. Chambers and Vickers indeed found greater gains in technique and more improved times during transfer, suggesting that bandwidth feedback and questioning have positive effects on performance, coach–athlete relationships, and overall development.

Development and training bring up questions related to youth sport and early specialization. Côté and colleagues' developmental perspective on expertise is particularly relevant (Côté, Baker, & Abernethy, 2003, 2007; Soberlak & Côté, 2003). These researchers confirm that deliberate practice is important in the development of expertise, but that play has an important role in development, and they caution against overly early specialization and structured practice. Their research indicates that experts spend more time in deliberate play from ages 6 to 14 but emphasize multiple activities and do not shift the majority of time to deliberate practice until later. Côté and associates (2003) conclude as follows:

> Early sport diversification, high amounts of deliberate play, child-centered coaches and parents, and being around peers who are involved in sport all appear to be essential characteristics of environments for young children that encourage their later investment in deliberate practice. (p. 110)

Baker and Young (2014) reviewed 20 years of research on deliberate practice and the development of expertise. They confirmed the importance of deliberate practice, but noted gaps in the literature and the need for stronger research designs.

Based on a review of the related literature, the International Society of Sport Psychology developed a position stand (Côté, Lidor, & Hackfort, 2009) that calls for early sampling in childhood as the base for both elite and recreational sport. That statement sets forth seven postulates on the role of sampling and deliberate play, as opposed to specialization and deliberate practice, during childhood to promote continued participation and elite performance in sport.

Attentional Control Strategies

As discussed in the preceding sections, attention and cognition are key aspects of sport and exercise behaviors, and the development and use of cognitive skills can enhance physical activity experiences. This section focuses on strategies for attention and thought control, and in the next section we turn to imagery, one of the most popular cognitive techniques. Nideffer's (1976a) model of attentional styles is the basis for some popular attentional control interventions, and Nideffer himself was among the first to use cognitive interventions in sport psychology. This section includes Nideffer's (1993) attentional control training as well as self-talk and cognitive restructuring techniques.

Attentional Control and Concentration

Concentration implies control of attention. Instructors often tell participants, "Keep your eye on the ball" or "Focus on the feelings." As with most psychological skills, it is much easier to tell someone to concentrate than to convey how to do it. Concentration is not an innate ability but a skill acquired through training and practice.

Nideffer (1993) proposed that people can improve their ability to use and shift attentional

Application Point

Developing Sport Experts

Research indicates that deliberate practice is important, and many people believe that early specialization in a sport is necessary to develop expertise. Considering the research on youth development and sport expertise, how would you advise youth sport coaches and parents who want to start young children on the path to becoming sport experts?

styles through ACT. Attentional control training includes the technique of centering, which involves relaxing the muscles, breathing deeply, and focusing on feelings with exhalation. This training also involves assessing individual attentional strengths and weaknesses, the attentional demands of the sport, and the situation and personal characteristics that affect behavior, and then developing an intervention program. Attentional control training requires instruction and practice, but there are many simpler concentration strategies that are also useful.

Williams, Nideffer, Wilson, and Sagal (2015) highlight ACT and also describe several strategies that physical activity participants could easily use. These strategies, listed next, are grouped as external (avoiding distractions) or internal (staying centered). Williams and colleagues refer to athletics, but these strategies can also be applied to children in physical education, adults in fitness programs, or clients in rehabilitation programs.

External Strategies to Minimize Distraction

- Dress rehearsal. Dress rehearsal, with such elements as music, uniforms, announcements, and lights matching competition conditions, is particularly effective.

- Rehearsal of simulated competition experiences. As with dress rehearsal, athletes practice concentrating and dissociating from disruptive stimuli. Simulated competition might involve tapes of competition sounds or crowd noises.

- Mental rehearsal. Mental rehearsal, visualization, and imagery are some of the most widely used and useful cognitive strategies. Imagery, which is covered in more detail in the next section, may be used for controlling attention and practicing concentration.

Internal Strategies to Stay Focused

- Attentional cues and triggers. Many athletes use verbal or kinesthetic cues to focus concentration or retrigger lost concentration. For example, a free throw shooter may focus on the rim, or a swimmer might focus on the feel of the hand pulling through the water.

- Centering. Centering is helpful in controlling emotion and focusing on relevant cues. Centering is a conscious process in which you adjust weight around your center of mass (the intersection of a line from head to toe, with a horizontal line that has half your weight above and half below) to feel centered and in control.

- Tic-toc. Tic is any thought that is irrelevant to what you need to do (e.g., thinking about the previous event). Switch to toc—actions needed right now.

- Turning failure into success. With this strategy, participants mentally rehearse a successful performance immediately after a failure. After a disastrous free exercise routine, for instance, a gymnast might immediately visualize the great routine of the previous meet.

- Biofeedback. Biofeedback (e.g., EEG) may be used to show how thoughts affect the body, to monitor relaxation, to identify stressful points during imagery, and to facilitate concentration training. For example, biofeedback might be used while an athlete is thinking of an anxiety-provoking situation to illustrate the effects of thoughts on the body. Biofeedback is common in rehabilitation settings and might easily be used to practice cognitive control.

- Increasing focusing and refocusing skills. Focus training involves bringing attention back when it starts to wander, as in meditation, or as discussed earlier, in mindfulness training. Williams and colleagues (2015) suggest four techniques.

  - Mindfulness is popular in research and practice. When using mindfulness as a simple focusing technique, the person sits quietly and tries to stay focused on a single thought. People often focus on their breath, and it is important to stay nonjudgmental (don't worry if your mind wanders, just bring it back). Mindfulness and related techniques are often incorporated into exercise programs. Not only can mindfulness training enhance the exercise itself, but it can help participants develop useful attentional and emotional control skills.

  - With the technique called one pointing, the person looks at an action photo or an object (e.g., a tennis ball) and keeps the focus on that one point.

  - The grid exercise is often used in psychological skills training. The grid (see figure 5.1, for example) is a 10-by-10 block of numbers ranging from 00 to 99 in random locations. The task is to mark off consecutive numbers from 00 to as high as possible within a given time, such as 2 minutes. The exercise can be varied through the use of distracting background sounds or different instructions (e.g., going backward). The point is to practice scanning and focusing (e.g., in soccer, players scan the field of play and then focus on the pass). However, as with most concentration exercises, the transfer value from the grid exercise to performance is questionable.

– Williams and coauthors (2015) suggest video games as a fourth technique for focusing and refocusing, and we might include varied computerized concentration exercises or apps. As with other focusing exercises, the transition from the computer exercise to the playing field can be a big leap. Exercises that incorporate some of these focusing techniques in the actual sport or exercise setting are likely to be more effective than exercises that do not have transitional steps to tie the skills to the activity.

• Developing preperformance and performance protocols. Williams and colleagues (2015) suggest that athletes might tune in to their ideal performance by associating concentration with certain performance rituals. Routines can be developed for warm-ups, practice, or specific times during performance. Once routines are consistently practiced, they may automatically trigger focused attention that leads to good performance. For example, Boutcher and Crews (1987) demonstrated that the use of a preshot concentration routine improved putting performance.

These are just a few examples; many athletes and exercisers have developed their own cognitive strategies and exercises.

Self-Talk

Self-talk occurs whenever a person thinks—whether the self-talk is spoken aloud or is silent—and makes perceptions and beliefs conscious.

Figure 5.1 Concentration Exercise Grid

Beginning with 00, put a slash through each number in the proper sequence.

84	27	51	78	59	52	13	85	61	55
28	60	92	04	97	90	31	57	29	33
32	96	65	39	80	77	49	86	18	70
76	87	71	95	98	81	01	46	88	00
48	82	89	47	35	17	10	42	62	34
44	67	93	11	07	43	72	94	69	56
53	79	05	22	54	74	58	14	91	02
06	68	99	75	26	15	41	66	20	40
50	09	64	08	38	30	36	45	93	24
03	73	21	23	16	37	25	19	12	63

Application Point

Concentration Strategies for Rehab

You are an athletic trainer working with a volleyball player who is beginning a six- to eight-week rehabilitation program. You have a plan for her exercises. You know that athletes are often distracted and not very focused on rehab exercises, so you want to add some cognitive strategies to help her get through the rehabilitation program. What cognitive strategies would you suggest to help the athlete stay focused on her rehab activities? List at least two specific strategies.

Self-talk may be classified as instructional or motivational. Most athletes and exercisers use self-talk, often as self-coaching, but there is little research or guidance on the technique. Hatzigeorgiadis, Zourbanos, Galanis, and Theodorakis (2011) conducted a meta-analysis and found a moderate positive effect of self-talk on performance, and more so for fine (rather than gross) motor skills and for novel (rather than well-learned) skills.

Uses of Self-Talk

Williams, Zinsser, and Bunker (2015) state that self-talk is the key to cognitive control. Self-talk occurs any time you give yourself instructions; reinforce or interpret your thoughts, feeling, or actions; or carry on an internal dialogue with yourself. They suggest that you can use self-talk for skill acquisition and performance, correcting bad habits, attentional control, changing affect–mood, and building self-confidence. As discussed in chapter 6, self-confidence is a psychological key to excellence and behavior change. As in the classic children's book *The Little Engine That Could*, if you keep repeating "I think I can," eventually you will make it up the hill.

Although most sport and exercise literature on cognitive skills and self-talk focuses on athletes, self-talk is equally applicable to exercise. As noted in chapter 6, self-efficacy is central in exercise adoption and adherence, and self-talk that builds confidence can help exercisers. Gauvin (1990) reports that persistent exercisers use positive and motivational self-talk, whereas dropouts and sedentary people use self-defeating and negative self-talk.

Effective Self-Talk

For self-talk to be effective, the user first must be aware of the self-talk and its effects. Williams and colleagues (2015) suggest that self-talk may be identified through retrospection (reflecting on exceptionally good or poor past performances and recalling the self-talk), imagery, and self-talk logs (daily records of self-talk that include details of the situation and the performance).

After identifying effective and ineffective self-talk patterns, one can modify them. Williams and colleagues (2015) offer common techniques for modifying self-talk:

- **Thought stopping.** The person uses a cue to interrupt unwanted thoughts as they occur. A common technique is to quickly and clearly say (or yell) "Stop!" as soon as that unwanted thought comes into the mind. Some people use visual cues (e.g., visualizing a red stoplight) or physical cues (e.g., snapping the fingers). Thought stopping is a great wake-up call, but you must then substitute a positive thought.

- **Changing negative thoughts to positive ones.** Switch from the negative thought to a constructive one. For example, after thinking, "I always hit into the lake on this hole," you would say "Stop!" Then you might think, "But when I take a smooth, easy backswing, I have a solid, straight drive." When standing at the tee, it's not easy to think of those positive substitute thoughts. Many consultants suggest making a list of typical negative thoughts and writing a positive substitute next to each one to make it easier to retrieve the replacement thoughts in stressful situations.

- **Countering.** Changing negative thoughts to positive ones is not effective if you don't believe what you're thinking. Countering is an internal debate, using reason to directly challenge self-defeating thoughts. For example, when the heart pounds and muscles tighten, saying "I am calm" is not likely to be effective. To counter the negative self-talk, you might say, "This happens to everyone; when I breathe easily and focus on my shot, I do fine."

- **Reframing.** People often view the world in narrow, rigid terms, and reframing changes that perspective. For example, the college freshman who starts off with a less than stellar season after a glorious high school record might reframe the situation as one for learning new skills and developing strategies for the higher-level play.

Self-Talk in Swim Class

Self-talk requires no special equipment or skills and can be used in many sport and exercise settings. It may be particularly useful for young children, and it can also be fun. Assume that you are the teacher of a children's beginning swimming class. Suggest several self-talk strategies the children could use to help them stay focused and develop skills.

Negative Self-Talk and Cognitive Restructuring

Many relatively simple techniques for modifying self-talk and developing concentration relate to cognitive restructuring, which was developed for clinical settings as part of Albert Ellis' rational emotional behavior therapy in the 1950s. According to Ellis (1982), among others, the many irrational or distorted thoughts that we all hold are debilitating, and might be the basis of depression or other clinical disorders. In sport and exercise, negative thoughts—such as "I'm nothing if I don't win this tournament," or "I can't run well if it's raining," or "I'll never be able to do this skill"—can interfere with performance and detract from the overall experience.

Key Point

Positive self-talk has positive effects whereas negative self-talk interferes with performance, but it's not easy to get rid of negative thoughts. Affirmations (positive thoughts) and cognitive restructuring, in which participants first recognize that negative thoughts are irrational and then identify constructive thoughts to replace them, can help.

The obvious answer is to get rid of negative thoughts, but that's not so easy. In cognitive restructuring, participants first recognize that such thoughts are irrational, identify constructive thoughts to replace them, and then practice rational, positive self-statements. Williams and colleagues (2015) suggest several strategies, including ABC cognitive restructuring, which involves (a) describing events that trigger negative thoughts, (b) recording specific negative self-talk, and (c) recording resulting feelings and behaviors. Then,

after completing the ABC steps, review to identify the irrational thinking, rebut the negative talk, and substitute more rational, positive thoughts. A simpler strategy, affirmations, involves constructing positive attitudes or thoughts (e.g., "I've got a smooth backswing," "I fly down the stretch"). Coping and mastery self-talk recordings, which essentially are affirmations and restructured thoughts, can also be used. For mastery, the athlete might imagine the ideal performance or recall a previous great performance and then write out a script of all the positive thoughts. After reviewing and modifying the script, he or she can make an audio recording. The recording might include music that elicits appropriate emotions, and the pace should permit visualization of the scenes. A coping recording is similar but is designed to help the person deal with anxiety or get through a difficult situation.

Imagery

Imagery might be considered part of attention, and imagery certainly can be considered a cognitive skill. Imagery is particularly prominent in sport and exercise psychology and merits a major section in this chapter. Individual differences are prominent in the work on attentional styles, but they have received less attention in relation to imagery. Instead, sport and exercise psychology focuses on the use of imagery techniques for performance enhancement.

What Is Imagery?

Imagery is one of the most often discussed and widely used cognitive processes in sport and exercise psychology. Imagery involves a particular type of attention—an internal, narrow focus—but is more than an attentional focus. Vealey and Forlenza (2015) describe imagery as "using one's senses to create or re-create an experience in the mind" (p. 240). Suinn (1993), one of the first psychologists to research and use psychological skills training with athletes, in discussing his visuomotor behavior rehearsal (VMBR) technique, described imagery as "a covert activity whereby a person experiences sensory-motor sensations that reintegrate reality experiences, and which include neuromuscular, physiological, and emotional involvement" (p. 499).

These descriptions, which are consistent with other sport and exercise literature on imagery, highlight several key aspects of imagery. First, imagery is a particular type of attention; with imagery, attention is internally (covertly, in the mind), narrowly focused. Second, imagery is not simply imagination; it is subject to conscious control (we create or reintegrate). And imagery is more than visual; imagery involves all senses—tactile, auditory, emotional, and, especially relevant for those in kinesiology, movement or kinesthetic sense.

Individual Differences in Imagery Ability

As early as the 1880s, Sir Francis Galton discussed imagery extensively and reported that he had given a questionnaire on imaging ability to a diverse sample (Burbridge, 1994). Many books on imagery have been written, and *Journal of Mental Imagery* has been published for some time.

Individual differences in imagery can be assessed in many ways, including objective, performance-based assessments, but most measures are self-report questionnaires. Many measures are multidimensional, recognizing that people have several imagery abilities. For instance, a person might be adept at picking out specific aspects of an image (e.g., seeing the position of a bat during a swing) but may develop grainy images rather than sharp, detailed images.

Craig Hall and colleagues have done some of the most extensive sport and exercise psychology research on imagery. Hall and colleagues (Hall, Pongrac, & Buckolz, 1985) developed the Movement Imagery Questionnaire (MIQ) and later the Imagery Use Questionnaire (IUQ) (Hall, Rodgers, & Barr, 1990) to assess athletes' use of imagery. Hall and colleagues also developed the Sport Imagery Questionnaire (SIQ; Hall, Mack, Paivio, & Hausenblas, 1998), which measures five types of imagery:

- Motivational specific (relates to specific goals and motivation)
- Motivational general—mastery (relates to coping and mastery of challenges)
- Motivational general—arousal (relates to emotional focus and control of anxiety or confidence)
- Cognitive specific (relates to the common use of imagery to develop and maintain skills)
- Cognitive general (relates to cognitive plans and strategies)

Hausenblas, Hall, Rodgers, and Munroe (1999) extended the SIQ model to exercisers and developed the Exercise Imagery Questionnaire (EIQ)

with similar types and uses. They found that, similarly to athletes, exercisers used imagery for both motivational and cognitive purposes. The EIQ structure is somewhat different from the SIQ and has three factors (energy, appearance, and technique).

Other than the SIQ and the related EIQ, sport and exercise psychologists have few measures of individual differences in imagery, but many consultants use some form of imagery assessment. For example, Vealey and Forlenza (2015) present a sport imagery evaluation that may be useful for self-assessment or for consultants working with athletes.

Sport and Exercise Psychology Research: Mental Practice Model

Although today imagery has a wide range of uses in sport and exercise psychology, including for attentional and emotional control, the early work focused on using imagery to practice motor skills; much of the support for imagery use comes from early work comparing mental practice with physical practice. Feltz and Landers (1983) provided a thorough review of that early literature on mental practice. Using meta-analysis, they reached several conclusions:

- Mental practice effects are primarily associated with cognitive–symbolic rather than motor elements of the task. Mental practice is especially useful for tasks involving movement sequences, timing, or cognitive problem solving.
- Mental practice effects are not limited to early learning; they are found in both early and later stages of learning and may be task specific. Imagery may be useful both in early learning and with more familiar tasks but may operate differently at various stages of learning.
- It is doubtful that mental practice effects are produced by low-gain innervation of muscles to be used during actual performance. Although Suinn (1983) and others report muscle activity during imagery, Feltz and Landers found no evidence for the claim that low-gain neuromuscular activity accounts for mental rehearsal effects. Instead, imagery appears to elicit general muscle innervation.
- Mental practice assists the performer in psychologically preparing for the skill to be

performed. The general muscle innervation might set appropriate tension levels and attentional focus.

Key Point

Feltz and Landers' (1983) meta-analysis led to several conclusions, including the conclusion that mental practice primarily affects cognitive–symbolic elements of the task and that the effects are not limited to early learning.

Other research has taken varied approaches and extended beyond mental practice. Still, research is limited in comparison to the applied literature on imagery in psychological skills training.

Imagery Theory

Although research is limited, several theories provide guidance and direction. Before the Feltz and Landers (1983) review, the psychoneuromuscular theory and the symbolic learning theory were dominant. Since then, several sport and exercise psychologists have adopted Lang's (1979) bioinformational theory or have focused on psychological states (Bhasavanija & Morris, 2014; Vealey & Forlenza, 2015).

- **Psychoneuromuscular theory.** Psychoneuromuscular theory, alluded to in Feltz and Landers' third conclusion, is also referred to as muscle memory. Jacobson (1931) first reported that imaginary movements produced muscle innervation similar to those produced in the actual movement. Suinn (1983) observed muscle activity (EMG) patterns during imagery that paralleled those during a ski run; but generally there is little support for the psychoneuromuscular theory.
- **Symbolic learning theory.** According to symbolic learning theory, imagery works like a blueprint to develop a mental code for movements. Much sport and exercise psychology research on imagery is consistent with symbolic learning, but we have no convincing tests of the theory.
- **Bioinformational theory.** Lang's (1977, 1979) psychophysiological information-processing theory assumes that an image is a function-

ally organized set of propositions. When imaging, we activate stimulus and response propositions, which implies that imagery training should include not only conditions of the situation (e.g., the setting), but also the behavioral, psychological, and physiological responses in that situation. Thus, we might think of response sets (Vealey & Forlenza, 2015) rather than simple responses.

- **Psychological states.** Psychological states or mental sets do not refer to a specific theory but explain imagery effects by referring to optimal arousal or attentional states. As we discuss in later chapters, imagery may be effective for controlling emotions to maintain an optimal psychological state, but that is not a theory to explain how imagery might affect performance.

Despite the prominence of imagery in the sport and exercise psychology literature, we can draw few conclusions about how it works. Generally, imagery seems to be one way to facilitate skill learning and performance. Many participants in physical activity find imagery effective, and sport and exercise psychology research on imagery training is accumulating.

Models for Imagery Use

Martin, Moritz, and Hall (1999) reviewed the literature and offered a model that provides a guide for imagery use in sport (see figure 5.2). The model incorporates the sport situation, the type of imagery used, and imagery ability as factors that influence imagery use. Martin and colleagues discuss three broad categories of imagery use: skill and strategy learning and performance, cognitive modification, and arousal and anxiety regulation. We usually think of imagery as mental practice for skills. However, imagery is also useful for developing cognitive skills, as discussed in the previous sections, as well as for emotional control. Moreover, as the model suggests, competitive sport is not the only situation in which imagery may be useful. Training and rehabilitation are specifically included in the model, and both practice and rehabilitation settings are promising but underused settings for imagery and cognitive skill use. The imagery types are those from the SIQ, and Martin and colleagues also include individual differences in imagery abilities.

Holmes and Collins (2001) developed the PETTLEP model, based on functional equivalence, to provide guidance for using imagery. PETTLEP

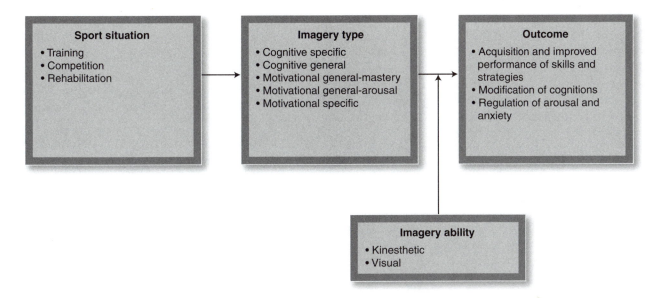

Figure 5.2 Applied model of mental imagery use in sport.

refers to seven practical issues (Physical, Environment, Task, Timing, Learning, Emotion, and Perspective) that must be considered for effective imagery use. Importantly, all aspects of the imagery should simulate the real performance situation as much as possible (that's functional equivalence). Wakefield, Smith, Moran, and Holmes (2013) reviewed the literature using the PETTLEP model and reported that several studies found interventions using PETTLEP effective. They concluded that overall, research supports PETTLEP imagery with a wide range of tasks and populations. They also noted gaps and some mixed findings, and suggested that it may be behavioral matching between imagery and action that underlies the results.

Imagery for Rehab

Application Point

Imagery can be used for practicing mental skills and emotional control as well as for practicing sport skills, and it has been underused in exercise and rehabilitation. List three ways in which a client in a rehabilitation program could use imagery to facilitate rehab exercises and return to full activity.

Using Imagery

As discussed earlier, imagery involves using all the senses to mentally create or recreate an experience. As we have already seen, imagery can be

effective for practicing other psychological skills such as modifying self-talk, practicing concentration, and building confidence. In an excellent review of imagery use in sport, Weinberg (2008) asked the question, Does imagery work? He noted that imagery has been widely used with athletes, often as part of more comprehensive psychological skills training, and that the literature suggests the helpfulness of imagery for performance and in developing other psychological skills. Weinberg also noted that the research evidence is not very strong. Most of the literature is on using imagery in mental skill training, with few controlled studies that get at how imagery works and what might make imagery more effective.

Now we consider using imagery in more detail. Gould, Voelker, Damarjian, and Greenleaf (2014) and Vealey and Forlenza (2015) reviewed the literature and drew upon their experiences to provide guidelines and exercises for imagery training; see those sources for more detailed information. Both focus on using imagery with athletes, and most research on imagery focuses on imagery and sport performance; but imagery can be just as useful in physical education, youth programs, and exercise or physical therapy settings. Imagery, as well as other cognitive skills, is increasingly used in training and rehabilitation.

In one of the first investigations of imagery with injured athletes, Ievleva and Orlick (1991) found that imagery helped athletes cope with pain, as well as stay motivated and positively involved in their sport and in the rehabilitation process. Other researchers and sports medicine professionals suggest that imagery may even help in the healing process. In their chapter on psychological strategies, Shaffer and Wiese-Bjornstal (1999) note possible roles of cognitive strategies, and they suggest that imagery has several roles for injured athletes. Injury imagery helps in reading the body and reactions to the injury; skill imagery helps in the practice of skills; and rehabilitation imagery helps in the healing process by promoting a positive mindset, keeping the athlete engaged in the rehabilitation process, and even influencing physiological function. Athletic trainers are increasingly using imagery and cognitive skills in their work with athletes and in educational programs. In a chapter on psychosocial strategies for athletic training, Hamson-Utley, Arvinen-Barrow and Granquist (2015) discuss using imagery to maintain focus and stay positive during sport injury rehabilitation and specifically cite healing imagery, pain-management imagery, rehabilitation process imagery, and performance imagery as useful strategies.

Imagery can be used, and is used, by participants in many sport and exercise settings. As with any cognitive skill, we do not just want to use imagery, but to use it effectively. Following are guidelines to help you, as a performer or as a professional working with others, use imagery effectively.

Guidelines for Using Imagery Effectively

For effective use of imagery, Gould and colleagues (2014) suggest the following:

- **Practice imagery regularly.** Like other psychological skills, imagery is developed through training and continued practice.

- **Use all senses to enhance image vividness.** Imagery is more than vision, and it is more effective when the image recreates all the sensations. Kinesthetic sense is particularly relevant for physical activities.

- **Develop imagery control.** Control is the key to psychological skills; practice controlling images.

- **Use both internal and external perspectives.** When Mahoney and Avener (1977) reported that elite gymnasts used more internal (performer's perspective) imagery than external (observer's perspective) imagery, many consultants advised athletes always to use an internal perspective. Most now recognize that advice should vary with the person, the activity, and the situation.

- **Facilitate imagery through relaxation.** As with concentration, imagery combined with relaxation is more effective than imagery alone.

- **Develop coping strategies through imagery.** Generally, positive imagery is preferable, but imagery can also be used to develop coping strategies and skills (e.g., coming back after a poor performance).

- **Use imagery in practice as well as competition.** Athletes are more likely to use cognitive techniques for competition than in practices. However, physical practice is the place to practice psychological skills, and these skills can make practice more fun and more effective.

- **Use DVDs or audiotapes to enhance imagery skills.** DVDs and tapes (and surely there's an imagery app) may be helpful and may add novelty to practices. Many resources are available, but it may be even better to make your own specific imagery script and record that. Try doing that in the lab at the end of the chapter.

- **Use triggers or cues to facilitate imagery quality.** Words, phrases, or objects may aid imagery, just as cues may aid concentration.

- **Emphasize dynamic kinesthetic imagery.** Dynamic imagery focusing on the kinesthetic feel of movements may help recreate the physical experience.

- **Imagine in real time.** Slowing down or speeding up may be useful in imagery training, but most imagery should match real time and speed.

- **Use imagery logs.** Logs can help people monitor progress, remember cues, or stay with a training program.

- **Consider the developmental level of participants.** Even young children can use imagery, but they are not likely to use imagery in the same way as the athletes on the college soccer team.

These guidelines can help anyone develop more effective imagery strategies, whether in extensive training or in occasional sport and exercise activities.

Imagery Practice— Make It Real

To practice making your imagery vivid and real, imagine you are in a fitness center about to begin your workout on a treadmill (or bike, stepper—your choice). Imagine the setting; use all your senses and put yourself there. When you have a vivid image of yourself in the setting, imagine getting on the treadmill and moving into your workout routine. Keep it real—in real time, use all your senses, and especially use your kinesthetic sense and imagine how you feel as you go through your workout.

Imagery Training Programs

For consultants helping athletes or other clients over time, imagery training may well be included. Vealey and Forlenza, as well as Gould and colleagues (2014), suggest similar four-phase models for imagery training with athletes. Note that their approach is just as appropriate for working with clients in other activity settings, and keep in mind that any training must be adjusted for the individual and the situation. Gould and coauthors and Vealey and Forlenza label the phases slightly differently, but they follow the same steps and offer similar advice. The first step is to introduce the client to imagery, assess the situation and client skills, and set up realistic expectations. Training then moves into basic skills, and then to using imagery in the sport or activity. The last phase involves monitoring, evaluating, and revising imagery.

1. **Awareness, realistic expectations, and education.** Help the client develop awareness and realistic expectations. Imagery is no quick and easy road to success—it takes practice. It is not a substitute for physical practice but a skill to enhance practice and performance.

2. **Imagery skill evaluation and development.** People vary in their imagery skills and styles. Evaluating imagery skills can increase awareness of skills and help the consultant work with the person to develop appropriate training strategies.

3. **Using imagery.** Basic training emphasizes vividness, controllability, and sensory awareness. Vividness training might start with simple exercises, such as imagining a childhood bedroom, to develop clearer, more vivid images. With controllability training, participants learn to regulate images, such as speeding up and slowing down while imagining running. Sensory awareness or self-awareness training involves becoming more aware of underlying thoughts and feelings that affect performance. Vealey and Forlenza suggest a series of exercises to help with the ability to experience different senses, emotions, and perspectives during imagery.

4. **Imagery evaluation, adjustment, and refinement.** Once imagery skills are developed, they can be used for many purposes, including practicing physical skills or strategies, correcting errors, practicing emotional control, and developing confidence. Vealey and Forlenza provide several excellent examples of exercises and guidelines for imagery training and use. The final step is evaluating whether imagery training has met its goals and whether refinements and adjustments are needed. It is best to evaluate and consider modifications throughout the program. No two people are alike, and variations and adjustments are expected in imagery training. Moreover, imagery does not automatically work, even with the best of intentions and adherence to guidelines.

Putting It Into Practice

Summary

Attention and cognitive skills are prominent in sport and exercise psychology, but research is limited. The expanding research from a psychophysiological perspective and the work on cognition and expertise are adding to our understanding of cognitive processes in physical activity. Cognitive-control strategies are popular and often effective in sport and exercise. Sport and exercise psychologists consistently emphasize the importance of controlling attention and thoughts, and participants use techniques such as thought stopping, cognitive restructuring, and imagery. Most sport and exercise psychologists advise individual assessments, evaluation, and modifications with cognitive skill training.

Review Questions

1. Define attention.
2. Describe Nideffer's two-dimensional model of attention.
3. Discuss the research on attentional style and sport performance.
4. Explain how experts differ from nonexperts in attention and cognitive skills.
5. Discuss the theories used to explain how imagery works.
6. Describe two specific concentration strategies that could be used in sport and exercise.
7. Identify common guidelines for using imagery effectively.

Recommended Reading

- Abernethy, B., Maxwell, J.P., Masters, R.S.W., van der Kamp, J., & Jackson, R.C. (2007). Attentional processes in skill learning and expert performance. In G. Tenenbaum & R.C. Eklund (Eds.), *Handbook of sport psychology* (3rd ed., pp. 245-263). Hoboken, NJ: Wiley. Abernethy has conducted considerable research on the role of attention and cognitive strategies of elite performers. This chapter summarizes work by motor behavior and sport psychology scholars, and it provides a solid review with suggestions for continuing work.

- Beilock, S.L. (2010). *Choke: What the secrets of the brain reveal about getting it right when you have to.* New York: Free Press. Beilock is a leading cognitive psychology researcher, and her work on attention and performance is especially relevant in sport and exercise psychology. In this book, she presents the latest research in a readable format that will help researchers, performers, and professionals who work with them better understand why we choke and what we can do about it.

- Essig, K., Janelle, C.M., Borgo, F. & Koester, D. (2014). Attention and neurocognition. In A.G. Papaionnou & D. Hackfort (Eds.), *Routledge companion to sport and exercise psychology: Global perspectives and fundamental concepts* (pp. 253-271). London: Routledge. The chapter by Essig and coauthors provides a nice overview of the current perspectives and research on attention; it includes more on neuroscience and psychophysiology than most sport and exercise psychology reviews.

- Vealey, R.S., & Forlenza, S.T. (2015). Understanding and using imagery in sport. In J.M. Williams & V. Krane (Eds.), *Applied sport psychology: Personal growth to peak performance* (7th ed., pp. 240-273). New York: McGraw-Hill. In the seventh edition of Williams' applied sport psychology book, Vealey and Forlenza update earlier chapters on imagery and sport. The chapter provides a good overview of research and theories to help you understand imagery, as well as helpful guidelines for using imagery.

- Williams, J.M., Nideffer, R.M., Wilson, V.E., & Sagal, M-S. (2015). Concentration and strategies for controlling it. In J.M. Williams & V. Krane (Eds.), *Applied sport psychology: Personal growth to peak performance* (7th ed., pp. 304-325). New York: McGraw-Hill. This chapter presents an up-to-date overview of attention and concentration, along with helpful suggestions for practice.

Create and Use an Imagery Script

For this lab, you are to create and use an imagery script for a specific skill or task. Follow numbers 1 through 4 to create your imagery script; then use and evaluate your imagery script (numbers 5 and 6).

1. Basic picture. Choose a specific skill or task (e.g., golf putting, basketball free throw, specific exercise routine, dance steps, preparing for a 10K race). Then outline all the components of the skill (steps in the skill, lead-up, and follow-up); these are the behaviors to be emphasized and imagined.

2. Add details. Add details for the skill and setting such as color, audience, weather, and movement qualities (e.g., speed of movement) to the script. Consider all senses (sight, sound, and especially movement sense).

3. Put yourself into it. Add the kinesthetic (movement) feelings, physical–body responses, and emotions. Use verbs or action words such as "feel," "do," "think," "see," and words that describe actions or emotions such as "tense," "careful," "alert," and "smooth."

4. Refine and write up the script. Put all the descriptions together and add transitions. Read it to yourself and try to imagine the event in all its sensory, action, and emotional detail. Do you feel as if you are actually executing the skill or experiencing the event? If not, reexamine the descriptors and action words to see if they accurately reflect the sensations associated with this action.

5. Learn it. When you have a suitable script, learn it and practice it by reading it, having someone read it for you, or recording it to use for your imagery training.

6. Use and evaluate your imagery script. After you have practiced and learned your script, use it at least two times with your activity and answer the following questions.

   a. How did using imagery affect you and your performance? Did it help at all—in performance, psychological state, preparation, specific moves, and so on?

   b. How easy or difficult was it to use imagery with your activity? What was easy or difficult?

   c. How could you revise your script or change your practice to make it more helpful (e.g., add details, change components, revise timing or transitions)?

Self-Perceptions

Chapter Objectives

After studying this chapter, you should be able to

- define the different approaches to the study of self-perceptions,

- describe the multidimensional views of the self and the related sport and exercise psychology work on physical self-concept and related constructs, and

- trace the development of self-efficacy theories and apply them to the promotion of self-esteem and physical activity–related behaviors and performance.

People's perceptions of themselves and what they believe they can accomplish in sport, academics, work, and life influence their performance, feelings, and thoughts. More positive feelings about oneself are associated with more positive outcomes. For example, higher self-esteem is associated with lower anxiety and greater optimism, adaptability, life satisfaction, happiness, and ability to cope with stress, whereas lower self-esteem is associated with depression, suicide ideation, disordered eating, and delinquency (Horn, 2004). These results parallel those found in physical activity, where people who reported more positive thoughts about themselves also tended to report higher levels of performance, motivation, physical activity, self-pride, and happiness and less boredom and anxiety (Craft, Magyar, Becker, & Feltz, 2003; Crocker & Kowalski, 2000; Georgiadis, Biddle, & Chatzisarantis, 2001; Hardy, Hall, Green, & Greenslade, 2014; Tod, Hardy, & Oliver, 2011; Tremblay, Inman, & Willms, 2000; Weiss & Ferrer-Caja, 2002).

Given these findings, it is not surprising that physical activity specialists such as teachers, coaches, athletic trainers, and personal trainers are interested in helping their students, athletes, and clients feel good about themselves so that they will have more positive attitudes toward physical activity and be more motivated to be physically active. Take a moment to consider how you might help the following people.

1. Christie, a 10-year-old girl, began playing soccer two years ago when she asked her parents if she could join the local recreational soccer league. Her parents were thrilled and were hopeful that the experience would help build her self-esteem. Although she voluntarily plays soccer each year and is as capable as most of the other players in the league, she exhibits low self-confidence and has an overall unhappy demeanor when it comes to actually playing in a game. In practice and in games, she gives up easily. Her parents are convinced that soccer will never do anything for their daughter's self-esteem. If you were the soccer coach, what would you do to help Christie view herself in a more positive light, both as a person and as a soccer player?

2. Marcus, a top tennis recruit at a nationally ranked university, was playing his first college match. Up two sets and ahead 4-2 in the third set, Marcus was on top of the world feeling competitive at the college level. Racing to return a shot, Marcus felt a sudden snap—he had ruptured his Achilles tendon and had to forfeit the match. His postsurgery rehabilitation program was effective but slow. Over time, Marcus began to question his ability to recover and his worth as an athlete. He wonders aloud who he will be and what he will do without tennis. If you were a physical therapist, what would you do to help Marcus overcome his despair and continue his rehabilitation efforts?

3. A recent medical checkup revealed that Jordan's blood pressure and cholesterol levels were rising. Her doctor, who had been suggesting that she increase her physical activity, is now warning Jordan that if she doesn't attempt to take control of her health through behavioral changes, she will be on medication within three months. With this wake-up call, Jordan wants to start exercising. As you are one of the best personal trainers in town, she comes to you for help. A former college athlete, Jordan is extremely disappointed in herself for letting her health and fitness levels get this bad, and she doubts that she will ever be able to regain what she once had. How will you help Jordan have a more positive view of herself and feel more confident about her ability to be physically fit?

Now that you have generated some solutions for helping the people described in these scenarios, the next step is to explain why these solutions will work. This is where greater knowledge of self-perceptions is helpful. A working knowledge of the self gives you insight into how people evaluate their abilities and their self-worth. It also provides you with an understanding of how external factors such as significant others can affect the self-evaluation process. It is this knowledge that will allow you to evaluate the effectiveness of the solutions you generated and, if needed, to refine or discard the ideas you have generated in order to create more effective ones.

Self-Perceptions Terminology

Self-perceptions are most broadly defined as people's thoughts, attitudes, and feelings about themselves in general or about their skills, abilities, and characteristics in a particular achievement domain (Horn, 2004). Two of the earliest self-perceptions studied were self-esteem (a.k.a., self-worth) and self-concept. William James (1890, 1892) discussed the development of a sense of global self-worth from more specific self-judgments. C.H. Cooley (1902), on the other hand, proposed that self-concept was formed through social interaction, and he introduced the notion of reflected appraisal and the term *looking-glass self.*

Although the terms are often used interchangeably, self-concept is the overall perception, or the descriptive aspect, of the self (e.g., I am compassionate, writing is my strength, free throw shooting is my weakness), whereas self-esteem is the evaluative aspect of the global self. These evaluations can be positive or negative (e.g., I am worthy, I am a failure). The distinction between self-concept and self-esteem is convenient for discussing the various aspects of the self; but in reality, these terms are difficult to separate because people's descriptions of themselves are so emotionally charged (Harter, 1999). The evaluative component usually is the key for study of the self. In the following sections, we explore various ways of viewing the self.

Self-Schema and Identity

Self-schema and identity are two widely studied self-perceptions within sport and exercise. Both reflect personal beliefs about the self, and each serves to organize behaviors in ways that are consistent with how people view themselves. We turn now to defining these constructs and outlining the role they play in directing sport and exercise behaviors.

Exercise Schema

According to Markus (1977), self-concept is a complex, multifaceted, dynamic system that consists of unique collections of cognitive representations of the self, called *schemata* (plural form of *schema*), that represent self-beliefs related to domain-specific attributes and abilities (e.g., athlete schema). Self-schemata are active, dynamic self-representations that are derived from past experiences and that organize and direct behaviors. Self-schemata allow for information retrieval and processing, as well as reaction to information.

People have many self-schemata that work together in a self-system. We can have schemata relative to exercise, body weight, independence, and academic performance (see Stein, Roeser, & Markus, 1998). Some self-schemata are more salient than others. For example, the athlete schema may be highly salient and a dominant influence for some but not for others. Schemata that are less salient and less elaborate have less influence. We are more apt to find a person who has a stronger exercise schema than athlete schema in the gym working out rather than on the playing field.

Application Point

Competing Self-Schemata

Kim and John are both athlete and math schematics. They are both on the school basketball and math teams. Kim's athlete schema is stronger than her math schema, whereas the opposite is true for John. They discover that the math bowl is scheduled on the same day as a basketball game. What event do you think Kim attended? What about John?

Although people possess numerous self-schemata, it is unlikely that everyone possesses self-schemata relative to every attribute in a domain. People can be schematic, aschematic, or nonschematic for a particular attribute in a domain (Kendzierski, 1988). For example, exercise schematics view exercise as highly and personally descriptive and as important to their overall sense of self. Exercise aschematics may moderately identify with exercise but do not believe the attribute is important to their self-concept. Nonexercise schematics do not identify with exercise participation, but they do believe that the attribute is important to their self-concept. People's schema types are related to their behavior. For example, Kendzierski's work (1988, 1994) has demonstrated that exercise schematics process information differently from others and are likely to exercise more than nonexercise schematics. Subsequent studies with predominantly college-aged students have shown that exercise schematics exercise more frequently, perform more exercise activities, and are more likely to start an exercise program in comparison to nonexercise schematics and aschematics. Exercise schematics also plan to exercise, strategize overcoming obstacles to exercise, report more exercise-related behavior, expend more calories, and perceive themselves as more fit than do those with a nonexercise schema (Estabrooks & Courneya, 1997; Kendzierski, 1988; Kendzierski, Furr, & Schiavoni, 1998; Yin & Boyd, 2000).

While much of this research has focused on younger adults, Whaley and Ebbeck (2002) reported that only 6 of 13 older adults who had been exercising for more than two years were schematic for exercise. Six of the remaining seven did not fall into any of the three categories defined by Kendzierski. All six considered exercise to be important to their self-concept, but *"exercise"* was only moderately descriptive. The older adult participants explained that exercisers are younger or exercise all the time. Whaley and Ebbeck suggested that the exercise behaviors of older adults did not fit into how society views an exerciser. These results highlight the influence of social context on self-concept.

Since the introduction of her research on exercise schema, Kendzierski and colleagues have developed a broader physical activity self-definition (PASD) model. In this model, participation in physical activity is a necessary, but not sufficient, requisite for developing physical activity–related identities. Individuals will have more salient PASD if they enjoy physical activity, want to participate and try to participate in it, and have a high commitment and the ability to participate (Kendzierski & Morganstein, 2009).

Schemata and other self-definitions are conceptions of the self in the present and are thought to influence behavior and future-oriented self-conceptions, called *possible selves* (Markus & Nurius, 1986). Possible selves are positive and negative self-images people have about future versions of themselves (Oyserman, Bybee, & Terry, 2006). Markus and Nurius (1986) discuss possible selves as important motivators that serve as a bridge between the present and the future. For example, a golfer who conceives of becoming a professional golfer (hoped-for self) may develop a more elaborate golfer schema, a sense of mastery and confidence, and specific goals and strategies. A person who fears losing motor functioning (feared self) may do home exercises. Various conditions are needed to maximize the relationship between possible selves and behavior. For example, possible selves are thought to be most effective when the hoped-for and feared selves are balanced (Oyserman & Markus, 1990). A person who hopes to be active and fears becoming sedentary may be more likely to exercise than one who only hopes to be active but does not fear becoming a couch potato.

Whaley (2004) suggests that possible selves influence behavior when people are confident that they can successfully execute a behavior and believe that achievement of the possible self is likely. The more elaborate and accessible the possible selves are, the more effective they are thought to be (Ruvolo & Markus, 1992). Imagery is a viable method for developing elaborate, accessible, possible selves in order to develop competence. Imagery helps when it is specific, or detailed, and we can see ourselves performing the behavior—we can see that it's possible.

Markus (1977) contends that only a subset of the self, not all self-knowledge, is active at any given time. This concept of the working self continually varies as it regulates behavior (con-

trols and directs actions). The immediate social situation affects the working self, which in turn affects behavior. For example, take DeAnne, an athlete schematic who has the opportunity to play recreational softball after years of not competing but chooses not to play because she fears looking unathletic. The invitation to play itself evokes DeAnne's athlete schema, and because she hasn't played for years it evokes the feared unathletic self. Her decision is a function of her working self-concept. Perhaps if the invitation had been made by family at a reunion, DeAnne would have played. Understanding the working self helps to explain that the self is dynamic without being inconsistent.

Social influence extends to social groups or culture. Markus (1977) discussed two views of the self that differ across cultures—independent and interdependent. The independent view (e.g., individual achievement, self-focused, private, direct) dominates North American culture, including its sport culture. Other cultures, such as most in Asia, take an interdependent view and see the self in relation to others (e.g., linked, relational, indirect, cooperative). In the United States, the typical athlete and exerciser schemata fit the independent view. We see athletes as independent, competitive, individual achievers, and if that does not fit with one's gender or cultural identity then one may not easily see oneself as an athlete—it's not a possible self. The exerciser schema may not be competitive, but it is independent as well as white and middle class, and exercise may be seen as self-indulgent to cultures with more community identity.

Exercise Identity

In addition to the work on exercise schema and possible selves, research has looked at the related construct of *exercise identity*. According to identity theory (Burke, Owens, Serpe, & Thoits, 2003; Burke & Reitzes, 1981), individuals will engage in behaviors that are consistent with their self-identity, especially when a particular identity is very salient (important) to a person's self-concept. Most research examining exercise identity has measured the construct using the Exercise Identity Scale developed by Anderson and Cychosz (1994). Individuals are more likely to have higher self-efficacy and engage more frequently in exercise when exercise identity is a central aspect of their overall self-concept. Exercise identity can change over time; people who participate in physical activity programs can develop a more salient exercise identity, which in turn predicts future exercise participation (Cardinal & Cardinal, 1997). Because identity has been shown to predict current and future exercise participation, practitioners should consider the role that identity plays in their clients' adoption and maintenance of physical activity behaviors.

Some researchers have started to examine exercise identity within a motivational framework, specifically using self-determination theory (see chapter 8). Strachan, Fortier, Perras, and Lugg (2012) found that a higher exercise identity was associated with more autonomous regulation of exercise behaviors. In particular, when people feel competent in their physical activities, are able to choose their own activities, and feel connected with other people through their activity experiences, they are more likely to identify as exercisers, have greater self-determined motivation, and participate in exercise more often (Springer, Lamborn, & Pollard, 2013; Vlachopoulos, Kaperoni, & Moustaka, 2011).

Athletic Identity

Athletic identity is another popular self-perception studied in sport and exercise contexts. Brewer, Van Raalte, and Linder (1993) defined athletic identity as the degree to which a person identifies with the athletic role and looks to others for acknowledgment of that role. A person with a strong athletic identity has an athlete self-schema and processes information from an athletic perspective. For example, people with strong athletic identities might think about how their eating and sleeping habits affect performance. Brewer and colleagues developed the Athletic Identity Measurement Scale (AIMS), and initial findings suggested that people establish strong athletic identities through the development of skills, confidence, and social interactions during sport. Further, a strong, exclusive athletic identity may predispose athletes to emotional difficulties when they cannot participate. A study on marathon runners showed that runners with higher athlete identities are more committed and better performers but are not more likely to neglect other aspects of their life compared to runners with lower athlete identities (Horton & Mack, 2000). Having a strong athletic identity is not always advantageous, however. For example, strong identification with the athlete role can interfere with planning for life beyond college (Lally & Kerr, 2005). As such, there are both positive and negative aspects of a salient athletic identity. Brewer and colleagues suggested in the title of their seminal article that the construct could be viewed as either "Hercules' muscle" or "Achilles' heel."

As conceived by Brewer and colleagues (1993), athletic identity is multifaceted, inclusive of (1) social identity, or the strength with which athletes identify with the athletic role; (2) exclusivity, or the degree to which athletes rely solely on the athletic setting for identity; and (3) negative affectivity, or negative emotional responses to not being able to train or compete. Athletic identity has been a central construct of interest in sport psychology research over the years, including its relationship to injury recovery (e.g., Brewer, Cornelius, Stephan, & Van Raalte, 2010; Lockhart, 2010; Manuel et al., 2002; Podlog et al., 2013) and transition to life after retirement from sport (e.g., Douglas & Carless, 2009; Lally, 2007; Lally & Kerr, 2007).

The social group of which one is a member (i.e., culture) is important to consider in regard to athletic identity. Research has also shown that men have stronger athletic identities than women (although not among elite athletes), and Mexican Americans are more likely to have stronger athletic identities than Caucasians and African Americans (see Wiese-Bjornstal, 2004). Further, not only do black athletes have stronger athletic identities than white athletes (Brown et al., 2003), but race and athletic identity converge in given situations to influence cognitions. Although black and white Division I college athletes had similar beliefs about racial discrimination, there were differences in beliefs with respect to athletes' racial and athletic identities. When white and black athletes with high and low athletic identities were compared, black athletes with high athletic identities were the most likely to believe that racial discrimination was no longer a problem, and black athletes with low athletic identities were the least likely to think this. In addition to highlighting the social nature of the self, these findings likely demonstrate the concept of the working self. Athletes' thoughts about racial discrimination were a function of their racial and athletic identities.

Though athletic identity is likely to be a salient part of self-concept for many athletes, identity can change over time. Research shows that athletic identity decreases after retirement from sport (Houle, Brewer, & Kluck, 2010). It is likely that as identity changes occur through retirement from competitive sport, related behaviors such as participation in sport and physical activity may also change. For example, in a study by Reifsteck,

Gill, and Brooks (2013), which looked at the relationship between athletic identity and physical activity, former student-athletes reported engaging in lower levels of physical activity compared to when they were in college. Stephan, Torregrosa, and Sanchez (2007) suggest that changes in activity levels through the transition may have a negative impact on retired athletes' identity and self-worth, and they recommend transitional programs to help better prepare athletes for the transition to life after competitive sport.

Application Point

Transitioning Out of Sport

Matt is a college athlete finishing his final year of eligibility. Being a collegiate baseball player is a central part of his self-identity. What psychological skills and strategies would you use to help him prepare for his transition out of college sport?

Theories on self-schema and identity are helpful in practice because they force us to recognize that the dimensions of the self do not work in isolation from each other (i.e., the self is dynamic and whole), and that the self does not function in isolation from its social context (i.e., the self is a social construct). With an understanding of the working self, it may be easier to accept that behavior is a reflection of the working self and all that comes with it. The complex, dynamic, fluid, and social aspects of the self will be important as we turn our attention to the structure of the self.

Multidimensional Self-Perceptions

Early perspectives emphasized a unidimensional, global view of the self in which aspects contributing to one's global self-esteem could not be differentiated. For example, Coopersmith (1967) viewed self-concept as a unitary construct, and his widely used measure combines items reflecting self-evaluations across many life domains as though they contribute equally to self-esteem. Others (e.g., Harter, 1983) have criticized this, arguing for a multidimensional approach. They argue that people do not value all domains equally; rather, self-evaluations of each of the multiple domains combine in a unique way to form self-esteem.

In what areas of life do your accomplishments mean the most to you—when you excel academically, athletically, socially, in your work, in relationships, in creative arts? How might you have answered this question five years ago? Do you think you will answer any differently five years from now? Understanding the multidimensional nature of self-esteem enables practitioners to better understand what life domains contribute to self-esteem and how these change over time.

Harter's Model of Perceived Competence: A Multidimensional Approach

Susan Harter (1990), who advocates a multidimensional and developmental approach to self-perceptions, has been particularly influential in our discipline. From a multidimensional and developmental perspective, the relationship between the domains and global self-esteem, the number of domains contributing to overall self-esteem, and the content of these domains change throughout life (Harter, 1999; Horn, 2004). Children as young as 4 to 7 years make self-judgments in five domains: cognitive competence, physical competence, physical appearance, social acceptance, and behavioral conduct. However, children are not capable of making overall judgments of their global self-worth. In this way, young children have a unidimensional perspective of self. With greater cognitive maturity, children aged 8 to 12 make more reliable judgments in the domain areas and are able to form an overall judgment of self-worth. In this way, older children have developed a multidimensional perspective, and the domains are linked with, but independent from, global self-esteem.

Harter (1990) suggests further developmental changes in self-perceptions, adding close friendship, romantic appeal, and job competence domains for adolescents. According to Harter, college students make clear differentiations among scholastic competence, intellectual ability, and creativity; but for slightly older adults, a single dimension of intelligence suffices.

Relative to the physical self, physical appearance remains a relevant subdomain throughout the life span. In contrast, athletic competence is replaced by leisure activities and health status in late adulthood (see Harter, 1999; Horn, 2004). Without multidimensional models such as Susan Harter's, explaining such variations of self-esteem would not be possible.

Hierarchical Models of Self-Concept and Self-Esteem

Multidimensional models have been expanded to include a hierarchical structure. Shavelson, Hubner, and Stanton (1976) proposed a multifaceted, hierarchical model with global self-concept at the top level, which is the most stable and resistant to the influence of external forces (see also Harter, 1999; Horn, 2004; Marsh & Craven, 2006). At the next level, academic self-concept and three nonacademic components—social self-concept, emotional self-concept, and physical self-concept—form the basis of the global self-concept. These lower-level, domain-specific self-concepts are less stable and resistant to external forces than the global self-concept. Each of these four components, in turn, includes subdomains based on evaluations of behavior in specific situations. For example, academic self-concept includes subdomains of language arts, history, math, and science, and physical self-concept includes physical ability and physical appearance.

Focusing on Physical Self-Concept

Herbert Marsh argues for a focus on the specific domain of interest rather than on global self-concept (Marsh & Craven, 1997). Marsh (Marsh, 1997; Marsh & Craven, 2006) and Ken Fox (Fox, 1990, 1998; Fox & Corbin 1989) have contributed substantially to our understanding of the physical self. Both used the Shavelson model as a blueprint but found the physical self to be more complex than that which can be captured with two subareas. In Fox's three-tier hierarchical model, global self-esteem is at the top. Physical self-worth, at the next level, is based on the four subdomains of sport competence, attractive body, physical strength, and physical condition. Physical self-worth mediates the relationship between self-esteem and the four subdomains. Although the hierarchical structure of self-concept is a pervasive perspective today, some research questions it (e.g., Kowalski, Crocker, Kowalski, Chad, & Humbert, 2003).

Fox developed a measurement tool, the Physical Self-Perception Profile (PSPP), for assessing the physical self. It includes the following subscales:

- **Sport competence (sport):** Perceptions of sport and athletic ability, ability to learn sport skills, and confidence in the sport environment
- **Physical condition (condition):** Perceptions of physical condition, stamina, and fitness; ability to maintain exercise; and confidence in the exercise and fitness setting
- **Body attractiveness (body):** Perceived attractiveness of figure or physique, ability to maintain an attractive body, and confidence in appearance
- **Physical strength (strength):** Perceived strength, muscle development, and confidence in situations requiring strength
- **Physical self-worth (PSW):** General feelings of happiness, satisfaction, pride, respect, and confidence in the physical self

The inclusion of physical self-worth underscores that the physical subdomains cannot simply be summed to obtain the physical self-worth score. Fox and Corbin (1989) provided evidence for the sensitivity, reliability, and stability of the subscales; confirmed the subscale factor structure; and reported associations of the subscales with physical activity involvement to provide initial validity support. Sonstroem, Speliotis, and Fava (1992) subsequently found that the PSPP showed strong internal consistency, separated exercisers from nonexercisers, and predicted degree of exercise involvement among adults, and they recommended its continued use.

Marsh (Marsh, 1996; Marsh, Richards, Johnson, Roche, & Tremayne, 1994) used psychometric techniques to develop the Physical Self-Description Questionnaire (PSDQ), a multidimensional physical self-concept measure with 11 scales: strength, body fat, activity, endurance and fitness, sport competence, coordination, health, appearance, flexibility, global physical self-worth, and global esteem. Marsh and colleagues provided good psychometric support for the measure. They confirmed its validity by correlating PSDQ subscales with external criterion measures of body composition, physical activity, endurance, strength, and flexibility.

Consistent with the hierarchical models (e.g., Shavelson et al., 1976), Fox and Marsh contend that the subdomains are further divided into more situation-specific areas. For example, sport competence can be divided into a facet (e.g., basketball ability), a subfacet (e.g., shooting ability), and self-efficacy or situation-specific confidence (e.g., "I can make this free throw"). Further, these more dynamic, lower-level self-perceptions affect their more stable, higher-order counterparts. These lower-level self-perceptions (e.g., confidence and self-efficacy) are discussed later in the chapter.

Sonstroem and Morgan (1989) made the nature of the relationship among the higher- and lower-order self-perceptions more explicit in their model, similar to that of Fox (1990) and Marsh (1990). They proposed the following:

1. Physical fitness is more highly related to physical self-efficacy than to physical competence, physical acceptance, and global self-esteem.

2. Physical self-efficacy is more highly related to physical competence than to physical acceptance or global self-esteem.

3. Physical competence is more highly related to global self-esteem than is physical self-efficacy or physical fitness.

Figure 6.1 combines and summarizes the models put forth by Fox and Corbin and Sonstroem and Morgan. Global self-esteem is influenced by physical self-worth—or acceptance, which is influenced by an individual's perceptions of his or her physical abilities and appearance. As

discussed later in this chapter, exercise has been shown to be related to improved self-esteem. This positive outcome is likely to occur through the process by which exercise interventions lead to improved physical functioning, which results in enhanced self-efficacy and improvements in the physical subdomains. This in turn leads to greater physical self-worth and, ultimately, self-esteem.

Further developing the understanding of self-esteem, Marsh (Marsh, Chanal, & Sarrazin, 2006; Marsh & Craven, 2006) argue that achievement is influenced by both a domain-level self-worth (e.g., physical self-worth) and performance, which are mutually reinforcing. Thus, physical performance influences physical self-worth and physical self-worth influences performance.

Enhancing Self-Esteem Through Physical Activity

Application Point

Alexis, who is only 10 years old, suffers from an overall poor self-esteem. Because she is well coordinated and likes to dance, her parents think that dance classes will bolster her low self-esteem. Considering the nature of self-esteem and the structure of the physical self, what do you think of her parents' idea, and why? How might her self-esteem be enhanced, and why would this be likely to happen?

Research on Physical Self-Concept

Earlier reviews of research on psychological benefits of physical activity (e.g., Folkins & Sime, 1981) suggested that vigorous exercise and enhanced fitness might positively affect mood and self-concept. Recent multidimensional self-perception measures allow consideration of more specific relationships among self-perceptions and physical activity, and they may be especially useful with the growing interest in health-oriented exercise and the psychological benefits of physical activity.

Among the many psychological benefits that can be gained from a physically active lifestyle, the greatest impact of exercise may be on self-esteem (Spence, McGannon, & Poon, 2005). Studies on the relationship between self-concept and exercise indicate a positive relationship (e.g., Asci, 2003; Taylor & Fox, 2005). Consistent with the hierarchical model of self-esteem, body esteem shows stronger relationships with fitness than global self-concept, and physical strength and body fat percentage are two physical measures

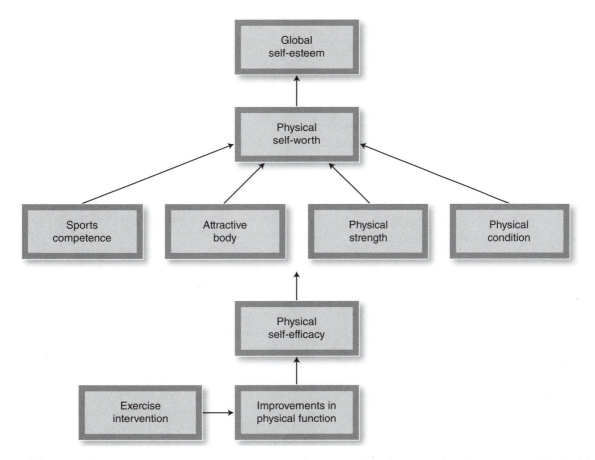

Figure 6.1   The influence of exercise interventions on self-esteem. Exercise and related changes to physical function and appearance influence more immediate psychological outcomes, which are related to the more stable global outcomes like self-esteem.

Adapted, by permission, from K.R. Fox and C.B. Corbin, 1989. "The physical self-perception profile: Development and preliminary validation," *Journal of Sport & Exercise Psychology 11*: 408-430.

that particularly relate to self-concept. Berger and McInman (1993) report that longitudinal or intervention studies on exercise are more mixed. However, participation in resistance exercise and aerobic activity have both been shown to improve self-esteem (Campbell & Hausenblas, 2009). Berger, Pargman, and Weinberg (2007) suggest that the neuropsychological, biochemical, and social cognitive characteristics of aerobic activities are the reason for their effectiveness. They also suggest that exercisers' motives play a role. They cite research revealing that exercisers with health and fitness motives experienced increases in self-esteem more than those with physical appearance motives.

Overall, sport, exercise, and physical activity programs do not have strong effects on global self-worth. As noted in previous chapters, general personality is not likely to change with short-term programs. However, activity programs may well influence specific perceptions of physical com-

petence or body concept. Fox's (2000) review of research on exercise and self-esteem found that 80 percent of studies demonstrated improvements in physical self-worth, with half of the included studies showing improvements in self-esteem. Self-esteem may improve as a result of improved self-efficacy, improved body image, or both through participation in exercise. Those with low self-esteem may have the most to gain from participation in exercise (McAuley, Mihalko, & Bane, 1997). Multidimensional measures may help us further investigate these effects. More specific perceptions of self-efficacy for specific tasks are even more amenable to change. We will consider those self-perceptions later in this chapter. Also, quality of life and psychological well-being, which are discussed in later chapters, encompass mood and emotion, as well as personality and self-concept. For instance, recent work by Legrand (2014) suggests that the positive changes in physical self-perceptions and self-esteem experienced by women of low socioeconomic status after participating in an exercise intervention may account for reduction in symptoms of depression.

Body Image

Body image is a specific self-perception related to physical activity that remains salient throughout the life span. Perceptions of the physical body are part of self-concept. Body perceptions play an important role in physical self-concept, and both Fox (1990) and Marsh (1990, 1996) include body image in their models. Moreover, body image is particularly relevant to sport and exercise psychology work on eating disorders and related concerns with participants in physical activity.

Body image, or our feelings about our body and its function, is subjective and derived from our own self-perceptions as well as the perceptions of others. Poor body image is often associated with anxiety, depression, low self-esteem, eating disorders, and alcohol or drug use.

Body perceptions and measures of body image have been associated with self-concept for some time. Early measures include the Body Cathexis Scale (BCS; Secord & Jourard, 1953) and the Body-Esteem Scale (BES). Other research on body image is grounded in self-presentation (Leary, 1992) and self-esteem literature. Self-presentation theory suggests that as social beings, people desire to make a positive impression and are selective in the self-information they present to others (see Martin Ginis, Lindwall, & Prapavessis, 2007; Prapavessis, Grove, & Eklund, 2004). When people want to present a favorable body image but fear negative evaluation by others, they experience social physique anxiety (SPA). Hart, Leary, and Rejeski (1989), who developed the Social Physique Anxiety Scale (SPAS), provided evidence that the SPAS demonstrates good internal consistency, test–retest reliability, and correlations with other body image and esteem measures and public self-consciousness.

In a review, Rodin and Larson (1992) concluded that cultural and social factors emphasize unrealistic body shapes and that thinness is joined by fitness within the body shape ideal. Developmental factors conspire against females since physical maturation conflicts with the prevailing cultural imperative. Rodin and Larson further concluded that athletes in particular face extraordinary cultural and psychological pressures to maintain an ideal body and that such pressures may lead to eating disorders and substance abuse. Reel and Gill (1996) found strong relationships between both SPAS and body dissatisfaction and eating behavior, suggesting that body image is an important predictor.

Eating disorders are more common among women than among men (cf. Martin Ginis et al., 2007). Body image concerns are not unique to women, however. In fact, research suggests that body image disturbance is increasing in prevalence among boys and young men (see Field et al., 2014). Male bodybuilders with higher SPA are more likely to use anabolic steroids than those with lower SPA (cf. Martin Ginis et al., 2007). Nonetheless, females generally are more concerned with body image than males (Hart et al., 1989) and have been found to have greater SPA (cf. Prapavessis et al., 2004). This is not surprising given the societal image of the ideal female body and the emphasis on physical attractiveness in media coverage of women's sport (see Gill, 2002, 2007). Ultimately, body image concerns affect both men and women, though cultural expectations of what constitutes an ideal body differ by gender.

Participation in aerobic and strength training can improve body image. However, some individuals with poor body image avoid physical activity because it draws attention to the body, further compounding the issue. Some forms of sport and physical activity, such as gymnastics, wrestling, figure skating, and competitive bodybuilding, may especially emphasize participants' body size or appearance, which may lead some athletes to engage in risky diet or exercise strategies to change their bodily appearance or weight. Reel, Galli and their colleagues (2010, 2011, 2013, 2014) have developed two versions (i.e., male athlete and female athlete versions) of the Weight Pressures in Sport scale to assess the various pressures athletes experience to lose weight or change their body in order to improve performance and gain societal acceptance. These pressures may include pressures from coaches about weight (e.g., "My coach encourages athletes on my team to drop pounds") and pressures regarding appearance and performance (e.g., "My performances would improve if I lost 5 pounds").

Self-Confidence and Self-Efficacy

Self-confidence and self-efficacy may be the most critical self-perceptions in sport and exercise psychology. Many top athletes exude confidence. Muhammad Ali and Joe Namath were known for their colorful and convincing boasts. When commenting about his status as a top wide receiver in 2001, the controversial Terrell Owens said, "To be honest, I think I'm a little better than [Randy] Moss. I bring a lot more to the table than he does" (Kroichick, 2001). Though male athletes have been perceived as more likely to be boastful publicly, female athletes have also been outspoken in their self-confidence. United States National Team soccer goalkeeper Hope Solo, described as arrogant by some critics, received quite a bit of notoriety for her comments throughout the 2012 Olympics: "I don't care how people perceive me. I am who I am. And I'm here to win" (Kiszla, 2012).

Athletes recognize the value of a positive attitude, and we tell performers, "Think like a winner" or "Believe in yourself." As noted in chapter 4, the most consistent difference between elite athletes and those who are less successful is that elite athletes possess greater self-confidence (e.g., Gould, Weiss, & Weinberg, 1981; Mahoney & Avener, 1977). Is self-confidence really that important? If so, can we enhance an athlete's confidence? If confidence increases, will athletes perform better, enjoy the activity more, or experience other benefits? Sport and exercise psychologists have applied Bandura's self-efficacy model and social cognitive theory to address these questions, and the work continues to advance in many directions.

Bandura's Self-Efficacy Theory

Albert Bandura (1977b, 1982, 1986, 1997) proposed an elegant model of self-efficacy and behavior. Consistent with models of self-esteem, self-efficacy is a situation-specific form of self-confidence, or the belief that one is competent and can do whatever is necessary to achieve expected outcomes. Self-efficacy may fluctuate greatly, whereas self-confidence is a more global and stable personality characteristic. A high school wrestler in a tournament might feel confident or efficacious going into the first match. If he goes into the final period behind on points, feeling tired, and seeing the opponent looking fresh and eager, he may quickly feel much less confident.

Key Point

Self-efficacy is a situation-specific form of self-confidence, or the belief that one is competent and can do whatever is necessary to achieve expected outcomes. Self-confidence is a more global and stable personality characteristic, whereas self-efficacy may fluctuate greatly.

For Bandura, self-efficacy predicts actual performance when necessary skills and appropriate incentives are present. He suggests that efficacy expectations are the primary determinants of choice of activity, level of effort, and degree of persistence. High-efficacious people seek challenges, try hard, and persist, whereas low-efficacious people tend to avoid challenges, give up, and become more anxious or depressed when faced with adversity. Self-efficacy theory implies that various strategies used by coaches, instructors, and performers affect performance and behavior because they affect self-efficacy—the critical mediating variable.

So far we have considered self-efficacy as an individual characteristic, but Bandura has also suggested the possibility of a collective form of efficacy. Collective efficacy is the shared belief of group members in their joint capabilities as a group to execute a task successfully. It involves the coordinated use of individual resources. Such a notion seems particularly applicable to sport teams. Bandura suggests that aggregating individual members' judgments about the group's capabilities is appropriate when assessing collective efficacy in groups requiring greater coordinated efforts (e.g., an American football team), whereas an aggregate of individuals' self-efficacy is sufficient for groups requiring less coordinated efforts (e.g., a wrestling team). In a review of the literature on collective efficacy in sport, Meyers and Feltz (2007) also conclude that aggregating individual athletes' self-efficacy is not appropriate for highly interdependent tasks.

Research on Sources of Self-Efficacy

Efficacy expectations develop through four primary types (or "sources") of information: performance accomplishments, vicarious experiences, emotional–physiological states, and verbal persuasion. Changes in self-efficacy, in turn, influence actual behavior. Performance accomplishments, or mastery experiences, provide the most dependable information and have the most powerful effects on self-efficacy. In practicing your serve, if you repeatedly view yourself as successful, self-efficacy will increase, whereas repeatedly viewing yourself as unsuccessful will result in lower self-efficacy. Feltz and Lirgg (2001) contend that the power of performance accomplishments depends on the perceived difficulty of the task, effort expended, guidance received, and degree to which the performer views the required ability as innate versus learned.

Vicarious experiences involve watching someone else accomplish the skill (a model). Demonstrations are often used to teach sport skills, and seeing someone else perform can give athletes confidence. Several studies have demonstrated the effectiveness of modeling (see McCullaugh & Weiss, 2001), particularly models who are similar to the observer (George, Feltz, & Chase, 1992; Weiss, McCullaugh, Smith, & Berlant, 1998). Self-modeling, or watching your own correct performance or the best parts of your performance, is also thought to affect self-efficacy. The use of imagery experiences, or simply imagining yourself correctly performing a specific skill, can also serve as a vicarious experience that may help improve self-efficacy for that particular skill (Feltz & Riessinger, 1990).

Verbal persuasion is often used to boost confidence. Teachers and coaches encourage performers with statements such as, "You've got the talent; I know you can do it." Others' evaluations or expectations as well as our own self-talk are forms of verbal persuasion. The use of positive self-talk that is either instructional or motivational while one is learning or executing a skill can improve self-efficacy (Hardy et al., 2005). For example, volleyball players who use instructional self-talk while practicing their serves experienced improved self-efficacy and performance (Zetou, Vernadakis, Bebetsos, & Makraki, 2012).

Bandura suggests that physiological and emotional states, or more precisely, perceptions of arousal, affect behavior through efficacy expectations. A person's physiological state is a function of the autonomic response associated with fear or readiness. If you notice your heart pounding and your knees shaking just before a match, you likely will feel less confident than if your heart were beating strongly and you felt steady. A person's interpretation of his or her physiological arousal may affect efficacy (e.g., do the butterflies in your stomach mean you are nervous, or excited?). Emotional state, or mood, is also associated with self-efficacy. Treasure, Monson, and Lox (1996) found that the higher a wrestler's positive emotional states were (e.g., determined, excited, inspired), the greater the self-efficacy; the higher the negative emotional states, the lower the self-efficacy. Further, the higher the precompetition self-efficacy, the better the wrestler's performance.

Key Point

There are four sources of self-efficacy: performance accomplishment, vicarious experiences, verbal persuasion, and physiological and emotional states. Past performance and vicarious experiences are likely to influence self-efficacy more than verbal persuasion and physiological or emotional states. Having been successful at a particular task in the past is the strongest source of self-efficacy for completing the task in the future.

In discussing sources of collective efficacy, Feltz and Lirgg (2001) suggest that self-efficacy and collective efficacy might share similar sources. At the group level, these sources include performance accomplishment, vicarious experience, verbal persuasion, and physiological and emotional states. For example, if team members repeatedly and collectively perceive team success, the efficacy of the group will probably increase. Likewise, seeing another team beat an upcoming opponent may enhance the group's collective efficacy. In addition, leader effectiveness may influence collective efficacy through minimization of coordination losses and verbal persuasion. Booing or cheering fans and positive or negative press have also been suggested as possible sources of collective efficacy.

Research on Self-Efficacy in the Physical Domain

Over the last two decades, self-efficacy theory has been applied more widely in exercise activities and sport. Based on Feltz and Lirgg's (2001) cogent review of self-efficacy in sport settings, we conclude the following. First, most of the studies show a significant or at least a moderate relationship between self-efficacy and performance. Second, self-efficacy is a stronger predictor of performance than other variables. Third, self-efficacy predicts performance, but performance is a stronger predictor of self-efficacy. Finally, self-efficacy is associated with anxiety, emotions, win orientation, and sport confidence. Collective efficacy may predict team performance more than self-efficacy.

In rehabilitation settings, self-efficacy is also a determinant of behavior. For example, Ewart, Taylor, Reese, and DeBusk (1983) reported that postmyocardial infarction (PMI) patients who were more efficacious about their physical capabilities exerted more effort, recovered faster, and returned to normal activities more quickly. Ewart and colleagues (1986) also demonstrated that PMI patients' efficacy predicted exercise compliance, whereas physical capabilities did not. Taylor, Bandura, Ewart, Miller, and DeBusk (1985) reported that not only patients' efficacy but also their spouses' efficacy predicted cardiac function.

Many studies support strong links between self-efficacy and physical activity. McAuley and his colleagues have conducted several leading studies in this area, and his reviews (McAuley, 1992, 1993; McAuley, Pena, & Jerome, 2001) summarize that work. Self-efficacy predicted exercise behavior in college undergraduates (Dzewaltowski, 1989; Dzewaltowski, Noble, & Shaw, 1990); it predicted exercise adherence for middle-aged adults (McAuley, 1993); and it related to physical activity in a community sample (Sallis et al., 1986). These studies suggest that self-efficacy theory may contribute substantially to our understanding of exercise behavior in both asymptomatic and diseased populations (McAuley, 1993). Physical activity also influences self-efficacy. Acute (e.g., McAuley et al., 1999; McAuley, Lox, & Duncan, 1993; Rudolph & McAuley, 1995) and chronic (Kaplan, Atkins, & Reinsch, 1984; Kaplan, Ries, Prewitt, & Eakin, 1994; Ries, Kaplan, Limberg, & Prewitt, 1995) exposure to exercise resulted in increased self-efficacy. Participation in physical activity can also improve self-efficacy among older adults (McAuley et al., 2006).

Application Point

Improving Self-Efficacy for Injury Recovery

Jamal is in rehabilitation after surgery to repair his anterior cruciate ligament. He has expressed doubts in his ability to fully recover and fears he will never return to game play. How do you think Jamal's attitude will affect his recovery, and why? Also, give three suggestions for bolstering Jamal's self-efficacy.

Self-Efficacy Measures

Self-efficacy by definition is unstable and situation specific. Bandura (1977a, 1986) argued (and most researchers agree) that self-efficacy measures should be microanalytic, assessing efficacy along three dimensions: level, strength, and generality.

- **Level** reflects the expected performance attainment or number of tasks that can be completed. For example, in Feltz's (1984) diving studies, performing the back dive from the board was the highest level, whereas jumping feet first from the side of the pool was a lower level. Components of a complex skill, or lead-up activities, might reflect levels.

- **Strength** represents the certainty with which the person expects to attain each level successfully. Typically, strength of efficacy is measured on a percentage scale, with 100 percent reflecting absolute certainty. On the diving task, a person might be 100 percent certain of successfully jumping off the side of the pool but only 20 percent certain of successfully completing a back dive from the board.

- **Generality** refers to the number of domains in which people consider themselves efficacious. For example, gymnastics efficacy might generalize from efficacy for floor exercise to efficacy for the balance beam and uneven parallel bars.

Because self-efficacy measures refer to specific tasks and situations, they vary widely across studies. Strength is usually the key measure, and most studies use the percentage format. Levels are also common, but they are not as critical as strength. For example, Feltz (1984) focused on the strength of efficacy for the ultimate task (back dive from the board) for her main tests of self-efficacy theory. Generality is even rarer in self-efficacy measures and research.

In addition to measuring qualities like the level, strength, and generality of self-efficacy, we can also measure specific types of self-efficacy (McAuley, White, Mailey, & Wojcicki, 2012). Common types include task-specific self-efficacy ("I believe I can complete 10 repetitions lifting this weight"), adherence self-efficacy ("I believe I can stick to my exercise program for the next six months"), and barriers self-efficacy ("I believe I can exercise regularly when the weather is bad"). Marcus, Selby, Niaura, and Rossi (1992) developed a five-item self-efficacy measure that has since been widely adopted in physical activity research. This short questionnaire measures people's confidence in their ability to persist with their regular exercise behaviors in various situations, such as when a person is tired, in a bad mood, or on vacation, or when the weather is bad or personal time is limited. The interested reader is encouraged to review Marcus and Forsyth's (2009) text,

Motivating People to Be Physically Active, which provides more detailed information, examples, and specific items for measuring self-efficacy.

Given what you have learned about self-efficacy, how might you enhance the self-confidence and efficacy among the people with whom you work and play?

Key Point

Bandura (1977a, 1986) argued that self-efficacy measures should assess efficacy along three dimensions: level, strength, and generality. Specific types of self-efficacy can also be measured, including barriers, task-specific, and adherence self-efficacy.

Putting It Into Practice

Summary

Self-perception is one of the most active research areas in sport and exercise psychology today. The work on physical self-concept has adopted the multidimensional and sport-specific frameworks that have advanced other areas of personality and individual differences. That approach provides stronger conceptual frameworks and sounder measures that allow us to investigate multifaceted relationships among self-perceptions and sport and exercise behaviors. Self-efficacy theory has been useful in the investigation of many behaviors, and sport and exercise psychology has moved from self-efficacy work with sport to a wide range of exercise and activity settings. Moreover, self-efficacy theories and research findings offer practical suggestions for enhancing performance and exercise as well as maintaining health-related activities.

Review Questions

1. Define *self-perceptions*.
2. Define *self-schema* and explain what it means to be schematic, aschematic, and non-schematic.
3. Explain the significance of Harter's model of perceived competence.
4. Describe hierarchical models of self-concept and explain the characteristics of and relationships among the levels.
5. Define and contrast *self-efficacy* and *self-confidence*.
6. What are the main sources of self-efficacy?
7. Describe the three dimensions along which self-efficacy should be analyzed.

Recommended Reading

- Harter, S. (1999). *Construction of the self: A developmental perspective.* New York: Guilford Press. This book traces changes in the structure and content of self-concept in children from a young age through adolescence. It focuses on the progression of individuals' competency-related self-assessment and how factors including significant others, gender, and culture shape these self-assessments.

- Kendzierski, D., Furr, R.M., & Schiavoni, J. (1998). Physical activity self-definitions: Correlates and perceived criteria. *Journal of Sport and Exercise Psychology, 20,* 176-193. Grounded in self-schema theory, this article investigates the criteria for self-definitions in a variety of physical activities (e.g., weightlifting, basketball, exercise) and factors associated with these self-definitions. Results reveal that participants described themselves based on behavioral criteria more than affective criteria.

- Legrand, F.D. (2014). Effects of exercise on physical self-concept, global self-esteem, and depression in women of low socioeconomic status with elevated depressive symptoms. *Journal of Sport and Exercise Psychology, 36*(4), 357-365. doi: 10.1123/

jsep.2013-0253. This study examines the impact of exercise on physical self-worth, self-esteem, and depression in a group of low-income women participating in a seven-week exercise intervention. Results show that physical self-worth was affected first, while reductions in depressive symptoms occurred in subsequent weeks, suggesting that changing self-perceptions through exercise interventions may improve mental health.

LAB

Building Self-Efficacy

Self-efficacy is confidence in one's ability to successfully perform a specific behavior. According to Bandura, self-efficacy predicts behavior, including activity choice, effort, and persistence. As the adage goes, if you think you can, you can! This lab provides an opportunity to apply self-efficacy theory to sport and exercise settings. To complete the lab, fill out the Building Self-Efficacy Worksheet.

Building Self-Efficacy Worksheet

1. Choose a specific activity setting (e.g., a new personal training client worried about getting started with an exercise routine; a physical education student struggling to learn a new skill in class). Activity setting: _____

   _____

   _____

2. Briefly define and describe the four sources of self-efficacy, and give one specific example of how each of the four sources could be used to foster self-efficacy for a client, student, or athlete within your specific sport or exercise activity.

Source	Definition	Example
1.		
2.		
3.		
4.		

Motivation

In part III we turn to motivation, a big and important topic. Motivation refers to the "why" of behavior: Why does one 12-year-old love soccer with her friends while her brother prefers working out on his own? Why does one client persist and progress in his training program while another client puts in little effort? As seen in earlier chapters, behavior is determined (or motivated) by both personal characteristics and environmental factors—remember B = f(P, E).

Part III covers the major theories of and approaches to motivation. First, chapter 7 gives us the basics of behavioral motivation, which focuses on the "E" or environment in motivation, with an emphasis on goals and behavior management. Then we turn to the social cognitive theories and models, which emphasize person characteristics and perceptions in motivation. Chapter 8 begins with discussion of enjoyment and commitment and focuses on the social cognitive models that dominate the sport and exercise psychology research on motivation. Chapter 9 focuses on motivational orientation, including research on achievement and goal orientations in sport and exercise. Finally, chapter 10 brings the behavioral and cognitive approaches together and applies integrated models to promoting and maintaining physical activity behavior.

Behavioral Approaches

Chapter Objectives

After studying this chapter, you should be able to

- define basic behavior terminology, including *reinforcement, punishment,* and *shaping,*

- explain how to set effective (SMART) goals,

- explain the steps in implementing a behavioral plan, and

- understand how kinesiology professionals can use behavioral strategies and approaches to help participants develop skills and maintain physical activity.

Consider these scenarios. The star athlete has had knee surgery and needs months of rehabilitation. The 55-year-old man is told by his physician that he is at risk for a heart attack and must start exercising. The young gymnast is overwhelmed when performing in front of a large audience at her first meet, doesn't live up to expectations, and considers quitting.

How does the trainer help the athlete stick to the prescribed rehabilitation regimen? How does the exercise instructor help the client start and stay with an exercise routine? How does the coach help the gymnast overcome the setback and focus on her performance? These are all questions of motivation. Motivation refers to the why of behavior. More specifically, motivation refers to the intensity and direction of behavior. That is, why do people do what they do (direction), and why do they put in effort and persist (intensity). Ultimately, motivation is self-motivation, but trainers, instructors, and coaches can apply motivational theories and models to help the athlete stick to rehab, help the client develop an exercise routine, or help the young gymnast persist.

As explained in this chapter, one answer is using principles of behavior theory. Behavioral approaches emphasize the "E" in B = f(P, E) and largely ignore person factors. Behavioral approaches emphasize changing the environment because behavior is determined primarily by its consequences. In other words, behavior is strengthened when rewarded and weakened when punished or ignored. But, before we can use behavioral approaches, we must first specify the behavior we want to change. That is, we set goals for behavior. Thus, we begin the chapter with goal setting.

Goals and Goal Setting

Goals are so common that they are almost unavoidable. Participants usually hold multiple goals, and even if they do not form goals, teachers, coaches, exercise instructors, family, or friends often set goals for them. Common as they are, though, goals are not automatically effective. It is much easier to set goals than to make them work effectively.

Simply, a goal is something that a person is trying to accomplish. Typically goals set a target behavior or a standard of excellence. For example, you might set a goal to cut three strokes off your golf game, to walk 1 mile (1.5 kilometers) every day next week, or to finish your first 10K run. Not only are goals common, they work; goals can

help improve performance and change behavior. Before continuing with this chapter, go to the Application Point and think about your goals.

List Your Goals

What are your goals? List two or three goals that you have. List goals that are important to you, and try to include one that is related to physical activity. Look at the goals you listed. How often do you really think about these goals? Do you take any active steps to reach your goals? If you are like most people you don't think about your goals very much, and you don't use them to guide your behavior. In this section we focus on setting effective goals, and then we cover behavioral approaches that can help you reach your goals.

Although goals are common, goals do not automatically change behavior or enhance performance. Some goals are more effective than others. First, we can classify goals as process, performance, or outcome goals. Outcome goals, which are standards of performance or desired results, are most common. Most likely your goals are outcome goals. Outcome goals can help us see where we want to go, but they are not very effective in changing behavior. Performance goals, which focus on improvement relative to one's own performance, and process goals, which focus on processes, procedures, or steps during performance, are more effective. Freund and Hennecke (2015) reviewed the literature and concluded that focusing on *how* (process focus) is more effective in goal pursuit and attainment than an outcome focus, particularly when a high level of skill or self-regulation is required to achieve the goal. Typical performance goals in sport demand skill, and exercise and physical activity goals require self-regulation.

Check your goals again. Can you change an outcome goal into a more effective goal by focusing on more specific performance or process goals that might move you closer to your outcome goal? In the following section we review the literature on effective goal setting and offer guidance on setting effective, SMART goals in sport and exercise.

Locke and Latham's Model of Goal Setting

Goal setting has been a popular research topic in psychology since the 1960s, when Locke began his influential studies. The literature reviewed by Locke and colleagues in 1981 indicated consistent benefits of goal setting for performance, and updated reviews (e.g., Locke & Latham, 1990, 2002) continue to confirm the benefits. That research has extended into sport and exercise psychology, and goal setting is one of the most common psychological interventions in sport and exercise settings. See reviews by Weinberg (2014), Burton and Weiss (2008), or Gould (2015) for more details on that work.

Locke and Latham's extensive research confirmed their primary prediction that specific, difficult (but realistic) goals enhance performance more than vague, easy (e.g., "Do your best") goals or no goals at all. As well as goal difficulty and goal specificity, they also cite goal valence (positive–negative) and goal proximity (short-term or long-term) as key attributes related to goal effectiveness. Just as specific, moderately difficult goals are more effective than vague or easy goals, positive goals that specify what you want to accomplish rather than what you want to avoid are more effective. In terms of proximity most scholars advocate short-term goals, which are more flexible and controllable and help to demonstrate progress and develop confidence. However, long-term goals also have an important role.

As well as identifying attributes, Locke and Latham identified mechanisms and proposed that goals work by directing attention, energizing and mobilizing effort, enhancing persistence, and developing and using relevant knowledge and strategies. They also suggested moderators. Specifically, goal effectiveness may depend on commitment, feedback, and task complexity. Goals are more effective when people see them as important and attainable and thus are more committed. Goals are also more effective when people get feedback, which may enhance confidence as well as allow for adjustments. When tasks are more complex and require higher skill (like most sport skills), new strategies may be needed before goal setting has motivational effects.

Key Point

Locke and Latham proposed that goal setting enhances performance by directing attention, mobilizing effort, enhancing persistence, and developing new learning strategies. Goal effectiveness may depend on ability, commitment, feedback, and task complexity.

Goal Setting in Sport and Exercise

Sport and exercise psychology research suggests that goal setting is popular and often effective, although goal setting in sport is often less effective than in the work settings used in much of the goal-setting research. Goal setting is one of the most common psychological interventions used with athletes. Weinberg, Burton, Yukelson, and Weigand (1993) surveyed athletes at three universities and found that virtually all the athletes set goals, and most considered goal setting to be moderately to highly effective.

Reviews by Burton and Weiss (2008), Gould (2015), and Weinberg (2014) confirm that specific, difficult, challenging goals improve performance more than vague or no goals, but other results are inconsistent. Kyllo and Landers (1995) used meta-analysis techniques and concluded that setting goals generally has a small effect on performance and that moderate, absolute, and combined short- and long-term goals are associated with the greatest effects. Several studies have used goal-setting interventions over an extended time. For example, Wanlin, Hrycaiko, Martin, and Mahon (1997) found that a goal-setting "package" including short- and long-term goals, along with other behavioral strategies, was effective in improving speed skaters' desirable behaviors (e.g., working harder and staying on task) as well as performance. Similarly, Vidic and Burton (2010) found that an eight-week goal-setting program improved confidence and performance of collegiate tennis players. Although most of the sport and exercise psychology research involves athletes, goal setting has also been used in a variety of physical activity settings. As discussed in chapter 10, goal setting is often used in exercise interventions and physical activity promotion, usually in combination with other behavioral and cognitive strategies. Danish and colleagues (Danish, Nellen, & Owens, 1996; Papacharisis, Goudas, Danish, & Theodorakis, 2005) used goal setting to develop life skills in youth sport programs with underserved youth.

Goal-Setting Principles

The extensive psychology research on goal setting, the more limited sport and exercise psychology research, and the reports of consultants who have conducted goal-setting interventions provide guidelines for setting goals effectively. The following principles, drawn from Weinberg (2014) and Gould (2015), are representative:

- **Set specific goals in measurable and behavioral terms.** One of the most consistent research findings is that specific goals enhance performance more than vague or no goals. Set specific goals, such as improving from 70 to 85 percent on free throws or walking 1 mile (1.5 kilometers) five days next week.

- **Set realistic but challenging goals.** Goals should be challenging but attainable.

- **Set short-term as well as long-term goals.** Athletes and exercisers typically have long-term goals, which provide a destination. However, short-term goals are needed to provide feedback about progress, allow for adjustment of goals, and generally keep people on track to meet their long-term goals.

- **Set goals for both practice and competition.** Practice goals can help focus attention and effort, develop strategies, and create a more realistic and motivating situation.

- **Ink it, don't think it—record goals.** Many authors advocate writing down and recording goals. Moreover, goals should be placed where they will be visible and salient. Goals can be "written" on a smartphone or in the cloud as long they are easily accessible.

- **Develop goal achievement strategies.** Identify strategies for reaching goals. For example, how might you improve free throw percentage? Perhaps you could change your technique or use specific practice drills.

- **Set process and performance goals as well as outcome goals.** Focus on process and performance rather than outcomes. The best way to win the gold (reach a desired outcome) is to focus on performance and process goals.

- **Set positive (vs. negative) goals.** Set goals in positive terms (e.g., increase free throw percentage by 10 percent, go to exercise class three days this week) that tell you what to do, rather than what not to do.

- **Set group as well as individual goals.** Most of our research and interventions focus on individual goals. But group goals, and individual goals that focus on the person's contribution to the group goal, are particularly useful with teams and group activities.

- **Provide support for goals.** Social support plays a role in goal attainment; coaches and instructors who show a genuine concern for participants provide goal support.

- **Evaluate goals.** Coaches, instructors, and trainers should provide feedback on goal effectiveness as well as on actual performance and should guide participants in revising goals.

Common Goal-Setting Problems

Of course, no goal-setting intervention is perfect. Some common problems in goal setting, again from Weinberg (2014) and Gould (2015), are as follows:

- **Failure to monitor goal progress and modify unrealistic goals.** People often start off strong but then fade. Reevaluation can help keep people motivated and on track.

- **Failure to recognize individual differences.** People differ, and goal setting should differ from person to person. Your exercise goals need not be the same as those of your younger, more fit best friend. Similarly, coaches and instructors should help individualize goals rather than assume that one goal fits all.

- **Setting goals that are too general or setting only outcome goals.** As noted earlier, people often set general, vague goals (e.g., "Improve my game"). Specific, measurable (SMART) goals emphasizing process and performance are more effective.

- **Setting too many goals.** People often set too many goals and have difficulty monitoring and tracking them. Help participants set priorities and focus on only a few initial goals.

Get SMART and SMARTER About Goals

Many resources on goals and goal setting draw from the literature and advocate SMART goals. SMART is an acronym that can help you set effective goals for yourself or when working with others.

SMART Goals

- **Specific:** The key principle. Specific, explicit, numerical goals are more effective than "do your best" goals. They are easier to identify, and you know when they are achieved. (Specific is key, but we could add an extra "S" [to get SSMART] for Self-determined. As we discuss in the next chapter, self-determined goals foster intrinsic motivation.)

- **Measurable:** Goals must measurable, so that you can see improvement.
- **Action oriented:** The participants must know exactly what they must do. Goals are actions or behaviors, and they are positive (what to do) rather than negative (what not to do).
- **Realistic:** Goals should be realistic yet challenging—a key to effective goals, but a tough balance.
- **Time based:** Set definitive time limits for each goal.

SMART goals set the target. Often, our targets in sport and exercise settings are far off, and as noted in connection with the principles and discussed in the following section, it is important to develop a goal plan and to monitor, evaluate, and revise goals as needed. So, we add "E" (for Evaluate) and "R" (for Revise) to get SMARTER over the long term.

SMARTER Goals

SMARTER goals build from the same list that makes up the SMART goals and add the following:

- **Evaluate:** Use feedback and adjust goals (do they still fit the SSMART principles?).
- **Revise:** Change if needed; set new goals once you have reached your original goal.

Application Point

SMART Goal Setting

You are a personal trainer, and Amy is your new client. Amy is an office manager at a local business. She was a high school athlete, but has done little exercise and has gained weight over the last 10 years. At your first meeting, Amy says, "I want to get back in shape, like when I was a high school athlete, by my 10th reunion, six months from now." Given that statement, how SMART is Amy's current goal plan? Explain how it is or isn't SMART. Then, as the professional, help her develop a SMARTER goal plan. Specifically, help Amy identify a SMART long-term goal (six months or longer). Then, identify two short-term goals that build toward that long-term goal. Again, try to make these SMART goals.

From Goal Setting to Goal Striving: Action Plans

As the goal-setting principles and SMARTER goals guidelines suggest, goal setting in physical activity settings typically extends over an extended time. For example, a client might have a goal of running a marathon within a year, and athletes continually work to develop and improve skills. Their goals may be SMART, but they are far off, and such long-term goals are not very effective in changing behavior. To reach long-term goals, a more specific action plan is needed. The strategy of combining short-term goals with those long-term goals, as suggested in some of the sport and exercise psychology research, can help. One strategy is to develop a goal staircase.

For example, if you are a personal trainer working with the client who wants to run a marathon a year from now, you can help the client set up a goal staircase. Start by helping the client make the long-term goal (running the marathon) as specific and SMART as possible. Then, help the client think about the steps that will lead up to that long-term goal. Work back from that long-term goal to short-term goals (and always SMART goals). Once you and the client have a reasonable set of SMART steps, focus on the most immediate short-term goal (e.g., goal for the coming week). Follow the goal principles, and be sure to get SMARTER and evaluate and revise as the client moves up the steps. Some setbacks or skipped steps are likely, and readjusting the goals along the way can smooth the path to the long-term goal.

Moving from goal setting to goal striving calls for a wider range of strategies. Behavioral approaches, covered in the rest of the chapter, are particularly useful in helping people stay on track to reach long-term goals.

Behavioral Basics

As most people learn in beginning psychology, the two basic behavioral processes are classical conditioning and operant conditioning. Classical conditioning involves learning by association with existing involuntary, reflective responses, whereas operant conditioning involves learning new skills and changing behavior. Operant conditioning is the more relevant process for physical activity behavior and thus is the focus of this chapter.

Key Point

Classical conditioning involves learning by association with existing involuntary, reflective responses, whereas operant conditioning involves learning new skills and changing behavior.

Classical conditioning is widely known through the work of Ivan Pavlov. A Nobel Prize–winning Russian physiologist, Pavlov made his name in psychology somewhat serendipitously after noticing that his dogs began to salivate at the sound of an assistant approaching with food. Pavlov then set up his classical-conditioning experiment. Classical conditioning begins with an existing (unconditioned) stimulus–response connection. In this case, the dog naturally salivates in response to food. To begin classical conditioning, Pavlov sounded a tone immediately before presenting the food. After several trials, the dog began to salivate at the tone regardless of whether the food followed. We now have a conditioned stimulus–response connection, developed by association. The tone is the conditioned stimulus, and the salivation response to the tone is the conditioned response. Classical conditioning is seldom used intentionally as an instructional strategy, but it does occur in sport and exercise, as well as in everyday life.

Today, most behavioral approaches and techniques are based on principles of operant conditioning. Operant conditioning does not depend on an existing stimulus–response connection, but it can be used to learn new skills or modify behavior. Behavioral management is effective, gives the person control, emphasizes learning, and is relatively easy to use. Behavior management includes numerous techniques, many of which are discussed here along with practical applications.

Basic Principles: Reinforcement and Punishment

To understand behavioral approaches, we start with the basics. The most basic principle of behavior management or operant learning, as in B.F. Skinner's widely recognized work, is that behavior is determined by its consequences. The basic consequences of any behavior are reinforcement or punishment. The key to behavior change is reinforcement. *Reinforcement* is any stimulus, event, or condition that immediately follows a response and increases the frequency of that response. That is, reinforcement is anything that strengthens a behavior. Common reinforcers include tangible rewards such as trophies, certificates, T-shirts, and scholarships, as well as nontangible rewards such as praise, cheers from the crowd, or comments on one's fit and healthy look. Successful performance itself is a common reinforcer; seeing the ball go through the basket or jogging that extra mile may reinforce specific behaviors. In these examples, behaviors are reinforced through provision of something positive such as praise or awards. This is termed *positive reinforcement*.

Key Point

Reinforcement is any stimulus, event, or condition that immediately follows a response and increases the frequency of that response. Positive reinforcement occurs when behaviors are reinforced through the provision of something positive. Negative reinforcement occurs when behaviors are strengthened through the removal of something negative.

Behaviors also can be strengthened through the removal of something negative or aversive. This is called *negative reinforcement*. Negative reinforcement is less obvious than positive reinforcement, but it does occur. For example, a coach may stop playing loud, annoying music only after the athletes have completed the required number of sit-ups. If you learned to dive into the water the way most beginners do, you probably took some painful belly flops. When you finally performed the dive correctly, you did not feel the usual pain. Removal of the pain negatively reinforced the correct diving technique. People may find negative reinforcement confusing because we often use the term *negative reinforcement* when we mean *punishment*. Remember, negative reinforcement is reinforcement—an operation that increases the strength of a behavior.

Punishment is any event or condition that follows a behavior and decreases the strength of the behavior. Punishment is the opposite of reinforcement, and punishment can occur through the presentation of something negative or through the withdrawal of something positive. Critical comments on poor play, penalties for improper behavior, and being faked out by an opponent may punish the preceding behaviors. Parents often withdraw privileges to punish undesirable behavior. Similarly, coaches may bench a player for skipping practice sessions.

Although it seems logical that we should punish undesirable behaviors as much as we reinforce desirable behaviors, this is not the case. Instead, a positive approach emphasizing reinforcement is preferable. Punishment should be used only when a behavior must be stopped, for example when someone's behavior is endangering him- or herself or others. If used, punishment should be immediate and clearly linked to the behavior, not the person. Rarely do we really need to stop behaviors in physical activity settings, and attempts to use punishment often backfire. Attention given to the unruly student can serve as a reinforcer, and the threat of punishment can lead students to avoid us and the activity. Punishment does not teach behaviors; it teaches people to avoid punishment. Most of the time, teachers and coaches want to teach or modify behavior, and reinforcement is more effective.

Key Point

Punishment is an aversive condition that follows a behavior and decreases rather than increases the strength of the behavior. Although punishment is effective in certain situations, a system involving reinforcements is preferable.

As shown in figure 7.1, the two basic behavioral operations are reinforcement and punishment. Reinforcement entails presenting something positive (positive reinforcement) or taking away something negative (negative reinforcement) in order to increase the preceding behavior. Punishment entails presenting something negative or taking away something positive in order to decrease the preceding behavior.

Implementing a Behavior Plan

Using behavioral approaches effectively involves incorporating the basic principles into a behavioral action plan. Whether you are planning to manage your own behavior or helping a client, there are several steps in implementing a behavioral plan.

1. Clarify the problem and set goals.
2. Define (specific, observable) target behaviors.
3. Identify the starting and maintaining conditions of the target behavior (A-B-C model, explained later in this section).
4. Design a behavior modification plan (use A-B-C model).
5. Implement the plan.
6. Evaluate and revise the plan.

Clarify the Problem and Set Goals: Get Specific, Be SMART

As noted in the goal-setting section, people often have vague goals that are outcomes rather than behaviors (e.g., "I can't concentrate on the game," "I want to get in shape"). The first step is to *get specific*. By specifying the problem, both the client and the consultant will be working on the same challenge.

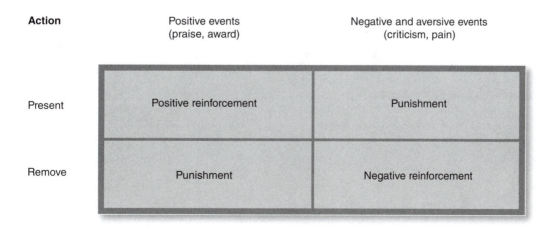

Action	Positive events (praise, award)	Negative and aversive events (criticism, pain)
Present	Positive reinforcement	Punishment
Remove	Punishment	Negative reinforcement

Figure 7.1 Reinforcement and punishment.

For instance, when an athlete describes difficulties with concentration, what does that really mean? When is the athlete having difficulty focusing? What exactly is the athlete having problems focusing on? What does "get in shape" mean for the client? By clearly defining the problem, we are able to tailor the behavior plan to the client's concerns.

Once the problem is clarified, specific goals need to be formulated. As discussed earlier, goals should be SMART—specific and in measurable, behavioral terms. That is, goals are specific target behaviors, and the behavioral action plan is a way to reach those goals. Consultants may give guidance, but goals must be the participant's goals, and similarly the behavioral plan is the participant's plan.

Define Target Behaviors: Get More Specific

A target behavior is a specific aspect of the problem that is clearly defined and easily measured. A client might have trouble completing a moderately intense workout three times a week. A personal trainer might sit down with the client and help him or her define a more specific target workout behavior. For instance, a specific target behavior might be completing two sets of 15 repetitions on each station of a weight training circuit during a workout. These target behaviors are narrow in scope, clearly defined using unambiguous language, and appropriate for the person. The more specific, the better.

The behavior must also be measurable, and measurement must begin before the action plan is put into place in order to set the baseline. The baseline is how often the target behavior occurs in a natural setting before the behavioral plan begins. For instance, the client who wants to increase the number of sets during each workout would have to monitor the number of sets performed before implementing a plan developed with the trainer.

Key Point

When designing a target behavior, it is important to select behaviors that the athlete or exerciser can actively work toward rather than a behavior that the person should not do.

When identifying a target behavior, it is important to select a behavior that the participant can actively work toward (something to do) rather than a behavior that the person should not do. For example, rather than a goal of not focusing on the crowd, a more effective goal would be to focus on a particular spot in the stadium each time the athlete becomes distracted. Telling a person not to do something does not provide a target and may prompt negative behavior. For example, do not think about a pink elephant for the next 2 minutes, or do not pick your head up on the golf swing. Make your target behaviors ones that you can actively perform.

Identify Conditions of the Target Behavior (A-B-C Model)

The next step is determining why the person maintains the current behaviors. For instance, why does the cardiac rehabilitation client not follow through on his exercise routine? This step requires an in-depth look at the client and the behavior.

A good way to understand behaviors is through the A-B-C model. The *A* stands for the antecedents, or the events that occur before the behavior. The *B* stands for the behavior itself. The *C* stands for the consequences, or the events that occur as a result of the behavior. Both antecedents and consequences can maintain a behavior. Antecedents are triggers or cues for the behavior. For instance, think about how your behavior differs when you are sitting in class, at a party, or on the sport field. Each environment has antecedents that trigger specific behaviors. Consequences determine whether the behavior will occur again. If the consequences of a behavior are aversive or negative (i.e., punishment), the behavior is less likely to be repeated. Conversely, if the consequences are positive (i.e., reinforcement), the behavior is likely to occur again. Consequences may occur immediately or be delayed, and they can happen directly to the person, to other people, or to the environment as a result of the person's behavior. For instance, a consequence of being late to practice might mean the whole team has to do push-ups.

A thorough assessment of the A-B-Cs (antecedents, behavior, consequences) is key to implementing an effective behavioral plan. This assessment can be done in a variety of ways and is most effective with multiple forms of assessment. Multiple reporters could include the client, the coach or trainer, teammates, friends, and family. Multiple aspects of the behavior may include overt behavior (e.g., number of sets), inner thoughts and emotions, and perhaps even physiological responses (e.g., heart rate).

Behavior can be assessed in several ways. One method is an interview with questions emphasizing the *what, when, where, how,* and *how often* of the behavior. In addition, a client may complete self-report inventories about current behaviors. Inventories are helpful, provided that the person answers the questions honestly and that the inventory actually measures what you want it to measure (e.g., anxiety in a game situation).

Another method is to actually observe the behavior. Coaches or consultants might watch an athlete during competition, practice, or even outside of the sport setting, noting the athlete's activities or using checklists and behavior rating scales.

Finally, and most importantly, individuals can record their own behaviors. Self-monitoring has several advantages over the other assessment techniques. For one, it allows the person to record both overt and covert behaviors, including thoughts about the behavior that an observer could not get. Most important, self-monitoring puts the person in control. Self-monitoring can help you see the antecedents and consequences of your behaviors, which in turn can suggest strategies for changing behavior. A consultant might well help a client self-monitor behavior, then work with the client to review and use those findings to set up a specific behavioral plan.

Some evidence indicates that simply the act of self-recording has a positive impact on performance. McKenzie and Rushall (1974) found that self-recording increased attendance and the number of practice laps taken by young swimmers. Critchfield and Vargas (1991) confirmed those

results and additionally found that self-recording was more effective than other interventions. Polaha, Allen, and Studley (2004) found that self-monitoring was effective in the development of swimming skills and concluded that self-monitoring is one of the simplest and most effective methods of behavioral change.

One drawback to self-monitoring behavior is the chance that the person may be inaccurate or biased in the reporting. Multiple assessments (formal records, other observers) can counter that while maintaining the benefits of self-monitoring.

At this point, you have clarified the problem and formed goals, defined a target behavior, and identified maintaining conditions. Now, how do you actually change behavior?

Design a Behavioral Plan

To change behavior, we go back to the A-B-C model. That is, we change the target behavior by changing the conditions (antecedents and consequences) that maintain it. Many conditions may maintain a behavior, which is why it is crucial that those conditions be thoroughly and carefully identified. For instance, the cardiac rehab client may stay late at work, like to spend time with family, or perhaps view exercise as punishing and thus does not follow through on his workout regimen. We can change antecedents (avoid those cues or events that lead to skipping exercise or add cues that prompt exercise); and it is a good idea to use effective antecedents, but most behavioral plans focus on the consequences, particularly reinforcement. For the cardiac rehab client, we want to reinforce exercise behavior and make the experience more rewarding, which will increase compliance.

Reinforcement

The key aspect of behavior management is reinforcement of the desired target behavior. Again, reinforcement is any stimulus, event, or condition that immediately follows and strengthens a specific behavior. Positive reinforcers are most effective, and rewards must be reinforcing to the person and administered in effective ways. For some participants, rewards such as T-shirts or snacks may be effective, but others may find improved fitness and appearance more powerful reinforcers. Money is often seen as a reward, but it might not be rewarding for some people, and it has other drawbacks. You can never assume that a particular consequence will serve as a reinforcer. Furthermore, what is reinforcing to one person may not be reinforcing to another. For example, one exerciser may like music during workouts while another finds it annoying; one athlete may welcome a coach's constant comments while a teammate becomes anxious and makes errors.

Reinforcers may be tangible, such as money, food, or awards, or social and intangible, such as attention, praise, and recognition from others. For instance, when the leaders of an exercise class announce the names of those who had perfect attendance for the month, they are reinforcing participants for adherence.

Public posting of records can be an effective reinforcer. Brobst and Ward (2002) found that public posting, along with goal setting and feedback, was effective in improving athletic performance both during and after the intervention. Social reinforcers are easy to administer and effective.

Finally, you can schedule rewarding activities following completion of a task that is less rewarding. This strategy, termed the *Premack principle*, allows people to engage in behaviors they want to do only after doing behaviors they do not want to do. For instance, after completing a challenging new exercise routine, a personal trainer might ask the client to pick a favorite exercise to finish the session.

Effective administration of reinforcers is also important. The reinforcer may be immediate, and generally immediate reinforcers are more effective, but both immediate and long-term reinforcers may be included in a behavior plan. For instance, a consultant could write a behavioral contract with a cardiac rehab client that includes a list of the behaviors the client needs to accomplish, how many tokens earned for each behavior, a list of rewards, and how many tokens needed to earn a reward. These tokens may be eventually exchanged for movie tickets, exercise clothes, or other rewards.

A Caution About Using Reinforcement

Although reinforcement is a key principle in behavior plans, and positive reinforcers are effective, rewards, particularly monetary rewards and costly reinforcers, can create problems. As we will see in the next chapters, rewards can undermine or reduce motivation when participants see themselves as working for the reward. That is, the rewards become controlling, which detracts from self-motivation. For example, in a review of worksite incentives for exercise behaviors, Strohacker, Galarraga, and Williams (2014) found that incentives were helpful during the intervention but not in sustaining exercise behaviors. Less valuable rewards are often just as effective and not likely to be seen as controlling behavior.

Most behaviorists advocate that teachers and coaches use positive reinforcement extensively. Positive reinforcement is more than standing by and saying, "Nice work." It is most effective when applied immediately and consistently, and when both the teacher and student know what specific behaviors are being reinforced. Guidelines for effective reinforcement include (a) reinforcing immediately, (b) reinforcing consistently (especially in early learning stages), (c) reinforcing effort and behavior and not outcomes (successful outcomes such as scoring a goal or finishing a 5K run are reinforcers in themselves), and (d) using occasional or intermittent reinforcement even after skills are well learned or behaviors are established. Teachers often focus on correcting errors and ignore students who create no problems, which may lead those students to change behaviors in undesirable ways.

Shaping: Reinforcing Steps

Many of the target behaviors in physical activity settings are not simple behaviors that we can immediately reinforce. Often the targets are exercise training, lifestyle activity patterns, or specific skills that require extensive practice. For example, if you are working with a beginning tennis player on the topspin serve and wait for the student to do the serve correctly before giving reinforcement, you will wait a long time. The student would likely get frustrated and not show much improvement. Rather than wait for the desired behavior, you can use a more effective behavioral strategy to gradually shape behavior over time. *Shaping* is the reinforcement of successive approximations of the final desired performance. It is a key technique in sport and exercise because most physical skills, routines, and behavioral patterns develop gradually through progressive steps. For instance, shaping can help a tennis player learn a particular serve or help an older adult develop a consistent exercise routine. Effective teachers identify successive steps and reinforce participants as they move toward the correct performance.

Komaki and Barnett (1977) used positive reinforcement and shaping to improve the performance of youth football players on three specific plays. Each play was broken down into specific steps, and the coach modeled the correct movements and provided detailed instruction on specific target behaviors. Performance improved about 20 percent after the reinforcement was systematically applied on each play. Fitterling and Ayllon (1983) found that detailed behavioral instruction helped ballet students increase the time they met target behaviors from 13 to 88 percent for the skills that were measured. Other studies have shown that the systematic use of reinforcement improved performance in gymnastics, swimming, baseball, golf, and tennis (Smith, Smoll, & Christensen, 1996).

Shaping Rehab Behavior

Shaping is a particularly useful behavioral technique for developing skills, maintaining physical activity behaviors, or progressing through rehabilitation exercises. As a therapist, how could you use shaping to help a client recovering from knee surgery progress through an exercise rehabilitation program leading to recovery of full range of motion and normal activity? Identify steps in the program and the reinforcement strategies you might use.

Application Point

Implement the Plan

Once the goals and the behavior plan are set, whether the plan is self-set or agreed upon by a client and consultant, the plan begins on an agreed-upon date. The plan is continually monitored and adjusted over time. For instance, if the goals change or life circumstances prevent certain activities, the goals and activities would need to be revised.

Evaluate the Plan

Evaluation begins with implementation of the behavioral plan and continues with revisions to ensure that the plan is effective in moving toward the target goal. If the target behavior is not reached, it may be time to reexamine the A-B-C variables maintaining the behavior and perhaps find another strategy. Again, assessment and monitoring of progress are needed. Whether that progress is a higher batting average, increased attendance at an exercise program, or successful progression through rehabilitation, you should be able to measure success.

Behavioral Approaches in Professional Practice

Behavioral approaches can be used effectively in a wide variety of kinesiology settings, including physical education, sport, fitness, and rehabilitation exercise. For example, behavioral strategies play a key role in helping people start and maintain lifestyle physical activity. We'll return to behavioral approaches when we discuss the role of behavioral strategies in integrated models of physical activity behavior in chapter 10. The following sections of this chapter focus on behavioral approaches in coaching. Specifically, we highlight Tharp and Gallimore's early work and Smith and Smoll's continuing work on youth sport coaching, one of the most extensive and influential research-into-practice examples in sport and exercise psychology.

Tharp and Gallimore's Research on John Wooden's Coaching Behavior

One of the first attempts to assess coaching behavior was Tharp and Gallimore's (1976) observational study of John Wooden, perhaps the most successful coach in college basketball. Before retiring in 1975, Wooden coached the UCLA (University of California, Los Angeles) men's basketball teams to 10 national championships in 12 years, a record no one else has approached. Tharp and Gallimore's coding system incorporated standard teaching behavior categories such as reward and punishment (verbal or nonverbal praise or scolds), instruction (statements about what to do or how to do it), and modeling (demonstration), as well as a few categories created for Wooden's behavior, such as hustles (statements to activate or intensify previously instructed behaviors). The authors observed and coded 2,326 teaching behaviors over 30 hours of practice in the 1974 to 1975 season.

The most striking finding was the predominance of instruction. Despite the UCLA team's experience and high skill level, more than 50 percent of Wooden's behaviors were specific instructions. Counting other informational acts, such as modeling and reinstruction, about 75 percent of Wooden's behaviors provided instruction, most of which involved basic basketball skills.

The authors found that Wooden seldom used praise, scolding, or nonverbal punishment. Keep in mind that the UCLA basketball players received tremendous praise and public acclaim, and certainly their many successes were rewarding. Most students and athletes do not have this history of success and rewards, and we should not assume that limiting praise is an effective coaching technique. The most extensive research on coaching behavior, discussed in the following section, indicates that effective coaches give considerable praise and encouragement and rarely use punitive behaviors (Smith & Smoll, 1997, 2012).

Gallimore and Tharp (2004) revisited Wooden's remarks to better understand the qualitative aspect of his coaching rather than simply counting his behaviors. The analysis showed that Wooden employed many of the aforementioned behavior strategies. He had an extensive, detailed plan for daily practices that he based on continual evaluation of individual and team development and performance. He made specific individual and team goals, allowing him to anticipate and understand what his players would do or fail to do.

Wooden went to practices with note cards describing the details of a skill the players needed to work on. Examples include moves for a particular position on the court and specific offensive and defensive mechanics that each player needed to master. He explained to the researchers, "I could track the practice of every single player for every single practice session he participated in while I was coaching him" (p. 126). He looked for small improvements over time, understanding that big improvements do not happen quickly. With his detailed skills training, positive reinforcement, and constant reevaluation of both player and team goals, Wooden clearly was skilled at using behavioral approaches, as well as a successful coach.

Key Point

The most extensive research on coaching behavior indicates that effective coaches give considerable praise and encouragement and rarely use punitive behaviors. The three-step feedback sandwich, when a positive, action-oriented instruction is sandwiched between two encouraging statements, is particularly effective.

Smith and Smoll's Work on Coaching Behavior

Ron Smith and Frank Smoll began systematically studying coaching behavior over 35 years ago, and they have extended that long-term research into educational and applied programs for coaches, parents, and the general public. In later chapters we focus more on coach–athlete relationships. In this chapter we focus on their work on the assessment of coach behaviors and identification of effective behavioral approaches for coaches.

Smith, Smoll, and Hunt (1977) began their work by developing an observational system, the Coaching Behavior Assessment System (CBAS), to quantify coaching behaviors. After observing and analyzing the behaviors of coaches in several sports, Smith and colleagues generated the 12 categories of coaching behaviors in the CBAS. Those coaching behaviors fall into two major classes: reactive behaviors and spontaneous behaviors.

Reactive behaviors are reactions to players' behaviors, specifically to desirable performances, mistakes, and misbehaviors. Mistakes are common and tend to elicit the most coaching behaviors. Following are the specific coach reactive behaviors.

- Responses to desirable performance
  - Reinforcement: verbal or nonverbal positive rewarding action
  - Nonreinforcement: failure to respond to good performance
- Responses to mistakes
  - Mistake-contingent encouragement: encouragement following a mistake
  - Mistake-contingent technical instruction: instructing on how to correct a mistake
  - Punishment: verbal or nonverbal negative reaction to mistake

- Punitive technical instruction: instruction given in a punitive manner
- Ignoring mistakes: failure to respond to mistakes
- Responses to misbehavior
  - Keeping control: reactions to maintain order

Spontaneous behaviors are not reactions but are initiated by the coach. Spontaneous coach behaviors may be game related or irrelevant to the game. Following are the specific spontaneous behaviors.

- Game related
  - General technical instruction: spontaneous instruction in techniques and strategies (not following a mistake)
  - General encouragement: spontaneous encouragement
  - Organization: assigning duties, responsibilities, positions, and so on
- Game irrelevant
  - General communication: interactions unrelated to the game

To use the CBAS, observers check the appropriate category for each observed behavior. The proportions of behaviors in the 12 categories are used to measure coaching style. Smith and colleagues (1977) demonstrated that the CBAS is easy to use, includes most coaching behaviors, has good reliability, and shows individual differences among coaches. In general, coaches use considerable reinforcement and instruction, but styles differ, most notably in the amount of instruction and proportion of positive behaviors and punitive behaviors.

The CBAS enabled researchers to investigate practical questions, such as whether differences in coaching behaviors affect players, and if so, whether coaches can be trained to use effective behaviors. Smith, Smoll, and Curtis (1978) used the CBAS to assess behaviors of Little League coaches and compared those behaviors with players' attitudes, enjoyment, and self-esteem.

In general, the coaches took a positive approach, using a great deal of reinforcement, technical instruction, and general encouragement. The players perceived coaching behaviors accurately, but the coaches' perceptions of their own behaviors were not accurate; they did not know which behaviors they used most often. Those results

imply that the first step in a coach training program should be to make coaches aware of their actual behaviors. That knowledge alone may be sufficient to positively modify the behaviors of many well-intentioned coaches who do not realize how much reinforcement or instruction they actually provide.

Understanding effective coaching behaviors is essential before implementing a behavioral plan. As you might expect, coaches who used more reinforcement and encouragement and fewer punitive behaviors were better liked. Contrary to the belief that children just want to have fun and don't care about skill development, coaches who used more instruction also were better liked. A positive approach combining instruction with encouragement related not only to participants' liking for the coach but also to their liking for the activity and teammates, as well as to a greater increase in self-esteem over the season.

You might think that coaches who used the positive approach won more games and that success led to positive player attitudes. However, coaching behaviors did not relate to win–loss records, and players did not like winning coaches any better than losing coaches. The best-liked coaches actually had a slightly, but not significantly, lower win percentage (0.422) than the least-liked coaches (0.545).

Smoll and Smith have not only continued their research but, more importantly, they extended their work into behavioral interventions for youth sport coaches and made their work widely available to coaches, parents, and the general public—with more impact than much of our research. For example, their book *Sport Psychology for Youth Coaches* (Smith & Smoll, 2012) offers sound evidence-based advice in readable form, and their Youth Enrichment in Sports website offers a wealth of information and resources. We cover positive youth development in more detail in later chapters. Here, we focus on guidelines for effective coaching behaviors, which are relevant across the wide range of coaching, teaching, and other professional settings. Specifically, Smith and Smoll advocate a positive behavioral approach.

The positive approach includes liberal use of positive reinforcement, encouragement, and sound technical instruction. Punitive responses are discouraged. The positive approach should be applied not only to skill development but also to desirable responses such as teamwork and sportsmanship. One effective way to implement the positive approach is through the feedback sandwich.

In this three-step approach, a positive, action-oriented instruction is sandwiched between two encouraging statements. For example, after your shortstop has bobbled a grounder, immediately give a sincere, encouraging statement: "Nice try. You got into position well." Then, give a corrective instruction: "Next time, put your glove on the ground and look the ball into it." Finally, finish off with another encouraging statement: "Hang in there. You'll get it."

Using the Feedback Sandwich in Coaching

Smith and Smoll's research with CBAS and coach training supports the positive approach, but it's not always easy to use this approach in practice. Assume that you are coaching a community soccer team of 10- to 12-year-olds. Several players are out of position and missing passes. How could you use the feedback sandwich with these players?

Self-Regulation and Habits

Much of this chapter discusses how teachers, coaches, and consultants can use behavioral approaches in professional practice. Reviews of behavioral approaches often leave the impression that behavioral techniques are something we do to others. In fact, the most effective uses of behavioral techniques are for self-regulation. That is, we use goals and behavioral approaches to regulate our own behavior and reach our goals. As mentioned in the section on SMART goals, self-determined goals are desirable and more motivating than goals set by others. Coaches, trainers, and consultants who are knowledgeable about goal setting and behavioral approaches can help students and clients set effective goals and behavioral plans, but self-monitoring and self-regulation of behavior are critical for success.

Self-regulation is particularly relevant when people are trying to start and maintain physical activity and exercise programs. Behavioral approaches are good ways to turn behavioral goals into habits. Maintaining regular physical activity is not easy, but when physical activity becomes a habit, or an automatic response, people do not need to think about it or plan for it and are more active. Several studies (e.g.,

Rhodes & De Bruijn, 2010; Wood & Neal, 2007) confirm that habits relate to physical activity behavior, and in a meta-analysis, Gardner, de Bruijn, and Lally (2011) found a medium-strong relationship between physical activity and habit strength. Rebar, Elavsky, Maher, Doerksen, and Conroy (2014) found that habits were particularly good predictors of activity on days when intentions were weak. Intentions fluctuate; some days you just don't feel like getting up and going to the gym. But if you have a strong habit, you don't keep thinking about it. You grab your workout gear and just do it.

Key Point

Behavioral approaches are good ways to turn behavioral goals into habits. Maintaining regular physical activity is not easy, but when physical activity becomes a habit, or automatic response, people do not need to think about it or plan for it and are more active.

Self-regulation, using behavioral strategies, helps turn our behavior into habits, and it can help us stick with exercise when program leaders and consultants are no longer there to keep us on track. De Bruin and coauthors (2012) acknowledged the large gap between intentions and health behaviors, and specifically found that while intentions predicted behavior, self-regulatory processes added to the prediction of exercise and may mediate the intention–behavior relationship. Dishman, Jackson, and Bray (2014) reported that the use of self-regulatory behavioral processes (e.g., reinforcement, cues) predicted exercise adherence. Mann, de Ridder, and Fujita (2013) reviewed the research on the role of self-regulation of health behavior in goal setting and goal striving. They concluded that there is no one answer for all people in all settings, but recommended several strategies. Specifically, they recommended that goals for health and physical activity behavior be consistent with other personal goals. In addition, they suggested identifying opportunities and planning appropriate behaviors while also considering barriers and prospective actions, developing habits, and deliberately redirecting attention and behavior away from tempting alternatives (e.g., sleeping in, skipping workouts for social events).

Putting It Into Practice

Summary

Behavioral techniques, which emphasize the role of the environment and behavioral contingencies, are the basics of behavior management. Operant conditioning and related behavior modification techniques can be highly effective with specific sport skills and targeted physical activity behaviors. These are the steps to implementing a behavioral plan:

1. Clarify the problem and form goals.
2. Define target behaviors.
3. Identify the maintaining conditions of the target behavior.
4. Design a behavioral plan.
5. Implement the plan.
6. Evaluate and revise the plan.

Overall, the most effective way to change behavior is through specific skill instruction and positive reinforcement.

The most effective behavioral approaches in sport and exercise psychology are more comprehensive behavioral programs with considerable variation, modification, and individualization over time. Behavioral techniques are the basics of effective practice needed by every teacher, coach, and consultant. But no practitioner can be effective in a multifaceted setting with only the basics. Behavioral basics are adapted, modified, and used in conjunction with other approaches that accommodate particular individual and physical activity contexts.

Review Questions

1. Explain the steps in implementing a behavior plan with an athlete or exerciser.
2. Define *reinforcement* and identify possible reinforcers for athletes and exercisers.
3. Define *punishment*. Explain why experts are cautious about using punishment.
4. Discuss guidelines for using reinforcement effectively.
5. Define *shaping* and give an example of how it might be used with a sport or exercise activity.
6. Summarize the findings of behavior modification research in sport and exercise settings.
7. Describe how Smith, Smoll, and colleagues used the Coaching Behavior Assessment System (CBAS) to quantify the behaviors of youth sport coaches, and discuss their findings on effective coach behaviors.

Recommended Readings

- Gould, D.R. (2015). Goal setting for peak performance. In J.M. Williams & V. Krane, *Applied sport psychology: Personal growth to peak performance* (7th ed., pp. 188-206)). New York: McGraw-Hill. This chapter provides an excellent overview of sport and exercise psychology work on goal setting and guidelines for effective goal setting in sport settings.

- Smith, R.E. (2015). A positive approach to coaching effectiveness and performance enhancement. In J.M. Williams & V. Krane, *Applied sport psychology: Personal growth to peak performance* (7th ed., pp. 40-56). New York: McGraw-Hill. This chapter provides an excellent overview of behavioral techniques and approaches as well as positive approaches in coaching.

- Smith, R.E., & Smoll, F.L. (1997). Coaching the coaches: Youth sports as a scientific and applied behavioral setting. *Current Directions in Psychological Science, 6,* 16-21.

Smith and Smoll's extensive research and related coach development training are a model of sport and exercise psychology research and practice. They have combined research on coaching behaviors with training programs from their beginning work in the 1970s, and they continue to provide new ideas and inspiration. This article summarizes their extensive work and provides an overview of their Coach Effectiveness Training (CET) program.

Manage Your Exercise Behavior

Behavioral techniques are helpful tools for any kinesiology professional, and they can also be used by students, athletes, or clients to self-regulate their own behaviors. If you can help participants develop effective self-regulatory behavioral skills, they can use those skills beyond the immediate program. Not only is self-regulation effective, but the sense of control is likely to be more motivating than if all reinforcement comes from the professional. To help you understand self-regulation, set up a behavioral program for your own exercise behavior. No doubt you engage in some type of exercise or physical activity, and most likely you do not always stick to your routine. Refer to the steps in implementing a behavioral plan, the principles of reinforcement, and the guidelines in this chapter. Then follow the procedure to set up a plan to monitor and reinforce your exercise behavior.

1. Starting point and goal. First, clarify your starting point and goal. Your goal is the specific target behaviors that you want to modify. Be sure these are specific, observable behaviors that you could measure and track. Identify the starting conditions (A, B, C). What are the current antecedents (A: conditions, triggers, incentives, barriers) and consequences (C: outcomes that reinforce or punish behavior) that affect your current behavior (B)? These are what you'll focus on in your plan.

2. Design your behavior plan. Considering the current A (antecedents) and C (consequences), develop a plan to modify your target behavior.
   - How could you modify or use antecedents (e.g., cues, conditions) to modify your behavior (give at least one specific way)?
   - Focus on consequences and use principles of effective reinforcement for the main plan. The plan should include specific reinforcers; how, when, and where you'll use them; how you'll record and monitor behavior (e.g., logs, record sheets); noting exactly what target behaviors you'll record); and expected outcomes.

   Effective reinforcers need not (and should not) be expensive or elaborate. Records of progress, a pat on the back, and a relatively inexpensive reward (e.g., a nickel in a jar every time you do the correct behavior) are often more effective and more motivating.

3. Implement and evaluate the plan. Use your plan (record and monitor your behaviors at least two separate times), and do a brief evaluation by addressing the following questions:
   a. How well did the plan work (Was the plan effective? Was it workable?)?
   b. What would you change to improve the plan (give at least one specific suggestion).

For added benefits and insights, continue to follow your plan (with revisions) and regulate your exercise behavior for at least a week. It's not easy, and you will want to evaluate and revise your plan. Good luck!

Chapter 8

Cognitive Approaches to Motivation

Chapter Objectives

After studying this chapter, you should be able to

- discuss the primary reasons why people participate in physical activity,

- explain the sport commitment model and its application to exercise,

- explain the role of enjoyment in sport commitment,

- describe the relationship between extrinsic rewards and intrinsic motivation,

- explain the components of self-determination theory, and

- apply key concepts of motivation to enhance participation in sport and physical activity settings.

Behavioral approaches assume that all behavior is determined by past reinforcements and present contingencies. In contrast, cognitive approaches assume that people are active perceivers and interpreters of information and that cognitive processes are the key to understanding motivation and behavior. That is, people's reasons and motives drive their behavior.

Participation in physical activity reflects one's motivation. We look at the activities in which people engage, how hard they try, and how long they persist in the face of a challenge and failure. Then we make judgments about their motivation. We can go beyond behavioral observations into individuals' cognitive processes by asking them why they participate in these activities. Early participation motivation researchers did just this. As you will see in this chapter, people participate in physical activity for a variety of reasons, and their reasons are similar regardless of age.

Knowing the reasons people participate provides us with a starting point for understanding an individual's motives, but does little to answer practical questions related to motivation such as these: What does it take to be committed? Does it really matter if we enjoy what we are doing? Does giving people rewards for their behavior and performances foster motivation, or turn play into work? The information in this chapter can help answer these questions. We begin with the early research on participation motivation.

Participation Motivation

In the 1970s and 1980s, sport psychologists asked youth sport participants their reasons for participating in and withdrawing from sport (see Weiss & Williams, 2004, for a review). Using the Participation Motivation Questionnaire (PMQ), Gill, Gross, and Huddleston (1983) found that the reasons young athletes gave fell into four general categories: fun, competence, affiliation, and fitness. That is, kids participated because (a) it is fun, (b) they like to strive to achieve and experience feelings of competence, (c) they want to be with their friends and meet new people, and (d) they want to increase or maintain their fitness. Several others used the PMQ or a modified version of it with other youth sport samples and obtained similar results (e.g., Gould, Feltz, & Weiss, 1985; Klint & Weiss, 1986). Another review of this literature reveals that these motives for participation, along with parent interaction, remain valid for today's youth (see Bailey, Cope,

& Pearce, 2013). Studies with college-aged and adult participants reveal that although variations have emerged, the general pattern of reasons is consistent (e.g., Campbell, MacAuley, McCrum, & Evans, 2001).

While there appears to be good reason for participation in physical activity, and despite its benefits, not everyone sticks with it. Approximately one-third of all participants in organized youth sports drop out each year (Burton, O'Connell, Gillham, & Hammermeister, 2011). As noted in chapter 10, the number of people who engage in physical activity at the level needed to obtain health benefits is conservatively estimated at 50 percent (Lox, Martin Ginis, & Petruzzello, 2014), and it is commonly reported that 50 percent of adults who begin an exercise program drop out within three to six months (Buckworth, Dishman, O'Connor, & Tomporowski, 2013).

Some of the reasons given for withdrawing from youth sport involve negative experiences such as lack of fun and playing time, coach-related problems, time requirements, overemphasis on winning, and other things to do (see Weiss & Amorose, 2008, for a review). However, Sapp and Haubenstricker (1978) found that such negative experiences accounted for less than 15 percent of the reasons kids gave for dropping out. More often, potential youth dropouts cited other interests and work-related issues as the reasons why they stopped. It is also important to note that some of the people we label as dropouts may remain active in another sport, exercise, or type of physical activity (see Weiss & Amorose, 2008).

This early descriptive research on participation motivation laid a foundation for the more theoretical research on motivation in the last three decades. Current research stemming from participation motivation focuses on commitment, enjoyment, and self-determination.

Reluctant Exercisers

Application Point

Many of Siobhan's clients are reluctant exercisers. They come to her, a personal trainer, because they know they should be more physically active, but they just don't like to exercise. As a result, many stop coming after three months. Given what you have learned about participation motivation, what suggestions do you have for Siobhan as she strives to keep her clients active?

Sport and Exercise Commitment

In the quest to understand youth sport participants' motivation, Scanlan and her colleagues have investigated the concept of sport commitment (e.g., Carpenter, Scanlan, Simons, & Lobel, 1993; Scanlan, Simons, Carpenter, Schmidt, & Keeler, 1993; Scanlan, Russell, Beals, & Scanlan, 2003; Scanlan, Russell, Scanlan, Klunchoo, & Chow, 2013). Sport commitment is a motivational force that reflects a person's desire and resolve to continue participation in sport (Scanlan, Carpenter, Schmidt, Simons, & Keeler, 1993). As conceptualized, it is a dynamic, psychological state of mind that influences behavior in the form of choice, effort, and persistence in relation to a specific physical activity, or in general, or in relation to a group of people such as a team. In the most recent model (Scanlan et al., 2003) six factors are theorized to determine a person's commitment:

- **Sport enjoyment** is defined as positive feelings about playing, such as feelings of fun, pleasure, or enjoying their experiences.
- **Valuable opportunities** involve the important opportunities that can be experienced only through continued participation and that would be missed if one were to quit. Examples are playing time and team camaraderie.
- **Other priorities** reflect the attractiveness or importance of other life responsibilities and activities that make participation difficult. For example, teenaged athletes may find having a paying job more important. Adults may find balancing family, work, and sport obligations difficult.
- **Personal investments** are the personal resources a person puts into an activity that cannot be recovered if participation ends. Examples are the time, energy, and monetary expense that cannot be returned if one stops participating. It is important to note that most of the research has measured personal investment as how much someone has invested (how much he or she has given to sport) rather than as the loss of investment (how all that effort would be wasted if the person quits). Because of this, the term personal investments in this text reflects how much one has invested.

- **Social constraints** reflect expectations that create feelings of obligation to others such as parents, peers, and coaches to continue involvement in sport.
- **Social support** involves the support and encouragement players perceive for their participation from others such as coaches, parents, and peers.

Positive relationships between commitment and five of these six factors are predicted, along with one negative association (i.e., other priorities). Specifically, participants who report the greatest enjoyment, personal investments, valuable opportunities, social constraints, and social support, and who do not perceive other, more attractive or pressing priorities, are expected to have the greatest commitment and thus be most apt to work hard and persist in physical activity.

Research with groups differing in gender, race or ethnicity, age, playing level, and type of sport has, for the most part, shown the sport commitment model to be relevant to diverse groups (see Weiss & Amorose, 2008). In general, research has supported the integrity of the sport commitment model, with enjoyment, personal investments, and valuable opportunities being strong predictors of commitment (see Weiss & Amorose). Participants reporting the greatest commitment are those most apt to enjoy sport participation, perceive substantial personal investment in the sport, and perceive that there are valuable opportunities in their participation.

Key Point

Participants who enjoy sport participation, perceive that they have made a substantial personal investment in the sport, and perceive that there are valuable opportunities in their participation report the greatest commitment to their sport.

Recently, Scanlan and colleagues (Scanlan, Russell, Magyar, & Scanlan, 2009) have emphasized that for some determinants to actually relate to commitment, athletes must view them as relevant. For example, athletes' commitment will be positively affected by personal investments and social constraints only when and if they perceive that they have put too much into their sport (personal investment) or that quitting would disappoint significant others (social constraints).

Likewise, athletes' commitment will be negatively affected by other priorities only if they perceive the existence of other, competing obligations that are compelling or pressing.

The idea that other priorities lessen commitment and that social constraints enhance commitment only when they are seen as relevant is a reasonable explanation for some of the inconsistent research findings. For example, other priorities have been shown to significantly and negatively predict sport commitment in adult and high school athletes, but not younger athletes. That is, among high school and adult athletes, those who report having other priorities or opportunities are more likely to report low commitment than those who do not, yet no relation is found between other priorities and sport commitment in younger athletes. This may be because, in comparison to adults, younger athletes do not have many important life responsibilities that compete with their participation in sport (Scanlan, Simons, Carpenter, Schmidt, & Keeler, 1993).

Another example pertains to the relationship between social constraints and commitment. Despite the predicted positive relationship between social constraints and sport commitment, researchers found either no relationship or small negative relationships between these variables (see Weiss & Amorose, 2008). The reason may be that sport, for most youth and nonprofessional adults, is volitional and enjoyable. They are not obligated (Carpenter et al., 1993). This sentiment was explicitly expressed by members of an adult elite–amateur New Zealand rugby team who stated they didn't *have* to play. They play because they want to (Carpenter & Coleman, 1998; Scanlan et al., 2009).

Want to (Volitional) Versus Have to (Obligatory) Commitment

The idea that some people play sport because they want to and some play because they feel they have to has been an element in the sport commitment literature for a long time. Schmidt and Stein (1991) introduced these concepts, which have been given various names (e.g., attraction based and entrapment based). For ease of our discussion, we use the terms volitional commitment and obligatory commitment.

Not only has terminology varied, but the ways in which people have investigated commitment have differed. For example, several researchers have used determinants of commitment in an attempt to profile young, high-caliber athletes as volitional or obligated (Raedeke, 1997; Weiss & Weiss, 2003; Weiss & Weiss, 2006). The volitional commitment profile has emerged as the most theoretically sound and consistent. Individuals with this profile were the most intrinsically and least extrinsically motivated (Weiss & Weiss, 2003), the most committed (Weiss & Weiss, 2006), and the least burned out (Raedeke, 1997).

In contrast to the profile approach, Young and Medic (2011) assessed the degree to which adult master swimmers reported that they participated because they chose to and because they felt obligated to. The statements "I am determined to keep doing my sport" and "I feel that my sport involvement is a duty" are examples of volitional and obligatory commitment, respectively. Young and Medic found that swimmers who felt increasingly obligated to continue to swim were more apt to perceive the benefits of their participation (valuable opportunities), acknowledge more competing priorities, and report feeling more socially constrained. In this research, different sources of social constraints, such as spouse, coach, and children, were assessed and found to be related to obligatory commitment. This indicates that the source of people's feelings of obligation to participate may provide greater insight into the nature or level of their commitment or both (see also Casper & Stellino, 2008; Weiss & Weiss, 2007).

Consistent with previous research on commitment, but in contrast to obligatory commitment, swimmers reporting higher volitional commitment reported greater enjoyment and personal investment in their sport than those with lower volitional commitment. Also, those scoring high on volitional commitment were least likely to perceive having other priorities competing with their sport participation.

Exercise Commitment

Research on sport commitment led some to investigate commitment to exercise (Gabriele, Gill, & Adams, 2011; Wilson et al., 2004). In this research, the term enjoyment in sport commitment research was changed to "satisfaction," and the idea of functional and obligatory commitment was retained. Similar to what was seen with the sport commitment model research, satisfaction and personal investment were the strongest and most consistent predictors of functional commitment to exercise. The results relative to obligatory commitment were partially consistent with Young and Medic's

(2011) findings in that other priorities and social constraints related to obligatory commitment. But in the end, only functional commitment was related to behavior-related constructs. This finding shows the versatility of the sport commitment model in explaining physical activity behavior, including exercise.

From a practical standpoint, individuals who report greater enjoyment for their sport or exercise experience and perceive that they have personally invested more in their sport, are more committed to exercising volitionally and more apt to exercise than those reporting less enjoyment and personal investment. The same is true for sport commitment. For both sport and exercise settings, enjoyment is the strongest and most consistent predictor of commitment.

Key Point

From a practical standpoint, individuals who report greater enjoyment of their sport or exercise experience and perceive that they have personally invested more in their activity are more committed to playing sport or engaging in exercise volitionally and more apt to play or exercise than those reporting less enjoyment and personal investment.

What Does It Take to Be Committed to Sport and Exercise?

Mary and Sam are 16 years old and have been competitive swimmers since they were 8. They are currently on their high school swim team. Each attends practice every day, works hard, and persists in efforts to excel. There is a difference between them, though. Mary is eager for practice to start and talks of wanting to swim. Sam, on the other hand, doesn't seem to have the same desire, and he talks of having to go to practice. Speculate on Mary's and Sam's commitment using the information on sport commitment.

Sources of Sport Enjoyment

There is no doubt that enjoyment is an important motivational factor in sport and exercise. It is such a strong and consistent predictor of commitment that some have argued that enjoyment mediates the relationship between the determinants of sport and commitment (Weiss, Kimmel, & Smith, 2001). Also recall from the participation motivation section of this chapter that enjoyment is a primary reason people give for participation in physical activity.

Before her work on commitment, Scanlan investigated athletes' sources of enjoyment (see Scanlan, Carpenter, Lobel, & Simons, 1993; Scanlan, Stein, & Ravizza, 1989; Scanlan & Lewthwaite, 1986). She and her research teams found that both young, male recreational athletes (Scanlan et al., 1993) and older, female elite athletes (Scanlan et al., 1989) enjoyed sport because of the competence- (e.g., mastery, winning) and social-related (e.g., friendship, family and coach interactions, recognition for their accomplishments) opportunities. The elite female athletes also reported enjoying skating because of love for the feeling of movement in skating. Collectively, this research indicates that youth and adults can find sport enjoyable when it provides opportunities for achievement or skill mastery, social affiliation, movement, or some combination of these. The findings on enjoyment we have discussed are notable, particularly when we also consider people's reasons for being physically active.

Take a moment to compare the sources of enjoyment found by Scanlan and colleagues with the reasons people give for participation. What similarities do you see? See if you can use the information presented thus far in this chapter to defend this statement: "If physical activity experiences can be designed to meet the four primary reasons people give for their physical activity participation in the form of social, achievement, and movement-related opportunities, participants will be more likely to enjoy their physical activity experiences, be committed to them because they want to be, and in the end be physically active."

To help you consider these questions, let's take a look at the relationships proposed by Weiss and Amorose (2008) in figure 8.1. They suggest that physical accomplishments, opportunities for social affiliation, and sensations inherent in movement experiences influence sport enjoyment—which in turn affects sport commitment, which then influences physical activity behavior. How clearly can you see the relationships between participation motives, enjoyment, commitment, and motivated behavior in this model?

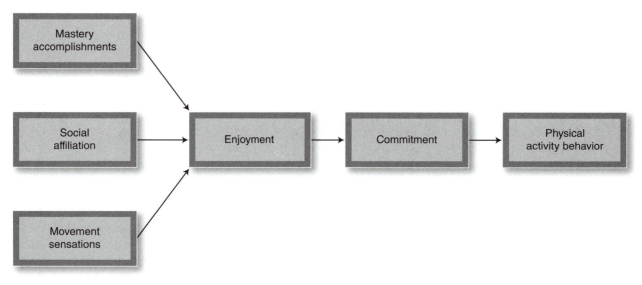

Figure 8.1 Sources of and consequences of enjoyment.

Self-Determination Theory

The preceding sections address the importance of enjoyment and satisfaction in promoting continued involvement in sport and exercise at all ages. We turn now to a broader framework of human behavior that focuses on intrinsic enjoyment and the importance of fostering motivation that is *self-determined.*

Self-determination theory (SDT), which was introduced by Deci and Ryan in 1985, is a metatheory that provides a framework for understanding the reasons underlying people's behaviors. Unlike most other theories of motivation that ask *how* motivated a person is (i.e., the amount of motivation), SDT focuses on *what* motivates a person (i.e., the type of motivation). In recent years, SDT has become one of the most popular theories of motivation and has been applied to many contexts, including sport, exercise, and physical activity settings (Ryan, Williams, Patrick, & Deci, 2009). Understanding motivation and behavior requires consideration of individual differences and situational factors. The work by Deci and Ryan and subsequent research provide an explanation for the relationship between these factors and motivation, and it can be applied to generate strategies for creating motivating environments.

Continuum of Self-Determined Motivation

According to SDT, there are two main types of motivation: intrinsic and extrinsic. People are intrinsically motivated to participate in behaviors that are inherently interesting and enjoyable. With intrinsic motivation, the regulatory process is completely internal. Behaviors are fully assimilated with one's sense of self in the absence of any separable consequences.

On the other hand, people can be extrinsically motivated to engage in a behavior when doing so leads to another desired outcome. These extrinsic reasons for motivation may vary along a continuum of behavioral regulation that ranges from totally external and controlling, on one end, to more self-determined and volitional on the other end. A subtheory of SDT, organismic integration theory, outlines this variation in extrinsic motivation:

- *Integrated regulation.* This is the most internalized form of extrinsic motivation and occurs when behavioral regulations have been fully integrated with the self. For instance, a basketball player continues to train for the sport because it is congruent with his self-identity.

- *Identified regulation.* The participant values the behavior and the behavior is internally regulated, but it is not fully assimilated into the participant's sense of self. For instance, a recreational runner completes her daily miles because she values the health benefits of running.

- *Introjected regulation.* The contingent consequences regulating the behavior are partially internalized. The behaviors are often performed for ego-involving reasons (e.g., pride, self-presentation) or to avoid guilt. For instance, an individual goes to the gym because he knows he will feel bad about himself if he misses his training session.

- ***External regulation.*** This is the least autonomous form of behavioral regulation, in which behavior is controlled by external forces such as rewards or punishment. For instance, a patient who recently suffered a heart attack participates in cardiac rehab exercises because her doctor mandates it.

Amotivation is at the lowest end of the SDT motivation continuum. Amotivation reflects a lack of intention, regulation, and self-determination regarding a behavior. People may lack motivation to engage in physical activity because they do not believe they are capable of being physically active (low self-efficacy; see chapter 6) or because they don't believe engaging in the behavior will lead to a valuable outcome. See figure 8.2 for an illustration of the motivation continuum outlined in SDT.

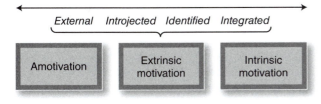

Figure 8.2 Self-determination theory motivation continuum.

Thogersen-Ntoumani and Ntoumanis (2006) found that long-term exercisers (i.e., exercising for more than six months) had higher intrinsic motivation for exercise, higher identified and introjected regulation, lower external regulation, and less amotivation. Participants with higher self-determined motivation also had greater intentions to exercise in the future, higher self-efficacy to overcome barriers to exercise, and enhanced physical self-worth. Considerable research supports the tenets of behavioral regulation in SDT and the importance of self-determined motivation in exercise contexts (e.g., Edmunds, Ntoumani, & Duda, 2006; Markland & Tobin, 2004; Thogersen-Ntoumani & Ntoumanis, 2006), though additional research has challenged the proposed continuum structure (Chemolli & Gagne, 2014).

Need Satisfaction and Self-Determined Motivation

Research grounded in SDT extends earlier research on intrinsic motivation by delineating the relationship between perceptions of competence, autonomy, and relatedness with more and less self-regulated forms of motivation, as well as the relationship between these forms of motivation and subsequent outcomes. While physical activity–related behaviors are not always intrinsically motivating, basic psychological needs theory, another subtheory of SDT, suggests that people can move up the continuum toward self-determination when certain psychological needs, which are basic to all people, are satisfied. Fulfilling the basic psychological needs of *autonomy* (personal choice), *competence* (demonstrated skill), and *relatedness* (connection to others) fosters greater internalization of the behavior and, subsequently, more self-determined motivation and greater physical activity participation (Barbeau, Sweet, & Fortier, 2009; Edmunds et al., 2006).

Given the key role of these basic needs, coaches and physical educators should create environments that cultivate autonomy, competence, and relatedness to promote greater enjoyment and continued involvement among their athletes and students. Studies by Gillet and colleagues (2010) and Amorose and Anderson-Butcher (2015) suggest that when coaches engage in greater autonomy-supportive behaviors (e.g., provide choice, acknowledge athletes' feelings, and avoid controlling behaviors; see Mageau & Vallerand, 2003), their athletes are more likely to have greater self-determined motivation, higher needs satisfaction, and lower burnout. Other researchers (Standage, Duda, & Ntoumanis, 2003) have found that autonomy-supportive climates positively relate to perceived competence, autonomy, and relatedness and, in turn, more internally regulated forms of motivation and intentions to participate in physical activity. Consistent with these findings, Hollembeak and Amorose (2005) found that male and female athletes who viewed their coaches as focusing more on training and instruction than on mistakes were more intrinsically motivated than those who perceived their coaches as less instructive, more mistake oriented, and more autocratic.

Further, Rodgers and Loitz (2009) suggest that fitness professionals can enhance motivation among their exercise clients by celebrating meaningful successes, providing options in their exercise routine, and connecting them with other clients. Similarly, Podlog and Eklund (2007) discuss issues of competence, autonomy, and relatedness following sport injury. Allowing athletes to have some control over the timetable for returning to play following an injury, rebuilding athletes' self-confidence in their physical abilities, and helping injured athletes remain connected to their team and involved in their sport in meaningful ways may promote positive return-to-sport outcomes. Clearly, SDT and its constructs have useful application in a variety of sport, exercise, and fitness settings.

Key Point

Creating an environment that fosters needs satisfaction leads to more positive motivational outcomes. Specifically, people are likely to have higher self-determined motivation when they are able to feel in control, competent, and connected to others through their activity experiences.

Application Point

Satisfying Psychological Needs in Physical Activity Settings

Adam is a third-grade student in your physical education class. You notice that Adam often seems shy in class, usually stands in the back of the line for each activity, and gives up easily. How might you build Adam's competence, autonomy, and relatedness so that he might enjoy your class more and be eager to participate?

Identity and Self-Determined Motivation: Research Into Practice

In recent years, integrated approaches for understanding sport, exercise, and physical activity behaviors have been developed by combining SDT with other relevant theories. Reifsteck, Gill, and Labban (2016) connected exercise identity (see chapter 6) with SDT to examine the physical activity behaviors of former college athletes. They developed and tested a model showing that former athletes who have higher exercise identity also have higher self-determined motivation for exercise and participate in more physical activity. Preliminary evidence suggested that self-determined motivation, and identified regulation in particular, mediated the relationship between exercise identity and behavior. In other words, former athletes who have a salient exercise identity may be more physically active after college in part because they are motivated by person-

ally valued goals. Using this theoretical model, Reifsteck and her research team developed the Moving On! program (see AthletesMovingOn.org), which helps student-athletes transition to a healthy lifestyle after college sports. The program includes cognitive behavioral strategies that enhance self-determined motivation for lifetime physical activity and healthy eating. During the program, transitioning student-athletes learn about guidelines and benefits for health-related physical activity and healthy eating, reflect on how these behaviors fit with their views of themselves for the future, practice setting effective goals, and participate in lifetime activities such as yoga in order to develop competence in a range of fun, health-enhancing activities outside of sport.

To Reward or Not Reward? That Is the Question

Self-determination theory's focus on cultivating intrinsic motivation raises an interesting question when it comes to the use of behavioral strategies discussed in chapter 7. Applying operant conditioning principles, we often use rewards and punishments for modifying behavior. We give our dog a treat when he correctly performs the trick we taught him, and we put children in "time-out" when they misbehave. We are providing rewards and punishments to reinforce good behavior and eliminate bad behavior.

The practical question concerns what happens when we combine extrinsic rewards with intrinsic motivation. At first glance, the answer would seem to be the more motivation, the better. Extrinsic rewards can be powerfully motivating. If we add extrinsic rewards to an activity that is already intrinsically motivating (e.g., giving special awards to all children who compete in an intramural track meet), we might suspect that those rewards should increase the total motivation. We assume that at worst, extrinsic rewards would have no effect and that they certainly could do no harm. Such conventional wisdom held until the mid-1970s, when researchers shocked the psychological community with studies on rewards and intrinsic motivation (e.g., Lepper & Greene, 1975). Recall that relying on external rewards and punishments (external regulation) falls low on the SDT motivation continuum. In the absence of these external factors, motivation is likely to be diminished if the reasons for participating in the behavior are not internalized. Further, extrinsic motivation may, in fact, undermine intrinsic motivation, as shown in a study titled "Turning Play Into Work" by Lepper and Greene (1975). Lepper and Greene found that children who participated in a novel activity expecting an extrinsic reward (i.e., the chance to play with highly attractive toys) showed less subsequent interest in the activity than those who had not expected a reward. In other words, being offered a reward actually decreased their intrinsic motivation.

Additionally, Deci and Ryan's (1985) research has demonstrated that both working for rewards and working under threat of punishment reduce intrinsic motivation. Both of these conditions are common in physical activity settings—some young people play sport to gain approval of a parent; older adults often adhere to exercise regimes under doctors' orders; and many college athletes get up before sunrise to train for the weekend victory. If the goal is to foster intrinsic motivation, should we award certificates when students reach physical fitness test standards? Should we give T-shirts to everyone who finishes the community 5K run-walk? Should we pay people to play? Such questions do not have simple yes-or-no answers. Rewards may undermine intrinsic motivation, but they can also modify behaviors and performance in positive ways.

Cognitive evaluation theory, which is a subtheory of self-determination theory (Deci & Ryan, 1985; Ryan & Deci, 2000), explores the factors, such as rewards, that affect intrinsic motivation. Deci and Ryan (1985) postulate that people have a propensity to seek out interesting ventures and engage in optimally challenging tasks. People are by nature intrinsically motivated, and this motivation is grounded in the psychological need to feel competent and autonomous. To develop fully, all people need to perceive themselves as effective in their environment and as acting freely. According to this theory, intrinsic motivation exists in contexts in which people feel competent when engaging in an interesting, challenging task on their own volition.

Cognitive evaluation theory suggests that when determining effects on intrinsic motivation, perception is the key. Interpretation of external events is critical—it is not the event itself, but the person's interpretation of it that matters. Deci and Ryan (1985) propose that events have both a controlling aspect and an informational aspect. The controlling aspect can undermine autonomy. If the controlling aspect of an event is high, then the person perceives it as controlling. When running a race for a T-shirt, exercising to please another person, or adhering to a home exercise program to avoid feelings of guilt, the T-shirt, the other person, or the guilt is controlling the action. Thus, the controlling aspect is high and feelings of autonomy are low. On the other hand, if the T-shirt, pleasing the other person, or staying guilt-free is not the controlling force, the controlling aspect is low and feelings of autonomy are high.

Key Point

The higher the controlling aspect of a reward, the more intrinsic motivation is undermined. If the controlling aspect of the reward is low, then participants do not see the reward as affecting their behavior and thus self-determination is high.

The informational aspect affects feelings of competence. An event with high informational value can provide either positive information about skills, abilities, and behaviors that enhances feelings of competence or negative information that detracts from such feelings. For example, receiving a patch for attaining a certain level on a physical fitness test provides positive information and enhances feelings of competence. In most sport and exercise situations, however, tangible rewards are given to a select few, and those who strive for but do not obtain rewards may receive negative information that decreases their feelings of competence and thus their intrinsic motivation.

Most events have both controlling and informational aspects, but the two aspects vary in salience. For example, tangible rewards, such as trophies and money, tend to have a highly salient controlling aspect, whereas verbal feedback seems less controlling. Rewards given for specific performance standards have more informational value than rewards distributed on the basis of ambiguous criteria. Additionally, the same event can be viewed differently by different people. For example, one person may perceive a reward primarily as informational, whereas another may perceive the reward primarily as controlling.

Rewards do not automatically undermine intrinsic motivation any more than they automatically enhance motivation. The practical question, then, is not whether we use rewards and reinforcers, but how we should use them. The individual's interpretation of the reward is critical. Carefully chosen rewards may encourage people to participate in new activities in which they can develop a sense of competence and intrinsic motivation. Rewards may also provide valuable competence information in ongoing activities, especially if they are given for the attainment of clearly specified goals that are perceived as within reach of participants. Coaches and instructors who rely on encouragement and reinforcement, emphasize the process rather than the outcome, and use rewards as symbols of accomplishments rather than to control behavior may find extrinsic rewards useful.

Putting It Into Practice

Summary

Cognitive approaches to motivation emphasize the role of perceptions and interpretations in participation and behavior. Early research found that reasons for participating fall into four categories: fun, competence, affiliation, and fitness. Scanlan and colleagues developed a model with enjoyment, personal investments, valued opportunities, and social support leading to, and other priorities detracting from, sport commitment. Later research differentiated volitional (want to) and obligatory (have to) commitment, and it found that enjoyment and personal investment related to volitional commitment in sport and exercise.

Self-determination theory, the dominant model in sport and exercise psychology research today, puts motivation on a continuum from amotivation, through extrinsic motivation, to the most self-determined form of motivation—intrinsic motivation. Self-determination theory further suggests that satisfaction of the basic needs for competence, autonomy, and relatedness fosters intrinsic motivation and long-term participation in sport and exercise. The collective work on self-determined motivation suggests that we should help participants set their own challenging, realistic goals so that their accomplishments will elicit feelings of competence, personal control, and the desire to continue pursuing sport and exercise activities.

Review Questions

1. What are the main reasons that people participate in physical activity according to the early participation motivation research?
2. What are the determinants of sport commitment in Scanlan and colleagues' (2003) model?
3. Explain the difference between volitional and obligatory commitment.
4. Explain the relationship between individual needs satisfaction and the continuum of motivation in SDT.
5. Do rewards enhance or undermine intrinsic motivation? In your answer, discuss the controlling and informational aspects of rewards and explain how they each affect intrinsic motivation.

Recommended Reading

Scanlan and colleagues have been developing and applying their sport commitment model for over 20 years. Check the 1993 article for the original model that was developed and used with youth sports. Then, see the 2013 article for an updated model that has been applied with elite athletes.

- Scanlan, T.K., Carpenter, P.J., Schmidt, G.W., Simons, J.P., & Keeler, B. (1993). An introduction to the Sport Commitment Model. *Journal of Sport and Exercise Psychology, 15*(1), 1-15.
- Scanlan, T.K., Russell, D.G., Scanlan, L.A., Klunchoo, T.J., & Chow, G.M. (2013). Project on Elite Athlete Commitment (PEAK): IV. Identification of new candidate

commitment sources in the sport commitment model. *Journal of Sport and Exercise Psychology, 35*(5), 525-535.

Self-determination theory is a complex metatheory with many subtheories and may seem overwhelming to a reader who is new to this literature. Rodgers and Loitz provide an easy-to-understand overview of SDT within a health and fitness context. They suggest specific strategies for creating a climate that is supportive of self-determined motivation among exercise clients.

- Rodgers, W.M., & Loitz, C.C. (2009). The role of motivation in behavior change: How do we encourage our clients to be active? *ACSM's Health Fitness Journal, 13*(1), 7-12. doi: 10.1249/FIT.0b013e3181916d11

LAB

Improving Adherence by Promoting Self-Determination

Self-determination theory (Deci & Ryan, 1985; Ryan & Deci, 2000) suggests that motivation exists along a continuum, with people's reasons for engaging in a behavior ranging from totally external to fully self-determined and volitional. Fulfilling the basic psychological needs of autonomy, competence, and relatedness can move individuals up the motivation continuum toward more self-determined motivation (Edmunds et al., 2006). Review the key points of SDT and respond to the following questions:

1. Describe the continuum of motivation. Specifically, list and define (in your own words) the six points along the continuum (from amotivation to intrinsic motivation).

2. List and define (in your own words) the three basic psychological needs.

3. Assume that you are an athletic trainer working with a freshman volleyball player, Maya, who was injured during the last game of the season. Maya is not motivated to participate in rehab. She often shows up late to her sessions and doesn't put forth her full effort in the exercises. Having never dealt with a serious injury before, she seems discouraged by the long road ahead and feels disconnected from her teammates because she is no longer able to participate in practice with them. In what ways could you enhance Maya's feelings of competence, autonomy, and relatedness in order to improve her motivation for sticking to the rehab plan? Identify at least two specific strategies for enhancing each of the three needs.

4. Now evaluate the strategies you identified to see if they may also have an impact on Maya's enjoyment of and commitment to her motivation for adhering to her rehab plan.

Achievement Motivation

Chapter Objectives

After studying this chapter, you should be able to

- discuss attribution theory in relation to achievement behavior in sport and exercise,

- describe learned helplessness and its relationship to attributions and mindsets,

- explain the role of competence and valence of competence in motivation for physical activity,

- explain the relationship between individual motivation characteristics and environmental conditions, and

- apply key concepts of attribution and achievement goal theory to enhance participation in sport and physical activity.

People participate in physical activity for a host of reasons. Many participants are interested in achievement. We may wonder why some people take on challenges, work hard, and persist whereas others avoid challenge, exert little effort, and give up easily. We may also question why some athletes are devastated by a loss and others take it in stride, or why some people eagerly approach competition and others avoid it. Achievement behavior is central to sport and exercise endeavors, and understanding individual differences in motivational orientations is a key to understanding achievement.

Achievement motivation theorists take a cognitive approach and assume that individuals are intentional and goal directed. People set goals and strive to achieve them. Achievement of one's goal is the basis by which people determine if they have succeeded or failed. Our achievement goals, the meaning we give to them, and the reasons we attribute to the outcome influence our achievement-related behaviors.

As you read this chapter, consider how achievement motivation can help you understand the physical activity experiences of two different people. Ximena and Rika, two ninth-graders, are best friends and do everything together, except when it comes to physical activity. Although Rika is more capable, Ximena is the one who embraces physical activity. In physical education, Ximena is always eager to participate, chooses personally challenging tasks, tries hard, and persists in the face of objective failure (i.e., losing a game, being slow to pick up a skill). It seems that Ximena likes physical activity, and regardless of her poor showing relative to her peers, she anticipates future success. In contrast, Rika, who could experience greater objective success, avoids participation. When obligated to play, she chooses either the easiest task possible or tasks that no one could do. For example, when given time to practice basketball, Rika spends most of her time dribbling and passing the ball to others. She usually attempts only half-court shots. When encouraged to shoot a variety of shots, she shoots bank shots about 2 feet (0.5 meter) from the basket. She expects to fail and seems to dread physical education.

Achievement goals likely have different meanings for Ximena and Rika, and they likely attribute the causes of their failures differently. Keep Ximena and Rika in mind as you read this chapter. Let's explore their potential differences first through the concept of attributions.

Attributions and Physical Activity

After action is taken and the outcome is determined, people attempt to explain the outcome—their success or failure. These perceived reasons, or attributions, given to explain the outcome affect motivation. Thus, they are important in the self-regulation of goal-directed behavior (see Hunt, Turner, Polatojko, Bottari, & Dawson, 2013, for a review). Attribution theories focus on people's interpretations of the reasons for unexpected, negative, or important outcomes. The attributions we make about our successes and failures affect our future behavior (e.g., effort and persistence), as well as our thoughts and feelings about our performance. If you are unable to do the shot put in physical education class, you behave differently depending on why you think you cannot do it. For instance, if you think you need practice, you might keep trying. If you think you need instruction, you might ask the teacher for guidance. Or, if you think you are just too weak and uncoordinated, you might give up and try the long jump instead.

Key Point

Attributions are the perceived causes of events and outcomes. Attribution theories focus on people's interpretations of the reasons for unexpected, negative, or important outcomes. The attributions we make about the outcome of our own and others' behaviors affect our future behaviors and interactions with others.

The attributions that we make about the outcome for others and that others make about us also affect future behaviors and interactions. If you go up for a rebound and unexpectedly get elbowed by an opponent, you react differently depending on whether you think the elbowing was intentional or accidental. A physical therapist who thinks her client cannot walk independently because they are not strong enough responds differently than one who thinks her clients are lazy and neglectful. Coaches think about the reasons their teams win and lose, and they act on the basis of those attributions in preparing for future contests.

Weiner's Model of Achievement Attributions

Although he was not the first person to propose a theoretical model of attributions, Weiner (1986, 1992, 2000) has done the most to bring attribution theory to prominence. Weiner suggested that, when faced with a performance outcome that is negative (e.g., failure), unexpected (e.g., an unexpected win), or important (failure on a mobility test needed for returning to independent living), people question why the outcome occurred. Why did I fail? Why did I win? Before reading on, think about the last time you performed successfully in your favorite sport or exercise activity. What was the main reason for your success? Now think about the last time you had an unsuccessful performance. What was the main reason for your lack of success?

The responses people give to these questions, their attributions, influence their motivation and motivated behavior via their feelings (affect) and expectations for future success and failure. For example, Jayla attributes her progress (i.e., a success) to her hard work and, in turn, feels a sense of pride and expects to be successful in the future. As a result, she strives to improve in her rehabilitation program. Anthony attributes his failure to a lack of ability and as a result is frustrated and sees no hope for improvement. Thus, he rarely comes to rehab, and when he does, he doesn't work very hard. The essential difference between high and low achievers such as Jayla and Anthony is a difference in attribution patterns.

The first step to understanding the effects of attributions on motivation is identifying the attributions that people actually make. According to Weiner, your responses will probably fall into one of four categories: ability, effort, luck, and task difficulty. Ability includes attributions such as "I'm not very good at tennis" or "I'm naturally gifted." Effort might include statements such as "We were not really up for the game" or "I never gave up when it got tough." Luck attributions include random events and environmental factors (e.g., "We got the breaks," "They had the ref on their side"). Task difficulty includes attributions relating to the opponent (e.g., "They were a ranked team") and to the task itself (e.g., "The moves were just too complicated"). Although other attributions exist, particularly in sport (Holt & Morley, 2004; Roberts & Pascuzzi, 1979), these four categories cover most reasons.

The four attributions themselves are not the critical consideration; the personal meaning they hold for each individual is (Weiner, 1979; Biddle, Hanrahan, & Sellars, 2001). The personal meaning individuals give to their attributions for success and failure is the driving force of motivation. Weiner's original model classified attributions along two dimensions: locus of causality and stability (see table 9.1). *Locus of causality* refers to the location of the cause—is it internal or external to the performer? Natural ability and effort are examples of internal attributions because they are personal characteristics that reside in the individual, whereas luck and task difficulty are considered more environmental or situational characteristics and are thus external attributions. *Stability* refers to the duration of the cause. Is it likely to change over time (unstable), or is it likely to remain the same (stable)? Ability and task difficulty are stable. For example, your tennis ability does not change much from one match to the next, and the height of the net will not change. On the other hand, effort and luck may change; you might be more up for the next match and try harder, or you might get the breaks on line calls. Natural ability is an internal, stable factor; effort is internal and unstable; task difficulty is external and stable; and luck is external and unstable.

Later, Weiner added a third dimension—controllability—to distinguish between factors that are internal but uncontrollable and those that are internal and controllable. Table 9.2 illustrates this three-way classification. We have all known people who had a natural ability for a particular activity, such as the person who picks up a golf club for the first time and swings it as though he has done it all his life. This natural ability is internal, but not something we can control. Personal effort, on the other hand, is an internal quality we can control. Effort is controllable, but since we cannot control someone else's effort, that can be either an internal or an external attribution. Before reading on, look over the reasons you gave for your last success

Table 9.1 Weiner's 2×2 Classification Scheme for Causal Attributions

	Internal	External
Stable	Ability	Task difficulty
Unstable	Effort	Luck

Table 9.2 Weiner's 2×2×2 Classification Scheme for Causal Attributions

		Locus of causality			
		Internal		External	
		Stable	Unstable	Stable	Unstable
Controllability	Controllable	Stable effort	Unstable effort	Others' stable effort	Others' unstable effort
	Uncontrollable	Ability	Mood	Task difficulty	Luck

and failure and see where your attributions fit in Weiner's classification.

If you monitor the comments of winning and losing players and coaches for a while, you will notice that external attributions (e.g., lucky breaks, officials' calls, the weather) usually come from the losing side. You likely never hear a winning coach state that the team won because of a referee's decision. This tendency to attribute success internally and failure externally is called self-serving bias because those attributions help us feel better about ourselves. For example, you will probably feel better about winning the 800-meter run if you attribute your win to your own effort than if you attribute it to your rival's injury. Alternatively, this attributional bias may exist simply because people plan to be successful. We tend to seek challenges for which we have the ability to succeed and then work hard to achieve them. Failure, on the other hand, isn't usually planned, so when we search for why we failed it makes sense that we look outside of ourselves. Hanrahan and Biddle (2008) refer to this as the cognitive explanation.

Key Point

People tend to attribute success internally and failure externally. Some refer to this as self-serving bias because it maximizes feelings of pride and minimizes feelings of shame. Others think it happens because people tend to strive for challenges for which they have the ability to succeed and then work hard to achieve them. Thus, failure is unexpected, and people naturally look outside of themselves for the cause.

According to Weiner (1986, 2000), the stability dimension relates to expectations for future success or failure. Stable attributions lead us to

expect the same outcome over time, whereas unstable attributions lead us to expect different outcomes. If you think your team won the volleyball match because yours is the best team in the league, you will expect to keep on winning. If you think you failed the high jump because the skill is too challenging given your level of ability, you will expect to continue failing. Conversely, if you won the match because of a fluke, you cannot be confident of future victories; and if you think you were unable to do the high jump because you misjudged your takeoff, you can change in the future and thereby maintain hope for future success.

The locus of causality and controllability dimensions relate to intrapersonal feelings. Specifically, Weiner contends that locus of causality relates to feelings of pride. People take more pride in successes that they earn than in those that are due to external factors. Feelings of shame in the face of failure are a function of a combination of locus of causality and controllability. Failure due to a "stupid mistake" elicits feeling of shame because the error was the person's fault (internal) and could have been avoided (controllable). It does not feel as bad to fail because of poor officiating as it does to lose because you gave up at the end. Thus, attributing success internally and failure externally and as uncontrollable is thought to be self-serving because it maximizes feelings of pride and minimizes feelings of shame.

In addition to our intrapersonal feelings, controllability also affects our feelings and moral judgments about others. An athlete's coach is likely to experience anger when witnessing a "stupid mistake," especially if it was made in an important game, leading to a negative outcome, and the athlete could have avoided making it but didn't. However, if the coach attributed the negative outcome to the athlete's lack of ability, which cannot be altered, the athlete would not be seen as personally responsible, and the coach is more likely to be sympathetic than angry.

In general, then, the attributional dimensions affect thoughts, feelings, and behaviors as follows:

- Stability relates to future expectations. We expect similar outcomes with stable attributions and changeable outcomes with unstable attributions.

- Locus of causality relates to feelings of pride and shame. We experience stronger feelings with internal attributions than with external attributions.

- Locus of causality and controllability relate to feelings of shame, guilt, and humiliation. We experience stronger negative feelings when we attribute our failure to internal and controllable factors.

- Controllability relates to negative feelings about others. We feel anger when we hold people accountable for a negative outcome that could have been avoided and sympathy if we believe preventing the error was beyond their control.

Learned Helplessness and Mindsets

The research findings just discussed support the work of Carol Dweck and her colleagues (see Dweck, 2000, 2006, 2012), who examined how people react to and cope with failure. Dweck identified two distinct patterns of reactions to failure on a difficult puzzle task (e.g., Diener & Dweck, 1978, 1980; Dweck, 1975). She describes one, labeled *learned helplessness*, as the acquired belief that one has no control over negative events or that failure is inevitable. Dweck (2000) characterizes the helpless student as one who attributes failure on a task to stable, uncontrollable factors such as a lack of intelligence, poor memory, or low ability; many such students don't think they can be successful in the future, and they experience negative affect. They tend to exaggerate their failures, lose sight of their successes, and become off-task, and their performance declines.

In contrast, mastery-oriented students see failure as a temporary setback due to unstable, controllable factors such as working hard to find a solution or slowing down and working more carefully. They persist in the face of failure as they self-instruct, try to do better, remain confident in their future success, and stay positive.

Dweck (2006, 2012) has expanded her research on attributions to people's basic beliefs or mindsets. People have two types of mindsets that guide their behavior. People with a growth mindset (or incremental mindset) believe that abilities and characteristics can change or be developed, whereas people with a fixed mindset (or entity mindset) believe that abilities and characteristics are fixed and cannot be changed. An adaptive-mastery orientation reflects a growth mindset, whereas learned helplessness reflects a fixed mindset. Dweck's continuing research extends the role of mindsets to personal and group relationships, productivity, and health behaviors, as well as achievement. Her 2006 book, *Mindset*, summarizes that work with examples and practical applications.

Attributions and Learned Helplessness Research in Physical Activity Settings

In reviewing the literature, Hanrahan and Biddle (2008) identified two areas of attributional research that have shown relatively consistent results. First, they concluded that the attributional bias, whether it is interpreted via the self-serving bias or the cognitive explanation, has been a consistent finding across a variety of sports. Moreover, this attributional bias exists even when people do not know how successful they have actually been, and it exists in coaches and spectators. In general, athletes attribute their success to internal, personal factors (e.g., ability, effort) and failure to external factors.

Second, Hanrahan and Biddle (2008) concluded that, in the sport setting, people can learn to change their attributions. This is particularly relevant to those who react to failure with a learned helpless attitude. Learned helplessness has been found in middle school physical education students (Martinek & Griffith, 1994; Martinek & Williams, 1997; Walling & Martinek, 1995) and sport participants (Prapavessis & Carron, 1988). For example, Johnson and Biddle (1988) examined attributions for success and failure on a balancing task. People who gave up easily (learned helpless) were more likely to make negative self-statements and to attribute their failure to lack of ability and task difficulty than did those who persisted longer. Those who persisted longer made more strategy-related statements.

Key Point

There are two key points in one here. One, the attributional bias has been a consistent finding across a variety of sports. Athletes tend to attribute their success to internal, personal factors (e.g., ability, effort) and failure to external factors. Second, people can learn to change their attributions to be more motivationally adaptive.

Attribution retraining has been shown to be effective among recreational (Orbach, Singer, & Murphey, 1997; Orbach, Singer, & Price, 1999), novice (Rascle, Le Foll, & Higgins, 2008), and competitive (Parkes & Mallett, 2011) athletes. This research has shown that reframing failure attributions to more internal, controllable, or unstable factors resulted in greater expectancy for success, more positive emotions, and improved performance. For example, Orbach and colleagues (1999) investigated the influence of an attribution training program for novice tennis players who were making dysfunctional attributions. Participants were placed into one of three groups. One group was taught to make more functional attributions. Specifically, they were told that their poor performances were based on controllable and unstable factors such as effort or game strategy used. Thus their performance could be improved over time. The other group was taught more dysfunctional attributions. They were told that their performances were based on uncontrollable and stable factors such as the lack of ability. Thus some people would just naturally perform better than others.

The results showed that those who learned more functional attributions had higher expectations for success and experienced more positive emotions than those who made more dysfunctional attributions. Furthermore, participants made these attributions for other tennis tasks and continued to make functional attributions for at least three weeks after the study. These results demonstrate that physical activity leaders can help people make motivationally adaptive attributions.

Attributional retraining can be effective even after a one-time occurrence. Rascle and coauthors (2008) got novice golfers to make more functional attributions, have greater expectations for success, and practice more after providing the golfers with a one-time bout of attribution feedback between practice sessions. Similar to the athletes in Orbach and colleagues' study, these golfers were told that the cause of their performance "reflected mostly internal, controllable, and unstable factors, such as your concentration, effort and the strategy [they] used to try to succeed in the task or other factors internal" (p. 160). The researchers emphasized that these causes were controllable and could change over time.

Attributions are important for self-regulation in rehabilitation settings, and this research supports the impact of stable and internal attributions on negative affect. For example, stable attributions associated with chronic disease were related to depression-related symptoms among patients with coronary heart disease (Sanjua'n, Arranz, & Castro, 2014). Internal attributions for failure predicted anxiety and depression (Bennett, Howarter, & Clark, 2013). The researchers for both of these studies recommend attributional retraining, which is discussed later in this chapter.

Attributions in Rehab

After suffering a stroke, Sara is in a skilled nursing facility until she can regain motor functioning. She is working with a physical therapist to relearn to walk. This is hard for Sara, and she is not always successful. When she cannot accomplish the task, she is embarrassed, laments that she'll never be able to walk again, and ends her physical therapy session early. When she is successful, she seems to dismiss it as something that probably will never happen again and continues to fear that she will never walk again. What type of attributions is she making when she is successful and when she fails? What advice would you give to Sara's physical therapist that might help Sara make more adaptive attributions?

The attributions we make to explain an event outcome, particularly when we fail, have an impact on our affect, behavior, and cognitions, but they are not the only valid explanations for individual differences in achievement behavior. Some theories emphasize personality and others stress perceptions and interpretations, but nearly all stem from the classic work of Atkinson (1964, 1974). We'll now explore the differences between Ximena and Rika through theories of achievement motivation.

Atkinson's Theory of Achievement Motivation

Atkinson's theory of achievement motivation is an interaction model that specifies personality and situational factors as determinants of achievement behavior in precise, formal terms. Atkinson extended the work of Murray (1938), who first discussed achievement motivation as a personality factor. He defined the need to achieve as the desire

> to accomplish something difficult. To master, manipulate or organize physical objects, human beings, or ideas. To do this as rapidly and as independently as possible. To overcome obstacles and attain a high standard. To excel one's self. To rival and surpass others. To increase self-regard by the successful exercise of talent. (p. 164)

Atkinson (1964, 1974) further delineated achievement motivation as a combination of two personality constructs: the motive to approach success (or the capacity to experience pride in accomplishment) and the motive to avoid failure (or the capacity to experience shame in failure). People experience both. In some situations, we strive for success, and in others, we strive to avoid failure; we feel good when we accomplish something and bad when we fail. Atkinson distinguished high and low achievers based on those two motives. High achievers have high motive to approach success and a low motive to avoid failure. High achievers seek out challenging achievement situations without worrying about possible failures. Low achievers have the reverse pattern. They have lower motive to approach success, worry about failure a great deal, and avoid achievement situations.

Atkinson also incorporated situational factors into the explanation of achievement motivation. He posited that task difficulty, or the probability of success, and incentive value of success in any given situation would affect performers' motivation. According to Atkinson, the lower the probability of success, the greater the incentive value. To illustrate, an average tennis player has a slim chance against top professional Novak Djokovic or Serena Williams but would be elated to win a game. In this example, the incentive value is high. At the other extreme, a top-seeded professional player would not be inspired by the prospect of playing the average player.

According to Atkinson (1964, 1974), the tendency to approach success is a function of the person's motive to approach success and the situational factors. High achievers are most likely to strive to achieve when their motive for success is high and there is a 50 percent chance of success, which would make the victory the most rewarding. People with a strong motive to avoid failure tend to avoid these situations. When forced into an achievement situation, a low achiever will choose either very easy (high probability of success) or very difficult (low probability of success) tasks.

Achievement Goal Theory

Many theorists have built on Atkinson's foundation by developing multidimensional approaches that consider personality, development, and environment. Over the last 35 years, cognitive approaches have dominated achievement research. Bernard Weiner (1974) sparked a dramatic change in the study of motivation when he proposed that high and low achievers think differently and therefore act differently. Since then, several multidimensional achievement goal approaches have emerged to explain achievement behaviors such as task choice, behavioral intensity, and persistence (e.g., Dweck, 2000; Elliot, 1999; Maehr & Nicholls, 1980; Nicholls, 1989). Despite their differences, they all contend that people are intentional and goal directed and that the goal in achievement settings (e.g., rehabilitation, fitness, sport) is to demonstrate ability and avoid appearing incompetent. In achievement settings, people experience feelings of success when they demonstrate high ability (i.e., meet their goal) and failure when they do not. Early research found that people's perceptions of success and failure were not synonymous with winning and losing (e.g., Spink & Roberts, 1980). Success and failure depend on how one defines ability, which in turn depends on personal, developmental, and situational factors. One's definition of competence is important in understanding achievement motivation.

Key Point

Although achievement goal theorists have distinct perspectives, they all contend that people are intentional and goal directed in achievement contexts. The goal in achievement settings is to demonstrate one's ability and avoid appearing incompetent.

With the distinctions among achievement goal perspectives comes a distinct terminology. For example, Dweck talks of mastery and performance goals, whereas Nicholls talks of task and ego goals. Additionally, achievement goals have been studied at two levels of analysis. At the situational level, the term *goal involvement* is used to indicate the "right now" nature of the goal. At the dispositional level, the term *goal orientation* is used to refer to one's tendency to strive for the different types of goals. While the distinctions between the nature of goals and terminology have theoretical importance, they are beyond the scope and purposes of this book. For our purpose, these constructs are more similar than different. Instead of making distinctions among theories, we discuss the general motivational processes and remove the theory-specific language as much as possible. For example, we avoid the involvement–orientation distinction by couching our discussion in the pursuit of achievement goals rather than one's goal involvement or goal orientation. We associate self-referenced and norm-referenced definitions of competence with the terms *mastery* and *performance achievement goals*. Lastly, instead of attempting to distinguish between the various terminologies used to refer to the two primary types of motivational climate, we use the terms *task-* and *ego-involving climate*.

Competence and Achievement Goals

Dweck's work on learned helplessness and mastery-oriented achievement-related reactions to failure was part of a larger investigation into why people of equal ability react so differently. She, like others, discovered that people define competence differently and use different criteria to judge their competence, which in turn has implications for individuals' achievement-related self-perceptions, beliefs, feelings and emotions, and behavior.

According to Nicholls (1989), young children cannot differentiate competence from task difficulty, luck, and effort; they have an undifferentiated conception of ability. For them, competence is demonstrated relative to one's own past performance via gains in task mastery or personal improvement. With the use of using an undifferentiated conception of ability, goals are mastery focused and are associated with the belief that competence can increase with effort (Sarrazin et al., 1996).

By age 11 or 12, most children have the cognitive maturity to differentiate ability from task difficulty, luck, and effort. They understand ability as capacity relative to others and that capacity limits the impact of effort. They can understand that when two players perform equally well on a task, the player who exerts the least effort is the most competent. In this way, judgments about one's competence are norm (other) referenced and goals are performance oriented. Performance goals are associated with the belief that competence is stable and cannot be changed (Sarrazin et al., 1996).

Research in the physical domain has supported this developmental progression (see Weiss & Williams, 2004, for a review). And, once capable of a differentiated conception of ability, individuals may choose to use that or an undifferentiated conception of ability (see Roberts, Treasure, & Conroy, 2007), which would explain why adolescents and adults can have either a mastery or performance focus in any given situation (goal involvement) (e.g., Harwood & Swain, 1998; Smith & Harwood, 2001) or across various situations (goal orientation) (see Roberts, 2012). Further research, grounded in Dweck's work, has shown a relationship between definitions of competence and achievement goals (e.g., Stenling, Hassmén, & Holmström, 2014).

Achievement goals are associated with achievement-related affect, behaviors, and cognition (Nicholls, 1989; Dweck, 2000, 2006). Specifically, Nicholls hypothesized that individuals with a mastery goal focus, regardless of their level of perceived competence, would exhibit adaptive achievement behaviors, such as selecting challenging tasks, trying hard, and persisting in the face of failure. In contrast, individuals with a performance goal focus, particularly those low in perceived competence, would exhibit maladaptive achievement behaviors, such as selecting easy or difficult tasks and exhibiting low effort and persistence, as well as anxiety. Research has provided support in the physical domain (for reviews see Harwood, Spray, & Keegan, 2008; Roberts et al., 2007). Specifically, mastery goals have been found to relate to (a) the belief that hard work leads to success and that sport promotes a strong work ethic; (b) adaptive learning strategies such as practice, and positive emotions such as enjoyment, satisfaction, and interest; and (c) motivated behavior such as persistence, effort, and performance (Biddle, Wang, Kavussanu, & Spray, 2003; Duda, 2005). Conversely, performance goals have been shown (a) to relate to beliefs that social status is a primary purpose of sport participation; (b) to be associated with performance strategies designed to make one look able (Biddle et al., 2003; Duda, 2005); and (c) to anxiety (Roberts et al., 2007).

The Valence of Competence

Early achievement motivation theorists (Atkinson, 1964, 1974; Dweck & Elliot, 1983; Dweck & Leggett, 1988) recognized that people can strive to avoid appearing incompetent (avoidance motivation) just as much or even more than they can strive to demonstrate their competence (approach motivation). Until recently, though, the concept of avoidance motivation had been largely ignored (see Harwood et al., 2008). Andrew Elliot (1999) reminded us that the valance of competence, or the degree to which one is striving to approach success or avoid failure, also has implications for achievement behavior. With this added dimension, Elliot and McGregor (2001) formulated a 2×2 achievement goal framework, including two definitions of competence (mastery and performance goals) and of the valence of competence (approach and avoidance). Table 9.3 illustrates four different achievement goals found in this taxonomy.

Individuals striving to demonstrate their competence are approach focused. *Approach goals* reflect people's motivation to strive for self-referenced competence by demonstrating mastery relative to their own past performances or task achievement (mastery approach) or normative competence by outperforming others (performance approach). Conversely, individuals striving to avoid the appearance of incompetence are avoidance focused. *Avoidance goals* reflect one's motivation to avoid self-referenced incompetence (mastery avoidance) or normative incompetence (performance avoidance). Here are some examples. Dejha is training in hopes of increasing her strength so she can leave the nursing facility and live independently (mastery approach). Lindsey is training to win a race (performance approach). Logan, afraid that he cannot complete the task

of 25 pull-ups (mastery avoidance), selects the push-up task instead (mastery approach). Nick complains of leg cramps and quits as Michael overtakes him in the race (performance avoidance).

According to Elliot (1997, 1999) people pursue these four goals for a number of reasons (antecedents), including individual difference (e.g., need to achieve, perceived competence, conception of ability, fear of failure, need for approval, perfectionism) and environmental (e.g., motivational climate, reward structures, instruction) factors. The reasons influence goal adoption, which in turn directs achievement-related behaviors, affect, and cognitions (Elliot, 1997). In essence, goals mediate the relationship between goal antecedents (e.g., fear of failure) and achievement outcomes. Research in the physical domain has supported this (e.g., Conroy & Elliot, 2004; Cury, Elliot, Sarrazin, Da Fonseca, & Rufo, 2002; Nien & Duda, 2008; Puente-Diaz, 2013). For example, Nien and Duda explored the relationships among perceived competence, fear of failure, achievement goals, and motivation. As predicted, they found that perceived competence was positively related to both (i.e., mastery and performance) approach goals, and fear of failure was positively related to performance approach and both (i.e., mastery and performance) avoidance goals. In turn, mastery approach was positively related to intrinsic motivation; performance–avoidance goals were positively associated with extrinsic motivation; and both avoidance goals were positively associated with the lack of motivation. It can be concluded that perceived competence increases the likelihood that one will adopt approach goals, and that the fear of failure increases the likelihood that one will adopt avoidance goals and performance–approach goals.

Adoption of mastery–approach goals is likely to increase the chance that one will be intrinsically motivated. Adoption of performance–avoidance

Table 9.3 Elliot and McGregor's (2001) 2×2 Achievement Goal Framework

		Definition of competence	
		Mastery (self-referenced)	Performance (normative)
Valence of competence	Approaching competence	Mastery–approach goals (MAp)	Performance–approach goals (PAp)
	Avoiding incompetence	Mastery–avoidance goals (MAv)	Performance–avoidance goals (PAv)

goals increases the chance that one will be extrinsically motivated. Adoption of avoidance goals, regardless if they are mastery or performance focused, also increases the likelihood that one will lack motivation. Similar results pertaining to fear of failure and avoidance goals and performance–approach goals were obtained by Puente-Diaz (2013). However, fear of failure, which is expected to energize, was negatively related to mastery–approach goal focus. Conroy and Elliot (2004) suggested that mastery–approach goals may protect individuals from developing a fear of failure.

A growing body of research in the physical domain has been addressing the antecedents, processes, and outcomes associated with achievement goals from a 2×2 achievement goal framework (e.g., Gao, Podlog, & Harrison, 2012; Su, McBride, & Xiang, 2015; Wang, Biddle, & Elliot, 2007). This body of research consistently shows that mastery–approach goals are the most motivationally adaptive, whereas performance–avoidance goals are generally maladaptive in sport and physical education. Mastery–approach goals have been found to be related to positive self-perceptions, intrinsic motivation, reduced anxiety, and better performance (Lochbaum & Smith, 2015); performance–avoidance goals have been associated with higher anxiety, as well as lower perceived competence, lower self-determined motivation, and lower performance (for reviews see Harwood et al., 2008; Lochbaum & Gottardy, 2014; Roberts et al., 2007). However, the research on performance–approach goals is not as consistent. For example, Lochbaum, Podlog, Litchfield, Surles, and Hilliard (2013) found that a performance–approach goal was beneficial to long-term exercise. The motivational profiles associated with performance approach and mastery avoidance have been mixed and likely relate to mediating and moderating factors. For example, gender was found to moderate the relationship between mastery–avoidance goals and anxiety, with females more likely to adopt mastery–avoidance goals and experience greater cognitive anxiety than males (e.g., Stenling et al., 2014).

Key Point

This body of research consistently shows that mastery–approach goals are the most motivationally adaptive, whereas performance–avoidance goals are generally maladaptive in sport and physical education.

This growing body of research not only informs our practice as physical activity specialists; it also informs theory. A paper by Mascret, Elliot, and Cury (2015) explored the utility of an extended 3×2 framework, in which mastery goals are broken into task-referenced goals (e.g., completing a task) and self-referenced goals (e.g., improving). Given the limited research on this, we hold further discussion for another time. For now, let's turn our attention to the second aspect of achievement motivation that Atkinson (1964, 1974) identified: situational factors.

Mastery Focus in Exercise Class

Application Point

Marsha and Darius are in the same exercise class at their local gym. To switch things up, their trainer asks the exercise group to pair up for a core strength circuit-training competition. The first team to complete the circuit wins. Marsha and Darius are similar in many ways. For example, they both have very poor core strength. One difference is that Marsha is highly mastery–approach focused, whereas Darius is predominantly performance–avoidance focused. How might they feel about today's lesson, what type of partner might they choose, and how might they behave during the activity? Explain your answers.

Motivational Climate

Recall that Atkinson (1964, 1974) and motivation theorists echoed the idea of the important role that situational factors play in adopting a goal and engaging in particular behaviors (Ames, 1984; Dweck & Leggett, 1988; Elliot, 1997, 1999). Most of the research exploring situational and environmental factors in achievement motivation in the physical domain stems from the early work of Carole Ames (1984; Ames & Ames, 1981; Ames & Archer, 1988; Ames, 1992). Ames (1984) identified two types of situations, each created by others (e.g., teacher, coach, therapist, peer), called competitive and individualistic reward structures. In competitive reward structures, only the winner receives an award. In contrast, in individualistic reward structures, personal improvement is the standard for achievement and thus awards are available to multiple people. To put this in achievement goal theory terms, these different reward structures, when salient to the learner, are thought to elicit different definitions of competence. For example, individualistic reward structures appear to encourage people to become involved in the task and the pursuit of mastery goals, whereas competitive reward structures encourage people to focus on enhancing their ego through superior performance relative to others and the pursuit of performance goals. Though they did not conduct a study on reward structures per se, Wulf and Lewthwaite (2009) demonstrated that inducing a particular definition of competence (i.e., conception of ability) via instruction can affect learning. After receiving instructions for a novel balance task that emphasized the ease of improvement with practice, adult performers mastered the task to a greater degree than those who received instructions that emphasized ability as capacity.

The assumption in the study of reward structures (as initiated by others) is that these climates dictate participants' achievement goals. This approach fails to consider the individuals' perceptions of the environment. Is it possible to be in a competitive reward structure (e.g., a race) and still pursue mastery goals? Taking this into account, Ames (1992) coined the term *motivational climate* to refer to individuals' perception of the reward structure. Task-involving climates are characterized by the perception that success and competence are judged via self-referenced criteria. Individuals are in task-involving climates when they perceive that improvement, learning, and effort are valued. Ego-involving climates, on the other hand, are characterized by the perception that success and competence are judged based on norm-referenced criteria. Individuals in ego-involving climates perceive that comparing favorably to or outperforming others (normative competence) is valued. Research shows a positive relationship between motivational climate and achievement goals (see Roberts, 2012). Specifically, those who perceive task-involving climates also tend to define competence in self-referenced terms and pursue mastery goals, whereas those who perceive ego-involving climates tend to define competence as normative performance and seek performance goals (see Roberts). Task- and ego-involving climates are perceptions that tend to correlate negatively and moderately. Practically speaking, this indicates that if physical activity leaders are seen as promoting effort, learning, and improving, they are less likely to be seen as rewarding the winners.

Based on their review of the motivational climate literature, Harwood and colleagues (2008) concluded that task-involving climates were associated with positive–adaptive motivational patterns, whereas ego-involving climate are "often associated with undesirable beliefs and patterns of behavior" (p. 178). In a subsequent systematic review of the interpersonal correlates of motivational climate, Harwood, Keegan, Smith, and Raine (2015) obtained similar results and concluded that those perceiving task-involving climates demonstrate a range of highly adaptive motivational profiles. Perceptions of a task-involving climate are associated with positive patterns (e.g., perceptions of competence, confidence and self-esteem, self-determined motivation, persistence) and negatively related with maladaptive patterns (e.g., norm-referenced competence, negative affect) (see also Roberts, 2012). Conversely, perceptions of an ego-involving climate related to constructs such as negative affect and amotivation.

While individuals in ego-involving climates, particularly those with a performance–approach goal focus, may engage in adaptive motivational patterns, Harwood and colleagues (2015) concluded that it is those perceiving a task climate who "engage in sport and physical activity favorably" (p. 19). To illustrate, perceptions of a task-involving climate appear to encourage prosocial behavior and sportspersonship such as respect for the rules and others (e.g., Miller, Roberts, & Ommundsen, 2004). Allen and her colleagues (Allen, Taylor, Dimeo, Dixon, & Robinson, 2015) found that elite athletes who perceived a greater task-involving climate were less likely to endorse the use of performance-enhancement drugs. It is reasonable, then, to suggest that designing an environment to be task involving may foster greater moral reasoning and behavior in athletes.

Three important points about motivational climate have been discussed thus far. One, motivational climate is initiated by others but perceived by the participant. Two, motivational climate and individuals' definitions of competence are related. Three, motivational climate is associated with achievement-related affect, behavior, and cognitions. Given the positive processes and outcomes associated with task-involving climate and defining competence in mastery terms, it is reasonable that physical activity leaders such as teachers, coaches, trainers, and therapists would be interested in creating task-involving climates as a means of fostering a mastery focus and a positive physical activity experience.

Initial investigations into the role that motivational climate plays in shaping individuals' tendency to be mastery focused revealed that task-involving climates predicted changes in end-of-season mastery (e.g., Waldron & Krane, 2005; Williams, 1998). Building on this, Gano-Overway and colleagues (Boyce, Gano-Overway, & Campbell, 2009; Gano-Overway & Ewing, 2004) found that motivational climate had the greatest impact on students' achievement goal focus when the goal focus and climate were in opposition. Specifically, students and student-athletes with a low mastery focus were more mastery focused after being exposed to a task-involving climate over time. Additionally, students and athletes who were mastery focused and perceived a low task-involving climate were less mastery focused by the end of the semester or season. Similar trends held true for performance goals and ego-involving climates. Collectively, the results of these studies revealed that task-involving climates related positively to individuals' end-of-season perceived competence and self-regulated practice strategies. These findings suggest that perceptions of a task-involving climate may influence individuals' goal focus over time and lead to adaptive motivational outcomes (see also Braithwaite, Spray, & Warburton, 2011).

Collectively, this research provides reason for creating task-involving climates in physical activity. One approach has been to employ principles that have become known by the acronym TARGET (see Roberts, 2012). Applying these principles to create a task-involving climate involves the following:

Task—Designing tasks that are appropriately challenging, varied, and skill mastery based

Authority—Providing participants with leadership and decision-making opportunities that involve self-regulation (e.g., choice)

Recognition—Recognizing students for their individual progress and improvement in private

Grouping—Providing students with group and mixed-level cooperative learning opportunities

Evaluation—Evaluating students on task mastery, improvement, and effort

Time—Providing participants with self-paced, self-directed, and adequate time to learn

Applying TARGET principles has been shown to be effective (Braithwaite et al., 2011; Roberts, 2012). In their meta-analytic review, Braithwaite and colleagues found that intentional creation and implementation of a task-involving motiva-

tional climate grounded in TARGET principles had a positive effect on, among other variables, physical education students' attitude, health and fitness, performance, and anxiety.

TARGET-guided motivational climate interventions have also been shown to be effective in sport contexts. Coaches adopted more task-involving behaviors and athletes perceived the climate to be more task involving and less ego involving after coach training that entailed analysis of coach behavior and multiple, individual, reflective discussions and behavioral critique of coach behavior relative to TARGET (Hassan & Morgan, 2015). Other more established and formal coach education programs include elements of TARGET, such as the Fundamentals of Coaching (found on the National Federation of State High School Associations [NFSH] website) and Mastery Approach to Coaching Sport (MACS; found on the Youth Enrichment in Sports website under Coach Education). MACS is based on years of research out of the University of Washington (see Smoll & Smith, 2015, for a review).

Application Point

TARGET the Climate in Physical Education

Zina teaches physical education and loves it. She is a dedicated teacher who strives to create environments in which all of her students want to learn and improve. She is finding that her efforts are falling short with Will. She is concerned that he has low perceived competence and is approach–avoidance focused. She wonders if he is learned helpless. Provide specific suggestions grounded in TARGET to foster a greater mastery–approach focus in Will.

Overall, there appears to be good reason for physical activity leaders to create task-involving climates that emphasize effort, learning, and improvement and thus foster mastery goal focus, which in turn provides greater opportunity for athletes to feel successful and develop adaptive motivational patterns. However, as noted in the Youth Enrichment in Sport education program, coaches are not the only ones who play a role in creating a motivational climate. We must also consider the role that others, such as parents and peers, play in creating motivational climates (e.g., Davies, Babkes-Stellino, Nichols, & Coleman, 2016; Leo, Sanchez-Miguel, Sanchez-Oliva, Amado, &

Garcia-Calvo, 2015; Smoll, Smith, & Cumming, 2007; Vazou, Ntoumanis, & Duda, 2006; Waldron & Krane, 2005). Broadly, the collective results of other-initiated climates parallel those of coach-initiated climates. Task-involving climates are more motivationally adaptive than ego-involving climates. What we consider most valuable in this line of research is the finding that parents appear to be more influential than the coach or peers among youth sport athletes (Atkins, Johnson, Force, & Petrie, 2015; O'Rourke, Smith, Smoll, & Cumming, 2014). Smoll and Smith appear on target when including Mastery Approach to Parenting in Sports in their YESports program.

Putting It Into Practice

Summary

To understand achievement behavior, we must consider individual differences. Cognitive motivation theorists focus on people's perceptions in achievement settings. Success attributions that are stable foster expectations for future success. Failure attributions that are internal and controllable elicit negative emotions related to guilt and shame. These expectations and emotions have implications for future achievement behavior. Achievement goal theorists incorporate personal definitions of success and failure. Some people focus on winning and outperforming others (performance), whereas others focus on task mastery (mastery goals). With a mastery goal focus comes a greater opportunity to experience adaptive achievement motivation. Using TARGET principles to create a task-involving climate has shown promise in fostering adaptive definitions of competence and achievement goals. This work is being extended from coach- to parent- and peer-initiated climates. Continued research may provide a greater understanding of the role of individual differences and contextual factors in people's motivation in sport and exercise settings.

Review Questions

1. Describe attributions and explain their role in achievement motivation.
2. Describe Weiner's $2 \times 2 \times 2$ classification scheme of causal attributions.
3. Define learned helplessness.
4. Discuss the purpose and effectiveness of attributional retraining programs.
5. Explain the role of personality and situational factors in Atkinson's theory of achievement motivation.
6. Compare and contrast the definitions of competence in mastery and performance achievement goals.
7. Discuss the role of valence of competence in achievement goal theory.
8. Explain the role of motivational climate in achievement motivation.
9. Compare and contrast task- and ego-involving climates.

Recommended Reading

- Dweck, C.S. (2006). *Mindset: The new psychology of success.* New York: Ballantine Books. In this book, Dweck shares her work, conclusions, and applications of the work on achievement behavior. She explains how conceptions of ability (mindset) guide decisions in our lives and have different motivational outcomes. She explains how a growth mindset leads to success in business, personal relationships, parenting, and athletics. Throughout the book she provides "how to" tips for changing mindset, concluding with success stories.

- Elliot, A.J. (1999). Approach and avoidance motivation and achievement goals. *Educational Psychologist, 34,* 169-189. In this article, Elliot overviews his initial reconceptualization of achievement motivation, which tackles the complex relationships among goal orientations, perceived competence, and motivation with greater deliberation than earlier achievement motivation theories. Elliot discusses the motivational correlates of mastery, performance–approach, and performance–avoidance orientations. This is a good starting point for learning about the 2×2 achievement goal framework.

Fostering Achievement Motivation

For this lab, let's revisit Ximena and Rika from earlier in this chapter. Ximena and Rika, two ninth-graders, are best friends and do everything together, except when it comes to being physically active. Although Rika is more capable in a variety of activities, Ximena embraces physical activity. In physical education, Ximena is always eager to participate, chooses personally challenging tasks, tries hard, and persists in the face of objective failure (i.e., losing a game, being one of the slowest to pick up a skill). It seems that Ximena likes physical activity, and regardless of her poor showing relative to her peers, she anticipates future success. In contrast, Rika, who could experience greater objective success, avoids participation. When obligated to play, she chooses either the easiest task possible or tasks that no one could do. For example, when given time to practice basketball, Rika spends most of her time dribbling and passing the ball to others. She usually attempts only half-court shots. When encouraged to shoot a variety of shots, she shoots bank shots about 2 feet (0.5 meter) from the basket. She expects to fail and seems to dread physical education.

Use your knowledge of attributions, achievement goals (definitions of competence and valence of competence), and motivational climate to create an achievement motivation profile for each girl. Then, provide suggestions to their physical education teacher for encouraging Ximena's adaptive motivational profile and fostering a more adaptive motivational profile for Rika.

Chapter 10

Integrated Approaches to Physical Activity Behavior

Chapter Objectives

After studying this chapter, you should be able to

- discuss the health benefits of physical activity,

- describe physical activity patterns in the general population and differences across various demographics (e.g., gender, age, ethnicity),

- discuss the motivational theories and models that have been applied to exercise behavior,

- understand the role of the physical and social environment in the development and maintenance of physical activity behavior,

- explain how integrative models, such as the transtheoretical model, can be used to promote physical activity as a lifestyle behavior,

- explain the principles of health coaching and the motivational interviewing approach to communicating with clients, and

- identify the characteristics of exercise dependence and strategies for referral.

This chapter focuses on motivation for continued participation in physical activity—why people begin and why they stay involved in exercise. We look most closely at physical activity as a lifestyle behavior, which is essential in health promotion and fitness programs, important in physical education and youth sport, and relevant even in competitive athletics. For instance, highly competitive athletes may emphasize achievement and performance and thus have difficulty maintaining activity patterns when they leave their competitive sport and no longer have the same motivational incentives to be active (Reifsteck, Gill, & Labban, 2016; Sorenson, Romano, Azen, Schroeder, & Salem, 2015).

Maintenance, rather than peak performance, is the overriding goal of lifestyle physical activity, and participants typically engage in varied activities rather than focusing on one sport or event. Indeed, that variation often is intentional in order to achieve health and fitness goals. Just as activities are varied, participants are much more diverse than the athletes in select sports. This chapter focuses on typical adult fitness participants, a diverse population in itself, as well as children, older adults, and clients in a variety of clinical and health promotion programs.

Physical Activity for Health and Well-Being

Lifestyle physical activity is increasingly promoted in the media, as well as in health and kinesiology resources. The U.S. Department of Health and Human Services (USDHHS) published Physical Activity Guidelines for Americans in 2008 and the updated Healthy People 2020 objectives in 2010. The focus of these guidelines and objectives is to improve Americans' health, fitness, and quality of life through daily physical activity. The Centers for Disease Control and Prevention (CDC) website also has a section that offers resources and information on physical activity.

Physical inactivity has been linked to nearly all major health problems, including increased risk for heart disease, diabetes, osteoporosis, and negative psychological conditions such as depression and anxiety (USDHHS, 2008), whereas regular physical activity is associated with a reduction in all-cause mortality, cardiovascular disease, and obesity (Kesaniemi et al., 2001). Further benefits of an active lifestyle include improved physical function and independent living, as well as decreased likelihood of depression.

Key Point

Physical inactivity has been linked to most major health problems, including heart disease, diabetes, osteoporosis, and negative psychological conditions such as depression and anxiety.

The interest in physical activity and health promotion is not limited to the United States. The World Health Organization (WHO) includes physical activity as a public health priority, and the WHO website contains information on physical activity and health that parallels U.S. reports. Physical inactivity is a major health problem around the world, and WHO estimates that over 80 percent of the world's adolescent population does not get enough physical activity to meet recommendations. Globally, adults in developed countries are the most likely to be inactive. Like the CDC, the American College of Sports Medicine (ACSM), and many governmental and professional organizations in North America, WHO promotes physical activity and offers recommendations for both individuals and public policies.

The USDHHS and ACSM recommend at least 30 minutes of moderate physical activity on most, if not all, days of the week (or minimum of 150 minutes total per week), yet data from population-based surveys consistently show that the majority of the U.S. population is insufficiently active. Less than half of the U.S. population meets physical activity guidelines, and less than 20 percent meet recommendations for both aerobic and muscle strengthening activities, with higher rates of inactivity among those who are older, racial or ethnic minorities, female, less educated, overweight, or have a history of being physically inactive. Physical activity patterns of childhood and adolescence begin the lifetime patterns that promote health in adulthood, but unfortunately, the evidence indicates that activity declines in adolescence, particularly for girls (CDC, 2014).

Key Point

The USDHHS and the ACSM recommend at least 30 minutes of moderate physical activity most days of the week (a minimum of 150 minutes per week), but most Americans do not meet these minimum guidelines.

Lox, Martin Ginis, and Petruzzello (2014) summarize the epidemiological data on physical activity patterns around the world as follows:

- The number of people worldwide who exercise at even the minimal level to achieve physical benefits is low (conservatively estimated at 50 percent); at least 25 percent do not exercise at all.

- Participation in physical activity declines linearly across the life span, and time spent in sedentary activities increases.

- Males are more likely to engage in vigorous activity, although women engage in as much moderate physical activity as men.

- Differences are small, but low-income groups and ethnic minority groups tend to participate in less physical activity than the overall population.

- The higher the education level, the greater the participation in physical activity. Although not as strong, a similar relationship exists between income level and physical activity.

Moreover, 50 percent of adults who start to exercise in fitness programs drop out within six months, and as Buckworth, Dishman, O'Connor, and Tomporowski (2013) note, this high dropout rate has not changed over the last several decades.

Much of the interest in physical activity motivation stems from increasing public recognition of the health benefits of exercise coupled with the fact that most people do not act on that recognition. Given this global lack of physical activity participation, the ability to understand and apply sport and exercise psychology principles is important for professionals seeking to promote health-related physical activity programs.

Theories and Models of Physical Activity Behavior

Much of the early research on participation motivation was descriptive and focused on identifying reasons young people engaged in youth sport. Unlike the largely descriptive research on youth sport motivation, the work on physical activity participation motivation is largely theory based. Because behavior change and maintaining activity are the main concerns, the models draw heavily upon behavioral and social cognitive models that have been applied to other health behaviors.

This section summarizes the main theoretical models and then provides applications of integrated models in physical activity interventions and health promotion programs. Specific details of motivational research and theories discussed in previous chapters (e.g., behavioral approaches in chapter 7, self-determination theory in chapter 8) are not repeated here but are highlighted as part of the integrated model for professional practice.

Health Belief Model

The health belief model developed by Rosenstock (1974) includes four major components:

- Perceived susceptibility, or the assessment of risk for the particular health threat
- Perceived severity of the health threat
- Perceived benefits of taking action to reduce the threat
- Perceived barriers to or costs of the action

The health belief model has considerable support in relation to health behaviors and medical compliance but limited application to exercise and physical activity. The strongest support has been found for components related to other theories. Specifically, perceived barriers, which relates to social cognitive theory, has stronger support than other components.

Theories of Reasoned Action and Planned Behavior

The attitude-based theories of reasoned action (TRA; Fishbein & Ajzen, 1974) and planned behavior (Ajzen, 1985) have received more attention in research on exercise behavior. Both propose that intentions are the main determinants of behavior. That is, to predict whether people will exercise, ask them whether they intend to exercise. Behavioral intentions, in turn, are determined by attitudes toward the behavior, along with subjective social norms. The theory of planned behavior (TPB) moves beyond reasoned action by adding the notion of perceived behavioral control. Perceived behavioral control is similar to self-efficacy (as discussed in chapter 6) in that it involves perceptions that one has the ability to carry out the behavior. When people have positive attitudes toward physical activity, believe that their peers are physically active, and feel capable of being physically active, then they are more likely to have intentions to be physically active, which in turn increases the likelihood that they will

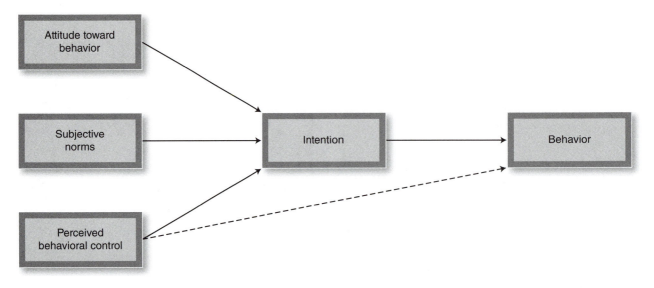

Figure 10.1 Conceptual model for the theory of planned behavior.

participate in physical activity. Unlike attitudes and social norms, which influence behavior only through intentions, perceived behavioral control is proposed to also directly influence behavior (shown as the dashed line in figure 10.1).

Several sport and exercise psychology researchers have applied reasoned action or planned behavior to understand and predict exercise behavior (e.g., Courneya, Estabrooks, & Nigg, 1997; Godin, 1993; McAuley & Courneya, 1993). Meta-analyses by Downs and Hausenblas (2005) and Hagger, Chatzisarantis, and Biddle (2002) support the TPB, finding that the most important predictor of physical activity is intention and that attitude and behavioral control predict intention. Subjective norm has not received consistent support in physical activity research, and Courneya, Plotnikoff, Hotz, and Birkett (2000) advocate substituting social support as the social influence predictor in the TPB model.

Social Cognitive Theory

Various social cognitive approaches to motivation (see chapter 8) have been applied to many health behaviors, including exercise behavior. Social cognitive theory (SCT; Bandura, 1986) is one of the most widely studied and applied theories of human behavior and has been used often in interventions to promote exercise adherence. Underlying this theory is the principle of triadic reciprocal determinism, in which individual behaviors, cognitions, and environmental factors all interact to influence each other. Individuals learn behaviors through other people who model

and reinforce the behavior. Exercise and other health behaviors are influenced by people's knowledge about health risks and the benefits of engaging in healthy behaviors, their self-efficacy (belief in their ability to engage in healthy exercise behaviors), their outcome expectations (belief that exercising will lead to a desired outcome), and perceived social and structural facilitators or impediments to changing their exercise behaviors (Bandura, 2004). As discussed in chapter 6, the role of self-efficacy is central to this framework. The concept of self-efficacy has received considerable attention in sport and exercise psychology research and has been incorporated into other theories such as the transtheoretical model (discussed later in this chapter).

On the basis of earlier work with other health behaviors (e.g., weight management, smoking cessation), Marcus, Selby, Niaura, and Rossi (1992) developed a five-item self-efficacy measure for exercise that includes the situational factors of negative affect, resisting relapse, and making time for exercise. As discussed in chapter 6, considerable literature supports the role of self-efficacy and social cognitive theory in sport and exercise behavior. For example, Jerome and McAuley (2013) demonstrated that self-efficacy was associated with enrollment and participation in an exercise program among adults. Maddison and Prapavessis (2004) found that self-efficacy predicted exercise adherence in cardiac rehab patients. Kroll and colleagues (2012) reported that self-efficacy predicted exercise behaviors among individuals with spinal cord injuries.

Several researchers have applied social cognitive models and found self-efficacy to be a strong predictor of physical activity in various populations, including persons who are obese (Dallow & Anderson, 2003) and people with physical disabilities (Cardinal, Kosma, & McCubbin, 2004). McAuley, Jerome, Marquez, Elavsky, and Blissmer (2003) confirmed the reciprocal efficacy–behavior relationships of SCT in reporting that previous exercise behavior predicted efficacy and future exercise behavior in older adults. At the other end of the age range, Lubans and Sylva (2006) applied SCT in a physical activity intervention with high school students. At the end of the program, the intervention group reported both more physical activity and greater self-efficacy for exercise than the control group.

Key Point

Several researchers have applied social cognitive models and found self-efficacy to be a strong predictor of physical activity in various populations, including people who are obese, people with physical disabilities, college students, and middle-aged adults.

Relapse Prevention Model

Regardless of how people start exercising, relapse is a problem, as it is for most health behaviors (Brownell, Marlatt, Lichtenstein, & Wilson, 1986). As noted earlier, about 50 percent of exercise program participants typically drop out within six months. Sallis and colleagues (1990) found that 40 percent of exercisers experienced relapse (stopped exercising for at least three months) and that 20 percent had three or more relapses. In relapse-prevention training, exercisers learn to view exercise as a continuum, to recognize and avoid risk situations, and sometimes to try a planned relapse. The principles of relapse prevention include identifying high-risk situations (e.g., a change in work hours) and then problem solving for those high-risk situations (e.g., when it starts to snow, walk inside the local mall).

When exercisers experience a relapse, they must deal with the abstinence violation effect (AVE), which is the belief that one slip means doom (e.g., one cookie ruins your diet, one missed exercise class and you're a couch potato).

Brownell (1989) differentiates among lapse (slip), relapse (string of lapses), and collapse (giving up and returning to past behaviors). Brownell advocates helping people become aware of AVE and the differences among lapses, relapses, and collapses in order to reduce recidivism. Marcus and colleagues (2000) suggest that the relapse-prevention model can be a useful framework for understanding the lapse-to-collapse process in exercise behavior.

Integrated Approaches to Physical Activity Promotion

Many practitioners and programs incorporate both cognitive approaches and behavioral techniques that draw from multiple theories. Given the diversity of participants, multifaceted programs with varied strategies are most likely to meet participants' needs and preferences. Focusing on older adults' physical activity behavior, Grodesky, Kosma, and Solmon (2006) specifically advocated the transtheoretical model as an overall guiding framework and incorporated elements of both the theory of planned behavior and self-determination theory within a comprehensive approach. We now turn our attention to these integrated approaches.

The Transtheoretical Model

Several researchers have advocated integration of the many available theoretical approaches. At this time, the most useful approach for practicing professionals may be the transtheoretical model (TTM; Prochaska & DiClemente, 1983), applied to exercise behavior by Bess Marcus and colleagues (e.g., Marcus, Rossi, Selby, Niaura, & Abrams, 1992; Marcus & Forsyth, 2009). Generally, the TTM helps us understand the relationship between individual readiness and actual exercise behavior, and it provides guidance for intervention programs aimed at increasing physical activity. According to the model, people progress through certain stages of change, applied to exercise (Marcus, Rossi, et al., 1992):

1. **Precontemplation:** Precontemplators do not exercise and do not intend to do so within the next six months.
2. **Contemplation:** Contemplators do not exercise but intend to start within six months.
3. **Preparation:** Preparers are exercising but not regularly (regular activity is defined as three

or more times per week for 20 minutes or longer if vigorous intensity, or 30 accumulated minutes or more per day on five or more days per week if moderate intensity).

4. **Action:** People at the action stage exercise regularly but have done so for less than six months.

5. **Maintenance:** Individuals at the maintenance stage have been exercising regularly for more than six months.

Key Point

The transtheoretical model helps us understand the relationship between individual readiness and actual exercise behavior, and it provides guidance for intervention programs aimed at increasing physical activity.

Marcus also relates the decisional balance and self-efficacy constructs to stages of change. *Decisional balance* refers to the process of weighing perceived relative costs (e.g., loss of time that could be devoted to other things; gym membership fees) and benefits (e.g., improved health and quality of life) of engaging in exercise. In relation to stages, the decisional balance typically favors the costs (i.e., perceived costs of becoming active outweigh perceived benefits of exercise) in the precontemplation and contemplation stages, crosses over in the preparation stage, and it favors benefits over costs in the action and maintenance stages (i.e., perceived benefits gained from an active lifestyle outweigh the potential costs) (Marcus, Rakowski, & Rossi, 1992; Prochaska et al., 1994). In terms of self-efficacy, over several studies (Marcus, Eaton, Rossi, & Harlow, 1994; Marcus & Owen, 1992; Marcus, Pinto, Simkin, Audrain, & Taylor, 1994; Marcus, Selby, et al., 1992), Marcus and colleagues have found a positive relationship between enhanced self-efficacy and greater readiness for change. Later in this chapter, we discuss specific applications of TTM that have been effective in the promotion of physical activity.

Social–Ecological Models

Much of the research and theorizing on physical activity promotion in sport and exercise psychology have focused on intervening at the individual level by modifying psychological determinants of behavior. However, as discussed in chapter 1, both personal and environmental factors interact to influence behavior. Social–ecological models move beyond social cognitive and behavioral theories that focus on the individual to a broader emphasis on the social environment and environmental interventions that can influence physical activity for the larger community. In particular, social–ecological models often focus on the built environment, such as housing patterns, walkways, and trails, as well as public policies.

Sallis, Bauman, and Pratt (1998) developed a social–ecological model for physical activity that suggests coordination and planning efforts among agencies (e.g., transportation, urban planning, schools) in order to facilitate policies and practices that support physical activity. Although social–ecological models are broad and offer few clear, testable predictions, they provide guidance for promoting physical activity and health at the community level. Specifically, such models suggest that physical activity can be increased by improving the availability of facilities and programs and supporting active transportation such as walking and biking.

The CDC clearly advocates such approaches, and its website includes suggestions and resources for developing active environments that promote physical activity. Additionally, objective 15 of the Healthy People 2020 objectives for physical activity is to "increase legislative policies for the built environment that enhance access to and availability of physical activity opportunities." Specific goals to be met within this overarching objective include improving policies around community spaces, streets, and transportation options that make opportunities for physical activity more widely available and easily accessible.

Interest in environmental and policy strategies to promote physical activity has grown over the last few years, as has the evidence that supports such approaches. Environmental and policy approaches are especially important because they can benefit everyone within the environment, including those at high risk for inactivity. Strategies include providing access to facilities and programs and supporting social environments that favor activity such as walking and bicycle trails, public funding for facilities, zoning and land use that facilitate activity in neighborhoods, mall walking programs, and building construction that encourages physical activity. Such approaches hold particular promise and should be taken into account in the design of community-based physical activity interventions. The CDC and the Healthy People websites provide links to related tools and resources that complement their efforts to create an active environment. Two important resources include Active Living Research and Active Living by Design, funded by the Robert Wood Johnson Foundation. Active Living by Design is a program that establishes and evaluates innovative approaches to increase physical activity through community design, public policies, and communications strategies.

Evidence to support such broad-based programs is growing. The Robert Wood Johnson Foundation has sponsored several Active Living Research conferences over the past decade, and more researchers have taken an ecological approach in their work. Taylor, Poston, Jones, and Kraft (2006) advocate environmental justice, referring to efforts to address disproportionate harmful environmental conditions experienced by low-income and racial and ethnic minority populations, and they provide evidence of the challenges faced in efforts to become active (e.g., higher crime rates; lack of sidewalks, safe places, and recreational facilities). Heath and colleagues (2006) identified two interventions that were effective in promoting physical activity: community-scale and street-scale urban design and land-use policies and practices. Cohen and colleagues (2006) found that distance to school was inversely related to moderate-to-vigorous physical activity in adolescent girls, with those more than 5 miles (8 kilometers) away the most adversely affected.

Bartholomew (2015) points out that much of the research in this area has focused on creating a supportive environment that allows people to be more active. However, a potentially more impactful approach might be to construct an environment where it is difficult for people to remain inactive. Bartholomew also argues that in order for ecological interventions to be successful long-term, researchers must consider the motivations of those responsible for implementing environmental changes (e.g., local policy makers, school administrators). As the title of his article suggests, we know that the environment changes people's behaviors—but who changes the environment? Clearly, physical activity promotion is a multifaceted concern, and we cannot ignore the profound influence of the social and physical environment.

Application Point

Promoting Physical Activity in the Community

Kinesiology professionals can and should promote physical activity in their larger communities as well as in professional practice. A neighborhood group interested in promoting physical activity is meeting at the school where you are a physical education teacher, and the group asks for your advice. What will you say? Consider social–ecological models and suggest specific policy and environmental changes to promote physical activity in the community.

Using Integrated Models: A Practical Guide

The TTM incorporates cognitive theories and behavioral strategies, emphasizes the need to individualize interventions, considers environmental barriers, and provides a useful guide for developing effective programs. Marcus and colleagues have gone beyond proposals to carry out interventions based on the TTM (see Marcus & Forsyth, 2009). In the Imagine Action campaign, 610 adults enrolled through worksites in response to community announcements, receiving a six-week intervention consisting of stage-matched self-help materials, a resource manual, weekly fun walks, and activity nights. The manual for contemplators was called *What's in It for You*, which is the critical question at that stage. Similarly, the preparation manual was *Ready for Action*, and the manual for those in action was *Keeping It Going*. Following the intervention, 30 percent of those in contemplation and 61 percent of those in preparation progressed to action. An additional 31 percent of those in contemplation progressed to preparation, whereas only 4 percent of those in preparation and 9 percent in action regressed. A subsequent controlled, randomized-design investigation of a stage-matched intervention at the workplace (Marcus, Emmons, et al., 1994) was also successful, with more subjects in the stage-matched group demonstrating stage progression at the three-month follow-up. In contrast, more subjects in the standard-care group displayed stage stability or regression.

Marcus and Forsyth (2009) compiled research and theoretical work into a practical guide called *Motivating People to Be Physically Active*. The guide emphasizes stages of change as an individual-difference variable and suggests behavioral and cognitive strategies, as well as social support and environmental approaches, to promote physical activity. Sources of information and guidelines for the general public, such as Corbin and colleagues' (2008) fitness and wellness manual and the CDC website, reference Bess Marcus' extensive research and recommend a similar approach. Project Active (Dunn et al., 1999) has successfully applied the model in a community-based physical activity program.

Marcus and Forsyth (2009) use the stages of change model as a framework for individualizing intervention strategies. People are at different stages depending on their current level of physical activity. The main point for professionals is that intervention programs should match the stage of change; that is, programs and strategies should be tailored to the individual, situation, and context.

Processes of behavior change are strategies and techniques for modifying behaviors. Processes fall into two categories: cognitive and behavioral. Cognitive processes involve thinking and awareness and include increasing knowledge, being aware of risks, caring about consequences to others, comprehending benefits, and increasing healthy opportunities. Behavioral processes involve action and include substituting alternatives, enlisting social support, rewarding yourself, committing yourself, and reminding yourself.

Programs based on this model match interventions to the participant's stage of readiness. In general, cognitive strategies are more useful for people in the early stages (precontemplation, contemplation), whereas people at later stages (preparation, action, and maintenance) use mostly behavioral strategies. Within that general framework, Marcus and Forsyth (2009) provide more specific examples and suggestions for consultants or fitness professionals who want to help clients use these strategies in the process of behavior change. Many of the specific strategies draw upon the behavioral and cognitive strategies and psychological skills discussed in the previous sections of this chapter. Strategies that are appropriate for the current stage help the person take positive steps toward fitness while overcoming barriers and building confidence. The Marcus and Forsyth book is readable and practical, as well as based on current theory and empirical evidence. It is highly recommended as a guide for sport and exercise psychology professionals working with individual clients, groups, or community programs to promote healthy physical activity.

Moving to the Next Stage

Your school is starting an after-school program for overweight middle school students, and you are on the team that is developing the program. Your team is using the integrated transtheoretical model as a guide. Your task is to design specific strategies and activities to include in the program. Participants are likely to be in early stages of exercise, so focus on strategies to move from contemplation and preparation toward action and maintenance. Include at least two specific behavioral strategies and two specific cognitive strategies, along with a rationale.

Increasingly, health and fitness organizations such as the ACSM are emphasizing integrated theoretical approaches to promote exercise adherence among clients. *ACSM's Guidelines for Exercise Testing and Prescription* (ACSM, 2017) includes a chapter devoted to behavioral theories and strategies to promote exercise. Many of the theories discussed in this textbook are also highlighted in the ACSM handbook. The ACSM guide outlines specific strategies to target relevant constructs from each theory and suggests ways to match those strategies with clients' stages of change. For instance, if a cardiac rehab client complains of not being motivated to exercise, a fitness professional might evaluate the client's stage of change (TTM), discuss the client's perceptions about the likelihood that a second heart attack will occur (health belief model), and reinforce outcome expectations that regular exercise can decrease the client's risk for another incident (SCT). Ultimately, by understanding and incorporating strategies that reflect behavior change theories, health fitness professionals can more effectively promote their clients' adoption and maintenance of exercise behaviors in order to optimize impact on health outcomes.

Physical Activity and Health Coaching

While several theories and integrated approaches have been outlined, Brawley, Gierc, and Locke (2013) questioned whether kinesiologists are truly ready to counsel individuals through the process of successfully adopting and maintaining healthy physical activity behaviors. Brawley and colleagues suggest that kinesiologists are the "front line troops" in the efforts to enhance people's motivation to make important health behavior changes. Cognitive behavioral and self-regulatory strategies such as setting goals, providing feedback, monitoring goal progress, and enhancing self-efficacy have been shown to be effective at promoting physical activity behavior change. While kinesiology students are well versed in skills related to physical training and fitness, kinesiologists are not sufficiently educated in or prepared for the practice of applying these cognitive behavioral strategies to promote adherence. In particular, most kinesiology students do not have the opportunity to actually practice relevant psychosocial skills during their educational training, which limits their potential effectiveness as practitioners. In recent years, however, the practice of "health coaching" has started to integrate theories, principles, and skills from sport and exercise psychology into the broader fields of public health and kinesiology.

Health coaches guide clients to develop the knowledge, skills, and confidence to achieve their health-related goals. Health coaching is a client-centered approach that puts the needs and agency of the client at the forefront of the relationship. Sforzo, Moore, and Scholtz (2015) outline the "4 Cs" of health coaching skills for exercise professionals, including connection, curiosity, confidence, and change. *Connection* involves using mindful listening skills and reflections, being nonjudgmental and compassionate toward clients, and fostering positivity. *Curiosity* relies on the health coach asking provocative questions to help clients set their own agenda and develop autonomous motivation for change. *Confidence* relates to building clients' self-efficacy for achieving their desired health goals, including helping clients develop self-determined goals and identify multiple avenues to meet those goals. Finally, *change* entails helping clients develop a vision for their future by setting realistic goals and holding them accountable.

One of the hallmarks of health coaching is the incorporation of *motivational interviewing*. Motivational interviewing helps elicit behavior change by helping clients explore and resolve ambivalence (Rollnick & Miller, 1995). For instance, a person who is considering becoming more physically active may have both positive feelings (e.g., I will be healthier if I exercise) and negative feelings (e.g., Exercise requires too much of my time) related to making this change. Motivational

interviewing is centered on the belief that motivation for change must come from the client (i.e., autonomous), and the coach–client relationship is defined as a partnership in which the coach is not positioned as the expert. Key motivational interviewing tools include listening without judgment (empathic counseling); acknowledging resistance to change and encouraging client commitment (rolling with resistance); instilling confidence in the client (supporting self-efficacy); and helping clients identify discrepancies between their current and desired behaviors in order to motivate change (developing discrepancies) (Mears & Kilpatrick, 2009).

Two specific communication strategies characteristic of this approach include the use of reflections and open-ended questions. Reflections are short summary statements of what the client has just said, allowing clients to hear their own words. Open-ended questions cannot be answered with a simple yes or no response and often start with words or phrases like "What," "How," "In what way," and "Tell me more." Examples of how you might respond to a client's statement with either a reflection or open-ended question follow.

> Client statement: *I just don't feel like I have the time to exercise. I work two jobs and have kids to take care of.*
>
> Reflection: *It's hard for you to find time to exercise.*
>
> Open-ended question: *Tell me about a day last week when you were able to find time to exercise . . .*

Reflections and open-ended questions shift the conversation from simply telling clients what to do to guiding them toward finding the answers for themselves. Both of these strategies build connection with the client and prompt the client to share additional information and insights.

Motivational interviewing techniques have been incorporated by exercise professionals to promote both exercise adherence (Mears & Kilpatrick, 2009) and weight loss (Whiteley & Milliken, 2011). Meta-analytic findings show that motivational interviewing is effective at improving clients' diet and exercise behaviors (Burke, Arkowitz, & Menchola, 2003). Mears and Kilpatrick (2009) offer several practical recommendations for exercise professionals who wish to incorporate aspects of motivational interviewing and self-determination theory—which, as discussed in chapter 8, has a similar focus on developing autonomous motivation. These recommendations include empowering clients by providing a rationale for why a specific exercise is important to their goals; establishing moderately difficult goals that foster both motivation and confidence; allowing clients to choose their own activities to enhance autonomy; building relationships with others through exercise to provide social support and accountability; and offering positive feedback about client progress to increase self-efficacy. Ultimately, integrating health coaching practices and motivational interviewing techniques can help exercise professionals assist their clients in achieving self-identified health outcomes and making lasting behavior changes.

Excessive Participation: Exercise Dependence

The majority of this chapter focuses on encouraging participation in physical activity. Indeed, this is a major concern for public health promotion, and significant efforts have been appropriately devoted to addressing the issue. Although not nearly as prevalent in the general population as the ill effects of sedentary behavior, excessive exercise, at the opposite extreme, may also become health damaging. Athletes may train excessively (overtrain), resulting in negative mental health (e.g., depression, tension, fatigue, reduced energy) as well as poorer performance. As Raglin and Moger (1999) note, the switch to negative mood states is related to the training load and in extreme cases can result in clinical depression.

Exercise dependence is more often associated with participants who are not competitive athletes and whose excessive exercise is not associated with training to enhance performance. Hausenblas and Symons Downs (2002a, p. 90) define exercise dependence as "a craving for leisure-time physical activity, resulting in uncontrollable excessive exercise behavior that manifests itself in physiological . . . and/or psychological . . . symptoms." As the definition indicates, it is not simply the amount or level of exercise, but the dependence (craving) and inability to control behavior that characterize the syndrome. In their review, Hausenblas and Symons Downs (2002a) further delineate the characteristics of exercise dependence as follows:

- **Tolerance:** An increased amount of exercise is needed to achieve the desired effect.
- **Withdrawal:** Withdrawal symptoms are felt when exercise is missed.

- **Intention effect:** Exercise lasts longer than was originally intended.
- **Loss of control:** Unsuccessful effort is made to control or cut back on the amount of exercise.
- **Time:** Lots of time is spent in activities necessary for obtaining exercise.
- **Conflict:** Important social or relationship activities are given up because of exercise.
- **Continuance:** Exercise is maintained in spite of knowing that it is problematic.

Hausenblas and Symons Downs' description brings some clarity to the literature. They have also developed and validated an exercise dependence scale based on clinical criteria for substance dependence (Hausenblas & Symons Downs, 2002b). Excessive exercise has been termed *compulsion*, *dependence*, and *obsession* but might also be characterized as *commitment* or a *healthy habit*. Early literature focused on running addiction, which Sachs (1981) defined as a psychological or physiological addiction to regular running that is characterized by withdrawal symptoms after 24 to 36 hours without running. Morgan (1979) suggested that addicted runners believe they need to exercise and cannot live without running daily; if deprived of exercise, they experience withdrawal symptoms including anxiety, restlessness, guilt, irritability, tension, and discomfort, as well as apathy, sluggishness, lack of appetite, sleeplessness, and headaches. Thompson and Blanton (1987) proposed a psychophysiological explanation, hypothesizing that exercise dependence is mediated by adaptive reductions in sympathetic output during exercise, which results from increased efficiency of energy use with exercise training.

Several studies suggest that many regular exercisers fit the addiction criteria. For example, Kagan and Squires (1985) found that college students who exercised regularly tended to fit an addictive personality, and Robbins and Joseph (1985) reported that over 50 percent of runners in a large sample experienced deprivation sensations when unable to run.

Not only has excessive exercise been discussed as a problem in itself, but some reports have linked excessive exercise with anorexia nervosa and bulimia. Yates, Leehey, and Shisslak (1983) interviewed 60 obligatory runners and suggested similarities to anorexia nervosa patients. Blumenthal, O'Toole, and Chang (1984), on the other hand, found that obligatory runners generally fell within the normal range of behavior whereas people with anorexia did not. In a follow-up article, Blumenthal, Rose, and Chang (1985) argued against a psychopathological or disease model of habitual running. Although most research does not link excessive exercise to clinical disorders, Pierce (1994) differentiated primary and secondary exercise dependence based on the exercise objective. In primary exercise dependence, exercise is an end in itself, whereas in secondary exercise dependence, exercise is a means to control body composition (i.e., weight or appearance). Excessive exercisers may well display unhealthy behaviors, particularly disordered eating, and professionals should be alert for signs of exercise dependence.

Key Point

Excessive exercise participation, sometimes termed *addiction, dependence,* or *commitment,* has been discussed as a problematic behavior. Some reports have also linked excessive exercise with eating disorders.

If you suspect that a friend or a client you are working with has become dependent on exercise to the point that it interferes with his or her functioning in daily life, you should consider referring the person to a mental health professional. To initiate the referral process, it is important to recognize signs that a referral is needed and to identify an appropriate professional to whom you can refer the person (e.g., college campus counseling center, community counselor). When raising the issue with a friend or client, explain why you feel the referral should be made and be sensitive to the person's concerns about being referred (Van Raalte & Andersen, 2014). In some instances, a person might not go through with the referral, so you may need to follow up with the individual

and revisit the conversation. To help remember these tips, Van Raalte and Andersen (2014, p. 347) created the REFER acronym:

Recognize that a referral is needed.

Explain the referral process.

Focus on feelings. Discuss the referral in a clear, caring, and supportive manner.

Exit if emotions are too intense. You can return to the topic when things calm down.

Repeat (and follow up) as needed. It often takes more than one suggestion for a referral to be accepted and acted on.

For more information about how to talk with a friend about a mental health issue or how to connect people to get help, visit the U.S. Department of Health and Human Services mental health website.

Application Point

Identifying the Signs of Exercise Dependence

As a kinesiology professional, you may well encounter students or clients who exercise excessively. If you suspected that your client at a performance training facility was developing exercise dependence, what signs or behaviors would you look for?

Whether considering those who engage in excessive exercise or the vast majority who do not participate in sufficient physical activity for health and well-being, we are ultimately dealing with human behavior. Sport and exercise psychology, which focuses on behavior in exercise and sport settings, can contribute to the development of effective programs and practices that promote healthy physical activity. In the end, the issue is behavior, and, most often, motivation for starting and maintaining physical activity behaviors.

Putting It Into Practice

Summary

This chapter focuses on participation motivation and interventions for promoting lifestyle physical activity. Although lifestyle physical activity differs from the sport and exercise behaviors emphasized in other chapters, motivation models and research can be applied to enhance continuing participation in physical activity. Indeed, effective application of behavioral and cognitive strategies within a theoretical framework is essential for effective programs.

Several motivational theories have been applied to physical activity participation and maintenance, and integrated models that incorporate both cognitive and behavioral strategies are the most useful. The TTM, which integrates theoretical perspectives and combines cognitive and behavioral strategies, has been successfully used in interventions and community programs to help people move through beginning stages to physical activity maintenance. Social–ecological models that focus on the social and physical environment have been especially useful in community- and population-based promotion of physical activity. In health promotion programs, the overriding goal is maintaining activity rather than continually striving to achieve performance standards.

Interventions that help participants focus on lifestyle activity are more likely to be effective. Behavioral strategies and social cognitive approaches that center on recognizing health and fitness benefits, overcoming barriers, and developing self-control and perceived competence in a supportive environment are particularly appropriate. Specific behavioral and cognitive strategies used within an integrative model that matches strategies to the individual can help participants overcome barriers, develop confidence, and gain greater health and wellness through fitness activities.

Review Questions

1. Describe the overall physical activity patterns in the United States. How do these patterns differ by age and gender?

2. What are the main components of the TRA and TPB? How do these theories explain exercise behavior?

3. List the five stages of change in the TTM. Explain how behavioral and cognitive processes can be matched to stages to help people progress through the stages.

4. What is the relapse-prevention model? How does it apply to exercise behavior?

5. Describe social–ecological models of physical activity behavior and explain how they include the physical and social environment.

6. Outline the key characteristics of the health coaching framework and motivational interviewing approach. How might these qualities differ from the way kinesiologists and exercise professionals typically approach physical activity behavior change?

7. What are some of the characteristics of exercise dependence? When and how should you refer a client who you suspect is exercise dependent?

Recommended Reading

Bess Marcus and her colleagues have done considerable research on exercise motivation, applying the TTM to enhance exercise participation in various populations. The first reference (Bock et al., 2014) provides an overview of that work and approaches for promoting physical activity. For those interested in more direct applications, read the Marcus and Forsyth book, which provides a guide to the basic principles and focuses on promoting physical activity with individuals, groups, community programs, and public health campaigns.

- Bock, B.C., Linke, S.E., Napolitano, M.A., Clark, M.M., Gaskins, R.B., & Marcus, B.H. (2014). Exercise initiation, adoption, and maintenance in adults: Theoretical models and empirical support. In J.L. Van Raalte & B.W. Brewer (Eds.), *Exploring sport and exercise psychology* (3rd ed., pp. 163-189). Washington, DC: APA.

- Marcus, B.H., & Forsyth, L.H. (2009). *Motivating people to be physically active* (2nd ed.). Champaign, IL: Human Kinetics.

In this article in the American College of Sports Medicine's popular *Health and Fitness Journal*, Sforzo and colleagues outline the emerging field of healthy coaching and its application for exercise professionals working with fitness clients.

- Sforzo, G.A., Moore, M., & Scholtz, M. (2015). Health and wellness coaching competencies for exercise professionals. *ACSM's Health and Fitness Journal, 19*(2), 20-26.

In addition to applying integrated psychological models, physical activity and health professionals are increasingly taking a broader view to promote active living among the wider population. For more information, check the tools and resources section at the Active Living website.

- The Robert Wood Johnson Foundation. www.activelivingresearch.org.

Counseling Clients Through Behavior Change: Practicing Health Coaching Skills

Brawley and colleagues (2013) questioned whether kinesiologists are ready to counsel individuals in successfully adopting and maintaining physical activity behaviors. As a future professional, ask yourself the following question: Are you ready to coach clients through healthy behavior change? Effective health coaching involves using important communication and listening skills. In this lab, you have the opportunity to practice these skills so you can be better prepared to empower clients to achieve their personal wellness goals.

1. Before beginning the lab, review the section "Physical Activity and Health Coaching" in this chapter, as well as the specific information about using reflections and open-ended questions.
2. Find a partner (e.g., a classmate, friend, or family member). Ask the person to tell you about a challenging situation that happened to him or her recently at work, in school, or in relation to physical activity.
3. For the first 2 minutes of the conversation, you (the "coach") can use only reflection statements while your partner (the "client") tells you his or her story. You cannot ask any questions during these 2 minutes. After 2 minutes have passed, you may begin to incorporate open-ended questions for an additional 2 minutes.
4. Reflecting on your experience in this activity, respond to the following questions:
   a. What was this experience like for you? What about the conversation was easy or difficult?
   b. How did this conversation differ from the way you typically communicate with others?
   c. Ask your partner to describe what it was like to have this conversation with you in comparison to one in which you had just told your partner the best way to handle the challenging situation. Summarize your partner's reactions.
   d. How might these listening skills be useful to you when interacting with future clients, students, or athletes in your professional setting?

PART IV

Emotions, Stress, and Coping

Emotion is the A, or affect component, in the ABCs of psychology. Affect encompasses all the feelings and moods that are part of human behavior. Emotion has a long history in psychology, but researchers have devoted more attention to the B and C components—behavior and cognition—and left the messier emotions for the poets and philosophers. Emotion is pervasive and obvious in the real world, including the sport and physical activity world. Much past sport and exercise psychology research on emotion has focused on competitive anxiety, but the research is expanding to include a wider range of emotions and physical activity settings. Chapter 11 covers the emotion basics—terminology and the major models of emotion—and then reviews the extensive sport and exercise psychology research on the emotion–performance relationship. Chapter 12 focuses on the rapidly growing research on the reverse relationship, the influence of physical activity on emotion and mental health. Chapter 13 covers stress models and emphasizes the role of emotional control and stress management in physical activity settings.

Chapter 11

Emotions and Performance

Chapter Objectives

After studying this chapter, you should be able to

- understand emotion and define related terms (affect, emotion, mood),

- explain the Lazarus model of emotion as a multidimensional process,

- understand positive emotions and explain how positive emotions differ from negative emotions,

- explain the anxiety–performance models used in sport and exercise psychology, and

- discuss the research on patterns of anxiety in relation to performance.

Emotion is everywhere. We recognize the thrill of victory and the agony of defeat in Olympic competitors and in 10-year-old soccer players. You might feel exhilarated after a daily run or embarrassed when looking in the mirror at the fitness center. Emotions in sport and exercise reflect all the complexities of psychology and behavior. They combine the biological, psychological, and social in a complex, dynamic mix that adds to life—but frustrates scientists.

Scholars cannot ignore such a pervasive and powerful aspect of behavior as emotion, and the psychology literature has considerable emotional content. William James discussed emotion more than 100 years ago, and since then psychologists have offered theories and empirical observations from varied perspectives. Anxiety and stress are the most prominent emotion topics in sport and exercise psychology, but research is expanding to a broader range of emotions and processes.

First, we will look at emotion basics—terms and definitions related to affect and emotion—and highlight positive emotions. Then we will cover the emotion and stress models that help us understand the role of emotion in sport and exercise. These models guide research on physical activity and emotion, as well as our use of emotional control and stress management in professional practice.

Emotion Concepts and Definitions

Emotion is a messy research topic, and the related terminology is just as messy. As Reeve (2005) noted, everyone knows what emotion is, but the definition is problematic. Reeve included four aspects of emotion—bodily arousal, social expressive, sense of purpose, and feelings—and stated the following:

> Emotions are short-lived, feeling-arousal-purposive-expressive phenomena that help us adapt to the opportunities and challenges we face during important life events. (p. 294)

Plutchik (2003) listed several definitions, starting with James in 1884 and moving through the major conceptual works on emotion over the next 100 years. Most psychologists recognize both physiological and psychological components of emotion and consider emotion to be a process rather than a static state. However, psycholo-

gists differ on the details of the process and the relative roles of physiological and social cognitive processes. Concise definitions cannot capture the complexity of emotions. Kleinginna and Kleinginna's (1981) all-embracing definition reflects many of the emotion models:

> Emotion is a complex set of interactions among subjective and objective factors, mediated by neural/hormonal systems, which can (a) give rise to affective experiences such as feelings of arousal, pleasure/displeasure; (b) generate cognitive processes; (c) activate widespread physiological adjustments to the arousing conditions; and (d) lead to behavior that is often, but not always, expressive, goal-directed, and adaptive. (p. 58)

Key Point

Emotion is a complex phenomenon that cannot easily be defined. Simply, emotions are short-lived feeling states that occur in response to events, but most psychologists recognize both physiological and psychological components of emotion and consider emotion to be a process rather than a static state.

As Reeve, Plutchik, and the previous definition suggest, emotion is a complex phenomenon that cannot easily be defined. For our purposes, we will draw from the major theoretical work and define emotion in simple terms as follows. *Emotions* are short-lived feeling states that occur in response to events. However, emotions are not simple, and as Reeve notes, emotion is more than the sum of its parts. Before considering models of emotion that provide guiding frameworks, we will clarify related terms used in sport and exercise psychology.

Although in common usage we use the word "emotion" to refer to all feeling states, we should clarify the distinctions between emotion and the related terms—affect, mood, and arousal. First, *affect*, the *A* of psychology's ABCs, is the general umbrella term for feeling states. Affect includes emotions and also includes moods. As defined earlier, emotions are short-lived feeling states in response to events. Moods are also feeling states, but they differ from emotion in duration, intensity, antecedent, and action. In contrast to emotions, moods are more enduring (duration), are less intense, usually do not have identifiable causes, and do not prompt specific actions.

Arousal is a term associated with emotion, but arousal is not emotion. Arousal, defined as a general state of activation ranging on a continuum from deep sleep to extreme excitement, is the intensity dimension of behavior. Arousal per se is neither positive nor negative. Arousal or activation is a part of emotion, but without direction and related cognition; arousal itself is not emotion. For example, anxiety, one of the most widely studied emotions, is typically defined as arousal with a negative (avoidance) direction—you might worry about making an error (and want to avoid it) as your heart races, your hands sweat, and you breathe heavily. *Anxiety*, then, is an emotion. Other emotions (joy, anger, sadness, and so on) also are characterized by arousal, but the related cognitions are quite different and specific to the emotion. Indeed, those thoughts or cognitions are key in identifying our emotions.

Key Point

Arousal is defined as a general state of activation ranging on a continuum from deep sleep to extreme excitement. Arousal is not an emotion. Anxiety, which is a feeling state characterized by high arousal and cognitive worry, is an emotion.

Positive and Negative Emotions—Accent on Positive

Anxiety is an often-studied emotion, particularly in sport and exercise psychology. What are the other emotions? Take a minute and list as many emotions as you can. As with many questions in this text, there is no one correct answer. Reeve (2005) notes that various scholars have identified 2 to 10 primary emotions, along with a host of other emotions. Fear, joy, sadness, and anger are on nearly every list, including five of the emotions starring in the (2015) Disney-Pixar film, *Inside Out* (the film also casts disgust as its fifth emotion); but given that psychology scholars have not agreed upon a list, we do not specify one here. Regardless of the number of primary emotions, many emotions exist.

Identify Your Emotions

Application Point

Think about the emotions you experience in physical activity. Imagine (use your imagery skills from chapter 5) that you are participating in an important event in your favorite sport or activity—try to really put yourself in the activity and imagine your feelings. Then, look back: Were you anxious, excited, confident, frustrated? Identify your emotions (could be several different ones). How did your emotions change over the course of the activity? How did your emotions affect you physically, mentally, and with regard to your behavior?

All lists of emotions, including those in the sport and exercise psychology literature, are heavy with negative emotions—anxiety, anger, depression, envy, and so on. Joy jumps in, but otherwise research and practice focus on negative emotions. Here we'll give positive emotions time in the spotlight. The positive psychology movement reminds us that positive emotions deserve equal attention in research and professional practice. Positive emotions are especially relevant to sport and exercise psychology because physical activity is promoted as a path to positive health and personal growth.

Barbara Fredrickson, the leading psychology researcher on positive emotions (2001, 2013a), describes positive emotions as markers of optimal functioning and argues that cultivating positive emotions is a way to foster psychological growth and physical health. She suggests that positive emotions have been neglected in psychology because definitions and models of emotion were developed to fit the negative emotions. Positive emotions are different; they are more general and diffuse and less closely tied to specific action tendencies (e.g., fight or flight).

Fredrickson offers an alternative *broaden-and-build* theory of positive emotions. That is, positive emotions broaden people's momentary thought–action repertoires and build enduring personal resources. Negative emotions narrow options—to fight or flee. Positive emotions such as joy, interest, serenity, pride, gratitude, love, or contentment do not provoke a specific response; many actions are possible and appealing. The broadening tendency of positive emotions builds enduring resources. Of particular note to those of us in kinesiology, Fredrickson cites play as an example, noting that play builds physical resources, as we often argue in kinesiology, and also builds social resources (social bonds, attachments) and intellectual resources (creativity).

Fredrickson (2001, 2013a, 2013b), along with her colleagues and other positive psychology researchers, have amassed a considerable body of research confirming the benefits of positive emotions for physical and mental health. Research also suggests that interventions and simple strategies to increase positive emotions have benefits. Links to the research, along with more accessible summaries of the information and practical suggestions, can be found at the positivity ratio website or Fredrickson's Positive Emotions and Psychophysiology Laboratory (PEP Lab) website. The positivity ratio refers to the 3:1 ratio of positive emotions to negative emotions that Fredrickson recommended for benefits. The mathematics behind the ratio have been criticized, and rightly so. Emotions are complex processes, and it is unlikely that any equation could capture the influence of emotions on our health and behavior. Still, as Fredrickson (2013b) rightly countered in an update, considerable evidence supports the key point that positive emotions are good for physical and mental health and relationships. Regardless of the specific ratio, the practical guideline is that we, as professionals working with others and for ourselves, should spend as much or more time fostering positive emotions as we do controlling negative emotions.

Positive Emotions in Sport and Exercise

To date, few sport and exercise psychology researchers have followed Fredrickson's work, but positive emotions are gaining attention. To understand emotion in kinesiology, we must give equal attention to positive emotion. McCarthy (2011) argued that research on the benefits of positive emotions for self-efficacy, motivation, attention, problem solving, and coping is particularly promising. We could even argue that positive emotion is more important than anxiety and negative emotion. Most people do not participate in exercise and sport to reduce stress (although that is a valued benefit), but because they feel better and because physical activity is fun!

Just as joy is the one positive emotion typically cited in psychology, joy or enjoyment has received attention in sport and exercise psychology. Within sport and exercise psychology, the most notable lines of research on positive emotions are the work of Tara Scanlan on enjoyment in sport and Csikszentmihalyi's long-term work on flow, which

has inspired several sport and exercise psychology researchers. That research is reviewed in the following section.

Enjoyment in Sport

Tara Scanlan is one of the few sport and exercise scholars to give equal attention to positive and negative aspects of emotion. Scanlan's work focuses on youth development and includes extensive research on stress and anxiety, as well as equally extensive and more current work on sport enjoyment (Scanlan, Babkes, & Scanlan, 2005) and commitment, as discussed in chapter 8. In line with the emotion theme of this chapter, Scanlan and Simons (1992, p. 202) defined enjoyment as a positive affective response to the sport experience that reflects generalized feelings such as pleasure, liking, and fun.

Kimiecik and Harris (1996) attempted to provide a framework for positive emotions in physical activity. They defined enjoyment with an adaptation of Csikszentmihalyi's flow definition as "an optimal psychological state that leads to performing an activity primarily for its own sake and is associated with positive feeling states" (p. 256).

Although current models of affect and emotion include positive dimensions, we do not have measures of positive emotions to match the carefully developed and validated (and often sport-specific) measures of anxiety. Several studies of enjoyment have used open-ended measures in a more qualitative approach (e.g., Scanlan, Stein, & Ravizza, 1989). Others have used simple measures developed for specific studies. Kendzierski and DeCarlo (1991) developed the 18-item Physical Activity Enjoyment Scale (PACES) and provided initial evidence for its reliability and validity with college students. Crocker, Bouffard, and Gessaroli (1995) subsequently failed to support its unidimensional structure, but PACES is still one of the most widely used measures of enjoyment in our research. Mullen and colleagues (2011) validated the PACES with older adults and found that a revised, shortened eight-item version was psychometrically strong and recommended for use.

In reviewing the literature on sport enjoyment, Scanlan and colleagues (2005) classified the sources of enjoyment as intrapersonal, situational, and significant others. Intrapersonal sources include perceived ability, mastery, motivational goal orientation, personal movement experiences, and personal coping and emotional release through sport. Specifically, research indicates that enjoyment is associated with perceived high ability, mastery experiences, higher task orientation, movement sensations, and emotional release.

Situational sources include competitive outcomes, achievement process, recognition, and opportunities. Not surprisingly, winning is associated with enjoyment, but the relationship is not as strong or absolute as one might assume. Several studies cited in Scanlan and colleagues' review showed that postgame stress was related to enjoyment regardless of win–loss outcomes. Being engaged in competition (playing) was associated with enjoyment, as were social recognition and opportunities to travel.

Finally, significant-other sources of enjoyment involve positive perceptions of interactions and feedback from coaches, parents, and peers. Many sources of enjoyment have parallel sources of stress, and those are classified into the same three categories in Scanlan and colleagues' (2005) review. As the authors conclude, the diverse sources of enjoyment make it easy to tap a number of them to maintain motivation and activity. Notably, the researchers emphasized enjoyment rather than stress in their conclusions. In line with positive psychology, we might emphasize positive emotion in professional practice to promote physical activity and health for all participants.

Any discussion of positive emotion in sport and exercise must be about fun. Enjoyment is a proxy term for fun, but fun can mean many things. As noted in chapter 8, when youth are asked why they participate in sport, fun is the top answer. But what is fun? Visek and colleagues (2015) addressed that question with physical activity participants and developed the multidimensional Fun Integration Theory (FIT). Using hierarchical cluster analyses of 81 specific fun determinants, they developed the pictorial "FUN MAPS" with four overarching fundamental tenets over 11 fun dimensions: (a) context (e.g., games and practice), (b) internal (e.g., learning, improving), (c) social (e.g., team dynamics, friendship), and (d) external (e.g., positive coaching).

Flow in Sport

Csikszentmihalyi's work on flow has contributed a great deal to positive psychology and our understanding of intrinsic motivation, and several researchers have specifically explored flow states with sport and exercise participants. Flow occurs when the person is totally connected to the performance in an activity in which skills equal challenges (Csikszentmihalyi, 1975, 1990). Csikszentmihalyi used innovative experience sampling and in-depth methods to develop his conceptualization of the optimal flow experience and its antecedents. In the original flow model, flow occurs when perceived challenges are in balance with perceived skills; when challenges are too high, anxiety results, and when they are too low, boredom results. The updated model (Nakamura & Csikszentmihalyi, 2005) expands to include a wider range of emotions. In the expanded model, we consider not only whether challenges and skills are equal or balanced, but also if they are high or low. More intense reactions occur as challenge and skill move farther from average levels, toward high or low ends. Flow is experienced when perceived challenges and perceived skills are both above average, and apathy is experienced when both are below average. High challenge and low skill leads to anxiety, whereas low challenge and high skill leads to relaxation. Flow is clearly a positive emotional state—perhaps the ultimate positive state.

Most participants at any level in any physical activity can relate to flow. Athletes may recall a peak experience—a time when everything came together and they were totally immersed in the activity. Sue Jackson started from Csikszentmihalyi's model and used in-depth interviews along with more typical survey approaches to identify characteristics and antecedents of flow with athletes (Jackson, 1995), and Jackson and Marsh (1996) developed the Flow State Scale (FSS). The nine scales of the 36-item FSS represent the dimensions of flow identified by Csikszentmihalyi, and Jackson and Marsh provided good psychometric evidence for the scales and the FSS. These are the nine dimensions of flow:

- **Challenge–skill balance:** The person perceives a balance between the challenges of a situation and his or her skills, with both at a high level.
- **Action–awareness merging:** Involvement is so deep that it becomes spontaneous or automatic.
- **Clear goals:** Clearly defined goals give the person a strong sense of knowing what to do.
- **Unambiguous feedback:** The person receives immediate and clear feedback, usually from the activity itself.
- **Concentration on task at hand:** Total concentration on the task occurs.
- **Sense of control:** The person experiences a sense of exercising control but without actively trying to exert control.

- **Loss of self-consciousness:** Concern for the self disappears as the person becomes one with the activity.
- **Transformation of time:** Time alters perceptibly, either slowing down or speeding up.
- **Autotelic experience:** An autotelic experience is intrinsically rewarding, done for its own sake.

Key Point

Flow occurs when the performer is totally connected to the performance in a situation in which skills equal challenges and both perceived challenges and perceived skills are above average. Flow is perhaps the ultimate positive emotional state.

Swann, Keegan, Piggott, and Crust (2012) reviewed the research on flow in sport and summarized the factors that facilitate flow as having appropriate focus, optimal preparation, and optimal situational conditions. The work of Scanlan, Jackson, and others provides direction and measures for the continuing exploration of flow and enjoyment, as well as highlighting positive emotions and fun in sport and exercise psychology.

Emotion Models

Emotions are complicated, and accordingly, the explanations and models of emotion are multidimensional and complex. This section reviews the major historical perspectives on emotion and focuses on Lazarus' model, which is widely used and useful for sport and exercise psychology.

Early Models of Emotion and Stress

In his 1884 essay, "What Is an Emotion?" William James proposed, "My theory is that the bodily changes follow directly the perception of the exciting fact, and that our feeling of the same changes as they occur is the emotion" (p. 204). Danish scientist Lange (1885) presented similar views, and the theory is known as the James-Lange theory. Walter Cannon (1929) challenged this focus on physiology, but the most notable counter to the physiologically oriented James-Lange theory is the cognitive approach of Schachter and Singer (1962), who emphasized the cognitive labeling of emotion. In their classic experiments, subjects

received either injections of epinephrine that created physiological arousal or a placebo. Then, the researchers manipulated the circumstances—specifically the behavior of a confederate. Some subjects knew about epinephrine's effects but others did not and had no obvious label for their emotion. Without a ready explanation, subjects used situational cues to label their emotion. Thus, Schachter and Singer proposed that emotion involves an interaction of cognition with physiological state.

Key Point

According to the James-Lange theory, bodily sensations stem directly from perceptions, and our awareness of the physiological changes is emotion. Schachter and Singer (1962), on the other hand, proposed an interaction of cognition with physiological state.

Psychologists continue to debate the roles of physiology and cognition, and models have become increasingly complex and typically add a social dimension. Richard Lazarus, the leading researcher in stress, emotion, and coping, provided an encompassing model that approaches emotion as a multidimensional, dynamic process rather than an easily identified state.

Lazarus' Model of Emotion

Lazarus' model provides a guiding framework for most psychology work on emotion, stress, and coping, including sport and exercise work. In his early writing on stress (the precursor to his emotion model), Lazarus (1966) emphasized *cognitive appraisal*. That is, actual events, such as waiting for the serve in a close tennis match, pose a potential threat. But only when we think about it—during cognitive appraisal—do we perceive a threat that then leads to an emotional response, such as anxiety.

Lazarus has maintained this cognitive emphasis but has also expanded the model greatly. Lazarus (1991, 1993) describes emotion as including an appraisal, outcome tendencies, a psychological response, and a subjective experience, with all this translated into coping processes after the appraisal. In a simplified version of Lazarus' model, the emotion process begins with an event, then moves to cognitive appraisal, then leads to the emotional response, which includes both physiological and psychological responses; that response then affects behavior. Also, note that the process is not all one-way, but includes two-way (recursive) relationships and behavior "feeding back" to affect the situation. It is not easy to illustrate the complex dynamics of the model, but Lazarus (1991, p. 210) listed five principles underlying his cognitive–relational theory of emotion:

- **System principle.** Emotion is an organized process with many interdependent variables.
- **Process principle.** The emotion process involves both flux (change) and structure with stable person–environment relationships, resulting in recurrent emotional patterns.
- **Developmental principle.** Biological and social variables influence emotional development and change.
- **Specificity principle.** The emotion process is distinct for each emotion.
- **Relational meaning principle.** Emotions are defined by unique relational meanings—core relational themes for each emotion. Emotional meaning is constructed by cognitive appraisal.

Key Point

Lazarus' encompassing model approaches emotion as a multidimensional, dynamic process rather than an easily identifiable state. Sport and exercise psychology scholars have moved to similar multidimensional models that better fit the complexities of emotion.

Over 30 years of stress and emotion research, Lazarus moved to a more social, dynamic model with emphasis on recursive relationships, dynamic process, and social context. The story of emotion in sport and exercise psychology began with simpler anxiety–performance models, progressed to cognitive approaches emphasizing perceptions (similar to appraisal in Lazarus' model), and has now moved to more dynamic, multidimensional approaches that better fit the complexities of emotion.

The most useful models highlight cognitive appraisal in a complex multidimensional system of interrelated psychobiological variables that highlights the importance of individualizing

applications and considering the social context. Given the almost limitless possibilities, the emotion process is different for everyone, even in the same situation. This is one of the most important practical implications of the research on stress and emotion. Emotion and stress are individualized and contextualized, and sport and exercise psychologists cannot apply universal strategies to all. The importance of individualizing training and intervention is a key element of stress management as discussed in chapter 13. In the remainder of this chapter, we focus on the most extensive research on emotion in sport and exercise psychology—the research on emotion and performance.

Emotions and Performance

The emotion–performance relationship is a prominent research and practical concern in sport and exercise psychology. Pregame rituals and pep talks to get players psyched up are assumed to enhance performance, but do they work? Most of us can recall times when a pep talk helped or when an athlete responded to the big game with the best performance of the season. The Olympic Games certainly induce high emotion, and the pressure and excitement of the Games seem to elicit a large share of record-breaking performances and personal bests.

However, you can probably recall other times when performers have choked under pressure. I once coached a team of seventh-grade girls who demonstrated modest basketball skills in practices and intramural games. When faced with competition against a team from another school, those same players completely missed the basket on shots, dribbled off their feet, threw passes into the bleachers, and managed to go through the game without scoring a basket. Clearly, a "psych-up" speech would have only made the situation worse.

Coaches who hold the image of a stirring Knute Rockne pep talk as the key to mental preparation might be surprised to learn what Rockne actually said about such tactics. In December 1924, Coleman Griffith wrote to Rockne to ask about his motivational tactics. Rockne replied as follows.

Dear Mr. Griffith:

I feel very grateful to you for having written me, although I do not know a great deal about psychology. I do try to pick men who like the game of football and who get a lot of fun out of playing. I never try to make football hard work. I do think our team plays good football because they like to play and I do not make any effort to key them up, except on rare, exceptional occasions. I keyed them up for the Nebraska game this year, which was a mistake, as we had a reaction the following Saturday against Northwestern. I try to make our boys take the game less seriously than, I presume, some others do, and we try to make the spirit of the game one of exhilaration and we never allow hatred to enter into it, no matter whom we are playing.

Thanking you for your kindness, I am
Yours cordially,

Knute Rockne

From the Coleman Griffith Collection, University Archives, University of Illinois at Urbana-Champaign.

People have done strange things to psych up athletes even though such tactics often psych them out. Many beginning coaches turn to these approaches at the very times they are least likely to help—when the situation has already raised emotion levels. How can such contrary psych-up and psych-out results be explained? Much sport and exercise psychology research focuses on that question, and most of that research has narrowly focused on the anxiety–performance relationship. Moreover, until recently, that research on anxiety and performance did not incorporate cognitive appraisal, and anxiety was typically conceptualized and measured more narrowly, as arousal.

Again, arousal is not an emotion; arousal is the general state of activation. Arousal is reflected in Hans Selye's (1956) *general adaptation syndrome*—the fight-or-flight response of the autonomic nervous system that we all experience in stressful situations. You know you are stressed when you breathe rapidly, your heart pounds, your hands sweat, your stomach does flips, your knees turn to jelly, and your mouth feels like cotton. That heightened physiological arousal is associated with anxiety, but anxiety also has a cognitive component.

The cognitive component of anxiety typically involves worrying about performance. A softball player experiencing physiological arousal may also think about the mistakes made last game, worry about everyone watching, and be aware of feeling anxious. Even noncompetitive activities may create both arousal and worry. A child in an elementary physical education class wants to please the teacher and not be the last one through

the obstacle course; an adult in a corporate fitness program does not want to appear out of shape in front of colleagues. That combination of physiological arousal and cognitive worry is the emotion of anxiety, often called *state anxiety*. As discussed in chapter 4, *trait anxiety* is a personality disposition to feel anxious in a wide range of situations; trait anxiety is not an emotion.

Cognitive and Somatic Anxiety

Application Point

You are an athletic trainer working with an athlete who is completing rehab and getting ready to return to activity. The athlete is clearly anxious about returning to play. How might the athlete be experiencing cognitive anxiety (what is the athlete thinking or worried about)? How might the athlete be experiencing somatic (physical) anxiety? How might cognitive and somatic anxiety affect the athlete's return to activity? As the athletic trainer, how might you work with the anxious athlete?

In our research, state anxiety has been assessed with physiological measures (e.g., heart rate, galvanic skin response) and behavioral observations, but most often with self-report measures, such as the state anxiety inventory of the State-Trait Anxiety Inventory (STAI) (Spielberger, Gorsuch, & Lushene, 1970). Some self-report measures assess physiological (somatic) anxiety and cognitive worry on separate dimensions; and as discussed in the following section, those separate measures are particularly important for research on anxiety–performance. Martens and his colleagues (Martens, Vealey, & Burton, 1990) developed the Competitive State Anxiety Inventory-2 (CSAI-2), which assesses cognitive worry and somatic anxiety on separate scales. The CSAI-2 has been widely used in research on the anxiety–performance relationship.

Anxiety–Performance Models and Research

Sport and exercise psychology researchers have applied models from psychology and developed a large body of literature on the emotion–performance relationship, but that research is largely limited to research on arousal and anxiety. In psychology, the dominant early models were drive theory, which holds that increased arousal increases performance of the dominant response, and the inverted-U hypothesis, which predicts that performance is best at a moderate optimal level and progressively worsens with either increases or decreases in arousal.

Drive Theory

Drive theory, as developed by Hull (1943) and modified by Spence (1956), is complex, but we'll consider a simple version: $P = f(H \times D)$. Performance (P) is a function of habit (H) times drive (D). Drive is essentially arousal, and habit refers to learned responses. The more a response has been reinforced, the greater its habit strength and the more likely it will occur. Essentially, this theory proposes that as drive increases (as when one is facing competition), learned, habitual responses are more likely to occur. The basic relationship is linear: As arousal increases, performance increases. But drive theory is not that simple. Overall performance does not necessarily improve. Instead, performance of the person's dominant response improves. Performance improves only if the dominant and most likely response is correct performance. Until athletes become proficient at a skill and have automatic expert responses, they are more likely to make mistakes than to do everything right.

For example, for the perfect golf swing, the golfer must have proper body alignment; shift weight correctly; keep the body and club in proper alignment throughout the swing; and perform the backswing, forward swing, and follow-through with the correct length, in the correct plane, and at an optimal speed. Unless you are an accomplished golfer with a grooved swing, your dominant response is not likely to be the correct swing. As arousal increases, such as in a club match, you are likely to revert to your dominant, error-ridden swing even more than usual. Perhaps you will swing too fast, swing out too much, and slice more than usual. In contrast, a professional golfer has performed each shot so often that the correct swing is the automatic, dominant response, and thus increased arousal improves performance. Drive theory predictions for motor performance can be summarized as follows:

- Increased arousal or drive increases the likelihood that the dominant response will occur.
- If a skill is relatively simple or is well learned, the dominant response is the cor-

rect response, and increased arousal will improve performance.

- If a skill is complex (as most motor skills are) and not well learned, the dominant response is an incorrect response and thus increased arousal will impair performance.

Inverted-U Theory

The inverted-U theory is a popular alternative explanation of the arousal–performance relationship. The inverted-U proposes that performance is best at a moderate optimal level of arousal and declines as arousal increases or decreases from that optimal level. The inverted-U model makes sense and fits our observations. People need some arousal to perform at their best; those who are too mellow give subpar performances. However, with too much arousal, performers are tense and prone to errors.

Although the inverted-U theory makes intuitive sense, controlled tests of the curvilinear relationship are difficult, and empirical support is limited. The original inverted-U research of Yerkes and Dodson (1908) involved lab-based, experimental animal research. Martens and Landers (1970) tested the inverted-U theory by having junior high school boys perform a tracking task under low-, moderate-, and high-stress conditions. The resulting performance scores formed an inverted-U pattern, with best performances in the moderate stress condition.

Key Point

Drive theory proposes that as drive increases (as when one is facing competition), learned responses are more likely to occur. The basic relationship is linear: As arousal increases, performance increases. The inverted-U theory proposes that performance is optimal at a moderate level of arousal and declines as arousal increases or decreases from that optimal level.

Sonstroem and Bernardo (1982) confirmed the inverted-U pattern in a field study with female university basketball players. The best performances were associated with moderate state anxiety and the poorest performances with high state anxiety. Sonstroem and Bernardo also found that the inverted-U was more pronounced for high-competitive, trait-anxious athletes, illustrating individual differences. Given the same situation, such as a club tennis match, one player might be below optimal arousal and need to psych up a bit, whereas another player might need to calm down to play in top form.

As well as differing from person to person, optimal levels may vary across tasks and skills. For example, putting in golf has a low optimal arousal level. Golfers perform best with low arousal, and even slight increases may disrupt their concentration and performance. Weightlifting has a higher optimal arousal level.

Performance is optimal at a moderate level of arousal, but optimal levels vary across tasks and people. We cannot predict precise optimal arousal levels for each performer in each task. Practically, we might better direct our efforts at helping performers recognize their own optimal states in varying situations.

Sport and exercise psychologists have tested and debated drive versus inverted-U. The inverted-U has intuitive appeal, and drive theory is cited in some work (e.g., audience effects on performance). However, neither is prominent in current research, and both miss one key element—cognitive appraisal.

Hanin's Individualized Zones of Optimal Functioning

Yuri Hanin (1989, 1995), who began his influential sport and exercise psychology work in the 1970s, proposed an alternative that relates to the inverted-U model but emphasizes individual differences. Hanin proposes that athletes have a zone of optimal functioning that is unique to the individual and can be identified through retrospective analyses and systematic multiple observations of athletes' state anxiety and performance levels. Thus, the model is the Individualized Zone of Optimal Functioning, or IZOF. Hanin developed his model in the former Soviet system with its emphasis on applied work with elite athletes. The IZOF model therefore has practical appeal as well as some empirical support. Hanin and Syrja (1996) extended the IZOF model beyond anxiety to patterns of emotions, moving closer to current emotion models.

Ruiz, Raglin, and Hanin (2015) reviewed the research and use of IZOF. They noted that over 35 years of research has accumulated, idiographic measures have been developed, and the focus on individualized patterns has evolved from a focus on anxiety to incorporate a wider range of emotions.

Multidimensional Anxiety–Performance Models

Multidimensional models and measures dominate current sport and exercise psychology work on competitive anxiety. Research during the development of the CSAI-2, as well as considerable subsequent work, suggests that cognitive worry and somatic anxiety show different patterns of change over time. In two studies with gymnasts and wrestlers, Martens and colleagues (1990) found that cognitive anxiety and self-confidence remained relatively stable before competition whereas somatic anxiety rapidly increased as time to competition neared. Gould, Petlichkoff, and Weinberg (1984) substantiated these trends with high school volleyball players who completed the CSAI-2 starting one week, 48 hours, 24 hours, 2 hours, and 20 minutes before competition. As predicted, only somatic anxiety increased over time. These results suggest more complex multidimensional models of anxiety–performance relationships.

Multidimensional Anxiety and Performance

On the basis of multidimensional anxiety theory, Martens and colleagues (1990) predicted that cognitive anxiety would be a stronger predictor of performance than would somatic anxiety because somatic anxiety dissipates at the onset of competition. However, in their study with golfers, CSAI-2 scores did not predict performance. Burton (1988) used the CSAI-2 and more precise performance measures with intercollegiate swimmers over a season. Burton predicted an inverted-U relationship between somatic anxiety and performance but a negative linear relationship between cognitive anxiety and performance. The results confirmed those predictions and supported the application of multidimensional anxiety theory to competitive sport.

Gould, Petlichkoff, Simons, and Vevera (1987) used a similar intraindividual approach to compare CSAI-2 scores and shooting performance at a police training institute. The results supported the inverted-U relationship of somatic anxiety and performance but did not show a relationship between cognitive anxiety and performance. As Martens and colleagues (1990) noted in their review of the CSAI-2 research, we cannot draw definitive conclusions, and the inconsistent results prompted consideration of other, more elaborate multidimensional models of the anxiety–performance relationship.

Rather than consider multiple dimensions separately, later models have incorporated interactions. As an example of one simple interaction, if cognitive anxiety is positive (e.g., confidence, no worry), then somatic anxiety or physiological arousal is positively related to performance. On the other hand, if cognitive anxiety is negative (e.g., high worry), then somatic anxiety and performance are negatively related. Although this is not a theory, reversal theory as proposed by Kerr (1997) is similar.

Reversal Theory

Reversal theory, first advanced as a general framework for arousal and emotional affect (Apter, 1984), holds that the relationship between arousal and affect depends on one's cognitive interpretation of arousal (again, cognitive appraisal is the key). High arousal may be interpreted in positive terms as excitement, or in negative terms as anxiety. Similarly, low arousal may be interpreted as relaxation (positive) or boredom (negative). Both arousal and interpretive affect vary on a continuum, and reversal theory also adds that a person may switch from one interpretation to the other—a reversal. Kerr (1985, 1997) has adapted reversal theory to competitive anxiety with arousal and cognitive dimensions. Perhaps the most important guidelines from reversal theory are that arousal may be either positive or negative and that cognitive interpretation makes all the difference in the anxiety–performance relationship.

Similarly, Jones (1995) has suggested that anxiety, which is typically viewed as only negative, may be interpreted as positive or negative. More specifically, Jones proposed that anxiety interpreted positively is facilitative and may enhance performance whereas anxiety interpreted negatively is debilitative. Hanton and Jones (1999a, 1999b), in two studies with swimmers, found that swimmers who learned to perceive anxiety as facilitative improved performance.

Key Point

Reversal theory holds that the relationship between arousal and affect depends on one's cognitive interpretation of arousal. High arousal may be interpreted positively (excitement) or negatively (anxiety). Low arousal may also be interpreted positively (relaxation) or negatively (boredom).

Catastrophe Model of Anxiety

Catastrophe theory has been applied to competitive anxiety by several sport psychologists, particularly Lew Hardy (1990, 1996). The catastrophe model includes an interaction similar to the simple interaction discussed at the beginning of this section, but it is more complex, with three-dimensional, nonlinear relationships. In the catastrophe model the interaction is three-way, as performance changes depend on the interaction of physiological arousal and cognitive anxiety.

Catastrophe theory suggests that when cognitive worry is low, as arousal increases, performance increases up to a point and decreases thereafter (as in the inverted-U). However, when cognitive worry is high, the arousal–performance curve is no longer the smooth inverted-U curve. Instead, as arousal goes beyond the optimal level, performance drops abruptly as the athlete goes over the edge—in other words, a catastrophe occurs. Moreover, athletes who have gone over the edge and tried to return to an optimal level cannot simply go back on the same path. Instead, they must go back to much lower anxiety levels in order to get on track and then gradually build arousal

Key Point

Catastrophe theory suggests that when cognitive worry is low, as arousal increases, performance increases up to a point and decreases thereafter (as in the inverted-U), but when cognitive worry is high, as arousal moves beyond the optimal level, performance drops abruptly as the athlete goes over the edge—a catastrophe occurs. Moreover, athletes who have gone over the edge and tried to regain control cannot simply go back on the same path. Instead, they must go back to much lower anxiety levels in order to get on track and then gradually build arousal again.

again. These statements seem reasonable, but showing the process on the model and demonstrating it empirically are a challenge, to say the least. Figure 11.1, *a* and *b*, depicts catastrophe predictions under high and low cognitive worry as just described, but predictions are not that simple. The mathematics are complex, and testing the relationships requires multiple, precise, consistent, and valid measures of both anxiety and performance—something easier said than done.

Hardy (1996) clarified the catastrophe model, and his interpretation, informed by his extensive research with the model and with competitive anxiety, provides a helpful guide for researchers who wish to apply catastrophe theory. The following key predictions provide guidance in understanding the catastrophe model (Hardy, 1996).

- **Interactive effects:** First, the model describes combined, interactive effects of cognitive anxiety and physiological arousal on performance. The model proposes that high cognitive anxiety will lead to enhanced performance when physiological arousal is low (e.g., days before competition) but will lead to impaired performance when physiological arousal is high (e.g., on game day). Edwards and Hardy (1996) provided some support for interactive effects in a study of netball players using a modified CSAI-2 with a directional scale assessing the facilitative or debilitative interpretation of anxiety. They found the predicted interaction; the combination of low physiological arousal and high cognitive anxiety led to better performance than low physiological arousal and low cognitive anxiety. However, the combination of high physiological arousal and high cognitive anxiety led to worse performance than that of high physiological arousal and low cognitive anxiety.

- **Facilitative versus debilitative effects:** In contrast to most views that cognitive worry is always debilitating, Hardy emphasizes that cognitive anxiety can sometimes enhance performance. Specifically, the model predicts that performers' best performances should be better and their worst performances worse when they perform under high cognitive anxiety than under low cognitive anxiety. Edwards and Hardy did not find any directional facilitative effects in their study, but earlier work (Hardy & Parfitt, 1991; Hardy, Parfitt, & Pates, 1994) supported this hypothesis.

- **Hysteresis effects:** The third feature, hysteresis, is particularly intriguing. Hysteresis is a mathematical term, and in the model it implies that the graph of performance against physiological arousal follows a different path when arousal is increasing than when arousal is decreasing. Performance increases linearly as arousal increases until arousal peaks and performance suddenly drops off sharply. As the athlete tries to gain control and decrease arousal, performance does not jump back up but stays low and begins to rise gradually only as arousal returns to much lower levels. Hysteresis explains the sudden drop-off or choking phenomenon, and the differing paths have implications for practical questions related to control and recovery.

In discussing practical applications of the catastrophe model, Hardy (1996) highlights the notion that cognitive anxiety is not necessarily detrimental to performance. Cognitive anxiety is most

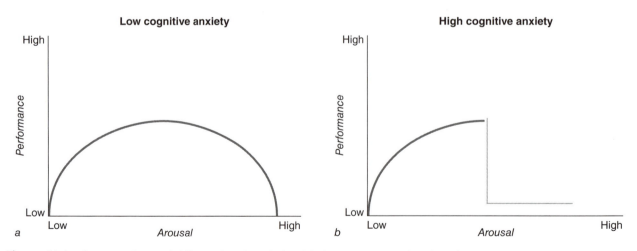

Figure 11.1 Catastrophe model illustrating the relationship between arousal and performance when cognitive worry is low and when cognitive worry is high. *(a)* When cognitive anxiety is low, somatic anxiety is associated with performance in inverted-U manner. *(b)* When cognitive anxiety is high, somatic anxiety can have catastrophic effects.

likely to be beneficial when performers have low physiological arousal and interpret their anxiety as beneficial. In the real world, those conditions may be difficult to achieve. Second, Hardy notes that if cognitively anxious performers become too physiologically aroused, they will reach a choke point and performance will drop suddenly and dramatically. Recovery will be faster if cognitive anxiety and physiological arousal are addressed simultaneously. Hardy proposes a multimodal stress management approach (i.e., addressing both cognitive and physiological anxiety), advising coaches and sport psychologists to use psyching-up strategies with great caution. Although cognitive anxiety and physiological arousal can be beneficial, there's a fine line between peak performance and disaster.

Anxiety Patterns and Performance

Multidimensional models capture the complexities of the anxiety–performance relationship, but most of the related research looks at anxiety only once, typically just before performance. Another line of research adds greater insights by looking at anxiety and emotion over time. Psychologist and parachutist Walter Fenz (1975, 1988) added important insights with his innovative studies of parachute jumpers. Fenz went out into the field, or rather into the air, and recorded changes and

patterns over time. Over several studies using varied methods and measures of emotion, the findings were consistent. Good performers and experienced jumpers did not differ from poorly skilled or novice jumpers in absolute levels. Instead, they differed in anxiety patterns over time (figure 11.2).

Fenz found that heart rates of poor performers increased from arrival at the airport to the time of the jump. Good performers increased in arousal at first, but peaked earlier and gradually decreased in arousal so that they were at moderate levels at the time of the jump. In another study (illustrated in figure 11.2), using self-reported ratings of anxiety, experienced jumpers had higher anxiety levels the day before the jump, but then decreased and at were at their lowest levels at the time of the jump. Novice jumpers, in contrast, started lower but then increased and were at peak anxiety levels right at the time of performance. Interestingly, after jumping, experienced jumpers increased (likely preparing for landing), whereas novices dropped back to low levels. Fenz's work suggests that the difference between better and poorer performers is not a difference in absolute levels but a difference in the ability to control emotion. Good performers seem to bring anxiety under control so that they are experiencing moderate levels at the time of performance.

Additional studies suggest that emotional control can be disrupted even in experienced, skilled performers. Fenz (1975) reported that one

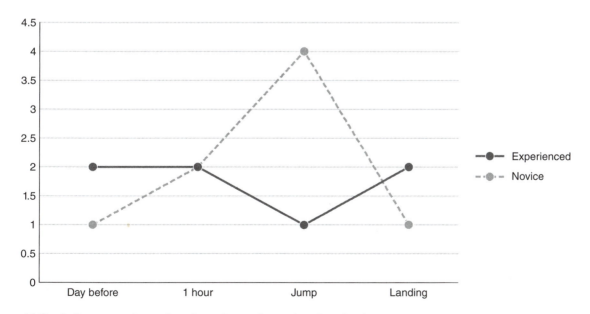

Figure 11.2 Self-report ratings of anxiety of experienced and novice jumpers.
Based on Fenz 1975.

experienced jumper broke an ankle on a jump. Upon returning, this jumper reverted to the novice's pattern of continual increases in arousal until the jump. Athletes returning to competition after injury might well exhibit similar patterns. In another study, an experienced jumper was told his chute could malfunction during any of the next 10 jumps. Although the jumper had an emergency chute and knew emergency procedures, the perceived threat (cognitive appraisal) of malfunction led to arousal patterns for those 10 jumps that were similar to those of novices, with continual increases to a peak at the time of the jump.

In one particularly encouraging training study, Fenz (1988) taught anxiety-control techniques (such as those described in chapter 13) to novice jumpers before their first jump. Even in their first jumps, the trained group demonstrated the controlled arousal pattern of the experienced jumpers. Fenz reported that the experimental jumpers had more fun during their training, and several eventually became experienced skydivers, suggesting that emotional control training may benefit even novice athletes.

As part of their study of Olympic qualifiers and nonqualifiers, Mahoney and Avener (1977) examined anxiety patterns over time. Retrospective reports revealed that the qualifiers' anxiety levels were just as high as or higher than those of nonqualifiers before performance, but qualifiers reported lower anxiety than nonqualifiers during performance. As with the parachutists, the better performers seemed to bring anxiety under control at the right time.

Mahoney (1979) suggested that differences in cognitive patterns, specifically precompetition thoughts, accompany the reported differences in anxiety patterns. The qualifiers seemed to approach competition with a task orientation and to focus their energy and attention on the task. In contrast, nonqualifiers worried more about being anxious. One Olympic qualifier described high anxiety, but then shifted his thoughts from the worry to the performance:

I get out there and they're waiting for me and all I can think is how scared I am. Twelve years I've worked to lay my life on the line for 30 seconds. Then I try to concentrate—"O.K., this is it; it's now or never. Let's pay attention to your tuck, stay strong on the press-out, and be ready for that dismount." I just start coaching myself. (Mahoney, 1979, p. 436)

Individual differences in competitive anxiety and the ability to control anxiety are major concerns in competitive sport programs, and indeed, in all physical activity settings. Many consultants spend considerable time helping participants learn to control anxiety.

Key Point

In general, the early anxiety–performance literature suggests that performance is best at a moderate level of arousal, although the precise optimal level varies among individuals, tasks, and situations, as well as with cognitive interpretations. The ability to control anxiety is a key factor that separates better and poorer performers.

Current research on emotion and performance in sport and exercise psychology has expanded beyond anxiety and performance. The IZOF model and related research consider multiple emotions and interactions. Although research on other emotions is limited, it is emerging. Woodman and colleagues (2009) used Lazarus' cognitive motivational–relational (CMR) theory, which proposes that different emotions have different core relational themes describing person–behavior interactions. Woodman's group specifically looked at the influence of happiness, hope, and anger on performance. In line with Lazarus' themes, they found that anger improved muscular peak force performance, whereas hope improved reaction-time performance in soccer players.

Putting It Into Practice

Summary

Emotion pervades all physical activities, and explanations of sport and exercise behavior that omit the emotional component are incomplete and rather dull. Emotion is a complex biopsychosocial process. Sport and exercise psychology research focuses on negative emotions, particularly anxiety, but the research on physical activity and emotion is expanding to a wider range of emotions and beginning to address positive emotions. People might respond to physical activity with joy or hope or find themselves in a flow state. More encompassing approaches such as Lazarus' (1991) multidimensional model or emotion as a process provide guidance.

Much sport and exercise psychology research has focused on the relationship of emotion to performance, and specifically the research on anxiety and performance. Early work suggested that performance is best at an optimal level of arousal, but optimal levels vary with the individual, activity, and situation. Research examining anxiety patterns over time reveals that the ability to control anxiety is crucial in separating better and poorer performers.

Review Questions

1. Define *emotion*, and explain how it is related to and different from arousal, affect, and mood.

2. Explain the major historical perspectives on emotion, including the James-Lange theory, Schachter and Singer's cognitive approach, and Lazarus' model of emotion.

3. Explain Fredrickson's theory of positive emotions and explain how positive emotions differ from negative emotions.

4. Define *flow*. Describe Csikszentmihalyi's model and Jackson's work on flow with athletes.

5. Compare and contrast drive theory and the inverted-U hypothesis as explanations of the anxiety–performance relationship. How does the IZOF theory differ from the inverted-U?

6. Describe the current multidimensional anxiety–performance models used in sport and exercise psychology, including the catastrophe model.

7. Describe the findings from Fenz's (1975, 1988) work on emotion and anxiety with parachute jumpers. How do experienced and novice jumpers differ? What are the implications for emotional control strategies?

Recommended Reading

- Csikszentmihalyi, M. (1990). *Flow: The psychology of optimal experience.* New York: Harper & Row. Csikszentmihalyi is widely cited for his innovative work on flow state. Many sport and exercise psychology students are drawn to his work, with good reason—they find new ideas and directions.

- Fredrickson, B.L. (2013a). Positive emotions broaden and build. In E.A. Plante & P.G. Devine (Eds.), *Advances in experimental social psychology* (Vol. 47, pp. 1-53). San Diego: Academic Press. This chapter reviews Fredrickson's influential work on positive emotions. Also, check the positivity ratio website.

- Hardy, L. (1996). Testing the predictions of the cusp catastrophe model of anxiety and performance. *The Sport Psychologist, 10,* 140-156. Hardy is a leader in applying catastrophe theory to anxiety and sport performance. Although catastrophe theory is mathematically and theoretically complex, this article is one of the most readable and understandable presentations. If you are interested in anxiety and performance, you would do well to read this article even if you do not specifically test catastrophe theory.

- Lazarus, R.S. (1993). From psychological stress to the emotions: A history of changing outlooks. *Annual Review of Psychology, 44,* 1-21. Lazarus has been a leading scholar on stress and coping since the 1960s. His most recent work emphasized the broader complexities of emotion. This review presents some of his many insights into moving from stress to emotions.

- Martens, R., Vealey, R.S., & Burton, D. (1990). *Competitive anxiety in sport.* Champaign, IL: Human Kinetics. Martens and colleagues began the move toward sport-specific constructs and measures with the development of the SCAT and followed with the development of a multidimensional sport-specific state anxiety measure. This book presents the background literature and information on the SCAT and CSAI-2 measures.

- Scanlan, T.K., Babkes, M.L., & Scanlan, L.A. (2005). Participation in sport: A developmental glimpse at emotion. In J.L. Mahoney, R.W. Larson, & J.S. Eccles (Eds.), *Organized activities as contexts of development* (pp. 275-309). Mahwah, NJ: Erlbaum. Scanlan is one of the few sport and exercise psychology scholars to devote attention to both positive (enjoyment) and negative (stress and anxiety) emotions. Much of her research is with young people, and this chapter summarizes the developmental research on stress and emotion in sport.

LAB

Physical Activity and Positivity

This lab focuses on positive emotion and draws from Barbara Fredrickson's (2009) book *Positivity* and the positivity ratio website, as well as the text chapter. For this lab, you will first assess your own positivity ratio and how that varies with your activities. Then, summarize your responses and consider applications in professional practice.

1. *Positivity ratio log.* Complete and score the positivity ratio two times for two different days (use the positivity ratio website). As well as determining your "ratio," do a brief log of your activities for that 24-hour period (list the main activities you did over the day before you did the ratio). Include the logs, as well as your overall positivity ratio scores, with the lab.

2. *Summary.* Write up a summary that includes a description of how your daily activities, and specifically physical activity, relate to your positivity. Refer to your positivity ratios and logs, but also consider your other experiences. What raises your positivity (activities, settings, and so on)? How does physical activity relate to your positivity? What could you do to raise your positivity (give at least two specific things you could do)?

Physical Activity, Emotion, and Mental Health

Chapter Objectives

After studying this chapter, you should be able to

- understand the circumplex model of affect,
- discuss the research on physical activity and mental health, and
- discuss the research on physical activity and cognition.

This chapter covers the relationship between physical activity and emotion. In chapter 11 we looked at the relationship of emotion to performance. Here, we look at the relationship in the other direction—the role of physical activity in emotion and mental health. First we cover models and measures of affect, focusing on the circumplex model and the related research on affect during exercise. Then we review the rapidly expanding research on physical activity and mental health, including research on exercise and cognition.

Physical Activity and Emotion

Research on physical activity and emotion is not new (for an early review, see Folkins & Sime, 1981). However, as with the work on emotion–performance discussed in chapter 11, the bulk of that work has emphasized negative emotion. In their review on the affective benefits of aerobic exercise, Tuson and Sinyor (1993) concluded that acute exercise may be associated with reduced anxiety but does not appear to influence other affective states. They also reported that although many explanations and mechanisms have been suggested, none has been supported.

That conclusion still holds, but the research has grown considerably. There is more evidence linking physical activity and fitness to emotions and mental health, and the research includes a wide range of participants in clinical and nonclinical settings. Overall, the growing research in this area confirms the popular belief that people feel better after exercise. However, the research reveals more complex relationships, and it raises more questions just as it offers more insights.

One area that has advanced greatly is our understanding of emotions and affect during exercise. Following an overview of the models and measures of affect, we focus on the extensive research of Ekkekakis and colleagues, who have continued to advance our understanding of exercise and affect.

Models and Measures of Emotion and Affect

Despite interest in the emotional benefits of physical activity, the research is limited and not at all consistent. Most research is narrowly focused on negative emotions, specifically anxiety. Gauvin and Brawley (1993) suggested that sport and exercise psychology adopt more encompassing conceptual models, such as Russell's (1980) model, which represents affect along two dimensions: hedonic tone (pleasure–displeasure) and activation (arousal–sleepiness). On the affect grid (Russell, Weiss, & Mendelsohn, 1989), respondents mark a square on a 9-by-9 grid to indicate affect state along those dimensions.

The affect grid is seldom used in sport and exercise psychology, but researchers have followed a similar two-dimensional approach. Hardy and Rejeski (1989) used the Feeling Scale (FS; Rejeski, Best, Griffith, & Kenney, 1987), a bipolar scale reflecting how good or bad one feels during exercise, and they also used the rating of perceived exertion (RPE), which might be considered similar to activation. Increased exercise intensities related to decreases on the FS and increases in RPE. The FS is among the few measures of emotion developed for exercise, and such measures are critical for extending our understanding of exercise and emotion.

The RPE, developed in the 1960s by Borg (1973, 1998), is widely used in exercise physiology research, but it was not designed as a measure of emotion or within any psychological framework. A comprehensive review (Robertson & Noble, 1997) indicates the use of several forms of RPE, most commonly the 15-category scale (from 6 = no exertion at all to 20 = maximal exertion). As a physiologist, Borg took a psychophysical perspective, and the RPE scales correspond to increases in heart rate with increases in exercise intensity. Thus, RPE reflects activation or arousal. Most current work adopting the two-dimensional model uses the Felt Arousal Scale (FAS; Svebak & Murgatroyd, 1985), which more clearly reflects the arousal dimension.

Watson and Tellegen's (1985) two-factor model of affect and the related Positive and Negative Affect Schedule (PANAS; Watson, Clark, & Tellegen, 1988), which includes scales for positive affect and for negative affect, have been used in several studies in physical activity settings (e.g., Crocker, 1997; Crocker & Graham, 1995). However, McAuley and Courneya (1994) suggested that the PANAS may be limited for exercise settings and pointed out that research on physical activity and affect is limited by the emphasis on negative emotions. For example, one of the most popular measures of affect, the Profile of Mood States (POMS); McNair, Lorr, & Droppleman, 1971), assesses five negative moods (tension, depression, anger, fatigue, confusion) and only one positive mood (vigor). As McAuley and Courneya note, psychological health includes both positive and negative affect.

McAuley and Courneya (1994) developed the Subjective Exercise Experiences Scale (SEES), with positive and negative factors corresponding to psychological well-being and psychological distress, as well as a third factor representing subjective indicants of fatigue. The initial work provided validity evidence, and the SEES is an easy-to-use and useful measure for investigating questions about emotion and physical activity. Similarly, Gauvin and Rejeski (1993) developed the Exercise-Induced Feeling Inventory (EFI), a 12-item inventory with four subscales: positive engagement, revitalization, tranquility, and physical exhaustion.

Circumplex Model of Affect

Ekkekakis and Petruzzello (1999, 2002) offer the most extensive conceptual work on emotion in sport and exercise psychology, and their circumplex model of affect is a useful base for research on physical activity and emotion. Like the Russell (1980) and Watson and Tellegen (1985) models, Ekkekakis and Petruzzello's circumplex model has two dimensions—an activation or arousal dimension and a valence (positive–negative) dimension—that result in four quadrants (see figure 12.1):

- Positive–activated (energy, excitement)
- Positive–unactivated (relaxation, calm)

- Negative–unactivated (boredom, fatigue)
- Negative–activated (anxiety, tension)

The circumplex model dominates research on physical activity and affect, and Ekkekakis is the leading researcher in that area. The model and related measures that can be used to monitor affect over time have contributed greatly to our understanding of physical activity and affect. People often report feeling better after exercise, but simply measuring affect after exercise misses the affect changes during exercise that can greatly influence physical activity behavior.

Research on Physical Activity and Affect

Ekkekakis and Petruzzello (1999), who developed the circumplex model, applied the model and related measures to investigate affect throughout exercise. People vary along each dimension, and affect state depends on both dimensions. For example, if you are sitting in a class, your arousal or activation level is likely very low. Your positive–negative valence could be negative if you're worried about a test, positive if you're interested in the topic, or in the middle. Affect can change quickly. If your instructor announces a pop quiz, your arousal levels likely would increase and you could feel more positive or more negative depending on your thoughts about the pop quiz. In the research with exercise, the one-item FAS

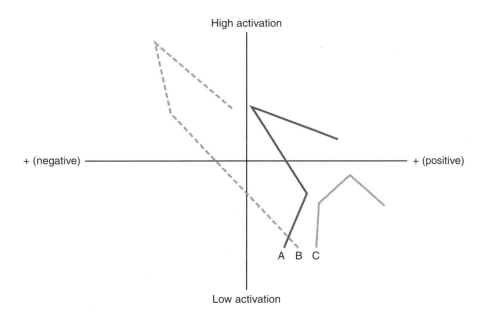

Figure 12.1 The circumplex model of affect with two dimensions: activation (low–high) and valence (negative–positive). The three lines, A, B, and C, illustrate changes in affect over an exercise session for three different individuals.

measures arousal, and the one-item FS measures valence. These simple measures allow for monitoring of affect during an exercise session, which provides more insight into the exercise–affect relationship.

Generally, the early research suggested that moderate-intensity exercise results in greater positive-valenced affective states, such as energy or vigor. With high-intensity exercise, negative affect states may increase while positive affect decreases, especially with people who are less fit. The implications for exercise programs are clear—moderate-intensity exercise is likely to make people feel better and thus keep them coming back. On the other hand, if the trainer pushes high-intensity exercise, clients may feel worse and drop out.

That conclusion still holds, but the research has grown considerably. Backhouse, Ekkekakis, Biddle, Foskett, and Williams (2007) used the circumplex model and related measures to track participants at eight points throughout an exercise session. Their most striking finding was the wide individual variation in patterns. Most people start at low arousal levels and slightly positive feeling states; arousal increases and valence tends to become more negative during exercise; and most people become more positive at the end. But there are wide variations, and no two patterns looked alike. Some of the participants changed a lot in arousal while others changed little, and valance changes were even more varied. Some participants stayed positive while others quickly became negative and never returned to positive affect. Backhouse and colleagues suggested that the "feel good" effect may be an artifact of just measuring pre–post affect, failing to measure negative affect changes, and using only aggregate group data without considering individual differences.

See figure 12.1 for examples of different individual patterns of affect change during exercise. In the figure, person A exhibits a common pattern of increasing arousal throughout exercise while feeling state becomes more positive, then slightly more negative, and back to more positive after exercise. Person B (perhaps less fit) also increases in arousal, but feeling state moves into the negative area and remains negative. Person C (perhaps very fit and engaging in easy walking) increases only slightly in arousal and also increases in positive feeling state and stays positive throughout exercise. Hyde, Conroy, Pincus, and Ram (2011) examined the "feel good" effect

of free-time physical activity using the four quadrants. They found that physical activity related to the pleasant–activated quadrant, but not the other three. That is, active people spent more time in the pleasant–activated quadrant than less active people. They also found within-person effects, in that on days when people were more active, they spent more time in the pleasant–activated quadrant.

Ekkekakis, Hargreaves, and Parfitt (2013), in a review of the research on exercise–affect, summarized the main results of 50 years of research as (a) recognition that exercise can have a positive, meaningful influence on affect; and (b) incorporation of affect in exercise prescription guidelines. They also cited emerging research directions including focusing on mechanisms, individual differences, exercise in treatment of addictions, and connections between affect and cognition.

In another review, Ekkekakis, Parfitt, and Petruzzello (2011) similarly summarized the research findings and more explicitly called for incorporating affect in exercise prescriptions. Specifically they called for a tripartite rationale for exercise intensity prescriptions. Typical exercise guidelines, such as those issued by the American College of Sports Medicine, are based on two considerations—effectiveness (improved fitness) and injury risk. Ekkekakis and colleagues (2011) argue that exercise prescriptions should also consider affective responses, so that the exercise prescription is manageable for the person and likely to be followed. As Ekkekakis and coauthors (2011) suggest, the most important message for professionals in the exercise and physical activity setting is to bring in psychology and specifically consider the individual's characteristics and affect state. Indeed, psychological factors may well be more important than physical factors in promoting exercise adherence and lifetime physical activity.

As well as the continuing research on exercise and affect state, research on the role of physical activity in stress responses and mental health has expanded rapidly in recent years. That research includes a wide range of participants in clinical and nonclinical settings. Overall, the research confirms popular beliefs in the benefits of physical activity for mental health, but specific relationships have not been delineated, and we know little about the exact processes and the many variations. The following section reviews that growing body of research.

Application Point

Positive Affect in Exercise Programs

Consider the circumplex model and research on exercise and emotions (both positive and negative). What are the implications for an exercise instructor in a community-based physical activity program with participants who are low fit and low active? Assuming you want participants to have a positive experience and stick with the program, what types of activities would you offer, and how would you organize your program?

Physical Activity and Stress Responses

One research line involves physical activity as a mediator between stress and illness (or health). Do people who are more physically fit have less response to stress, and might that help prevent illness or injury? The simple answer is yes, but it is not that simple. Not all studies show benefits, and questions remain about processes, mechanisms, and variations.

Much research demonstrates benefits of physical activity and fitness. Crews and Landers' (1987) meta-analysis indicated that exercise leads to less stress reactivity and faster recovery from stress responses. In their meta-analysis, Long and van Stavel (1995) concluded that exercise training had low to moderate positive effects on anxiety reduction and that adults with more stressful lifestyles benefited more from exercise training. Forcier and colleagues (2006), in a meta-analysis on fitness and cardiovascular reactivity, found that fitness was associated with reduced reactivity. However, in their review, Jackson and Dishman (2006) found no reduced reactivity and slightly faster stress recovery. With research on training effects, Spaulding, Lyon, Steel, and Hatfield (2004) found that aerobic training improved fitness and had a stress-buffering effect on reactivity and recovery. Similarly, Heydari, Boutcher, and Boutcher (2013) found a positive effect of high-intensity interval training on stress reactivity and recovery. In summarizing the research on physical activity and stress responses, Lox, Martin Ginis, and Petruzzello (2014) concluded that while the evidence is not totally consistent, it is likely that exercise is useful in reducing stress responses. Whether that is mainly reduced reactivity or faster recovery is unclear.

An intriguing line of research on psychoneuro-immunology has demonstrated that stress affects immune function, and immune function may be the key link between stress and illness. Of relevance to sport and exercise psychology, Hong and Mills (2006) suggest that regular exercise may lead to adaptations that protect against stress-induced immune suppression, and Hamer and Steptoe (2007) found that increased fitness was related to decreased inflammatory responses to stress.

Even if physical activity does not have a clear biological effect, it can serve as a coping mechanism in recovery and rehabilitation (e.g., physical activity programs with cancer or acquired immunodeficiency syndrome [AIDS] patients). In extensive research using exercise programs with human immunodeficiency virus (HIV) and AIDS patients, LaPerriere and colleagues (LaPerriere et al., 1990, 1991) reported that exercise reduced depression.

Following LaPerriere's lead, Lox, McAuley, and Tucker (1995) examined the influence of an exercise intervention on psychological well-being with an HIV-1 population. Both aerobic and weight-training exercise enhanced physical self-efficacy, positive and negative mood (assessed with PANAS), and life satisfaction. These research programs and related practical applications do not simply look at biological medical outcomes; instead, they consider the whole person. Psychological well-being is a key part of health and medical research, and many programs are examining connections between psychology and health in innovative ways.

Research on physical activity and stress continues, and generally it suggests that exercise is beneficial, leading to less negative and more positive emotional responses for a variety of people in clinical and nonclinical settings. Latimer and Martin Ginis (2005), for example, found that people with spinal cord injury had reduced stress and less perceived pain with an exercise program. Courneya and colleagues (Courneya et al., 2003; Courneya, Mackey, & Jones, 2000) have conducted extensive research with cancer patients and survivors demonstrating the benefits of physical activity.

Key Point

Research on physical activity and stress suggests that exercise is beneficial, leading to less negative stress responses and more positive emotional responses for people in clinical and nonclinical settings.

Physical Activity and Mental Health

Mental health is increasingly recognized as a major health issue, even in youth and college student-athletes, and physical activity is increasingly considered in the prevention and treatment of mental health disorders, as well as in the promotion of positive mental health. Mental health and mental disorders might best be viewed as a continuum, with optimal, positive mental health at one end and clinical mental health disorders at the other end. Notably, a large part of the population falls between the extremes. Many people fall short of optimal mental health and have some mental health issues but do not reach the level of clinical diagnoses. While physical activity may well be useful for people with diagnosed clinical disorders, perhaps the greatest role of physical activity is in moving people along the continuum closer to the optimal level.

Overall, public heath reports indicate that about 20 to 25 percent of the population will experience mental health disorders in their lifetime, and anxiety and depression are the most common disorders. Accordingly, much of the research on physical activity and mental health focuses on depression and anxiety. Notably, both anxiety and depression fall along the mental health continuum. That is, people may have depressed mood or issues with anxiety without meeting criteria for clinical disorders. Thus, physical activity may be particularly helpful in prevention of clinical anxiety and depression, and it may also be considered an alternative treatment.

The National Athletic Trainers' Association (NATA) published a consensus statement with recommendations related to psychological concerns of collegiate student-athletes. The executive summary has been published (Neal et al., 2013), and the full report is available at the NATA website (click on News & Publications, then Statements, then Consensus, then Inter-Association Recommendations 2013). The report cites the relatively high rates of mental illness in the population and notes that the rate for 18- to 25-year-olds is higher than rates for older adults. More importantly, the report begins by stating that the full range of mental health concerns found in the general student population can also be seen in collegiate student-athletes. Athletic trainers often have little education or experience with psychology and mental health, but they are often in a good posi-

tion to recognize mental health issues. The NATA consensus statement includes a list of behaviors to monitor that may reflect psychological concerns, as well as information and guidelines on related psychological services and referral. The report concludes by stating that the most important factors in helping a student-athlete with a psychological concern are education, early recognition of a potential problem, and effective referral into the mental health care system. The conclusions also recommend downloading and sharing the full report with coaches, athletic staff, and related campus offices and services; helping athletes with psychological concerns is a team effort. Sport and exercise psychology training can help athletic trainers and other professionals working with people in sport and exercise programs recognize mental health issues and also use psychological and behavioral strategies to promote positive mental health.

Physical Activity and Anxiety

Much of the sport and exercise psychology research on emotion–performance focuses on anxiety, and anxiety is also one of the prominent topics in research on the physical activity–mental health relationship. Research suggests that physical activity can aid in prevention and treatment of anxiety. In their meta-analysis, Petruzzello, Landers, Hatfield, Kubitz, and Salazar (1991) confirmed that aerobic exercise is associated with reductions in anxiety. More specifically, acute exercise was associated with reduced state anxiety, and chronic exercise was related to lower trait anxiety. In a review, Landers and Petruzzello (1994) found that physically fit people have less anxiety than those who are unfit. Goodwin (2003), using data from a national survey, found physical activity to be associated with a reduced chance of anxiety disorders, suggesting a preventive role for physical activity. Brunes, Augestad, and Gudmundsdottir (2013), in a large Norwegian study, found physical activity associated with reduced risk of anxiety disorders.

As well as the Petruzzello and colleagues meta-analysis, several studies suggest that physical activity can be effective in treating anxiety disorders. Broocks and colleagues (1998) and Meyer and colleagues (1998) found that exercising led to improvements in panic disorder patients. Several reviews (Asmundson et al., 2013; Bartley, Hay, & Bloch, 2013; Jayakody, Gunadasa, & Hosker, 2014) conclude that exercise is at least as effective as other treatments for anxiety disorders.

Physical Activity and Depression

Depression is one of the most common mental health issues, and much of the research on physical activity and mental health focuses on depression. Depression can be a transient mood state or a more serious clinical disorder. An early meta-analysis of the exercise and depression literature (North, McCullagh, & Tran, 1990) indicated that exercise decreased depression and was as effective as traditional therapies. The evidence has continued to accumulate with both clinically depressed and nonclinical participants. Craft and Landers (1998) conducted a meta-analysis of training studies with clinically depressed participants and reported a larger effect size than did North and colleagues. Motl, Birnbaum, Kubik, and Dishman (2004) examined changes in physical activity levels and depression in a large study with adolescents over two years. They found that more active adolescents had less depression and that change in activity related to change in depression. Those who became more active had less depression, whereas lower activity related to higher depression levels.

Mammen and Faulkner (2013), in a systematic review of prospective, longitudinal studies on physical activity for the prevention of depression, found good evidence that physical activity levels are associated with lower risk of depression. They suggested that physical activity is an effective mental health promotion strategy in reducing risk of depression.

Several studies have involved older adults and people with chronic illness or injury. Martin Ginis and colleagues (2003) used exercise training with people with spinal cord injury and found lower depression. Exercise has also been found to result in lower depression with older adults (Mobily, Rubenstein, Lemke, O'Hara, & Wallace, 1996), with chronic obstructive pulmonary disease (COPD) patients (Emery, Schein, Hauck, & MacIntyre, 1998), and with breast cancer survivors (Segar et al., 1998). Heller, Hsieh, and Rimmer (2004) compared an experimental exercise program with a control condition for adults with Down syndrome and found that exercise led to increased life satisfaction and lower depression.

Blumenthal has done much of the research on exercise and depression, including the Duke SMILE (Standard Medical Intervention & Long-term Exercise) studies. Blumenthal, Smith, and Hoffman (2012) summarized the research on exercise as a treatment for depression and offered practical suggestions. As Blumenthal and colleagues (2012) noted, extensive research indicates that exercise is a viable alternative treatment for depression. Exercise was just as effective as standard clinical treatment, and in a follow-up study, exercise participants had less relapse than those in the standard treatment. As Blumenthal and coworkers noted, issues related to which type and dose of exercise are most effective are open questions. Most research has used aerobic activity, but resistance exercise may also be effective, and mindful exercise (e.g., tai chi, yoga) is promising.

Key Point

As summarized by Blumenthal and colleagues (2012), research indicates that exercise is a viable alternative treatment for depression and just as effective as standard clinical treatment. Which type and dose of exercise are most effective are open questions. Most research has used aerobic activity, but resistance exercise may also be effective, and mindful exercise (e.g., tai chi, yoga) is promising.

How Physical Activity Affects Mental Health

Overall, the research indicates that physical activity can play an important role in the prevention and treatment of mental health disorders, as well as in promoting positive mental health. Still, many more questions remain as to the most beneficial forms of exercise and the explanations or mechanisms underlying benefits. Boutcher (1993) categorized explanations for the benefits of exercise into physiological and psychological mechanisms and concluded that no proposed mechanism had convincing support. He suggested that several physiological and psychological factors might be involved and that the process may vary from person to person.

Other reviews (e.g., Lox et al., 2014) offer slightly different lists but do not make many more conclusive statements about underlying mechanisms. Several researchers cited in this section called for more research on mechanisms, and many scholars conclude that multiple mechanisms are involved and that different mechanisms and processes likely underlie different emotions (e.g., mechanisms for effects on depression may differ from mechanisms for effects on stress response). Continuing research may well lead to a complex mix of multidimensional processes, which matches the complexity of emotion and provides a better guide than simpler mechanistic explanations.

Physical Activity and Cognition

In addition to specific effects on stress response, anxiety, and depression, researchers have found that physical activity relates to cognitive function. Indeed, exercise and cognition is one of the "hot" research topics in sport and exercise psychology, with tremendous advances in that body of research in recent years. Several meta-analyses have found a positive relationship between physical activity and cognitive function among older adults (Colcombe & Kramer, 2003; Etnier et al., 1997). Kramer and Hillman (2006) reviewed the research from a psychobiological perspective and suggested that exercise effects are the most beneficial for cognitive tasks that involve executive control, especially for persons who are elderly. Research is continuing to add to our understanding and to open new questions. Chaddock, Voss, and Kramer (2012) reviewed the literature on children and older adults, the two segments of the population that seem to show the greatest benefits. They concluded that in children, both physical activity and fitness are associated with better academic performance and cognitive processes. They further suggested brain volume and function as potential mechanisms underlying cognitive performance differences. For older adults, physical activity is associated with better performance on varied cognitive tasks as well as less risk of cognitive impairment, with less brain tissue loss and increased brain function efficiency as possible mechanisms.

Chronic Effects

Etnier (2014), one of the leading researchers on exercise and cognition, summarized the research and concluded that the evidence supporting the beneficial effects of both chronic (long-term) and acute (immediate) exercise for cognitive performance is robust. As earlier reviews indicated, children and older adults particularly benefit. As with other research on physical activity and mental health, most studies use aerobic exercise, but resistance exercise and mindful exercise also are promising options.

Some cognitive decline is normal with aging, but cognitive impairment, and particularly Alzheimer's disease (AD), are major health concerns with our aging population. In a review of the research on physical activity in the prevention of AD, Etnier (2015) reported that evidence from randomized controlled trials (RCTs) supports the protective effect of physical activity on cognitive performance, and evidence from prospective studies supports reduced risk of cognitive decline ranging from 28 to 45 percent. Furthermore, although findings are not completely consistent, research with people at genetic risk for AD shows the greatest benefits.

Acute Effects

Chronic exercise of any type seems to be beneficial, but issues related to exercise type and dose are more unsettled for acute (immediate) exercise effects. Chang, Labban, Gapin, and Etnier (2012) conducted a meta-analysis on the effects of acute exercise on cognitive performance. As they noted, most of the existing research suggests a small positive effect on immediate cognitive performance. Chang and colleagues confirmed the small positive effect, but also found that exercise duration, intensity, type of cognitive performance, and fitness were significant moderators. In her review of the research Etnier (2014) reported that some studies suggest 30 minutes of exercise at higher intensity may be better for information processing, while moderate intensity is better for executive function. However, research on dose of acute exercise that is most beneficial for performance on varied cognitive tasks is still a work in progress.

Chang and Etnier (2015) edited a special issue of *Journal of Sport and Health Science* on acute exercise and cognitive function. Their editorial and several articles in that issue reached conclusions similar to those of Chang and colleagues (2012), with some updates. They noted that several reviews and meta-analyses confirmed that acute exercise has a positive effect on cognition, particularly executive function, while also suggesting several mediators and moderators. Research using neuropsychological approaches and mechanisms is advancing our understanding and opening more questions. Piepmeier and Etnier (2015) reviewed the literature on brain-derived neurotropic factor (BDNF) as a potential mechanism for acute effects. They concluded that the role of BDNF in cognitive performance is well supported, and exercise has been shown to increase BDNF.

However, the full exercise–BDNF–cognitive performance relationship has only recently been explored, and further research is needed. Tomporowski, McCullick, Pendleton, and Pesce (2015) reviewed the literature and concluded that both acute and chronic exercise enhance children's cognition. They further noted that while there is a clear causal link between exercise and children's cognition, the link between exercise-induced changes in cognition and academic performance is less clear.

As with most research on physical activity and emotion, most work on exercise and cognition uses aerobic exercise. Gothe, Pontifex, Hillman, and McAuley (2013) looked at the acute effect of yoga on executive function. They found that cognitive performance after yoga was significantly better than performance after aerobic exercise as well as compared to the baseline. Performance in the aerobic condition did not differ from the baseline, in contrast to other research on acute exercise. These authors' findings suggest the need to further investigate mindful exercise and the promise of that endeavor. Overall, it seems that some exercise, particularly at moderate levels, has a positive effect, but the research does not allow more specific prescriptions.

Physical Activity and Academic Performance

Research on exercise and cognition is particularly relevant to issues related to physical activity and academic performance. As Chaddock and colleagues (2012) noted, physical activity and fitness are associated with better academic performance, and reviews of the research suggest that both chronic and acute physical activity are related to better cognitive performance. However, most of the evidence is cross-sectional, and we do not have RTCs or strong evidence to support benefits of physical activity for academic performance. Eveland-Sayers, Farley, Fuller, Morgan, and Caputo (2009) examined physical fitness and academic achievement in elementary children. They found one-mile run times and muscular fitness related to mathematics scores; and when considering gender, significant effects were found for girls but not for boys. Their results suggest some links between fitness and academic achievement. Castelli, Hillman, Buck, and Erwin (2007) found aerobic fitness positively related to math and reading performance, and Pontifex and colleagues (2011) found that more fit children had

better cognitive function. Hillman and coworkers (2009) found acute effects on children's cognitive control and academic performance after exercise.

Key Point

As summarized by Chaddock and colleagues (2012), research indicates that physical activity and fitness are associated with better academic performance, and that both chronic and acute physical activity are related to better cognitive performance. However, most research on academic performance is cross-sectional. Tomporowski and colleagues (2015) suggested that the association between exercise and academic performance is complex and likely influenced by multiple mediators and moderators.

Howie and Pate (2012) reviewed the research and noted that a large portion of the related articles had been published in the last five years. They noted that the quality of the research was improving but that results were inconsistent. Most studies do show a positive effect of physical activity, but stronger studies are needed to identify the types and doses of activity needed to yield academic improvements. Tomporowski and colleagues (2015), in their review, suggested that the association between exercise and academic performance is complex and likely influenced by multiple mediators and moderators. They further called for considering metacognition, which reflects an individual's understanding of what is known and how to use that knowledge as a mediator to advance our understanding of physical activity and academic performance.

Physical Activity and Quality of Life

Much of the work on physical activity and mental health focuses on prevention and treatment of mental health problems, but in taking a more positive approach, we turn to the other end of the mental health continuum—optimal mental health and quality of life. A significant body of research, including systematic reviews and meta-analyses, confirms that physical activity enhances quality of life (e.g., Berger & Tobar, 2007; Bize, Johnson, & Plotnikoff, 2007; Gillison, Skevington,

Sato, Standage, & Evangelidou, 2009; McAuley & Elavsky, 2006; Rejeski, Brawley, & Shumaker, 1996). In their seminal review, Rejeski and colleagues (1996) noted that quality of life (QoL), a key concern in health-related research and practice, has not been clearly conceptualized and measured. Instead, studies have used various measures, typically focusing on negative emotions. Rejeski and colleagues described QoL as a subjective, multidimensional construct but focused on health-related quality of life (HRQoL) as a more restricted construct, referring to those dimensions of QoL that are related to health.

Since then, the distinction between HRQoL and QoL has blurred, and the evidence that physical activity promotes QoL has continued to accumulate. For example, Schechtman and Ory (2001) conducted a meta-analysis on the effects of exercise on older adults and found a modest improvement in QoL. Schmitz, Kruse, and Kugler (2004) found that higher levels of physical activity were associated with higher health-related QoL in a survey of people with mental disorders.

Lee and Russell (2003) investigated physical activity and mental health with a large sample of Australian women and found that higher levels of physical activity were associated with higher scores on all mental health variables. Further, women who had made a transition from some physical activity to none showed negative changes in emotional well-being, whereas those who maintained or adopted physical activity had better outcomes. Stathi, Fox, and McKenna (2002) used a qualitative approach and concluded that physical activity contributes to the mental health of older adults through maintenance of a busy and active life, mental alertness, a positive attitude toward life, and avoidance of stress, negative function, and isolation.

Despite the seemingly consistent results, the approaches to QoL are not at all consistent. There are no guiding theoretical frameworks, and QoL measures range from Diener's (1984; Diener, Emmons, Larsen, & Griffin, 1985) widely used Satisfaction with Life Scale to aggregate measures of separate components of QoL and extend to related constructs (e.g., depression) as markers of QoL. The most commonly used QoL measures, such as the Medical Outcomes Study 36-item Short Form Health Survey, commonly called the SF-36 (Ware, 2000), were designed for medical research and clinical purposes and did not emerge from a conceptual base. Several

years ago we began a line of research on physical activity and QoL to address the gap in QoL models and measures that are relevant for sport and exercise psychology.

Quality of Life Model for Sport and Exercise Psychology

Although the literature does not provide conceptual frameworks or agreed-upon definitions of QoL, we can find several common themes. First, QoL is multidimensional, with physical, social, and psychological or emotional dimensions nearly always included. Quality of life is also subjective; that is, QoL is the individual's perception rather than an objective, external measure. Most current work on QoL also takes a positive approach and refers to the definition of health in the preamble to the constitution of the World Health Organization (WHO, 1946): "Health is a state of complete physical, mental, and social well-being, and not merely the absence of disease or infirmity."

Key Point

Quality of life reflects positive health and may be defined as a subjective, multidimensional, integrative construct that reflects optimal health and psychological well-being. In Gill and colleagues' (2011) hierarchical model, subdomains of physical, social, emotional, cognitive, and spiritual well-being contribute to an integrative subjective well-being.

Drawing from the literature as well as the WHO model and definition, we began our research by defining QoL as follows: QoL is a subjective, multidimensional, integrative construct that reflects optimal health and psychological well-being (Gill et al., 2011, p. 184). We then began with a working conceptual model with subdomains of physical, social, emotional, cognitive, and spiritual well-being contributing to an integrative QoL (see figure 12.2).

Quality of Life Assessment for Sport and Exercise Psychology

After reviewing the literature and related measures, we developed our initial measure of QoL based on our model. We conducted several studies over several phases with a wide range of

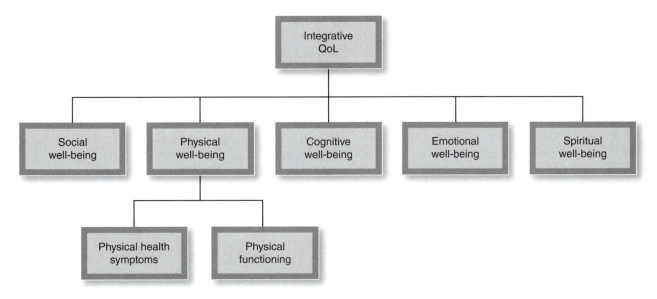

Figure 12.2 Conceptual model of quality of life. The model reflects our definition of QoL as a multidimensional, integrative construct with physical, social, emotional, cognitive, and spiritual well-being contributing to integrative quality of life.

community participants. The resulting 32-item QoL survey fit with our model and demonstrated good psychometric properties. Physical, social, emotional, spiritual, and functional well-being, as well as integrative QoL, emerged as separate domains. Although we initially thought the physical domain might subdivide into physical health, functional activities of daily living (ADL), and physical fitness, physical fitness did not emerge as a separate domain but was subsumed under physical health. On the QoL measure, a simple 1 to 5 scale ranging from poor to excellent is used to rate the QoL statements addressing, for example, physical health and well-being (physical), ability to think (cognitive), and social relationships (social) (see Gill et al., 2011, for details and the full QoL measure).

After publishing the QoL survey, we continued research with several different samples using a test–retest design and comparing our QoL survey with other measures including the SF-36 (Gill, Reifsteck, Adams, & Shang, 2015). These results confirmed the structural model and subdomains as well as reliability. Our QoL survey also had slightly stronger psychometric properties than the SF-36 and had stronger correlations with related measures. Gill and colleagues (2015) concluded that when assessing QoL in physical activity and health promotion contexts, the QoL survey has the edge over the SF-36. Colleagues in Korea (Park, Lyu, Jang, Kim, & Gill, 2015) followed similar steps in developing and validating a Korean version of the QoL survey.

As we were developing the survey measures, we also took a different approach and focused on participants' views of physical activity and QoL. With several samples of community and student participants we asked open-ended questions: What is quality of life, and how is physical activity related to quality of life? We also asked those same open-ended questions in several focus groups from community programs. In describing quality of life, participants generally discussed all aspects of the model. As we would expect, participants cited physical well-being as part of QoL, but emotional and social well-being were cited just as often, with spiritual, cognitive, and specific mention of functional well-being also common. Notably, especially in focus groups, participants specifically discussed QoL as integrative and cited multiple dimensions. Of more interest to those of us in kinesiology were responses to the question about physical activity and QoL. We would expect people to cite benefits to physical health and well-being, and our findings confirmed that. More importantly, participants cited emotional benefits just as often, with social, spiritual, and cognitive benefits also cited (Gill et al., 2013). Participants in the focus groups explicitly described multiple integrative benefits.

These findings based on participant views have implications for programs and professional practice. Typical physical activity programs focus on physical fitness and training, using the common FITT (frequency, intensity, time, type) prescription model. Given that participants in most programs, like those in our research, are not focused on fitness training but on QoL, kinesiology professionals might be wise to design programs targeting all domains. As Ekkekakis and colleagues (2011) called for considering affect in exercise prescription, we suggest considering participants' multidimensional QoL in physical activity programming.

Application Point

Enhancing Quality of Life in Rehab

As an exercise therapist in a cardiac rehabilitation (CR) setting, your clients will be concerned about QoL as well as their physical recovery. Considering the QoL model, how could you enhance specific aspects of QoL through the CR exercise program?

Putting It Into Practice

Summary

Sport and exercise psychology addresses the relationship between physical activity and emotion in both directions. Early work focused on anxiety and performance. More recently, research has shifted to look at the reverse relationship—physical activity's effects on emotion. Application of the circumplex model with continued monitoring of affect state during exercise has revealed variations in patterns and deepened our understanding, with implications for professional practice.

Research on the role of physical activity in mental health and cognition has expanded greatly in recent years and continues to expand. That research confirms the benefits of physical activity for mental health, particularly for stress responses and depression. A growing body of research confirms both chronic and acute benefits on cognitive function and suggests that physical activity aids academic performance, but many questions remain. The continuing research suggests that professionals working in physical activity programs should consider participants' affect state and move beyond the focus on fitness training to target the range of psychosocial outcomes to increase adherence, promote lifetime physical activity, and enhance participants' QoL.

Review Questions

1. Describe the circumplex model of affect. Use that model to explain how affect might change over time for a person walking at a moderate pace for 30 minutes, and for a person doing a $\dot{V}O_2$ max test to exhaustion.
2. Discuss the research on physical activity in the prevention and treatment of depression.
3. Discuss the research findings on both acute and chronic exercise and cognitive performance.
4. Describe the QoL model. How does physical activity relate to QoL domains?

Recommended Reading

- Blumenthal, J.A., Smith, P.J., & Hoffman, B.M. (2012). Is exercise a viable treatment for depression? *ACSM's Health and Fitness Journal, 16*(4), 14-21. Blumenthal is a leading researcher in behavioral medicine and specifically on the role of exercise in prevention and treatment of depression. This article summarizes related research and offers recommendations for professional practice.
- Ekkekakis, P., Hargreaves, E.A., & Parfitt, G. (2013). Invited guest editorial: Envisioning the next fifty years of research on the exercise-affect relationship. *Psychology of Sport and Exercise, 14,* 751-758. Ekkekakis developed the circumplex model and applied it to investigate exercise and affect. This invited review summarizes research on exercise and affect and offers directions for continuing research.
- Etnier, J.L. (2014). Research . . . How fun is that? Interesting questions relative to the effects of exercise on cognitive performance. *Kinesiology Review, 3,* 151-160. Etnier is

one of the main researchers addressing exercise and cognition. This article, based on an invited senior scholar lecture, summarizes much on the related research as well as promising research directions.

- Gill, D.L., Chang, Y-K., Murphy, K.M., et al. (2011). Quality of life assessment in physical activity and health promotion. *Applied Research in Quality of Life, 6*, 181-200. doi: 10.1007/s11482-010-9126-2. This article presents the QoL model and QoL survey measure. Gill and colleagues (2015) include additional psychometric evidence and findings from that QoL survey.
- Hardy, L. (1996). Testing the predictions of the cusp catastrophe model of anxiety and performance. *The Sport Psychologist, 10*, 140-156. Hardy is a leader in applying catastrophe theory to anxiety and sport performance, and this article is one of the most readable and understandable presentations.
- Martens, R., Vealey, R.S., & Burton, D. (1990). *Competitive anxiety in sport.* Champaign, IL: Human Kinetics. Martens and colleagues began the move toward sport-specific constructs and measures with the development of the SCAT and followed with the development of a multidimensional sport-specific state anxiety measure. This book presents the background literature and information on the SCAT and CSAI-2 measures.

LAB

Exercise and Affect

This lab focuses on physical activity and emotion and specifically changes in affect state or emotion during exercise. Review the section on the circumplex model and exercise and affect. Then, for this lab, first assess your own affect state three times (before, during, and after exercise) using the Feeling Scale (FS) and Felt Arousal Scale (FAS) ratings. Then summarize how physical activity relates to your affect state, and finally, discuss how you could apply this information as an exercise instructor in a cardiac rehab program.

1. *FS and FAS.* First, you are to complete the FS and FAS ratings three times— before, during, and after an exercise or activity session. Each is a simple one-item rating (see Rating Scales Worksheet). Identify the activity (time, location, type of activity), and record your before, during, and after FS and FAS ratings. If you wish, you can graph your three sets of scores by creating a two-dimensional circumplex model (as in figure 12.1) and placing your three scores on the model.

2. *Summary.* Then, write up a summary describing your emotions in relation to your exercise or physical activity. How did your FS or FAS scores change over the session? Did you move through different places on the circumplex? In addition to your responses on this lab exercise, think about how your emotions change during other physical activities. How does exercise affect your emotional state or mood—at the time of the activity, immediately after activity, and later through the day?

3. *Application.* For this part of the lab, assume that you are an exercise instructor working in a cardiac rehab program.

    a. Consider participants' emotions. What emotions are likely in your setting? How might emotions or feelings change over a typical activity session? How might emotions vary among different participants?

    b. We want participants to "feel good" about the activity. What could you do in your program (interactions with participants, structure, environment, activities, and so on) to help participants feel good (experience positive feeling states)? Describe your general approach and include at least three specific suggestions.

Rating Scales Worksheet: Feeling Scale and Felt Arousal Scale

The Feeling Scale (FS) measures the valence dimension of affect—how pleasant, unpleasant, or good–bad you feel. The Felt Arousal Scale (FAS) measures the arousal or activation dimension.

Activity time: _____

Activity location: _____

Type of activity: _____

Feeling Scale (Valence, Positive–Negative Rating)

−5	−4	−3	−2	−1	0	1	2	3	4	5
Very bad		Bad			Neutral			Good		Very good

Felt Arousal Scale

1	2	3	4	5	6
Low arousal					High arousal

Record Your Responses

Estimate how aroused you feel during each part of the exercise session.

	Feeling scale	Felt arousal scale
Before exercise session	_____	_____
During exercise session	_____	_____
After exercise session	_____	_____

From D.L. Gill, L. Williams, and E.J. Reifsteck, 2017, *Psychological Dynamics of Sport and Exercise,* 4th ed. (Champaign, IL: Human Kinetics).

Stress and Stress Management

Chapter Objectives

After studying this chapter, you should be able to

- explain the benefits of practicing stress management for performance and wellness,

- identify several stress models and discuss their use in sport and exercise psychology,

- describe several stress management techniques, including meditation and progressive muscle relaxation, and

- provide examples of cognitive–behavioral approaches to stress management.

Emotions and stress are common and powerful in physical activity. Both participants and the professionals who work with them can use emotional control and stress management to enhance the physical activity experience. The emotion models and related research discussed in chapter 11 provide some guidance. Emotion is a complex process, and competitive anxiety has both physiological and cognitive components. Stress management or emotional control strategies may address either or both components at any stage of the process. Because optimal emotional states vary across people, tasks, and situations, the key factor for good performance, positive experiences, and overall health is the ability to manage stress. Many of the cognitive interventions, such as imagery, discussed in chapter 5, can also be useful in stress management. Other techniques focus more specifically on the physiological aspect of stress and emotion, while more comprehensive intervention programs combine cognitive strategies with physiological relaxation techniques.

Research on stress management does not allow us to say with certainty which stress management techniques are most effective for specific people in specific situations or to identify the best way to develop emotional control. However, the growing literature, combined with practical information from sport and exercise psychology consultants, provides guidance and a starting point.

Importance of Stress Management

We begin by exploring why it is important for participants to develop stress management skills. As discussed in chapter 11, some level of physiological arousal is necessary to mobilize energy and perform physical activities. A person who is below an optimal arousal level during a practice session, a repetitive workout, or a match against a weaker opponent might want to increase arousal. More often, however, participants want to lower arousal, and that is not easy. Competition or any performance evaluation increases anxiety, and typical warm-up activities increase physiological activity. When arousal increases beyond the optimal level, emotional control is needed. Most strategies for stress management involve relaxation.

In competitive anxiety, physiological arousal typically is accompanied by cognitive worry, and increased cognitive worry is associated with lower self-confidence and poorer performance. Tactics for increasing arousal may be useful in nonstressful teaching and practice situations, but those strategies need not have anxiety-provoking implications that increase cognitive worry. Even with physiological arousal, the benefits are limited. The autonomic stress responses (e.g., increased heart rate, sweating) have no functional value for most physical activities and can actually be detrimental. Stressing the cardiovascular system more than necessary can induce early fatigue and decrease endurance, and increased muscle tension creates problems.

In addition to the detrimental effects of overarousal, initial increases in either physiological arousal or cognitive worry can quickly create a negative thought–anxiety cycle. In a stressful situation such as competition, evaluation in physical education, or the presence of spectators in an exercise class, an initial increase in cognitive anxiety occurs along with the physiological changes associated with the stress response. Even slight changes, such as increased muscle tension, can interfere with coordination. Perhaps you are playing shortstop in baseball and bobble the first ball hit to you because you are thinking about the last time this batter hit one by you. Making that error increases cognitive worry and further heightens physiological arousal, decreasing your concentration and increasing the probability of more errors. Unless you can break out of the negative cycle by controlling your worry and physiological arousal, you're in for a long afternoon. Effective stress management skills are the key to breaking the negative cycle.

In sport and exercise psychology, research on emotional control and stress management often focuses on athletes and performance enhancement. However, emotional control can also enhance performance in physical education classes, recreational sport, and exercise programs. Moreover, many people engage in physical activity to help relieve stress. Teaching stress management in sport and exercise programs can not only enhance the activity experience but also build emotional control skills for life enhancement.

Managing Stress in Sport

How do you deal with stress and stay calm under pressure? Imagine you are coaching a high school basketball team. How might you feel stress? What thoughts or physical stress responses do you experience, and how would you deal with them? How could learning how to manage stress be helpful to you and the players on the team?

Beyond the challenges that stress presents in sport and exercise settings specifically, prolonged stress can negatively affect physical and mental health more broadly. Hans Selye greatly influenced our modern understanding of stress when he introduced the general adaptation syndrome (GAS) in the 1930s (Selye, 1936) to explain the stress response and its related effects. According to the GAS model (Selye, 1946), our bodies automatically have an initial physical reaction to a perceived stressor (alarm stage), and the "fight-or-flight" response (e.g., increased adrenaline and cortisol) is initiated to prepare the body to leap into action. If the experience of stress is not immediately resolved, the body begins to adapt or resist (stage of resistance). With prolonged exposure to stress, the body's resistance to the stress weakens (stage of exhaustion). At this point, immune function is compromised and individuals can eventually become susceptible to illness and the development of chronic diseases.

In his book *Why Zebras Don't Get Ulcers*, Robert Sapolsky (2004) explains the role of stress in chronic diseases like diabetes, heart disease, and depression. Sapolsky argues that people develop these diseases in part because the human body is not designed to deal with the prolonged stress placed on it in modern society. From an evolutionary standpoint, like zebras and other animals, humans were built to deal with more short-term episodes of stress (e.g., running away from a lion) that are resolved quickly in comparison to the chronic life stressors that people face today—which don't often have a quick resolution. In a report titled "Stress in America" released annually by the American Psychological Association (APA) since 2007, the APA (2016) contends that stress levels remain at higher than healthy levels among Americans. While chronic stress continues to be a key health issue, Americans typically do not engage in healthy stress management strategies, like taking advantage of the stress-buffering benefits of physical activity (Clay, 2011). Instead, many people compound the problem by indulging in unhealthy behaviors such as overeating, skipping meals, or misusing drugs and alcohol. To reverse this trend, several models and techniques outlined in the following sections can be applied to help people better manage their stress in order to enhance their performance and experiences in sport, exercise, and physical activity, as well as in their general health and well-being.

Stress Models in Sport and Exercise Psychology

Several sport and exercise psychology researchers have developed models that incorporate the key elements of the Lazarus emotion model (see chapter 11). The models are multidimensional, include physiological and cognitive components, start with a situation or stressor, highlight cognitive appraisal, and include recursive relationships in a dynamic process. Emotional control and stress management are key aspects of applied sport and exercise psychology. The models reviewed in this section provide a framework and guide for using techniques effectively to improve performance, facilitate injury prevention and recovery, promote exercise adherence, and generally enhance the physical activity experience for participants.

Smith's Cognitive–Affective Model of Stress and Stress Management

One of the earliest and most influential models in sport and exercise psychology is Ron Smith's (1980) cognitive–affective stress model. The model (figure 13.1) highlights cognitive appraisal, includes multiple interrelated variables, and involves a process that changes over time. The top half of the model is the same as the Lazarus model, discussed in chapter 11. External events, specifically demands and resources in the situation, may trigger stress, but appraisal is the key to the person's response. The emotional response has physiological and psychological correlates that affect behavior and consequences. Cognitive appraisal of the situation and coping ability interact with emotional responses within the central stress appraisal process, which then results in certain behaviors, particularly task and coping behaviors. The bottom half of the model shows how cognitive and relaxation skill interventions can be applied for stress management. Cognitive skills can be applied to the cognitive appraisal, whereas relaxation skills can be applied to the physiological response. As discussed later in the chapter, cognitive and relaxation skills are combined into an integrative coping response in Smith's stress management training program. Smith's model provides the basis for many stress management techniques used in sport and exercise psychology.

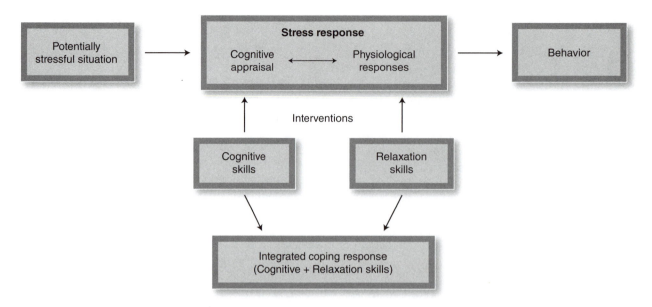

Figure 13.1   Mediational model of stress underlying Smith's cognitive–affective stress management program (Smith, 1980).

Adapted, by permission, from R.E. Smith, 1980, A cognitive-affective approach to stress management training for athletes. In *Psychology of motor behavior and sport-1979*, edited by C.H. Nadeau et al. (Champaign, IL: Human Kinetics), 56.

Key Point

Smith's (1980) cognitive–affective stress model fits with the Lazarus model and provides the framework for stress management training involving both cognitive and behavioral strategies.

Stress and Burnout

In addition to providing a framework for stress management, Smith's model has been adapted for burnout and injury in sport. Smith's (1986) burnout model parallels the stress model. Indeed, burnout is a form of stress. The Smith burnout model, as well as most related work in sport and exercise psychology, follows Maslach and Jackson (1986), who developed the most widely used model and measure of burnout. Burnout is a consequence of prolonged stress that may result in

- emotional exhaustion,
- depersonalization (distancing oneself from others), and
- reduced sense of meaning or personal accomplishments.

Maslach and Jackson's (1986) Burnout Inventory assesses these three dimensions. As in the Lazarus and Smith models, the burnout process begins with a stressful situation. As the person perceives overload, helplessness, or lack of accomplishments, the appraisal interacts with physical symptoms, including tension, depression, or fatigue, which results in the multidimensional burnout syndrome. Vealey, Udry, Zimmerman, and Soliday (1992) used Smith's model as a framework and supported the mediating role of cognitive appraisal in coach burnout. Kelley and Gill (1993) also supported the main relationships of the model. Specifically, satisfaction with social support, low experience, and gender (being female) were related to stress appraisal and perceived stress, which in turn predicted burnout.

Raedeke (1997) adapted Maslach's framework to burnout in sport, defining athletic burnout as a multidimensional syndrome characterized by emotional and physical exhaustion, reduced sense of accomplishment, and sport devaluation. DeFreese, Raedeke, and Smith (2015) reviewed the literature on athlete burnout citing the Smith (1986) and Raedeke (1997) foundational work. They noted that burnout has been explained from four perspectives: overtraining (discussed in chapter 4), stress (discussed here), and self-determination theory and sport entrapment (both discussed in chapter 8). Much of the related research focuses on stress and stress models and suggests reducing stressors and developing coping resources as interventions.

Raedeke and Smith (2004) used Smith's stress and burnout model as a guide to investigate the role of coping resources and social support in the stress–burnout relationship with age-group swimmers. They found that perceived stress, general coping behaviors, and social support satisfaction were related to burnout. As the models suggest, coping resources and social support mediated the stress–burnout relationship.

Key Point

Burnout is a consequence of prolonged stress that may result in emotional exhaustion, depersonalization, and a reduced sense of meaning or personal accomplishments. In several research studies, stress appraisal predicted all burnout components. Raedeke and Smith (2004) found that coping resources and social support mediated the stress–burnout relationship with age-group swimmers.

Stress and Injury

The psychology of injury has become a popular research and applied area within sport and exercise psychology, and that work is guided by emotion and stress models. Mark Anderson and Jean Williams (Andersen & Williams, 1988) first adapted the stress model to sport injuries and

rehabilitation. Their model (see figure 13.2) reflects the key aspects of Lazarus' emotion model and is similar to Smith's stress management model. Again, the process begins with a potentially stressful situation, but the key to the stress process (and injury) is the interaction of cognitive appraisal and physiological processes. As with the stress and burnout models, the stress response is influenced by personal (e.g., hardiness, trait anxiety) and situational (e.g., history of stressors, social support) factors, and also by coping resources. The authors have continued their work; models have been updated (Williams & Andersen, 1998; Wiese-Bjornstal, Smith, Shaffer, & Morrey, 1998), and researchers from both sports medicine and psychology have applied the models to investigate psychological aspects of injury.

The most current adaptations of the stress–injury models are biopsychosocial models that bring in sociocultural factors, and the models have been applied to injury response and recovery as well as injury risk. Brewer, Anderson, and Van Raalte's (2002) biopsychosocial model of rehabilitation adds sociological factors, as well as psychological and biological factors, influencing the stress and injury rehabilitation process. Wiese-Bjornstal (2010), one of the leading researchers in psychology of injury, explicitly advocated a biopsychosocial framework to advance our understanding of sport injury as a stressful event associated with complex risks, consequences, and outcomes. She presented the consensus view that

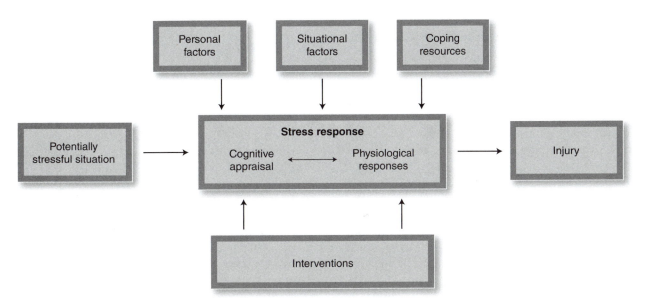

Figure 13.2 Williams and Andersen's (1988) model of injury antecedents.

Adapted, by permission, from M. Andersen and J. Williams, 1988, "A model of stress and athletic injury: Prediction and prevention," *Journal of Sport and Exercise Psychology* 10(3): 297.

a complex mix of psychological, sociocultural, and biomedical issues affects sport injury risk, response, and recovery.

Stress is central in all of the models. Thus, stress management is key in injury risk, response, and recovery. As the models suggest, that may involve cognitive and relaxation skills to deal with the stress response. Also, coping resources come into play as an antecedent affecting the appraisal process and subsequent stress response. Coping resources extend beyond cognitive and relaxation skills to a broader range of resources and strategies that people use to deal with stress.

Coping With Stress

According to Richard Lazarus and Susan Folkman's (1984) transactional model of stress and coping, stress results from an imbalance between the perceived demands of a potentially stressful situation and available resources to deal with those demands. Specifically, we experience stress when the pressure of a situation exceeds our ability to cope. Thus, the interpretation of the stressful event is more important than the event itself. Like beauty, stress is in the eye of the beholder.

In response to the perceived stress, people engage in coping behaviors, classically defined as "a process of constantly changing cognitive and behavioral efforts to manage specific external and/or internal demands or conflicts appraised as taxing or exceeding one's resources" (Lazarus & Folkman, 1984, p. 141). People cope with stress in many different ways, some of which are more effective than others. Coping responses are most commonly classified using Lazarus and Folkman's (1984) distinction between emotion-focused coping and problem-focused coping.

Emotion-focused coping involves managing the negative emotions that are associated with stressful circumstances. This way of coping might include emotional control strategies like relaxation or meditation, as well as less formal strategies such as watching a movie to get your mind off the errors you made in your last game or seeking emotional support from a friend.

Problem-focused coping involves efforts to actually address the problems that cause people to feel stressed. It includes strategies such as time management, goal setting, weighing alternatives, and developing action plans.

Problem-focused coping is useful when you can do something about the situation. Emotion focused-coping can be helpful when there is nothing you can do about the situation. For example, if you are feeling stressed about upcoming exams and assignments and also trying to fit in your exercise and time for your family, some problem-focused coping may help. You might set priorities, schedule specific times for your exercise, join a study group, or plan a family get-together after exams. Note that some emotion-focused coping might also be helpful in this case. On the other hand, if you just lost the tennis match after double-faulting on match point, you can't change that. Emotion-focused coping, even something as simple as a few deep breaths, will be more useful. When you can't change the situation, you can try to change your reaction.

Some scholars and measures (e.g., Endler & Parker, 1994; Kowalski & Crocker, 2001) include avoidance coping, which is a subscale in the Lazarus and Folkman model, as a separate, third form. *Avoidance coping* is basically not dealing with the stress. For example, students faced with the stress of multiple upcoming exams and other demands might give up trying and go out with friends. Substance abuse can be a form of avoidance coping.

Several questionnaires have been developed to measure the various coping strategies people use, such as the Ways of Coping (WOC) scale (Lazarus & Folkman, 1985) and the Coping Orientations to Problems Experienced (COPE) scale (Carver, Scheier, & Weintraub, 1989). Kowalski and Crocker (2001) developed the Coping Functions Questionnaire (CFQ), which assesses the three broad categories of emotion-based, problem-based, and avoidance coping, specifically for sport.

Key Point

When a situation is perceived as stressful, a person will engage in coping behaviors in an attempt to manage the demands of the situation. These behaviors may be categorized as problem-focused or emotion-focused strategies.

Research has investigated the role of coping in physical activity settings, particularly in stressful situations such as sport injury and recovery. Udry (1997) investigated the coping strategies used by athletes recovering after knee surgery. During recovery, athletes most frequently used instrumental, or problem-focused, strategies like seeking out advice from a health care provider to alleviate stress. Further, instrumental coping predicted greater adherence to the rehabilitation program. In another study, Johnson and Ivarsson (2011) found that greater negative life stress, higher anxiety, and use of negative or ineffective coping skills collectively predicted injury occurrence among Swedish high school soccer players. These findings and others suggest that stress and emotion models offer a useful framework for research and practice regarding sport injury and rehabilitation.

Coping With Injury

As an athletic trainer, you would be likely to encounter athletes coping with injuries in many ways. List examples of both emotion-focused and problem-focused coping strategies, as well as avoidance coping, that injured athletes might use. Be specific and note both effective strategies and strategies that are less likely to be effective.

Application Point

Stress Management Techniques

While tackling a stressful problem head-on through problem-focused coping strategies is often the most effective way to alleviate long-term stress, we sometimes find ourselves in situations that are likely to remain stressful regardless of our preparation—for instance, shooting a penalty kick at the end of the game to win the championship, recovering from an unexpected injury, or participating in an exercise class for the very first time. Several useful techniques can be practiced to help individuals better manage their emotional and physical response to stress in various physical activity settings.

Educational Stress Management

One simple but effective stress management technique is learning about anxiety and its impact on performance. Many performers mistakenly believe that high arousal is necessary to perform well and that they should prepare by psyching up. However, the optimal state for most sport and exercise activities is one of relaxed concentration. Carl Lewis, who demonstrated peak performance under pressure when he won four gold medals at the 1984 Olympics, described his running as follows: "When I run like Carl Lewis, relaxed, smooth, easy, I can run races that seem effortless to me and to those watching" (Callahan, 1984, p. 52).

Of course, Carl Lewis put in tremendous effort and worked hard to develop his skills. But at the time of competition, he reduced his physiological arousal to achieve a relaxed state. Athletes and exercisers must be alert and attentive, but they should also be free of excess muscle tension and worry. In short, they should be in control. Most stress management techniques aim to achieve this controlled, relaxed state.

Key Point

Many performers mistakenly believe that high arousal is necessary, but the optimal state for most sport and exercise activities is one of relaxed concentration.

Sometimes simply telling people about the importance of relaxation and control is enough to eliminate ineffective approaches. For example, a baseball player may try to deal with a batting slump by increasing tension and arousal, or a well-intentioned coach might put extra pressure on the athlete, thereby aggravating a negative thought–anxiety cycle. Information about negative effects of muscle tension and overarousal and about the importance of relaxed concentration may make participants aware of the desired psychological state and encourage alternative tactics.

Cognitive Stress Management Techniques

Simple cognitive techniques, such as thought stopping and many of the cognitive interventions discussed in chapter 5, can be applied to control anxiety and manage stress. Mahoney (1979) and Fenz (1975, 1988) both reported that successful performers who were able to control anxiety were more task oriented. Helping athletes shift their focus from negative thoughts to specific actions might well enhance performance. When recognizing a negative thought such as "My feet are rooted to the floor," the person might stop the negative thought and substitute a positive statement, such as "I'm relaxed and ready to move."

Similarly, attentional control strategies might help an anxious person direct attention away from worry and onto something else. For example, a basketball substitute waiting to enter the game might focus on the movement of an opposing forward along the baseline. As discussed in chapter 5, many athletes use imagery to mentally practice moves or routines, and imagery can also serve as a relaxation technique. Simply imagining a calm, peaceful scene may allow a person to mentally transcend a stressful situation and gain control. As in the process of counterconditioning, in which one response is substituted for another, it is impossible to be both relaxed and anxious at the same time. Pictures, audio, or videos may be helpful in prompting relaxing imagery. Mindfulness exercises are also becoming increasingly popular in the world of sport to improve focus and manage stress–arousal levels.

Relaxation Exercises

The most widely recognized stress management techniques work directly on regulating arousal. Relaxation techniques include simple breathing exercises, progressive relaxation, meditation, and variations of these.

Breathing Exercises

One of the simplest but most effective relaxation techniques is slow, deep breathing. Increased respiration rate is part of the autonomic stress response, and respiration is one of the physiological responses easy to control; controlling heart rate or body temperature is much more difficult. In his work with parachute jumpers, Fenz (1975) reported that respiration rate tended to come under control earlier in the jump sequence, whereas other physiological responses, including heart rate and palmar sweating, remained at high levels longer. This suggests that controlling breathing might be an effective way to initiate relaxation.

Breathing techniques emphasize slow, deep breathing. One technique is to breathe in slowly and deeply while counting to four, hold the breath briefly, and then exhale slowly for four counts. A consultant might help by starting the exercise and counting aloud. Many other relaxation techniques incorporate similar breathing. Both progressive relaxation and meditation include attention to slow, deep breathing.

Progressive Muscle Relaxation

Progressive muscle relaxation (PMR), originally developed by Jacobson (1938), is one of the most popular relaxation techniques used today. Although relatively simple, it requires practice. The technique involves the progressive tensing and relaxing of various muscle groups. An example is included with the lab at the end of the chapter. The underlying notion behind this form of somatic relaxation is that an anxious mind cannot exist in a relaxed body. When our muscles are tense and breathing is rapid, our minds interpret these physiological feelings as stress, but when we are physically relaxed and our breathing is calm, the mind follows suit.

Sport and exercise psychology consultants use progressive relaxation extensively when helping clients develop psychological skills. Typically, a consultant conducts several sessions, giving cues to tense and then relax specific muscle groups. The first sessions may take 45 minutes or longer, but as clients become more proficient, sessions become shorter as muscle groups are combined and as the tension phase is gradually reduced and finally omitted. The goal is for the person to learn to recognize subtle levels of muscle tension and to relax those muscles at will. For example, the exerciser in a spinning class who notices tightness in the neck and shoulders can then focus attention on those muscles, relax them, and refocus on the task.

People can learn PMR with the aid of instructions, handouts, or audio guides. Many athletes and exercisers already use versions of progressive relaxation. The 10K runner who shakes out his muscles just before the event and the basketball player who tightens her shoulders and lets them drop while preparing for a free throw are using a form of progressive relaxation. Readers who wish to know more about progressive relaxation should refer to the recommended readings at the end of this chapter.

Meditation

As a stress management technique, PMR involves relaxing the muscles and letting the mind follow ("body-to-mind" approach). Meditation techniques work the other way, relaxing the mind and letting the body follow ("mind-to-body" approach). When worries and anxiety fill our minds, muscles tend to tighten and breathing rate increases. On the other hand, when we are able to relax our minds, such as through mindfulness techniques like meditation, the body also begins to relax. Meditation generally involves a relaxed, passive focusing of attention and an avoidance of tension and strain. Often the person who is meditating simply focuses on breathing with no analytic thought, judgment, or special effort.

Key Point

As a stress management technique, progressive relaxation involves relaxing the muscles and letting the mind follow. Meditation techniques work the other way, relaxing the mind and letting the body follow.

Benson's (1976) relaxation response is an easy and popular technique. To use the Benson method, practitioners first find a quiet setting without distractions and then attend to their breathing. Benson suggests silently repeating any nonstimulating word with each exhalation to help maintain attention. Hanton, Mellalieu, and Williams (2015) suggest using the word "*calm*" or a word or sound of your choice. Meditation involves passive attention. Neither the mind nor the body is active. You simply attend to breathing, and when attention wanders, bring the focus back to breathing without straining or worrying about it. Hanton and colleagues (2015, p. 224) offer these directions for a meditation exercise:

1. Sit quietly in a comfortable position and close your eyes.
2. Deeply relax all muscles, beginning at the top of your head and progressing to your feet (or feet to head if preferred), and keep them relaxed.
3. Concentrate on your breathing as you breathe easily and naturally through your nose. With each breath out, silently say the word "*calm*" or some other word or nonsense sound.
4. When you finish, sit quietly for several minutes, at first with your eyes closed and later with your eyes open. Wait a few minutes before standing up.

Do the exercise for about 5 minutes at first and build to 15 to 20 minutes with practice. Don't worry about whether you are successful in achieving a deep level of relaxation—just remain passive and let relaxation happen. Practice the technique once or twice daily, but wait at least an hour after any meal, because digestive processes seem to interfere with the relaxation response.

Autogenic Training

Autogenic training, developed in the 1930s by Johannes Schultz in Germany (Hanton et al., 2015), is similar to meditation and is a form of autohypnosis, or self-hypnosis. As in meditation, attention is passive and one lets the feelings happen. However, autogenic training takes several months and proceeds through six stages as

On-the-Go Stress Management Techniques: There's an App for That!

With continued growth in the technological capacity of smartphones and tablets, learning how to manage stress is becoming easier and more accessible than ever before. Countless apps, such as Headspace (mindfulness), Relax Me (progressive muscle relaxation), and Breathing Zone (breathing), to name a few, can be downloaded to a mobile device and used anywhere at any time. Apps like these provide step-by-step instructions, audio, videos, or some combination of these, that guide the user through various stress management techniques. The advent of mobile apps is also making even complex techniques more accessible. Biofeedback, which is used to increase people's awareness and control of their bodily functions such as heart rate and breathing, has typically relied on electrical sensors and expensive equipment. Now, smartphones can provide some simple tricks, like reading your heart rate and monitoring breathing. These days there is little excuse not to incorporate stress management techniques into one's daily life, as they are literally at one's fingertips.

the person tries to induce sensations of warmth and heaviness.

Given the extensive time demands of autogenic training and its lack of direct connection to sport and exercise, it has not been the relaxation technique of choice. It is more popular in Europe, and for people who like the idea of hypnosis, autogenic training, with its focus on physical sensations, may be particularly appealing.

Cognitive–Behavioral Stress Management

The cognitive and relaxation techniques covered so far are all relatively simple techniques that require no special training. More elaborate and comprehensive stress management may be appropriate, especially when a consultant works with a person over a longer time frame. Some athletes have used hypnosis or biofeedback for stress management. These both require special training and extended time to be effective. The most popular stress management programs in educational and clinical psychology work combine behavioral relaxation exercises with cognitive interventions.

Suinn's Visuomotor Behavior Rehearsal Technique

Combining progressive relaxation and imagery exercises, psychologist Richard Suinn (1976, 1983, 1993) developed his visuomotor behavior rehearsal (VMBR) technique. As described by Suinn (1976, 1993), VMBR is a covert activity whereby a person experiences sensorimotor sensations that reintegrate reality experiences and that include neuromuscular, physiological, and emotional involvement. It involves two steps: relaxation training and imagery rehearsal. In VMBR, unlike mental practice, relaxation is an essential step that always precedes imagery. Practitioners use all senses to reexperience an event and actually feel as though they are in the situation, performing the activity. In VMBR, the images that are produced and the actions that occur are subject to control.

In his 1993 review, Suinn cites several case examples and research studies illustrating the effectiveness of VMBR with athletes. He notes that VMBR is a training tool that must be applied in accordance with known principles of skill acquisition, skill building, and skill enhancement. Suinn's use of VMBR with Olympic skiers was among the first and most widely cited psychological skills programs. The combination of relaxation and cognitive intervention remains a popular model for psychological skills training.

Smith's Cognitive–Affective Stress Management Program

Smith's (1980) stress model provides a guide for stress management programs in sport and exercise. Recall that in the model, the stress process begins with an external situation and individual characteristics and then adds cognitive appraisal and physiological components that interact to influence responses and behavior. Stress management may work in any part of the model, including the initial conditions. For example, youth sport programs that provide behavioral guidelines for parents or even spectators aim to reduce situational stressors. Similarly, exercise classes designed for specific groups, such as older adults, single-sex groups, or overweight adolescents, may reduce stress for participants.

Specific cognitive interventions, such as thought stopping or imagery, work on the cognitive component, whereas relaxation techniques focus on the physical component. Cognitive–behavioral programs, such as VMBR and Smith's cognitive–affective stress management program, include both cognitive and relaxation skills in more comprehensive programs. Smith's program incorporates progressive relaxation, emphasizes breathing cues as a relaxation technique, and uses either cognitive restructuring or self-talk as the cognitive component. The key skill in Smith's program is the integrated coping response, which combines relaxation with cognitive restructuring. Smith's stress management program is based on earlier work, particularly Meichenbaum's (1977) stress inoculation training.

Smith's cognitive–affective stress management training follows Meichenbaum's stress inoculation model with some variations, and Smith (1980) has specifically applied the model with athletes. However, the model fits anyone developing stress management skills. Smith's program typically follows these steps:

1. *Pretreatment assessment.* Before any training, the first step is to assess the situation and individual characteristics. For example, what specific situations bring out excessive anxiety? What physiological symptoms dominate? Some of the measures discussed in chapter 11 (e.g., CSAI-2, SAS) might be used, as might reports or observations.

2. *Treatment rationale.* The consultant and client develop a plan, and the consultant presents the rationale. This is the education phase, giving the client information and an explana-

tion for the training. Most sport and exercise psychology consultants emphasize that the client must believe in and commit to the training for it to be effective.

3. **Skill acquisition.** During skill acquisition, which continues over several sessions, the client learns the integrated coping response. Specifically, the person learns relaxation and cognitive coping techniques and combines them into the integrated coping response. Smith uses progressive relaxation exercises, and similar to Meichenbaum, emphasizes breathing as a relaxation cue. Cognitive coping emphasizes cognitive restructuring and includes self-statements similar to those used in stress inoculation training. Smith notes that for some people, particularly young athletes, simple self-instruction statements may be more effective than cognitive restructuring, and cognitive skills might involve either of those strategies.

4. **Skill rehearsal.** As with the application training step of stress inoculation, the person practices coping skills in stressful situations. However, here Smith departs from the stress inoculation model in advocating practice in situations that are more stressful than the problem situation. Smith aims to induce affect (hence the term *cognitive–affective*) that is greater than the person will deal with in actuality. For example, the person might imagine the worst possible scenario, develop all the affect (worry and physiological arousal) that accompanies that situation, and then use the integrated coping skills to control the affect. Training as a clinical psychologist is essential for these procedures. A typical educational sport psychology consultant would not attempt to induce extreme anxiety and affect.

5. **Evaluation.** No effective program stops at training, and Smith recognizes the role of evaluation in applied work. Evaluation is important in order for the client to determine whether training is effective, to make modifications and adjustments, and to maintain skills. Evaluation is also important for the sport and exercise psychologist to develop and refine skills and programs, as well as for the field of sport and exercise psychology to build the knowledge base and provide guidance for others.

Putting It Into Practice

Summary

Stress and emotion are everywhere in sport, exercise, and life in general. Stress management techniques are key psychological skills in many interventions that promote improved performance and overall health. Stress has cognitive and physiological components, and stress management encompasses both cognitive and physical relaxation techniques. Cognitive interventions discussed in chapter 5, such as imagery, are effective techniques. Physical relaxation techniques, like breathing exercises and progressive relaxation, are also effective strategies for managing stress.

Sport and exercise psychology consultants working with participants often use more comprehensive stress management programs, such as Smith's cognitive–affective stress management training. These programs typically include both cognitive and physical relaxation techniques within a training program that progresses from initial assessment and education through skill development and practice sessions, application of the skills in sport and exercise settings, and evaluation of the stress management program.

Review Questions

1. Identify several benefits of practicing stress management.

2. Define *burnout* and explain the role of cognitive appraisal in burnout models and stress and injury models.

3. Compare educational stress management techniques, cognitive stress management techniques, and relaxation exercises.

4. Describe progressive relaxation, meditation, and breathing exercises as stress management techniques, and explain how they could be used in sport and exercise settings.

5. Outline the elements of Suinn's VMBR technique and Smith's cognitive–affective stress management training.

Recommended Reading

- Hanton, S., Mellalieu, S., and Williams, J.M. (2015). Understanding and managing stress in sport. In J.M. Williams & V. Krane (Eds.), *Applied sport psychology: Personal growth to peak performance* (7th ed., pp. 207-239). New York: McGraw-Hill. This chapter provides a good overview of stress management techniques that can be used in many sport and exercise settings, including several body-to-mind and mind-to-body techniques.

- Sapolsky, R.M. (2004). *Why zebras don't get ulcers* (3rd ed.). New York: Holt Paperbacks. This book by Stanford scientist Robert Sapolsky provides an easy-to-read and witty explanation of the science behind stress. Sapolsky describes how stress is experienced differently in humans than in animals (i.e., why zebras don't get ulcers but humans do), the increased risk for certain chronic diseases resulting from prolonged stress, the link between stress and depression, and the application of stress management principles for coping with stress.

- Smith, R.E. (1980). A cognitive-affective approach to stress management training for athletes. In C.H. Nadeau, W.R. Halliwell, K.M. Newell, & G.C. Roberts (Eds.), *Psychology of motor behavior and sport—1979* (pp. 54-72). Champaign, IL: Human Kinetics. This article is more than 35 years old, but its presentation of Smith's cognitive–affective stress management model and his approach to professional practice is still a classic model for sport and exercise psychologists and consultants who want to be effective practitioners.

LAB

Using and Evaluating Stress Management Techniques

Relaxation exercises consist of both body-to-mind techniques (e.g., progressive muscle relaxation) and mind-to-body techniques (e.g., meditation). For this lab activity, you will first practice each kind of technique on your own and then apply this experience to describe how stress management techniques may be used in a professional setting.

1. Do a progressive muscle relaxation (PMR) exercise. You can use the example provided following this lab or search for other examples online, such as YouTube videos. Complete the pre- and postratings in the Evaluation of Relaxation Techniques form to rate your experience.

2. Do Benson's relaxation response exercise. To find examples that will guide you in completing this exercise, follow the simple steps provided in the "Meditation" section in this chapter or search online for related resources using the key phrase "Benson relaxation response." Record your pre–post ratings and overall evaluation using the Evaluation of Relaxation Techniques form.

3. Identify a specific sport- or exercise-related professional setting, such as physical education, physical therapy, or personal training. Describe how and why stress management might be helpful for the participants in this setting (why, when, how they could use it; what it could do for them). In your response, identify two specific techniques or exercises discussed in this chapter and explain how you might use them with these participants.

Progressive Muscle Relaxation Example

Progressive muscle relaxation involves progressively tensing and then relaxing muscle groups. As you are doing PMR, pay attention to the feelings of tension and relaxation. The following muscle sequence includes 16 muscle groups. The PMR exercise can be shortened by combining muscle groups. For example, you might combine the foot and leg muscles into one group. As you practice, you can shorten the sessions. The goal of PMR is to learn to recognize tension in any muscle and then be able to relax the muscle.

As you progress through the sequence, tense each muscle group for about 5 seconds. Then relax that muscle group for about 10 seconds while paying attention to the feelings in the muscle group.

PMR Sequence

1. Right foot
2. Right lower leg and foot
3. Entire right leg
4. Left foot
5. Left lower leg and foot
6. Entire left leg
7. Right hand
8. Right forearm and hand
9. Entire right arm
10. Left hand
11. Left forearm and hand
12. Entire left arm
13. Abdomen
14. Chest
15. Neck and shoulders
16. Face

From D.L. Gill, L. Williams, and E.J. Reifsteck, 2017, *Psychological Dynamics of Sport and Exercise*, 4th ed. (Champaign, IL: Human Kinetics).

Evaluation of Relaxation Techniques

Complete this form for each exercise in steps 1 and 2 of the Using and Evaluating Stress Management Techniques lab.

Name _____ Date _____

Technique used (e.g., PMR; Benson's) _____

Presession Ratings

What is your relaxation level before doing the technique? To what degree do you feel each of the following right now, prior to beginning your relaxation session?

	Not at all						Very much
Tightness or tension in muscles	1	2	3	4	5	6	7
General physiological arousal	1	2	3	4	5	6	7
Worry or anxiety	1	2	3	4	5	6	7

Take your pulse (heart rate) (e.g., at the wrist for 60 seconds) and record here: _____

Describe your general emotional (physiological and mental) state right now:

Postsession Ratings

What are your relaxation levels after doing the technique? To what degree do you feel each of the following right now, immediately after your relaxation session?

	Not at all						Very much
Tightness or tension in muscles	1	2	3	4	5	6	7
General physiological arousal	1	2	3	4	5	6	7
Worry or anxiety	1	2	3	4	5	6	7

Take your pulse (heart rate) (e.g., at the wrist for 60 seconds) and record here: _____

Describe your general emotional (physiological and mental) state right now:

General Evaluation

Provide a general evaluation and reaction to this session and the technique.

From D.L. Gill, L. Williams, and E.J. Reifsteck, 2017, *Psychological Dynamics of Sport and Exercise*, 4th ed. (Champaign, IL: Human Kinetics).

Social Processes

PART V

Earlier chapters focused on the individual in sport and exercise settings. In part V, we look at the bigger picture and view the individual in relation to others. Specifically, we consider how others such as teachers and coaches, therapists and athletic trainers, family and friends, and teammates and group members, as well as the larger social context, influence individual behavior, interpersonal interactions, and group processes.

Chapter 14 covers the broad topic of social influence, including the influence of others as spectators, participants, instructors, and leaders. Chapter 15 takes a more developmental view with a focus on aggression, social behavior, and positive youth development in physical activity settings. The last two chapters move even further from the individual to the social context. Chapter 16 addresses group dynamics and interpersonal processes, including leadership and team building. The final chapter considers social diversity, emphasizing gender and cultural relations as well as the promotion of cultural competence and inclusive physical activity.

Social Influence

Chapter Objectives

After studying this chapter, you should be able to

- identify ways in which the presence of others can influence sport and exercise performance,

- understand the concept of modeling and how significant others can affect sport and exercise behavior, and

- identify the three main types of social support.

Social influence, which was a central topic in the early sport and exercise psychology research of the 1960s and 1970s, remains prominent today because nearly all physical activities involve social behavior. Much sport activity involves competition, which is social by definition. Noncompetitive activities such as physical education classes, fitness programs, recreational sport, and rehabilitation exercise usually involve social interaction. Similarly, exercise instructors and sport leaders exert social influence when they give directions, watch us perform, and tell us how we are doing. We often perform in front of family, friends, and the general public. Classmates see whether we can do a cartwheel, and colleagues in the aerobic exercise group notice if we're out of shape. Additionally, we learn by watching others.

In this chapter, we consider the major types of social influence that have been addressed in sport and exercise psychology research. We focus on social influence on the individual, including the presence of others and the more active influence of social support and modeling (learning through observation).

Social Facilitation

Social facilitation is the influence of the presence of others on performance, including audience (i.e., spectators simply observing) and coaction (i.e., people doing the same thing at the same time) effects. Social facilitation is one of the oldest research topics in social psychology. Triplett (1898) found that paced times were faster (by about 35 seconds per mile) than unpaced times and that competitive times were fastest of all. He also found that children winding a fishing reel were faster when they worked in pairs than when they worked alone. Triplett proposed that the presence of others arouses competitive drive, releases energy, and enhances performance.

Expanding on Triplett's work, Allport (1924) coined the term *social facilitation* to refer to performance improvements due to the presence of others. Allport did, however, recognize that the presence of others did not always improve performance, but sometimes hindered performance.

Zajonc (1965) proposed that drive theory (discussed in chapter 11) explained these apparent contradictory findings. He posited that

- the presence of others, either as an audience or as coactors, creates arousal or drive;
- increased arousal increases the likelihood

that the person's dominant response will occur;

- if the skill is simple or well learned, the dominant response is the correct response and performance improves (facilitation); and
- if the skill is complex and not well learned, the dominant response is an incorrect response and performance is impaired.

Subsequent research with motor tasks (e.g., Martens, 1969; Martens & Landers, 1972) confirmed Zajonc's predictions: The presence of an audience or coactors creates arousal, which impairs learning but facilitates performance after the task is well learned.

Key Point

Social facilitation is the influence of the presence of others on performance, including audience and coaction effects.

According to Zajonc (1965), the mere presence of others creates arousal that affects performance. Cottrell (1968) challenged that, arguing that evaluation apprehension was the key to heightening of arousal and changes in performance. Neither drive theory nor evaluation apprehension has stirred much interest since the 1970s, and sport and exercise psychology research has turned to more social cognitive approaches.

Research on Social Facilitation and Physical Activity

More recent research in sport and exercise psychology confirms that the presence of others influences sport and exercise behavior. In a review chapter, Martin Ginis and Mack (2012) stated that the exercise literature is consistent in showing that people tend to exercise harder when they know other people are watching. The authors discussed this from a self-presentational perspective, suggesting that increased effort and behavior changes are a form of impression management. They conducted a meta-analysis of five studies meeting their criteria and found small to moderate effects on objective measures of effort (e.g., weight lifted). For example, Rhea, Landers, Alvar, and Arent (2003) found that people lifted more weight in the presence of an audience than when alone. Grindrod, Paton, Knez, and O'Brien (2006) compared the 6-minute walk distance in alone and group conditions. Both men and women walked greater distances in the group than when alone.

Feltz and colleagues (Feltz, Kerr, & Irwin, 2011) examined the Kohler effect with coactors who were virtually present. The Kohler effect occurs when weaker individuals in a group expend more effort and perform better than when alone. The effect may be due to upward social comparison, or alternatively due to social indispensability when the individual is especially aware of his or her contribution to the group. The Kohler effect presumably occurs with conjunctive tasks, in which a group's performance depends on the weakest group member. Feltz and colleagues (2011) looked at individual exercise performance under four conditions: alone control, coaction, additive, and conjunctive. Task persistence was greater in all three experimental conditions compared to the individual control. The conjunctive condition was no more motivating than the additive or coactive condition, suggesting that working out with a virtually present superior partner improves persistence on an exercise task.

In a subsequent study, Irwin, Scorniaenchi, Kerr, Eisenmann, and Feltz (2012) used a similar design to look at aerobic exercise with a virtual partner under coactive, conjunctive, and individual conditions. Performance was best in the conjunctive condition and worst in the individual condition, and the authors concluded that exercising with a virtual partner can improve performance on an aerobic exercise task.

The Home Advantage

One interesting and practical phenomenon related to social facilitation, the home advantage, lingers today. We often assume that the home audience provides support and facilitates performance, but the evidence is not so clear. Schwartz and Barsky (1977) first documented the home advantage with professional and collegiate men's team sports. Teams won games more often at home than away for all sports, and the home advantage was greatest for the indoor sports (hockey and basketball). Varca (1980) observed that home and away basketball teams did not differ on field goal or free throw percentage; instead, the home team demonstrated more functionally aggressive behavior (e.g., steals, blocked shots, rebounds), whereas the away team demonstrated more dysfunctionally aggressive behavior (e.g., fouls).

Courneya and Carron (1992) reviewed more than 30 studies, concluding that the likelihood of home teams winning ranged from 55 percent (effect size = 0.07) for baseball to 69 percent (effect size = 0.38) for soccer. They also noted that these largely descriptive studies did not address possible reasons for a home advantage. Carron and his colleagues (Carron, Loughhead, & Bray, 2005) concluded that location factors such as crowd density, unfamiliarity with playing conditions, and inconvenience of traveling contribute to the home advantage.

Continuing research confirms that the home advantage exists, but sometimes playing in front of the supportive home crowd is a disadvantage. Baumeister (1984; Baumeister & Steinhilber, 1984) argued that the opportunity to win a championship in front of the home crowd would increase self-consciousness and disrupt skilled performance. Data from World Series baseball and professional basketball confirmed Baumeister's views; home teams tended to choke in the final, decisive game.

The most recent work confirms the home advantage and suggests some moderating effects, but the research remains largely descriptive. Jamieson (2010) conducted a meta-analysis with an emphasis on potential moderators. A significant home advantage (home teams won about 60 percent of the time) was observed over all conditions, with some moderating effects; the home advantage was greater in earlier time eras (pre-1950) and in sports with shorter seasons. Allen and Jones (2014b) looked at the home advantage over 20 seasons in the English Premier League. They found a home advantage (home teams winning about 60 percent of the time) that was consistent over time, but the advantage was greater for low-ability teams than for high-ability teams. Jones (2013) reviewed the home advantage for individual sports, finding a significant home advantage for subjectively evaluated sports such as diving, gymnastics, and figure skating, but weak and inconsistent effects for other individual sports (e.g., tennis, golf). Allen and Jones (2014a), noting the consistently reported home advantage, reviewed research on the three main conceptual models: (a) game-location factors (as Carron et al., 2005, suggested), (b) protective response to territorial incursion, and (c) involuntary attentional shifts. They found some support for all three and advocated an integrative approach looking at how audience support affects physiological reactivity, attention, stress responses, and decision making.

Application Point

The Home Advantage

This coming weekend your local high school is hosting two important events: a soccer game and a tennis match. In both events, your team, the Hawks, is competing with its arch rival, the Eagles. The two teams have similar season records and have split (1-1) against each other. Your friends are convinced that the Hawks will win because they will have the home advantage. How do you respond when they ask you if you think the home advantage will help the Hawks win? Explain your response, giving your reasoning, and consider whether the home advantage will be the same for both tennis and soccer.

Social Reinforcement and Performance

Research on social reinforcement in sport and exercise psychology followed the same designs and is a variation of the research on social facilitation. In social reinforcement, audience members play an active (although limited) role, consisting of evaluative comments and actions such as verbal praise, criticism, and body language (smiles, frowns, gestures). Most audiences in sport and exercise settings provide social reinforcement, so it was logical to extend social influence to include this evaluative component.

Early social reinforcement work using novel complex motor tasks failed to find social reinforcement effects (e.g., Martens, 1972). Martens suggested that performers received better and more specific information from the task itself than from social reinforcement, which provided only redundant information that did not help improve performance. Also, on most sport and exercise tasks, and even the motor tasks in these experiments, most people want to perform well, and social reinforcement will not add much motivation.

To investigate the informational and motivation effects, Gill and Martens (1975) created four conditions: social reinforcement (praise for good scores, negative comments for poor scores); knowledge of results with precise error scores; social reinforcement and knowledge of results; and control (no social reinforcement or knowledge of results). Both social reinforcement and knowledge of results improved performance, and the group receiving both performed best. Surprisingly, the group with only social reinforcement performed better than the group with only knowledge of results, suggesting that social reinforcement provided sufficient information and possibly had a motivational effect.

Overall, the research suggests that social reinforcement may have an informational effect when other information sources are absent, and it may have a motivational effect when the activity is not intrinsically motivating. However, the effects were small, and the experimental situations were quite artificial. The limited influence does not imply that social reinforcement is undesirable. No studies showed detrimental effects, and social reinforcement has other benefits. Social reinforcement is related to social support and is a key component of effective teaching and leadership behaviors.

In a meta-analysis on social influence and exercise, Carron, Hausenblas, and Mack (1996) identified four sources of social influence, including family, important others (e.g., friends, colleagues), instructors and other professionals, and other participants. They concluded that social influence has a small to moderate positive effect (effect size from 0.20 to 0.50) on exercise behaviors, cognitions, and affect. However, the larger effects did not involve traditional social reinforcement or audience influences but rather support of family and important others. Sport and exercise psychology has moved well past the controlled lab experiments of the early research. The current work on social support moves to real sport and exercise settings and more complex social interactions.

Social Cognitive Theory

Social facilitation and reinforcement, home advantage, and social support help explain the emergence of behavior in different social settings and are consistent with Bandura's (1977, 1986) views on the process by which people learn social behavior. According to Bandura, the situation in which people find themselves affects their behavior. You may behave differently in the classroom than you do in the gym or differently with your parents than you do with your friends. Variations in the environment that change the way people view the situation can influence behavior. For example, shooting a free throw early in the game is different than shooting a free throw with the scored tied and no time remaining in the game. Behavior, though, is not merely a function of situation and the person in that situation. Rather, behavior, the person, and the situation constantly influence each other. A change in one affects the others.

With a specific focus on social behavior, Bandura posited that we learn social behavior through direct reinforcement and observational learning. Given the detailed discussion of reinforcement in chapter 7, we turn our attention here to observational learning. Observational learning is known by many names, such as imitation, vicarious learning, action observation, and modeling. In this text, observational learning refers to processes of observing. The term modeling and its derivatives refer to the act of demonstrating a behavior.

Observational Learning

People learn by observing others. Physical activity specialists such as therapists, teachers, coaches, and trainers rely on learners to learn by watching, and it is common for these physical activity specialists to model the behavior they want to see replicated. While modeling, observation, and imitation are necessary components of observational learning, they alone are not sufficient. Effective skill acquisition requires the transfer of information from the instructor to the learner (Horn & Williams, 2004). Learning requires cognitive processing of information from the observed behavior. This processing of information results in a cognitive representation of the action that serves as a reference of correctness by which learners can evaluate their behavioral outcome. Learning by observation involves a mediational process in which information processing mediates the relationship between the demonstration and the resulting learner behavior. According to Bandura, effective demonstration influences behavior, among other things, through a four-component mediational process called cognitive mediation theory (Magill, 2011). The first two processes, attention and retention, relate to learning or acquisition of skill. The second two processes, motor production and motivation, relate to actual performance of the skill.

The attention process involves the observation of a model and extraction of information gleaned from that model. Learning from observation requires attention to and accurate perception of the significant features of the modeled behavior. If your tennis instructor demonstrates a backhand return but you are watching the ball instead, you may not pick up the key elements of the stance, swing, and follow-through. Many factors, including characteristics of the model, the observer,

and the skill, can affect the attention process. Models usually present more information than an observer, especially a beginner, can process effectively, so observational learning can be enhanced by channeling attention to critical features of the demonstrated skill. Thus, the instructor should use cues or techniques to direct the learner's attention to key elements of the skill (Coker, 2015).

People not only must attend to the model, they must remember the modeled behavior. The *retention process* involves developing symbolic representations of the skill that serve as internal models for later action. Activities that aid retention, particularly rehearsal and labeling, can facilitate the development of this representation (Magill, 2011). For example, mentally rehearsing the tennis serve immediately after the observation may strengthen the performer's image of the skill. Good instructors are masters at giving just the right cues or phrases to help performers code the skill in memory. For example, dance students usually remember steps with phrases such as "step–together–step."

In addition to attending to relevant information and retaining the representation of a skill, performers must match their actions to the internal representation of correct performance. This *motor reproduction process* is not easy. First, people must have the physical capability to reproduce the action. Most people can watch Michael Jordan slam-dunk a basketball and retain a clear image of how to perform that skill but will never do a slam dunk. Even a capable learner does not immediately imitate a complex golf swing or a complicated gymnastics move. After the internal representation of a skill is formed and retained, performers self-correct and practice with an instructor's feedback in order to gradually match actual performance to the given image. Physical capability, the ability to retain appropriate responses, and accurate feedback are important considerations in the motor reproduction phase.

The final component in Bandura's model is the *motivation process*. We do not imitate everything we learn through observation. External reinforcement (reinforcement to the performer), vicarious reinforcement (reinforcement to the model), and self-reinforcement all help determine which behaviors we will imitate. When you see a teammate elude a defender with a particular dribbling move, you have incentive to imitate that move. Likewise, if your instructor praises you for getting the idea of a demonstrated serve, you will probably keep trying to do it.

Though originally focused on behavior (and though the preceding examples focus on behavior), observational learning is as powerful in transmitting values, beliefs, and attitudes as it is in transmitting behavior (Bandura, 1986). Furthermore, social cognitive theory acknowledges that people have personal control over their behavior. The mere observation of a behavior does not always result in a specified social value, belief, attitude, or behavior.

Key Point

Four processes are involved in observational learning. Two, attention and retention, relate to learning or acquisition of skill; and two, motor reproduction and motivation, determine actual performance of the acquired skill.

Sport and Exercise Psychology Research on Observational Learning

Skill acquisition and performance, development and execution of strategy, and enhancement of psychological skills that facilitate performance are the primary reasons people use observational learning. Research shows that observational learning is particularly effective relative to skill acquisition and performance and to psychological factors related to performance (see Ste-Marie et al., 2012, for a review). Motor skill acquisition and refinement effects have been found in sport training (e.g., Baudry, Leroy, & Chollet, 2007) and resistance training (e.g., Ram, Riggs, Skaling, Landers, & McCullagh, 2007) and in rehabilitation settings (e.g., Maddison, Prapavessis, & Clatworthy, 2006).

Key Point

Research shows that observational learning is particularly effective relative to skill acquisition and performance and to psychological factors related to performance.

Relative to skill acquisition, which is the most common reason for learning through observation (Cumming, Clark, Ste-Marie, McCullagh, & Hall, 2005), the effective use of models contributes to movement outcome (time walked, number of successful serves) and movement dynamics (e.g., power, velocity) (Ashford, Bennett, & Davids, 2006; Ashford, Davids, & Bennett, 2007). For example, Sakadjian, Panchuk, and Pearce (2014) examined the effects of observational learning on power clean form and performance in terms of time. One group of Australian rules footballers, who were inexperienced with the power clean, were taught this lift via traditional methods including instruction and feedback. In addition to these traditional methods, the other group watched a video of an expert model performing a power clean. The researchers found that while both groups improved, those who watched the model improved their technique faster than those who received instruction and feedback only. Moreover, they discovered that better technique was associated with greater performance in the form of power generation. While effective for both skill acquisition and performance, meta-analytic research shows that observational learning is more effective for movement dynamics than outcome (Ashford et al., 2006).

Though the findings are equivocal (see Ste-Marie et al., 2012), observational learning has also been shown to be effective with psychological skills, such as self-efficacy (see McCullagh & Weiss, 2001). Self-efficacy is of particular interest because Bandura (1986) theorized that one way in which observational learning enhances behavior is by enhancing one's self-efficacy, particularly for those new to a skill.

To examine the effects of modeling on skill acquisition and self-efficacy, Weiss, McCullagh, Smith, and Berlant (1998) used videotaped and similarly aged mastery and coping models when teaching novice and fearful youngsters to swim. Mastery models verbalized confident statements and demonstrated correct swimming skill performances. The skill performance of the alternating male and female coping models was only partially correct. Throughout the video, their comments moved from reflecting a "can't do" attitude, in which they verbalized doubts about their ability, to comments reflecting coping (e.g., "I'll try my best"), to comments reflecting greater confidence and a "can do" attitude. Results revealed that skill performance and self-efficacy increased for both the mastery and coping model groups. Research has also shown beneficial effects of observational learning on other psychological variables such as satisfaction and motivation (e.g., Clark & Ste-Marie, 2007). The efficacy of mastery models has been examined in the rehabilitation setting as well (e.g., Paquette, Egan, & Martini, 2013).

In addition to demonstrating the effectiveness of observational learning on skill and psychological development, Weiss and colleagues (1998) illustrate something about the type of models used. Although it is intuitive to assume that skilled models would be the best type of model because they would provide the most accurate cognitive representation of the skill, research has not consistently supported this assumption. This makes sense in that it is possible to watch an expert and think, "There is no way I could do that!"

Research has shown that performance can improve with models who are perceived as similar to the learner (e.g., Gould & Weiss, 1981; McCullagh, 1987). As Weiss and colleagues (1998) demonstrated, a coping or learning model can be effective. This is likely because fearful, anxious, and confident students related to a coping model who was similar in age and who was also just learning to swim. Age and gender are other important model characteristics to consider when using observational learning (e.g., Law & Hall, 2009; for reviews see also McCullagh & Weiss, 2001; Ste-Marie et al., 2012).

As in most observational learning studies, videotaped models were used in the studies highlighted in this section. While live models have been shown to be effective when teaching motor skills (e.g., Feltz, Landers, & Raeder, 1979), Lhhuisset and Margness (2016) found that videotaped models were more effective than live models when teaching new complex skills. Based on motor learning literature, they suggested that the live model provides too much information, distracting the learner from seeing the relevant aspects of the movement that novices need in order to reproduce the movement.

Models: The Self and Socializing Agents

The previous sections provide evidence for modeling effects. But just who are these models? Research has mainly focused on parents, peers, and coaches, the primary socializing agents who can influence cognitions, affect, behaviors, and overall self-concept throughout life. Research has also shown that we can learn from ourselves. In this section of the chapter, we discuss both the self and others. We begin with the self because the research is limited to modeling effects, and then we move on to discuss significant others as social influences.

Self-as-Model

Although observational learning is often thought of as observing others, modern technology provides for the opportunity to observe ourselves. Self-observation is thought to be especially effective because research in the physical domain has highlighted the importance of model similarity in performance and psychological responses. Using one's self as a model could involve still pictures, but the most common form of self-as-model is video.

Self-as-model can be broken down into two different categories: self-observation and self-modeling. Self-observation involves watching oneself execute skills and behaviors and then self-critiquing the performances. Self-modeling involves individuals watching themselves perform a correct or adaptive behavior of which they are capable. This can be accomplished via positive review, which involves editing the videotape to obtain a positive review capturing only the best performance out of many. Alternatively, the feedforward technique involves the removal of performance errors so people watch themselves performing behaviors beyond their capabilities.

McCullagh, Ste-Marie, and Law (2014) contend that self-observation is more appropriate for intermediate and advanced performers, who can interpret the information from the observation and use it for performance enhancement, than for beginners. With most complex skills, beginners are unable to detect and correct errors and need guidance from others (Coker, 2015). Self-modeling has been shown to be effective with beginners as well as more advanced performers, but the findings have been equivocal (McCullagh et al., 2014). Of the two forms of self-modeling, feedforward versus positive review, the feedforward technique has been shown to be more effective. McCullagh and colleagues suggest that confounding factors such as skill type, skill level, and intervention length should be considered in future research to better understand this.

Socializing Agents

As we move on to issues of socializing agents, remember that observational learning is one way in which socializing agents influence the cognitions, affect, and behavior of those around them, and they are one among many aspects within a person's socializing environment. Social influence has been studied from various perspectives, such as relationships, leadership, and motivational climate (parent, peer, and coach initiated). In this chapter we focus primarily on the relationship aspect of socialization. Socializing agents affect people's self-perceptions, attitudes, values, beliefs, and the behaviors of others (Fredricks & Eccles, 2005); and people can also affect the attitudes, values, beliefs, and behaviors of their significant others (e.g., Dorsch, Smith, & McDonough, 2009). Parents, peers, and coaches or teachers are important socializing agents who through social interaction shape others' behaviors and perspectives (for reviews see Horn & Horn, 2007; Partridge, Brustad, & Stellino, 2008; Sheridan, Coffee, & Lavallee, 2014). Researchers have also begun to examine siblings as socializing agents.

Parents

Parents play a significant role in the socialization of their children into sport and physical activity (see Partridge et al., 2008). Parents are often the ones who introduce and provide access to the sport experience, help to interpret their children's sport experience, and serve as role models (see Fredricks & Eccles, 2004; Sheridan et al., 2014). An example of parental socialization comes from Kremer-Sadlik and Kim (2007), whose analysis of videotaped family interactions during their children's sport participation and TV viewing of sports revealed parental influence via modeling, inquiry about their children's actions and thoughts, and instruction.

Parental influence comes from parents' beliefs, values, and attitudes about physical activity based on their own physical activity behavior. These are transmitted to their children and can affect how children perceive their sport experience (see Fredricks & Eccles, 2004; Horn & Horn, 2007, for reviews). In their review, Horn and Horn (2007) found evidence that parents' general belief systems do relate to children's belief systems and

their behavior. The more children perceive that their parents value sport participation, the more likely they are to perceive themselves as competent, value their own sport participation, and actually participate (see also Eccles & Harrold, 1991; Fredricks & Eccles, 2005). Support for this was demonstrated by Kimiecik and Horn (2012); they found that schoolchildren who reported higher scores (denoting that their parents exemplified values of confidence, independence, and doing one's best) reported greater perceived fitness competence than children reporting lower scores. Additionally, Ullrich-French and Smith (2006) found that perceived quality relationships with mothers and fathers predicted youth sport participants' perceived competence. Young females with parents they describe as warm, involved, and supportive have the best chance of heightened levels of self-esteem, sport enjoyment, and perceived physical competence (Atkins, Johnson, Force, & Petrie, 2013). Given the power of perceived competence relative to continued sport participation (e.g., Ullrich-French & Smith, 2009), parents can positively influence their children's continued participation in physical activity by fostering their children's perceptions of competence.

Children of parents who perceive them as competent and who have high expectations are advantaged, but it is also possible to hold expectations that are too high. Parents are aware that they are socializing agents for their children and develop emotional ties to their children's sport participation, which appears to strengthen as the children's participation continues (Dorsch et al., 2009). Longer participation in sport requires greater parental tangible and emotional investment (Sheridan et al., 2014). It may be this type of strong emotional attachment that leads some parents to have a more negative socializing effect on their child. Athletes identified the following as negative parent behaviors: being negative and critical, being overly pushy, being controlling, and overemphasizing winning—which resembles an authoritarian style of parenting and parent-initiated performance climate. Youth sport athletes report increases in parent-initiated performance climates over time (Le Bars, Gernigon, & Ninot, 2009). Regardless of the reason and although this is not the norm (Camiré, 2014), parents can play a negative socializing role in children's youth sport experience, which can result in athlete stress and withdrawal from sport (Sheridan et al., 2014) and inhibit athlete development (Lauer, Gould, Roman, & Pierce, 2010). For more on potential harmful effects of youth sport participation, see Bean, Fortier, Post, and Chima (2015).

Youth athletes have reported their preference for parents to focus on effort rather than outcome and not interfere with coaches or referees or draw attention to themselves during competitions. They also noted preferences for positive, realistic feedback about their performances (Knight, Neely, & Holt, 2011). One way to circumvent attrition from sport is for parents to create a mastery climate in which their pattern of behavior denotes the high value they place on personal improvement, mastery and concerted effort, and persistence. Schwebel, Smith, and Smoll (2016) found that parent-initiated climate as measured by the Perceived Parent Success Standards Scale was related to positive athlete outcomes such as lower anxiety and higher self-esteem. Le Bars and colleagues (2009) found that elite athletes who persisted were more likely to perceive a parent-initiated mastery climate. Harwood and Knight (2015) argue that parenting athletes requires a unique knowledge set, and they call for sport organizations to provide parent assistance to help parents gain a greater understanding of their role in their athlete's social network (see also Knight & Holt, 2014; Saelens & Kerr, 2008) and optimize the youth sport experience (see Bean et al., 2015).

Siblings

Parents are not the only socializing agents within the family. Parental influence is typically stronger in childhood, whereas sibling influence has been shown to be stronger in adolescence. Siblings also play a role in shaping attitudes, cognitions, and behaviors relative to physical activity. Siblings can be a positive social influence, introduce their younger siblings to sport, and serve as role models (see Horn & Horn, 2007, for a review).

Research in sport also reveals the paradoxical nature of sibling relationships (Blazo, Czech, Carson, & Dees, 2014; Davis & Meyer, 2008; Trussell, 2014). From interviews with community-level youth sport participants, Trussell found that siblings' involvement in youth sports influences sibling relationships and interactions and contributes to the meaning of their sport involvement. Youth sport participation both strengthens and challenges sibling relationships and their experiences in sport. On one hand, it serves to enhance their connection and shared sense of identity, and older siblings positively influenced younger siblings' sport participation. On the other hand, older siblings' teasing can diminish younger siblings' sport experience. From their interviews with National Collegiate Athletic Association (NCAA) Division I athletes, Davis and Meyer concluded that rivalry and closeness and displays of both positive social regard and disregard toward their sibling-athlete exists among NCAA Division I same-sex sibling competitors. Tension and negative emotion are particularly prevalent when younger siblings are seen as the better athlete.

Of all the primary socializing agents studied in sport psychology, we know the least about siblings. With the greater attention to issues of family (e.g., Saelens & Kerr, 2008), an increase in the number of studies on siblings, and Taylor and Collins' (2015) call for studying the family and family system as they pertain to talent development, sibling research at all levels of physical activity is ripe for future research endeavors.

Peers

The role of peers in sport and physical activity has a long history (e.g., Gill, Gross, & Huddleston, 1983). Children indicate that being with friends is an important aspect of their physical activity (e.g., Humbert et al., 2006; Salguero, Gonzalez-Boto, Tuero, & Marquez, 2003), that participation in sport is a way to develop friendships (see Smith, 2007), and that peer comparison is an important source of competence information (see Horn, 2004). Research has also shown that conflict resolution via dialogue with peers can positively influence children's moral development (e.g., Romance, Weiss, & Bockoven, 1986).

Despite the importance of peers in youth sport, the systematic study of peer groups, relations, or interactions in sport began only around the turn of this century with the work of Weiss and colleagues (Smith, 1999; Weiss & Smith, 2002; Weiss, Smith, & Theeboom, 1996). This work focused on peer relationships in the form of friendship and peer acceptance. Friendship is an interpersonal construct that involves having a close, mutual, dyadic relationship. Friendship has three dimensions: reciprocity and interaction, friend characteristics, and friendship quality (denoting the warmth of the relationship) (Smith, 2007; Smith & McDonough, 2008). Specific friend characteristics become more important with age (Weiss & Smith, 2002). There are six dimensions of friendship: quality self-esteem enhancement and support, loyalty and intimacy, pleasant play or companionship, things in common, conflict, and conflict resolution (Weiss & Smith, 1999). This early research revealed that youngsters perceive friendship in both positive and negative terms. For instance, children liked their best friends but recognized their faults. Participants liked the loyalty when their best friends stuck up for them and, not surprisingly, did not like to be betrayed. Betrayal included such things as a best friend "pay[ing] more attention to another friend" (Weiss et al., 1996, p. 371). Lastly, participants did not like conflict with their best friends, but they noted that conflict was rare and easy to resolve.

Peer acceptance pertains to peer group relations and is synonymous with social status (worthiness) and popularity (likeability) within a group (Smith, 2003). Peer acceptance is linked with athletic ability (see Weiss & Stuntz, 2004). Generally, good athletes are accepted by their peers.

Research on peer relationships in sport has demonstrated that peer acceptance and friendship quality are meaningful constructs in physical activity. Adaptive peer relationships have been shown to have a positive association with motivation, participation, and physical activity levels (see Sheridan et al., 2014). Smith (1999) found that adolescents who have close personal friendships within physical activity are more apt to like the activity, to be more motivated to achieve through hard work, and to be active participants. Additionally, those participants who reported greater self-worth were also more apt to have a sense of pride and confidence in physical activity endeavors.

Peer relationships are associated with competence-related beliefs as well as self-determined motivation, enjoyment, feelings of self-esteem, sport commitment, and social physique anxiety (Cox, Ullrich-French, Madonia, & Witty, 2009; Horn, 2004; McDonough & Crocker, 2005; Ullrich-French & Smith, 2006; Weiss & Smith,

2002). For example, Smith and colleagues (Smith, Ullrich-French, Walker, & Hurley, 2006) found that participants with an adaptive peer relationship profile characterized by perceptions of acceptance, friendship quality, and low friendship conflict reported higher perceived competence, enjoyment, and self-determined motivation as well as lower anxiety and self-presentational concerns relative to sport than those with a maladaptive profile. The maladaptive profile was characterized by low perceptions of peer acceptance and positive friendship quality, with high perceptions of friendship conflict.

The majority of the peer relationship literature has focused on benefits of positive peer relationships, resulting in a lack of understanding of the negative aspects involving conflict. Conflict is an important part of friendship (Weiss & Smith, 1999; Weiss et al., 1996), but conflict resulting in relational aggression that attempts to undermine another's social structure can lead to negative psychological outcomes such as fear of negative evaluation, feelings of loneliness, and attempts to avoid social endeavors (Storch & Masia-Warner, 2004). This is particularly true for females during adolescence (Partridge & Knapp, 2016).

In an attempt to better understand peer conflict, Partridge and Knapp (2016) interviewed 15 female high school athletes about their interpersonal interactions and experiences with their teammates. They discovered three primary sources of conflict: jealousy over skill level and relationships with boys, personal characteristics such as attitudes of superiority and importance, and influence of parents and the presence of cliques. Conflict manifested itself in the forms of indirect, sport-specific, and direct victimization. Indirect victimization was delivered through behaviors that circuitously conveyed the message that a teammate was not liked (e.g., dirty looks, rumors, laughing to make fun of her). Sport-specific victimization came in the form of excluding a teammate from participation, for example, refusing to pass her the ball. In cases of direct victimization, the message that a teammate was not liked was delivered overtly and to her face. Females on the team noted that conflict interfered with team communication, performance, and team cohesion; that it heightened competitive anxiety; and that it resulted in myriad negative emotional outcomes such as sadness, embarrassment, anger, and frustration. In terms of interpersonal relations, victims of bullying reported weaker connections with peers, whereas perpetrators reported weaker relationships with the coach (Evans, Alder, MacDonald, & Cote, 2016).

Bullying and victimization are prevalent social phenomena (Storch & Masia-Warner, 2004). Though less so than in the larger school setting (Evans et al., 2016), they do occur in sport and other physical activity settings (e.g., O'Conner & Graber, 2014; Shannon, 2013). When discussing ways to reduce conflict, female athletes in the Partridge and Knapp study acknowledged that conflicts sometimes got out of control because the men who coached them didn't understand female interactions; they said that explicit rules about how to handle interpersonal conflict (e.g., leave the conflict at the door) were best, and they appreciated team-building initiatives. In their review of literature, Smith and McDonough (2008) also alluded to team-building experience for promoting physical activity as well as peer modeling.

Other peer research points to the virtues of fostering a mastery peer-created climate in which improvement, effort, and support are valued (see Vazou, Ntoumanis, & Duda, 2007, for more details). Mastery peer-created motivational climates have been shown to positively relate to physical self-esteem, enjoyment, sport commitment, team cohesion, intrinsic motivation, and persistence (Garcia-Calvo, et al., 2014; Jõesaar, Hein, & Hagger, 2011; Vazou, Ntoumanis, & Duda, 2006) and negatively relate to burnout (Smith, Gustafsson, & Hassmén, 2010).

Key Point

Research has revealed both beneficial and harmful effects of peer relationships. To increase the probability of positive peer relationships, research points to the potential utility of explicit coach expectations, team-building exercises, peer modeling, and fostering a mastery peer-created climate.

Coaches and Teachers

Much has been written about coach leadership (see chapter 16 in this text) and coaching effectiveness (see chapter 7 in this text as well as Horn, 2004, and Smith & Smoll, 2007). Smith and Smoll offer the only coaching training program (Mastery Approach to Coaching [formerly Coach Effectiveness Training]) that is both grounded in and supported by research. Go to YESports (Youth

Enrichment in Sport) for more information on Mastery Approach to Coaching. Their training program has demonstrated positive self-esteem, anxiety reduction, enjoyment, team and coach attractiveness, and retention effects for youth sport participants (see Smith & Smoll, 2007, for a review). The coach is a powerful socializing agent who influences athlete motivation, participation, satisfaction, burnout, and psychosocial development and dropout (see Sheridan et al., 2014, for a review). In this section, we examine the socializing role of coaches and physical activity teachers through the lens of relational coaching and caring climates.

Relational Coaching Relational coaching involves the relationship between a coach and athlete that gives rise to performance and satisfaction. Interpersonal relationship is a key ingredient, and together with effective technical coaching, it results in effective coaching (Jowett & Shanmugam, 2015). It is in the coach–athlete relationship that coaches' and athletes' cognition, affect, and behavior are interconnected (Jowett, 2007). In their review, Jowett and Shanmugam identified four elements of a quality coach–athlete relationship: (1) interpersonal closeness, involving mutual trust and respect, caring and support, and attraction; (2) mutual commitment for a close and long relationship; (3) behaviors that are complementary or cooperative; and (4) the degree to which the coach and athlete perceive common ground about the nature of their relationship (co-orientation). According to Jowett, research has shown that the quality of the coach–athlete relationship is positively related to satisfaction with the relationship and positive athlete outcomes associated with affect, self-perceptions, motivation, and team cohesion.

Given the volume of research on relational coaching (see Jowett & Shanmugam, 2015, for a review), we discuss two studies to illustrate the nature of the concept. Davis, Jowett, and Lafrenière (2013) used attachment theory to investigate the correlation between coach–athlete relationship quality and satisfaction. They found that the higher the coach–athlete relationship quality, as perceived by both the coach and the athlete, the greater relationship satisfaction on the part of both parties. They also discovered a negative relationship between athletes' avoidant attachment style and quality of the coach–athlete relationship, which suggests that high levels of avoidant attachment (i.e., athletes' need for closeness, support, and protection with their coach was not met) may lead to lower levels of relationship quality. In this study, relationship quality was measured using the Coach-Athlete Relationship Questionnaire, which taps into the four elements of relational coaching.

Key Point

Higher coach–athlete relationship quality as perceived by both the coach and the athlete leads to greater relationship satisfaction on the part of both parties.

Those findings were supported by Davis and Jowett (2014), who examined athlete attachment styles, relationship quality, and athletes' well-being in the form of positive and negative affect. In this study, relationship quality was assessed in terms of social support, importance of the relationship, and conflict. The authors found that an avoidant attachment was negatively related to all three components of relationship quality, whereas a secure attachment style was positively related to perceptions of social support and importance of the relationship, and negatively related to conflict. In turn, relationship quality in terms of lower conflict was associated with more positive and less negative affect. Collectively, the research on relational coaching demonstrates that the quality of the athlete–coach relationship is important to those involved in sport.

Caring Climates   Caring climate is also a relational psychological construct. A caring climate is one that is perceived as inviting, safe, and supportive and one in which a person feels valued and respected (Newton, Fry, et al., 2007). Caring climates have been investigated in sport (e.g., Fry & Gano-Overway, 2010), exercise (Brown & Fry, 2014a), and physical education (Gano-Overway, 2013).

Research on caring climate in youth sport has demonstrated personal and relationship-related benefits (Fry & Gano-Overway, 2010; Newton, Fry, et al., 2007; Newton, Watson, et al., 2007). For example, Newton, Fry, and colleagues (2007) found that youth sport participants coached by individuals trained in a caring climate scored higher in their intentions to play again the following year and in empathy than those coached by individuals using traditional teaching methods. Fry and Gano-Overway (2010) found that youth athletes who perceived a greater caring climate

reported more positive attitudes toward their coach and greater sport enjoyment and commitment.

In the fitness setting, perceptions of a caring climate combined with a mastery climate were positively related to feelings of hope and happiness and physical self-concept (Brown & Fry, 2014b). As discussed in more detail in chapter 15, Gano-Overway (2013) has found perceptions of a caring climate related to middle school physical education students' empathy and appropriate social behavior. The research on caring climate in physical activity is still in its infancy, but the collective results of the existing research indicate the potential beneficial effects of this type of climate.

Interactive Influence of Socializing Agents

It is important to note that the findings we present in this section do not capture the dynamics or interactive effects of these socializing agents. However, there is a growing body of literature that considers the influences of peers and teachers (e.g., Cox & Ullrich-French, 2010), parents and coaches (e.g., Schwebel et al., 2016), and coach–athlete and peer relationships (e.g., Riley & Smith, 2011). As these studies begin to explore the combined and interactive influences of these socializing agents, their results, regardless of the specific socializing agents and relationships investigated, continue to support the conclusion that positive and supportive relationships with parents, siblings, peers, coaches, and teachers have multiple cognitive, affective, and behavioral benefits for physical activity participants.

Key Point

Parents, siblings, peers, coaches, and teachers are important socializing agents who, through social interaction, have multiple cognitive, affective, and behavioral benefits for physical activity participants.

Social Support

Social support is a familiar term, referring to the support of others, but more specific definitions are useful for research and practice. Some research has operationally defined social support as the number of people who provide support. With advances in research and conceptual models, social support is viewed as a multidimensional social process, and the quality of support is more important than quantity of social contacts. Here, we use Shumaker and Brownell's (1984) definition of social support as "an exchange of resources between at least two individuals perceived by the provider or the recipient to be intended to enhance the well-being of the recipient" (p. 13).

Types of Social Support

Shumaker and Brownell defined social support as a social influence process, which is consistent with current research and theory. Social support is prominent in the sport and exercise psychology research on social influence, and it is relevant in professional practice. Social support is common in sport and exercise and particularly relevant in athletic training and rehabilitation.

Social support providers include teachers and coaches, teammates, and group members and extend outside the specific activity setting to family, friends, and health care providers. Providers communicate social support through their behaviors, and behaviors constitute social support when the recipient perceives them as enhancing well-being. Sarason, Sarason, and Pierce (1990) argue that perceived social support is the key contributor to health and well-being.

Those social support behaviors take many forms, and several models and measures have been used to classify and measure social support. The most common way to classify social support is into these three broad types:

- Tangible (or instrumental) support—involves tangible or direct assistance (e.g., driving a friend to rehab, assisting a student with a task)
- Informational support—involves giving directions, suggestions, or advice (e.g., explaining how to do a specific skill, giving tips for exercising at home)
- Emotional support—involves expressing encouragement, empathy, or concern (e.g., comforting a teammate after a bad game, encouraging an exerciser who is having difficulty)

Some researchers have expanded or subdivided these three forms of social support. Wills and Shinar (2000) included emotional, tangible, and informational and also added two other forms of social support:

- Companionship support—involves participating with someone (e.g., being a running buddy, accompanying a friend to yoga class)
- Validation support—involves comparison to gauge or confirm thoughts, feelings, or problems (e.g., exercising in a cardiac rehab group)

The Rosenfeld and Richman (1997) model, which has been used in research with injured athletes, expands social support behaviors to eight forms:

- **Listening support:** Others listen to you without giving advice or being judgmental.
- **Emotional support:** Others comfort and care for you and indicate they are on your side.
- **Emotional challenge:** Others challenge you to evaluate your attitudes, values, and feelings.
- **Task appreciation:** Others acknowledge your efforts and express appreciation for the work you do.
- **Task challenge:** Others challenge your way of thinking about your work in order to stretch you, motivate you, and lead you to greater creativity, excitement, and involvement.
- **Reality confirmation:** Others are similar to you, see things the way you do, and help you confirm your perception of the world.
- **Tangible assistance:** Others provide you with financial assistance, products, or gifts.
- **Personal assistance:** Others provide services or help, such as running errands or offering expertise, to help you accomplish your tasks.

Key Point

Shumaker and Brownell (1984) define social support as "an exchange of resources between at least two individuals perceived by the provider or the recipient to be intended to enhance the well-being of the recipient" (p. 13). Most scholars agree that social support involves direct assistance (tangible support), advice (informational support), or encouragement (emotional support).

Those expanded models provide finer distinctions and have been used as the base for some measures of social support. Still, the three main types can subsume the expanded ones. Companionship fits with emotional support, and validation provides information. Listening, emotional support, emotional challenge, and task appreciation can all fit with emotion, whereas task challenge and reality confirmation provide information, and tangible and personal assistance are tangible support. Regardless of the specific details of the measures, most scholars agree that social support involves direct assistance (tangible support), advice (informational support), or encouragement (emotional support).

Measures of Social Support

Several measures of social support have been developed, including some specifically designed for sport and exercise settings. Most measures ask respondents to rate the availability of, or satisfaction with, different types of support. Two of the most commonly used measures in psychology are the Social Support Questionnaire (SSQ; Sarason, Levine, Basham, & Sarason, 1983) and the Social Provisions Scale (SPS; Cutrona & Russell, 1987). Both have been used in research in sport and exercise psychology. Also, the Social Support Survey (SSS; Richman, Rosenfeld, & Hardy, 1993), which was developed for social work, follows the Rosenfeld and Richman model and has been used in several studies with athletes.

As well as the general measures, several social support measures have been developed or adapted for research in sport and exercise settings. Chogahara (1999) developed a multidimensional scale assessing both positive and negative social influences specifically for physical activity with older adults. The three positive scales assess companionship, informational, and esteem (emotional) support. All three social support scales were positively associated with physical activity variables. The negative scales are not really social support (they aren't intended as or perceived as support), but they are reminders that not all social influence is positive or supportive.

Freeman, Coffee, and Rees (2011) also developed the Perceived Available Support in Sport Questionnaire (PASS-Q) based on social support in sport research. They confirmed the proposed four-factor structure of the PASS-Q, which assesses emotional, esteem, informational, and tangible support. In a second study they found that higher levels of all four types of perceived support were associated with higher self-confidence and lower levels of burnout in competitive athletes.

Sport and Exercise Psychology Research on Social Support

In one of the earlier studies, Rosenfeld, Richman, and Hardy (1989), using an earlier version of the Richman and colleagues (1993) measure, investigated student-athletes' social support networks. They found that athletes' support networks consisted of coaches and teammates who provided mostly task challenge support, friends who provided mostly listening support, and parents who provided mostly task appreciation support.

Sarason and colleagues (1990) summarized social support research using the SSQ, including research in sport. For example, Kelley and Gill (1993) used the SSQ to investigate the role of social support in stress and burnout with collegiate coaches. They found that satisfaction with social support was related to perceived stress and that perceived stress in turn predicted burnout.

Duncan and McAuley (1993) used the SPS to investigate social support, self-efficacy, and exercise behaviors with sedentary, middle-aged men and women. Social support had a direct effect on self-efficacy, which in turn predicted exercise behavior. Duncan and McAuley noted the importance of matching support to needs and monitoring changes over time. Several subsequent researchers have echoed those cautions. Different people have different needs for support, and needs change with the situation and over time. For example, the beginner in the cardiac rehab program likely needs more informational support than the long-term participant.

Research on social support within sport and exercise psychology has expanded beyond these early studies to investigate social support in a wide range of sport and physical activity settings. Considerable research draws from the health psychology research to consider social support in physical activity programs related to health promotion.

Social Support and Physical Activity

The influence of parents, coaches, and peers in youth sports is covered in other sections of this chapter. Social support is a key component of social influence in youth sport and in youth physical activity more generally. Ferreira and colleagues' review (2007) showed that social support from parents and other family members was positively related to physical activity in adolescents. Davison, Cutting, and Birch (2003) investigated social support and physical activity in young girls. They found that mothers gave more instrumental support, whereas fathers gave more validation support, and both types of parental support were related to higher physical activity. Mendonça, Cheng, Mélo, and de Farias (2014) conducted a systematic review of the research on physical activity and social support in adolescents. Based on the 75 articles that met inclusion criteria, social support was positively and consistently associated with activity of adolescents. More overall social support, as well as more support from parents, friends, and family, was related to higher physical activity levels.

Key Point

Based on a systematic review of 75 articles, Mendonça and colleagues (2014) concluded that social support was positively and consistently associated with activity of adolescents. More overall social support, as well as more support from parents, friends, and family, was related to higher physical activity levels.

The sources of support are different, but the relationships are similar with adult exercisers. Molloy, Dixon, Hamer, and Sniehotta (2010) found higher levels of social support at time 1 were associated with greater physical activity at time 2, seven weeks later, in Scottish university students. Kouvonen and colleagues (2012) found emotional and instrumental support at baseline related to changes in physical activity in British adults over a five-year period. Among those insufficiently active at baseline, those with high instrumental support were more likely to be sufficiently active at the follow-up. For those sufficiently active at baseline, those with high levels of both instrumental and emotional support were more likely to maintain activity at follow-up.

Just as parent and family support was related to physical activity with youth, spouse or partner support has been shown to be related to physical activity with adults. Gellert, Ziegelmann, Warner, and Schwarzer (2011) found that older adults who participated in an exercise intervention with a partner or spouse increased more in physical activity than those without a partner. Hong and

colleagues (2005) found that when spouses or partners in cardiac rehab had similar exercise levels, social support was related to exercise behavior; but when couples did not have similar exercise levels, no relationship between support and exercise behavior was found.

Exercise Leaders and Social Support

Exercise leaders and health professionals are important sources of support for physical activity. As discussed in chapter 16, social support behaviors are key components of effective leaders. Effective exercise leaders provide emotional support (e.g., encouragement), tangible support (e.g., assisting with exercise, providing appropriate equipment), and informational support (e.g., instruction on proper form) in the exercise setting and advice for exercising outside of the formal class.

Lox, Martin Ginis, and Petruzzello (2014) summarized the research on exercise leaders and concluded that participants who have socially supportive instructors report the following positive effects:

- Greater exercise self-efficacy
- More energy and enthusiasm
- Less postexercise fatigue
- Less concern about embarrassing themselves and trying new things
- More enjoyment
- Greater confidence in the instructor's capabilities
- Stronger intentions to join future exercise classes
- Better exercise adherence

Other health care providers, particularly physicians, can provide social support for physical activity, although few do so. Katz, Shuval, Comerford, Faridi, and Njike (2008) found that adults who received very brief physical activity counseling from a physician increased in physical activity 6 and 12 months later compared to a control group. Fortier and colleagues (2011) used a partnered approach with brief counseling from a physician and six added sessions with a physical activity counselor. Those with the added counseling had increased physical activity over a three-month period.

Social Support in Group Programs

Brawley, Flora, Locke, and Gierc (2016) argue that using groups in physical activity programs provides social support. Specifically, they advocate the Group-Mediated Cognitive Behavioral (GMCB) intervention model, which incorporates evidence-based cognitive behavioral strategies in a group setting. Their meta-analytic summary of results with the GMCB indicates that it is effective in enhancing adherence and physical function and at the social cognitive level. Of particular relevance here, GMCB intervention increases social support compared to control, and that social support is a key element of the program.

Social support is a key component of physical activity programs with clinical populations. As noted earlier, social support has been associated with adherence and positive outcomes in cardiac rehab settings. In a series of studies, Sabiston, McDonough, and Crocker (2007) looked at psychosocial experiences of breast cancer survivors in a dragon boat program. Their initial interviews revealed that the dragon boat program facilitated social support among participants, and specifically did that through common challenges and understanding of survivorship. McDonough, Sabiston, and Crocker (2008) interviewed participants at the beginning and end of a season focusing on body image and social support. They found more positive self-perceptions of strength and fitness, with a shift toward discussing body image in terms of fitness rather than appearance and weight. Social support was clear as the women reported connecting with others who understood the experience and sharing information.

In a subsequent report based on interviews at five times over two seasons, McDonough, Sabiston, and Ulrich-French (2011) explored development of social relationships, social support, and posttraumatic growth. They found four profiles of social and posttraumatic growth: (a) "developing a feisty spirit of survivorship" (progressive improvements in social relations, support, and growth); (b) "I don't want it to be just about me" (focus on supporting others); (c) "it's not about the pink, it's about the paddling" (emphasis on physical activity rather than dwelling on cancer); and (d) "hard to get close" (experiences that limit positive outcomes). The first two reflect clear social support and highlight the relationship as participants both received and provided social support, which was related to posttraumatic growth. The third profile emphasizes the unique contribution of physical activity in giving participants a more positive focus rather than dwelling on cancer, as often occurs in cancer-specific support groups. The final profile has more negative connotations, and serves as a reminder that some participants face barriers and that not all social influence is positive. The authors specifically suggested participative leadership and autonomy support (controlling practices had negative effects) as helpful strategies. The link to posttraumatic growth is a novel finding, and it suggests that building social support within physical activity is particularly helpful with similar participant groups.

Social Support in Injury Risk and Response

Social support is particularly applicable to sport injury and rehabilitation (Hardy & Crace, 1993). Health psychology research (e.g., Cohen, 2004; Shumaker & Brownell, 1984) indicates that social support plays a role in stress reduction and health promotion. Several sport and exercise psychology researchers have looked at the role of social support in sport injury and rehabilitation using the framework of the stress–injury models (Williams & Andersen, 1998; Wiese-Bjornstal, Smith, Shaffer, & Morrey, 1998) discussed in chapter 13. As those models suggest, stress plays a major role in injury risk, response, and recovery. Social support can serve a direct role in stress reduction, or it can have a buffering role in coping with the negative effects of stress (e.g., Cohen, 2004). In the stress–injury models, social support is a key coping resource in reducing injury risk and also in coping with stress in injury response and recovery.

Key Point

Social support can serve a direct role in stress reduction, or it can have a buffering role in coping with the negative effects of stress. In the stress–injury models, social support is a key coping resource in reducing injury risk and also in coping with stress in injury response and recovery.

Research in both sports medicine and sport and exercise psychology confirms the role of social support in injury risk, response, and recovery. Granquist and Stadden (2015) provide a nice overview of the research on social support and injury, along with recommendations for athletic trainers working with injured athletes. Athletes have many sources of social support, including coaches, family, and teammates, but athletic trainers are particularly important with injury.

Clement and Shannon (2011) investigated athletes' perceptions of social support from teammates, coaches, and athletic trainers following injury. Athletes perceived social support from athletic trainers as more important, and they were more satisfied with the support from trainers than that from coaches or teammates. Yang, Peek-Asa, Lowe, Heiden, and Foster (2010) looked at social support patterns before and after injury with a large sample of collegiate athletes. Male athletes had more sources of support, whereas female athletes were more satisfied with the support they received. The researchers also found changes in social support after injury. Athletes reported relying more on coaches, athletic trainers, and physicians and also reported greater satisfaction with support from friends, coaches, athletic trainers, and physicians after injury.

Bone and Fry (2006) looked at perceived social support from athletic trainers and athletes' beliefs related to rehab. They found that social support was related to more positive beliefs about rehab for athletes with severe injuries. They concluded that when severely injured athletes perceive that their trainers provide strong social support, they are more likely to believe in the rehab process. Rees, Mitchell, Evans, and Hardy (2010) looked at social support and injury response in high- and low-performance (level) athletes. With high-performance athletes, they found a direct effect of social support on injury response (less negative responses). With low-performance athletes they found a buffering effect in that the detrimental effects of stress were reduced with social support,

but with low stress, social support was relatively unimportant.

As Granquist and Stadden (2015) conclude, social support is an important coping resource related to injury, and the athletic trainer plays a key social support role for injured athletes. Athletic trainers can provide tangible support (e.g., personal assistance with exercises), informational support (e.g., information about the injury and rehab process), and emotional support (e.g., listening, showing care). Other sports medicine professionals in other settings would be well advised to follow those suggestions and incorporate social support strategies. Go to the application point and try to apply the research and recommendations on social support to working with an injured athlete. Remember to consider the needs of the athlete, and remember that needs and social support change over time.

Social Support in the Training Room

Application Point

Assume you are an athletic trainer working with a collegiate basketball player recovering from recent knee surgery. This is her first week in the training room with you. She plans to be back in full practice and competition when the league season begins, but she has four or five weeks of rehab before that. How could you provide tangible, informational, and emotional support for this athlete in your training room? Give specific examples of each of the three types. Then, assume that she has made good progress and is near the end of her rehab. Give specific examples of how you would provide each of the three types of support considering that her needs may have changed.

Putting It Into Practice

Summary

Social influence is prominent in sport and exercise, but we have abandoned the limited approaches of the early research on social facilitation and moved to more process-oriented and multifaceted approaches. Audiences and instructors are not passive evaluators or simply providers of reinforcement. Effective social influence can enhance physical activity for all participants. Social support, which may be emotional (encouragement), tangible (direct assistance), or informational (advice), is related to physical activity in both youth and adults, and social support is particularly applicable to injury and rehabilitation. Through modeling, people learn social behaviors for sport and exercise participation.

Most commonly, people learn through reinforcement and observation. We tend to act in a way we will be rewarded for, and we imitate those we wish to learn from. Parents, peers, and coaches and exercise leaders are the primary significant others in physical activity settings.

Review Questions

1. Define social facilitation.
2. Describe how Zajonc applied drive theory to explain social facilitation effects.
3. Trace the research documenting evidence of the home advantage.
4. Contrast social facilitation and social reinforcement.
5. Explain how modeling affects behavior by relating the concepts of attention processes, retention processes, motor reproduction processes, and motivation processes, and provide support for modeling effects.
6. Identify the four types of models discussed in this chapter and explain how they can influence physical activity–related cognitions and behaviors in young athletes.
7. Identify the three types of social support, and give examples of how each could be used in an exercise class.

Recommended Reading

- Brawley, L.R., Flora, P.K., Locke, S.R., & Gierc, M.S. (2016). Social influence in promoting change among older adults: Group-mediated cognitive behavioral interventions. *Kinesiology Review, 5,* 39-49. In this article the authors describe and summarize research using Group-Mediated Cognitive Behavioral (GMCB) interventions with older adults. They argue that social influence provided by the group is a key component of effective physical activity interventions. They also discuss translation of GMBC into real-world programs.

- Jamieson, J. (2010). The home field advantage in athletics: A meta-analysis. *Journal of Applied Social Psychology, 40,* 1819-1848. http://dx.doi.org/10.1111/j.1559-1816.2010.00641.x. This article presents a meta-analytic summary of the home advantage, with an emphasis on the role of potential moderators. The home advantage continues to be a topic of interest, but the research is largely descriptive.

- Jowett, S., & Shanmugam, V. (2015). Relational coaching in sport: Its psychological underpinnings and practical effectiveness. In R. Schinke, K.R. McGannon, & B. Smith (Eds.), *Routledge international handbook of sport psychology.* New York: Routledge. This book chapter introduces readers to the concept of relational coaching, overviews the research on coach–athlete relationship quality, and discusses a communication model for enhancing the relationship quality.

Social Influence to Enhance Physical Activity

This chapter brings together theories and research on social influence. For this lab, use the chapter material to develop a plan that uses a variety of social influence strategies to enhance physical activity performance and attitudes.

The local park and recreation department is planning its annual campaign to increase the membership. This year the department is particularly interested in targeting family memberships, and the director wants to ensure that worthwhile programs are available to families. As the exercise and fitness specialist, you've been asked to develop the Families Together and Active program. The primary goals of your program are to improve participants' health and fitness and to foster positive attitudes toward physical activity. Present your program to the director. Include a brief description of the program and explain how the program is designed to meet its goals.

Hints: Refer to the theories and research on social influence that guide your program. Identify elements of the program that should lead to positive attitudes and physical activity behavior, and explain why this is so; also refer to research that supports the effectiveness of the program. Be specific about how you would use social support and observational learning, keeping in mind the focus on families, and note how you would consider relationships (parent–child, peers, and so on) in your program.

Chapter 15

Aggression and Social Development

Chapter Objectives

After studying this chapter, you should be able to

- define aggression,

- explain several theories of aggression,

- understand the role of individual and social–environmental factors in antisocial and prosocial behavior, and

- understand positive youth development and how it can be encouraged in sport and physical activity programs.

Sport and exercise are largely social activities that involve social behaviors, and those social behaviors include both antisocial (e.g., aggression) and prosocial (e.g., helping) behaviors. In this chapter we first focus on aggression, the most visible antisocial behavior in sport. We clarify terminology, then cover theories and research on aggression. We then look at moral behavior, including antisocial and prosocial behavior, in sport and physical activity. Finally, we end on a positive note, considering social development in sport and physical activity programs.

Defining Aggression

Aggressive behavior is obvious in competitive sport as we see basketball players fight for rebounds or runners throw elbows and jostle for position in a race. Fights are common in ice hockey, and you may have read about more violent incidents at soccer matches around the world. Of course, not all aggressive sport behavior is this violent or egregious. Many forms of aggressive behavior are accepted and even promoted as part of the game.

Using the term *aggression* to refer to such a wide range of behaviors can cause confusion. Value judgments and emotional connotations further cloud our understanding. We encourage so-called good aggressive tactics, but we find violent aggressive acts shocking. We can better explain aggression if we do not think of aggression as good or bad but simply as behavior that we want to understand.

Before we discuss theories and research, we need to clarify terms. We can all agree that it's aggression when an angry batter rushes the pitcher after a close pitch, tackles him, and pummels him until he's pulled off by others. What about the pitcher who threw the pitch that nearly hit the batter? Is that aggression?

How do you define aggression? Take a minute and write down a definition that clearly delineates behaviors that you consider aggression. Now, let's see how well your definition works as you read about the playoff game between two youth ice hockey teams, the Blue Bombers and the Red Barons.

> Andre, one of the Bombers' top players, slams Derek, a Baron forward, into the boards to keep him away from the puck (a perfectly legal move). Derek retaliates by swinging his stick and smashing Andre in the ribs (not a perfectly legal move). When the

same thing occurs later in the game, Derek again tries to retaliate by swinging his stick at Andre, but Andre skates away and Derek misses.

> Viktor, Andre's younger brother and the least skilled Bomber player, gets into the game for his required ice time in the final minute. Viktor is defending the goal as Baron forward Monica skates toward it to take a shot that could tie the game. Viktor tries to take the puck away from Monica, catches his stick on her skate, and accidentally trips her. Missing her chance to make the tying goal and become the first girl to score a hat trick in a playoff game, Monica jumps up and yells at Viktor that he's a wimp who "should stick to figure skating." Liam, Monica's father and the Barons' assistant coach, sees his team's championship hopes end as the time runs out, and he smashes his clipboard over the bench.

How many of these incidents do you consider to be aggression? Does your definition clearly separate aggressive from nonaggressive incidents? Do you define legal tactics as aggression? What about accidental injuries? What if someone tries to hit you but misses? Can aggression be verbal? Is throwing a clipboard aggression? Not everyone will agree on the answers to all of these questions. Most people agree that when Derek swings his stick at Andre and misses, it is aggression, but Viktor's accidental tripping of Monica is not. Most definitions of aggression include this notion of the intent to harm. Baron and Richardson (1994) offered the following widely cited definition: "Aggression is any form of behavior directed toward the goal of harming or injuring another living being who is motivated to avoid such treatment" (p. 7).

In another review, Bushman and Huesmann (2010) more concisely noted that aggression is generally defined as any behavior that is intended to harm another person who does not want to be harmed. That definition raises several key points. First, aggression is behavior. It is not an attitude, emotion, or motive. Anger and thoughts might play a role in aggressive behavior, but they are not defining characteristics. Second, aggression is directed or intentional behavior. Third, aggression involves harm or injury. Unlike violence, which refers to aggression with more extreme physical harm as the goal, aggression can be verbal (e.g., yelling, name calling) or relational (e.g., intentionally harming a person's social relationships, inclusion within a group) as well as physical. Aggression involves living beings; smashing a clipboard or kicking a bench is not aggression. Finally, the definitions limit aggression to incidents in which the victim wants to avoid the harm.

Key Point

Aggression is generally defined as any behavior that is intended to harm another person who does not want to be harmed. That definition raises several key points. Aggression is behavior. It is not an attitude, emotion, or motive. Aggression is intentional, not accidental. The intent is to harm another person who wants to avoid harm.

Aggression can be categorized as hostile or instrumental depending on the end goal and the presence of anger (Bushman & Anderson, 2001). Behavior performed for the sole purpose of causing harm and done with anger is hostile aggression; both the intent and the end goal are to cause harm, and the behavior is often impulsive or reactive. Intentionally harmful behavior performed as a means to achieve a nonaggressive goal is instrumental aggression, as seen in the hockey player who slams the opponent into the boards to keep him away from the puck. The behavior is intentional, but the end goal is to get the puck. The distinction between hostile and instrumental aggression seems clear, but in practice it's not so easy to determine.

Theories of Aggression

The aggression literature is rich in theory. Because of its prevalence and social implications, people want to know why aggression occurs and how it can be controlled. Explanations of aggression fall into three major categories: instinct theories, drive theories, and social learning theories.

Instinct Theories

Instinct theories propose that aggressiveness is an innate characteristic: We are born with an instinct that makes aggressive behavior inevitable. The main proponents of this approach are Konrad Lorenz (1966) and others who assert that aggression is an innate fighting instinct developed through evolution. Much of this literature draws comparisons between humans and other species. Ardrey (1966), for example, discusses the tendency of animals to defend their territory with aggressive behaviors and notes that humans do the same thing. For example, do you feel an aggressive urge if a stranger bypasses all the empty tables to sit right next to you?

According to Lorenz, the fighting instinct spontaneously generates aggressive energy that builds up, like steam in a boiler, until it is released through an aggressive act. The more built-up energy there is, the more easily the aggressive behavior is triggered, and the more potentially destructive the outburst. Instinct theory suggests that the best way to prevent destructive violence is to ensure that people release aggressive energy in less destructive ways such as competitive sport. Lorenz asserted that

---

Is It Aggression?

You call it—violence, hostile aggression, instrumental aggression, or not aggression?
These examples are designed to help you become more familiar with the concepts.
Do not worry if your classmate has a different answer. The key here is to be able to defend your call knowledgeably.

- A basketball coach breaks a chair in protesting a disputed call.

- A pitcher throws a fastball that gets away from her and hits the batter.

- Behind by two strokes on the 18th hole, a golfer deliberately coughs as her opponent tees off in hopes of throwing her off her shot.

- A race car driver spins out of control around a curve and hits the car of a competitor, paralyzing the competitor for life.

- A boxer knocks out his opponent with a crushing blow to the head.

- A personal trainer yells at his client—"You're lazy and you'll never lose weight if you don't get to work."

- An athlete in the training room quickly jumps ahead of a teammate (rival for starting position) to grab an open spot so that she can get her workout done first.

sport is an outlet for aggressive energy, and Storr (1968) presented the following view:

> It is obvious that the encouragement of competition in all possible fields is likely to diminish the kind of hostility which leads to war rather than to increase it . . . . Rivalry between nations in sport can do nothing but good. (p. 132)

Although the idea that sport has cathartic value and allows participants to vent aggressive energy has appeal, the instinct theory with its venting model has no research support (e.g., Berkowitz, 1993; Bushman & Huesmann, 2010). Are athletes who participate in the most aggressive competitive sports the calmest and least aggressive people off the field? Perhaps some are, but this generalization would not hold across many comparisons.

Frustration–Aggression Drive Theory

Drive theory has more credibility among psychologists. The most notable drive approach is the frustration–aggression theory of Dollard, Dobb, Miller, Mowrer, and Sears (1939). They proposed that frustration always leads to some form of aggression, and aggression always stems from frustration. Frustration, which arises when a person is blocked from achieving a goal, creates an aggressive drive, which in turn facilitates aggressive behavior.

The proposition that frustration always leads to aggression fits with many of our personal experiences in sport, but there are many exceptions, and it is not widely advocated today. Current models emphasize situational cures, learning, and cognition.

Key Point

The frustration–aggression drive theory holds that frustration always leads to some form of aggression, and aggression always stems from frustration. That theory is not widely accepted today, and current models emphasize situational cures, learning, and cognition.

Aversive Stimulation Theory

Retaining some elements of frustration–aggression theory while also incorporating learning theory and cognitive psychology, Leonard Berkowitz (1962, 1989, 1993, 2008) proposed that frustra-

tion creates a readiness for aggressive behavior. Frustration is not a sufficient cause for aggression, however, and readiness for aggression is not a drive that must be released. Instead, learning and situational cues determine whether aggressive behavior actually occurs.

Berkowitz is one of the most productive researchers in aggression. In a typical experiment, a subject was angered or not angered and then given the opportunity to commit aggression against a victim, usually by administering shocks. Within that framework, Berkowitz examined several cues and situational factors. People who were angered usually gave more shocks, but situational cues exerted an even greater influence. Watching an aggressive film, the presence of aggressive weapons, and characteristics of the victim that were associated with aggression (such as being a boxer and having the same name as an aggressive character in a film) all increased aggressive behavior.

Social Learning Theories

Proponents of the social learning perspective, most notably Albert Bandura (1973), assert that aggression is learned social behavior that is acquired, elicited, and maintained in the same manner as other social behaviors. According to Bandura, we learn aggressive behaviors through direct reinforcement and observational learning. As early behaviorists demonstrated, reinforcement (as discussed in chapter 7) can teach and change behaviors.

Clearly, many aggressive behaviors are reinforced in sport. For example, fans cheer when a hockey player slams an opponent into the boards, and giving an opponent a hard elbow may keep that opponent off the player's back for the rest of a basketball game. Sometimes the reinforcement is less obvious. Perhaps the youth soccer coach and league rules discourage aggression, but when Alan gets home his parents tell him he did a great job intimidating the opposing forward with his tough, aggressive play. Bandura recognized the role of such direct reinforcement but argued that observational learning, or modeling (discussed in chapter 14), was more powerful with social behaviors.

In Bandura's classic "Bobo doll" studies (Bandura, 1965; Bandura, Ross, & Ross, 1963a, 1963b), children watched a model playing with various toys. In one condition, the model threw and punched the Bobo doll while making statements such as "Sock him in the nose" and "Hit him down," whereas another model did not demonstrate aggressive behaviors. Observing an aggressive model, whether live or on film, invari-

Key Point

Proponents of the social learning perspective assert that aggression is a learned social behavior that is acquired, elicited, and maintained in the same manner as other behaviors. According to Bandura (1973), we learn aggressive behaviors through direct reinforcement and observational learning.

ably increased the children's aggressive behavior. Seeing an aggressive model receive a reward or praise especially elicited aggressive behavior, whereas children who saw an aggressive model punished did not display as much aggressive behavior. When those same children were offered rewards for imitating the aggressive model, however, they displayed just as much aggressive behavior as those who had seen the aggressive model rewarded. Rewards and punishments to the model influenced the children's actual display of aggressive behaviors, but apparently all of the children learned the behaviors. Bandura suggested that the children made cognitive inferences about the behaviors and consequences, and those inferences influenced later behaviors. For more, look at the American Psychological Society (APS) website for an interview with Bandura on the classic "Bobo doll" research.

Unlike instinct and drive theories, social learning theory does not propose any constant drive toward aggression. Instead, people learn aggression through reinforcement and modeling, and their learning and cognitions influence subsequent aggressive behavior. Social learning theory is the most optimistic approach to aggression and violence. If people can learn aggressive responses to certain situations and cues, they can also learn nonaggressive responses to those situations. Whereas instinct and drive theories see aggression as inevitable, social learning theory suggests that aggression is learned and can be controlled.

Aggression and Sport

Sport and exercise psychology research on aggression has taken several routes. Some have examined aggression in sport as a catharsis that releases aggressive impulses and reduces aggressive behavior in nonsport settings. Others have examined the antecedents and consequences of aggression in sport. Still others have looked at aggression in relation to moral behavior.

Sport as a Catharsis for Aggression

Although many contend that sport acts as a catharsis for aggressive behavior, the evidence does not support such claims. As noted earlier, instinct theories support sport as a catharsis, and the original frustration–aggression hypothesis implies that sport acts as a catharsis by releasing the aggressive drive. Those theories are not major forces in today's aggression literature, and neither social learning theory nor Berkowitz's aversive stimulation theory supports catharsis. Both Bandura (1986) and Berkowitz (1993) argue that learning and reinforcement of aggressive behavior should increase rather than decrease the probability of later aggressive behavior.

Even though evidence indicates that aggressive sport has no cathartic value, participating in vigorous activity often seems to help when we are angry. Perhaps vigorous exercise is a nonaggressive way of venting that reduces the probability of further aggressive actions. Again, the research evidence suggests otherwise. Bushman and Huesmann (2010) summed up the research by stating that venting doesn't work even for people who believe in venting or feel better after venting; it has the opposite effect—it increases aggression.

Ryan (1970) compared the aggressive behaviors of people in a control condition to behaviors of those who engaged in vigorous physical activity (pounding a mallet), and they found no support for a cathartic effect. Zillmann, Katcher, and Milavsky (1972) compared people who were provoked and then exercised on a bicycle ergometer or performed a nonarousing task. Not only did the results fail to support catharsis, but the people who exercised behaved more aggressively than those who performed the nonarousing activity. Bushman (2002) asked angered participants to hit a punching bag with rumination (thinking about the person who angered them) or hit the punching bag with distraction (thinking about being fit). Then they got the chance to administer loud blasts of noise to the person who angered them. A control group had no punching bag. Rumination increased rather than decreased anger, and doing nothing (no punching bag) was more effective than venting anger. As Bushman and Huesmann (2010) concluded, exercise may be good for the heart, but it's not good for reducing anger; exercise increases arousal rather than decreasing it, and increased arousal is related to aggression.

Sport as Catharsis

A know-it-all friend explains to you that American football is such a violent game because players build up a lot of emotion in the off-season when they have no outlets. Football lets players blow off the excess energy that builds up in them. Thus, violence is not only inevitable—it's a good thing. Explain to your friend in a brief yet convincing way how this is faulty thinking.

Antecedents of Aggression in Sport

Why do we see aggression in sport? In line with Berkowitz's theory, sport and exercise often increase arousal and frustration, which can increase the likelihood of aggression. In line with both Berkowitz's and Bandura's views, situational cues, learning, and cognitions that prompt aggression are common in sport. Kavussanu and Tenenbaum (2014) note that athletes expect reinforcement for aggression; they cite both individual-difference factors and social–environmental factors associated with aggression. Kirker, Tenenbaum, and Mattson (2000) referred to the socializing environment, including game importance, fan reaction, and moral atmosphere of the team. For example, aggression is more likely when people perceive their teammates to be supportive of aggression (Stephens, 2001, 2004; Stephens & Kavanagh, 2003).

Michael Smith, who has written extensively about aggression in youth ice hockey (Morra & Smith, 1996; Smith, 1988), argues that violence is caused by the influence of the professional game. The hockey system encourages aggressive behavior as a way to advance to higher levels. Significant others (parents, coaches, teammates) praise aggressive acts, and the media rewards such behavior by focusing on violent incidents.

Individual-difference factors include personal expectancies, judgments, motivational orientations, and emotions. For example, players express less guilt for aggressive behavior in sport than in other contexts, and Ryan, Williams, and Wimer (1990) found that players who judged aggressive actions as legitimate engaged in more aggressive behaviors. Motivational orientation has been linked to aggression in several studies, with task orientation related to more prosocial attitudes and more ego-oriented athletes more likely to

view injuring an opponent as a legitimate behavior (Duda, Olson, & Templin, 1991; Stephens, 2004).

Stanger, Kavussanu, McIntyre, and Ring (2016) investigated the empathy–aggression relationship, which is well documented in aggression research, and they also looked at the mediating role of emotion and the moderating role of gender in athletes under high and low provocation. In line with previous research, empathy reduced aggression at low provocation for men and for women in both conditions. In addition, guilt mediated the effect of empathy on aggression at low provocation for men, whereas anger had no mediating effects. Those findings confirmed that empathy inhibits aggression, also confirmed that provocation and gender moderate the relationship, and further indicated that guilt has a mediating role.

Consequences of Aggression

Not much has changed in the research on the relationship between aggression and performance from earlier editions of this text. Although many athletes and coaches still believe that aggression on the field leads to better performance, research does not bear this out. To the contrary, hostile aggression may create anger and arousal that interfere with attention and performance.

Ruiz and Hanin (2011) looked at the impact of anger on performance. As with other research on emotion and performance (see chapter 11), they found large interindividual variability in anger intensity; the anger intensity levels associated with best and worst performance were low, moderate, or high for different athletes. For best performances, anger was perceived as increasing energy, whereas in worst performances, anger reflected ineffective generation and use of resources. Results also suggest that the negative consequences of aggression may extend beyond immediate performance effects.

Key Point

Although many athletes and coaches still believe that aggression on the field leads to better performance, research does not support this belief. To the contrary, hostile aggression may create anger and arousal that interfere with attention and performance.

Psychological Skills to Reduce Aggression

The bulk of the research on aggression and sport argues for reducing aggression. For example, Lauer and Paiement (2009) argue that the effects of aggression go well beyond performance and that the negatives far exceed the positives. They particularly cite high injury rates as a significant consequence, as well as the concern that aggressive behavior may transfer to other situations.

Gee and Potwarka (2014) noted that the increasing concerns related to aggression, anger, and violence, along with declines in youth sport participation, have put "cleaning up" competitive sport on the agenda for many sport organizations and programs. On the basis of the related research and theories, they offered specific recommendations for controlling aggression by helping athletes develop emotional control and cognitive skills. They first discussed strategies for avoiding retaliation, as provocation is a key trigger for aggression in sport, and recommended a three-step approach. First, identify triggers (e.g., trash talk). Second, help athletes identify their emotional state. Then, when athletes can identify their triggers and feelings of frustration or anger, provide them with skills and strategies to address these emotional states, such as self-talk or rehearsal training. As well as helping athletes develop skills and strategies to use in competition, Gee and Potwarka also recommended using strategies to deal with precompetition anxiety, which has been linked to anger and risk for aggression, such as relaxation and cognitive strategies discussed in chapter 13. Finally, they noted that as well as working directly with athletes, we can work at the macro level to change the sport context.

Lauer and Paiement (2009), drawing from the same literature, developed the Playing Tough and Clean Hockey Program to reduce aggressive behavior in youth hockey. In the program, tough and clean hockey was defined as playing physical (tough) hockey within the rules (clean). Of particular relevance for this chapter, playing within the rules without intent to harm or injure an opponent (aggression) was emphasized. The authors focused on reducing aggressive responses to provocation, using emotional and cognitive skills much as suggested by Gee and Potwarka (2014), and they implemented the program over a 10-week period with three youth hockey players identified as often exhibiting aggressive behavior. Their results showed improvements for all three players, particularly in retaliatory and major aggressive acts.

The Playing Tough and Clean Hockey Program was based on relevant theory and research, well planned, and conducted over an extended time, but the key technique was the relatively simple 3 Rs routine. The 3 Rs routine is a great example of Psychological Skills Training (PST). Psychological Skills Training typically involves combining cognitive skills, such as self-talk or imagery, with emotional control skills, such as progressive muscle relaxation, over an extended time. In this case, self-talk and cues were combined with deep breathing in the 3 Rs routine. Following are the stages and techniques in the 3 Rs.

1. **Respond.** The first R is respond. As the authors told the hockey players, you will be provoked and feel frustrated. Rather than try to repress the emotion, do respond or react—feel the emotion, but then let it go. They worked with each player to identify a cue word or trigger (e.g., "ignore it") to use in the first step.

2. **Relax.** The second R is relax. After responding, feeling the emotion, and then letting it go, the next step is to control the emotional response. As we learned in chapter 13, that can be as simple as taking a slow, deep, relaxing breath. This is what was used in the program, a centering breath along with a cue (e.g., "calm").

3. **Refocus.** The final R is refocus—get back on task, back in the game. Again, a cue or trigger (e.g., "play your game") was used.

Lauer and Paiement (2009) worked with each athlete to develop his own cues and routines and then practice using the 3 Rs in program sessions and on the ice in practices and games. The technique is relatively simple, but as with any skill, practice is important. In the actual event, things

Key Point

The 3 Rs routine (Lauer & Paiement, 2009) is an example of Psychological Skills Training (PST). Psychological Skills Training typically involves combining cognitive skills, such as goal setting, self-talk, or imagery, with emotional control skills, such as progressive muscle relaxation or meditative relaxation, over an extended time.

move quickly, and the routine must be well learned and relatively automatic to be effective. The 3 Rs routine can be adapted and used effectively in many sport and physical activity settings. To illustrate, go to the Application Point and develop a 3 Rs routine that you could use with a rehab client.

3 Rs in Rehab

Assume you are an athletic trainer working with a soccer player in rehab. She is in the first week of a six- to eight-week rehab program and is eager to get back with her team. This is her first major rehab, and she gets angry and frustrated in sessions when she can't do exercises. Thus, she doesn't complete exercises or make progress.

As the trainer, how could you apply the 3 Rs to help the soccer player control her emotion and get through rehab successfully? Explain how each of the 3 Rs could be applied. Be specific and give details on the 3 Rs routine.

Moral Behavior in Sport and Physical Activity

Most current research on aggression in sport and exercise psychology extends to a broader range of moral behavior, emphasizing developmental, individual, and situational influences. Two major lines of research are those of Bredemeier and Shields, who take a developmental approach, and Kavussanu and colleagues' extensive research on aggression and moral behavior in sport.

As discussed by Kavussanu (2014), moral behavior comprises behaviors in the moral domain that have consequences for others—moral behaviors are social behaviors. Moral behaviors may be antisocial, that is, behaviors intended to harm or disadvantage others, or prosocial—behaviors intended to help or benefit others. Clearly, aggression is antisocial behavior. Antisocial behavior extends beyond aggression to include behaviors that do not cause physical or psychological harm to others, such as faking an injury to gain advantage. Antisocial and prosocial behavior are not opposites on a continuum, but they are relatively independent, suggesting that the developmental pathways and antecedents may be different. In this section we review the literature related to moral development and the factors that influence moral behavior in sport and physical activity.

Key Point

As discussed by Kavussanu (2014), moral behavior comprises behaviors in the moral domain that have consequences for others; moral behaviors are social behaviors. Moral behaviors may be antisocial, that is, behaviors intended to harm or disadvantage others, or prosocial, behaviors intended to help or benefit others.

Developmental Approach to Morality and Aggression in Sport

Bredemeier and Shields (1995, 2014; Shields & Bredemeier, 2014) focused on the development of aggression and moral behavior and applied Haan's (1991) interactional model, which emphasizes moral reasoning and balancing interests of self and others. That is, people reason about why they act as they do, and as they mature, moral reasoning becomes more comprehensive and complex, typically moving from self-concern to other-concern to principled social welfare. However, the context of sport may promote a morality different from that of everyday life.

Bredemeier and Shields (1986, 2014) proposed a theory of "*game reasoning*," or bracketed morality. Game reasoning suggests that athletes use a different (and lower) stage of reasoning in sport than they do in other contexts, and research supports that contention. Bredemeier and Shields (1986, 1995) asked high school and collegiate basketball players, swimmers, and nonathletes to respond to hypothetical dilemmas in sport and daily life and found that the athletes used lower levels of moral reasoning in sport.

This is not to say that sport is free from moral confines. Although bracketed from everyday life, sport does call for moral reasoning and action. The developmental level of moral reasoning is one factor, but moral behavior in sport and physical activity is also influenced by the social context.

Importantly, Shields and Bredemeier (2014) apply the theories and research to promote moral reasoning and reduce aggressive, antisocial behavior. Specifically, they call for dialogue as a key strategy. That is, coaches, youth leaders, or parents should engage participants in discussion about moral issues to promote higher levels of reasoning and reduce antisocial behavior.

Antecedents of Moral Behavior in Sport and Physical Activity

Maria Kavussanu and colleagues have conducted much of the major research on aggression and moral behavior in sport and exercise psychology (e.g., Kavussanu, Stamp, Slade, & Ring, 2009). That research has identified both individual and situational factors as antecedents of aggressive behavior and also includes the development of a measure, the Prosocial and Antisocial Behavior in Sport Scale (Kavussanu & Boardley, 2009; Kavussanu, Stanger, & Boardley, 2013). Kaye and Hoar (2015) subsequently developed the Antisocial Sport Behaviors Survey to assess the many antisocial behaviors in sport.

The main individual factors that have been identified in the research are goal orientations and moral disengagement. As discussed in chapter 9, goal orientation refers to the extent to which an individual is task oriented (self-referenced, focusing on mastery and improvement) or ego oriented (focused on comparison to others and competitive outcomes). Generally, research indicates that those who are high in task orientation are more likely to engage in prosocial behaviors whereas those high in ego orientation are more likely to engage in antisocial behaviors.

Moral disengagement refers to cognitive mechanisms that people use to justify antisocial behavior without experiencing negative emotions (e.g., guilt). For example, athletes might displace responsibility to the coach, blame the victim, or downplay the negative consequences. More specifically, moral disengagement refers to the eight mechanisms identified by Bandura (1991): moral justification, euphemistic labeling, advantageous comparison, displacement of responsibility, diffusion of responsibility, distortion of consequences, dehumanization, and attribution of blame. As Boardley (2014) explains, all are present in sport, and the combined use of multiple mechanisms can increase the overall effect.

Of course, moral disengagement is related to antisocial behavior. For example, Corrion, Long, Smith, and d'Arripe-Longueville (2009) investigated moral disengagement with adult elite basketball and tae kwon do athletes. They found that the athletes used all eight forms of moral disengagement as reasons for their transgressive behavior, with displacement of responsibility, attribution of blame, distortion of consequences, and diffusion of responsibility used far more frequently than the other mechanisms. Board-ley and Kavussanu (2007, 2011) have reviewed the research and developed a measure of moral disengagement in sport. d'Arripe-Longueville, Corrion, Scoffier, Roussel, and Chalabaev (2010) used that measure and found that moral disengagement mediated the relationship between self-regulatory efficacy (confidence in ability to regulate negative emotion) and both cheating and prosocial behavior.

Key Point

Moral disengagement refers to cognitive mechanisms, and specifically the eight mechanisms identified by Bandura (1991) that people use to justify antisocial behavior. Corrion and colleagues (2009) found that athletes use moral disengagement mechanisms to explain their antisocial behaviors.

Shields, Funk, and Bredemeier (2015) examined predictors of moral disengagement with a large sample of university athletes. They found that gender, contesting orientation, moral identity, and one form of moral attentiveness predicted moral disengagement. And, as bracketed morality suggests, moral attentiveness was lower in sport than in everyday life.

The social environment also has a strong influence on moral behavior. As Bredemeier and Shields' (1986, 2014) concept of game reasoning suggests, the sport context clearly has unique moral features. For example, sport competition has opposing teams and pursuit of self-interest is expected, and moral responsibility is concentrated in the roles of officials.

Kavussanu, Boardley, Sagar, and Ring (2013) investigated bracketed morality with male and female participants in sport and university contexts. They found higher prosocial behavior toward teammates and higher antisocial behavior toward opponents in sport than toward other students. They further found that effects were partially mediated by moral disengagement and ego orientation. Kavussanu and Ring (2016) also found students more likely to act antisocially and less likely to act prosocially toward opponents in sport than toward other students. The difference for antisocial behavior was fully mediated by moral judgment, whereas the difference for prosocial behavior was partially mediated. The authors suggested a more nuanced aspect to bracketed morality that considers in-group loyalty in and out of the sport context.

Motivational climate is one environmental factor that has received research attention. As discussed in chapter 9, motivational climate parallels goal orientation, but climate is environmental and typically is created by coaches, teachers, or parents. Competitive outcomes are emphasized in a performance climate, whereas mastery and improvement are emphasized in a mastery climate. Research shows that a mastery climate is associated with prosocial behavior and performance climate with antisocial behavior. Although most sport and exercise psychology research on moral behavior involves aggression in sport, research has been extended to other physical activity settings and a wider range of moral behaviors, including bullying.

Bullying

Bullying is clearly antisocial behavior and relevant to sport and exercise psychology; much bullying takes place in schools, often in sport and physical activity settings. Hymel and Swearer (2015), in an introduction to a special issue of *American Psychologist* on school bullying, defined bullying as "a subcategory of interpersonal aggression characterized by *intentionality, repetition,* and an *imbalance of power,* with abuse of power being a primary distinction between bullying and other forms of aggression" (p. 293).

Gano-Overway and her colleagues (Fry & Gano-Overway, 2010; Gano-Overway, 2013; Gano-Overway et al., 2009) have conducted several studies on prosocial and antisocial behavior, focusing on the climate, and specifically on a caring climate, in which each participant is treated in a caring, supportive manner. More explicitly, Fry and Gano-Overway (2010) described the caring climate as an overarching context characterized by engrossment (listening, accepting, and attending), motivational displacement (honoring interests, supporting and helping achieve goals, empowering), and respect (trust, sensitivity). Research in nonsport settings suggests that a caring climate reduces bullying, and one key mechanism is through the development of empathy.

Gano-Overway and colleagues (2009) looked at the role of caring climate on prosocial and antisocial behaviors with a large sample of participants in the National Youth Sport Program, and also looked at self-regulatory efficacy and empathic self-efficacy as mediators. As expected,

perceived caring climate positively related to prosocial behavior and negatively predicted antisocial behavior. Furthermore, mediation effects suggested that the caring climate develops youths' ability to self-regulate positive affect, which in turn enhances their belief in their ability to empathize. As the authors concluded, through the intentional structuring of a youth sport context perceived as caring, youth reap not only physical benefits but also important social, emotional, and psychological benefits.

Gano-Overway (2013) looked at the relationship between caring climate, empathy, prosocial behaviors, and antisocial behaviors with middle school physical education students. Perceived caring climate positively predicted prosocial behavior and cognitive empathy and negatively predicted antisocial behavior, including bullying. Both boys and girls who perceived the climate as more caring were less likely to engage in antisocial behavior and more likely to engage in prosocial behavior. Gano-Overway concluded that creating a caring climate is one way in which physical education teachers can promote positive behavior.

Key Point

In a caring climate, each participant is treated in a caring, supportive manner. Gano-Overway (2013) found that perceived caring climate positively predicted prosocial behavior and cognitive empathy and negatively predicted antisocial behavior, including bullying.

We are concerned about bullying because of its immediate negative effects, but also because of the long-term consequences. Long-term effects on health and well-being are well documented; and of particular concern for sport and exercise psychology, bullying in school can have long-term effects on physical activity. Kestila and colleagues (2015) looked at childhood adversities and socioeconomic status as predictors of physical activity with a large sample of young adults (age 18-29) from the Finnish Health 2000 Study. They found only a few of the 11 childhood adversities they examined predicted activity, but bullying stood out. Having been bullied at school was associated with inactivity independently of other childhood circumstances and education. The researchers concluded that bullying at school can have long-lasting effects on physical activity levels.

In reviewing what we know and need to know about the serious issue of school violence, Bushman, Newman, and Calvert (2016) concluded that prevention should be a national priority. They cited interventions that focus on the development of self-control skills and social competence skills as promising approaches. While school violence is a more pressing issue than aggression in sport, the antecedents and promising approaches are similar. Helping youth (or adults) develop emotional and cognitive control skills is a key strategy for reducing antisocial behavior and promoting prosocial behavior. Similarly, the development of social competence (empathy, perspective taking, conflict management) can enhance social development in sport and physical activity as in any social context. These skills are fostered in a positive, caring climate. In the next section, we focus more specifically on positive social development through physical activity.

Positive Social Development Through Physical Activity

The sport and exercise psychology work on positive social development focuses on youth programs and overlaps with the research on moral behavior discussed in the preceding section. For example, Shields and Bredemeier (2014) have extended their research to character development, which includes intellectual character (e.g., curiosity, critical thinking), civic character (e.g., social organization, rights and responsibilities), and performance character (e.g., resilience, emotional control), as well as moral character. Similarly, the Fair Play for Kids program draws on the moral behavior and development literature.

Fair Play for Kids incorporates fair play principles (e.g., respect for rules and others, self-control) into all classroom settings. Gibbons, Ebbeck, and Weiss (1995) investigated the effects of Fair Play for Kids on the moral judgment, reasoning, intention, and behavior of fourth and sixth graders. They assigned groups as control classes, Fair Play for Kids curriculum in physical education classes only, and Fair Play for Kids curriculum in all classes. After seven months, both treatment groups scored higher than the control groups on moral judgment, reasoning, intention, and behavior. In a follow-up study, Gibbons and Ebbeck (1997) found higher moral judgment, intention, and behavior in only four months and

concluded that the systematic implementation of effective teaching strategies led to student growth in moral reasoning.

Don Hellison's (2011) Teaching Personal and Social Responsibility program was one of the earliest to focus on social development through physical activity. The most recent sport and exercise psychology research focuses on positive youth development (PYD), with much of that research conducted by Dan Gould, Maureen Weiss, and their colleagues. Other related projects have extended to broader social development, such as sport for peace or community development. These programs and related research are reviewed in the following sections.

Teaching Personal and Social Responsibility

Don Hellison was involved in positive social development through physical activity long before positive youth development was a common topic in sport and exercise psychology. More than 40 years ago he began his career in physical education with a focus on character development and a passion for helping urban, at-risk youth. Today, the needs are still clear, and the issues are not confined to inner cities.

On the basis of his experience and his commitment to help students, Hellison (2011) developed a model called *Teaching Personal and Social Responsibility (TPSR)*. In the early stages (e.g., Hellison, 1983) he focused on two personal well-being values (effort and self-direction) and two social well-being values (respect for others and caring about others) in a loose progression moving from respect at level 1 to caring and helping at level 4. Level 5, outside the gym, was soon added, and the model has continued to develop and change. Hellison (2011) calls TPSR a theory-in-practice because the framework is constantly being tested in practice, even years since its creation. Teaching Personal and Social Responsibility has been applied in several youth development programs, some adhering closely to the model and others taking positive youth development in different directions. The following section outlines the TPSR framework and related research.

TPSR Framework

The TPSR framework includes core values and assumptions and the levels of responsibility, and it moves into program leader responsibilities, program format, strategies, problem solving, and assessment. Hellison (2011) characterizes the core value underlying the program as putting kids first or being youth centered. Holistic self-development is a complementary value, with physical development taking place along with emotional, social, and cognitive development in TPSR. As a final value, Hellison characterizes TPSR not as a way of teaching but as a way of being.

Levels of responsibility are the most visible and widely cited part of TPSR. The five levels and the components of each (Hellison, 2011) are as follows:

- Level I: *Respecting the rights and feelings of others.* Components of respect are self-control, right to peaceful conflict resolution, and right to be included and to have cooperative peers.
- Level II: *Effort and cooperation.* The components are self-motivation, exploration of effort and new tasks, and getting along with others.
- Level III: *Self-direction.* The components are on-task independence, goal-setting progression, and courage to resist peer pressure.
- Level IV: *Helping others and leadership.* The components are caring and compassion, sensitivity and responsiveness, and inner strength.
- Level V: *Transfer outside the gym.* The components are trying these ideas in other areas of life and serving as a positive role model for others, especially for younger kids.

In Hellison's cumulative approach, each higher level encompasses all lower levels. People can, and often do, function at multiple levels. For example, a student may engage in self-directed play and cooperate with others one minute and shout at and blame another player the next minute.

As Hellison (2011) notes, although levels hold center stage, TPSR is broader and more nuanced, relying on leader responsibilities. In TPSR, leaders guide and gradually shift responsibility so that students have opportunities to feel empowered, purposeful, and connected to others as well as to experience responsible behavior, persevere, and acknowledge activities that impinge upon others.

Teaching Personal and Social Responsibility usually starts with brief relational time before the actual lesson begins, with awareness talks in which students learn about the importance of the levels. During the lesson, in which physical activity takes the most time, students experience the levels in action. For example, students may play an inclusion game to stress that everyone has a right to participate. Opportunities for individual decision making, such as choosing activities, are built into instruction. The lessons always close with reflection time in which students discuss the degree to which they have been respectful of others, involved in the program, self-directed, and helpful to others.

TPSR Research

Research on TPSR has been encouraging. In a review of 26 programs, Hellison and Walsh (2002) concluded that participants in TPSR programs demonstrated greater respect and feelings for others, were willing to try hard and work together, and were more self-directed in the physical activity setting. They added the caution that the TPSR model must be faithfully implemented and that the results of their review provide greater evidence that the program is worth doing than it does that the program is working.

Additional studies since then (Hellison & Wright, 2003; Walsh, 2008; Wright & Burton, 2008) provide further evidence that the TPSR program is effective in developing skills. Transfer of TPSR skills outside the gym is the most challenging level, and support for transfer is limited. Walsh, Ozaeta, and Wright (2010) found that youth were able to transfer some TPSR goals to the school context when the instructors used deliberate strategies to promote transfer. Other research, however, found difficulties with transfer despite positive changes in the program (Martinek, Schilling, & Johnson, 2002; Schilling, Martinek, & Carson, 2007).

In light of the challenges, Martinek and Lee (2012) proposed a framework for transfer of values with three interconnected elements: (a) participants' awareness of values, (b) school's awareness and support of program goals, and (c) a set of transfer strategies. Jacobs and Wright (2016) suggest imagery as a promising strategy and offer practical suggestions for youth leaders to use to promote transfer of life skills.

Transfer from programs to life is a major issue for all positive youth development programs. Turnnidge, Côté, and Hancock (2014) outline some of the issues and challenges with transfer. Although the research does not point to specific recommendations, it is clear that the environment and supportive relationships are important. Turnnidge and colleagues also note the importance of fostering continued participation and providing opportunities for excitement, skill development, and connections with peers. As they concluded, sport participation may be a beneficial, but insufficient, factor in promoting positive development.

Positive Youth Development

Hellison's TPSR program clearly targets youth development, but positive youth development (PYD) within sport and exercise psychology is a more recent area drawing from developmental psychology. According to Weiss and Wiese-Bjornstal (2009), in a comprehensive review of related research, positive youth development involves the development of personal skills or assets that youth need in order to become successfully functioning members of society. Furthermore, PYD programs emphasize developing these skills within positive, supporting climates. As Weiss and Wiese-Bjornstal observed, effective youth development programs emphasize three main components: (a) personal or life skills development; (b) positive adult, peer, and community relationships; and (c) a climate focused on learning, mastery, and autonomy support.

Key Point

Effective positive youth development programs emphasize (a) personal or life skills development; (b) positive adult, peer, and community relationships; and (c) a climate focused on learning, mastery, and autonomy support.

PYD Framework

The leading researchers and frameworks (e.g., Gould & Carson, 2008; Petitpas, Cornelius, Van Raalte, & Jones, 2005; Weiss, 2011) that guide current PYD work draw from a few sources. The first, Benson's (2006) developmental assets, includes 20 internal or personal assets (e.g., integrity, self-esteem, competence) and 20 external or social assets (e.g., family support, positive peer influence). The second, Lerner's 5 Cs approach (Lerner, Almerigi, Theokas, & Lerner, 2005), includes character, caring, competence, confidence, and connection, with a sixth C, contribution, added as a result of demonstrating all five Cs. The final framework is Larson's developmental or growth experiences. In Larson's (2000) developmental model, youth develop personal skills (e.g., initiative, problem solving) and interpersonal skills (group process skills, peer relationships)

through growth experiences. In all of these approaches, PYD, in line with positive psychology, focuses on developing strengths.

The sport and exercise psychology work on PYD follows that framework in focusing on the development of personal and interpersonal skills or assets and creating a supportive, learning-oriented climate. Several programs have been developed, and research provides evidence of program effectiveness. However, as Dzewaltowski and Rosenkranz (2014) noted, although there is evidence to inform practice, consensus is lacking on the definition and outcomes of PYD. As nearly everyone who has developed programs or conducted research related to PYD has stated, youth sport programs do not automatically result in positive outcomes; character is not "caught" in youth sport, but must be taught by trained, informed leaders. Sport-related interventions can promote positive development, but only when interventions are intentionally designed to do so.

PYD Research

Gould, Cowburn, and Shields (2014) summarized the evidence on psychological and social outcomes of youth sport participation, noting that there is good evidence for psychological and social benefits, such as enhanced confidence, prosocial values, positive affect, formation of positive relationships, and teamwork skills.

Several studies have used the Youth Experiences Scale (Hansen & Larson, 2007), which assesses a wide range of developmental outcomes, with youth sport (Gould & Carson, 2011; Gould, Flett, & Lauer, 2012; Larson, Hansen, & Moneta, 2006). Those results show that young athletes learn personal skills (e.g., setting goals, exerting effort, problem solving, time management), as well as social skills (e.g., compromising, giving and receiving feedback, leadership).

However, research also has identified negative outcomes including stress, burnout, and lowered motivation. In their review, Eime and coauthors (2013) concluded that there is substantive evidence for many psychological and social benefits, but cautioned that the evidence is limited and largely cross-sectional, with no randomized controlled studies.

Gould and colleagues (2014) highlighted the importance of the climate in achieving positive outcomes. Specifically, as already noted, a mastery motivational climate and a caring climate have both been associated with positive developmental outcomes.

In one of the few comprehensive evaluations of PYD programs, Weiss, Stuntz, Bhalla, Bolter, and Price (2013) conducted a longitudinal evaluation of The First Tee program. The First Tee is a sport-based PYD program teaching life skills and promoting positive psychosocial and behavioral outcomes through the sport of golf. Their findings provide evidence that The First Tee has a positive effect on promoting life skills and core values among youth participants within a golf context and also in the transfer to other domains. The authors further suggested that the program is effective because of the synergy among the context (golf), external assets (delivery by trained coaches), internal assets (life skills guided by intentional curriculum), and development outcomes.

PYD Programs

Overall, PYD programs are in line with developmental theories and research, and the research within sport and exercise psychology provides evidence that well-designed programs that intentionally target psychological and social development in a mastery-oriented, caring climate do indeed foster positive developmental skills.

We must not lose sight of physical development. Positive youth development includes physical development, and indeed, that is a primary and unique target for physical activity programs. Dzewaltowski and Rosenkranz (2014) argue that PYD should more explicitly focus on physical activity as the primary outcome to promote lifelong participation. As Weiss and Wiese-Bjornstal (2009) emphasized, physical competencies contribute to psychosocial development and commitment to physical activity. Fundamental motor skills are prerequisite to mastering sport-specific skills; and more importantly, physical skills and physical literacy are keys to maintaining lifelong physical activity with all its related health benefits. Weiss (2011) contends that PYD should include both motor skills development and physical activity and health goals.

Developmental Model of Sport Participation

That reminder of our focus on physical activity recalls the work on the development of talent or expertise in sport discussed in chapter 5. Côté and colleagues (Côté, Baker, & Abernethy, 2007; Côté, Hancock, & Abernethy, 2014) proposed the Developmental Model of Sport Participation (DMSP) with the following three stages.

1. Sampling years (age 6-13). Emphasis is on play and a wide range of activities.
2. Specializing years (age 13-15). Youth invest significantly more time and effort in a few sports, with a balance between deliberate play and practice.
3. Investment years (ages 15-20). The focus switches to achieving elite levels in one sport with considerable time and effort dedicated to deliberate practice.

As Côté and colleagues demonstrated, that developmental model works for most elite athletes. Whereas a few specialize very early successfully, many more reach elite levels with the DMSP. More relevant here, the DMSP is clearly the better path for the vast majority of youth participants who will never reach elite levels. In this stage, the emphasis is on fun and sampling a range of sport and physical activities. By emphasizing play (vs. practice and training) and offering encouragement and support in the early years, parents and leaders provide opportunities for children to develop fundamental motor skills while also enhancing motivation and positive attitudes. Even through the later stages, emphasis on developing physical skills and literacy within holistic PYD models will better serve the wide range of youth participants.

Social Development Across the Life Span

Although PYD and most developmental physical activity programs focus on youth, neither physical nor social development ends at adolescence. Physical activity programs can promote the development of personal and social life skills throughout the life span. Indeed, the psychological and social benefits of physical activity are often both motivating factors and sustaining outcomes in adult physical activity programs. Chinkov and Holt (2016) investigated the transfer for life skills through participation in Brazilian jujitsu with Canadian adults (age 19-54). Participants reported that involvement in jujitsu had changed their lives, specifically citing acquisition of four life skills: respect for others, perseverance, self-confidence, and healthy habits. These findings are very similar to those with youth programs. Furthermore, participants cited the head instructors and peers as creating the atmosphere for learning life skills.

Returning to the DMSP and athletes, we do not need to stop at age 20, but we can take a PYD approach with adult sport participants, even elite athletes. Indeed, we rarely think about the development of elite athletes after they reach the elite level; but in fact, nearly all of them will end their elite athletic participation, often abruptly. We might well focus on the development of social and life skills to foster more positive transitions throughout the life span. Within sport and exercise psychology, increasing attention is being paid to athletes' career transitions as they move out of the elite or mastery years in their sport. That attention does not match the attention to the early developing years, but it's a promising area for both research and applied programs. If we look at the developing years with the DMSP narrowing from sampling to investment, we might well look at the later years as a broadening out from the intense focus on training in one sport to wider activities, as well as to the continuing development of personal and social life skills.

Stambulova and Wylleman (2014), who have both done considerable research and applied work with athletes at different career stages, propose taking the long view of multiyear transitions and a holistic life span perspective that considers life issues beyond sport. Their multilevel, holistic model can be applied with athletes at any stage, from youth through college and through the adult years. Too often we neglect the psychosocial development of athletes, and even their physical development, with early overspecialization.

Research by Reifsteck and colleagues (Reifsteck, Gill, & Brooks, 2013; Reifsteck, Gill, & Labban, 2016) indicates that former college athletes are no more active than other college graduates, and they often have difficulty transitioning from intense focused training and competition to lifestyle physical activity. Former athletes who have more self-determined motivation and a broader self-identity as an exerciser (vs. a narrow athlete identity) are more likely to engage in continuing physical activity. In light of that, Reifsteck and colleagues are continuing their research and developing transition programs aimed at helping college athletes transition to a healthy lifestyle.

Sport and Social Missions

The role of sport and physical activity in social development has extended beyond individual social skills to broader social missions. As discussed in an International Society of Sport Psychology (ISSP) position stand (Schinke, Stambulova, Lidor, Papaioannou, & Ryba, 2016), sport and exercise psychology is expanding to social missions that aim to promote social change leading to betterment for individuals, groups, communities, countries, and world regions. Social missions through sport include PYD, but they also extend to broader social issues such as sport for peace or sport for cultural exchange and social justice.

As Schinke and colleagues note, a longstanding belief in the social virtues of sport has led to the use of sport for social integration and building community. They also note, however, that sport can foster violence, exploitation, discrimination, and nationalism. Critical sport studies scholars have rightly criticized sport for development programs, particularly those that go into underdeveloped countries or target underserved populations with little understanding of the particular cultural context. As with the PYD programs discussed earlier, programs with social missions must be intentionally designed to achieve positive outcomes and avoid negative consequences, with particular attention to the needs and cultural context of participants.

Key Point

Social missions through sport include PYD, but they also extend to broader social issues such as sport for peace or sport for cultural exchange and social justice. As with PYD, programs with social missions must be intentionally designed to achieve positive outcomes and avoid negative consequences, with particular attention to the needs and cultural context of participants.

In the ISSP position stand, Schinke and colleagues (2016) offer the following principles for high-quality sport for development projects: (a) planning by first understanding the needs of those involved and then setting up relevant goals to meet those needs, (b) understanding and considering the historical–social context of the participants, (c) taking an inclusiveness approach, (d) recognizing indirect as well as direct influences on participants, (e) using culturally relevant theories and methods that fit the participants and their context, and (f) continuous reflection on the process. These are big challenges. Following are a few examples of programs with social missions attempting to meet those challenges.

Maro, Roberts, and Sorensen (2009) developed a community-based soccer program in Tanzania aimed at reducing the high rate of human immunodeficiency virus (HIV) infection in youth age 15 to 25. In the program, peer coaches were trained to teach not only soccer skills, but also HIV/ acquired immunodeficiency syndrome (AIDS) prevention strategies. The project also involved a soccer group with a mastery motivational climate and two control groups, one receiving regular school education on the topic and another with no education. HIV/AIDS education was more effective with the two soccer groups. Lidor and Blumenstein (2011) also used soccer in a sport-for-peace program aimed at building bridges between Jewish and Arab cities in Galilee. That program is based on the principles of neutrality (no political agendas), inclusion, respect, trust, and responsibility—values similar to those emphasized in the TPSR and PYD programs.

Whitley, Forneris, and Barker, who have each been involved in community-based youth development programs using TPSR or PYD life skills approaches, have outlined issues and challenges involved in implementing, sustaining, and evaluating programs in a series of articles (Forneris, Whitley, & Barker, 2013; Whitley, Forneris, & Barker, 2014, 2015). Although each of the programs faced some unique challenges, common challenges arose that are faced by many programs with social missions. Similarly, many of the recommendations, or lessons learned, reflect those discussed in the ISSP position statement. For example, Forneris and colleagues (2013) recommended

involving community members in the planning and implementation and maintaining consistent contact with leaders and organizations during and after the program. Training for all staff, recruiting bilingual leaders, and having resources for leaders are also in line with ISSP recommendations. Sustaining the program is always an issue and an especially important one for social development programs. Challenges, such as building strong relationships with community partners, knowledge translation, and funding, may be addressed with strategies of planning, capacity building, recruitment, and evaluation.

Blom and colleagues (2015) described their experiences with U.S. and international sport for development and peace programs. On the basis of their experiences they highlighted the importance of establishing partnerships, developing curriculum, training program staff, monitoring and evaluation, and sustaining programs. All these recommendations and the ISSP position stand call for advance planning, continuing involvement of community partners, culturally relevant approaches, and continued reflection and evaluation. Perhaps one of the strongest recommendations for anyone considering such a program is to go in with the long view—start by planning for a program that will continue and be self-sustaining even if you are no longer there.

Putting It Into Practice

Summary

Many have written about aggression in sport, but systematic research is limited. Aggression is defined as an intentional act designed to harm other people. The strongest theoretical work and research suggest that emotions, particularly frustration and anger, play a role, but learning and situational cues have a stronger influence. Aggression is learned through the observation and reinforcement of aggressive behaviors. Research does not support the popular notion that sport acts as a catharsis to release aggressive urges. Instead, it is likely that aggression in sport increases the probability of aggressive behaviors in both sport and nonsport settings. Research on aggression and moral behavior in sport and exercise psychology suggests that individual factors, specifically motivational orientation and moral disengagement, as well as the climate, are antecedents of aggression.

Youth sport and physical activity programs can foster confidence, prosocial behavior, teamwork skills, and continued physical activity, but positive social development does not occur automatically in youth sport programs. Research within sport and exercise psychology provides evidence that well-designed programs intentionally targeting psychological and social development in a mastery-oriented, caring climate foster positive personal and social developmental skills.

Review Questions

1. Define aggression as the term is used in this text.
2. Explain how instrumental aggression and hostile aggression differ.

3. Describe the original frustration–aggression drive theory of aggression, as well as Berkowitz's revised and more widely accepted theory.

4. Explain Bandura's social learning theory of aggression.

5. What does research show regarding the idea that sport can act as a catharsis for aggression?

6. Explain how Lauer and Paiement used the 3 Rs routine to help youth ice hockey players deal with emotions and reduce aggressive behavior.

7. Explain how game reasoning or bracketed morality relates to aggression in sport.

8. Identify the primary individual factors and social–environmental factors related to moral behavior in sport and physical activity.

9. Identify the five levels in Hellison's Teaching Personal and Social Responsibility model, and explain how a youth leader might develop a lesson in line with model.

10. Discuss the role of a mastery climate and a caring climate in positive youth development.

Recommended Reading

- Gano-Overway, L.A., Newton, M., Magyar, T.M., Fry, M.D., Kim, M., & Guivernau, M. (2009). Influence of caring youth sport contexts on efficacy-related beliefs and social behaviors. *Developmental Psychology, 45*, 329-340. doi:10.1037/a0014067. Gano-Overway and colleagues have conducted several studies looking at the role of the climate on social behaviors. This article demonstrates the influence of a caring, supportive climate in reducing antisocial behavior and promoting prosocial behavior in youth sport.

- Lauer, L., & Paiement, C. (2009). The Playing Tough and Clean Hockey Program. *Sport Psychologist, 23*(4), 543-561. Lauer and Paiement apply research and models of aggression in a practical program to help youth ice hockey players deal with emotions and control aggression.

- Schinke, R.J., Stambulova, N.R., Lidor, R., Papaioannou, A., & Ryba, T.V. (2016). ISSP position stand: Social missions through sport and exercise psychology. *International Journal of Sport and Exercise Psychology, 14*(1), 4-22. doi: 10.1080/1612197X.2014.999698. The ISSP position stand provides a good overview of the expanding sport and exercise psychology programs with social missions. The position stand highlights challenges with such programs and also offers recommendations to address challenges.

After-School Program to Promote Positive Youth Development

For this lab, refer to the chapter material on aggression, moral behavior, and positive youth development to develop a plan for an after-school physical activity program to reduce aggression and promote prosocial behavior and positive social development.

In response to an increase in violence by students after school, the middle school principal has decided to start an after-school physical activity program so students will have something to do before their parents come home from work. You have been hired by the principal to create the program. Your mandate is to create a physical activity program that reduces antisocial behavior and builds positive personal and social skills. The principal wants to see more positive social behavior when students are playing sports and less in-school fighting.

Present your program to the principal. Include your overall approach and rationale, your target behaviors and expected outcomes, and specific strategies.

In your plan, refer to the theories and models that guide your program (e.g., PYD, TPSR) and research that supports your program. Be specific and detailed in identifying strategies you will use to create a climate that will promote positive social behaviors both on and off the playing field.

Group Dynamics

Chapter Objectives

After studying this chapter, you should be able to

- understand group dynamics concepts and models as they relate to sport and physical activity,

- explain the relationship of individual capabilities and motivational processes to group performance,

- explain several leadership models used in sport and exercise psychology,

- describe transformational leadership and its four primary components,

- understand the relationship between group cohesion and group performance, and

- explain team-building models and research related to sport and exercise settings.

Most sport and physical activities involve groups. People play on volleyball teams, learn motor skills in physical education, join fitness clubs, and participate in yoga classes. Sport and exercise psychologists might pose many questions about groups and group processes. How does turnover of team members affect performance? Does leader behavior affect adherence to exercise programs? Will a team-building session increase cohesion and performance of the soccer team? Answers to these types of questions are few. The traditional social psychology literature on groups typically ignores physical activity, and the organizational models are far removed from the unique relationships of sport teams and exercise groups. Groups by definition involve interaction, and the dynamic nature of group processes makes it difficult to draw clear conclusions. Still, the sport and exercise psychology literature on group dynamics provides guidelines for enhancing the experience for participants in sport and exercise groups.

Group Dynamics Concepts and Models

First, we should define *group*. Certainly a professional basketball team, a youth soccer team, and the noon exercise club are groups. What about several people jogging on the same route or the crowd at a football game? Most people who have written about groups agree that a collection of individuals does not make a group—interaction is the defining feature. Group members must be aware of each other, relate to each other in some way, and be able to interact with each other through group processes. In his classic definition, McGrath (1984, p. 7) stated, "Groups are those social aggregates that involve mutual awareness and potential interaction." In a review chapter on group behavior and performance, Hackman and Katz (2010, p. 1210) offered the following definition: "A group is an intact social system, complete with boundaries, interdependence for some shared purpose, and differentiated member roles."

Sport and exercise psychology research on groups adopts similar definitions. Carron and Eys (2012, p. 14) define a sport group as

> a collection of two or more individuals who possess a common identity, have common goals and objectives, share a common fate, exhibit structured patterns of interaction and modes of communication, hold common

perceptions about group structure, are personally and instrumentally interdependent, reciprocate interpersonal attraction, and consider themselves to be a group.

For our purposes, most sport teams, exercise groups, and physical activity classes meet these criteria, and application of a group dynamics framework may help us understand sport and exercise groups.

Group Models

McGrath's (1984) conceptual framework provides the framework for most of the psychology literature on group dynamics. Interaction, the defining characteristic of a group, is the central element of the model. The rest of the model specifies factors that both influence, and are influenced by, those interactive processes. Individual characteristics influence group structures; environmental properties affect the group task and situation; and those factors collectively influence the setting in which group interaction takes place. All those components influence the interaction process, which in turn may influence the group members, the environment, and the relationships in the group.

Key Point

According to McGrath's conceptual framework, individual characteristics influence group structures, environmental properties affect the group task and situation, and those factors collectively influence the setting in which group interaction takes place. All those components influence the interaction process, which in turn may influence the group members, the environment, and the relationships in the group.

For example, consider a soccer team. Players have varying individual characteristics, including physical characteristics, specific soccer skills, goals and motivational orientations, cognitive skills, competitive experiences, and so on. Those individual characteristics affect group structures, such as starting positions, leadership roles, and offensive and defensive plays. Also, the environment, such as the opponent, field conditions, and weather, might influence positioning and strategies. The ongoing interaction and game progress may then change the environment, individuals, and relationships. For example, the player who is having a great day may get the ball more often and play with enhanced confidence.

Widmeyer, Brawley, and Carron (2002) offered a linear model that has guided much of the sport and exercise psychology research on group dynamics. Like McGrath, Widmeyer and colleagues include individual attributes and the environment as starting input components. These influence group structure, which influences group cohesion, which then influences group processes. Finally, group processes influence group and individual outputs. Group cohesion stands out in this framework, reflecting the prominence of group cohesion in the sport and exercise psychology literature. Current work on team building, discussed later in the chapter, moves cohesion to the output side of the model, reflecting the mutual relationships and dynamic nature of group processes.

Group Characteristics

The definition of a group cited earlier incorporates several group characteristics, including mutual awareness, shared goals, and structured interactions. Sport and exercise groups vary on characteristics, and group characteristics influence group processes and outcomes. Characteristics that describe sport and exercise groups (Carron & Eys, 2012; Eys, Burke, Dennis, & Evans, 2015) include the following:

- **Common fate:** The outcome, success or failure, is shared by group members.
- **Interpersonal attraction and mutual benefit:** Group membership is enjoyable and rewarding.
- **Social structure:** Pattern of relationships is stable, including norms and roles specific to the group.
- **Interdependence:** Members rely on each other to achieve goals.
- **Common identity and self-categorization:** Members perceive themselves as group members.

Sport and exercise groups vary on these characteristics, and that variation has implications for group processes and performance. Interdependence, which varies a great deal among sport and exercise groups, has been investigated in relation to individual and team outcomes. For example, Bruner, Eys, Evans, and Wilson (2015) found higher perceptions of interdependence related to greater social identity with high school team

sport athletes. Martinez and Tindale (2015) found that interdependence moderated the relationship between organizational citizenship (helping behavior) and performance; helping behavior predicted performance, but the effect differed between softball and tennis teams.

Evans, Eys, and Bruner (2012) argued that group dynamics and interdependence are important in individual as well as team sports. As in their title, seeing the "we" in "me" sports can add to our understanding. Evans and Eys (2015) looked at the role of interdependence within individual sport teams. They found that participants who worked together on collective tasks or had shared team outcomes perceived greater interdependence, which in turn related to increased cohesion and satisfaction.

All of the group characteristics together make up "groupness" (Spink, Wilson, & Priebe, 2010). All groups have some degree of groupness, but the amount varies. Certainly a high school basketball team has a great deal of groupness, perhaps more than the tennis team, and more than the yoga class at the recreation center. Still, groupness is present in the yoga class, and Spink and colleagues (2010) found that enhanced perceptions of groupness were associated with attendance in exercise settings.

Group Norms and Roles

As well as characteristics of the group, group norms and roles play an important part in group dynamics. In general, norms reflect what is accepted, appropriate, or valued behavior. Norms are not formal laws or rules, but informal and often unstated standards of behavior expected of group members. In sport and exercise settings, norms often relate to interpersonal behavior such as punctuality, practice behavior, or communication styles.

Roles have received more attention than norms in sport and exercise psychology, particularly in relation to sport teams. In general, roles are behaviors expected of those in specific positions within a group. Those roles include formal roles, such as team captain or spiker and setter in volleyball, and informal roles, such as enforcer or social leader. Cope, Eys, Beauchamp, Schinke, and Bosselut (2011) identified 12 informal roles on sport teams and found that informal roles were most often discussed with reference to individual (e.g., satisfaction) and group (e.g., cohesion) contexts. The important role elements for sport teams (Eys et al., 2015) are as follows:

- **Role clarity or ambiguity:** degree of understanding of one's role responsibilities; ambiguity refers to a lack of clear, consistent information regarding one's role
- **Role acceptance:** willingness to carry out one's role responsibilities
- **Role efficacy:** beliefs about one's capabilities to carry out role responsibilities
- **Role conflict:** incongruent or conflicting expectations of others about the role
- **Role overload:** too many roles or inability to prioritize appropriately
- **Role satisfaction:** how happy one is with the given role
- **Role performance:** one's behaviors pertaining to role responsibilities

Role ambiguity has received the most attention in sport and exercise psychology. Beauchamp, Bray, Eys, and Carron (2002) proposed a model and measure, the Role Ambiguity Scale, noting that athletes need to understand four aspects of their role: (a) scope of responsibilities, (b) specific behaviors needed to carry out the role, (c) how they will be evaluated, and (d) consequences of not fulfilling role responsibilities. Subsequent research indicated that athletes who understand their roles better (less ambiguity) are more satisfied (Eys, Carron, Bray, & Beauchamp, 2003), have less anxiety (Beauchamp, Bray, Eys, & Carron, 2003), and view their teams as more cohesive (Bosselut, McLaren, Eys, & Heuzé, 2012).

Group Performance

All of the group characteristics, as well as group processes, affect group performance, and group performance is a pressing practical concern in sport and exercise psychology. Perhaps the maxim most accepted by researchers and practitioners is that the best players make the best team. In general, this rule undoubtedly holds; five intercollegiate basketball players will consistently defeat five intramural players. However, the relationship between individual abilities and group performance is far from perfect. You probably can recall instances when teams with all the talent to win the championship did not, or times when teams without individual stars performed exceptionally well as a group. Simply summing the abilities of individual group members does not accurately describe group performance. We must also consider the group process—interaction.

Steiner's Model of Individual–Group Performance

Steiner (1972) proposed a model of the individual–group performance relationship, expressed as follows:

Actual productivity = potential productivity – losses due to faulty process

Potential productivity, which is the group's best possible performance, depends on the group's resources and task demands. Resources comprise all the relevant knowledge and skills of individual members. Individual ability, demonstrated by individual performance, is the most important resource of most sport groups. As in the maxim, the best players make the best team, but Steiner's model goes beyond the maxim. Task demands—the rules and requirements of the task—determine which resources are relevant to performance. For example, height is a much more relevant resource for volleyball than for track. When a group effectively uses its available resources to meet task demands, its actual productivity approaches its potential.

In Steiner's model, a group's actual performance falls short of its potential (we're never perfect) because of faulty process. The process includes all individual and interactive actions by which a group transforms its resources into a collective product or performance—putting it all together. Process losses fall into two categories:

- Coordination losses occur when poor timing or ineffective strategies detract from the group's potential, such as when a basketball team fails to get the ball to the top scorer.
- Motivational losses occur when group members slack off or give less than their best effort.

These process losses are critical considerations in work with sport and exercise groups. Coaches have some influence on group resources when they recruit individual talent or provide instruction to improve individual skills, but resources and task demands are relatively stable. The main task of a coach or group leader is to reduce process losses by developing organizational strategies that decrease coordination losses and by maintaining optimal motivation levels.

Process losses and the strategies for reducing them vary with the task. Activities requiring considerable interaction or cooperation, such as basketball, are more susceptible to coordination losses than are activities demanding less interaction,

Reaching Your Group Potential

Application Point

You are coaching the dance team at your middle school. The team will perform at regional, state, and national events. Keeping in mind the resources and task demands, identify some possible coordination losses and motivational losses that might affect the dance team's performance. Be specific. Then, identify strategies you might use to reduce those process losses so the team reaches its potential.

such as swimming. Consequently, the basketball coach emphasizes strategies and drills to achieve precise timing and team movement patterns. The swimming coach may try to develop efficient transitions among relay members but spends little time on interactive skills. Regardless of the level of interaction, all teams and groups must avoid motivation losses to reach their potential. Much of the research on individual and group performance focuses on motivation within the group process.

Ringelmann Effect

Much of the research on group process and performance originates in an obscure, unpublished study of individual and group performance on a rope-pulling task. More than 100 years ago, Ringelmann (cited in Ingham, Levinger, Graves, & Peckham, 1974; Kravitz & Martin, 1986) observed that groups pulled with more force than individuals did, but not with as much force as would be predicted by adding individual scores. The average individual force in two-person groups was 93 percent of the average individual force, and for eight-person groups it was 49 percent. This phenomenon of average individual performance decreasing with increases in group size is called the *Ringelmann effect*.

No one actually studied the Ringelmann effect until Ingham and colleagues (1974) resurrected the original Ringelmann paradigm with updated controls. Experiment 1, with individuals and groups of two, three, four, five, and six people, partially replicated the Ringelmann effect. The average performance dropped with two-person and three-person groups but then leveled off, with the average performance in six-person groups at 78 percent of the average solo performance.

Ingham and colleagues then eliminated the coordination requirements of the group task to see whether the Ringelmann effect was attribut-

able to coordination losses or motivation losses. In experiment 2, only one subject actually pulled on the rope, but through use of blindfolds and trained confederates who pretended to pull, subjects were led to believe they were performing in groups of one to six members. The results were virtually identical to those of experiment 1. The authors concluded that the decreases in average performance were due to motivational losses within groups.

Social Loafing and Social Incentives in Groups

In the 1970s, Latane, Williams, and Harkins undertook a systematic investigation of group performance, and in light of the Ingham and colleagues' (1974) findings, they dubbed the motivational losses in groups *social loafing*. Their first study (Latane et al., 1979), which used clapping and shouting as group tasks, confirmed the Ringelmann effect: The average sound produced per person decreased to 71 percent in two-person groups and 40 percent in six-person groups. In a second experiment, instructions and background noise played through earphones led subjects to believe they were clapping or shouting in groups when in fact they were performing alone (pseudogroups). Performance dropped even in the pseudogroups. Because coordination losses (e.g., interfering sound waves) were eliminated, Latane and colleagues concluded that the performance drop was due to motivation losses—social loafing. The greater performance drop for actual groups represented a combination of coordination losses and motivation losses.

Key Point

The phenomenon of average individual performance decreasing with increases in group size is called the *Ringelmann effect*. Ingham and colleagues and Latane and coauthors found performance decreases even when coordination losses were eliminated, and they called such motivational losses in groups *social loafing*.

Latane and colleagues proposed that identifiability of individual performance is critical for reducing social loafing (Williams, Harkins, & Latane, 1981). When individual efforts are lost in the crowd, performance decreases. In two experiments, Williams and colleagues demonstrated that when group members believed their individual outputs were identifiable (i.e., known to others), social loafing was eliminated.

If monitoring individual performance can eliminate social loafing, perhaps other tactics can reverse the effect and provide social incentives to individuals in groups. Sport teams certainly seem to provide social incentives. Latane and colleagues noted the common belief that athletes perform better in a relay or in a group than alone and examined social loafing and identifiability in a sport setting.

They first checked individual and relay times at an intercollegiate swim meet and found no social loafing. Instead, relay times were faster than individual times. Faster starts in relays could account for the difference, so they designed an experiment to test their observations (Williams, Nida, Baca, & Latane, 1989). In an experimental competition, 16 members of an intercollegiate team swam both as individuals and as one member of a relay team. Starts were standardized to the faster relay starts, and identifiability was manipulated by announcing or not announcing lap times. Results revealed an interaction between identifiability and individual-relay conditions. Under low identifiability, individual times (61.34 seconds) were faster than relay times (61.66), implying social loafing. Under high identifiability, individual times (60.95) were slower than relay times (60.18). Not only was social loafing eliminated, but the group seemed to provide a social incentive. Time differences were small. However, such small differences often determine places in competitive events.

Research on social loafing and group performance has continued. Karau and Williams (1993, 1995) reviewed more than 80 studies on social loafing, which they defined as "a reduction in motivation and effort when individuals work collectively compared to when they work individually or coactively." (p. 134). Their meta-analysis yielded a moderate effect size of 0.44, and they found social loafing consistently across a wide variety of tasks and populations.

Key Point

Karau and Williams' (1993) collective effort model (CEM) proposes that individuals will exert effort on a collective task only to the degree to which they expect their efforts to help them obtain valued outcomes that are important, meaningful, or intrinsically satisfying.

As an integrative framework, Karau and Williams (1993) offered the collective effort model (CEM), which proposes that individuals will exert effort on a collective task only to the degree to which they expect their efforts to help them obtain valued outcomes that are important, meaningful, or intrinsically satisfying.

Karau and Williams (1995) suggest that social loafing is reduced in the following situations:

- When individuals believe that others can evaluate their collective performance
- When people work in smaller groups
- When people perceive their contributions to the collective product as unique
- When people have a standard with which to compare their group's performance
- When people work on tasks that are intrinsically interesting, meaningful, important to others, or high in personal involvement
- When individuals work with people they respect or in a situation that activates a salient group identity
- When individuals expect their coworkers to perform poorly
- When people have a dispositional tendency to view favorable collective outcomes as valuable and important

Most studies of group performance do not involve physical activity. Moreover, in focusing on social loafing, the research is one-sided; social incentives have been ignored. Initiatives related to team building, discussed later in the chapter, may help us move in that direction.

As suggested at the beginning of this section, even the apparently straightforward relationship of individual abilities to group performance is not so straightforward. Swaab, Schaerer, Anicich, Ronay, and Galinsky (2014) specifically looked at the relationship between talent and team performance across five studies. They first confirmed that people believe there is a linear, near-perfect relationship between talent and performance—the best individuals make the best team. They predicted that talent facilitates performance only up to a point, and they further predicted that task interdependence is a key determinant of when talent becomes detrimental. The results of three archival studies confirmed their predictions in that the too-much-talent effect emerged when teams were interdependent (international football–soccer, basketball) but not independent (baseball). The basketball results also established the mediating role of team coordination. The authors concluded that when teams need to come together, more talent can tear them apart.

Group processes and the social context must be considered to understand team performance, and group dynamics are just as important in considering nonperformance outcomes. Even those who work with highly competitive, task-oriented teams often engage in team-building activities to improve group communication or cohesion. Professionals in physical education, recreational activities, and exercise programs may be even more concerned with interpersonal relationships. The following sections focus on interpersonal relationships, particularly leadership and cohesion, in sport and exercise groups.

Leadership in Sport and Physical Activity

Leadership is a traditional topic in group dynamics, and sport and exercise psychology has adapted some of that work. Although we often think of the team coach, class instructor, or exercise director as the leader, leadership is not simply a characteristic of a single person. Instead, leadership is a complex social relationship. As Hogg (2010) noted in a social psychology handbook chapter, influence is the key defining feature of leadership. Chemers (2001, p. 376) defined leadership as "a process of social influence through which an individual enlists and mobilizes the aid of others in the attainment of a collective goal. Similarly, but more concisely, Barrow (1977) defined leadership as "the behavioral process of influencing individuals and groups toward set goals" (p. 232).

Early research on leadership emphasized common characteristics of great leaders, or the great-man theory of leadership (indeed it was a theory of great men—no women were included). Similar to early trait personality research, the leadership trait work yielded few conclusive findings. Trait models have long been out of favor and never received much attention in sport and exercise psychology.

Fiedler's (1967) contingency model of leadership effectiveness, which guided much of the early work, is an interaction model that classifies leaders as task oriented (primarily focused on performance) or person oriented (primarily concerned with interpersonal relationships), and it proposes that leader effectiveness depends on situation favorableness. According to Fiedler, task-oriented leaders are more effective in both the most

favorable and least favorable situations, whereas person-oriented leaders are more effective in moderately favorable situations. Fielder's model was the leader in the 1970s, but the variables are difficult to assess and findings were inconclusive. More important, its appropriateness for sport and exercise groups is questionable.

Leadership theories have evolved from the early trait theories through behavioral, situational, and interactional models to transformational leadership theory, which is currently garnering considerable attention in sport and exercise psychology. The following sections cover the major leadership models in the sport and exercise psychology literature, beginning with the mediational models that have mainly been applied to coaching behavior.

Mediational Model of Leadership

Mediational models consider relationships among situational, individual, cognitive, and behavior variables. Within sport and exercise psychology, much of the leadership research focuses on coach behavior. Coach behavior is discussed in chapter 7 on behavioral approaches and in chapter 14 on social influence. Here we highlight the leadership role.

Smoll and Smith (1989), who have done extensive work on coach behaviors with youth sport, expanded that work into a mediational model of leadership. In the model, which expands from behavioral to more social cognitive approaches, the influence of coach behaviors is mediated through the athletes' perceptions and recall of those behaviors. Coach (leader) behavior is determined by individual-difference variables (e.g., coaches' beliefs about what a coach should do), situational factors (e.g., game status), and coaches' perceptions of athletes' attitudes. Athletes' perceptions and recall are also determined by individual and situational variables, as well as by the coaches' actual behaviors. The model is the basis of Smith and Smoll's (2012) coach effectiveness training, discussed in earlier chapters. Thelma Horn's (2008) coaching effectiveness model is similar but adds more explicit antecedents and mediational pathways to coach behavior. Again, more detail on Horn's model and research on coach behavior is presented in chapter 14.

Chase (2010) took a social cognitive approach to leadership in arguing that sport coaching and leadership training should focus on developing a "growth mindset." Carol Dweck's (2006) extensive research on mindsets, made more accessible in her 2006 book, stems from cognitive motivation and attribution research (discussed in chapter 8). More specifically, Dweck differentiates a growth mindset, a belief that we can change, improve, and grow in abilities, from a fixed mindset, a belief that our abilities and characteristics are fixed and cannot be changed. People with a growth mindset are more likely to persist, put in effort, believe they can overcome obstacles, and ultimately succeed, whereas those with a fixed mindset are more likely to give up when faced with failure. Considerable research supports that basic premise, and it also suggests that interventions to help people, especially youth, develop growth mindsets are effective. Chase applies that logic to leadership, suggesting that coaches with a growth mindset can transform themselves and believe in their ability to influence the transformation of others.

Within sport and exercise psychology, the leadership work of Chelladurai and colleagues is prominent. Chelladurai's model draws from earlier leadership models and has been revised to include elements of transformational leadership. Chelladurai's model and related research are reviewed in the following section, and a later section covers more current transformational leadership research within sport and exercise psychology.

Chelladurai's Multidimensional Model of Leadership

Chelladurai and colleagues conducted a systematic investigation of leadership with several studies over several years (see Chelladurai, 1984, 1990, 2007, 2014). Chelladurai's (1984) multidimensional model of leadership considers the influence of situation, leader, and member characteristics on leader behaviors and the subsequent influence of leader behaviors on group performance and satisfaction. The model includes three states of leader behaviors: (a) required behavior, mainly defined by the situation, such as the type of task or age level of the group; (b) preferred behavior, which refers to the followers' preferences; and (c) actual behavior, which is how the leader actually behaves. The major proposition of the model is the congruence hypothesis. That is, optimal performance and satisfaction are realized when the three states of leader behavior are congruent. In other words, the more the leader's actual behaviors match the preferences of group members and situation requirements, the better the group's performance and the greater the group members' satisfaction.

Key Point

According to Chelladurai's multidimensional model of leadership, the more the leader's actual behaviors match the preferences of group members and situation requirements, the better the group's performance and the greater the group members' satisfaction.

As an initial step, Chelladurai and Saleh (1980) developed the Leadership Scale for Sports (LSS). In a test of the congruence prediction, Chelladurai (1984) reported that the discrepancy between preferred and actual leader behavior was related to satisfaction. Athletes in wrestling, basketball, and track and field preferred an emphasis on training and instruction, and the more the coach matched those preferences, the greater the athletes' satisfaction. Basketball players were more satisfied when positive feedback met or exceeded their preferences, but athletes in wrestling and track were not. Considerable research has been done with the model and the LSS, much confirming the congruence hypothesis with regard to preferred and actual (usually perceived) behaviors.

In 2007, Chelladurai made a significant revision to the model, incorporating the concept of transformational leadership. That was added in recognition that successful coaches articulate a new mission and convince members of its importance and their capacity to achieve it. That addition acknowledges current trends in leadership theory and research, as discussed in the following section.

Transformational Leadership

Transformational leadership has become the number one approach to leadership in social psychology and in sport and exercise psychology research (Beauchamp & Morton, 2011; Morton, Sylvester, Wilson, Lonsdale, & Beauchamp, 2014; Sterrett & Janssen, 2015). Transformational leadership theory was conceptualized by Bass (1985; Bass & Riggio, 2006), who differentiated transformational leadership from transactional leadership.

Transactional leadership relies on contingent reward and behavioral approaches (carrot and stick approach). Transformational leadership involves inspiring, motivating, and encouraging others. Bass describes this as an augmentation effect in that transformational leadership builds upon and goes beyond transactional behaviors.

As such, transformational leadership is similar to motivational interviewing and health behavior coaching, which, as described in chapter 10, are client centered and focus on eliciting behaviors rather than prescribing or directing. Similarly, transformational leaders inspire and motivate others to seek and achieve higher standards.

These are the four primary components of transformational leadership:

- **Idealized influence:** Leaders are role models, "practicing what they preach."
- **Inspirational motivation:** Leaders provide a clear vision and instill confidence and optimism.
- **Intellectual stimulation:** Leaders challenge and engage others in decision making.
- **Individualized consideration:** Leaders attend to each individual's needs and abilities.

Key Point

Transformational leadership involves inspiring and motivating others to seek and achieve higher standards. The four primary components of transformational leadership are idealized influence, inspirational motivation, intellectual stimulation, and individualized consideration.

Several studies within sport and exercise psychology suggest that transformational leadership is beneficial to individuals and groups. Charbonneau, Barling, and Kelloway (2001) found that university athletes who perceived that their coach used transformational leadership behaviors had better performance, with the relationship mediated by intrinsic motivation. Rowold (2006) looked at transactional and transformational leadership behaviors in martial arts and found that transformational behaviors added to the influence of transactional behaviors on student perceptions of coach effectiveness. Callow, Smith, Hardy, Arthur, and Hardy (2009) found that ultimate Frisbee players' perceptions of transformational leadership behaviors were related to team cohesion, and they also found that performance level had a moderating effect. That is, some specific behaviors were more influential with high-performance athletes and others with lower-level athletes. Tucker, Turner, Barling, and McEvoy (2010) looked at transformational leadership and aggression in youth hockey. They found

that transformational leaders modeled prosocial behaviors and players demonstrated fewer aggressive behaviors.

Transformational leadership has not been applied as widely in exercise settings, but research on social supportive leader behaviors (e.g., Bray, Millen, Eidsness, & Leuzinger, 2005; Turner, Rejeski, & Brawley, 1997; see chapter 14) suggests that effective leaders use behaviors associated with transformational leadership (e.g., individual attention; positive, encouraging feedback). Beauchamp, Welch, and Hulley (2007) looked at transactional and transformational behaviors in exercise leaders. Although transformational behaviors did not have added effects, they suggested that the limited opportunities for transformational leader–member interactions in the exercise setting may be the reason. More promising effects have been found in physical education, a setting with many more opportunities for transformational interactions.

Beauchamp and Morton (2011) reviewed the literature on transformational teaching, concluding that transformational leadership, as displayed by physical education teachers, leads to greater physical activity behavior. Morton, Keith, and Beauchamp (2010) found that perceived transformational teaching was related to more positive student attitudes, motivation, and both in-class and leisure-time physical activity. Beauchamp and colleagues (2010) developed a measure of transformational teaching and found that adolescents' perceived teacher transformational behaviors predicted positive affect and self-determined motivation.

Beauchamp, Barling, and Morton (2011) used an intervention to modify teachers' transformational behaviors in a randomized controlled trial. Adolescents in the intervention condition rated their teachers as displaying significantly higher levels of transformational teaching and reported significantly higher levels of self-determined motivation, self-efficacy, and intentions to be physically active than those in the control group. Also, the between-group differences in perceived transformational teaching and self-determined motivation remained at the second posttest.

Drawing on intervention-based work on transformational leadership in nonsport settings, as well as Beauchamp and colleagues' (2011) intervention study, Morton and coauthors (2014) offered the following recommendations for coaches:

- Treat players with respect to earn their respect (idealized influence).

- Lead by example (idealized influence).
- Remain optimistic and enthusiastic about what athletes can accomplish (inspirational motivation).
- Articulate a compelling vision—map out what you want athletes to do, not what you don't want them to do (inspirational motivation).
- Encourage athletes to provide input and feedback so that they are part of the decision-making process (intellectual stimulation).
- Try to understand each individual player and that player's specific strengths and weaknesses, and support his or her personal development (individualized consideration).

Transformational Leadership in Cardiac Rehab

Transformational leadership involves inspiring and motivating others to reach their potential. Review the four components of transformational leadership and Morton and colleagues' recommendations for coaches. Then, assume you are the exercise leader in a cardiac rehab program, and come up with a list at least five things you could do to be a transformational leader. Be specific, and include all four components in your list.

Application Point

Peer Leadership Within Groups

Leadership within sport and exercise psychology has largely focused on the coach and sometimes on the teacher or exercise leader. Leadership as a process and relationship, however, is not limited to one leader or coach. Within sport and exercise psychology, some researchers have looked at athlete and peer leadership (Loughhead, Mawn, Hardy, & Munroe-Chandler, 2014).

A few studies have considered leadership within sport teams. Glenn and Horn (1993) investigated leadership within female high school soccer teams. Coaches suggested that athlete leadership was associated with soccer skill, whereas peers identified several psychological characteristics, including self-esteem, psychological androgyny, and lower trait anxiety, in addition to soccer competence. Later research has suggested that playing time and starting status are key characteristics of athlete leaders (Loughhead, Hardy, & Eys, 2006;

Moran & Weiss, 2006), and Price and Weiss (2011) found peer leaders higher in perceived competence, behavioral conduct, intrinsic motivation, and peer acceptance compared to those rated lower on leadership. Research has gone beyond characteristics to look at relationships, finding that peer acceptance and social connectedness are important in good athlete leaders (Moran & Weiss, 2006; Price & Weiss, 2011).

Fransen, Vanbeselaere, De Cuyper, Vande Broek, and Boen (2014) distinguished four different leadership roles for athletes: (a) task leader, giving tactical advice; (b) motivational leader, encouraging teammates; (c) social leader, developing good team atmosphere; and (d) external leader, handling communications with management and media. Fransen, Haslam, and colleagues (2015) found that team members had greater team confidence and better performance when the athlete leader expressed higher confidence, and they further suggested that this effect was partially mediated by team members' increased team identification. They concluded that athlete leaders can shape team members' confidence and hence performance in both positive and negative ways.

Fransen, Van Puyenbroeck, and colleagues (2015) used social network analysis to investigate general leadership quality, and in a second study they focused on specific task, motivational, social, and external leader qualities. They found that the extent to which athletes felt connected with their leader was most predictive of athletes' perceptions of the leader's quality in each role. At the team level, teams with higher athlete leadership quality were more strongly connected.

Price and Weiss (2013) looked at both coach and peer leadership, applying transformational leadership theory with adolescent female soccer players. They found that coach leadership was more influential than peer leadership for predicting individual outcomes (perceived competence, enjoyment, intrinsic motivation) and collective efficacy. With regard to cohesion, peer leadership was more strongly related to social cohesion than was coach leadership, whereas peer and coach leadership were equally important for task cohesion. Their findings indicate that both coach and peer leaders influence individual and group outcomes, and that players may look to coach and peer leaders for different types of information. As they concluded, peers and coaches can be powerful, inspirational, and influential leaders, and effective leadership can promote positive youth development.

Cohesion in Sport and Exercise Groups

Cohesion is the most popular group dynamics topic in sport and exercise psychology, including continuing research on the cohesion–performance relationship and research on cohesion in exercise groups. Research suggests that cohesion benefits the group and group members, but relationships vary with individual and group characteristics and ever-changing group processes.

Cohesion: Definition and Conceptual Model

First, let's clarify the term *cohesion*. Within the group dynamics literature, "cohesion" and "cohesiveness" are used interchangeably, and many articles cite the classic definition of cohesiveness as "the total field of forces which act on members to remain in a group" (Festinger, Schachter, & Back, 1950, p. 164). This definition fits our understanding, but it is nearly impossible to operationalize, and it emphasizes individuals rather than group cohesion.

Within sport and exercise psychology, the major group dynamics and cohesion research began in the 1980s with the systematic research conducted by the Canadian trio of Bert Carron, Larry Brawley, and Neil Widmeyer (e.g., Carron, 1982; Carron, Widmeyer, & Brawley, 1985, 1988). They laid the groundwork by developing a conceptual framework and defining cohesion as "a dynamic process which is reflected in the tendency for a group to stick together and remain united in the pursuit of its instrumental objectives and/or the satisfaction of member affective needs" (Carron, Brawley, & Widmeyer, 1998, p. 213). Their definition incorporates some features particularly relevant to sport and exercise psychology.

First, cohesion is multidimensional, with many factors that relate to cohesion and differ across groups. Second, cohesion is dynamic, changing over time through group processes. Third, cohesion is instrumental; group members cohere for a purpose, whether to be part of a university basketball team or to maintain an exercise program. Fourth, cohesion has an affective dimension; even in highly task-oriented groups such as sport teams, social cohesion generally develops through interactions and communications.

Key Point

Carron, Widmeyer, and Brawley laid the groundwork for sport and exercise research on cohesion by developing a conceptual framework and defining cohesion as "a dynamic process which is reflected in the tendency for a group to stick together and remain united in the pursuit of its instrumental objectives and/or the satisfaction of member affective needs."

Carron and colleagues (e.g., Carron et al., 1985) proposed a multidimensional model that is the basis for most sport and exercise psychology work on cohesion. Their model incorporates two major aspects of cohesion: group objectives and perspectives. Group objectives can be classified as task or social. Task objectives focus on performance or productivity, whereas social objectives focus on group harmony and interpersonal relationships. Perspectives may be of the group as a whole (group integration) or members' individual attractions to the group. Group integration refers to the degree of closeness or unity in the group, whereas individual attractions refer to members' personal motivations or feelings toward the group. Combining the task–social objectives and group–individual perspectives gives us the four dimensions of cohesion as follows:

- **Group integration–task (GI-T):** the degree to which the group is united around task objectives
- **Group integration–social (GI-S):** the degree to which the group is united around social objectives
- **Individual attractions to the group–task (ATG-T):** group members' perceptions of their personal involvement with the task aspects of the group
- **Individual attractions to the group–social (ATG-S):** group members' perceptions of their personal involvement with the social aspects of the group

Measures of Cohesion

Most measures of cohesion used in sport and exercise psychology are based on the four dimensions of the Carron and colleagues (1985) model. The most widely used cohesion measure is the Group Environment Questionnaire (GEQ; Brawley,

Carron, & Widmeyer, 1987; Carron, Brawley, & Widmeyer, 2002; Carron et al., 1985). As in the conceptual model, the GEQ assesses both task and social cohesion from both group integration and individual attractions perspectives. Thus, the GEQ assesses the resulting four dimensions of cohesion:

- Group integration–task (GI-T) (e.g., our team is united in trying to reach its goals for performance)
- Group integration–social (GI-S) (e.g., our team members rarely party together—reversed)
- Individual attractions to the group–task (ATG-T) (e.g., I am unhappy with my team's level of desire to win—reversed)
- Individual attractions to the group–social (ATG-S) (e.g., some of my best friends are on this team)

The Group Environment Questionnaire is an 18-item, four-scale measure that has good internal consistency and is applicable to a variety of sport and exercise groups. The GEQ continues to be the most accepted and widely used measure of cohesion in sport and exercise psychology, and several related measures have been developed for different target groups.

Estabrooks and Carron (2000) adapted the GEQ to develop a cohesion measure more appropriate for exercise groups, the Physical Activity GEQ (PAGEQ), which has the same four subscales. Two measures have been developed for younger groups. The Youth Sport Environment Questionnaire (YSEQ) was developed specifically for youth ages 13 through 17 (Eys, Loughead, Bray, & Carron, 2009), and the Child Sport Cohesion Questionnaire (CSCQ) was developed specifically for younger (age 9-12) children (Martin, Carron, Eys, & Loughhead, 2012). Research, we should note, suggests that younger participants do not distinguish the group integration and individual attractions to group perspectives; thus it is recommended that only the task–social dimension be used with them (e.g., Eys et al., 2015). Both the YSEQ and CSCQ assess only the task and social dimension.

Correlates of Cohesion

As well as the conceptual model of cohesion, the model expands to antecedents and consequences, or more correctly, correlates of cohesion. Specifically, the model includes environmental, personal, leadership, and team factors that contribute to,

and are influenced by, cohesion. Notably, research and reviews of the cohesion research (e.g., Eys et al., 2015) suggest that these factors serve as both antecedents and consequences of cohesion, and the relationships are bidirectional and dynamic.

Environmental factors include proximity, group size, and distinctiveness. In terms of proximity, people who are physically close to each other tend to bond together, as do team members who live near each other or travel together. Distinctiveness from other groups also increases feelings of unity. Special privileges, club T-shirts, or group rituals might all enhance distinctiveness. Widmeyer, Brawley, and Carron (1990) found an inverted-U relationship between group size and social cohesion in intramural basketball, with moderate-sized groups showing greatest cohesiveness. However, Williams and Widmeyer (1991) found no relationship between group size and social cohesion with golf teams, and we cannot draw strong conclusions about size and cohesion.

Personal factors reflect individual abilities, attitudes, and commitment. Eys and colleagues (2015) suggest that the most important personal factor is satisfaction. Indeed, several studies show a positive relationship between satisfaction and cohesion. For example, Jeffery-Tosoni, Eys, Schinke, and Lewko (2011) found that youth athletes who perceived the group as more socially cohesive were more satisfied. Other personal sources of cohesion include similarity of group members, competitive state anxiety, degree to which members engage in social loafing, and commitment to the team. As discussed in chapter 15, many youth sport and physical activity programs focus on positive youth development (PYD) and fostering personal and social skills. Bruner, Eys, Wilson, and Côté (2014) looked at cohesion and PYD with a large sample of adolescent athletes. They found that higher perceptions of both task and social cohesion predicted greater personal and social skills and lower levels of negative experiences at the individual level.

Leadership factors reflect relationships with the coach or leader. Generally, a more democratic decision style (vs. an autocratic style) is related to cohesion. Also, as discussed earlier, transformational leadership behaviors are related to cohesion (Callow et al., 2009). Leaders also create the climate, and the climate influences cohesion. Both Eys and colleagues (2013) and Horn, Byrd, Martin, and Young (2012) found that both task and social cohesion were higher when the coach-initiated climate was characterized by task-related behaviors, or more mastery oriented. Given those findings, McLaren, Eys, and Murray (2015) conducted an intervention study with youth coaches. The motivational climate intervention was effective in increasing coaches' task-focused behaviors and positively influencing youth perceptions of both task and social cohesion.

Team factors relate to the group structure (roles and norms), group processes (goals, communication), and group outcomes. As discussed in the earlier section, research suggests that when people understand their roles (role clarity), accept their roles (role acceptance), and carry out their roles (role performance), groups are more effective, and as Eys and colleagues (2015) note, more cohesive. Research on norms is limited, but Gammage, Carron, and Estabrooks (2001) found norms associated with cohesion. Eys and coauthors (2015) note that establishing and emphasizing group goals promotes cohesion and suggest that group communication and cohesion are interrelated.

Key Point

Research suggests that when people understand their roles (role clarity), accept their roles (role acceptance), and carry out their roles (role performance), groups are more effective and more cohesive.

Communication is associated with cohesion in a circular way: Increased communication on task and social issues increases cohesion, and more cohesive groups have increased communication. Finally, performance success increases cohesion (Eys et al., 2015), as discussed in more detail in the following section.

The Cohesion–Performance Relationship

Despite more than 40 years of research on the relationship between cohesion and sport team performance, the evidence does not consistently support the intuitive assumption that cohesive teams win more games. Early research by Martens and Peterson with male intramural basketball players provided support for a positive relationship between cohesion and performance. Their first study (Martens & Peterson, 1971), which examined preseason cohesiveness as a determinant of team success, showed that high-cohesive teams

won more games than low-cohesive teams. The second study (Peterson & Martens, 1972), which investigated the influence of team success on postseason cohesiveness, showed that successful teams were more cohesive than less successful teams.

Several studies confirmed the positive relationship between cohesion and success with teams in various sports (e.g., Carron & Ball, 1977; Landers, Wilkinson, Hatfield, & Barber, 1982; Ruder & Gill, 1982; Williams & Hacker, 1982; Williams & Widmeyer, 1991). These studies seem to make a strong case, but other studies found either no relationship or negative relationships. Continuing research with updated models and measures has examined moderators, mediators, and causality to shed more light on the cohesion–performance relationship.

Causality is a key consideration: Does cohesion predict success, or does success predict cohesion? Some researchers attempted to get at causality by looking at the relationship in both directions. Bakeman and Helmreich (1975) and Carron and Ball (1977) applied the cross-lagged panel design to assess both cohesion and performance at two time points. In both cases they found that earlier performance predicted later cohesion, but they found no support for the influence of cohesion on later performance.

These findings do not necessarily imply that cohesion does not influence performance. Preseason measures are likely to be unreliable, and retrospective postseason measures may reflect the glow of success. Continuing research using stronger designs and measures indicates that the cohesion–performance relationship is more dynamic and complex than observations and the early research findings suggest. Mullen and Copper's (1994) review confirmed a stronger relationship from performance success to cohesion than from cohesion to success, but Carron, Colman, Wheeler, and Stevens (2002) found similar relationships in both directions in their meta-analysis.

The most recent reviews of the evidence (e.g., Eys et al., 2015) conclude that the cohesion–performance relationship is positive and bidirectional; greater cohesion leads to better performance, and better performance leads to cohesion. That conclusion holds across different sport types (e.g., independent, interdependent) and competitive levels. Several potential moderating variables have been examined, but only gender seems to moderate the relationship, with the cohesion–performance link stronger for female athletes.

Key Point

The most recent reviews of the evidence conclude that the cohesion–performance relationship is positive and bidirectional; greater cohesion leads to better performance, and better performance leads to cohesion. That conclusion holds across different sport types (e.g., independent, interdependent) and competitive levels.

Cohesion and Adherence

Investigations of cohesion in physical activity settings other than competitive sport are limited but expanding. In competitive sport settings, team performance is the primary outcome variable. With youth and recreational levels, developmental and psychosocial outcomes may be more important. In adult exercise settings, continued activity or adherence is often a key outcome. As discussed in the earlier section on correlates, cohesion is related to several psychosocial outcomes, including satisfaction and collective efficacy.

Burke, Carron, and Shapcott (2011) reviewed the literature on cohesion and exercise groups and reached four conclusions. First, exercise classes are groups, and examination of cohesion is worthwhile. Second, most people prefer exercising in groups versus alone. Third, research provides strong evidence of associations between perceptions of cohesion and physical activity–related behaviors, cognitions, and affective responses. Finally, research and meta-analytic summaries support the conclusion that exercising in a group is associated with adherence behavior.

Several studies indicate that cohesion facilitates exercise adherence. Studies with university classes indicate that participants who report higher cohesion attend more classes and are less likely to drop out (Carron et al., 1988; Spink & Carron, 1992, 1993). Task cohesion was the key dimension in university classes; but with a private health club, social cohesion was more important in predicting dropout rates (Spink & Carron, 1994). In their meta-analysis of social influence and exercise, Carron, Hausenblas, and Mack (1996) suggested that cohesion, especially task cohesion, influences exercise adherence. Dunlop, Falk, and Beauchamp (2013) extended that research by looking at changes over time with exercise classes. They found that social cohesion changed significantly over time and also varied between individuals over

time. Task cohesion stayed constant over time and relatively consistent across people and groups.

Overall, the sport and exercise psychology literature indicates that cohesion is positively related to sport and exercise behavior and also to group members' satisfaction, liking for the activity, and later participation in physical activity. The individual- and group-level benefits suggest that group leaders and participants would be wise to foster cohesion in sport and exercise groups. Interventions designed to increase cohesion and foster positive outcomes are promising, and team building is a particularly promising approach advocated by several group dynamics researchers.

Applying Group Dynamics Through Team Building

Team building puts group dynamics models and research into practice. Team building in sport and exercise psychology draws from organizational psychology, and that work is quite adaptable to physical activity settings. Coaches, teachers, exercise leaders, and other kinesiology professionals use team building. Also, researchers and consultants have applied team building in both sport and exercise settings.

Brawley and Paskevich (1997) summarized the organizational development definitions and concluded that team building is a method of helping the group to increase effectiveness, satisfy the needs of its members, or improve work conditions. In a more concise statement, Carron and Eys (2012) defined team building as "team enhancement for both task and social purposes" (p. 368).

Key Point

Team building can be characterized as team enhancement for both task and social purposes.

Team-Building Models

Most team-building models used in sport and exercise psychology stem from the cohesion model, and more specifically from Carron and Spink's (1993) team-building framework. Hardy and Crace (1997) noted that most models focus on enhancing team effectiveness by improving team processes. Although team performance is often the output of interest, cohesion is the primary target in Carron and Spink's framework. Here, team building is used to increase cohesion, which in turn improves group effectiveness or performance. With exercise groups we might substitute group maintenance for group effectiveness. The team-building process typically involves the group environment (distinctiveness), group structure (group norms and positions), and group process (interaction, communication, and sacrifices).

Team-Building Interventions

Team-building interventions aim to increase group effectiveness or maintenance by enhancing group cohesion. Carron and Spink's guiding model for team building involves four stages. The first three stages typically occur in a workshop with coaches or leaders. In the fourth stage, the coach or leader applies team-building strategies with the group members. The introductory stage and the conceptual stage give the coach or leader an overview of the benefits of cohesion and a frame of reference. The conceptual model identifies factors within each category that contribute to the development of cohesion. In the practical stage, coaches or leaders brainstorm to identify specific strategies to use for team building with their group. Finally, in the intervention stage, the coaches or leaders introduce and maintain the team-building protocols in the group setting.

Carron and colleagues (Carron & Spink, 1993; Carron, Spink, & Prapavessis, 1997) have used this intervention successfully with fitness classes and sport teams. With university aerobics classes (Carron & Spink, 1993), specific interventions addressed group environment, group structure, and group processes. Distinctiveness, the target of the group environment intervention, included such strategies as group names and T-shirts. Group structure interventions included both individual roles (e.g., pick spots) and group norms (e.g., establish partner goals). Group process interventions included sacrifices (e.g., regulars helping new people) and interaction and communication (e.g., taking turns in partner activities). The eight-week intervention increased group task cohesion. Continuing research and team-building interventions with other sport and exercise groups have provided promising results (see Eys et al., 2015, or Carron & Eys, 2012, for more detailed reviews).

Although Carron and Spink's four-phase model has been most often used in sport and exercise psychology, other team-building approaches have been used. Crace and Hardy (1997) take a values-based approach and emphasize awareness of individual and team values, identification of interfering factors, and development of interventions to improve mutual respect and cohesion. Similarly, Yukelson (1997) focuses on developing an effective team culture with open communication and offers several suggestions, such as getting to know each athlete as a unique individual and having regular team meetings designated as time to talk openly.

The Personal Disclosure–Mutual Sharing (PDMS) model, which is related to Yukelson's and Crace and Hardy's approaches, has been used as team-building invention in several studies. Dunn and Holt (2004) used PDMS with ice hockey players and reported benefits including increased understanding, cohesion, and confidence. Holt and Dunn (2006) replicated the PDMS intervention with an elite women's soccer team, finding similar benefits. Pain and Harwood (2009) found that their intervention, which was designed to encourage open discussion, led to improvements in perceptions of team functioning (cohesion, communication, and trust and confidence in teammates), training quality, self-understanding, player ownership, and team performance.

As well as the Caron and Spink model and PDMS approaches, other approaches to team building could be applied in sport and exercise settings. In a review, Martin, Carron, and Burke (2009) identified four forms of team-building interventions—interpersonal relations, goal setting, adventure, and omnibus. Interpersonal relations, which includes the Carron and Spink and PDMS models, is the most widely used in sport by far. Group goal setting is used next most often, and the omnibus approach, which draws from several different group dynamics principles, is used rarely.

Adventure approaches are seldom used in sport and exercise psychology interventions, but adventure experiences, challenge courses, experiential education, and related activities are often used in youth programs, in schools, and with business and organizational groups. Such programs typically involve challenges that can be met only by all group members working together cooperatively. Although such approaches have seldom been used in sport and exercise psychology research, many athletic programs take their athletes to ropes courses as team-building activities, and physical education classes often incorporate these types of team-building activities.

Several of the reviews (e.g., Eys et al., 2015) provide examples of team-building strategies based on the existing research. Following are examples for sport and exercise groups from the five categories of distinctiveness, individual positions, group norms, individual sacrifices, and interaction and communication:

- Distinctiveness
  - Sport: Provide unique identifiers such as T-shirts, logos, or mottoes.
  - Exercise: Have a group name; provide neon headbands or shoelaces; make up a class slogan.
- Individual positions
  - Sport: Create team structure with clearly differentiated roles.
  - Exercise: Provide specific positions for high-, moderate-, and low-impact exercisers.
- Group norms
  - Sport: Point out how individual contributions contribute to team success.
  - Exercise: Encourage members to become fitness buddies; set a goal for the group.
- Individual sacrifices
  - Sport: Ask veterans to sit out to give novices playing time.
  - Exercise: Ask regulars to help new people.
- Interaction and communication
  - Sport: Provide opportunities for athlete input.
  - Exercise: Use partner work; take turns showing moves.

Application Point

Building Your Team

You are coaching a regional softball team made up of players from several different teams that will go on to play in a state tournament. Thus, the players have not all been together on the same team before. Refer to the information on team building, and identify team-building strategies you might use with this team in your practice sessions and during the tournament. Be specific, and try to come up with a specific strategy in each of the five categories (distinctiveness, individual positions, group norms, individual sacrifices, and interaction and communication).

Putting It Into Practice

Summary

Most sport and physical activities involve groups. Groups involve interaction, and understanding interpersonal relationships and ongoing processes are keys to understanding groups. Group performance is the primary outcome for most sport groups, but effective group performance is more than gathering the most skilled individuals. Steiner's model of group performance is expressed as actual productivity (or performance) = potential productivity – process losses. Those process losses may be coordination losses or motivation losses. The main task of a coach or group leader is to reduce process losses by developing organizational strategies and maintaining optimal motivation levels.

Leadership is a key concern for coaches and teachers, but leadership is a complex social relationship and not a characteristic of one person. Leadership theories have evolved from the early trait theories through behavioral, situational, and interactional models to transformational leadership theory, which has garnered considerable attention in sport and exercise psychology. Transformational leadership, which involves inspiring and motivating others to seek and achieve higher standards, has been related to performance, motivation, and prosocial behaviors in sport, as well as to positive attitudes, motivation, and physical activity in physical education.

Cohesion, which reflects a group's tendency to remain united in pursuit of its goals, is a particularly popular topic in sport and exercise psychology. Cohesion is typically conceptualized and measured in line with Carron and colleagues' model, which classifies cohesion in terms of the group's objective (task or social) and perspectives (group as a whole, or individual attractions). Research and reviews conclude that the cohesion–performance relationship is positive and bidirectional; greater cohesion leads to better performance, and better performance leads to cohesion. Overall, the research indicates that cohesion is positively related to group members' satisfaction, liking for the activity, and later participation in physical activity, as well as to performance.

Team-building interventions aim to increase group effectiveness or maintenance by enhancing group cohesion. Team-building strategies, such as group names, group norms, sacrifices, interaction, and communication, have been used successfully to develop cohesion and enhance effectiveness of sport and exercise groups.

Review Questions

1. Define *group* as the term is used in sport and exercise psychology.
2. Explain Steiner's model of group performance, including the relationships among actual and potential performance and group processes.
3. Define the *Ringelmann effect* and its related term, *social loafing*.
4. Describe transformational leadership and identify its four components.
5. Describe Carron and colleagues' conceptual model with its four dimensions of cohesion.
6. Describe Carron and Spink's team-building framework.

Recommended Reading

- Beauchamp, M.R., & Morton, K.L. (2011). Transformational teaching and physical activity engagement among adolescents. *Exercise and Sport Sciences Reviews, 39*(3), 133-139. Transformational leadership, which involves inspiring and motivating others to seek and achieve higher standards, is the number one approach to leadership in group dynamics. In this article the authors review the literature and specifically apply transformational leadership to physical education and youth activity settings.

- Eys, M.A., Burke, S.M., Dennis, P., & Evans, B. (2015). The sport team as an effective group. In J.M. Williams & V. Krane (Eds.), *Applied sport psychology* (7th ed., pp. 124-139). New York: McGraw-Hill. This chapter provides an overview of the sport team as an effective group, including models of group processes, cohesion, leadership, and team building in sport groups.

- Price, M.S., & Weiss, M.R. (2013). Relationships among coach leadership, peer leadership, and adolescent athletes' psychosocial and team outcomes: A test of transformational leadership theory. *Journal of Applied Sport Psychology, 25*(2), 265-279. doi:10.1080/10413200.2012.725703. Price and Weiss connect transformational leadership with positive youth development in their research. Specifically, they looked at both coach and peer leadership and found that both play a role in young athletes' personal and social development.

Team Building in a Youth Activity Program

For this lab, you are to apply group dynamics, and specifically team building, in professional practice. Team building is often used to develop cohesion in sport teams. Team building is just as relevant to other areas of kinesiology practice, including physical education and exercise programs. For this lab, the imagined setting is an after-school activity program. And, in the spirit of group dynamics, you may want to work together with one or two friends or classmates to complete the lab.

Assume that you are one of the leaders of an after-school activity program at the middle school. This program targets students who are not involved in sport teams or other school clubs. Thus, as well as promoting physical activity, the program is a way to help students be more involved and connected with other students. The students are a diverse group of boys and girls with varying skill levels and interests. Your coleader suggested using team-building activities, and you agree. Address the following steps:

1. Why use team building? How might team building be beneficial to your program and to the individual students in the program?

2. What team-building approaches and strategies will you use? Refer to the examples in the chapter, but consider the unique characteristics of your class (e.g., individuals, structure, environment) and be creative.

3. Create a specific team-building activity that you could use with your program. Include background information and all instructions or guidelines for the activity (so that someone else could follow your instructions and do that activity). Revisit this chapter and go to team-building websites or resources for information and ideas, but create your own activity.

4. Optional: If you complete this lab as part of a class, teaching your activity to others in the class would be a good team-building follow-up to the lab.

Culture and Cultural Competence

Chapter Objectives

After studying this chapter, you should be able to

- describe culture and cultural identities,

- discuss the role of power and privilege in cultural relations,

- identify ways in which gender and cultural stereotypes can affect participants and professionals in sport and physical activity, and

- describe cultural competence and discuss its role in professional practice.

"How many goodly creatures are there here! How beauteous mankind is! O brave new world that has such people in it!" (from William Shakespeare's *The Tempest*, V, 1, 182). Over 400 years ago Shakespeare recognized and valued cultural diversity. Cultural diversity is much more evident and easily recognized today than it was in Shakespeare's time. Culture is ever present and powerful in sport and exercise. Participants are diverse in many ways, and physical activity takes place in a culturally diverse world. People carry their gender and cultural identities everywhere. And, importantly, our cultural identity affects our behaviors and interactions with others. In today's world it is essential that we recognize and value cultural diversity. One size does not fit all—in clothing or in our professional practice.

This chapter takes an encompassing view of culture and begins with some basic information and a guiding framework. Then the chapter reviews scholarship on gender and culture and offers directions for enhancing cultural competence in professional practice. The discussion should help you understand cultural diversity and the many ways in which the sport and exercise experience is shaped by the cultural context.

Culture: Basics and a Guiding Framework

In this first section, we will set the stage for a review of sport and exercise psychology scholarship on culture. First, we clarify terminology. Then we provide a guiding framework for understanding culture and moving toward cultural competence in professional practice.

Multicultural psychology may be defined as the "systematic study of behavior, cognition and affect in many cultures" (Mio, Barker-Hackett, & Tumambing, 2006, p. 3). *Culture*, however, is complex and not easily defined. Narrow definitions emphasize ethnicity, but we will adopt the common practice in multicultural psychology and broaden the definition to *shared values, beliefs, and practices of an identifiable group of people*. Thus, culture includes race and ethnicity, gender, language, spirituality, sexuality, and of particular relevance for sport and exercise, physicality (physical abilities and characteristics). Multicultural psychology further emphasizes intersections of identities and the totality of cultural experiences and contexts.

The multicultural psychology scholarship, along with the cultural sport studies literature, converges on common themes that form the guid-

Key Point

Culture refers to shared values, beliefs, and practices of an identifiable group of people, and thus it includes race and ethnicity, gender, language, spirituality, sexuality, and physicality (physical abilities and characteristics).

ing framework for this chapter. All emphasize multiple, intersecting cultural identities; highlight power relations; and call for social action and advocacy.

- *Multiple, intersecting cultural identities.* We all have gender, race and ethnicity, and other intersecting identities. The mix of intersecting identities is unique to each person and varies across individuals, time, and contexts. For example, when you are in circumstances in which you are the only person with your identity (e.g., the only girl on the youth baseball team, the only Latino in the spin class), that aspect of your identity is more salient.

- *Power relations.* Culture is more than categories. Culture is relational, and cultural relations involve power and privilege. That is, one group has power or privilege, and other groups lack privilege or are oppressed. Who makes the rules? Who is left out? In the U.S. Western culture, white and middle- and upper-class men typically have power.

- *Action and advocacy.* Understanding intersecting cultural identities and recognizing power and privilege in cultural relations lead to action for social justice. Action and advocacy call for professionals to develop their own cultural competencies and to work for social justice in our programs and institutions. Specifically, culturally competent kinesiology professionals take action to ensure that physical activity is inclusive and empowering for all participants.

Psychology has moved beyond its decidedly nonmulticultural past, described in Robert Guthrie's (2004, classic ed.) book *Even the Rat Was White*, first published in 1976. Psychology scholars have expanded multicultural research, and cultural competence is required in professional practice. Multicultural psychology scholars emphasize intersecting identities, as well as power and privilege in cultural relations, and call for moving from scholarship to social action.

Derald Wing Sue (2004), who has written extensively on multicultural psychology, argues that psychology must make the invisible visible—recognize white privilege and the culture-bound nature of our scholarship and practice—to advance its mission and enhance the health and well-being of all people. But moving beyond cultural boundaries and traditional approaches is no easy task. The sport and exercise context has clear cultural boundaries, and we must consider people in that context in order to understand their behavior.

Multicultural psychologists call for attention to power relations and social context but also retain concern for the individual. The combined focus on the individual and cultural relations may seem paradoxical, but that combination is the essence of a useful multicultural sport and exercise psychology. Psychology focuses on individual behavior, thoughts, and feelings, but we cannot fully understand the individual without considering the larger world, and that larger world involves culture. The goal is to apply our understanding to help people in the real world—to promote inclusive and empowering physical activity for all.

Key Point

Multicultural psychologists call for attention to power relations and social context but also retain concern for the individual. The combined focus on the individual and cultural relations may seem paradoxical, but it is the essence of a useful multicultural sport and exercise psychology.

Cultural Context of Sport and Exercise

Before reviewing the literature on cultural diversity, let's identify the cultural context of sport and exercise. As a warm-up, consider how culture might affect your thoughts, feelings, and behaviors in the following cases:

- A college soccer player who lacks control and is prone to angry outbursts explains this behavior by stating, "I really get into the game, and sometimes I just lose it."

- A middle school student in physical education is withdrawn and reluctant to get into the action despite good physical skills and your encouragement.

- An athletic trainer suspects that a figure skater may have an eating disorder, but the skater claims to be working to make it to nationals and get endorsements.

Imagine each case with a female and then with a male. Does gender influence your response to these cases? Do you think a teacher, coach, trainer, or parent would behave in the same way? What about other aspects of culture—would your responses vary if the participants were African American, Asian American, or immigrants from a non-Western cultural tradition? If you try to eliminate all considerations of culture and treat everyone the same, you will have difficulty. Again, culture affects our behaviors and interactions—gender makes a difference, and *race matters* (to borrow the title of Cornel West's 1993 book). Trying to treat everyone the same ignores cultural identities and does a disservice to the participants.

Cultural Diversity in an Activity Program

Assume that you are the activity director in a community recreation center. Identify various ways participants in your activity program might differ from you (consider gender, age, race and ethnicity, physical characteristics, and so on). Then identify ways in which participants are likely to differ from each other. No doubt you will have a long list. Participants are diverse, and that diversity affects behaviors and relationships.

Cultural Diversity in Sport and Physical Activity

Our world is shaped by our cultural identities and the cultural context. Physical activity participants are diverse, but not as diverse as the broader population. Until the 1970s, when an identifiable sport and exercise psychology emerged, "*athlete*" meant male athlete, and male athletes were not culturally diverse. School physical education and community recreational programs may come closer to reflecting community diversity, but all sport and exercise programs reflect cultural restrictions. Gender influence is particularly powerful and has some unique features in physical activity settings.

The physical education roots of sport and exercise psychology provide a unique gender context. Strong women leaders developed women's physical education as an alternative to men's physical education programs and provided a female-oriented environment long before the women's movement of the 1970s and before sport and exercise psychology was an identifiable area. At a 1923 conference, physical education leaders set guidelines that included putting athletes first, preventing exploitation, downplaying competition while emphasizing enjoyment and good sporting behavior, promoting activity for all rather than an elite few, and developing women as sport leaders. A related clarifying statement (from the National Amateur Athletic Federation [NAAF], 1930, p. 41) concluded with the classic line, "A game for every girl and every girl in a game." The 1972 passage of Title IX of the Education Amendments, the U.S. law that prohibits sex discrimination in educational institutions, marked the beginning of a move away from the early women's physical education model toward the competitive women's sport programs of today.

Participation of girls and women in youth and college sport exploded in the last generation. Still, the numbers of female and male participants are not equal. Sabo and Veliz (2012), in a nation-wide study of high schools, found that overall, boys had more sport opportunities than girls. Moreover, progress toward gender equity, which had advanced before 2000, had reversed since then, resulting in a wider gender gap. Geographic region and social class further affected sport opportunities, with urban schools and those with the least economic resources offering fewer athletic opportunities for all students.

Kanters, Bocarro, Edwards, Casper, and Floyd (2013) looked at the role of gender, race, ethnicity, and socioeconomic status in middle school sport participation and compared schools with interscholastic sports to those with intramural sports. Overall, more students participated in schools with intramural sports. Participation of girls was similar in the two groups of schools, but higher percentages of boys participated in intramural sports, and co-ed intramural sports were dominated by boys. Also, higher percentages of black students and lower-income students participated at intramural schools. The authors concluded that intramural sports were a promising strategy for increasing sport participation among all students and especially those from black and low-income households. They also suggested that segregated gender opportunities might encourage more girls to participate in intramural sports. Casper, Bocarro, Kanters, and Floyd (2011) looked at the constraints that limit adolescent sport participa-

tion and found cultural differences, with girls, Latinos, and lower socioeconomic status students reporting more constraints. To better understand gender and any aspect of culture, we must look beyond biology and simple dichotomous categories to cultural relations.

Citius, Altius, Fortius—the Olympic motto—translates as "Swifter, Higher, Stronger," underscoring the physical but also implying that sport is competitive and hierarchical. The average male may be taller, faster, and stronger than the average female, but biological sex is only part of the gender mix. All meanings, social roles, and expectations, as well as the standards of behavior, beauty, and power, are constructed in the cultural context. Sport does not have to be higher, faster, and stronger. Instead, it might call for fun, flair, and friendship. (I disclose my biases: I am not high, fast, strong—or competitive.)

Key Point

The average male may be taller, faster, and stronger than the average female, but biological sex is only part of the gender mix. Meanings, social roles, and expectations, as well as standards of behavior, beauty, and power, are constructed in the cultural context.

Cultural Diversity: Beyond the Numbers

In considering cultural diversity, it is important to go beyond participation numbers and categories to consider power and privilege, or who makes the rules. Sue (2004) illustrated the power differential in noting that although white males make up just 33 percent of the U.S. population, they hold 80 percent of tenured faculty positions, 92 percent of *Forbes* 400 CEO-level positions, 80 percent of House of Representatives seats, and 84 percent of Senate seats. And of special interest here, they make up 99 percent of athletic team owners. Although Sue's numbers are over 10 years old, the numbers today are much the same, especially in the athletic world.

Richard Lapchick has been monitoring gender and racial diversity in sport for several years, and his *Racial and Gender Report Card* shows racial and gender inequities, with little progress. The 2015 report card (Lapchick, 2015) indicates that African Americans are slightly overrepresented in

U.S. Division I athletics, mainly due to overrepresentation in basketball, but other racial and ethnic minorities are very underrepresented (see more statistics and reports at the Institute for Diversity and Ethnics in Sport [TIDES] website).

When we consider positions of power, diversity is virtually nonexistent. Before Title IX (1972), more than 90 percent of women's athletic teams were coached by women and had a woman athletic director. Today less than half of women's teams are coached by women (Acosta & Carpenter, 2014). White men dominate coaching, even of women's teams. Coaches of other racial and ethnic identities can hardly be counted, and administration remains solidly white male. The 2015 *Racial and Gender Report Card* indicated that whites held 90 percent of the athletic director positions, and less than 10 percent were women.

Although international data are lacking, the trends are similar (Norman, 2008), and the limited data available suggest even fewer women coaches at the youth level than at the collegiate and elite levels (Kamphoff & LaVoi, 2013; Messner, 2009). The 2012 London Olympics showcased women athletes and also demonstrated intersecting cultural identities and power relations. The United States sent more female than male athletes to London, but women were vastly underrepresented in several delegations; coaching positions are heavily dominated by men, and Olympic officials are not as diverse as the athletes. Clearly, elite sport is culturally elite.

Key Point

Before Title IX (1972), more than 90 percent of women's athletic teams were coached by women. Today, less than half of women's teams are coached by women (Acosta & Carpenter, 2014).

What about exercise and the wider range of physical activities? *Physical activity*, a more inclusive term, suggests diversity, but census data and public health reports indicate otherwise. Physical activity is limited by gender, race, socioeconomic status, and especially by physical attributes. In their chapter on physical activity epidemiology, Lox, Martin Ginis, and Petruzzello (2014) summarized research and large national surveys on physical activity trends from several countries. Evidence continues to show that physical activity decreases across the adult life span, with men more active than women, especially with regard to vigorous activity; racial and ethnic minorities and low-income groups are less active, and young adult women (particularly African American women) are among the most inactive populations in the United States (Kimm et al., 2002; Pate, Dowda, O'Neill, & Ward, 2007). The Centers for Disease Control and Prevention (CDC) tracks physical activity, and the CDC website provides updated data on trends in the United States as well as helpful information. Cultural constraints to physical activity extend around the world. The World Health Organization (WHO, 2014) identifies physical inactivity as a global health problem, noting that about 31 percent of adults are insufficiently active. Inactivity rates are higher in the Americas and Eastern Mediterranean and lowest in South East Asia, and men are more active than women in all regions.

Cultural Diversity in Sport and Exercise Psychology

Despite the diversity of participants and the need for cultural competence in professional practice, sport and exercise psychology has been slow to recognize and value cultural diversity. Research does not address diversity; professional practice focuses on elite sport; educational programs do not incorporate multicultural competencies; and sport and exercise psychology does not address social justice issues.

Duda and Allison (1990) first identified the lack of research on race and ethnicity, reporting that only 1 of 13 published theoretical papers and 7 of 186 empirical papers (less than 4 percent) considered race or ethnicity, and most of those were descriptions of the racial or ethnic composition of the sample. Ram, Starek, and Johnson (2004) reviewed articles in sport and exercise psychology journals between 1987 and 2000 for both race and ethnicity and sexual orientation content, and they confirmed the persistent void in the scholarly literature. They found that only 20 percent of the articles made reference to race or ethnicity and 1.2 percent to sexual orientation. More important, those few articles provided little analysis and few insights. Ram and colleagues concluded that there is no systematic attempt to include the experiences of marginalized groups.

Kamphoff and colleagues (Kamphoff, Gill, Araki, & Hammond, 2010) surveyed the Association for Applied Sport Psychology (AASP) conference program abstracts from the first conference in 1986 to 2007 and found that only about 10 percent addressed cultural diversity, and those few focused on sample comparisons and gender differences. Almost no abstracts addressed race, ethnicity, sexual orientation, social class, physical disabilities, or any other cultural diversity issue.

The AASP program content extends beyond the research to professional issues, but our findings suggest a continuing gap with little attention to the wider range of participants or multicultural issues. Just as conference programs reflect little diversity, professional organizations, much like elite sport, are dominated by white men. For example, the North American Society for Psychology of Sport (NASPSPA) started in 1965. Dorothy Harris, who served as its first woman president in 1974 to 1975, was one of very few early women leaders. The AASP began in 1985 with John Silva as president, followed by seven male presidents before Jean Williams became president in 1993. Similarly, the American Psychological Association (APA)-47 had all male presidents from 1986 until Diane Gill became president more than 10 years later. The International Society of Sport Psychology (ISSP), which was the first sport and exercise psychology organization, had all men presidents for over 25 years. Racial and ethnic diversity is still lacking today; nearly all of the presidents of these organizations have been North American or European and white. Vikki Krane and Diane Whaley conducted in-depth interviews with eight of the early women leaders who played influential roles in the development of sport and exercise psychology. In their first paper (Krane & Whaley, 2010) they documented the contributions in research, teaching, and service, highlighting the generations of students who had continued that active research and leadership. In the second article (Whaley & Krane, 2012), they described the challenges faced by these trailblazers and how they overcame them to move forward.

Butryn (2002), taking a critical perspective, focused on white privilege in consulting and specifically argued that confronting the "invisible knapsack of white privilege is essential for effective sport psychology consulting. Butryn used Peggy McIntosh's (1988) term invisible knapsack to refer to privileges that those of us who are white carry around with us but often don't recognize (they're invisible to us). For example, a white person is not likely to be followed or accused of shoplifting in a store. Butryn emphasized that we must recognize and consider these privileges when consulting. He

further reminded us that race is not just black and white; we must expand the discourse on race and privilege to the wider range of racial and ethnic identities.

Just as we have seldom addressed cultural issues, our major journals and conference programs have little international reach. Papaioannou, Machaira, and Theano (2013) surveyed six major journals from 1997 to 2011 and found that the vast majority (82 percent) were from English-speaking countries. Less than 4 percent were from the continents of Asia, Africa, and South America. They also examined the proceedings of the four World Congresses of Sport Psychology during that time and found less dominance, with less than half of the articles from English-speaking countries. They noted a high correlation between continents' representation on editorial boards and publications, suggesting possible systematic errors or bias in the review process. As with professional organizations, journal editorial boards have also been dominated by white men, with few women editors until very recently.

The *International Journal of Sport and Exercise Psychology* (*IJSEP*) recently (Schinke, Papaioannou, & Schack, 2016) addressed this problem with a special issue on sport psychology in emerging countries. One article in that issue (Sorensen, Maro, & Roberts, 2016) reported on gender differences in a community-based human immunodeficiency virus/acquired immune deficiency syndrome (HIV/AIDS) education intervention through soccer in Tanzania. The findings highlight cultural intersections and the importance of considering gender along with local culture in programs. Other articles in the special issue reported on active sport and exercise psychology research and educational programs in Botswana (Tshube & Hanrahan, 2016) and Brazil (Serra de Queiroz, Fogaça, Hanrahan, & Zizzi, 2016).

As an assignment in my graduate sport and exercise psychology class I ask students to review recent issues of the major sport and exercise psychology journals specifically to note cultural diversity content and author affiliations. To date, their findings have confirmed the earlier reports—we find little attention to diversity issues, and authors and editorial boards are dominated by English-speaking countries. To check for yourself, go to the Application Point and do your own survey of one of our journals. I hope you find that we are making some progress, but we have far to go.

Culture in Sport and Exercise Psychology Journals

Select one of our major journals (*JSEP, JASP, IJSEP, PSE, SEPP*). Review the articles in the most recent year for cultural diversity. Do the articles include diverse participants? Do any articles address cultural diversity issues? Check the authors—are they culturally diverse? How many are from non-English–speaking countries?

Considering our research, publications, professional organizations, and programs, cultural diversity is still marginalized, and our educational programs and professional practice are culturally elite. To apply our expertise to promote physical activity for all so that the health and well-being benefits are not limited to the elite, sport and exercise psychology must expand the research base on cultural diversity and adopt multicultural competencies for professional practice. To begin, we can draw from and expand upon related psychology scholarship on gender and culture.

Gender Scholarship in Sport and Exercise Psychology

We first focus on gender scholarship because gender is particularly prominent and relevant in sport and physical activity. Gender scholarship in sport and exercise psychology largely follows psychology, which has shifted from early research on sex differences and personality to more social perspectives and the current emphasis on intersecting identities and cultural relations. As Basow and Rubin (1999) explained, *gender* refers to the meaning attached to being female or male in a particular culture, and gender-role expectations vary with ethnicity, social class, and sexual orientation. This section highlights the gender scholarship that has most influenced sport and exercise psychology.

Maccoby and Jacklin's (1974) classic review exemplifies the psychology research on sex differences. Their main finding, which often is ignored, was that few conclusions could be drawn from the literature on sex differences. Similarly, Ashmore (1990) later concluded that average differences were elusive, and the evidence did not support

biological dichotomous sex-linked connections. Other reviews of the sex differences literature confirm those conclusions.

Hyde (2005) reviewed 46 meta-analyses of the extensive literature on sex differences and concluded that results support the *gender similarities hypothesis*. Males and females are more alike than different on psychological variables, and overstated claims of gender differences cause harm and limit opportunities. Reis and Carothers (2014) investigated the structure of sex differences, asking, Are they categorical, with distinct categories (as we stereotypically assume), or dimensional, with men and women falling along overlapping continuous dimensions? They concluded that the evidence clearly supports overlapping dimensions. Zell, Krizan, and Teeter (2015) followed Hyde's meta-analysis by using metasynthesis to evaluate the many meta-analyses that have been conducted on sex differences. They found that the vast majority of differences were small or very small and were constant across age, culture, and generations. They concluded that the findings provide compelling support for the gender similarities hypothesis.

Key Point

Reviews and meta-analyses of the extensive literature on sex differences in psychology (Hyde, 2005; Zell et al., 2015) provide strong support for the gender similarity hypothesis. That is, males and females are more alike than different on psychological variables. Overstated and unfounded claims of gender differences influence behaviors and limit opportunities for everyone.

After dismissing sex differences, many psychologists interested in gender followed Bem's (1978) lead. Importantly, Bem argued that biological sex, personality (masculine, feminine), and sexual orientation were not necessarily connected. Bem's work is a key step toward current views of gender identity and sexuality. The early work focused on personality, often using the Bem Sex Role Inventory (BSRI), which assesses masculine and feminine personalities on separate dimensions, and it suggested that androgyny (high levels of both) is desirable. More recently, the masculine and feminine categories and measures have fallen out of favor, and even Bem (1993) progressed to a more encompassing gender perspective. Still, much sport and exercise psychology gender research is based on that early work.

Several early studies (e.g., Harris & Jennings, 1977; Spence & Helmreich, 1978) reported that most female collegiate athletes were either androgynous or masculine, in contrast to non-athlete college females, who were most often classified as feminine. Koca and Asci (2005) surveyed a large Turkish sample of female elite athletes and nonathletes. As with Western samples, Turkish female athletes scored higher on masculinity and were more likely to be classified as androgynous, whereas nonathletes were most often classified as feminine. Koca and Asci noted that athletics is highly competitive and individual, and both female and male athletes must be competitive, assertive, independent, and willing to take risks—all characteristics classified as masculine. Overall, this research suggests that female athletes possess more masculine personality characteristics than do female nonathletes, but this is not particularly enlightening.

Social Perspectives and Gender Stereotypes

Today, most psychologists look beyond the male–female and masculine–feminine dichotomies to social cognitive models and cultural relations. Over 30 years ago, in *The Female World*, sociologist Jesse Bernard (1981) proposed that the social worlds for females and males are different even when they appear similar. In earlier times we created separate worlds with segregated physical education and sport programs. Still today, the social worlds are different for female and male youth soccer players, university athletes in the training room, and older adults in senior games.

Gender stereotypes are particularly pervasive and powerful in sport and physical activity. In her classic analysis, Eleanor Metheny (1965) identified gender stereotypes and concluded that it is not socially appropriate for women to engage in contests in which

- the resistance of the opponent is overcome by bodily contact,
- the resistance of a heavy object is overcome by direct application of bodily force, or
- the body is projected into or through space over long distances or for extended amounts of time.

Gender stereotypes did not fade away with the implementation of Title IX. Kane and Snyder (1989) confirmed gender stereotyping of sports and more explicitly identified physicality with emphasis on physical muscularity, strength, and power as the key feature. Mary Jo Kane, one of the leading sport studies scholars on gender, has continued her research with emphasis on the sport media. Early research (e.g., Kane & Parks, 1992; Messner, Duncan, & Jensen, 1993) showed that female athletes received much less coverage and different coverage than males, with the emphasis on athletic ability and accomplishments for men and on femininity and physical attractiveness for women.

Over 25 years later, even with increased participation of girls and women at all levels of sport, women still receive lower pay and fewer endorsements and are seldom in leadership positions, and the media coverage has not changed much. Cooky, Messner, and Hextrum (2013) found that televised coverage of women's sports was the lowest ever and concluded that the media built audiences for men's sport while marginalizing women's sport. In the most recent update of this 25-year longitudinal study, Cooky, Messner, and Musto (2015) found televised coverage of women's sport "dismally low," with no progress, and highlighted the stark contrast between the exciting, amplified delivery of stories about men's sport with the dull delivery of women's sport stories. As their title suggested, when it comes to televised sport—"It's Dude Time!" Media representations are a major source of stereotypes, and all evidence indicates that all forms of the media send the message that sport is for men.

Key Point

One prominent source of stereotypes and differential treatment is the media. Despite the increased participation of girls and women, research continues to show that female athletes receive much less coverage, and different coverage, with the emphasis on athletic ability and accomplishments for men and on femininity and physical attractiveness for women.

Stereotypes are a concern because we act on them, exaggerating minimal gender differences and restricting opportunities for everyone. Both girls and boys can participate in dance or baseball, and at early ages physical capabilities are similar. Yet children see female dancers and male baseball players as role models; peers gravitate to sex-segregated activities; and parents, teachers, and coaches support gender-appropriate activities. This cycle reflects the view that gender is socially constructed and highlights the power of cultural context.

Gender and Sport Media

Select a newspaper, television report, magazine, or website that covers a wide range of sports, and review the coverage of men and women. Note the proportion of the coverage of men compared with women and the type of coverage (e.g., references to accomplishments, personal lives, and gender marking). Did you find gender bias in this media coverage?

Application Point

Gender and Physical Self-Perceptions

Gender and culture are prominent in the continuing developmental psychology research on achievement and self-perceptions by Eccles and colleagues (e.g., Eccles, 1985; Eccles, Barber, Jozefowicz, Malenchuk, & Vida, 1999). Eccles and Harold (1991) confirmed that the developmental model holds for sport achievement, that gender influences children's sport achievement perceptions and behaviors at a young age, and that these gender differences seem to be the product of gender-role socialization. Eccles consistently finds larger gender differences in sport competence than in other domains. Moreover, even in sport, the gender differences in perceptions are much larger than the gender differences in actual sport-related skills.

Fredericks and Eccles' (2004, 2005) research on parental influence and youth sport involvement revealed that parents held gender-stereotyped beliefs and provided more opportunities and encouragement to sons than to daughters. In addition, the parents' perception of the child's ability had the strongest relationship to the child's beliefs and participation. The results confirmed that boys had higher perceived competence, value, and participation in sport despite the absence of gender differences in motor proficiency.

Considerable research shows that gender-related self-perceptions affect sport and physical activity behavior. Chalabaev, Sarrazin, Fontayne, Boiche, and Clément-Guillotin (2013) reviewed the literature on gender stereotypes and physical activity, confirming the persistent gender stereotypes in sport and the influence of stereotypes on participation and performance. For example, Jensen and Steele (2009) found that girls who experienced weight criticism and body dissatisfaction engaged in less vigorous physical activity; and Chalabaev, Sarrazin, and Fontayne (2009) found that stereotype endorsement (girls perform poorly in soccer) negatively predicted girls' performance, with perceived ability mediating the relationship.

Considering the gender issues in perceived sport competence and body image, physical activity has a tremendous potential to enhance girls' and women's sense of competence and control. Several studies (e.g., Craft, Pfeiffer, & Pivarnik, 2003) and Hausenblas and Fallon's (2006) meta-analysis confirm that physical activity leads to improved body image. Tiggemann and Williamson (2000), in one of the few studies including both women and men and a wide age range (16-60 years), found a negative relationship between exercise and self-perception for younger women but a positive relationship for mature women and both young and mature men. Their results suggest developmental changes over the age range as well as gender influences.

Conception and Ebbeck (2005) explored the role of physical activity with survivors of domestic abuse, women who clearly can benefit from programs that foster empowerment and competence. The participants reported that physical activity provided a sense of accomplishment, enhanced mental and physical states, and provided a sense of normality. Although the study was limited in scope, it offers promising directions for using physical activity to enhance the well-being of women in a particular cultural context. Overall, research suggests that physical self-perceptions are powerful and gender related, and that relationships vary with the activity and cultural context.

Gender, Physical Activity, and Youth Development

Several researchers and community service professionals have promoted sport and physical activity programs for youth development (as discussed in chapter 15). Research supports benefits for both girls and boys, with gender and cultural variations.

Miller, Sabo, Farrell, Barnes, and Melnick (1999) used data from the CDC 1995 Youth Risk Behavior Survey of culturally diverse high school students to address the practical question, Does sport reduce the risk of teen pregnancy? Girls who participated in sport were indeed at less risk for teen pregnancy, reporting lower rates of sexual experience, fewer partners, later age of first intercourse, higher rates of contraception use, and lower rates of past pregnancies. Boys in sport also reported higher contraceptive use, but on other measures they reported more sexual experience. Miller and colleagues suggested that athletic participation for girls leads to less adherence to conventional cultural scripts and more social and personal resources in sexual bargaining. Sport for boys provides similar resources but strengthens their commitment to traditional masculine scripts.

Notably, Miller and colleagues included a racially and ethnically diverse sample. In addition to the main results on sport and sexual behaviors, Miller and colleagues (1999) reported that males had higher sport participation rates than did females, and whites had the highest participation of three race and ethnic groups, with Hispanic youth reporting the lowest rates. To date, few studies within sport and exercise psychology have incorporated such diverse samples; but the growing work on youth development, which often focuses on underserved youth, brings that perspective and offers insights into the role of physical activity (see chapter 15 for more on youth development).

Erkut, Fields, Sing, and Marx (1996) described experiences (including sport experiences) that influence urban girls from across the United States representing five ethnic backgrounds (Native American, African American, Anglo-European American, Asian Pacific Islander, and Latina). When asked girls were asked, "What activities make you feel good about yourself?", athletics was the most common response, mentioned by nearly half (46 percent) of them. When they were asked what about the activity made them feel good, the most common response was mastery or competence (e.g., "I'm good at it"), followed by enjoyment. Erkut and colleagues' large, diverse sample and the many variations in findings highlight the importance of cultural contexts in the lives of these girls and suggest exciting directions for sport and exercise psychology.

A report for the Women's Sport Foundation, *Her Life Depends on It III* (Staurowsky et al., 2015), updated previous reports and confirmed that physical activity and sport provides the critical foundation that allows girls and women to lead healthy, strong, and fulfilled lives. The report, which reviewed over 1,500 studies, documented the important role of physical activity in reducing risk of major health issues (e.g., cancer, coronary heart disease, dementias) as well as depression, substance abuse, and sexual victimization. The report further concluded that all girls and women are shortchanged with respect to realizing the benefits of physical activity, and that females of color and those with disabilities face even greater barriers.

Sexuality and Sexual Prejudice

Sexuality and sexual orientation are clearly linked with gender and gender identity. Before we review the related scholarship, some clarification of terminology is in order. As discussed earlier, Bem (1978, 1993) noted that we often (and incorrectly) conflate biological sex, gender roles, and sexual orientation. For example, we assume that a male football player must have masculine personality characteristics and be heterosexual, but that is not necessarily true. Furthermore, male–female biological sex, masculine–feminine personality, and homosexual–heterosexual orientations are not the clear, dichotomous categories that we often assume. Even biological sex is not a clear dichotomy; many individuals (about 1 in 2,000) are born intersex, which includes a variety of conditions in which a person's sexual anatomy does not match the typical definitions of male and female (from Intersex Society of North America website). Clearly, individuals' gender identities, gender expressions, and sexual orientations are even more varied, and not necessarily linked. Still, when biological sex, gender expression, and sexual orientation do not line up with stereotypes, people face discrimination.

Gender identity is one's internal sense of being a boy or girl, woman or man. For transgender people, gender identity is not consistent with their biological sex or may be perceived as something other than male or female (Krane & Mann, 2014). Gender expression refers to how people convey gender, such as through clothing or behaviors. Sexual orientation or identity is based on one's emotional and sexual attraction, usually considered as heterosexual (opposite sex), homosexual (same sex), or bisexual (both).

Discrimination and prejudice on the basis of sexual orientation is often referred to as *homopho-*

bia. Herek (2000), a leading psychology scholar on lesbian, gay, and bisexual issues, prefers the broader term *sexual prejudice*, which suggests an attitude or evaluation of a social group that involves hostility or dislike. *Heterosexism* refers to the privilege of heterosexual people. *Sexual prejudice* is the more encompassing term, but related scholarship often refers to *homophobia* and *heterosexism*. As Krane and Mann (2014) point out, heterosexism is common in sport—we assume that people are heterosexual, and we discriminate against those who do not fit heterosexist stereotypes. Also, biological sex, gender identity, and sexuality are conflated in sport, and we clearly discriminate against transgender and transsexual people.

Messner (2002), a sport studies scholar, describes sport as a powerful socializing force and argues that homophobia leads all boys and men (gay or straight) to conform to a narrow definition of masculinity. Real men compete and avoid anything feminine that might lead them to be branded a sissy. Messner also links homophobia with misogyny; sport bonds men together as superior to women. We expect to see men dominate women, and we are uncomfortable with bigger, stronger women who take the active, dominant roles expected of athletes.

Despite the visibility of a few prominent gay and lesbian athletes and the recent, growing recognition of civil rights, many athletes go out of their way to fit heterosexual ideals. Sport is often stereotypically associated with lesbians, but there is no inherent relationship between sexual orientation and sport (no gay gene will turn someone into a softball player or figure skater). No doubt, homophobia has kept more heterosexual women than lesbians out of sport, and homophobia restricts the behavior of all women in sport. Moreover, as Messner (2002) suggests, homophobia probably restricts men in sport even more than it restricts women. Further work (e.g., Anderson, 2011) suggests that men, and particularly gay men, have more latitude in sport today, but sport is still a space of restricted masculinity and sexual prejudice.

Sexual Prejudice in Sport and Physical Activity

Vikki Krane and colleagues (2001; Barber & Krane, 2005; Krane & Barber, 2003; Krane & Mann, 2014; Krane & Symons, 2014) have done much of the work addressing gender, sexuality,

and heterosexism in sport and exercise psychology. As pointed out in several of those sources, discrimination on the basis of gender and sexual identity is common in sport and occurs at all levels. Such hostile climates have been reported around the world. For example, Shang and Gill (2012) found the climate in Taiwan athletics hostile toward those with nonconventional gender identity or sexual orientation, particularly male athletes.

Key Point

Discrimination on the basis of gender and sexual identity is common in sport and occurs at all levels. Such hostile climates have been reported around the world. For example, Shang and Gill (2012) found the climate in Taiwan athletics hostile for those with nonconventional gender identity or sexual orientation, particularly for male athletes.

Although research is limited, reports from the National Gay and Lesbian Task Force Policy Institute (Rankin, 2003) and Human Rights Watch (2001), as well as observations and anecdotal evidence, suggest that organized sport is a particularly hostile environment, and that fitness clubs, sports medicine facilities, and recreational physical activity programs do not welcome gay men and lesbians. Additional reports from the Gay, Lesbian, Straight Education Network (GLSEN) national surveys (Kosciw, Greytak, Bartkiewicz, Boesen, & Palmer, 2012) suggest that sport is a particularly hostile environment for lesbian, gay, bisexual, and transgender (LGBT) youth.

In one of the few empirical studies, Morrow and Gill (2003) reported that both physical education teachers and students witnessed high levels of homophobic and heterosexist behaviors in public schools, but teachers failed to confront those behaviors. The good news is that more than 75 percent of the teachers say that they want safe, inclusive physical education; the bad news is that more than 50 percent of those teachers report that they never confront homophobia.

In subsequent research, Gill, Morrow, Collins, Lucey, and Schultz (2006) examined attitudes toward racial and ethnic minorities, older adults, people with disabilities, and sexual minorities. Overall, attitudes of our preprofessional (exercise and sport science, recreation) students were markedly more negative toward both gay men and lesbians than toward other minority groups, with males especially negative toward gay men. Interestingly, on our demographic page, many students went out of their way to indicate that they were exclusively heterosexual, further confirming the stigma of gay or lesbian identity and social acceptance of sexual prejudice.

In 2013, GLSEN released a research brief on the experiences of LGBT students in school sport based on their 2011 national school survey data. The brief confirms that LGBT students face discrimination and bullying in physical education and school athletics and do not feel supported by school officials. In response to the continuing reports, GLSEN developed "Changing the Game: The GLSEN Sports Project" (search for the GLSEN website, then go to sports) to assist kindergarten through high schools with creating safe and respectful sport and physical education environments for LGBT students. As the GLSEN projects suggests, the situation for LGBT people has changed dramatically in recent years in society and even in sport. More prominent gay and lesbian athletes have come out, and more resources are available to promote inclusive practice in sport and physical activity settings.

Despite the progress, we still have far to go, particularly with the "T" part of LGBT. In a review of research on LGBT issues in sport psychology, Krane, Waldron, Kauer, and Semerjian (2010) found no articles focused on transgender athletes. As Lucas-Carr and Krane (2011) noted, transgender athletes are present at all levels of sport but largely hidden and silenced. Lucas-Carr and Krane's article focuses on increasing awareness and understanding among sport psychology professionals and offers advice on policies and practices. Hargie, Mitchell, and Somerville (2015) interviewed 10 transgender athletes and found common themes of intimidation, alienation, fear of public spaces, and overall effects of being deprived of the social, health, and well-being aspects of sport. As Lucas-Carr and Krane concluded, creation of safe and compassionate sport settings for all athletes, including trans athletes, is an ethical responsibility. Krane and colleagues, who have done much of the research in sport and exercise psychology, have also moved to social action and provided guidelines for considering gender and sexual identities in professional practice. And, on a promising note, several programs have been developed to promote inclusive sport climates. For example, Krane and Symons (2014) described several programs, including Fair go, sport!—an Australian social inclusion project focusing on gender and sexual diversity.

Sexual Harassment

Sexual harassment has clear gender and sexuality connotations, and considerable psychological research (e.g., Koss, 1990) and public attention demonstrate the prevalence of sexual harassment. Sport studies scholars have addressed these concerns, but the sport and exercise psychology literature has contributed little on this topic. Lenskyj (1992) linked sexual harassment to power relations and ideology of male sport and noted unique concerns for female athletes. Sport (as a nonfeminine activity) may elicit derisive comments; clothes are revealing; male coaches are often fit and conventionally attractive; female athletes spend much time training and less in general social activity; coaches are authoritarian; and for some sports, merit is equated with heterosexual attractiveness.

Interestingly, sexual harassment has received more attention at the international level than in the United States. Kari Fasting of Norway and Celia Brackenridge of the United Kingdom have led many of the related research and program efforts. The collective works of these scholars and others from varying perspectives and countries indicate that the sport climate fosters sexual harassment and abuse; that young, elite female athletes are particularly vulnerable; that neither athletes nor coaches have education or training about the issues; and that both research and professional development are needed in sport and exercise psychology to address the issues (Brackenridge, 2001; Brackenridge & Fasting, 2002; Fasting, Brackenridge, & Sundgot-Borgen, 2004; Fasting, Brackenridge, & Walseth, 2007). This research comes from several European countries and Australia, and Rodriguez and Gill (2011) reported similar findings with former Puerto Rican women athletes.

The International Olympic Committee (IOC) recognized the problem, and in a 2007 statement defined sexual harassment as "behavior towards an individual or group that involves sexualized verbal, nonverbal or physical behavior, whether intended or unintended, legal or illegal, that is based on an abuse of power and trust and that is considered by the victim or a bystander to be unwanted or coerced" (p. 3). Women are more likely to be harassed and men are more likely to be harassers, although it is not exclusively men harassing women, as the highly publicized Sandusky case at Penn State in the United States illustrates.

Clearly more research is needed. Sexual harassment probably occurs much more often in sport and exercise settings than we recognize. Fasting (2015) reviewed the sociology of sport research on sexual harassment. She summarized the research, noting that sexual harassment is widespread in sport, but also cited the challenges in conducting this research, including funding, access, and cooperation from athletes and perpetrators and ethical issues. On the positive side, she suggested building on the recent policies of major organizations such as the IOC to curb harassment and continue research to advance systematic knowledge. Both women and men must be aware of the issues, and other professionals should be enlisted to support educational efforts and action.

Race, Ethnicity, and Social Class

Duda and Allison (1990) and Ram and colleagues (2004) found a striking void in sport and exercise psychology on race and ethnicity, and Kamphoff and colleagues (2010) confirmed that the void extends to conference programs. Social class often is conflated with race and ethnicity, but it is qualitatively different. Class operates within all racial and ethnic groups and also interacts with gender; however, there is little research on social class in psychology and none within sport and exercise psychology. Thus, most of the research covered in this section, limited as it is, focuses on race and ethnicity and comes from psychology and sport studies.

First, a note on race and ethnicity is warranted. Race and ethnicity are often connected or used interchangeably, but race and ethnicity are not the same. We often associate race with biological markers such as facial features and skin color and associate ethnicity with cultural traditions of a nation or geographic region. Hazel Markus (2008), who is widely recognized for her cultural psychology scholarship, offered a unified theory of race and ethnicity. Markus, and most other scholars, agree that race is not a clear, biologically determined category as often assumed. Race and ethnicity are dynamic, historically derived and institutionalized ideas and practices. That is, race and ethnicity are not objective, identifying characteristics but the meanings that we associate with the characteristics, and those meanings often carry power or privilege.

Markus further suggested that race and ethnicity differ in that race is more often imposed and associated with differential power between groups, whereas ethnicity is more often a claimed identity associated with a sense of belonging and pride. The United States and many Western countries have a long history of racial discrimination that has not disappeared today, and cultural relations based on ethnicity may also involve discrimination. For example, as discussed earlier, white people are overrepresented in positions of power, such as political leaders, business leaders, and athletic administrators.

Sport Studies Scholarship on Race and Ethnicity

Sport studies scholarship shows that significant numbers of athletes are not white and middle class, yet power remains solidly white and middle and upper class. The popular media and some scholars have discussed such practices as stacking (i.e., assigning African Americans to certain peripheral positions and not to central roles), as well as the white male dominance of coaching and management positions.

Most of that research found that white players tended to hold central, controlling positions whereas African Americans held peripheral positions. Smith and Henderson (2000) argued that stacking reflects social isolation, marginalization, and systematic discrimination against African Americans. Jamieson, Reel, and Gill (2002) extended the stacking research to women's collegiate softball, finding different patterns. White women, as in previous studies, predominated in the most central position of catcher. As expected, African American women were stacked in the peripheral outfield positions, and so were Asian American women, in contrast to typical stereotypes. However, Latina players were stacked in the central positions of pitcher and infield, challenging the notion that all minority players are stacked in noncentral positions and calling for more complex cultural analyses.

In Brooks and Althouse's (2000) edited volume on racism in college athletics, Smith (2000) noted that community-based educational and sport structures have been the dominant support networks for African American female athletes, and the tradition of athleticism for women comes out of social acceptance of physicality and recognition of the inner strength of women. Corbett and Johnson (2000) similarly focused on the cultural context, calling attention to the overlooked heroines and continuing nonrepresentative media coverage. They cited the 1997 *Racial and Gender Report Card*, noting that black women held only 2.1 percent of the Division I head coaching positions for women's collegiate teams and only 1 percent of college athletic director positions. In the more recent *Racial and Gender Report Cards*, the numbers have not improved. Corbett and Johnson noted that the black community and networks of professionals provide a supportive environment. However, barriers persist, and the cultural context in sport continues to exclude women of color.

Psychology Scholarship on Health Disparities

The psychology scholarship on race and ethnicity is growing and beginning to take a multicultural perspective. The major lines of research that are relevant to sport and exercise psychology are research on health disparities and research on stereotypes and stereotype threat. Health disparities include any health differences linked with social or economic disadvantages. Health disparities are well documented, and reports indicate that health care is suboptimal for minorities and low-income people (go to the National Healthcare Quality & Disparities Reports website). For example, racial and ethnic minorities are more likely to be poor or near poor, and blacks, Native Americans, and Hispanics–Latinos all have had poorer quality of care and worse access to health care than whites, with no significant change over time.

Adler and colleagues (1994) called attention to the role of social class in health risk, health behaviors, and health care, and Contrada and colleagues (2000) summarized research indicating that racial and ethnic minorities face stress based on discrimination, stereotypes, and conformity pressures and that these stresses affect health and well-being. As Yali and Revenson (2004) suggest, with the changing population demographics, socioeconomic disparities are likely to have an even greater effect on health in the near future. Lott (2012), in a review based on her contributions to the social psychology of class, noted the research confirming that class predicts access to economic and political resources, a wide array of life experiences, and beliefs and values. She further noted that class is more than socioeconomic status, highlighting power relations, and that classism contributes to diminished opportunities for low-income families. In their review of the psychology research on socioeconomic status and health, Matthews and Gallo (2011) focused on the role of stress and highlighted related biomarkers and pathways.

Discrimination and related stress constitute one source of health disparities. As we saw in chapter 13, stress is linked to many negative health outcomes. And, according to the APA Stress in America survey (Bethune, 2016; full version at the APA website; go to Psychology Topics, then Stress), discrimination is a major source of stress, reported by nearly half of U.S. adults. More relevant to this section, black adults are most likely to report experiencing discrimination, and black, Asian, Hispanic, and Native American adults all report more discrimination than white adults and also that race is the main reason for discrimination.

In one of the few studies to look at race and ethnicity with exercise, Heesch, Brown, and Blanton (2000) examined exercise barriers with a large sample of women over age 40, including African American, Hispanic, Native American, and white women. They found several common barriers across racial and ethnic groups, but they also reported variations by racial and ethnic group and cautioned that their results and specific community needs preclude definitive guidelines for interventions.

Health disparities are relevant to sport and exercise psychology in that physical activity is a key health behavior. In one of the few studies to specifically look at social class and physical activity with a national database, Crespo, Ainsworth, Keteyian, Heath, and Smit (1999) found inactivity to be more common in less privileged social classes. Crespo (2005) later outlined the cultural barriers and called for professionals to consider unique needs and cultural constraints when giving advice on exercise. Given that physical activity is a key health behavior and that disparities in physical activity parallel disparities in health, kinesiology professionals who are aware of the health disparities research are better positioned to provide guidance on promoting physical activity for health and well-being.

Scholarship on Stereotypes and Stereotype Threat

Claude Steele (1997) has done extensive research on gender, racial, and ethnic stereotypes and the effects of *stereotype threat,* the fear of confirming negative stereotypes, on performance (Steele, Spencer, & Aronson, 2002). Steele's research indicates that stereotypes affect everyone, but the most devastating effects are on those minority group members who have abilities and are motivated to succeed. For example, assume that you are a student-athlete striving to get good grades and get into medical school. Your chemistry instructor thinks that all athletes care about are their sports and that they lack the intelligence and motivation for academic work. You have the ability and really want to get an A, but you are aware of the instructor's negative stereotype. That's stereotype threat. The threat may create anxiety, interfering with your performance in class.

Steele's research also suggests that even simple manipulations that take away the stereotype threat (e.g., instructors telling students that test scores are not related to race, or that athletes have always done well in their class) negate the stereotype effects. Stereotype threat has been widely researched and extended to sport. Beilock

and McConnell (2004) reviewed that literature, concluding that negative stereotypes are common in sport and lead to performance decrements, especially when the performers are capable and motivated.

The prevalence of negative stereotypes for racial and ethnic minorities, particularly African American athletes, is well documented. For example, Devine and Baker (1991) found that the terms *unintelligent* and *ostentatious* were associated with the category *black athlete,* and Krueger (1996) found that both black and white participants perceived black men to be more athletic than white men. Johnson, Hallinan, and Westerfield (1999) asked participants to rate attributes of success in photos of black, white, Hispanic, and composite male athletes. Success for the black athlete was attributed to innate abilities, whereas it was attributed to hard work and leadership ability for the white athlete. Interestingly, no stereotyping was evident for the Hispanic athlete. This may reflect lower visibility of Hispanics in sport and the fact that there is little sport research on racial and ethnic minorities other than African Americans; views seem limited to black and white. Both Harris (2000) and Sailes (2000) document persistent stereotypes and report that African American athletes are more likely than white athletes to have higher aspirations for professional sport and to see sport as a route to social mobility. These views may reflect stereotypes or barriers in other areas, but they certainly suggest cultural influences and power relations within sport.

More important, stereotypes affect behavior and relationships. Stone, Perry, and Darley (1997) had people listen to a college basketball game and evaluate players after being told that the player they were evaluating was black or white. Both white and black students rated black players as more athletic and white players as having more basketball intelligence. Stone, Lynch, Sjomeling, and Darley (1999) found that black participants performed worse on a golf task when told that the test was of sport intelligence, and white participants performed worse when told that the test was of natural ability. Stone (2002) continued this line of research with a study demonstrating that white athletes faced with stereotype threat were prompted to use self-handicapping behaviors.

Although much of the work on stereotype threat involves race and ethnicity, and that is particularly relevant for sport and physical activity, Steele and colleagues also found gender-related stereotype threat effects in academic settings.

Key Point

Steele and colleagues have done extensive research on stereotype threat (Steele, 1997; Steele et al., 2002). Stone and colleagues (1999) confirmed stereotype threat in sport when black participants performed worse after being told that the test they were taking was of sport intelligence, and white participants performed worse after being told that the test was of natural ability.

Heidrich and Chiviacowsky (2015) extended that research to motor tasks and found that female participants in the stereotype threat condition (in which they were told that women do worse than men) had lower self-efficacy and performed worse on a soccer task than those in the nonstereotype threat condition. Feltz, Schneider, Hwang, and Skogsberg (2013) looked at predictors of student-athletes' stereotype threat. They found that student-athletes do perceive stereotype threat in the classroom, and those with higher athletic identity perceived more threat. They also found that how athletes perceived their coach's regard for their academic ability affected their susceptibility and could serve as a buffer to stereotype threat.

Beilock and McConnell (2004) linked stereotype threat to attention (as discussed in chapter 5), suggesting that stereotype threat both fills working memory and entices the performer to pay more attention to step-by-step control. As Beilock and McConnell conclude, we know less about stereotype threat in physical domains than in cognitive areas. These authors also pointed out that people belong to multiple groups, and how they think about their group membership is critical. That raises the issue of intersections.

Ruth Hall, who is particularly eloquent on intersections of gender, race, and class in sport and exercise psychology, began a discussion of women of color in sport (Hall, 2001) with the following commentary:

Race and gender are firecrackers that ignite America's social conscience, rattle the cages that bind us—cages that block our passage to equality. It's a double whammy for African American female athletes since we aren't the dominant norm—we're not white. Race and racism loom large and throw a level playing field off kilter.

Many of us don't fit the Anglo mold. We stretch the parameters of gender roles by our presence, our physical appearance, and sometimes unorthodox style. We aren't "feminine," they say. Commentators describe figure skaters Debbie Thomas and Surya Bonaly and the tennis star Venus Williams as "athletic" "muscular" meaning "not feminine." We create dissonance with our skin color, body type, and facial features. We are the other. (Hall, 2001, pp. 386-387)

Although Hall's quote is over 15 years old, the stereotypes are still relevant and illustrate the intersections of gender and race in our sport culture.

Physicality and Weight Bias

Kinesiology professionals deal with physical activities, and thus physical abilities and characteristics are prominent. Moreover, opportunity is limited by physical abilities, physical skills, physical size, physical fitness, and physical appearance—collectively referred to here as *physicality*. Elite sport is elite in many ways, but it is especially physically elite. The increasing public attention to obesity has created a negative culture for people who are overweight or obese, and people with disabilities certainly are among those who are left out in sport and exercise. Indeed, exclusion on the basis of physicality is nearly universal in sport and physical activity, and this exclusion is a public health and social justice issue.

Physical Abilities and Disabilities

Physical activity professionals address physical disabilities with adapted activities, but they seldom address physicality as a cultural diversity issue. In discussing the role of physical activity in the health and well-being of those with disabilities, Rimmer (2005) notes that people with physical disabilities are among the most inactive segments of the population, arguing that organizational policies, discrimination, and social attitudes are the real barriers.

As part of our larger study on sexual prejudice, we (Gill, Morrow, Collins, Lucey, & Schultz, 2010) examined the climate for minority groups (racial and ethnic minorities, LGB people, older adults, and people with disabilities) in organized sport, exercise settings, and recreational settings. Notably, the climate was rated as most exclusionary for people with disabilities.

Olkin and Pledger (2003) called for disability studies in psychology paralleling the critical studies of gender and race and ethnicity in order to emphasize empowerment and social context for disability. Several sport studies scholars have addressed disability from a cultural relations perspective (e.g., DePauw, 1997; Henderson & Bedini, 1995). Semerjian (2010), one of the few scholars who has addressed disability issues in sport and exercise psychology, takes a critical cultural perspective and highlights the larger cultural context as well as the intersections of race, gender, and class with physicality. Testimony from people who have faced discrimination speaks clearly. Pain and Wiles (2006) conducted in-depth interviews with individuals with disabilities; following are quotes from three of their participants:

> I am frightened to go back about this wheelchair because they're always going on about my weight.

> They think that because you are in a wheelchair you haven't got a brain.

> I have got to say that actually every time you go outside your front door, life's really difficult. . . . Barriers all the way along, really. (Pain & Wiles, 2006, p. 4)

Physical diversity is more than ability or disability, and physicality is particularly relevant to sport and exercise psychology. Physical skill, strength, and fitness are key sources of restrictions, and physical appearance influences physical activity behaviors.

Obesity and Weight Bias

Physical size, particularly obesity, is a prominent source of social stigma and oppression, and with the current emphasis on the so-called obesity epidemic, stereotypes related to physical size are a particular concern for kinesiology professionals. Considerable research (e.g., Brownell, 2010; Puhl & Heuer, 2011) has documented clear and consistent stigmatization and discrimination in employment, education, and health care. Persons who are obese are targets for teasing, are more likely to engage in unhealthy eating behaviors, and are less likely to engage in physical activity than others (Faith, Leone, Ayers, Heo, & Pietrobelli, 2002; Puhl & Wharton, 2007; Storch et al., 2007). Check the Rudd Center for Food Policy & Obesity website for resources and information on weight bias in health and educational settings.

Importantly, kinesiology students and professionals who typically profess concern about obesity are just as likely as others to hold negative stereotypes and anti-fat bias. Greenleaf and Weiller (2005) found that physical education teachers held anti-fat bias and strong personal weight control beliefs (idea that people who are obese are responsible for their obesity). They also held higher expectations for young people of normal weight, and as discussed in the chapters on self-perceptions and motivation, expectations are strong determinants of behaviors and outcomes.

O'Brien, Hunter, and Banks (2007) also found anti-fat bias in physical education students, and they held greater bias than students in other health areas. They also had higher bias at year 3 than at year 1, suggesting that bias was not being countered in their preprofessional programs. Fontana, Furtado, Mazzararrdo, Hong, and Campos (2016) examined anti-fat bias in professors teaching physical education majors at several different universities and found that the professors exhibited anti-fat bias and disapproved of physical education teachers who were obese as role models.

Key Point

Physical size, particularly obesity, is a prominent source of social stigma and oppression. Kinesiology students and professionals are just as likely as others to hold negative stereotypes and anti-fat bias.

Anti-fat bias is also seen among fitness students and professionals. Chambliss, Finley, and Blair (2004) found a strong anti-fat bias among U.S. exercise science students, and Robertson and Vohora (2008) found a strong anti-fat bias among fitness professionals and regular exercisers in England. According to Donaghue and Allen (2016), personal trainers recognized that their clients had unrealistic weight goals, but still focused on diet and exercise to reach goals.

Negative stereotypes about people with obesity are so prevalent that we may not realize our biases. That is, we may have implicit, or unconscious, biases even if we do not explicitly recognize those biases. A great deal of research has been done on implicit biases and their effects (see the Project Implicit website and check your own implicit biases in the Application Point). Implicit biases are particularly likely with weight and size given the negative media messages, and implicit biases are just as likely to have harmful effects as explicit biases. Indeed, when we do not recognize our implicit biases, we do not take actions to counter them and they are especially likely to have harmful effects.

Check Your Weight Bias

Go to the Project Implicit website and take the implicit association test on weight. Most likely you will find that you have some implicit bias, and you may become more aware of how such biases may affect behaviors and interactions in kinesiology settings. Think about how you might counter that implicit bias to make an exercise program more welcoming for people who are obese. Check the Rudd Center for Food Policy & Obesity website for ideas.

Weight Stigma and Health Promotion

Anti-fat bias and weight discrimination among professionals have important implications for health promotion and may actually contribute to unhealthy behaviors and lower quality of life. The prevalence and acceptance of anti-fat bias create weight stigma and discrimination, which is associated with stress and many negative health outcomes.

Sutin, Stephan, and Terracciano (2015) looked at the role of weight discrimination with participants from two large U.S. national studies. They found that weight discrimination was associated with increased mortality risk, and that the association was stronger than that between mortality and other forms of discrimination. They concluded that weight discrimination not only is associated with poor health outcomes but also may shorten life expectancy.

Weight stigma is even associated with greater risk of obesity. That is, the more we stigmatize people who are obese, the greater the risk of obesity. Tomiyama and colleagues (2014) found that independent of abdominal fat, weight stigma was related to cortisol responses and oxidative stress, and perceived stress mediated the relationship. As well as their physiological effects, weight stigma and discrimination affect mental health and behaviors. Vartanian and Novak (2011) found that experiences with weight stigma had a negative impact on body satisfaction and self-esteem, and importantly for kinesiology, weight stigma was related to avoidance of exercise. They found that

weight stigma negatively influences motivation to exercise, particularly among those who have high internalized societal attitudes about weight.

Key Point

Weight discrimination not only is associated with poor health outcomes, but also may shorten life expectancy. As well as physiological effects, weight stigma and discrimination affect mental health and behaviors, including avoidance of exercise.

With all the negative media messages about weight and the prevalence of anti-fat bias, health and fitness professionals must be aware of weight stigma and its effects. Thomas, Lewis, Hyde, Castle, and Komesaroff (2010) conducted in-depth interviews with 142 adults in Australia who were obese regarding interventions for obesity. Participants supported interventions that were nonjudgmental and empowering; they were less likely to view as effective those interventions that were stigmatizing or that blamed and shamed individuals for being overweight. The authors concluded by calling for interventions that support and empower individuals to improve their lifestyle. Focusing on weight is not helpful. Hoyt, Burnette, and Auster-Gussman (2014) reported that the "obesity as disease" message may have benefits for body image but that it has negative effects for self-regulation. That is, people who are obese may feel more positive about their bodies, but they are less likely to engage in health-promoting behaviors. More positive approaches that take the emphasis off weight and highlight health gains are more promising.

This positive, empowering approach is exemplified in the Healthy at Every Size (HAES) programs. Mansfield and Rich (2013) critically examined health promotion programs and found the weight-centric approach more common but not very effective. Continuing research shows that significant weight loss is difficult to achieve and sustain; very few people can do it. The HAES framework is more inclusive, recognizes the limits of diet and exercise and the many factors that affect weight, and emphasizes health outcomes. Although many clients go to fitness programs and health clubs to lose weight, helping those clients shift their focus off the scale and onto their health gains (e.g., reduced blood pressure, ability to recover faster, less fatigue) will go far toward promoting health and well-being.

Intersections and Cultural Relationships Revisited

Most current scholarship emphasizes intersections of cultural identities and recognizes power in cultural relations. That is easily overlooked in reviews of literature on gender and race and ethnicity separately. In her 2008 article, Shields stated that intersectionality, which involves considering the complex interactions of cultural identities, has transformed gender research. In a subsequent introduction to a special issue on intersections of sexuality, gender, and race, Warner and Shields (2013) noted that intersectionality complicates thinking about sexual orientation, and indeed, intersectionality complicates thinking about any aspect of culture.

Ghavami and Peplau (2013) used an intersectional analysis to look at cultural stereotypes of groups varying by gender and ethnicity (Asian, black, Latino, Middle Eastern, white). They found that gender-by-ethnicity stereotypes contained unique elements that were not simply the result of adding gender and ethnic stereotypes. Also, stereotypes of ethnic groups were more similar to stereotypes of men than of women; and finally, stereotypes of men and women were most similar to those of white men and women and least similar to those of black men and women. The authors concluded that ethnic and gender stereotypes are complex and that intersections produce meaningful differences. Galinsky, Hall, and Cuddy (2013) looked at racial (Asian, black, white) and gender stereotypes related to interracial dating, leadership, and athletic participation. Overall, the Asian stereotype was viewed as more feminine and the black stereotype as more masculine compared to the white stereotype. In the analysis of college athletics, blacks were more heavily represented than were Asians in masculine sports.

Within sport and exercise psychology, Ruth Hall has most eloquently addressed the intersections of gender, race, and sexuality, whether drawing on her clinical experiences to discuss the role of exercise in therapy with African American women (Hall, 1998) or more explicitly trying to shake the foundation of sport and exercise psychology in discussing the marginalization of women of color in sport (Hall, 2001). Hall reminds us of key themes in this chapter—multiple, intersecting identities; power relations and privilege; and advocacy for social justice. Keep those themes in mind as we now turn to cultural competence.

Cultural Competence

Cultural competence, which refers to the ability to work effectively with people who are of a different culture, takes cultural diversity directly into professional practice. Culturally competent professionals act to empower participants, challenge restrictions, and advocate for social justice. Cultural competence applies not only to direct interactions with students and clients as teachers, trainers, or consultants, but also in our roles as researchers and scholars.

Cultural Sport and Exercise Psychology

Although the previous sections show a lack of attention to cultural diversity in our research, a few dedicated scholars have been developing cultural sport and exercise psychology in line with our guiding framework. Fisher, Butryn, and Roper (2003) and Ryba and Wright (2005) advocated a cultural studies perspective for sport psychology. Schinke and Hanrahan's (2009) edited text, *Cultural Sport Psychology*, brought together much of the initial scholarship. Ryba, Schinke, and Tenenbaum's (2010) edited volume, *The Cultural Turn in Sport Psychology*, moved to a more critical cultural studies perspective. It is too early to know if sport and exercise psychology has truly made a "cultural turn," but we do have some guides to work from.

Two of our journals devoted special issues to cultural sport psychology. The *International Journal of Sport and Exercise Psychology* special issue (Ryba & Schinke, 2009) highlighted the dominance of the Western worldview in our research and practice. Ryba and Schinke emphasized cultural praxis, referring to an active process of blending theory, lived culture, and social action in professional settings. Practical examples of cultural praxis are programs and campaigns aimed at reducing racism, such as the Fédération Internationale de Football Association (FIFA) *Say No to Racism* campaign or programs targeting sexual prejudice discussed earlier. The *Journal of Clinical Sport Psychology* special issue (Schinke & Moore, 2011) on culturally informed sport psychology called for understanding, respect, and integration of culture in professional practice.

The continuing work of these scholars gives culture and cultural diversity a greater presence in sport and exercise psychology and fits with the framework of this chapter. Cultural sport and exercise psychology calls for awareness of (and a critical look at) our own cultural identity; continuing reflection to gain a deeper understanding of culture within sport psychology; and, in line with the third theme, action for social justice. That brings us to the topic of cultural competence.

Cultural Competence for Professionals

Cultural competence is a professional competency required in psychology and many health professions. Cultural competence is essential for anyone working with others, and certainly in all professional kinesiology roles. It includes both understanding and action and is needed at both the individual and organizational levels. That is, professionals not only develop their own cultural competence, but also work to ensure that their educational programs, professional practices, and organizations are culturally competent.

Psychology has developed resources and actively promotes cultural competence. Most resources adopt a model developed by Stanley Sue (2006), one of the leading scholars in multicultural psychology. Cultural competence has three key components: awareness of one's own cultural values and biases, understanding of other worldviews, and development of culturally appropriate skills. Culturally competent professionals work to be conscious and mindful of their personal reactions, biases, and prejudices (i.e., awareness); recognize their client's worldview or cultural perspective and background (i.e., understand); and develop abilities that allow them to work effectively with people who are different from them (i.e., skills). Cultural competence is not static and might best be thought of as existing on a continuum; we continually strive for cultural competence.

Key Point

Cultural competence refers to the ability to work effectively with people who are of a different culture. Cultural competence has three key components: awareness of one's own cultural values and biases, understanding of other worldviews, and development of culturally appropriate skills.

The American Psychological Association recognized the key role of cultural competence in fulfilling the mission of psychology to promote health and well-being and developed the APA (2003) multicultural guidelines. Those guidelines call for psychologists to develop awareness of their own cultural attitudes and beliefs, understanding of other cultural perspectives, and culturally relevant skills. Furthermore, the guidelines call for action at the organizational level for social justice. We can move toward the goal of physical activity for the health and well-being of all by following those guidelines.

Sport and exercise psychology can also look to the Association for Applied Sport Psychology Ethics Code, Principle D: Respect for People's Rights and Dignity. That principle clearly calls for cultural competence, although the statement is not as strong or as detailed as the APA guidelines:

> AASP members accord appropriate respect to the fundamental rights, dignity, and worth of all people. They respect the rights of individuals to privacy, confidentiality, self-determination, and autonomy, mindful that legal and other obligations may lead to inconsistency and conflict with the exercise of these rights. AASP members are aware of cultural, individual, and role differences, including those due to age, gender, race, ethnicity, national origin, religion, sexual orientation, disability, language, and socioeconomic status. AASP members try to eliminate the effect on their work of biases based on those factors, and they do not knowingly participate in or condone unfair discriminatory practices. (available at the Association for Applied Sport Psychology website)

The International Society of Sport Psychology also developed and published an ISSP position stand on culturally competent research and practice in sport and exercise psychology (Ryba, Stambulova, Si, & Schinke, 2013). The article includes a review of the relevant scholarship as well as recommendations for culturally competent research and practice. In the closing section, it describes three major areas of cultural competence: cultural awareness and reflectivity, culturally competent communication, and culturally competent interventions. Awareness and reflectivity refers to recognition of between- and within-culture variations as well as reflection on both the client's and one's own cultural background. Culturally competent communication involves meaningful dialogue and shared language. Culturally competent interventions recognize culture while avoiding stereotyping, take an idiosyncratic approach, and stand for social justice.

William Parham (2005), a leader in APA multi-cultural programming as well as an active member of the sport and exercise psychology community, offered three useful guiding premises:

- Context is everything. First, context is key when one is providing services to diverse individuals (and all kinesiology professionals work with diverse individuals); history, economics, family, and social context are all relevant.

- Culture, race, and ethnicity as separate indices do little to inform us. Parham reminds us that cultural groups are not homogenous; every individual has a unique mix of cultural identities.

- Use paradigms reflecting differing worldviews. The typical U.S. worldview emphasizes independence, competitiveness, and individual striving. Emphasis on connectedness rather than separation, deference to higher power, mind–body interrelatedness rather than control, and a sense of "spirit-driven energy" may be more prominent in another's worldview.

Parham (2011) offered further helpful guides to enhance cultural competence resting on the following guiding premises: (a) The explanatory power of the scientific method relative to culture, race, and ethnicity is limited; (b) culture, race and ethnicity, gender, age, and other elements of personal identification are operative in every social and research-based interpersonal interaction; (c) the quality of the relationship represents a foundational ingredient in interpersonal interactions; (d) sport psychology has not moved along in advancing a cultural agenda; (e) context is very important; and (f) culture, race, and ethnicity as separate indices do little to inform us about within- and across-group variability.

Overall, Parham (2011) calls for "more of thee and less of me" in research and practice. That is, professionals are listening as much as (or more than) talking while engaging in culturally informed interactions. To understand and communicate effectively you must ask questions and listen more than you offer advice and directions.

Markus, Uchida, Omoregie, Townsend, and Kitayama (2006) provided evidence for diverse worldviews with their study of Japanese and American explanations of Olympic performances. They found that in Japanese contexts, agency (and performance) is construed as jointly due to athletes' personal attributes, background, and social–emotional experience. In American contexts, agency is construed as separate from background or social–emotional experience; performance is primarily due to personal characteristics. The authors further note that these differing explanations are reflected and fostered in the culture, particularly television reports. As Markus and colleagues (2006) suggest, we may all "go for the gold," but we go for it in different ways, and we value gold in different ways. We all live, act, and engage in physical activity within a cultural context, and that context affects our perceptions and interpretations (our worldview) as well as our behavior.

Cultural Competence: A Continuing Process

Given the role of physical activity in health, cultural competence is necessary for all kinesiology professionals. Cultural competence is integral to quality programs and effective practice, yet few kinesiology professional programs include multicultural competencies. For kinesiology professionals, cultural competence must be applied to all levels, including instruction, program development, hiring practices, and organizational policies and procedures.

Cultural competence may best be thought of as on a continuum or a developmental process; there are no quick fixes. You might try to move toward competence by adopting a culture-blind approach and treat everyone the same. That may seem desirable, but a culture-blind approach is a one-size-fits-all approach. Moreover, that one size invariably is the size of the dominant or privileged cultural group. Culture blindness is better than overt discrimination, but we can move up to a higher level of cultural competence. Cross, Bazron, Dennis, and Isaacs (1999) describe a continuum moving from the lowest level, cultural destructiveness, to the highest level, cultural proficiency:

- **Cultural destructiveness:** This is characterized by policies, actions, and beliefs that are damaging to cultures.

- **Cultural incapacity:** There is no intention to be culturally destructive, but there is a lack of ability to respond effectively to diverse people (e.g., bias in hiring practices, lowered expectations).

- **Cultural blindness:** This philosophy includes being unbiased and holding that all people are the same (e.g., encouraging assimilation, not valuing cross-cultural training, blaming people for not fitting in).

- **Cultural precompetence:** Desire exists, but there is no clear plan to achieve cultural competence.

- **Cultural competence:** Respect and recognition for diversity exists, as well as genuine understanding of cultural differences (e.g., seeking training and knowledge to prevent biases from affecting work, collaborating with diverse communities, willingness to make adaptations, continued training and commitment to work effectively with diverse groups).

- **Cultural proficiency:** Culture is held in high esteem and is understood to be an integral part of who we are (e.g., conducting research to add to the knowledge base, disseminating information on proven practices and interventions, engaging in advocacy with diverse groups that support the culturally competent system).

Key Point

Cultural competence may best be thought of as on a continuum or a developmental process; there are no quick fixes. Cross and colleagues (1999) describe a continuum moving from the lowest level, cultural destructiveness, to the highest level, cultural proficiency.

The Cross and colleagues (1999) model and APA multicultural guidelines reflect similar themes. That is, professionals recognize and value cultural diversity, continually seek to develop their multicultural knowledge and skills, translate those understandings into practice, and extend their efforts to advocacy by promoting organizational change and social justice. Remember that cultural competence

is a process. As with any skill, the adage "use it or lose it" holds. You must continue to practice and train to reach and maintain excellence.

Cultural competence at the individual level is a professional responsibility. The concept of inclusive excellence moves cultural competence to the institutional level and to social justice and advocacy. That is, we work for changes in organizations and policies that make our programs accessible and welcoming for diverse people. Inclusive excellence is promoted in higher education and characterized in this statement from the Association of American Colleges & Universities (AAC&U) website:

> . . . AAC&U understands diversity and equity as fundamental goals of higher education and as resources for learning that are valuable for all students, vital to democracy and a democratic workforce and to the global position and wellbeing of the United States. AAC&U's commitment to make excellence inclusive—to bring the benefits of liberal education to all students—is rooted deeply in commitment to a diverse, informed, and civically active society.

If we take inclusive excellence into kinesiology we recognize and value diversity and equity as goals that will enhance our programs and institutions, as well as bring the benefits of physical activity to participants. Therefore, we not only work to develop our individual cultural competencies, but also work for change at the institutional level to ensure that our programs are inclusive—and excellent.

Psychology and most health professions are far ahead of kinesiology in recognizing the essential role of cultural competence, and most health education programs address cultural competence in their curriculums (Luquis, Perez, & Young, 2006). The resources and guidance from these and other sources are starting points to help you develop your own cultural competencies and to ensure that kinesiology programs and institutions are inclusive and empowering for all participants.

Putting It Into Practice

Summary

Culture, which refers to shared beliefs and practices of an identifiable group of people, is ever present and powerful in sport and physical activity. One size does not fit all; gender makes a difference, race matters, and we cannot simply treat everyone the same. Gender and culture are best understood within a multicultural framework that recognizes multiple, intersecting identities; power relations; and the need for social action. Sport and exercise participants are culturally diverse in many ways, but others are excluded; and power (e.g., leadership roles) is primarily held by white, middle- to upper-class men.

Sport and exercise psychology scholarship on culture focuses on gender. Although participation of girls and women has increased dramatically in recent years, stereotypes and media representations convey the message that sport is still a masculine activity. Race, ethnicity, and socioeconomic status all limit opportunities. Today, with the increasing prevalence of and public attention to obesity, people who are overweight or obese are particularly subject to bias and discrimination in sport and physical activity settings. Cultural competence, which refers to the ability to work effectively with people who are of a different culture, is essential for professional practice in sport and exercise psychology and kinesiology. Individuals must develop cultural competencies, and all of us must advocate for social justice to expand our reach to those who are marginalized and to promote physical activity for the health and well-being of all.

Review Questions

1. Identify and briefly explain the three themes in the multicultural framework for this chapter.

2. Explain privilege in cultural relations. Give a specific example of "white privilege" in sport and physical activity.

3. Discuss the status of culture and cultural diversity in sport and exercise psychology journals and professional organizations.

4. Identify several forms of gender stereotypes and bias in media coverage of female and male athletes.

5. Define *stereotype threat* and explain how it might operate in physical activity settings.

6. Describe the research on stereotypes and biases related to obesity, and discuss implications of weight bias for physical activity programs.

7. Define *cultural competence* and identify the three general areas of multicultural competencies.

Recommended Reading

- American Psychological Association (APA). (2003). Guidelines on multicultural education, training, research, practice, and organizational change for psychologists. *American Psychologist, 58,* 377-402. This document is also available online at www.apa.org/pi under Multicultural Guidelines.

- Parham, W.D. (2011). Research vs. me-search: Thinking more of thee and less of me when working within the context of culture. *Journal of Clinical Sport Psychology, 5,* 311-324. Parham is a clinical psychologist with considerable experience in sport and exercise psychology. In this article, he offers insights and suggestions that can help any kinesiology professional become more culturally competent.

- Ryba, T.V., Stambulova, N.B., Si, G., & Schinke, R.J. (2013). ISSP position stand: Culturally competent research and practice in sport and exercise psychology. *International Journal of Sport and Exercise Psychology, 11,* 123-142. http://dx.doi.org/10.1080/1612197X.2013.779812. This article includes a review of relevant sport and exercise psychology scholarship as well as guidelines and recommendations for culturally competent research and practice.

Websites

- Institute for Diversity and Ethics in Sport (www.tidesport.org). The institute, directed by Richard Lapchick, serves as a comprehensive resource for questions related to gender and race in amateur, collegiate, and professional sport. Lapchick continues to monitor collegiate and professional sport and updates the *Racial and Gender Report Card* each year.

- Project Implicit (www.projectimplicit.net; https://implicit.harvard.edu/implicit). These sites include information from the research on implicit attitudes as well as demonstration tests of implicit attitudes. The first site is for general information and the other has demonstration tests.
- Rudd Center (www.uconnruddcenter.org). The Rudd Center for Food Policy & Obesity is a nonprofit research and public policy organization devoted to promoting solutions to childhood obesity, poor diet, and weight bias through research and policy.
- Tucker Center (www.cehd.umn.edu/tuckercenter). The Tucker Center for Research on Girls & Women in Sport at the University of Minnesota is an interdisciplinary research center focusing on how sport and physical activity affect the lives of girls and women.

LAB

Cultural Competence in Professional Practice

Select one of the following professional settings: an exercise and fitness center, an athletic training facility, or physical education in a public school. As a professional in that setting, you want to promote the health and well-being of your students or clients. To do that, you must be a culturally competent professional and your program must be inclusive and empowering. Most likely you did not get any multicultural training in your professional preparation, and your professional organizations do not have guidelines or resources. You are on your own (but you do have the information, resources, and examples from this chapter).

First, how would you develop your own cultural competencies? What resources might you go to, and what specific actions would you take to move up the cultural competence continuum? In your response, answer each of the following questions:

1. How could you enhance your *awareness* (give at least two specific ways)?
2. How could you enhance your *understanding* of your students' or clients' culture and worldviews (give at least two specific ways)?
3. How could you develop culturally relevant *skills* and strategies (give at least two specific examples)?

As well as your own individual cultural competencies, think about your program or organization and consider these questions:

1. How could your agency (school, facility, or program) be more culturally competent, or be a model of inclusive excellence?
2. How could you work with the other professionals to ensure that your program is inclusive and empowering for participants? (You might consider staff guidelines, program materials, available resources, and interpersonal relationships.)

In your response, include at least three specific strategies or recommendations that you would advocate for in your program.

References

Chapter 1

Haywood, K.M., & Getchell, N. (2014). *Life span motor development* (6th ed.). Champaign, IL: Human Kinetics.

Johnson, S.B. (2013). Increasing psychology's role in health research and health care. *American Psychologist, 68*, 311-321.

Lewin, K. (1935). *A dynamic theory of personality.* New York: McGraw-Hill.

Lewin, K. (1997). *Resolving social conflicts & Field theory in social science.* Washington, D.C.: American Psychological Association.

Schmidt, R.A., & Lee, T. (2014). *Motor learning and performance* (5th ed.). Champaign, IL: Human Kinetics.

Chapter 2

Association for the Advancement of Applied Sport Psychology (1986, Winter). Nags head meeting launches AAASP. *AAASP Newsletter, 1* (1), p. 1.

Cratty, B.J. (1967). *Psychology and physical activity.* Englewood Cliffs, NJ: Prentice Hall.

Fitz, G.W. (1895). A local reaction. *Psychological Review, 2*, 37-42.

Griffith, C.R. (1925). Psychology and its relation to athletic competition. *American Physical Education Review, 30*, 193-199.

Gill, D.L. (1986). *Psychological dynamics of sport.* Champaign, IL: Human Kinetics.

Gill, D.L. (1995). Women's place in the history of sport psychology. *Sport Psychologist, 9*, 418-433.

Gill, D.L. (1997). Measurement, statistics and research design issues in sport and exercise psychology. *Measurement in Physical Education and Exercise Science, 1*, 39-53.

Gould, D., & Pick, S. (1995). Sport psychology: The Griffith era, 1920-1940. *Sport Psychologist, 9*, 391-405.

Griffith, C.R. (1926). *Psychology of coaching.* New York: Scribners.

Griffith, C.R. (1928). *Psychology and athletics.* New York: Scribners.

Griffith, C.R. (1930). A laboratory for research in athletics. *Research Quarterly, 1*(3), 34-40.

Hall, G.S. (1908). Physical education in colleges. In *Report of the National Education Association.* Chicago: University of Chicago Press.

Harris, D.V., & Harris, B.L. (1984). *The athlete's guide to sports psychology: Mental skills for physical people.* New York: Leisure Press.

Johnson, W.R. (1949). A study of emotion revealed in two types of athletic sport contests. *Research Quarterly, 20*, 72-79.

Kenyon, G.S., & Grogg, T.M. (1970). *Contemporary psychology of sport.* Chicago: Athletic Institute.

Kornspan, A.S. (2012). History of sport and performance psychology. In S.M. Murphy (Ed.), *The Oxford handbook of sport and performance psychology.* Oxford: Oxford University Press. Oxford Handbooks Online (www.oxfordhandbooks.com). doi:10.1093/oxfordhb/9780199731763.013.0001

Krane, V., & Whaley, D. (2010). Quiet competence: Writing women into the history of sport and exercise psychology. *Sport Psychologist, 18*, 349-372.

Kroll, W., & Lewis, G. (1970). America's first sport psychologist. *Quest, 13*, 1-4.

Loy, J.W. (1974). A brief history of the North American Society for the Psychology of Sport and Physical Activity. In M.G. Wade & R. Martens (Eds.), *Psychology of motor behavior and sport* (pp. 2-11). Champaign, IL: Human Kinetics.

Martens, R. (1975). *Social psychology and physical activity.* New York: Harper & Row.

Martens, R. (1979). About smocks and jocks. *Journal of Sport Psychology, 1*, 94-99.

Martens, R. (1987a). *Coaches guide to sport psychology.* Champaign, IL: Human Kinetics.

Martens, R. (1987b). Science, knowledge and sport psychology. *Sport Psychologist, 1*, 29-55.

McCloy, C.H. (1930). Character building through physical education. *Research Quarterly, 1*, 41-61.

McCullagh, P. (1995). Sport psychology: A historical perspective. *The Sport Psychologist, 9*, 363-365.

Miles, W.R. (1928). Studies in physical exertion: I. A multiple chronograph for measuring groups of men. *American Physical Education Review, 33*, 361-366.

Miles, W.R. (1931). Studies in physical exertion: II. Individual and group reaction time in football charging. *Research Quarterly, 2*, 14-31.

Nideffer, R.M. (1976). *The inner athlete.* New York: Crowell.

Nideffer, R.M. (1985). *Athlete's guide to mental training.* Champaign, IL: Human Kinetics.

Ogilvie, B.C., & Tutko, T.A. (1966). *Problem athletes and how to handle them*. London: Pelham Books.

Orlick, T. (1980). *In pursuit of excellence*. Champaign, IL: Human Kinetics.

Patrick, G.T.W. (1903). The psychology of football. *American Journal of Psychology, 14*, 104-117.

Ryan, E.D. (1981). The emergence of psychological research as related to performance in physical activity. In G. Brooks (Ed.), *Perspectives on the academic discipline of physical education* (pp. 327-341). Champaign, IL: Human Kinetics.

Ryba, T.V., Stambulova, N.B., & Wrisberg, C. (2005). The Russian origins of sport psychology: A translation of an early work of A.C. Puni. *Journal of Applied Sport Psychology, 17*, 157-169.

Singer, R.N. (1968). *Motor learning and human performance*. New York: Macmillan.

Triplett, N. (1898). The dynamogenic factors in pacemaking and competition. *American Journal of Psychology, 9*, 507-553.

Vanek, M. (1985, Summer). A message from the president of ISSP: Prof. Dr. Miroslav Vanek. *International Society of Sport Psychology Newsletter, 1*, 1-2.

Vanek, M. (1993). On the inception, development and perspectives of ISSP's image and self-image. In S. Serpa, J. Alves, V. Ferreira, & A. Paula-Brito (Eds.), *Proceedings VIII World Congress of Sport Psychology* (pp. 154-158). Lisbon: International Society of Sport Psychology.

Wade, M.G., & Martens, R. (1974). *Psychology of motor behavior and sport*. Champaign, IL: Human Kinetics.

Whaley, D., & Krane, V. (2012). Resilient excellence: Challenges faced by trailblazing women in sport psychology. *Research Quarterly for Sport and Exercise, 83*, 65-76.

Wiggins, D.K. (1984). The history of sport psychology in North America. In J.M. Silva & R.S. Weinberg (Eds.), *Psychological foundations of sport* (pp. 9-22). Champaign, IL: Human Kinetics.

Williams, J.M. (Ed.). (1986). *Applied sport psychology: Personal growth to peak performance*. Mountain View, CA: Mayfield.

Chapter 3

APA Presidential Task Force on Evidence-Based Practice. (2006). Evidence-based practice in psychology. *American Psychologist, 61*, 271-285.

Boyer, E.L. (1990). *Scholarship reconsidered*. Princeton, NJ: Carnegie Foundation for the Advancement of Teaching.

Brustad, R. (2002). A critical analysis of knowledge construction in sport psychology. In T.S. Horn (Ed.), *Advances in sport psychology* (2nd ed., pp. 21-37). Champaign, IL: Human Kinetics.

Cacioppo, J.T., & Cacioppo, S. (2013). Social neuroscience. *Perspectives on Psychological Science, 8*, 667-669.

Carroll, L. (1992). *Alice's adventures in wonderland and through the looking glass*. New York: Dell Books. (Original work published 1865)

Champagne, F.A., & Mashoodh, R. (2009). Genes in context: Gene-environment interplay and the origins of individual differences in behavior. *Current Directions in Psychological Science, 18*, 127-131. doi:10.1111/j.1467-8721.2009.01622.x

Dewar, A., & Horn, T.S. (1992). A critical analysis of knowledge construction in sport psychology. In T.S. Horn (Ed.), *Advances in sport psychology* (pp. 13-22). Champaign, IL: Human Kinetics.

Dzewaltowski, D.A. (1997). The ecology of physical activity and sport: Merging science and practice. *Journal of Applied Sport Psychology, 9*(2), 254-276.

Dzewaltowski, D.A., Estabrooks, P.A., & Glasgow, R.E. (2004). The future of physical activity behavior change research: What is needed to improve translation of research into health promotion practice? *Exercise and Sport Sciences Reviews, 32*(2), 57-63.

Forscher, B.K. (1963). Chaos in the brickyard. *Science, 142*(3590), 339.

Gill, D.L. (1997). Sport and exercise psychology. In J. Massengale & R. Swanson (Eds.), *History of exercise and sport science* (pp. 293-320). Champaign, IL: Human Kinetics.

Kitayama, S. (2013, December). Mapping mindsets: The world of cultural neuroscience. Association for Psychological Science (APS). *Observer, 26*(10), 21-23.

Landers, D.M. (1983). Whatever happened to theory testing in sport psychology? *Journal of Sport Psychology, 5*, 135-151.

Lewin, K. (1935). *A dynamic theory of personality*. New York: McGraw-Hill. Lewin, K. (1948). *Resolving social conflicts*. New York: Harper & Row.

Lewin, K. (1951). *Field theory in social science*. New York: Harper & Brothers.

Mahoney, M.J. (1991). *Human change processes: The scientific foundations of psychotherapy*. New York: Basic Books.

Mahoney, M.J. (2005). Constructivism and positive psychology. In C.R. Snyder & S.J. Lopez (Eds.), *Handbook of positive psychology* (pp. 745-750). New York: Oxford University Press.

Martens, R. (1979). From smocks to jocks. *Journal of Sport Psychology, 1*, 94-99.

Martens, R. (1987). Science, knowledge and sport psychology. *Sport Psychologist, 1*, 29-55.

Oishi, S., & Graham, J. (2010). Social ecology: Lost and found in psychological science. *Perspectives on Psychological Science, 5*, 356-377. doi:10.1177/1745691610374588

Thomas, J.R., Nelson, J.K., & Silverman, S.J. (2011). *Research methods in physical activity* (6th ed.). Champaign, IL: Human Kinetics.

Chapter 4

Ahmetoglu, G., & Chamorro-Premuzic, T. (2013). *Personality 101.* New York: Springer.

Anderson, M.B. (2011). Who's mental? Who's tough and who's both? Mutton constructs dressed up as lamb. In D.F. Gucciardi & S. Gordon (Eds.), *Mental toughness in sport: Developments in research and theory* (pp. 69-88). Abington, UK: Routledge.

Araki, K., & Gill, D.L. (2012). Development and validation of the Sport Perfectionism Scale. In *Athletic insight's writings in sport psychology* (pp. 273-288). Hauppauge, NY: Nova Science.

Bandura, A. (1977). *Social learning theory.* Englewood Cliffs, NJ: Prentice Hall.

Butler, R.J., & Hardy, L. (1992). The performance profile: Theory and application. *Sport Psychologist, 6,* 253-264.

Carver, C.S., Scheier, M.F., Miller, C.J., & Fulford, D. (2009). Optimism. In S.J. Lopez & C.R. Snyder (Eds.), *Oxford handbook of positive psychology* (pp. 303-312). New York: Oxford University Press.

Cattell, R.B. (1943). The description of personality: Basic traits resolved into clusters. *Journal of Abnormal and Social Psychology, 8*(4), 476-506.

Chartrand, J., Jowdy, D.P., & Danish, S.J. (1992). The Psychological Skills Inventory for Sports: Psychometric characteristics and applied implications. *Journal of Sport and Exercise Psychology, 14,* 405-413.

Costa, P.T., Jr., & McCrae, R.R. (1985). *The NEO Personality Inventory manual.* Odessa, FL: Psychological Assessment Resources.

Coulter, T.J., Mallett, C.J., Singer, J.A., & Gucciardi, D.F. (2016). Personality in sport and exercise psychology: Integrating a whole person perspective. *International Journal of Sport and Exercise Psychology, 14*(1), 23-41. doi:10.1080/1612197X.2015.1016085

Crust, L. (2008). A review and conceptual re-examination of mental toughness: Implications for future researchers. *Personality and Individual Differences, 45*(7), 576-583.

Duckworth, A.L., Peterson, C., Matthews, M.D., & Kelly, D.R. (2007). Grit: Perseverance and passion for long-term goals. *Journal of Personality and Social Psychology, 92,* 1087-1101.

Dunn, J.G.H., Causgrove Dunn, J., & Syrotuik, D.G. (2002). Relationships between multidimensional perfectionism and goal orientations in sport. *Journal of Sport and Exercise Psychology, 24,* 376-395.

Eysenck, H.J. (1970). *The structure of human personality* (3rd ed.). London: Methuen.

Eysenck, H.J. (1991). Dimensions of personality: 16, 5, or 3?—criteria for a taxonomic paradigm. *Personality and Individual Differences, 12,* 773-790.

Fisher, A.C., Ryan, E.D., & Martens, R. (1976). Current status and future directions of personality research related to motor behavior and sport: Three panelists' views. In A.C. Fisher (Ed.), *Psychology of sport* (pp. 400-431). Palo Alto, CA: Mayfield.

Flett, G.L., & Hewitt, P.L. (2005). The perils of perfectionism in sports and exercise. *Current Directions in Psychological Science, 14,* 14-18.

Friedman, H.S., & Kern, M.L. (2014). Personality, well-being, and health. *Annual Review of Psychology, 65,* 719-742.

Galton, F. (1883). *Inquiries into human faculty and its development.* London: Macmillan.

Gould, D., Weiss, M., & Weinberg, R. (1981). Psychological characteristics of successful and nonsuccessful Big Ten wrestlers. *Journal of Sport Psychology, 3,* 69-81.

Griffith, C.R. (1926). *Psychology of coaching.* New York: Scribners.

Griffith, C.R. (1928). *Psychology and athletics.* New York: Scribners.

Gucciardi, D.F., & Gordon, S. (2009). Revisiting the performance profile technique: Theoretical underpinnings and application. *Sport Psychologist, 23,* 93-117.

Gucciardi, D.F., Gordon, S., & Dimmock, J.A. (2009). Development and preliminary validation of a mental toughness inventory for Australian football. *Psychology of Sport and Exercise, 10,* 201-209.

Hall, P.A., & Fong, G.T. (2013). Conscientiousness versus executive function as predictors of health behaviors and health trajectories. *Annals of Behavioral Medicine, 45,* 398-399.

Hall, H.K., Jowett, G.E., & Hill, A.P. (2014). Perfectionism: The role of personality in shaping an athlete's sporting experience. In A.G. Papaionnou & D. Hackfort (Eds.), *Routledge companion to sport and exercise psychology: Global perspectives and fundamental concepts* (pp. 152-168). London: Routledge.

Hewitt, P.L., & Flett, G.L. (1991). Perfectionism in the self and social contexts: Conceptualization, assessment, and association with psychopathology. *Journal of Personality and Social Psychology, 60,* 456-470.

Highlen, P.S., & Bennett, B.B. (1979). Psychological characteristics of successful and nonsuccessful elite wrestlers: An exploratory study. *Journal of Sport Psychology, 1,* 123-137.

John, O.P., Donahue, E.M., & Kentle, R.L. (1991). *The Big Five Inventory–versions 4a and 54.* Berkeley: University of California at Berkeley, Institute of Personality and Social Research.

Jones, G., Hanton, S., & Connaughton, D. (2002). What is this thing called mental toughness? An investigation of elite sport performers. *Journal of Applied Sport Psychology, 14,* 205-218. doi:10.1080/10413200290103509

Jones, G., Hanton, S., & Connaughton, D. (2007). A framework of mental toughness in the world's best performers. *Sport Psychologist, 21,* 243-264.

Kagan, J. (1994). *Galen's prophecy: Temperament in human nature.* New York: Basic Books.

Kagan, J. (2012). *Psychology's ghosts: The crisis in the profession and the way back.* New Haven, CT: Yale University Press.

Kobasa, S.C. (1979). Stressful life events, personality, and health: An inquiry into hardiness. *Journal of Personality and Social Psychology, 37,* 1-11.

Madrigal, L., Hamill, S., & Gill, D.L. (2013). Mind over matter: The development of the Mental Toughness Scale (MTS). *Sport Psychologist, 27,* 62-77.

Mahoney, M.J., & Avener, M. (1977). Psychology of the elite athlete: An exploratory study. *Cognitive Therapy and Research, 1,* 135-141.

Mahoney, M.J., Gabriel, T.J., & Perkins, T.S. (1987). Psychological skills and exceptional athletic performance. *Sport Psychologist, 1,* 181-199.

Martens, R. (1977). *Sport competition anxiety test.* Champaign, IL: Human Kinetics.

Martens, R., Vealey, R.S., & Burton, D. (1990). *Competitive anxiety in sport.* Champaign, IL: Human Kinetics.

Mayer, J.D. (2005). A tale of two visions: Can a new view of personality integrate psychology? *American Psychologist, 60,* 294-307.

McAdams, D.P. (2013). The psychological self as actor, agent, and author. *Perspectives on Psychological Science, 8,* 272-295. doi:10.1177/1745691612464657

McAdams, D.P., & Pals, J.L. (2006). A new big five: Fundamental principles for an integrative science of personality. *American Psychologist, 61,* 204-217.

McNair, D.M., Lorr, M., & Droppleman, L.F. (1971). *Manual for the Profile of Mood States.* San Diego: Educational and Industrial Testing Service.

Meyers, A.W., Cooke, C.J., Cullen, J., & Liles, L. (1979). Psychological aspects of athletic competitors: A replication across sports. *Cognitive Therapy and Research, 3,* 361-366.

Mischel, W. (1968). *Personality and adjustment.* New York: Wiley.

Mischel, W. (1973). Toward a cognitive social learning reconceptualization of personality. *Psychological Review, 80,* 252-283.

Morgan, W.P. (1978). Sport personology: The credulous-skeptical argument in perspective. In W.F. Straub (Ed.), *Sport psychology: An analysis of athlete behavior* (pp. 330-339). Ithaca, NY: Mouvement.

Morgan, W.P. (1980). The trait psychology controversy. *Research Quarterly for Exercise and Sport, 51,* 50-76.

Morgan, W.P., Brown, D.R., Raglin, J.S., O'Connor, P.J., & Ellickson, K.A. (1987). Psychological monitoring of overtraining and staleness. *British Journal of Sports Medicine, 21,* 107-114.

Nicholls, A.R., Polman, R.C., Levy, A.R., & Backhouse, S.H. (2008). Mental toughness, optimism, pessimism, and coping among athletes. *Personality and Individual Differences, 644,* 1182-1192. doi:10.1016/j.paid.2007.11.011

Ogilvie, B.C. (1968). Psychological consistencies within the personality of high-level competitors. *Journal of the American Medical Association, 205,* 156-162.

Raglin, J.S. (1993). Overtraining and staleness: Psychometric monitoring of endurance athletes. In R.B. Singer, M. Murphey, & L.K. Tennant (Eds.), *Handbook of research on sport psychology* (pp. 840-850). New York: Macmillan.

Rammstedt, B., & John, O.P. (2007). Measuring personality in one minute or less: A 10-item short version of the Big Five Inventory in English and German. *Journal of Research in Personality, 41,* 203-212.

Rand, K.L., & Cheavens, J.S. (2009). Hope theory. In S.J. Lopez & C.R. Snyder (Eds.), *Oxford handbook of positive psychology* (pp. 323-334). New York: Oxford University Press.

Rhodes, R.E. (2006). The built-in environment: The role of personality in physical activity. *Exercise and Sport Sciences Reviews, 34,* 83-88.

Rhodes, R.E. (2014). Personality traits and exercise. In R.C. Eklund & G. Tenenbaum (Eds.), *Encyclopedia of sport and exercise psychology* (pp. 539-542). Thousand Oaks, CA: Sage.

Rowley, A.J., Landers, D., Kyllo, L.B., & Etnier, J.L. (1995). Does the iceberg profile discriminate between successful and less successful athletes? A meta-analysis. *Journal of Sport and Exercise Psychology, 17*(2), 185-199.

Ryan, E.D. (1968). Reaction to "sport and personality dynamics." *Proceedings of the National College Physical Education Association for Men,* 70-75.

Scheier, M.F., Carver, C.S., & Bridges, M.W. (1994). Distinguishing optimism from neuroticism (and trait anxiety, self-mastery, and self-esteem): A reevaluation of the Life Orientation Test. *Journal of Personality and Social Psychology, 67,* 1063-1078.

Seligman, M.E.P. (2005). Positive psychology, positive prevention and positive therapy. In C.R. Snyder & S.J. Lopez (Eds.), *Handbook of positive psychology* (pp. 3-9). New York: Oxford University Press.

Sheard, M., & Golby, J. (2006). Effect of a psychological skills training program on swimming performance and positive psychological development. *International Journal of Sport Psychology, 4,* 149-169.

Smith, R.E., Schutz, R.W., Smoll, F.L., & Ptacek, J.T. (1995). Development and validation of a multidimensional measure of sport-specific psychological skills: The Athletic Coping Skills Inventory-28. *Journal of Sport and Exercise Psychology, 17,* 379-398.

Smith, R.E., Smoll, F.L., & Schutz, R.W. (1990). Measurement and correlates of sport-specific cognitive and somatic trait anxiety: The Sport Anxiety Scale. *Anxiety Research, 2,* 263-280.

Snyder, C.R., Harris, C., Anderson, J.R., et al. (1991). The will and the ways: Development and validation of an individual differences measure of hope. *Journal of Personality and Social Psychology, 60,* 570-585.

Spielberger, C.D. (1966). *Anxiety and behavior.* New York: Academic Press.

Stoeber, J. (2011). The dual nature of perfectionism in sports: Relationships with emotion, motivation, and performance. *International Review of Sport and Exercise Psychology, 4,* 128-145.

Stoeber, J. (2014). Perfectionism. In R.C. Eklund & G. Tenenbaum (Eds.), *Encyclopedia of sport and exercise psychology* (pp. 528-530). Thousand Oaks, CA: Sage.

Terry, P.C., Lane, A.M., & Fogarty, G.J. (2003). Construct validity of the POMS-A for use with adults. *Psychology of Sport and Exercise, 4,* 125-139.

Terry, P.C., Lane, A.M., Lane, H.J., & Keohane, L. (1999). Development and validation of a mood measure for adolescents. *Journal of Sports Sciences, 17,* 861-872.

Thomas, P.R., Murphy, S.M., & Hardy, L. (1999). Test of performance strategies: Development and preliminary validation of a comprehensive measure of athletes' psychological skills. *Journal of Sports Sciences, 17,* 1-15.

Tutko, T.A., Lyon, L.P., & Ogilvie, B.C. (1969). *Athletic Motivation Inventory.* San Jose, CA: Institute for the Study of Athletic Motivation.

Vanden Auweele, Y., De Cuyper, B.D., Van Mele, V., & Rzewnicki, R. (1993). Elite performance and personality: From description and prediction to diagnosis and intervention. In R.N. Singer, M. Murphey, & L.K. Tennant (Eds.), *Handbook of research on sport psychology* (pp. 257-289). New York: Macmillan.

Woodcock, C., Duda, J.L., Cumming, J., Sharp, L., & Halland, M.J.G. (2012). Assessing mental skill and technique use in applied interventions: Recognizing and minimizing threats to the psychometric properties of the TOPS. *Sport Psychologist, 26,* 1-15.

Chapter 5

Abernethy, B., Maxwell, J.P., Masters, R.S.W., van der Kamp, J., & Jackson, R.C. (2007). Attentional processes in skill learning and expert performance. In G. Tenenbaum & R.C. Eklund (Eds.), *Handbook of sport psychology* (3rd ed., pp. 245-263). Hoboken, NJ: Wiley.

Abernethy, B., & Russell, D.G. (1987). Expert-novice differences in an applied selective attention task. *Journal of Sport Psychology, 9,* 326-345.

Ahearn, C., Moran, A.P., & Lonsdale, C. (2011). The effect of mindfulness training on athletes' flow: An initial investigation. *Sport Psychologist, 25,* 177-189.

Allard, F., Graham, S., & Paarsalu, M.T. (1980). Perception in sport: Basketball. *Journal of Sport Psychology, 2,* 14-21.

Baker, J., & Young, B. (2014). Deliberate practice and expertise review. *International Review of Sport and Exercise Psychology, 7*(1), 135-157. doi.org/10.1080/1750984X.2014.896024

Beilock, S.L. (2010). *Choke: What the secrets of the brain reveal about getting it right when you have to.* New York: Free Press.

Beilock, S.L., & Carr, T.H. (2001). On the fragility of skilled performance: What governs choking under pressure? *Journal of Experimental Psychology: General, 130,* 701-725.

Beilock, S.L., & Gray, R. (2007). Why do athletes "choke" under pressure? In G. Tenenbaum & R.C. Eklund (Eds.), *Handbook of sport psychology* (3rd ed., pp. 425-444). Hoboken, NJ: Wiley.

Beilock, S.L., Wierenga, S.A., & Carr, T.H. (2003). Memory and expertise: What do experienced athletes remember? In J.L. Starkes & A. Ericsson (Eds.), *Expert performance in sports* (pp. 295-320). Champaign, IL: Human Kinetics.

Bhasavanija, T., & Morris, T. (2014). Imagery. In A.G. Papaionnou & D. Hackfort (Eds.), *Routledge companion to sport and exercise psychology: Global perspectives and fundamental concepts* (pp. 356-371). London: Routledge.

Boutcher, S.H. (2008). Attentional processes and sport performance. In T.S. Horn (Ed.), *Advances in sport psychology* (3rd ed., pp. 325-338). Champaign, IL: Human Kinetics.

Boutcher, S.H., & Crews, D.J. (1987). The effect of a preshot attentional routine on a well-learned skill. *International Journal of Sport Psychology, 18,* 30-39.

Boutcher, S., & Zinsser, N.W. (1990). Cardiac deceleration of elite and beginning golfers during putting. *Journal of Sport and Exercise Psychology, 12,* 37-47.

Brewer, B.W., & Buman, M.P. (2006). Attentional focus and endurance performance: Review and theoretical integration. *Kinesiologica Slovenica, 12,* 82-97.

Brick, N., MacIntyre, T., & Campbell, M. (2014). Attention and endurance activity: New paradigms and future directions. *International Review of Sport and Exercise Psychology, 7*(1), 106-134.

Burbridge, D. (1994). Galton's 100: An Exploration of Francis Galton's Imagery Studies. *The British Journal for the History of Science, 27,* (4), 443-463

Chambers, K.L., & Vickers, J.N. (2006). Effects of band-width feedback and questioning on the performance of competitive swimmers. *Sport Psychologist, 20,* 184-197.

Chase, W.G., & Simon, H.A. (1973). Perception in chess. *Cognitive Psychology, 4,* 55-81.

Côté, J., Baker, J., & Abernethy, B. (2003). A developmental framework for the acquisition of expertise in team sport. In J.L. Starkes & A. Ericsson (Eds.), *Expert performance in sports* (pp. 89-114). Champaign, IL: Human Kinetics.

Côté, J., Baker, J., & Abernethy, B. (2007). Practice and play in the development of sport expertise. In R. Eklund & G. Tenenbaum (Eds.), *Handbook of sport psychology* (3rd ed., pp. 184-202). Hoboken, NJ: Wiley.

Côté, J., Lidor, R., & Hackfort, D. (2009). ISSP position stand: To sample or to specialize? Seven postulates about youth sport activities that lead to continued participation and elite performance. *International Journal of Sport and Exercise Psychology, 9,* 7-17.

Crews, D.J., & Landers, D.M. (1991). *Cardiac pattern as an indicator of attention: A test of two hypotheses.* Manuscript submitted for publication.

Dewey, D., Brawley, L.R., & Allard, F. (1989). Do the TAIS attentional style scales predict how visual information is processed? *Journal of Sport and Exercise Psychology, 11,* 171-186.

Ellis, A. (1982). Self-direction in sport and life. *Rational Living, 17,* 27-33.

Essig, K., Janelle, C., Borgo, F., & Koester, D. (2014). Attention and neurocognition. In A.G. Papaionnou & D. Hackfort (Eds.), *Routledge companion to sport and exercise psychology: Global perspectives and fundamental concepts* (pp. 253-271). London: Routledge.

Feltz, D.L., & Landers, D.M. (1983). The effects of mental practice on motor skill learning and performance: A meta-analysis. *Journal of Sport Psychology, 5,* 25-57.

Gauvin, L. (1990). An experiential perspective on the motivational features of exercise and lifestyle. *Canadian Journal of Sport Sciences, 15,* 51-58.

Gill, D.L., & Strom, E.H. (1985). The effect of attentional focus on performance of an endurance task. *International Journal of Sport Psychology, 16,* 217-223.

Gladwell, M. (2008). *Outliers: The story of success.* Boston: Little, Brown.

Gould, D., Tammen, V., Murphy, S., & May, J. (1989). An examination of U.S. Olympic sport psychology consultants and the services they provide. *Sport Psychologist, 3,* 300-312.

Gould, D., Voelker, D.K., Damarjian, N., & Greenleaf, C. (2014). Imagery training for peak performance. In J.L. Van Raalte & B.W. Brewer (Eds.), *Exploring sport and exercise psychology* (3rd ed., pp. 55-82). Washington, DC: American Psychological Association.

Hall, C.R., Mack, D., Paivio, A., & Hausenblas, H.A. (1998). Imagery use in athletes: Development of the Sport Imagery Questionnaire. *International Journal of Sport Psychology, 29,* 73-89.

Hall, C.R., Pongrac, J., & Buckolz, E. (1985). The measurement of imagery ability. *Human Movement Science, 4,* 107-118.

Hall, C.R., Rodgers, W.M., & Barr, K.A. (1990). The use of imagery by athletes in selected sports. *Sport Psychologist, 4,* 1-10.

Hamson-Utley, J.J., Arvinen-Barrow, M. & Granquist, M.D. (2015). Psychosocial strategies: Effectiveness and application. In M. Granquist, J.J. Hamson-Utley, L.J. Kenow & J. Stiller-Ostrowski (Eds.) *Psychosocial strategies for athletic training.* (pp. 231-268). Philadelphia: F.A. Davis.

Hatfield, B.D., & Kerick, S.E. (2007). The psychology of superior performance: A cognitive and affective neuroscience perspective. In G. Tenenbaum & R.C. Eklund (Eds.), *Handbook of sport psychology* (3rd ed., pp. 84-109). Hoboken, NJ: Wiley.

Hatfield, B.D., Landers, D.M., & Ray, W.J. (1984). Cognitive processes during self-paced motor performance: An electroencephalographic profile of skilled marksmen. *Journal of Sport Psychology, 6,* 42-59.

Hatzigeorgiadis, A., Zourbanos, N., Galanis, E., & Theodorakis, Y. (2011). Self-talk and sports performance: A meta-analysis. *Perspectives on Psychological Science, 6,* 348-356. http://dx.doi.org/10.1177/174569161141313

Hausenblas, H.A., Hall, C.R., Rodgers, W.M., & Munroe, K. (1999). Exercise imagery: Its nature and measurement. *Journal of Applied Sport Psychology, 11,* 171-180.

Holmes, P.S., & Collins, D.J. (2001). The PETTLEP approach to motor imagery: A functional equivalence model for sport psychologists. *Journal of Applied Sport Psychology, 13,* 60-83.

Ievleva, L., & Orlick, T. (1991). Mental links to enhanced healing: An exploratory study. *Sport Psychologist, 5,* 25-40.

Jackson, S.A., & Kimiecik, J.C. (2008). The flow perspective of optimal experience in sport and physical activity. In T.S. Horn (Ed.), *Advances in sport and exercise psychology* (3rd ed., pp. 377-399). Champaign, IL: Human Kinetics.

Jacobson, E. (1931). Electrical measurement of neuromuscular states during mental activities. *American Journal of Physiology, 96.*

James, W. (1890). *The principles of psychology* (Vol. 1). New York: Holt.

Kabat-Zinn, J. (2005). *Coming to our senses: Healing ourselves and the world through mindfulness.* New York: Hyperion.

Landers, D.M. (1981). Arousal, attention and skilled performance: Further considerations. *Quest, 33,* 271-283.

Landers, D.M., Christina, B.D., Hatfield, L.A., Doyle, L.A., & Daniels, F.S. (1980). Moving competitive shooting into the scientists' lab. *American Rifleman, 128,* 36-37, 76-77.

Lang, P.J. (1977). Imagery in therapy: An information processing analysis of fear. *Behavior Therapy, 8,* 862-886.

Lang, P.J. (1979). A bio-informational theory of emotional imagery. *Psychophysiology, 16,* 495-512.

Lind, E., Welch, A.S., & Ekkekakis, P. (2009). Do "mind over muscle" strategies work? *Sports Medicine, 39,* 743-764.

Mahoney, M.J., & Avener, M. (1977). Psychology of the elite athlete: An exploratory study. *Cognitive Therapy and Research, 1,* 135-141.

Mann, D.T.Y., Williams, A.M., Ward, P., & Janelle, C.M. (2007). Perceptual-cognitive expertise in sport: A Meta-analysis. *Journal of Sport and Exercise Psychology, 29,* 457-478.

Martin, K.A., Moritz, S.E., & Hall, C.R. (1999). Imagery use in sport: A literature review and applied model. *Sport Psychologist, 13,* 245-268.

McPherson, S.L. (2000). Expert-novice differences in planning strategies during singles tennis competition. *Journal of Sport and Exercise Psychology, 22,* 39-62.

McPherson, S.L., & Kernodle, M.W. (2003). Tactics, the neglected attribute of expertise: Problem representations and performance skills in tennis. In J.L. Starkes & A. Ericsson (Eds.), *Expert performance in sports* (pp. 137-167). Champaign, IL: Human Kinetics.

Moore, L.J., Vine, S.J., Freeman, P., & Wilson, M.R. (2013). Quiet eye training promotes challenge appraisals and aids performance under elevated anxiety. *International Journal of Sport and Exercise Psychology, 11,* 169-183. doi:10.1080/1612197X.2013.773688

Morgan, W.P. (1981). Psychophysiology of self-awareness during vigorous physical activity. *Research Quarterly for Exercise and Sport, 52,* 385-427.

Morgan, W.P., Horstman, D.H., Cymerman, A., & Stokes, J. (1983). Facilitation of physical performance by means of a cognitive strategy. *Cognitive Therapy and Research, 7,* 251-264.

Morgan, W.P., & Pollock, M.L. (1977). Psychologic characterization of the elite distance runner. *Annals of the New York Academy of Sciences, 301,* 382-403.

Nideffer, R.M. (1976a). *The inner athlete.* New York: Crowell.

Nideffer, R.M. (1976b). Test of attentional and interpersonal style. *Journal of Personality and Social Psychology, 34,* 394-404.

Nideffer, R.M. (1993). Concentration and attention control training. In J.M. Williams (Ed.), *Applied sport psychology: Personal growth to peak performance* (2nd ed., pp. 243-261). Mountain View, CA: Mayfield.

Orlick, T., & Partington, J. (1988). Mental links to excellence. *Sport Psychologist, 2,* 105-130.

Salmon, P., Hanneman, S., & Harwood, B. (2010). Associative/dissociative cognitive strategies in sustained physical activity: Literature review and proposal for a mindfulness-based conceptual model. *Sport Psychologist, 24,* 127-156.

Schomer, H. (1987). Mental strategy training programme for marathon runners. *International Journal of Sport Psychology, 18,* 133-151.

Shaffer, S.M., & Wiese-Bjornstal, D.M. (1999). Psychosocial interventions in sports medicine. In R. Ray & D.M. Wiese-Bjornstal (Eds.), *Counseling in sports medicine* (pp. 41-54). Champaign, IL: Human Kinetics.

Sheehan, P.W., Ashton, R., & White, K. (1983). Assessment of mental imagery. In A.A. Sheikh (Ed.), *Imagery: Current theory, research, and application* (pp. 189-221). New York: Wiley.

Silva, J.M., & Applebaum, M.S. (1989). Association-dissociation patterns of United States Olympic marathon trial contestants. *Cognitive Therapy and Research, 13,* 185-192.

Smith, A.L., Gill, D.L., Crews, D.J., Hopewell, R., & Morgan, D.W. (1995). Attentional strategy use by experienced distance runners: Physiological and psychological effects. *Research Quarterly for Exercise and Sport, 66,* 142-150.

Soberlak, P., & Cote, J. (2003). The developmental activities of elite ice hockey players. *Journal of Applied Sport Psychology, 15,* 41-49.

Starkes, J.L., & Ericsson, A. (Eds.). (2003). *Expert performance in sports.* Champaign, IL: Human Kinetics.

Starkes, J.L., Helsen, W., & Jack, R. (2001). Expert performance in sport and dance. In R.N. Singer, H.A. Hausenblas, & C.M. Janelle (Eds.), *Handbook of sport psychology* (2nd ed., pp. 174-201). New York: Macmillan.

Stevinson, C.D., & Biddle, S.J.H. (1998). Cognitive orientations in marathon running and "hitting the wall." *British Journal of Sports Medicine, 32,* 229-235.

Suinn, R.S. (1983). Imagery and sports. In A.A. Sheikh (Ed.), *Imagery: Current theory, research, and application* (pp. 507-534). New York: Wiley.

Suinn, R.S. (1993). Imagery. In R.N. Singer, M. Murphey, & L.K. Tennant (Eds.), *Handbook of research on sport psychology* (pp. 492-510). New York: Macmillan.

Van Schoyck, S.R., & Grasha, A.F. (1981). Attentional style variations and athletic ability: The advantages of a sports-specific test. *Journal of Sport Psychology, 3,* 149-165.

Vealey, R.S., & Forlenza, S.T. (2015). Understanding and using imagery in sport. In J.M. Williams & V. Krane (Eds.), *Applied sport psychology: Personal growth to peak performance* (7th ed., pp. 240-273). New York: McGraw-Hill.

Vickers, J.N. (1996). Visual control when aiming at a far target. *Journal of Experimental Psychology: Human Perception and Performance, 22,* 342-354.

Vickers, J.N. (2004, January). The quiet eye: It's the difference between a good putter and a poor one. *Golf Digest,* 96-101.

Vickers, J.N. (2007). *Perception, cognition, and decision training: The quiet eye in action.* Champaign, IL: Human Kinetics.

Vickers, J.N. (2016). The quiet eye: Origins, controversies, and future directions. Kinesiology Review, 5, 119-128.

Vine, S.J., & Wilson, M.R. (2010). Quiet eye training: Effects on learning and performance under pressure. *Journal of Applied Sport Psychology, 22,* 361-376. doi:10.1080/10413200.2010.495106

Wakefield, C., Smith, D., Moran, A.P., & Holmes, P. (2013). Review of research on PETTLEP model of imagery. *International Review of Sport and Exercise Psychology, 6*(1), 105-121.

Weinberg, R. (2008). Does imagery work? *Journal of Imagery Research in Sport and Physical Activity, 3*(1), article 1.

Williams, J M., & Leffingwell, T.R. (2002). Cognitive strategies in sport and exercise psychology. In J.L. Van Raalte & B.W. Brewer (Eds.), *Exploring sport and exercise psychology* (2nd ed., pp. 75-98). Washington, DC: American Psychological Association.

Williams, J.M., Nideffer, R.M., Wilson, V.E., & Sagal, M-S. (2015). Concentration and strategies for controlling it. In J.M. Williams & V. Krane (Eds.), *Applied sport psychology: Personal growth to peak performance* (7th ed., pp. 304-325). New York: McGraw-Hill.

Williams, A.M., Ward, P., & Chapman, C. (2003). Training perceptual skill in field hockey: Is there transfer from the laboratory to the field? *Research Quarterly for Exercise and Sport, 74,* 98-103.

Wulf, G. (2012). Attentional focus and motor learning: A review of 15 years. *International Review of Sport and Exercise Psychology, 6*(1), 77-104. doi:10.1080/1750984x.2012.723728

Wulf, G. (2014). Attentional focus. In R.C. Eklund & G. Tenenbaum (Eds.), *Encyclopedia of sport and exercise psychology* (pp. 47-50). Thousand Oaks, CA: Sage.

Williams, J.M., Zinsser, N. & Bunker, L. (2015) .Cognitive techniques for building confidence and enhancing performance. In J.M. Williams & V. Krane (Eds.), *Applied sport psychology: Personal growth to peak performance* 7th ed., (pp. 274-303). New York: McGraw-Hill.

Chapter 6

Anderson, D.F., & Cychosz, C.M. (1994). Development of an exercise identity scale. *Perceptual and Motor Skills, 78,* 747-751.

Asci, F.H. (2003). The effects of physical fitness training on trait anxiety and physical self-concept on female university students. *Psychology of Sport and Exercise, 4,* 255-264.

Bandura, A. (1977a). Self-efficacy: Toward a unifying theory of behavioral change. *Psychological Review, 84,* 191-215.

Bandura, A. (1977b). *Social learning theory.* Englewood Cliffs, NJ: Prentice Hall.

Bandura, A. (1982). Self-efficacy mechanism in human agency. *American Psychologist, 37,* 122-147.

Bandura, A. (1986). *Social foundations of thought and action: A social cognitive theory.* Englewood Cliffs, NJ: Prentice Hall.

Bandura, A. (1997). *Self-efficacy: The exercise of control.* New York: Freeman.

Berger, B.G., & McInman, A. (1993). Exercise and the quality of life. In R.N. Singer, M. Murphey, & L.K. Tennant (Eds.), *Handbook of research on sport psychology* (pp. 729-760). New York: Macmillan.

Berger, B.G., Pargman, D., & Weinberg, R.S. (2007). *Foundation of exercise psychology.* Morgantown, WV: Fitness Information Technology.

Brewer, B.W., Cornelius, A.E., Stephan, Y., & Van Raalte, J. (2010). Self-protective changes in athletic identity following anterior cruciate ligament reconstruction. *Psychology of Sport and Exercise, 11*(1), 1-5. doi:10.1016/j.psychsport.2009.09.005

Brewer, B.W., Van Raalte, J.L., & Linder, D.W. (1993). Athletic identity: Hercules' muscles or Achilles heel? *International Journal of Sport Psychology, 24,* 237-254.

Brown, T.N., Jackson, J.S., Brown, K.T., Sellers, R.M., Keiper, S., & Manuel, W.J. (2003). "There's no race on the playing field." *Journal of Sport and Social Issues, 27,* 162-183.

Burke, P.J., Owens, T.J., Serpe, R.T., & Thoits, P.A. (2003). *Advances in identity theory and research.* New York: Kluwer Academic/Plenum.

Burke, P.T., & Reitzes, D. (1981). The link between identity and role performance. *Social Psychology Quarterly, 44,* 83-92.

Campbell, A., & Hausenblas, H.A. (2009). Effects of exercise interventions on body image: A meta-analysis. *Journal of Health Psychology, 14,* 780-793.

Cardinal, B.J., & Cardinal, M.K. (1997). Changes in exercise behaviour and exercise identity associated with a 14-week aerobic exercise class. *Journal of Sport Behavior, 20,* 377-386.

Cooley, C.H. (1902). *Human nature and the social order.* New York: Scribner.

Coopersmith, S. (1967). *The antecedents of self-esteem.* San Francisco: Freeman.

Craft, L.L., Magyar, T.M., Becker, B.J., & Feltz, D.L. (2003). The relationship between the Competitive State Anxiety Inventory-2 and sport performance: A meta-analysis. *Journal of Sport and Exercise Psychology, 25,* 44-65.

Crocker, P.R.E., & Kowalski, K.C. (2000). Children's physical activity and physical self-perceptions. *Journal of Sports Sciences, 18,* 383-394.

Douglas, K., & Carless, D. (2009). Abandoning the performance narrative: Two women's stories of transition from professional sport. *Journal of Applied Sport Psychology, 21,* 213-230. doi:10.1080/10413200902795109

Dzewaltowski, D.A. (1989). Toward a model of exercise motivation. *Journal of Sport & Exercise Psychology, 11,* 251-269.

Dzewaltowski, D.A., Noble, J.M., & Shaw, J.M. (1990). Physical activity participation: Social cognitive theory versus the theories of reasoned action and planned behavior. *Journal of Sport & Exercise Psychology, 12,* 388-405.

Estabrooks, P., & Courneya, K.S. (1997). Relationships among self-schema, intention, and exercise behavior. *Journal of Sport and Exercise Psychology, 11,* 408-430.

Ewart, C.K., Stewart, K.J., Gillian, et al. (1986). Usefulness of self-efficacy in predicting overexertion during programmed exercise in coronary artery disease. *American Journal of Cardiology, 57,* 557-561.

Ewart, C.K., Taylor, C.B., Reese, L.B., & DeBusk, R.F. (1983). Effects of early post myocardial infarction exercise testing on self-perception and subsequent physical activity. *American Journal of Cardiology, 51,* 1076-1080.

Feltz, D.L. (1984). Path analysis of the causal elements in Bandura's theory of self-efficacy and an anxiety-based model of avoidance behavior. *Journal of Personality and Social Psychology, 42,* 764-781.

Feltz, D.L., & Lirgg, C.D. (2001). Self-efficacy beliefs of athletes, teams, and coaches. In R.N. Singer, H.A. Hausenblas, & C.M. Janelle (Eds.), *Handbook of sport psychology* (pp. 340-361). New York: Wiley.

Feltz, D.L., & Riessinger, C.A. (1990). Effects of in vivo emotive imagery and performance feedback on self-efficacy and muscular endurance. *Journal of Sport and Exercise Psychology, 12,* 132-143.

Field, A.E., Sonneville, K.R., Crosby, R.S., et al. (2014). Prospective associations of concerns about physique and the development of obesity, binge drinking, and drug use among adolescent boys and young adult men. *JAMA Pediatrics, 168*(1), 34-39. doi:10.1001/jamapediatrics.2013.2915

Folkins, C.H., & Sime, W.E. (1981). Physical fitness training and mental health. *American Psychologist, 36,* 373-389.

Fox, K.R. (1990). *The Physical Self-Perception Profile manual.* DeKalb: Northern Illinois University, Office for Health Promotion.

Fox, K.R. (1998). Advances in the measurement of the physical self. In J.L. Duda (Ed.), *Advances in sport and exercise psychology measurement (pp. 295310).* Morgantown, WV: Fitness Information Technology.

Fox, K.R. (2000). Self-esteem, self-perceptions and exercise. *International Journal of Sport Psychology, 31*(2), 228-240.

Fox, K.R., & Corbin, C.B. (1989). The Physical Self-Perception Profile: Development and preliminary validation. *Journal of Sport and Exercise Psychology, 11,* 408-430.

Galli, N., Reel, J.J., Petrie, T.P., Greenleaf, C., & Carter, J. (2011). Preliminary development and validation of the weight pressures in sport scale for male athletes. *Journal of Sport Behavior, 34,* 47-68.

Galli, N., Petrie, T.A., Reel, J.J., Chatterton, J.M., & Baghurst, T.M. (2014). Assessing the validity of the weight pressures in sport scale for male athletes. *Psychology of Men & Masculinity, 15,* 170-180. doi: http://dx.doi.org.ezproxy.lib.utah.edu/10.1037/a0031762

George, T.R., Feltz, D.L., & Chase, M.A. (1992). The effects of model similarity on self-efficacy and muscular endurance: A second look. *Journal of Sport and Exercise Psychology, 14,* 237-248.

Georgiadis, M., Biddle, S., & Chatzisarantis, N. (2001). The mediating role of self-determination in the relationship between goal orientations and physical self-worth in Greek exercisers. *European Journal of Sport Science, 1,* 1-9.

Gill, D.L. (2002). Gender and sport behavior. In T.S. Horn (Ed.), *Advances in sport psychology* (2nd ed., pp. 355375). Champaign, IL: Human Kinetics.

Gill, D.L. (2007). Gender and cultural diversity. In G. Tenenbaum & R.C. Eklund (Eds.), *Handbook of s port psychology* (3rd ed., pp. 823-844). New York: Wiley.

Gould, D., Weiss, M., & Weinberg, R. (1981). Psychological characteristics of successful and nonsuccessful Big Ten wrestlers. *Journal of Sport Psychology, 3,* 69-81.

Hardy, J., Hall, C.R., Gibbs, C., & Greenslade, C. (2005). Self-talk and gross motor skill performance: An experimental approach? *Athletic Insight, 7*(2), 1-13.

Hardy, J., & Oliver, E.J. (2014). Positive thinking. In R.C. Eklund & G. Tenenbaum (Eds.), *Encyclopedia of sport and exercise* (pp. 543-545). Thousand Oaks, CA: Sage.

Hardy, J., & Oliver, E.J. (2014). Self-talk. In R.C. Eklund & G. Tenenbaum (Eds.), *Encyclopedia of sport and exercise* (pp. 659-662). Thousand Oaks, CA: Sage.

Hardy, J., & Oliver, E.J. (2014). Thought stopping. In R.C. Eklund & G. Tenenbaum (Eds.), *Encyclopedia of sport and exercise* (pp. 750-751). Thousand Oaks, CA: Sage.

Hart, E.A., Leary, M.R., & Rejeski, W.J. (1989). The measurement of social physique anxiety. *Journal of Sport and Exercise Psychology, 11,* 94-104.

Harter, S. (1983). Developmental perspectives on the self-system. In E.M. Hetherington (Ed.), *Handbook of child psychology: Social and personality development* (Vol. 4, pp. 275-385). New York: Wiley.

Harter, S. (1990). Causes, correlates and the functional role of global self-worth: A life-span perspective. In R.J. Sternberg & J. Kolligan (Eds.), *Competence considered* (pp. 67-97). New Haven, CT: Yale University Press.

Harter, S. (1999). *Construction of the self: A developmental perspective.* New York: Guilford Press.

Horn, T.S. (2004). Developmental perspectives on self-perceptions in children and adolescents. In M.R. Weiss (Ed.), *Developmental sport and exercise psychology: A lifespan perspective* (pp. 101-143). Morgantown, WV: Fitness Information Technology.

Horton, R.S., & Mack, D.E. (2000). Athletic identity in marathon runners: Functional focus or dysfunctional commitment? *Journal of Sport Behavior, 23,* 101-109.

Houle, J.L.W., Brewer, B.W., & Kluck, A.S. (2010). Developmental trends in athletic identity: A two-part retrospective study. *Journal of Sport Behavior, 33,* 146-159.

James, W. (1890). *The principles of psychology* (Vol. 1). New York: Holt.

James, W. (1892). *Psychology: Briefer course.* New York: Holt.

Kaplan, R.M., Atkins, C.J., & Reinsch, S. (1984). Specific efficacy expectations mediate exercise compliance in patients with COPD. *Health Psychology, 3,* 223-242.

Kaplan, R.M., Ries, A.L., Prewitt, L.M., & Eakin, E. (1994). Self-efficacy expectations predict survival for patients with chronic obstructive pulmonary disease. *Health Psychology, 13,* 366-368.

Kendzierski, D. (1988). Self-schemata and exercise. *Basic and Applied Social Psychology, 9,* 45-59.

Kendzierski, D. (1994). Schema theory: An information processing focus. In R.K. Dishman (Ed.), *Advances in exercise adherence* (pp. 137-159). Champaign, IL: Human Kinetics.

Kendzierski, D., Furr, R.M., & Schiavoni, J. (1998). Physical activity self-definitions: Correlates and perceived criteria. *Journal of Sport and Exercise Psychology, 20,* 176-193.

Kendzierski, D., & Morganstein. (2009). Test, revision, and cross-validation of the physical activity self-definition model. *Journal of Sport and Exercise Psychology, 31,* 484-504.

Kiszla, M. (2012, August 10). Mark Kiszla: Hope Solo backs up arrogance with golden goalkeeping. *Denver Post.* Retrieved from www.denverpost.com

Kowalski, K.C., Crocker, P.R.E., Kowalski, N.P., Chad, K.E., & Humbert, M.L. (2006). Examining the physical self in adolescent girls over time: Further evidence against the hierarchical model. *Journal of Sport and Exercise Psychology, 25,* 5-18.

Kroichick, R. (2001, August 27). License to thrill. *The Sporting News* [Online]. www.encyclopedia.com.

Lally, P. (2007). Identity and athletic retirement: A prospective study. *Psychology of Sport and Exercise, 8,* 85-99. doi:10.1016/j.psychsport.2006.03.003

Lally, P., & Kerr, G.A. (2005). The career planning, athletic identity, and student role identity of intercollegiate student athletes. *Research Quarterly for Exercise and Sport, 76,* 275-283. doi:10.1080/0270136 7.2005.10599299

Leary, M.R. (1992). Self-presentational process in exercise and sport. *Journal of Sport and Exercise Psychology, 14,* 339-351.

Legrand, F.D. (2014). Effects of exercise on physical self-concept, global self-esteem, and depression in women of low socioeconomic status with elevated depressive symptoms. *Journal of Sport and Exercise Psychology, 36*(4), 357-365. doi:10.1123/jsep.2013-0253

Lockhart, B.D. (2010). Injured athletes' perceived loss of identity: Educational implications for athletic trainers. *Athletic Training Education Journal, 5*(1), 26-31.

Mahoney, M.J., & Avener, M. (1977). Psychology of the elite athlete: An exploratory study. *Cognitive Therapy and Research, 1,* 135-141.

Manuel, J.C., Shilt, J.S., Curl, W.W., et al. (2002). Coping with sports injuries: An examination of the adolescent athlete. *Journal of Adolescent Health, 31*(5), 391-393.

Marcus, B.H., & Forsyth, L.H. (2009). *Motivating people to be physically active 2nd Edition.* Champaign, IL: Human Kinetics.

Marcus, B.H., Selby, V.C., Niaura, R.S., & Rossi, J.S. (1992). Self-efficacy and the stages of exercise behavior change. *Research Quarterly for Exercise and Sport, 63*(1), 60-66. doi:10.1080/02701367.1992.10607557

Markus, H. (1977). Self-schemata and processing information about the self. *Journal of Personality and Social Psychology, 35,* 63-78.

Markus, H., & Nurius, P. (1986). Possible selves. *American Psychologist, 41,* 954-969.

Marsh, H.W. (1990). A multidimensional, hierarchical self-concept: Theoretical and empirical justification. *Educational Psychology Review, 2,* 77-172.

Marsh, H.W. (1996). Construct validity of physical self-description questionnaire responses: Relations to external criteria. *Journal of Sport and Exercise Psychology, 18,* 111-113.

Marsh, H.W. (1997). The measurement of physical self-concept: A construct validity approach. In K.R. Fox (Ed.), *The physical self: From motivation to well-being* (pp. 27-58). Champaign, IL: Human Kinetics.

Marsh, H.W., Chanal, J.P., & Sarrazin, P.G. (2006). Self-belief does make a difference: A reciprocal effects model of the causal ordering of physical self-concept and gymnastics performance. *Journal of Sports Sciences, 24,* 101-111.

Marsh, H.W., & Craven, R.G. (1997). Academic self-concept: Beyond the dustbowl. In G. Phye (Ed.), *Handbook of classroom assessment: Learning, achievement, and adjustment* (pp. 131-198). Orlando, FL: Academic Press.

Marsh, H.W., & Craven, R.G. (2006). Reciprocal effects of self-concept and performance form a multidimensional perspective. *Perspectives on Psychological Science, 1,* 133-163.

Marsh, H.W., Richards, G.E., Johnson, S., Roche, L., & Tremayne, P. (1994). Physical Self-Description Questionnaire: Psychometric properties and multitrait-multimethod analysis of relations to existing instruments. *Journal of Sport and Exercise Psychology, 16,* 270-305.

Martin Ginis, K.A., Lindwall, M., & Prapavessis, H. (2007). Who cares what other people think. In G. Tenenbaum & R. Eklund (Eds.), *Handbook of sport psychology* (3rd ed., pp. 136-157). New York: Wiley.

McAuley, E. (1992). Understanding exercise behavior: A self-efficacy perspective. In G.C. Roberts (Ed.), *Motivation in sport and exercise* (pp. 107-127). Champaign, IL: Human Kinetics.

McAuley, E. (1993). Self-referent thought in sport and physical activity. In T.S. Horn (Ed.), *Advances in sport psychology* (pp. 101-118). Champaign, IL: Human Kinetics.

McAuley, E., Katula, J., Mihalko, S.L., et al. (1999). Mode of physical activity differentially influences self-efficacy in older adults: Latent growth curve analysis. *Journal of Gerontology, 54B,* P283-P292.

McAuley, E., Konopack, J.F., Motl, R.W., Morris, K.S., Doerksen, S.E., & Rosengren, K.R. (2006). Physical activity and quality of life in older adults: Influence of health status and self-efficacy. *Annals of Behavioral Medicine, 31*(1), 99-103.

McAuley, E., Lox, C.L., & Duncan, T. (1993). Long-term maintenance of exercise, self-efficacy, and physiological changes in older adults. *Journal of Gerontology, 48,* P218-P223.

McAuley, E., Mihalko, S.L., & Bane, S. (1997). Exercise and selfesteem in middleaged adults: Multidimensional relationships and physical fitness and selfefficacy influences. *Journal of Behavioral Medicine, 20,* 67-83.

McAuley, E., Pena, M.M., & Jerome, G.J. (2001). Self-efficacy as a determinant and outcome of exercise. In G.C. Roberts (Ed.), *Advances in motivation in sport and exercise* (pp. 235-261). Champaign, IL: Human Kinetics.

McAuley, E., White, S.M., Mailey, E.L., & Wojcicki, B.S. (2012). Exercise-related self-efficacy. In G. Tenenbaum, R.C. Eklund, & A. Kamata (Eds.), *Measurement in sport and exercise psychology* (pp. 239-250). Champaign, IL: Human Kinetics.

McCullaugh, P., & Weiss, M.R. (2001). Modeling: Considerations for motor skill performance and psychological responses. In R.N. Singer, H.A. Hausenblas, & C.M. Janelle (Eds.), *Handbook of sport psychology* (2nd ed., pp. 205-238). New York: Wiley.

Meyers, N.D., & Feltz, D.L. (2007). From self-efficacy to collective efficacy. In G. Tenenbaum & R.C. Elkund (Eds.), *Handbook of sport psychology* (3rd ed., pp. 799-819). New York: Wiley.

Oyserman, D., Bybee, D., & Terry, K. (2006). Possible selves and academic outcomes: How and when possible selves impel action. *Journal of Personality and Social Psychology, 90,* 188-204.

Oyserman, D., & Markus, H. (1990). Possible selves and delinquency. *Journal of Personality and Social Psychology, 59,* 112-125.

Pekmezi, D., Jennings, E., & Marcus, B.H. (2009). Evaluating and enhancing self-efficacy for physical activity. *ACSM's Health and Fitness Journal, 13*(2), 16-21.

Podlog, L., Gao, Z., Kenow, L., et al. (2013). Injury rehabilitation overadherence: Preliminary scale validation and relationships with athletic identity and self-presentation concerns. *Journal of Athletic Training, 48*(3), 372-381. doi:10.4085 1062-6050-48.2.20

Prapavessis, H., Grove, J.R., & Eklund, R. (2004). Self-presentational issues in competition in sport. *Journal of Applied Sport Psychology, 16,* 19-40.

Reel, J.J., & Gill, D.L. (1996). Psychosocial factors related to eating disorders among high school and college female cheerleaders. *Sport Psychologist, 10,* 195-206.

Reel, J.J., Petrie, P., SooHoo, S., & Anderson, C. (2013). Weight pressures in sport: Examining the factor structure and incremental validity of the weight pressures scale - females. *Eating Behaviors, 14*(2), 137-144.

Reel, J.J., SooHoo, S., Petrie, T., & Greenleaf, C. (2010). Slimming down for sport: Developing a weight pressures in sport measure for female athletes. *Journal of Clinical Sport Psychology, 4*(2), 99-111.

Reifsteck, E.J., Gill, D.L., & Brooks, D.L. (2013). The relationship between athletic identity and physical activity among former college athletes. *Athletic Insight, 5*(3), 271-284.

Ries, A.L., Kaplan, R.M., Limberg, T.M., & Prewitt, L.M. (1995). Effects of pulmonary rehabilitation on physiologic and pyschosocial outcomes in patients with chronic obstructive pulmonary disease. *Annals of Internal Medicine, 122,* 823-832.

Rodin, J., & Larson, L. (1992). Social factors and the ideal body shape. In K.D. Brownell, J. Rodin, & J.H. Wilmore (Eds.), *Eating, body weight, and performance in athletes* (pp. 146-158). Philadelphia: Lea & Febiger.

Rudolph, D.L., & McAuley, E. (1995). Self-efficacy and salivary cortisol responses to acute exercise in physically active and less active adults. *Journal of Sport and Exercise Psychology, 17,* 206-213.

Ruvolo, A.P., & Markus, H. (1992). Possible selves and performance: The power of self-relevant imagery. *Social Cognition, 10*(1), 95-124.

Sallis, J.F., Haskell, W.L., Fortmann, S.P., Vranizan, K.M., Taylor, C.B., & Solomon, D.S. (1986). Predictors of adoption and maintenance of physical activity in a community sample. *Preventive Medicine, 15,* 331-341.

Secord, P.F., & Jourard, S.M. (1953). The appraisal of body cathexis: Body cathexis and the self. *Journal of Consulting Psychology, 17,* 343-347.

Shavelson, R.J., Hubner, J.J., & Stanton, G.C. (1976). Self-concept: Validation of construct interpretations. *Review of Educational Research, 46,* 407-441.

Sonstroem, R.J., & Morgan, W.P. (1989). Exercise and self-esteem: Rationale and model. *Medicine and Science in Sports and Exercise, 21,* 329-337.

Sonstroem, R.J., Speliotis, E.D., & Fava, J.L. (1992). Perceived physical competence in adults: An examination of the Physical Self-Perception Scale. *Journal of Sport and Exercise Psychology, 10,* 207-221.

Spence, J.C., McGannon, K.R., Poon, P. (2005). The effect of exercise on global self-esteem: A quantitative review. *Journal of Sport and Exercise Psychology, 27,* 311-334.

Springer, J.B., Lamborn, S.D., & Pollard, D.M. (2013). The importance of basic psychological need satisfaction in developing the physically active self. *American Journal of Health Promotion, 27*(5), 284-293. doi:10.4278/ajhp.110211-QUAL-62

Stein, K.F., Roeser, R., & Markus, H. (1998). Self-schemas and possible shelves as predictors and outcomes of risky behaviors in adolescents. *Nursing Research, 47*(2), 96-106.

Stephan, Y., Torregrosa, M., & Sanchez, X. (2007). The body matters: Psychophysical impact of retiring from elite sport. *Psychology of Sport and Exercise, 8,* 73-83. doi:10.1016/j.psychsport.2006.01.006

Strachan, S.M., Fortier, S., Perras, G.M., & Lugg, C. (2012). Understanding variations in identity strength through identity theory and self-determination theory. *International Journal of Sport and Exercise Psychology, 11,* 1-13. doi:10.1080/1612197X.2013.749005

Taylor, C.B., Bandura, A., Ewart, C.K., Miller, N.H., & DeBusk, R.T. (1985). Exercise testing to enhance wives' confidence in their husbands' cardiac capabilities soon after clinically uncomplicated acute myocardial infarction. *American Journal of Cardiology, 55,* 635-638.

Taylor, A.H., & Fox, K.R. (2005). Effectiveness of primary care exercise referral intervention for changing physical self-perceptions over 9 months. *Health Psychology, 24,* 11-24.

Tod, D., Hardy, J., & Oliver, E. (2011). Effects of self-talk: A systematic review. *Journal of Sport and Exercise Psychology, 33,* 666-687.

Treasure, D.C., Monson, J., & Lox, C.L. (1996). Relationship between self-efficacy, wrestling performance and affect prior to competition. *Sport Psychologist, 10,* 73-83.

Tremblay, M.S., Inman, J.W., & Willms, J.D. (2000). The relationship between physical activity, self-esteem, and academic achievement in 12-year old children. *Pediatric Exercise Science, 12,* 312-323.

Vlachopoulos, S.P., Kaperoni, M., & Moustaka, F.C. (2011). The relationship of self-determination theory variables to exercise identity. *Psychology of Sport and Exercise, 12,* 265-272. doi:10.1016/j.psychsport.2010.11.006

Weiss, M.R., & Ferrer-Caja, E. (2002). Motivational orientations and sport behavior. In T.S. Horn (Ed.), *Advances in sport psychology* (2nd ed., pp. 101-183). Champaign, IL: Human Kinetics.

Weiss, M.R., McCullagh, P., Smith, A.L., & Berlant, A.R. (1998). Observational learning and the fearful child: Influence of peer models on swimming skill performance and psychological responses. *Research Quarterly for Exercise and Sport, 69,* 380-394.

Wiese-Bjornstal, D.M. (2004). From skinned knees and peewees to menisci and masters: Developmental sport injury psychology. In M.R. Weiss (Ed.), *Developmental sport and exercise psychology: A lifespan perspective* (pp. 525-568). Morgantown, WV: Fitness Information Technology.

Whaley, D. (2004). Seeing isn't always believing: Self-perceptions and physical activity behaviors in adults. In M.R. Weiss (Ed.), *Developmental sport and exercise psychology: A lifespan perspective* (pp. 289-311). Morgantown, WV: Fitness Information Technology.

Whaley, D.E., & Ebbeck, V. (2002). Self-schemata and exercise identity in older adults. *Journal of Aging and Physical Activity, 10,* 245-259.

Yin, Z., & Boyd, M.P. (2000). Behavioral and cognitive correlates of exercise self-schema. *Journal of Psychology, 134,* 269-282.

Zetou, E., Vernadakis, N., Bebetsos, E., & Makraki, E. (2012). The effect of self-talk in learning the volleyball service skill and self-efficacy improvement. *Journal of Human Sport and Exercise, 7*(4), 794-805. doi:10.4100/jhse.v7i4.349

Chapter 7

Brobst, B., & Ward, P. (2002). Effects of public posting, goal setting, and oral feedback on the skills of female soccer players. *Journal of Applied Behavior Analysis, 35,* 247-257.

Burton, D., & Weiss, C. (2008). The fundamental goal concept: The path to process and performance success. In T.S. Horn (Ed.), *Advances in sport psychology* (3rd ed., pp. 339-375). Champaign, IL: Human Kinetics.

Critchfield, T.S., & Vargas, E.A. (1991). Self-recording, instructions and public self-graphing: Effects on swimming in the absence of coach verbal interaction. *Behavior Modification, 15,* 95-112.

Danish, S.J., Nellen, V.C., & Owens, S.S. (1996). Teaching life skills through sport: Community-based programs for adolescents. In J.L. Van Raalte & B.W. Brewer (Eds.), *Exploring sport and exercise psychology* (2nd ed., pp. 205-225). Washington, DC: American Psychological Association.

De Bruin, M., Sheeran, P., Kok, G., et al. (2012). Self-regulatory processes mediate the intention-behavior relation for adherence and exercise behaviors. *Health Psychology, 31,* 695-703.

Dishman, R.K., Jackson, A.S., & Bray, M.S. (2014). Self-regulation of exercise behavior in the TIGER study. *Annals of Behavioral Medicine, 48,* 80-91.

Fitterling, J.M., & Ayllon, T. (1983). Behavioral coaching in classical ballet. *Behavior Modification, 3,* 345-368.

Freund, A.M., & Hennecke, M. (2015). On means and ends: The role of goal focus in successful goal pursuit. *Current Directions in Psychological Science, 24,* 149-153.

Gallimore, R., & Tharp, R. (2004). What a coach can teach a teacher, 1975-2004: Reflections and reanalysis of John Wooden's teaching practices. *Sport Psychologist, 18,* 119-137.

Gardner, B., de Bruijn, G.J., & Lally, P. (2011). A systematic review and meta-analysis of applications of the Self-Report Habit Index to nutrition and physical activity behaviors. *Annals of Behavioral Medicine, 42,* 174-187.

Gould, D.R. (2015). Goal setting for peak performance. In J.M. Williams & V. Krane (Eds.), *Applied sport psychology: Personal growth to peak performance* (7th ed., pp. 188-205). New York: McGraw-Hill.

Komaki, J., & Barnett, F.T. (1977). A behavioral approach to coaching football: Improving the play execution of the offensive backfield on a youth football team. *Journal of Applied Behavior Analysis, 10,* 657-664.

Kyllo, L.B., & Landers, D.M. (1995). Goal setting in sport and exercise: A research synthesis to resolve the controversy. *Journal of Sport and Exercise Psychology, 17,* 117-137.

Locke, E.A., & Latham, G.P. (1990). *A theory of goal setting and task performance.* Englewood Cliffs, NJ: Prentice Hall.

Locke, E.A., & Latham, G.P. (2002). Building a practically useful theory of goal setting and task motivation: A 35-year odyssey. *American Psychologist, 57,* 705-717.

Locke, E.A., Saari, L.M., Shaw, K.N., & Latham, G.P. (1981). Goal setting and task performance: 1969-1980. *Psychological Bulletin, 90,* 125-152.

Mann, T., de Ridder, D., & Fujita, K. (2013). Self-regulation of health behavior: Social psychological approaches to goal setting and goal striving. *Health Psychology, 32,* 487-498.

McKenzie, T., & Rushall, B. (1974). Effects of self-recording on attendance and performance in a competitive swimming training environment. *Journal of Applied Behavior Analysis, 7,* 199-206.

Papacharisis, V.P., Goudas, M., Danish, S.J., & Theodorakis, Y. (2005). The effectiveness of teaching a life skills program in a sport context. *Journal of Applied Sport Psychology, 17,* 247-254.

Polaha, J., Allen, K., & Studley, B. (2004). Self-monitoring as an intervention to decrease swimmers' stroke counts. *Behavior Modification, 28,* 261-275.

Rebar, A.L., Elavsky, S., Maher, J.P., Doerksen, S.E., & Conroy, D.E. (2014). Habits predict physical activity on days when intentions are weak. *Journal of Sport and Exercise Psychology, 36,* 157-165.

Rhodes, R.E., & de Bruijn, G.J. (2010). Automatic and motivational correlates of physical activity. Does intensity moderate the relationship? *Behavioral Medicine, 36,* 44-52.

Smith, R.E. (2015). A positive approach to coaching effectiveness and performance enhancement. In J.M. Williams & V. Krane (Eds.), *Applied sport psychology: Personal growth to peak performance* (7th ed., pp. 40-56). New York: McGraw-Hill.

Smith, R.E., & Smoll, F.L. (1997). Coaching the coaches: Youth sports as a scientific and applied behavioral setting. *Current Directions in Psychological Science, 6,* 16-21.

Smith, R.E., & Smoll, F.L. (2012). *Sport psychology for youth coaches: Developing champions in sports and life.* New York: Rowman & Littlefield.

Smith, R.E., Smoll, F.L., & Christiansen, D.S. (1996). Behavioral assessments and interventions in youth sport. *Behavior Modification, 20,* 3-44.

Smith, R.E., Smoll, F.L., & Curtis, B. (1978). Coaching behaviors in little league baseball. In F.L. Smoll & R.E. Smith (Eds.), *Psychological perspectives in youth sports* (pp. 173-201). Washington, DC: Hemisphere.

Smith, R.E., Smoll, F.L., & Hunt, E. (1977). A system for the behavioral assessment of athletic coaches. *Research Quarterly, 48,* 401-407.

Strohacker, K., Galarraga, O., & Williams, D.M. (2014). The impact of incentives on exercise behavior: A systematic review of randomized control trials. *Annals of Behavioral Medicine, 48,* 92-99.

Tharp, R.G., & Gallimore, R. (1976, January). What a coach can teach a teacher. *Psychology Today, 9,* 74-78.

Vidic, Z., & Burton, D. (2010). The roadmap: Examining the impact of a systematic goal-setting program for collegiate women's tennis. *Sport Psychologist, 26,* 469-477.

Wanlin, C.M., Hrycaiko, D.W., Martin, G.L., & Mahon, M. (1997). The effects of a goal-setting package on the performance of speed skaters. *Journal of Applied Sport Psychology, 9,* 212-228.

Weinberg, R. (2014). Goal setting in sport and exercise: Research to practice. In J.L. Van Raalte & B.W. Brewer (Eds.), *Exploring sport and exercise psychology* (3rd ed., pp. 33-54). Washington, DC: American Psychological Association.

Weinberg, R.S., Burton, D., Yukelson, D., & Weigand, D. (1993). Goal setting in competitive sport: An exploratory investigation of practices of collegiate athletes. *Sport Psychologist, 7,* 275-289.

Wood, W., & Neal, D.T. (2007). A new look at habits and the habit-goal interface. *Psychological Review, 114,* 843-863.

Chapter 8

Amorose, A.J., & Anderson-Butcher, D. (2015). Exploring the independent and interactive effects of autonomy-supportive and controlling coaching behaviors on adolescent athletes' motivation for sport. *Sport, Exercise, and Performance Psychology, 4*(3), 206-218. doi:10.1037/spy0000038

Bailey, R., Cope, E.J., & Pearce, G. (2013). Why do children take part in, and remain involved in sport? A literature review and discussion of implications for sports coaches. *International Journal of Coaching Science, 7,* 56-75.

Barbeau, A., Sweet, S.N., & Fortier, M. (2009). A path-analytic model of self-determination theory in a physical activity context. *Journal of Applied Biobehavioral Research, 14*(3), 103-118.

Buckworth, J., Dishman, R., O'Connor, P., & Tomporowski, P. (2013). *Exercise psychology.* Champaign, IL: Human Kinetics.

Burton, D., O'Connell, K., Gillham, A.D., & Hammermeister, J. (2011). More cheers and fewer tears: Examining the impact of competitive engineering on scoring and attrition in youth flag football. *International Journal of Sports Science and Coaching, 6*(2), 219-228.

Campbell, P.G., MacAuley, D., McCrum, E., & Evans, A. (2001). Age differences in motivating factors for exercise. *Journal of Sport and Exercise Psychology, 23,* 291-199.

Carpenter, P.J., & Coleman, R. (1998). A longitudinal study of elite youth cricketers' commitment. *International Journal of Sport Psychology, 29*(3), 195-210.

Carpenter, P.J., Scanlan, T.K., Simons, J.P., & Lobel, M. (1993). A test of the Sport Commitment Model using structural equation modeling. *Journal of Sport and Exercise Psychology, 15*(1), 119-133.

Casper, J.M., & Stellino, M.B. (2008). Demographic predictors of recreational tennis participants' sport commitment. *Journal of Park and Recreation Administration, 26*(3), 93-115.

Chemolli, E., & Gagne, M. (2014). Evidence against the continuum structure underlying motivation measures derived from self-determination theory. *Psychological Assessment, 26*(2), 575-585. doi:10.1037/a0036212

Deci, E.L., & Ryan, R.M. (1985). *Intrinsic motivation and self-determination in human behavior.* New York: Plenum Press.

Deci, E.L., & Ryan, R.M. (2000). The "what" and "why" of goal pursuits: Human needs and the self-determination of behavior. *Psychological Inquiry, 11,* 227-268.

Edmunds, J., Ntoumanis, N., & Duda, J. (2006). A test of self-determination theory in exercise. *Journal of Applied Social Psychology, 36*(9), 2240-2265.

Gabriele, J.M., Gill, D.L., & Adams, C.E. (2011). The roles of want to commitment and have to commitment in explaining physical activity behavior. *Journal of Physical Activity and Health, 8,* 420-438.

Gill, D.L., Gross, J.B., & Huddleston, S. (1983). Participation motivation in youth sports. *International Journal of Sport Psychology, 14,* 1-14.

Gillet, N., Vallerand, R.J., Amoura, S., & Baldes, B. (2010). Influence of coaches' autonomy support on athletes' motivation and sport performance: A test of the hierarchical model of intrinsic and extrinsic motivation. *Psychology of Sport and Exercise, 11,* 155-161. doi:10.1016/j.psychsport.2009.10.004

Gould, D., Feltz, D., & Weiss, M. (1985). Motives for participating in competitive youth swimming. *International Journal of Sport Psychology, 6,* 126-140.

Hollembeak, J., & Amorose, A.J. (2005). Perceived coaching behaviors and college athletes' intrinsic motivation: A test of self-determination theory. *Journal of Applied Sport Psychology, 17,* 20-36.

Howard, D.R. (1992). Participation rates in selected sport and fitness activities. *Journal of Sport Management, 6*(3), 191-205.

Klint, K.A., & Weiss, M.R. (1986). Dropping in and dropping out: Participation motives of current and former youth gymnasts. *Canadian Journal of Applied Sport Science, 11,* 106-114.

Lepper, M.R., & Greene, D. (1975). Turning play into work: Effects of adult surveillance and extrinsic rewards on children's intrinsic motivation. *Journal of Personality and Social Psychology, 31,* 479-486.

Lox, C.L., Martin Ginis, K.A., & Petruzzello, S.J. (2014). *The psychology of exercise* (3rd ed.). Scottsdale, AZ: Holcomb Hathaway.

Mageau, G.A., & Vallerand, R.J. (2003). The coach-athlete relationship: A motivational model. *Journal of Sports Sciences, 21,* 883-904. doi:10.1080/0264041031000140374

Markland, D., & Tobin, V. (2004). A modification to the Behavioural Regulation in Exercise Questionnaire to include an assessment of amotivation. *Journal of Sport and Exercise Psychology, 26,* 191-196.

Podlog, L.W., & Eklund, R.C. (2007). The psychosocial aspects of a return to sport following serious injury: A review of the literature. *Psychology of Sport and Exercise, 8*(4), 535-566. doi:10.1016/j.psychsport.2006.07.008

Raedeke, T.D. (1997). Is athletic burnout more than just stress? A sport commitment perspective. *Journal of Sport and Exercise Psychology, 19,* 396-417.

Reifsteck, E.J., Gill, D.L., & Labban, J.D. (2016). "Athletes" and "exercisers": Understanding identity, motivation, and physical activity participation in former college athletes. *Sport, Exercise, and Performance Psychology, 5*(1), 25-38. doi:10.1037/spy0000046

Rodgers, W.M., & Loitz, C.C. (2009). The role of motivation in behavior change: How do we encourage our clients to be active? *ACSM's Health Fitness Journal, 13*(1), 7-12. doi:10.1249/FIT.0b013e3181916d11

Ryan, R.M., & Deci, E.L. (2000). Intrinsic and extrinsic motivations: Classic definitions and new directions. *Contemporary Educational Psychology, 25,* 54-67. doi:10.1006/ceps.1999.1020

Ryan, R.M., Williams, G.C., Patrick, H., & Deci, E.L. (2009). Self-determination theory and physical activity: The dynamics of motivation in development and wellness. *Hellenic Journal of Psychology, 6,* 107-124.

Sapp, M., & Haubenstricker, J. (1978, April). *Motivation for joining and reasons for not continuing in youth sport programs in Michigan.* Paper presented at the meeting of the American Alliance for Health, Physical Education, Recreation and Dance, Kansa City, MO.

Scanlan, T.K., Carpenter, P.J., Lobel, M., & Simons, J.P. (1993). Sources of enjoyment of youth sport athletes. *Pediatric Exercise Science, 5*(3), 275-285.

Scanlan, T.K., Carpenter, P.J., Schmidt, G.W., Simons, J.P., & Keeler, B. (1993). An introduction to the Sport Commitment Model. *Journal of Sport and Exercise Psychology, 15*(1), 1-15.

Scanlan, T.K., & Lewthwaite, R. (1986). Social psychological aspects of competition for male youth sport participants: IV. Predictors of enjoyment. *Journal of Sport Psychology, 8,* 25-35.

Scanlan, T.K., Russell, D.G., Beals, K.P., & Scanlan, L.A. (2003). Project on Elite Athlete Commitment (PEAK): II. A direct test and expansion of the sport commitment model with elite amateur sportsmen. *Journal of Sport and Exercise Psychology, 25,* 377-401.

Scanlan, T.K., Russell, D.G., Magyar, M.T., & Scanlan, L.A. (2009). Project on Elite Athlete Commitment (PEAK): III. An examination of the external validity across gender, and the expansion and clarification of the sport commitment model. *Journal of Sport and Exercise Psychology, 30,* 685-705.

Scanlan, T.K., Russell, D.G., Scanlan, L.A., Klunchoo, T.J., & Chow, G.M. (2013). Project on Elite Athlete Commitment (PEAK): IV. Identification of new candidate commitment sources in the sport commitment model. *Journal of Sport and Exercise Psychology, 35*(5), 525-535.

Scanlan, T.K., Simons, J.P., Carpenter, P.J., Schmidt, G.W., & Keeler, B. (1993). The Sport Commitment Model: Measurement development for the youth-sport domain. *Journal of Sport and Exercise Psychology, 15*(1), 16-38.

Scanlan, T.K., Stein, G.L., & Ravizza, K. (1989). An in-depth study of former elite figure skaters: 2. Sources of enjoyment. *Journal of Sport and Exercise Psychology, 11,* 65-83.

Schmidt, G.W., & Stein, G.L. (1991). Sport commitment: A model integrating enjoyment, dropout, and burnout. *Journal of Sport and Exercise Psychology, 13,* 254-265.

Standage, M., Duda, J.L., & Ntoumanis, N. (2003). A model of contextual motivation in physical education: Using constructs from self-determination and achievement goal theories to predict physical activity intentions. *Journal of Educational Psychology, 95,* 419-439.

Thogersen-Ntoumani, C., & Ntoumanis, N. (2006). The role of self-determined motivation in the understanding of exercise-related behaviours, cognitions and physical self-evaluations. *Journal of Sports Sciences, 24*(4), 393-404. doi:10.1080/02640410500131670

Weiss, M.R., & Amorose, A.J. (2008). Motivational orientations and sport behavior. In T.S. Horn (Ed.), *Advances in sport psychology* (3rd ed., pp. 115-155). Champaign, IL: Human Kinetics.

Weiss, M.R., Kimmel, L.A., & Smith, A.L. (2001). Determinants of sport commitment among junior tennis players: Enjoyment as a mediating variable. *Pediatric Exercise Science, 1,* 131-144.

Weiss, W.M., & Weiss, M.R. (2003). Attraction- and entrapment-based commitment among competitive female gymnasts. *Journal of Sport and Exercise Psychology, 25,* 229-247.

Weiss, W.M., & Weiss, M.R. (2006). A longitudinal analysis of commitment among competitive female gymnasts. *Psychology of Sport and Exercise, 7,* 309-323.

Weiss, W.M., & Weiss, M.R. (2007). Sport commitment among competitive female gymnasts: A developmental perspective. *Research Quarterly for Exercise and Sport, 78,* 90-102.

Weiss, M.R., & Williams, L. (2004). The why of youth sport involvement: A developmental perspective on motivational processes. In M.R. Weiss (Ed.), *Developmental sport and exercise psychology: A lifespan perspective* (pp. 223-268). Morgantown, WV: Fitness Information Technology.

Wilson, P.M., Rodgers, W.M., Carpenter, P.J., Hall, C., Hardy, J., & Fraser, S.N. (2004). The relationship between commitment and exercise behavior. *Psychology of Sport and Exercise, 5,* 405-421.

Young, B.W., & Medic, N. (2011). Examining social influences on the sport commitment of Masters swimmers. *Psychology of Sport and Exercise, 12,* 168-175.

Chapter 9

Allen, J., Taylor, J., Dimeo, P., Dixon, S., & Robinson, L. (2015). Predicting elite Scottish athletes' attitudes towards doping: Examining the contribution of achievement goals and motivational climate. *Journal of Sports Sciences, 33,* 899-906. doi:10.1080/02640414.2014.976588

Ames, C. (1984). Conceptions of motivation within competitive and noncompetitive goal structures. In R. Schwarzer (Ed.), *Self-related cognitions in anxiety and motivation* (pp. 205-241). Hillsdale, NJ: Erlbaum.

Ames, C. (1992). Achievement goals, motivational climate, and motivational processes. In G.C. Roberts (Ed.), *Motivation in sport and exercise* (pp. 161-176). Champaign, IL: Human Kinetics.

Ames, C., & Ames, R. (1981). Competitive versus individualistic goal structures: The salience of past performance information for causal attributions and affect. *Journal of Educational Psychology, 73,* 411-418.

Ames, C., & Archer, J. (1988). Achievement goals in the classroom: Students' learning strategies and motivation processes. *Journal of Educational Psychology, 80,* 260-267.

Atkins, M.R., Johnson, D.M., Force, E.C., & Petrie, T.A. (2015). Peers, parents, and coaches, oh my! The relation of the motivational climate to boys' intention to continue in sport. *Psychology of Sport and Exercise, 16,* 170-180. doi:10.1016/j.psychsport.2014.10.008

Atkinson, J.W. (1964). *An introduction to motivation.* Princeton, NJ: Van Nostrand.

Atkinson, J.W. (1974). The mainsprings of achievement-oriented activity. In J.W. Atkinson & J.O. Raynor (Eds.), *Motivation and achievement* (pp. 13-41). New York: Halstead.

Bennett K.K, Howarter, A.D., & Clark J.M.R.. (2013). Self-blame attributions, control appraisals, and distress among cardiac rehabilitation patients. Psychology and Health, 28, 637-652, doi: 10.1177/2055102916632669

Biddle, S.J.H., Hanrahan, S.J., & Sellars, C.N. (2001). Attributions: Past, present, and future. In R.N. Singer, H.A. Hausenblas, & C.M. Janelle (Eds.), *Handbook of sport psychology* (2nd ed., pp. 444-471). New York: Wiley.

Biddle, S.J.H., Wang, J.C.K., Kavussanu, M., & Spray, C. (2003). Correlates of achievement goal orientations in physical activity: A systematic review of research. *European Journal of Sports Science, 3,* 1-19.

Boyce, B.A., Gano-Overway, L.A., & Campbell, A.L. (2009). Perceived motivational climate's influence on goal orientations, perceived competence, and practice strategies across the athletic season. *Journal of Applied Sport Psychology, 21,* 381-394. doi:10.1080/10413200903204887

Braithwaite, R., Spray, C.M., & Warburton, V.E. (2011). Motivational climate interventions in physical education: A meta-analysis. *Psychology of Sport and Exercise, 12,* 628-638. doi:101016/j.psychsport.2011.06.005

Conroy, D.E., & Elliot, A.J. (2004). Fear of failure and achievement goals in sport: Addressing the issue of the chicken and the egg. *Anxiety, Stress and Coping, 17,* 271-285.

Cury, F.D., Elliot, A.J., Sarrazin, P., Da Fonseca, D., & Rufo, M. (2002). The trichotomous achievement goal model and intrinsic motivation: A sequential mediational analysis. *Journal of Experimental Social Psychology, 38,* 473-481.

Davies, M.J., Babkes Stellino, M., Nichols, B.A., & Coleman, L.M. (2016). Other-initiated motivational climate and youth hockey players' good and poor sport behaviors. *Journal of Applied Sport Psychology, 28,* 78-96. doi:10.1080/10413200.2015.1071297

Diener, C.I., & Dweck, C.S. (1978). An analysis of learned helplessness: Continuous changes in performance, strategy, and achievement cognitions following failure. *Journal of Personality and Social Psychology, 36,* 451-462. doi:10.1037/0022-3514.36.5.451

Diener, C.I., & Dweck, C.S. (1980). An analysis of learned helplessness: II. The processing of success. *Journal of Personality and Social Psychology, 39,* 940-952.

Duda, J.L. (2005). Motivation in sport: The relevance of competence and achievement motivation. In A.J. Elliot & C.S. Dweck (Eds.), *Handbook of competence and motivation* (pp. 318-335). New York: Guilford Press.

Dweck, C.S. (1975). The role of expectations and attributions in the alleviation of learned helplessness. *Journal of Personal and Social Psychology, 31,* 674-685.

Dweck, C.S. (2000). *Self-theories: Their role in motivation, personality, and development.* Philadelphia: Psychology Press.

Dweck, C.S. (2006). *Mindset: The new psychology of success.* New York: Ballantine Books.

Dweck, C.S. (2012). Implicit theories. In P.A.M. Van Lange, A.W. Kruglanski, & E.T. Higgins, *Handbook of theories of social psychology* (pp. 43-61). London: Sage. doi:10.4135/9781446249222.n28

Dweck, C.S., & Leggett, E.L. (1983). A social-cognitive approach to motivation and personality. *Psychological Review, 95,* 256-269.

Dweck, C.S., & Leggett, E.L. (1988). A social-cognitive approach to motivation and personality. *Psychological Review, 95,* 256-259.

Elliot, A.J. (1997). Integrating "classic" and "contemporary" approaches to achievement motivation: A hierarchical model of approach and avoidance achievement motivation. In P. Pintrich & M. Maehr (Eds.), *Advances in motivation and achievement* (Vol. 10, pp. 143-179). Greenwich, CT: JAI Press.

Elliot, A.J. (1999). Approach and avoidance motivation and achievement goals. *Educational Psychologist, 34,* 169-189.

Elliot, A.J., & McGregor, H.A. (2001). A 2×2 achievement goal framework. *Journal of Personality and Social Psychology, 80,* 501-519. doi:10.1037/0022-3514.80.3.501

Gano-Overway, L.A., & Ewing, M.E. (2004). A longitudinal perspective of the relationship between perceived motivational climate, goal orientations, and strategy use. *Research Quarterly for Exercise and Sport, 75,* 315-325. doi:10.1080/02701367.2004.10609163

Gao, Z., Podlog, L., & Harrison, L. (2012). College students' goal orientations, situational motivation and effort/persistence in physical activity classes. *Journal of Teaching Physical Education, 31,* 246-260.

Hanrahan, S.J., & Biddle, S.J.H. (2008). Attributions and perceived control. In T.S. Horn (Ed.), *Advances in sport psychology* (3rd ed., pp. 99-114). Champaign, IL: Human Kinetics.

Harwood, C.G., Keegan, R.J., Smith, J.M.J., & Raine, A.S. (2015). A systematic review of the intrapersonal correlates of motivational climate perceptions in sport and physical activity. *Psychology of Sport and Exercise, 18,* 9-25. doi:10.1016/j.psychsport.2014.11.005

Harwood, C.G., Spray, C., & Keegan, R.J. (2008). Achievement goal theories in sport. In T.S. Horn (Ed.), *Advances in sport psychology* (3rd ed., pp. 157-185). Champaign, IL: Human Kinetics.

Harwood, C.G., & Swain, A.B.J. (1998). Antecedents of pre-competition achievement goals in elite junior tennis players. *Journal of Sports Sciences, 16,* 357-371.

Hassan, M., & Morgan, K. (2015). Effects of a mastery intervention programme on the motivational climate and achievement goals in sport coaching: A pilot study. *International Journal of Sport Science and Coaching, 10,* 248-503. doi:10.1260/1747-9541.10.2-3.487

Holt, N.L., & Morley, D. (2004). Gender difference in psychosocial factors associated with athletic success during childhood. *Sport Psychologist, 18,* 138-153.

Hunt, A.W., Turner, G.R., Polatojko, H., Bottari, C., & Dawson, D.R. (2013). Executive function, self-regulation and attribution in acquired brain injury: A scoping review. *Neuropsychological Rehabilitation, 23,* 914-932. doi:10.1080/09602011.2013.835739

Johnson, L., & Biddle, S.J.H. (1988). Persistence after failure: An exploratory look at "learned helplessness" in motor performance. *British Journal of Physical Education Research Supplement, 5,* 7-10.

Leo, F.M., Sanchez-Miguel, P.A., Sanchez-Oliva, D., Amado, D., & Garcia-Calvo, T. (2015). Motivational climate created by other significant actors and antisocial behaviors in youth sport. *Kinesiology, 47,* 3-10.

Lochbaum, M., & Gottardy, J. (2014). A meta-analytic review of the approach-avoidance achievement goals and performance relationships in the sport psychology literature. *Journal of Sport and Health Science, 17,* 1-10. doi:10.1016/j.jshs.2013.12.004

Lochbaum, M., Podlog, L., Litchfield, K., Surles, J., & Hilliard, S. (2013). Stage of physical activity and approach-avoidance achievement goals in university students. *Psychology of Sport and Exercise, 14,* 161-168.

Lochbaum, M., & Smith, C. (2015). Making the cut and winning a golf putting championship: The role of approach-avoidance achievement goals. *International Journal of Golf Science, 4,* 50-66.

Maehr, M.L., & Nicholls, J.G. (1980). Culture and achievement motivation: A second look. In N. Warren (Ed.), *Studies in cross-cultural psychology* (Vol. 3, pp. 221-267). New York: Academic Press.

Martinek, T., & Griffith, J.B. (1994). Learned helplessness in physical education: A developmental study of causal attributions and task persistence. *Journal of Teaching in Physical Education, 13,* 108-122.

Martinek, T., & Williams, L. (1997). Goal orientation and task persistence in learned helplessness and mastery oriented students in middle school physical education classes. *International Sports Journal, 1,* 63-76.

Mascret, N., Elliot, A.J., & Cury, F. (2015). Extending the 3x2 achievement goal model to the sport domain: The 3x2 achievement goal questionnaire for sport. *Psychology of Sport and Exercise, 17,* 7-14. doi:10.1016/j.psychsport.2014.11.001

Miller, B.W., Roberts, G.C., & Ommundsen, Y. (2004). Effect of motivational climate on sportspersonship among young male and female football players. *Scandinavian Journal of Medicine and Science in Sports, 14,* 193-202.

Murray, H.A. (1938). *Explorations in personality.* New York: Oxford University Press.

Nicholls, J.G. (1989). *The competitive ethos and democratic education.* Cambridge, MA: Harvard University Press.

Nien, C.L., & Duda, J.L. (2008). Antecedents and consequences of approach and avoidance achievement goals: A test of gender invariance. *Psychology of Sport and Exercise, 9,* 352-372. doi:10.1016/j.psychsport.2007.05.002

Orbach, I., Singer, R.N., & Murphey, M. (1997). Changing attributional style with an attribution training technique related to basketball dribbling. *Sport Psychologist, 11,* 294-304.

Orbach, I., Singer, R.N., & Price, S. (1999). An attribution training program and achievement in sport. *Sport Psychologist, 13,* 69-82.

O'Rourke, D.J., Smith, R.E., Smoll, F.L., & Cumming, S.P. (2014). Relations of parent- and coach-initiated motivational climates to young athletes' self-esteem, performance anxiety, and autonomous motivation: Who is more influential? *Journal of Applied Sport Psychology, 26,* 395-408. doi:10.1080/10413200.2014.907838

Parkes, J.F., & Mallett, C.J. (2011). Developing mental toughness: Attributional style retraining in rugby. *Sport Psychologist, 25,* 269-287.

Prapavessis, H., & Carron, A.V. (1988). Learned helplessness in sport. *Sport Psychologist, 2,* 189-201.

Puente-Diaz, R. (2013). Achievement goals and emotions. *Journal of Psychology, 147,* 245-259.

Rascle, O., Le Foll, D., & Higgins, N.C. (2008). Attributional retraining alters novice golfers' free practice behavior. *Journal of Applied Sport Psychology, 20,* 157-164.

Roberts, G.C. (2012). Motivation in sport and exercise from an achievement goal theory perspective: After 30 years, where are we? In G.C. Roberts & D.C. Treasure (Eds.), *Advances in motivation in sport and exercise* (3rd ed., pp. 5-58). Champaign, IL: Human Kinetics.

Roberts, G.C., & Pascuzzi, D. (1979). Causal attributions in sport: Some theoretical implications. *Journal of Sport Psychology, 1,* 203-211.

Roberts, G.C., Treasure, D.C., & Conroy, D.E. (2007). Understanding the dynamics of motivation in sport and physical activity: An achievement goal interpretation. In G. Tenenbaum & R.E. Eklund (Eds.), *Handbook of sport psychology* (3rd ed., pp. 3-30). Hoboken: NJ: Wiley.

Sanjua'n, P., Arranz, H., & Castro, A. (2014). Effect of negative attributions on depressive symptoms of patients with coronary heart disease after controlling for physical functional impairment. *British Journal of Health Psychology, 19,* 380-392. doi:10.1111/bjhp.12044

Sarrazin, P., Biddle, S., Famose, J.P., Cury, F., Fox, K., & Durand, M. (1996). Goal orientations and conceptions of the nature of sport ability in children: A social cognitive approach. *British Journal of Social Psychology, 35,* 399-414.

Smith, J.M.J., & Harwood, C.G. (2001, September). *The transiency of goal involvement states in match-play: An elite player case study.* Paper presented at the British Association of Sport and Exercise Sciences conference, Newport, RI.

Smoll, F., & Smith, R. (2015). Conducting evidence based coach-training programs: A social-cognitive approach. In J.M. Williams & V. Krane (Eds.), *Applied sport psychology: Personal growth to peak performance* (7th ed., pp. 359-382). Boston: McGraw-Hill.

Smoll, F.L., Smith, R.E., & Cumming, S.P. (2007, Summer). Effects of coach and parent training on performance anxiety in young athletes: A systemic approach. *Journal of Youth Development, 2,* Article 0701FA002.

Spink, K.S., & Roberts, G.C. (1980). Ambiguity of outcome and causal attributions. *Journal of Sport Psychology, 2,* 237-244.

Stenling, A., Hassmén, P., & Holmström, S. (2014). Implicit beliefs of ability, approach-avoidance goals and cognitive anxiety among team sport athletes. *European Journal of Sport Science, 14,* 720-729. doi:10.1080/17461391.2014.901419

Su, X., McBride, R.E., & Xiang, P. (2015). College students' achievement goal orientation and motivational regulations in physical activity classes: A test of gender invariance. *Journal of Teaching Physical Education, 34,* 2-17. doi:10.1123/jtpe.2013-0151

Vazou, S., Ntoumanis, N., & Duda, J.L. (2006). Predicting young athletes' motivational indices as a function of their perceptions of the coach- and peer-created climate. *Psychology of Sport and Exercise, 7,* 215-233.

Waldron, J.J., & Krane, V. (2005). Motivational climate and goal orientation in adolescent female softball players. *Journal of Sport Behavior, 28,* 378-392.

Walling, M., & Martinek, T. (1995). Learned helplessness: A case study of a middle school student. *Journal of Teaching in Physical Education, 14,* 454-466.

Wang, C.K., Biddle, S.J.H., & Elliot, A.J. (2007). The 2×2 achievement goal framework in a physical education context. *Psychology of Sport and Exercise, 8,* 147-168. doi:10.1016/j.pscyhsport.2005.08.012

Weiner, B. (1974). *Achievement motivation and attribution theory.* Morristown, NJ: General Learning Press.

Weiner, B. (1979). A theory of motivation for some classroom experiences. *Journal of Educational Psychology, 71,* 3-25.

Weiner, B. (1986). *An attributional theory of motivation and emotion.* New York: Springer-Verlag.

Weiner, B. (1992). *Human motivation.* Newbury Park, CA: Sage.

Weiner, B. (2000). Intrapersonal and interpersonal theories of motivation from an attribution perspective. *Educational Psychology Review, 12,* 1-14.

Weiss, M.R., & Williams, L. (2004). The *why* of youth sport: A developmental perspective on motivational processes. In M.R. Weiss (Ed.), *Developmental sport and exercise psychology: A lifespan perspective* (pp. 223-268). Morgantown, WV: Fitness Information Technology.

Williams, L. (1998). Contextual influences and goal perspectives among female youth sport participants. *Research Quarterly for Exercise and Sport, 69,* 47-57.

Wulf, G., & Lewthwaite, R. (2009). Conceptions of ability affect motor learning. *Journal of Motor Behavior, 41,* 461-467. doi:10.3200/35-08-083

Chapter 10

Ajzen, I. (1985). From intentions to actions: A theory of planned behavior. In J. Kuhl & J. Reckman (Eds.), *Action control: From cognition to behavior* (pp. 11-39). Heidelberg: Springer.

American College of Sports Medicine. (10th ed., 2017). *ACSM's guidelines for exercise testing and prescription.* Philadelphia: Wolters Kluwer/Lippincott Williams & Wilkins Health.

Bandura, A. (1986). *Social foundations of thought and action: A social cognitive theory.* Englewood Cliffs, NJ: Prentice Hall.

Bandura, A. (2004). Health promotion by social cognitive means. *Health Education and Behavior, 31,* 143-164. doi:10.1177/1090198104263660

Bartholomew, J.B. (2015). Environments change child behavior, but who changes environments? *Kinesiology Review, 4,* 71-76. doi:10.1123/kr.2014-0077

Blumenthal, J.A., O'Toole, L.C., & Chang, J.L. (1984). Is running an analogue of anorexia nervosa? *Journal of the American Medical Association, 252*(4), 520-523.

Blumenthal, J.A., Rose, S., & Chang, J.L. (1985). Anorexia nervosa and exercise: Implications from recent findings. *Sports Medicine, 2,* 237-247.

Bock, B.C., Linke, S.E., Napolitano, M.A., Clark, M.M., Gaskins, R.B., & Marcus, B.H. (2014). Exercise initiation, adoption and maintenance in adults: Theoretical models and empirical support. In J.L. Van Raalte

& B.W. Brewer (Eds.), *Exploring sport and exercise psychology* (3rd ed., pp. 163-189). Washington, DC: American Psychological Association.

Brawley, L.R., Gierc, M.S.H., & Locke, S.R. (2013). Powering adherence to physical activity by changing self-regulatory skills and beliefs: Are kinesiologists ready to counsel? *Kinesiology Review, 2,* 4-16.

Brownell, K.D. (1989). *The LEARN program for weight control.* Dallas: Brownell & Hager.

Brownell, K.D., Marlatt, G.A., Lichtenstein, E., & Wilson, G.T. (1986). Understanding and preventing relapse. *American Psychologist, 41,* 765-782.

Buckworth, J., Dishman, R.K., O'Connor, P.J., & Tomporowski, P.D. (2013). *Exercise psychology (2nd ed.).* Champaign, IL: Human Kinetics.

Burke, B.L., Arkowitz, H., & Menchola, M. (2003). The efficacy of motivational interviewing: A meta-analysis of controlled clinical trials. *Journal of Consulting and Clinical Psychology, 71,* 843-861.

Cardinal, B.J., Kosma, M., & McCubbin, J.A. (2004). Factors influencing the exercise behavior of adults with physical disabilities. *Medicine and Science in Sports and Exercise, 36,* 868-875.

Centers for Disease Control and Prevention (CDC). (2014). Facts about physical activity. Retrieved from https://www.cdc.gov/physicalactivity/data/facts.htm

Cohen, D.A., Ashwood, S., Scott, M., et al. (2006). Proximity to school and physical activity among middle school girls: The trial of activity for adolescent girls study. *Journal of Physical Activity and Health, 3*(Suppl. 1), S129-S138.

Corbin, C.B., Welk, G.J., Corbin, W.R., & Welk, K.A. (2008). *Concepts of fitness and wellness* (7th ed.). Boston: McGraw-Hill.

Courneya, K.S., Estabrooks, P.A., & Nigg, C.R. (1997). Predicting change in exercise stage over a 3-year period: An application of the theory of planned behavior. *Avante, 3,* 1-13.

Courneya, K.S., Plotnikoff, R.C., Hotz, S.B., & Birkett, N.J. (2000). Social support and the theory of planned behavior in the exercise domain. *American Journal of Health Promotion, 14,* 300-308.

Dallow, C.B., & Anderson, J. (2003). Using self-efficacy and the transtheoretical model to develop a physical activity intervention for obese women. *American Journal of Health Promotion, 17,* 373-381.

Downs, D.S., & Hausenblas, H.A. (2005). The theories of reasoned action and planned behavior applied to exercise: A meta-analytic update. *Journal of Physical Activity and Health, 2,* 76-97.

Duda, J.L., & Tappe, M.K. (1989). The Personal Incentives for Exercise Questionnaire: Preliminary development. *Perceptual and Motor Skills, 68,* 1122.

Dunn, A.L., Marcus, B.H., Kampert, J.B., Garcia, M.E., Kohl, H.W., & Blair, S.N. (1999). Reduction in cardiovascular disease risk factors: 6-month results from Project Active. *Preventive Medicine, 26,* 883-892.

Fishbein, M., & Ajzen, I. (1974). Attitudes toward objects as predictors of single and multiple behavioral criteria. *Psychological Review, 81,* 59-74.

Gill, D.L., Dowd, D.A., Williams, L., Beaudoin, C.M., & Martin, J.J. (1996). Competitive orientation and motives of adult sport and exercise participants. *Journal of Sport Behavior, 19,* 307-318.

Godin, G. (1993). The theories of reasoned action and planned behavior: Overview of findings, emerging research problems, and usefulness for exercise promotion. *Journal of Applied Sport Psychology, 5,* 141-157.

Grodesky, J.M., Kosma, M., & Solmon, M.A. (2006). Understanding older adults' physical activity behavior: A multi-theoretical approach. *Quest, 58,* 310-329.

Hagger, M.S., Chatzisarantis, N.L.D., & Biddle, S.J.H. (2002). A meta-analytic review of the theories of reasoned action and planned behavior in physical activity. *Journal of Sport and Exercise Psychology, 24,* 3-32.

Hausenblas, H.A., & Symons Downs, D. (2002a). Exercise dependence: A systematic review. *Psychology of Sport and Exercise, 3,* 89-123.

Hausenblas, H.A., & Symons Downs, D. (2002b). How much is too much? The development and validation of the Exercise Dependence Scale. *Psychology and Health, 17,* 387-404.

Heath, G.W., Brownson, R.C., Kruger, J., Miles, R., Powell, K.E., Ramsey, L.T.; and the Task Force on Community Preventive Services. (2006). The effectiveness of urban design and land use and transport policies and practices to increase physical activity: A systematic review. *Journal of Physical Activity and Health, 3*(Suppl. 1), S55-S76.

Jerome, G.J., & McAuley, E. (2013). Enrollment and participation in a pilot walking programme: The role of self-efficacy. *Journal of Health Psychology, 18*(2), 236-244. doi:10.1177/1359105311430869

Kagan, D.M., & Squires, R.L. (1985). Addictive aspects of physical exercise. *Journal of Sports Medicine, 25,* 227-237.

Kesaniemi, Y.K., Danforth, E., Jr., Jensen, M.D., Kopelman, P.G., Lefebre, P., & Reeder, B.A. (2001). Dose-response issues concerning physical activity and health: An evidence-based symposium. *Medicine and Science in Sports and Exercise, 33*(Suppl. 6), S351-S358.

Kroll, T., Kratz, A., Kehn, M., et al. (2012). Perceived exercise self-efficacy as a predictor of exercise behavior in individuals aging with spinal cord injury. *American Journal of Physical Medicine and Rehabilitation, 91*(8), 640-651. doi:10.1097/PHM.0b013e31825a12cd

Lox, C.L., Martin Ginis, K.A., & Petruzzello, S.J. (2014). *The psychology of exercise* (3rd ed.). Scottsdale, AZ: Holcomb Hathaway.

Lubans, D., & Sylva, K. (2006). Controlled evaluation of a physical activity intervention for senior school students: Effects of the lifetime activity program. *Journal of Sport and Exercise Psychology, 28,* 252-268.

Maddison, R., & Prapavessis, H. (2004). Using self-efficacy and intention to predict exercise compliance among patients with ischemic heart disease. *Journal of Sport and Exercise Psychology, 26*(4), 511-524.

Marcus, B.H., Dubbert, P.M., Forsyth, L.H., et al. (2000). Physical activity behavior change: Issues in adoption and maintenance. *Health Psychology, 19*(Suppl. 1), 32-41.

Marcus, B.H., Eaton, C.A., Rossi, J.S., & Harlow, L.L. (1994). Self-efficacy, decision making and stages of change: An integrative model of physical exercise. *Journal of Applied Social Psychology, 24,* 489-508.

Marcus, B.H., Emmons, K.M., Simkin, L.R., et al. (1994). Comparison of stage-matched versus standard care physical activity interventions at the workplace. *Annals of Behavioral Medicine, 16,* S035.

Marcus, B.H., & Forsyth, L.H. (2003). *Motivating people to be physically active.* Champaign, IL: Human Kinetics.

Marcus, B.H., & Forsyth, L.H. (2009). *Motivating people to be physically active* (2nd ed.). Champaign, IL: Human Kinetics.

Marcus, B.H., & Owen, N. (1992). Motivational readiness, self-efficacy and decision-making for exercise. *Journal of Applied Social Psychology, 22,* 3-16.

Marcus, B.H., Pinto, B.M., Simkin, L.R., Audrain, J.E., & Taylor, E.R. (1994). Application of theoretical models to exercise behavior among employed women. *American Journal of Health Promotion, 9,* 49-55.

Marcus, B.H., Rakowski, W., & Rossi, J.S. (1992). Assessing motivational readiness and decision-making for exercise. *Health Psychology, 11,* 257-261.

Marcus, B.H., Rossi, J.S., Selby, V.C., Niaura, R.S., & Abrams, D.B. (1992). The stages and processes of exercise adoption and maintenance in a worksite sample. *Health Psychology, 11,* 386-395.

Marcus, B.H., Selby, V.C., Niaura, R.S., & Rossi, J.S. (1992). Self-efficacy and the stages of exercise behavior change. *Research Quarterly for Exercise and Sport, 63,* 60-66.

Martin, J.E., & Dubbert, P.M. (1984). Behavioral management strategies for improving health and fitness. *Journal of Cardiac Rehabilitation, 4,* 200-208.

McAuley, E., & Courneya, K.S. (1993). Adherence to exercise and physical activity as health-promoting behaviors: Attitudinal and self-efficacy influences. *Applied and Preventive Psychology, 2,* 65-77.

McAuley, E., Jerome, G.J., Marquez, D.X., Elavsky, S., & Blissmer, B. (2003). Exercise self-efficacy in older adults: Social, affective and behavioral influences. *Annals of Behavioral Medicine, 25,* 1-7.

Mears, J., & Kilpatrick, M. (2009). Motivation for exercise: Applying theory to make a difference in adoption and adherence. *ACSM's Health and Fitness Journal, 12*(1), 20-26.

Morgan, W.P. (1979). Negative addiction in runners. *Physician and Sportsmedicine, 7*(2), 57-70.

Pierce, E.F. (1994). Exercise dependence syndrome in runners. *Sports Medicine, 18,* 149-155.

Prochaska, J.O., & DiClemente, C.C. (1983). Stages and processes of self-change of smoking: Towards an integrative model of change. *Journal of Consulting and Clinical Psychology, 51,* 390-395.

Prochaska, J.O., Velicer, W.F., Rossi, J.S., et al. (1994). Stages of change and decisional balance for twelve problem behaviors. *Health Psychology, 13,* 39-46.

Raglin, J.S., & Moger, L. (1999). Adverse consequences of physical activity: When more is too much. In J. Rippe (Ed.), *Lifestyle medicine* (pp. 998-1004). Malden, MA: Blackwell Scientific.

Reifsteck, E.R., Gill, D.L., & Labban, J.D. (2016). "Athletes" and "Exercisers": Understanding identity, motivation, and physical activity participation in former college athletes. *Sport, Exercise, and Performance Psychology, 5*(1), 25-38. doi:10.1037/spy0000046

Robbins, J.M., & Joseph, P. (1985). Experiencing exercise withdrawal: Possible consequences of therapeutic and mastery running. *Journal of Sport Psychology, 7,* 23-39.

Rollnick, S., & Miller, W.R. (1995). What is motivational interviewing? *Behavioural and Cognitive Psychotherapy, 23,* 325-334.

Rosenstock, I.M. (1974). Historical origins of the health belief model. *Health Education Monographs, 2,* 328-335.

Sachs, M.L. (1981). Running addiction. In M. Sacks & M. Sachs (Eds.), *Psychology of running* (pp. 116-127). Champaign, IL: Human Kinetics.

Sallis, J.F., Bauman, A., & Pratt, M. (1998). Environmental and policy interventions to promote physical activity. *American Journal of Preventive Medicine, 15,* 379-397.

Sallis, J.F., Hovell, M.F., Hofstetter, C.R., et al. (1990). Lifetime history of relapse from exercise. *Addictive Behaviors, 15,* 573-579.

Sforzo, G.A., Moore, M., & Scholtz, M. (2015). Health and wellness coaching competencies for exercise professionals. *ACSM's Health and Fitness Journal, 19*(2), 20-26. doi:10.1249/FIT.0000000000000109

Sorenson, S.C., Romano, R., Azen, S.P., Schroeder, E.T., & Salem, G.J. (2015). Life span exercise among elite intercollegiate student athletes. *Sports Health: A Multidisciplinary Approach, 7,* 80-86. doi:10.1177/1941738114534813

Taylor, W.C., Poston, W.S.C., Jones, L., & Kraft, A.K. (2006). Environmental justice: Obesity, physical activity and healthy eating. *Journal of Physical Activity and Health, 3*(Suppl. 1), S30-S54.

Thompson, J.K., & Blanton, P. (1987). Energy conservation and exercise dependence: A sympathetic arousal hypothesis. *Medicine and Science in Sports and Exercise, 19,* 91-99.

U.S. Department of Health and Human Services. (2015). MentalHealth.gov. www.mentalhealth.gov

U.S. Department of Health and Human Services, Office of Disease Prevention and Health Promotion. (2008). *2008 Physical activity guidelines for Americans.* Washington, DC: HHS.

U.S. Department of Health and Human Services, Office of Disease Prevention and Health Promotion. (2010). Healthy people 2020. Retrieved from www.healthy-people.gov

Van Raalte, J.L., & Andersen, M.B. (2014). Referral processes in sport psychology. In J.L. Van Raalte & B.W. Brewer (Eds.), *Exploring sport and exercise psychology* (3rd ed., pp. 337-350). Washington, DC: American Psychological Association.

Whiteley, J.A., & Milliken, L.A. (2011). Making weight loss a family affair. *ACSM's Health and Fitness Journal, 15*(2), 13-19.

World Health Organization. (2015). Physical activity. Retrieved from www.who.int/topics/physical_activity/en/

Yates, A., Leehey, K., & Shisslak, C.M. (1983). Running—an analogue of anorexia. *New England Journal of Medicine, 308,* 251-255.

Chapter 11

Apter, M.J. (1984). Reversal theory and personality: A review. *Journal of Research in Personality, 18,* 265-288.

Burton, D. (1988). Do anxious swimmers swim slower? Reexamining the elusive anxiety-performance relationship. *Journal of Sport & Exercise Psychology, 10,* 26-37.

Cannon, W.B. (1929). *Bodily changes in pain, hunger, fear and rage* (2nd ed.). New York: Appleton-Century-Crofts.

Crocker, P.R.E., Bouffard, M., & Gessaroli, M.E. (1995). Measuring enjoyment in youth sport settings: A confirmatory factor analysis of the Physical Activity Enjoyment Scale. *Journal of Sport and Exercise Psychology, 17,* 200-205.

Csikszentmihalyi, M. (1975). *Beyond boredom and anxiety.* San Francisco: Jossey-Bass.

Csikszentmihalyi, M. (1990). *Flow: The psychology of optimal experience.* New York: Harper & Row.

Edwards, T., & Hardy, L. (1996). The interactive effects of intensity and direction of cognitive and somatic anxiety and self-confidence upon performance. *Journal of Sport and Exercise Psychology, 18,* 296-312.

Fenz, W.D. (1975). Coping mechanisms and performance under stress. In D.V. Harris, R.W. Christina, & R.W. Landers (Eds.), *Psychology of sport and motor behaviour II* (pp. 3-24). University Park: Pennsylvania State University.

Fenz, W.D. (1988). Learning to anticipate stressful events. *Journal of Sport and Exercise Psychology, 10,* 223-228.

Fredrickson, B.L. (2001). The role of positive emotions in positive psychology: The broaden-and-build theory of positive emotions. *American Psychologist, 56,* 218-226. doi:10.1037/0003-066X.56.3.218

Fredrickson, B.L. (2013a). Positive emotions broaden and build. In P. Devine & A. Plant (Eds.), *Advances in experimental social psychology* (Vol. 47, pp. 1-53). San Diego: Academic Press. doi:10.1016/B978-0-12-407236-7.00001-2

Fredrickson, B.L. (2013b). Updated thinking on positivity ratios. *American Psychologist, 68,* 814-822. doi:10.1037/a0033584

Gould, D., Petlichkoff, L., Simons, J., & Vevera, M. (1987). Relationship between Competitive State Anxiety-2 subscale scores and pistol shooting performance. *Journal of Sport Psychology, 9,* 33-42.

Gould, D., Petlichkoff, L., & Weinberg, R.S. (1984). Antecedents of, temporal changes in, and relationships between CSAI-2 subcomponents. *Journal of Sport Psychology, 6,* 289-304.

Hanin, Y. (1989). Interpersonal and intragroup anxiety in sports. In D. Hackfort & C.D. Spielberger (Eds.), *Anxiety in sports: An international perspective* (pp. 19-28). Washington, DC: Hemisphere.

Hanin, Y. (1995). Individual zones of optimal functioning (IZOF) model: An idiographic approach to anxiety. In K. Henschen & W. Straub (Eds.), *Sport psychology: An analysis of athlete behavior* (pp. 103-119). Longmeadow, MA: Mouvement.

Hanin, Y., & Syrja, P. (1996). Predicted, actual, and recalled affect in Olympic-level soccer players: Idiographic assessments on individualized scales. *Journal of Sport and Exercise Psychology, 18,* 325-335.

Hanton, S., & Jones, G. (1999a). The acquisition and development of cognitive skills and strategies: I. Making the butterflies fly in formation. *Sport Psychologist, 13,* 1-21.

Hanton, S., & Jones, G. (1999b). The effects of a multimodal intervention program on performers: II. Training the butterflies to fly in formation. *Sport Psychologist, 13,* 22-41.

Hardy, L. (1990). A catastrophe model of performance in sport. In J.G. Jones & L. Hardy (Eds.), *Stress and performance in sport* (pp. 81-106). Chichester, England: Wiley.

Hardy, L. (1996). Testing the predictions of the cusp catastrophe model of anxiety and performance. *Sport Psychologist, 10,* 140-156.

Hardy, L., & Parfitt, C.G. (1991). A catastrophe model of anxiety and performance. *British Journal of Psychology, 82,* 163-178.

Hardy, L., Parfitt, C.G., & Pates, J. (1994). Performance catastrophes in sport. *Journal of Sports Sciences, 12,* 327-334.

Hull, C.L. (1943). *Principles of behavior.* New York: Appleton-Century-Crofts.

Jackson, S.A. (1995). Factors influencing the occurrence of flow state in elite athletes. *Journal of Applied Sport Psychology, 7,* 138-166.

Jackson, S.A., & Marsh, H.W. (1996). Development and validation of a scale to measure optimal experience: The flow state scale. *Journal of Sport and Exercise Psychology, 18,* 17-35.

James, W. (1884). What is emotion? *Mind, 9,* 188-204.

Jones, G. (1995). More than just a game: Research developments in competitive anxiety in sport. *British Journal of Psychology, 86,* 449-478.

Kendzierski, D., & DeCarlo, K.J. (1991). Physical activity enjoyment scale: Two validation studies. *Journal of Sport and Exercise Psychology, 13,* 50-64.

Kerr, J. (1997). *Motivation and emotion in sport: Reversal theory.* East Sussex, UK: Psychology Press.

Kerr, J.H. (1985). The experience of arousal: A new basis for studying arousal effects in sport. *Journal of Sports Sciences, 3,* 169-179.

Kimiecik, J.C., & Harris, A.T. (1996). What is enjoyment? A conceptual/definitional analysis with implications for sport and exercise psychology. *Journal of Sport and Exercise Psychology, 18,* 247-263.

Kleinginna, P.R., & Kleinginna, A.M. (1981). A categorized list of emotional definitions, with suggestions for a consensual definition. *Motivation and Emotion, 5,* 345-379.

Lange, C.G. (1885). *Om sindsbevaegelser. et psyko. fysidog. studie.* Copenhagen: Kronar.

Lazarus, R.S. (1966). *Psychological stress and the coping process.* New York: McGraw-Hill.

Lazarus, R.S. (1991). *Emotion and adaptation.* New York: Oxford University Press.

Lazarus, R.S. (1993). From psychological stress to the emotions: A history of changing outlooks. *Annual Review of Psychology, 44,* 1-21.

Mahoney, M.J. (1979). Cognitive skills and athletic performance. In P.C. Kendall & S.D. Hollon (Eds.), *Cognitive-behavioral intervention: Theory, research, and procedures* (pp. 423-443). New York: Academic Press.

Mahoney, M.J., & Avener, M. (1977). Psychology of the elite athlete: An exploratory study. *Cognitive Therapy and Research, 1,* 135-141.

Martens, R., & Landers, D.M. (1970). Motor performance under stress: A test of the inverted-U hypothesis. *Journal of Personality and Social Psychology, 16*, 29-37.

Martens, R., Vealey, R.S., & Burton, D. (1990). *Competitive anxiety in sport.* Champaign, IL: Human Kinetics.

McCarthy, P.J. (2011). Positive emotion in sport performance: Current status and future directions. *International Review of Sport and Exercise Psychology, 4*, 50-69.

Mullen, S.P., Olson, E.A., Phillips, S.M., et al. (2011). Measuring enjoyment of physical activity in older adults: Invariance of the physical activity enjoyment scale (PACES) across groups and time. *International Journal of Behavioral Nutrition and Physical Activity, 8*(103). doi:10.1186/1479-5868-8-103

Nakamura, J., & Csikszentmihalyi, M. (2005). The concept of flow. In C.R. Snyder & S.J. Lopez (Eds.), *Handbook of positive psychology* (pp. 89-105). New York: Oxford University Press.

Plutchik, R. (2003). *Emotions and life.* Washington, DC: American Psychological Association.

Reeve, J. (2005). *Understanding motivation and emotion* (4th ed.). Hoboken, NJ: Wiley.

Ruiz, M.C., Raglin, J.S., & Hanin, Y.L. (2015). The individual zones of optimal functioning (IZOF) model (1978–2014): Historical overview of its development and use. *International Journal of Sport and Exercise Psychology.* Advance online publication. doi.org/10.1080/1612197x.2015.1041545

Scanlan, T.K., Babkes, M.L., & Scanlan, L.A. (2005). Participation in sport: A developmental glimpse at emotion. In J.L. Mahoney, R.W. Larson, & J.S. Eccles (Eds.), *Organized activities as contexts of development* (pp. 275-309). Mahwah, NJ: Erlbaum.

Scanlan, T.K., & Simons, J.P. (1992). The construct of sport enjoyment. In G. Roberts (Ed.), *Motivation in sport and exercise* (pp. 199-215). Champaign, IL: Human Kinetics.

Scanlan, T.K., Simons, J.P., Carpenter, P.J., Schmidt, G.W., & Keeler, B. (1993). The Sport Commitment Model: Measurement development for the youth-sport domain. *Journal of Sport and Exercise Psychology, 15*, 16-38.

Scanlan, T.K., Stein, G.L., & Ravizza, K. (1989). An in-depth study of former elite figure skaters: 2. Sources of enjoyment. *Journal of Sport and Exercise Psychology, 11*, 65-83.

Schachter, S., & Singer, J. (1962). Cognitive, social and physiological determinants of emotional state. *Psychological Review, 69*, 378-399.

Selye, H. (1956). *The stress of life.* New York: McGraw-Hill.

Sonstroem, R.J., & Bernardo, P.B. (1982). Intraindividual pregame state anxiety and basketball performance: A re-examination of the inverted-U curve. *Journal of Sport Psychology, 4*, 235-245.

Spence, K.W. (1956). *Behavior theory and conditioning.* New Haven, CT: Yale University Press.

Spielberger, C.D., Gorsuch, R.L., & Lushene, R.E. (1970). *Manual for the State-Trait Anxiety Inventory.* Palo Alto, CA: Consulting Psychologists Press.

Swann, C., Keegan, R.J., Piggott, D., & Crust, L. (2012). A systematic review of the experience, occurrence, and controllability of flow states in elite sport. *Psychology of Sport and Exercise, 13*, 807-819.

Visek, A.J., Archrati, S.M., Mannix, H.M., McDonnell, K., Harris, B.S., & DiPietro, L. (2015). The fun integration theory: Toward sustaining children and adolescents sport participation. *Journal of Physical Activity and Health, 12*, 424-433. doi.org/10.1123/jpah.2013-0180

Woodman, T., Davis, P.A., Hardy, L., Callow, N., Glasscock, I., & Yuill-Proctor, J. (2009). Emotions and sport performance: An exploration of happiness, hope and anger. *Journal of Sport and Exercise Psychology, 31*, 169-188.

Yerkes, R.M., & Dodson, J.D. (1908). The relation of strength of stimulus to rapidity of habit formation. *Journal of Comparative and Neurological Psychology, 18*, 459-482.

Chapter 12

Asmundson, G.J.G., Fetzner, M.G., DeBoer, L.B., Powers, M.B., Otto, M.W., & Smits, J.A.J. (2013). Let's get physical: A contemporary review of the anxiolytic effects of exercise for anxiety and its disorders. *Depression and Anxiety, 30*, 362-373.

Backhouse, S.H., Ekkekakis, P., Biddle, S.J.H., Foskett, A., & Williams, C. (2007). Exercise makes people feel better but people are inactive: Paradox or artifact? *Journal of Sport and Exercise Psychology, 29*, 498-517.

Bartley, C.A., Hay, M., & Bloch, M.H. (2013). Meta-analysis: Aerobic exercise for the treatment of anxiety disorders. *Progress in Neuro-Psychopharmacology and Biological Psychiatry, 45*, 34-39.

Berger, B.G., & Tobar, D. (2007). Physical activity and quality of life. In G. Tenenbaum & R. Eklund (Eds.), *Handbook of research on sport psychology* (3rd ed., pp. 598-620). Hoboken, NJ: Wiley.

Bize, R., Johnson, J.A., & Plotnikoff, R.C. (2007). Physical activity and health-related quality of life in the general adult population: A systematic review. *Preventive Medicine, 45*, 401-415.

Blumenthal, J.A., Smith, P.J., & Hoffman, B.M. (2012). Is exercise a viable treatment for depression? *ACSM's Health and Fitness Journal, 16*(4), 14-21.

Borg, G. (1973). Psychophysical basis of perceived exertion. *Medicine and Science in Sports and Exercise, 14*, 377-381.

Borg, G. (1998). *Borg's perceived exertion and pain scales.* Champaign, IL: Human Kinetics.

Boutcher, S. (1993). Emotion and aerobic exercise. In R.N. Singer, M. Murphey, & L.K. Tennant (Eds.), *Handbook of research on sport psychology* (pp. 799-814). New York: Macmillan.

Broocks, A., Bandelow, B., Pekrun, G., et al. (1998). Comparison of aerobic exercise, chloripramine, and placebo in the treatment of panic disorder. *American Journal of Psychiatry, 155,* 603-609.

Brunes, A., Augestad, L.B., & Gudmundsdottir, S.L. (2013). Personality, physical activity, and symptoms of anxiety and depression: The HUNT study. *Social Psychiatry and Psychiatric Epidemiology, 48,* 745-756.

Castelli, D.M., Hillman, C.H., Buck, S.M., & Erwin, H.E. (2007). Physical fitness and academic achievement in third- and fifth-grade students. *Journal of Sport and Exercise Psychology, 29,* 239-252.

Chaddock, L., Voss, M.W., & Kramer, A.F. (2012). Physical activity and fitness effects on cognition and brain health in children and older adults. *Kinesiology Review, 1,* 37-45.

Chang, Y.K., & Etnier, J.L. (2015). Editorial: Acute exercise and cognitive function: Emerging research issues. *Journal of Sport and Health Science, 4,* 1-3.

Chang, Y.K., Labban, J.D., Gapin, J.I., & Etnier, J.L. (2012). The effects of acute exercise on cognitive performance: A meta-analysis. *Brain Research, 1453,* 87-101. doi:10.1016/j.brainres.2012.02.068

Colcombe, S., & Kramer, A.F. (2003). Fitness effects on the cognitive function of older adults: A meta-analytic study. *Psychological Science, 14,* 125-130.

Courneya, K.S., Friedenreich, C.M., Sela, R.A., Quinney, A., Rhodes, R.E., & Handman, M. (2003). The group psychotherapy and home-based (GROUP-HOPE) trial in cancer survivors: Physical fitness and quality of life outcomes. *Psycho-Oncology, 12,* 357-374.

Courneya, K.S., Mackey, J.R., & Jones, L.W. (2000). Coping with cancer: Can exercise help? *Physician and Sportsmedicine, 28,* 49-51, 55-56, 66-68, 71, 73.

Craft, L.L., & Landers, D.M. (1998). The effect of exercise on clinical depression and depression resulting from mental illness: A meta-analysis. *Journal of Sport and Exercise Psychology, 20,* 339-357.

Crews, D.J., & Landers, D.M. (1987). A meta-analytic review of aerobic fitness and reactivity to psychosocial stressors. *Medicine and Science in Sports and Exercise, 19,* S114-S120.

Crocker, P.R.E. (1997). A confirmatory factor analysis of the Positive Affect Negative Affect Schedule (PANAS) with a youth sport sample. *Journal of Sport and Exercise Psychology, 19,* 91-97.

Crocker, P.R.E., & Graham, T.R. (1995). Coping by competitive athletes with performance stress:

Gender differences and relationships with affect. *Sport Psychologist, 9,* 325-338.

Diener, E. (1984). Subjective well-being. *Psychological Bulletin, 95*(3), 542-575.

Diener, E., Emmons, R.A., Larsen, R.J., & Griffin, S. (1985). The Satisfaction with Life Scale. *Journal of Personality Assessment, 49*(1), 71-75.

Ekkekakis, P., Hargreaves, E.A., & Parfitt, G. (2013). Invited guest editorial: Envisioning the next fifty years of research on the exercise affect relationship. *Psychology of Sport and Exercise, 14,* 751-758. doi. org/10.1016/j.psychsport.2013.04.007

Ekkekakis, O., Parfitt, G., & Petruzzello, S.J. (2011). The pleasure and displeasure people feel when they exercise at different intensities. *Sports Medicine, 41*(8), 641-671.

Ekkekakis, P., & Petruzzello, S.J. (1999). Acute aerobic exercise and affect: Current status, problems and prospects regarding dose-response. *Sports Medicine, 28,* 337-374.

Ekkekakis, P., & Petruzzello, S.J. (2002). Analysis of the affect measurement conundrum in exercise psychology. *Psychology of Sport and Exercise, 3,* 35-63.

Emery, C.F., Schein, R.L., Hauck, E.R., & MacIntyre, N.R. (1998). Psychological and cognitive outcomes of a randomized trial of exercise among patients with chronic obstructive pulmonary disease. *Health Psychology, 17,* 232-240.

Etnier, J.L. (2014). Research . . . How fun is that? Interesting questions relative to the effects of exercise on cognitive performance. *Kinesiology Review, 3,* 151-160. doi.org/10.1123/kr.2014-0050

Etnier, J.L. (2015). Physical activity in the prevention of Alzheimer's disease. *Kinesiology Review, 4,* 28-38. doi.org/10.1123/kr.2014-0075

Etnier, J.L., Salazar, W., Landers, D.M., Petruzzello, S.J., Han, M., & Nowell, P. (1997). The influence of physical fitness and exercise upon cognitive functioning: A meta-analysis. *Journal of Sport and Exercise Psychology, 19,* 249-277.

Eveland-Sayers, B.M., Farley, R.S., Fuller, D.K., Morgan, D.W., & Caputo, J.L. (2009). Physical fitness and academic achievement in elementary school children. *Journal of Physical Activity and Health, 6,* 99-104.

Folkins, C.H., & Sime, W.E. (1981). Physical fitness training and mental health. *American Psychologist, 36,* 373-389.

Forcier, K., Stroud, L.R., Papandonatos, G.D., et al. (2006). Links between physical fitness and cardiovascular reactivity and recovery to psychological stressors: A meta-analysis. *Health Psychology, 25*(6), 723-739.

Gauvin, L., & Brawley, L.R. (1993). Alternative psychological models and methodologies for the study of exercise and affect. In P. Seraganian (Ed.), *Exercise psychology: The influence of physical exercise on psychological processes* (pp. 146-171). New York: Wiley.

Gauvin, L., & Rejeski, W.J. (1993). The Exercise-Induced Feeling Inventory: Development and initial validation. *Journal of Sport and Exercise Psychology, 15,* 403-423.

Gill, D.L., Chang, Y-K., Murphy, K.M., et al. (2011). Quality of life assessment in physical activity and health promotion. *Applied Research in Quality of Life, 6,* 181-200. doi:10.1007/s11482-010-9126-2

Gill, D.L., Hammond, C.C., Reifsteck, E.J., et al. (2013). Physical activity and quality of life. *Journal of Preventative Medicine and Public Health, 46,* S28-S34. doi: 10.3961/jpmph.2012.45.S.S1.

Gill, D.L., Reifsteck, E.R., Adams, M.M, & Shang, Y. (2015). Quality of Life Assessment for Physical Activity and Health Promotion: Further Psychometrics and Comparison of Measures. *Measurement in Physical Education and Exercise Science, 19,* 159-166. doi: 10.1080/1091367X.2015. 1050102.

Gillison, F.B., Skevington, S.M., Sato, A., Standage, M., & Evangelidou, S. (2009). The effects of exercise interventions on quality of life in clinical and healthy populations: A meta-analysis. *Social Science and Medicine, 68,* 1700-1710.

Goodwin, R.D. (2003). Association between physical activity and mental disorders among adults in the United States. *Preventive Medicine, 36,* 698-703.

Gothe, N., Pontifex, M.B., Hillman, C., & McAuley, E. (2013). The acute effects of yoga on executive function. *Journal of Physical Activity and Health, 10,* 488-495.

Hamer, M., & Steptoe, A. (2007). Association between physical fitness, parasympathetic control, and proinflammatory responses to mental stress. *Psychosomatic Medicine, 69,* 660-666.

Hardy, C.J., & Rejeski, W.J. (1989). Not what, but how one feels: The measurement of affect during exercise. *Journal of Sport and Exercise Psychology, 11,* 304-317.

Hardy, L. (1996). Testing the predictions of the cusp catastrophe model of anxiety and performance. *The Sport Psychologist, 10,* 140-156.

Heller, T., Hsieh, K., & Rimmer, J.H. (2004). Attributional and psychosocial outcomes of a fitness and health education program on adults with Down syndrome. *American Journal of Mental Retardation, 109,* 175-185.

Heydari, M., Boutcher, Y.N., & Boutcher, S.J. (2013). The effects of high-intensity intermittent exercise training on cardiovascular response to mental and physical challenge. *International Journal of Psychophysiology, 87,* 141-146.

Hillman, C.H., Pontifex, M.B., Raine, L.B., Castelli, D.M., Hall, E.E., & Kramer, A.F. (2009). The effect of acute treadmill walking on cognitive control and academic performance in preadolescent children. *Neuroscience, 159*(3), 1044-1054.

Hong, S., & Mills, P.J. (2006). Physical activity and psychoneuroimmunology. In E.O. Acevedo & P. Ekkekakis (Eds.), *Psychobiology of physical activity* (pp. 177-188). Champaign, IL: Human Kinetics.

Howie, E.K., & Pate, R.R. (2012). Physical activity and academic achievement in children: A historical perspective. *Journal of Sport and Health Science, 1,* 160-169. doi.org/10.1016/j.jshs.2012.09.003

Hyde, A.L., Conroy, D.E., Pincus, A.L., & Ram, N. (2011). Unpacking the feel-good effect of free-time physical activity: Between- and within-person associations with pleasant-activated feeling states. *Journal of Sport and Exercise Psychology, 33,* 884-902.

Jackson, E.M., & Dishman, R.K. (2006). Cardiorespiratory fitness and laboratory stress: A meta-regression analysis. *Psychophysiology, 43,* 57-72.

Jayakody, K., Gunadasa, S., & Hosker, C. (2014). Exercise for anxiety disorders: Systematic review. *British Journal of Sports Medicine, 48*(3), 187-196. doi:10.1136/bjsports-2012-091287

Kramer, A.F., & Hillman, C.H. (2006). Aging, physical activity and neurocognitive function. In E.O. Acevedo & P. Ekkekakis (Eds.), *Psychobiology of physical activity* (pp. 45-59). Champaign, IL: Human Kinetics.

Landers, D.M., & Petruzzello, S.J. (1994). Physical activity, fitness and anxiety. In C. Bouchard, R.J. Shepard, & T. Stephens (Eds.), *Physical activity, fitness and health: International proceedings and consensus statement* (pp. 868-882). Champaign, IL: Human Kinetics.

LaPerriere, A.R., Antoni, M.H., Schneiderman, N., et al. (1990). Exercise intervention attenuates emotional distress and natural killer cell decrements following notification of positive serologic status for HIV-1. *Biofeedback and Self-Regulation, 15,* 229-242.

LaPerriere, A.R., Fletcher, M.A., Antoni, M.H., Klimas, N.G., Ironson, G., & Schneiderman, N. (1991). Aerobic exercise training in an AIDS risk group. *International Journal of Sports Medicine, 12,* S53-S57.

Latimer, A.E., & Martin Ginis, K.A. (2005). The theory of planned behavior in prediction of leisure time physical activity among individuals with spinal cord injury. *Rehabilitation Psychology, 50,* 389-396.

Lee, C., & Russell, A. (2003). Effects of physical activity on emotional well-being among older Australian women: Cross-sectional and longitudinal analyses. *Journal of Psychosomatic Research, 54*(2), 155-160.

Long, B.C., & van Stavel, R. (1995). Effects of exercise training on anxiety: A meta-analysis. *Journal of Applied Sport Psychology, 7,* 167-189.

Lox, C.L., Martin Ginis, K.A., & Petruzzello, S.J. (2014). *The psychology of exercise: Integrating theory and practice* (4th ed.). Scottsdale, AZ: Holcomb Hathaway.

Lox, C.L., McAuley, E., & Tucker, R.S. (1995). Exercise as an intervention for enhancing subjective well-being in an HIV-1 population. *Journal of Sport and Exercise Psychology, 17,* 345-362.

Mammen, G., & Faulkner, G. (2013). Physical activity and the prevention of depression: A systematic review of prospective studies. *American Journal of Preventive Medicine, 45*(5), 649-657. doi. org/10.1016/j.amepre.2013.08.001

Martens, R., Vealey, R.S., & Burton, D. (1990). *Competitive anxiety in sport.* Champaign, IL: Human Kinetics.

Martin Ginis, K.A., Latimer, A.E., McKechnie, K., et al. (2003). Using physical activity to enhance subjective well-being among people with spinal cord injury. *Rehabilitation Psychology, 48,* 157-164.

McAuley, E., & Courneya, K.S. (1994). The subjective exercise experience scale (SEES): Development and preliminary validation. *Journal of Sport and Exercise Psychology, 16,* 163-177.

McAuley, E., & Elavsky, S. (2005). Physical activity, aging, and quality of life: Implications for measurement. In W. Zhu (Ed.), *Measurement issues and challenges in aging and physical activity research* (pp. 57-68). Champaign, IL: Human Kinetics.

McNair, D.M., Lorr, M., & Droppleman, L.F. (1971). *Manual for the profile of mood states.* San Diego: Educational and Industrial Testing Service.

Meyer, T., Broocks, A., Bandelow, B., Hillmer-Vogel, U., & Ruther, E. (1998). Endurance training in panic patients: Spiroergometric and clinical effects. *International Journal of Sports Medicine, 19,* 496-502.

Mobily, K.E., Rubenstein, L.M., Lemke, J.H., O'Hara, M.W., & Wallace, R.B. (1996). Walking and depression in a cohort of older adults: The Iowa 65+ Rural Health study. *Journal of Aging and Physical Activity, 4,* 119-135.

Motl, R.W., Birnbaum, A.S., Kubik, M.Y., & Dishman, R.K. (2004). Naturally occurring changes in physical activity are inversely related to depressive symptoms during early adolescence. *Psychosomatic Medicine, 66,* 336-342.

Neal, T.L., Diamond, A.B., Goldman, S., et al. (2013). Inter-association recommendations for developing a plan to recognize and refer student-athletes with psychological concerns at the collegiate level: An executive summary of a consensus statement. *Journal of Athletic Training, 48*(5), 716-720. doi:10.4085/1062-6050-48.4.13

North, T.S., McCullagh, P., & Tran, Z.V. (1990). Effects of exercise on depression. *Exercise and Sport Sciences Reviews, 18,* 379-415.

Park, S.Y., Lyu, M.J., Jang, J.Y., Kim, J., & Gill, D.L. (2015). Development and preliminary validation of Korean version of Quality of Life survey. *Korean Journal of Sport Psychology, 26*(1), 61-72.

Petruzzello, S., Landers, D.M., Hatfield, B.D., Kubitz, K.A., & Salazar, W. (1991). A meta-analysis on the anxiety-reducing effects of acute and chronic exercise: Outcomes and mechanism. *Sports Medicine, 11,* 143-182.

Piepmeier, A.T., & Etnier, J.L. (2015). Brain-derived neurotropic factor (BDNF) as a potential mechanism of the effects of acute exercise on cognitive performance. *Journal of Sport and Health Science, 4,* 14-23.

Pontifex, M.B., Raine, L.B., Johnson, C.R., et al. (2011). Cardiorespiratory fitness and the flexible modulation of cognitive control in preadolescent children. *Journal of Cognitive Neuroscience, 23,* 1332-1345.

Rejeski, W.J., Best, D.L., Griffith, P., & Kenney, E. (1987). Sex-role orientation and the responses of men to exercise stress. *Research Quarterly for Exercise and Sport, 58,* 260-264.

Rejeski, W.J., Brawley, L.R., & Shumaker, S.A. (1996). Physical activity and health-related quality of life. *Exercise and Sport Sciences Reviews, 24,* 71-108.

Robertson, R.J., & Noble, B.J. (1997). Perception of physical exertion: Methods, mediators, and applications. *Exercise and Sport Sciences Reviews, 25,* 407-452.

Russell, J.A. (1980). A circumplex model of affect. *Journal of Personality and Social Psychology, 57,* 491-502.

Russell, J.A., Weiss, A., & Mendelsohn, G.A. (1989). Affect grid: A single item scale of pleasure and arousal. *Journal of Personality and Social Psychology, 39,* 1161-1178.

Schechtman, K.B., & Ory, M.G. (2001). The effects of exercise on the quality of life of frail older adults: A preplanned meta-analysis of the FICSIT trials. *Annals of Behavioral Medicine, 23*(3), 186-197.

Schmitz, N., Kruse, J., & Kugler, J. (2004). The association between physical exercise and health-related quality of life in subjects with mental disorders: Results from a cross-sectional survey. *Preventive Medicine, 39*(6), 1200-1207.

Segar, M.L., Katch, V.L., Roth, R.S., et al. (1998). The effect of aerobic exercise on self-esteem and depressive and anxiety symptoms among breast cancer survivors. *Journal of Rheumatology, 10,* 2473-2481.

Spaulding, T.W., Lyon, L.A., Steel, D.H., & Hatfield, B.D. (2004). Aerobic exercise training and cardiovascular reactivity to psychological stress in sedentary young normotensive men and women. *Psychophysiology, 41,* 552-562.

Stathi, A., Fox, K.R., & McKenna, J. (2002). Physical activity and dimensions of subjective well-being in older adults. *Journal of Aging and Physical Activity, 10*(1), 76-92.

Svebak, S., & Murgatroyd, S. (1985). Metamotivational dominance: A multimethod validation of reversal theory constructs. *Journal of Personality and Social Psychology, 48,* 107-116.

Tomporowski, P.D., McCullick, B., Pendleton, D.M., & Pesce, C. (2015). Exercise and children's cognition: The role of exercise characteristics and a place for metacognition. *Journal of Sport and Health Science, 4,* 47-55.

Tuson, K.M., & Sinyor, D. (1993). On the affective benefits of aerobic exercise: Taking stock after twenty years of research. In P. Seraganian (Ed.), *Exercise psychology: The influence of physical exercise on psychological processes* (pp. 80-121). New York: Wiley.

Ware, J.E. (2000). SF-36 health survey update. *Spine, 25*(24), 3130-3139.

Watson, D., Clark, L.A., & Tellegen, A. (1988). Development and validation of brief measures of positive and negative affect. The PANAS scales. *Journal of Personality and Social Psychology, 54,* 1063-1070.

Watson, D., & Tellegen, A. (1985). Toward a consensual analysis of mood. *Psychological Bulletin, 98,* 219-235. World Health Organization. (1946). Preamble to the Constitution of the World Health Organization. Retrieved from www.who.int/governance/eb/who_constitution_en.pdf?ua=1

Chapter 13

American Psychological Association. (2016). Stress in America. Retrieved from www.apa.org/news/press/releases/stress/index.aspx

Andersen, M., & Williams, J. (1988). A model of stress and athletic injury: Prediction and prevention. *Journal of Sport and Exercise Psychology, 10,* 294-306.

Benson, H. (1976). *The relaxation response.* New York: William Morrow.

Brewer, B.W., Andersen, M.B., & Van Raalte, J.L. (2002). Psychological aspects of sport injury rehabilitation: Toward a biopsychosocial approach. In D.I. Mostofsky & L.D. Zaichkowski (Eds.), *Medical and psychological aspects of sport and exercise* (pp. 41-54). Morgantown, WV: Fitness Information Technology.

Callahan, T. (1984, July 30). No limit to what he can do. *Time,* pp. 52-59.

Carver, C.S., Scheier, M.F., & Weintraub, J.K. (1989). Assessing coping strategies: A theoretically based approach. *Journal of Personality and Social Psychology, 56,* 267-283.

Clay, R.A. (2011). Stressed in America. *Monitor on Psychology, 42*(1), 60.

DeFreese, J.D., Raedeke, T.D., & Smith, A.L. (2015). Athlete burnout: An individual and organizational phenomenon. In J.M. Williams & V. Krane (Eds.), *Applied sport psychology: Personal growth to peak performance* (7th ed., pp. 444-461). New York: McGraw-Hill.

Endler, N.S., & Parker, J.D.A. (1994). Assessment of multidimensional coping: Task, emotion, and avoidance strategies. *Psychological Assessment, 6,* 50-60.

Fenz, W.D. (1975). Coping mechanisms and performance under stress. In D.V. Harris, R.W. Christina, & R.W. Landers (Eds.), *Psychology of sport and motor behaviour II* (pp. 3-24). University Park: Pennsylvania State University.

Fenz, W.D. (1988). Learning to anticipate stressful events. *Journal of Sport and Exercise Psychology, 10,* 223-228.

Hanton, S., Mellalieu, S.D., & Williams, J.M. (2015). Understanding and managing stress in sport. In J.M. Williams & V. Krane (Eds.), *Applied sport psychology: Personal growth to peak performance* (7th ed., pp. 207-239). New York: McGraw-Hill.

Jacobson, E. (1938). *Progressive relaxation.* Chicago: University of Chicago Press.

Johnson, U., & Ivarsson, A. (2011). Psychological predictors of sport injuries among junior soccer players. *Scandinavian Journal of Medicine and Science in Sports, 21*(1), 129-136. http://doi.org/10.1111/j.1600-0838.2009.01057.x

Kelley, B.C., & Gill, D.L. (1993). An examination of personal/situational variables, stress appraisal, and burnout in collegiate teacher-coaches. *Research Quarterly for Exercise and Sport, 64,* 94-102.

Kowalski, K.C., & Crocker, P.E. (2001). Development and validation of the coping function questionnaire for adolescents in sport. *Journal of Sport and Exercise Psychology, 23,* 136-155.

Lazarus, R.S., & Folkman, S. (1984). *Stress, appraisal and coping.* New York: Springer.

Lazarus, R.S., & Folkman, S. (1985). If it changes, it must be a process: Study of emotion and coping during three stages of a college examination. *Journal of Personality and Social Psychology, 48,* 150-170.

Mahoney, M.J. (1979). Cognitive skills and athletic performance. In P.C. Kendall & S.D. Hollon (Eds.), *Cognitive-behavioral intervention: Theory, research, and procedures* (pp. 423-443). New York: Academic Press.

Maslach, C., & Jackson, S.E. (1986). *Maslach Burnout Inventory manual* (6th ed.). Palo Alto, CA: Consulting Psychologists Press.

Meichenbaum, D. (1977). *Cognitive-behavior modification.* New York: Plenum.

Raedeke, T.D. (1997). Is athlete burnout more than just stress? A sport commitment perspective. *Journal of Sport and Exercise Psychology, 19,* 396-417.

Raedeke, T.D., & Smith, A.L. (2004). Coping resources and athlete burnout: An examination of stress mediated and moderation hypotheses. *Journal of Sport and Exercise Psychology, 26,* 525-541. Sapolsky, R.M. (2004). *Why zebras don't get ulcers* (3rd ed.). New York: Holt Paperbacks.

Selye, H. (1936, July 4). A syndrome produced by diverse nocuous agents. *Nature, 138,* 32.

Selye, H. (1946). The general adaptation syndrome and the diseases of adaptation. *Journal of Allergy, 17*(4), 231-247.

Smith, R.E. (1980). A cognitive-affective approach to stress management training for athletes. In A. Nadeau (Ed.), *Psychology of motor behavior and sport* (pp. 54-72). Champaign, IL: Human Kinetics.

Smith, R.E. (1986). Toward a cognitive-affective model of athletic burnout. *Journal of Sport and Exercise Psychology, 8,* 36-50.

Suinn, R.S. (1976, July). Body thinking: Psychology for Olympic champs. *Psychology Today, 10,* 38-43.

Suinn, R.S. (1983). Imagery and sports. In A.A. Sheikh (Ed.), *Imagery: Current theory, research, and application* (pp. 507-534). New York: Wiley.

Suinn, R.S. (1993). Imagery: In R.N. Singer, M. Murphey, & L.K. Tennant (Eds.), *Handbook of research on sport psychology* (pp. 492-510). New York: Macmillan.

Udry, E. (1997). Coping and social support among injured athletes following surgery. *Journal of Sport and Exercise Psychology, 19,* 71-90.

Vealey, R.S., Udry, E.M., Zimmerman, V., & Soliday, J. (1992). Intrapersonal and situational predictors of coaching burnout. *Journal of Sport and Exercise Psychology, 14,* 40-58.

Wiese-Bjornstal, D.M. (2010). Psychology and socioculture affect injury risk, response, and recovery in high-intensity athletes: A consensus statement. *Scandinavian Journal of Medicine and Science in Sports, 20*(Suppl. 2), 103-111. doi:10.111/j.1600-0838.2010.01195.x

Wiese-Bjornstal, D.M., Smith, A.M., Shaffer, S.M., & Morrey, M.A. (1998). An integrated model of response to sport injury: Psychological and sociological dynamics. *Journal of Applied Sport Psychology, 10,* 46-69.

Williams, J.M., & Andersen, M.B. (1998). Psychosocial antecedents of sport injury: Review and critique of the stress and injury model. *Journal of Applied Sport Psychology, 10,* 5-25.

Chapter 14

Allen, M.S., & Jones, M.V. (2014a). The "home advantage" in athletic competitions. *Current Directions in Psychological Science, 23,* 48-53. doi:10.1177/0963721413513267

Allen, M.S., & Jones, M.V. (2014b). The home advantage over the first 20 seasons of the English Premier League: Effects of shirt colour, team ability and time trends. *International Journal of Sport and Exercise Psychology, 12*(1), 10-18. doi:10.1080/16121 97X.2012.756230

Allport, F.H. (1924). *Social psychology.* Boston: Houghton Mifflin.

Ashford, D., Bennett, S.J., & Davids, K. (2006). Observational modeling effects for movement dynamics and movement outcome measures across differing task constraints: A meta-analysis. *Journal of Motor Behavior, 38,* 185-205.

Ashford, D., Davids, K., & Bennett, S.J. (2007). Developmental effects influencing observational modelling: A meta-analysis. *Journal of Sports Sciences, 25,* 547-558. doi:10.1080/02640410600947025

Atkins, M.R., Johnson, D.M., Force, E.C., & Petrie, T.A. (2013). "Do I still want to play?" Parents' and peers' influences on girls' continuation in sport. *Journal of Sport Behavior, 36,* 329-345.

Bandura, A. (1977). *Social learning theory.* Englewood Cliffs, NJ: Prentice Hall.

Bandura, A. (1986). *Social foundations of thought and action: A social cognitive theory.* Englewood Cliffs, NJ: Prentice Hall.

Baudry, L., Leroy, D., & Chollet, D. (2007) The effect of combined self- and expert-modelling on the performance of the double leg circle on the pommel horse, Journal of Sport Sciences, 24, 1055-10633.doi.org/10.1080/02640410500432243

Baumeister, R.F. (1984). Choking under pressure: Self-consciousness and paradoxical effects of incentives on skillful performance. *Journal of Personality and Social Psychology, 47,* 610-620.

Baumeister, R.F., & Steinhilber, A. (1984). Paradoxical effects of supportive audiences on performance under pressure: The home field disadvantage in sports championships. *Journal of Personality and Social Psychology, 47,* 85-93.

Bean, C.N., Fortier, M., Post, C., & Chima, K. (2014). Understanding how organized youth sport may be harming individual players within the family unity: A literature review. *International Journal of Environmental Research and Public Health, 11,* 10226-10268. doi:10.3390/ijerph111010226

Blazo, J.A., Czech, D.R., Carson, S., & Dees, W. (2014). A qualitative investigation of the sibling sport achievement experience. *Sport Psychologist, 28,* 36-47. doi:10.1123/tsp.2012-0089

Bone, J.B., & Fry, M.D. (2006). The influence of injured athletes' perceptions of social support from ATCs on their beliefs about rehabilitation. *Journal of Sport Rehabilitation, 15,* 156-167.

Brawley, L.R., Flora, P.K., & Locke, S.R., & Gierc, M.S. (2016). Social influence in promoting change among older adults: Group-mediated cognitive behavioral interventions. *Kinesiology Review, 5,* 39-49.

Brown, T.C., & Fry, M.D. (2014a). Motivational climate, staff members' behaviors, and members' psychological well-being at a national fitness franchise. *Research Quarterly for Exercise and Research, 85,* 208-217. doi:1 0.1080/02701367.2014.893385

Brown, T.C., & Fry, M.D. (2014b). College exercise class climates, physical self-concept, and psychological well-being. *Journal of Clinical Sport Psychology, 8,* 299-313. doi:10.1123/jcsp.2014-0031

Camiré, M. (2014). Youth development in North American high school sport: Review and recommendations. *Quest, 66,* 495-511. doi:10.1080/00336297.201 4.952448

Carron, A.V., Hausenblas, H.A., & Mack, D. (1996). Social influence: A meta-analysis. *Journal of Sport and Exercise Psychology, 18,* 1-16.

Carron, A.V., Loughhead, T.M., & Bray, S.R. (2005). The home advantage in sport competitions: Courneya and Carron's (1992) conceptual framework a decade later. *Journal of Sports Sciences, 23,* 395-407.

Chogahara, M. (1999). A multidimensional scale for assessing positive and negative social influences on physical activity in older adults. *Journals of Gerontology Series B, Psychological Sciences and Social Sciences, 54*(6), S356-S367. doi:10.1093/geronb/54B.6.S356

Clark, S.E., & Ste-Marie, D.M. (2007). The impact of self-as-a-model interventions on children's self-regulation of learning and swimming performance. *Journal of Sports Sciences, 25,* 577-586.

Clement, D., & Shannon, V.R. (2011). Injured athletes' perceptions about social support. *Journal of Sport Rehabilitation, 20,* 457-470.

Cohen, S. (2004). Social relationships and health. *American Psychologist, 59,* 673-684.

Coker, C.A. (2015). *Motor learning and control for practitioners.* Scottsdale, AZ: Holcomb Hathaway.

Cottrell, N.B. (1968). Performance in the presence of other human beings: Mere presence, audience, and affiliation effects. In E.C. Simmer, R.A. Hope, & G.A. Milton (Eds.), *Social facilitation and imitative behavior* (pp. 91-110). Boston: Allyn & Bacon.

Courneya, K.S., & Carron, A.V. (1992). The home advantage in sport competitions: A literature review. *Journal of Sport and Exercise Psychology, 14,* 13-27.

Cox, A.E., & Ullrich-French, S. (2010). The motivational relevance of peer and teacher relationship profiles in physical education. *Psychology of Sport and Exercise, 11,* 337-344. doi:10.1016/j.psychsport.2010.04001

Cox, A.E., Ullrich-French, S., Madonia, J., & Witty, K. (2009). Social physique anxiety in physical education: Social contextual factors and links to motivation and behavior. *Research Quarterly for Sport and Exercise, 12,* 555-562. doi:10.1016/j.psychsport.2011.05.001

Cumming, J., Clark, S.E., Ste-Marie, D.M., McCullagh, P., & Hall, C. (2005). The functions of observational learning questionnaire (FOLQ). *Psychology of Sport and Exercise, 6,* 517-537. doi:10.1016/j.psychsport.2004.03.006

Cutrona, C.E., & Russell, D.W. (1987). The provisions of social relationships and adaptation to stress. In W.H. Jones & D. Perlman (Eds.), *Advances in personal relationships* (Vol. 1, pp. 37-67). Greenwich, CT: JAI Press.

Davis, L., & Jowett, S. (2014). Coach–athlete attachment and the quality of the coach–athlete relationship: Implications for athlete's well-being. *Journal of Sports Sciences, 32,* 1454-1464. doi:10.1080/02640414.2014. 898183

Davis, L., Jowett, S., & Lafrenière, M.K. (2013). An attachment theory perspective in the examination of relational processes associated with coach-athlete dyads. *Journal of Sport and Exercise Psychology, 35,* 156-167.

Davis, N.W., & Meyer, B.B. (2008). When sibling becomes competitor: A qualitative investigation of same-sex sibling competition in elite sport. *Journal of Applied Sport Psychology, 20,* 220-235. doi:10.1080/10413200701864817

Davison, K.K., Cutting, T.M., & Birch, L.L. (2003). Parents' activity-related parenting practices predict girls' physical activity. *Medicine and Science in Sports and Exercise, 35,* 1589-1595.

Dorsch, T.E., Smith, A.L., & McDonough, M.H. (2009). Parents' perceptions of child-to parent socialization in organized youth sport. *Journal of Sport and Exercise Psychology, 31,* 444-468.

Duncan, T.E., & McAuley, E. (1993). Social support and efficacy cognitions in exercise adherence: A latent growth curve analysis. *Journal of Behavioral Medicine, 16*(2), 199-218.

Eccles, J.S., & Harrold, R.D. (1991). Gender differences in sport involvement: Applying the Eccles' expectancy-value model. *Journal of Applied Sport Psychology, 3,* 7-35.

Evans, B., Alder, A., MacDonald, D., & Cote, J. (2016). Bullying, victimization and perpetration among adolescent sport teammates. *Pediatric Exercise Science, 28,* 296-303. doi:10.1123/pes.2015-0088

Feltz, D.L., Kerr, N.L., & Irwin, B.C. (2011). Buddy up: The Köhler effect applied to health games. *Journal of Sport and Exercise Psychology, 33,* 506-526.

Feltz, D.L., Landers, D.L., & Raeder, U. (1979). Enhancing self-efficacy in high avoidance motor tasks: A comparison of modeling techniques. *Journal of Sport Psychology, 1,* 112-122.

Ferreira, I., van der Horst, K., Wendel-Vos, W., Kremers, S., van Lenthe, F.J., & Brug, J. (2007). Environmental correlates of physical activity in youth – a review and update. *Obesity Reviews, 8,* 129-154. doi:10.1111/j.1467-789X.2006.00264.x

Fortier, M.S., Hogg, W., O'Sullivan, T.L., et al. (2011). Impact of integrating a physical activity counsellor into the primary health care team: Physical activity and health outcomes of the Physical Activity Counselling randomized controlled trial. *Applied Physiology, Nutrition, and Metabolism, 36*(4), 503-514. doi:10.1139/H11-040

Fredricks, J.A., & Eccles, J.S. (2004). Parental influences on youth involvement in sports. In M.R. Weiss (Ed.), *Developmental sport and exercise psychology: A lifespan perspective* (pp. 145-164). Morgantown, WV: Fitness Information Technology.

Fredricks, J.A., & Eccles, J.S. (2005). Family socialization, gender, and sport motivation and involvement. *Journal of Sport and Exercise Psychology, 27,* 3-31.

Freeman, P., Coffee, P., & Rees, T. (2011). The PASS-Q: The Perceived Available Support in Sport Questionnaire. *Journal of Sport and Exercise Psychology, 33*(1), 54-74.

Fry, M.D., & Gano-Overway, L.A. (2010). Exploring the contribution of the caring climate to the youth sport experience. *Journal of Applied Sport Psychology, 22,* 294-304. doi:10.1080/10413201003776352

Gano-Overway, L.A. (2013). Exploring the connections between caring and social behaviors in physical education. *Research Quarterly for Exercise and Sport, 84,* 104-114. doi:10.1080/02701367.2013.762322

García-Calvo, T., Leo, F.M., Gonzalez-Ponce, I., Sánchez-Miguel, P.A., Mouratidis, A., & Ntoumanis, N. (2014). Perceived coach-created and peer-created motivational climates and their associations with team cohesion and athlete satisfaction: Evidence from a longitudinal study. *Journal of Sports Sciences, 32,* 1738-1750. doi:10.1080/02640414.2014.918641

Gellert, P., Ziegelmann, J.P., Warner, L.M., & Schwarzer, R. (2011). Physical activity intervention in older adults: Does a participating partner make a difference? *European Journal of Ageing, 8,* 211-219. doi:10.1007/s10433-011-0193-5

Gill, D.L., Gross, J.B., & Huddleston, S. (1983). Participation motivation in youth sports. *International Journal of Sport Psychology, 14,* 1-14.

Gill, D.L., & Martens, R. (1975). The informational and motivational influence of social reinforcement on motor performance. *Journal of Motor Behavior, 7,* 171-182.

Gould, D., & Weiss, M.R. (1981). The effects of model similarity and model talk on self-efficacy and muscular endurance. *Journal of Sport Psychology, 3,* 17-29.

Granquist, M.D., & Stadden, S.A. (2015). Social support and the athletic trainer. In M.D. Granquist, J.J. Hamson-Utley, L.J. Kenow, & J. Stiller-Otrowski (Eds.), *Psychosocial strategies for athletic training* (pp. 209-228). Philadelphia: Davis.

Grindrod, D., Paton, C.D., Knez, W.L., & O'Brien, B.J. (2006). Six minute walk distance is greater when performed in a group than alone. *British Journal of Sports Medicine, 40,* 876-877. doi:10.1136/bjsm.2006.027904

Hardy, C.J., & Crace, R.K. (1993). The dimensions of social support when dealing with sport injuries. In D. Pargman (Ed.), *Psychological bases of sport injuries* (pp. 121-144). Morgantown, WV: Fitness Information Technology.

Harwood, C., & Knight, C.J. (2015) Parenting in youth sport: A position paper on parenting expertise. *Psychology of Sport and Exercise, 16,* 24-35. doi: 10.1016/j.psychsport.2014.03.001.

Hong, T.B., Franks, M.M., Gonzalez, R., Keteyian, S.J., Franklin, B.A., & Artinian, N.T. (2005). A dyadic investigation of exercise support between cardiac patients and their spouses. *Health Psychology, 24*(4), 430-434. doi:10.1037/0278-6133.24.4.430

Horn, T.S. (2004). Developmental perspectives on self-perceptions in children and adolescents. In M.R. Weiss (Ed.), *Developmental sport and exercise psychology: A lifespan perspective* (pp. 101-143). Morgantown, WV: Fitness Information Technology.

Horn, T.S. (2014). Developmental perspectives on self-perceptions in children. In M.R. Weiss (Ed.), *Developmental sport and exercise psychology: A lifespan perceptive* (pp. 101-144). Morgantown, WV: Fitness Information Technology.

Horn, T.S., & Horn, J.L. (2007). Family influences on children's sport and physical activity participation, behavior, and psychosocial responses. In G. Tenenbaum & R.C. Eklund (Eds.), *Handbook of sport psychology* (3rd ed., pp. 685-711). New York: Wiley.

Horn, R.R., & Williams, A.M. (2004). Observational learning: Is it time we took another look? In A.M. Williams & N.J. Hodges (Eds.), *Skill acquisition in sport: Research, theory, and practice* (pp. 175-206). New York: Routledge.

Humbert, M.L., Chad, K.E., Spink, K.S., et al. (2006). Factors that influence physical activity participation among high- and low-SES youth. *Qualitative Health Research, 16,* 467-483.

Irwin, B.C., Scorniaenchi, J., Kerr, N.L., Eisenmann, J.C., & Feltz, D.L. (2012). Aerobic exercise is promoted when individual performance affects the group: A test of the Kohler motivation gain effect. *Annals of Behavioral Medicine, 44,* 151-159. doi:10.1007/s12160-012-9367-4

Jamieson, J. (2010). The home field advantage in athletics: A meta-analysis. *Journal of Applied Social Psychology, 40,* 1819-1848. http://dx.doi.org/10.1111/j.1559-1816.2010.00641.x

Jõesaar, H., Hein, V., & Hagger, M.S. (2011). Peer influence on young athletes' need satisfaction, intrinsic motivation and persistence in sport: A 12-month prospective study. *Psychology of Sport and Exercise, 12,* 500-508. doi:10.1016/j.psychsport.2011.04.005

Jones, M.B. (2013). The home advantage in individual sports: An augmented review. *Psychology of Sport and Exercise, 14,* 397-404.

Jowett, S. (2007). Interdependence analysis and the 3+1Cs in the coach-athlete relationship. In S. Jowett & D. Lavallee (Eds.), *Social Psychology in Sport* (pp. 15-27). Champaign, IL: Human Kinetics.

Jowett, S., & Shanmugam, V. (2015). Relational coaching in sport: Its psychological underpinnings and practical effectiveness. In R. Schinke, K.R. McGannon, & B. Smith (Eds.), *Routledge international handbook of sport psychology* (pp. 471-484). New York: Routledge.

Katz, D.L., Shuval, K., Comerford, B.P., Faridi, Z., & Njike, V.Y. (2008). Impact of an educational intervention on internal medicine residents' physical activity counseling: The pressure system model. *Journal of Evaluation in Clinical Practice, 14,* 294-299.

Kelley, B.C., & Gill, D.L. (1993). An examination of personal/situational variables, stress appraisal, and burnout in collegiate teacher-coaches. *Research Quarterly for Exercise and Sport, 64,* 94-102.

Kimiecik, J., & Horn, T.S. (2012). Examining the relationship between family context and children's physical activity beliefs: The role of parenting style. *Psychology of Sport and Exercise, 13,* 10 18. doi:10.1016/j.psychsport.2011.08.004

Knight, C.J., & Holt, N.L. (2014). Parenting in youth tennis: Understanding and enhancing children's experiences. *Psychology of Sport and Exercise, 15,* 155-164. doi:10.1016/j.psychsport.2013.10.010

Knight, C.J., Neely, K.C., & Holt, N.L. (2011). Parental behaviors in team sports: How do female athletes want parents to behave? *Journal of Applied Sport Psychology, 23,* 76-92. doi.org/10.1080/10413200.2010.525589

Kouvonen, A., De Vogli, R., Stafford, M., et al. (2012). Social support and the likelihood of maintaining and improving levels of physical activity: The Whitehall II Study. *European Journal of Public Health, 22*(4), 514-518. doi.org/10.1093/eurpub/ckr091

Kremer-Sadlik, T., & Kim, J.L. (2007). Lessons from sports: Children's socialization to values through family interaction during sport activities. *Discourse and Society, 18,* 35-52.

Lauer, L., Gould, D., Roman, N., & Pierce, M. (2010). Parental behaviors that affect junior tennis player development. *Psychology of Sport and Exercise, 11,* 487-496. doi:10.1016/j.psychsport.2010.06.008

Law, B., & Hall, C. (2009). The relationships among skill level, age, and golfers' observational learning use. *Sport Psychologist, 23,* 42-58.

Le Bars, H., Gernigon, C., & Ninot, G. (2009). Personal and contextual determinants of elite young athletes' persistence or dropping out over time. *Scandinavian Journal of Medicine and Science in Sports, 19,* 274-285. doi:10.1111/j.1600-0838.2008.00786.x

Lhuisset, L., & Margnes, E. (2015). The influence of live- vs. video-model presentation on the early acquisition of a new complex coordination, *Physical Education and Sport Pedagogy, 20,* 490-502. doi: 10.1080/17408989.2014.923989

Lox, C.L., Martin Ginis, K.A., & Petruzzello, S.J. (2014). *The psychology of exercise* (3rd ed.). Scottsdale, AZ: Holcomb Hathaway.

Maddison, R., Prapavessis, H., & Clatworthy, M. (2006). Modeling and rehabilitation following anterior cruciate ligament reconstruction. *Annals of Behavioral Medicine, 31,* 89-98. doi:10.1207/s15324796abm3101_13

Magill, R.A. (2011). *Motor learning and control: Concepts and applications* (3rd ed.). New York: McGraw-Hill.

Martens, R. (1969). Effect of an audience on learning and performance of a complex motor skill. *Journal of Personality and Social Psychology, 12,* 252-260.

Martens, R. (1972). Social reinforcement effects on motor performance as a function of socio-economic status. *Perceptual and Motor Skills, 35,* 215-218.

Martens, R., & Landers, D.M. (1972). Evaluation potential as a determinant of coaction effects. *Journal of Experimental Social Psychology, 8,* 347-359.

Martin Ginis, K.A., & Mack, D. (2012). Understanding exercise behaviors: A self-presentational perspective. In G.C. Roberts & D.C. Treasure (Eds.), *Advances in motivation in sport and exercise* (3rd ed., pp. 327-355). Champaign, IL: Human Kinetics.

McCullagh, P. (1987). Model similarity effects on motor performance. *Journal of Sport Psychology, 9,* 249-260.

McCullagh, P., Ste-Marie, D., & Law, B. (2014). Modeling: Is what you see, what you get? In J.L. Van Raalte & B.W. Brewer (Eds.), *Exploring sport and exercise psychology* (3rd ed., pp. 139-162). Washington, DC: American Psychological Association. doi:10.1037/14251-007

McCullagh, P., & Weiss, M.R. (2001). Modeling: Considerations for motor skill and psychological responses. In R.N. Singer, H.A. Hausenblas, & C.M. Janelle (Eds.), *Handbook of sport psychology* (pp. 205-238). New York: Wiley.

McDonough, M.H., & Crocker, P.R.E. (2005). Sport participation motivation in young adolescent girls: The role of friendship quality and self-concept. *Research Quarterly for Exercise and Sport, 76,* 456-467.

McDonough, M.H., Sabiston, C.M., & Crocker, P.R.E. (2008). An interpretative phenomenological examination of psychosocial changes among breast cancer survivors in their first season of dragon boating. *Journal of Applied Sport Psychology, 20,* 425-440.

McDonough, M.H., Sabiston, C.M., & Ulrich-French, S. (2011). The development of social relationships, social support, and posttraumatic growth in a dragon boating team for breast cancer survivors. *Journal of Sport and Exercise Psychology, 33,* 627-648.

Mendonça, G., Cheng, L.A., Mélo, E.N., & de Farias, J.C., Jr. (2014). Physical activity and social support in adolescents: A systematic review. *Health Education Research 29*(5), 822-839. doi:10.1093/her/cyu017

Molloy, G.J., Dixon, D., Hamer, M., & Sniehotta, F.F. (2010). Social support and regular physical activity: Does planning mediate this link? *British Journal of Health Psychology, 15,* 859-870.

Newton, M., Fry, M., Watson, D., et al. (2007). Psychometric properties of the caring climate scale in a physical activity setting. *Revista de Psicologia del Deporte, 16,* 67-84.

Newton, M., Watson, D.L., Gano-Overway, L., Fry, M., Kim, M., & Magyar, M. (2007). The role of a caring-based intervention in a physical activity setting. *Urban Review: Issues and Ideas in Public Education, 39,* 281-299.

O'Connor, J.A., & Graber, K.C. (2014). Sixth-grade physical education: An acculturation of bullying and fear. *Research Quarterly for Exercise and Sport, 85,* 398-408. doi:10.1080/02701367.2014.930403

Paquette, G., Egan, M., & Martini, R. (2013). Peer mastery in addition to direct instruction post-stroke: A single-subject design. *Physical and Occupational Therapy in Geriatrics, 31,* 354-367.

Partridge, J.A., Brustad, R.J., & Stellino, M.B. (2008). Social influence in sport. In T.S. Horn (Ed.), *Advances in sport psychology* (3rd ed., pp. 270-291). Champaign, IL: Human Kinetics.

Partridge, J.A., & Knapp, B.A. (2016). Mean girls: Adolescent female athletes and peer conflict in sport. *Journal of Applied Sport Psychology, 28,* 113-127. doi:10.1080/10413200.2015.1076088

Ram, N., Riggs, S.M., Skaling, S., Landers, D.M., & McCullagh, P. (2007). A comparison of modeling and imagery in the acquisition and retention of motor skills. *Journal of Sports Sciences, 25,* 587-597.

Rees, T., Mitchell, I., Evans, L., & Hardy, L. (2010). Stressors, social support and psychological responses to sport injury in high- and low-performance standard participants. *Psychology of Sport and Exercise, 11,* 505-512.

Rhea, M.R., Landers, D.M., Alvar, B.A., & Arent, S.M. (2003). The effects of competition and the presence of an audience on weight lifting performance. *Journal of Strength and Conditioning Research, 17,* 303-306.

Richman, J.M., Rosenfeld, L.B., & Hardy, C.J. (1993). The social support survey: An initial evaluation of a clinical measure and practice model of the social support process. *Research on Social Work Practice, 3,* 288-311.

Riley, A., & Smith, A.L. (2011). Perceived coach-athlete and peer relationships of young athletes and self-determined motivation for sport. *International Journal of Sport Psychology, 42,* 115-133.

Romance, T.J., Weiss, M.R., & Bockoven, J. (1986). A program to promote moral development through elementary school physical education. *Journal of Teaching in Physical Education, 5,* 126-136.

Rosenfeld, L.B., & Richman, J.R. (1997). Developing effective social support: Team building and the social support process. *Journal of Applied Social Psychology, 9,* 133-153.

Rosenfeld, L.B., Richman, J.M., & Hardy, C.J. (1989). An examination of social support networks among athletes: Description and relationship to stress. *Sport Psychologist, 3,* 23-33.

Sabiston, C.M., McDonough, M.H., & Crocker, P.R.E. (2007). Psychosocial experiences of breast cancer survivors involved in a dragon boat program: Exploring links to positive psychological growth. *Journal of Sport and Exercise Psychology, 29,* 419-438.

Saelens, B.E., & Kerr, J. (2008). The family. In A.L. Smith & S.J.H. Biddle (Eds.), *Youth physical activity and sedentary behavior: Challenges and solutions* (pp. 267-294). Champaign, IL: Human Kinetics.

Sakadjian, A., Panchuk, D., & Pearce, A.J. (2014). Kinematic and kinetic improvements associated with action observation facilitated learning of the power clean in Australian footballers. *Journal of Strength Conditioning Research, 28,* 1613-1625.

Salguero, A., Gonzalez-Boto, R., Tuero, C., & Marquez, S. (2003). Identification of dropout reasons in young competitive swimmers. *Journal of Sports Medicine and Physical Fitness, 43,* 530-534.

Sarason, I.G., Levine, H., Basham, R., & Sarason, B. (1983). Concomitants of social support: The social support questionnaire. *Journal of Personality and Social Psychology, 44,* 127-139.

Sarason, I.G., Sarason, B.R., & Pierce, G.R. (1990). Social support, personality and performance. *Journal of Applied Sport Psychology, 2,* 117-127.

Schwartz, B., & Barsky, S.F. (1977). The home advantage. *Social Forces, 55,* 641-661.

Schwebel, F.J., Smith R.E., & Smoll, F.L. (2016). Measurement of perceived parental success standards in sport and relations with athletes' self-esteem, performance anxiety, and achievement goal orientation: Comparing parental and coach influences. *Child Development Research, 2016,* 1-13. doi:10.1155/2016/7056075

Shannon, C.S. (2013). Bullying in recreation and sport settings: Exploring risk factors, prevention efforts, and intervention strategies. *Journal of Parks and Recreation Administration, 31,* 15-33.

Sheridan, D., Coffee, D., & Lavallee, D. (2014). A

systematic review of social support in youth sport. *International Review of Sport and Exercise Psychology, 7,* 198-228. doi:10.1080/1750984X.2014.931999

Shumaker, S.A., & Brownell, A. (1984). Toward a theory of social support: Closing conceptual gaps. *Journal of Social Issues, 40,* 11-36.

Smith, A.L. (1999). Perceptions of peer relationships and physical activity participation in early adolescents. *Journal of Sport and Exercise Psychology, 21,* 329-350.

Smith, A.L. (2003). Peer relationships in physical activity contexts: A road less traveled in youth sport and exercise psychology research. *Psychology of Sport and Exercise, 4,* 25-39.

Smith, A.L. (2007). Youth peer relationships in sport. In S. Jowett & D. Lavallee (Eds.), *Social psychology in sport* (pp. 41-54). Champaign, IL: Human Kinetics.

Smith, A.L., & McDonough, M.H. (2008). Peers. In A.L. Smith & S.J.H. Biddle (Eds.), *Youth physical activity and sedentary behavior: Challenges and solutions* (pp. 295-320). Champaign, IL: Human Kinetics.

Smith, A.L., Gustafsson, H., & Hassmén, P. (2010). Peer motivational climate and burnout perceptions of adolescent athletes. *Psychology of Sport and Exercise, 11,* 453-460. doi:10.1016/j.psychsport.2010.05.007

Smith, R.E., & Smoll, F.L. (1997). Coaching the coaches: Youth sports as a scientific and applied behavioral setting. *Current Directions in Psychological Science, 6,* 16-21.

Smith, R. E., & Smoll, F. L. (2007). Social-cognitive approach to coaching behaviors. In S. Jowett & D. Lavallee (Eds.), *Social Psychology in Sport* (pp. 75-90). Champaign, IL: Human Kinetics.

Smith, A.L., Ullrich-French, S., Walker, E. II, & Hurley, K.S. (2006). Peer relationship profiles and motivation in youth sport. *Journal of Sport and Exercise Psychology, 28,* 362-382.

Ste-Marie, D.M., Law, B., Rymal, A.M., Jenny, O., Hall, C., & McCullagh, P. (2012). Observation interventions for motor skill learning and performance: An applied model for the use of observation. *International Review of Sport and Exercise Psychology, 5,* 145-176. doi:10.1080/1750984X.2012.665076

Storch, E.A., & Masia-Warner, C. (2004). The relationship of peer victimization to social anxiety and loneliness in adolescent females. *Journal of Adolescence, 27,* 351-362.

Taylor, R.D., & Collins, D. (2015). Reviewing the family unit as a stakeholder in talent development: Is it undervalued? *Quest, 67,* 330-343. doi:10.1080/00336 297.2015.1050747

Triplett, N. (1898). The dynamogenic factors in pacemaking and competition. *American Journal of Psychology, 9,* 507-553.

Trussell, D.E. (2014). Contradictory aspects of organized youth sport: Challenging and fostering sibling relationships and participation experiences. *Youth and Society, 46,* 801-818. doi:10.1177/0044118X124 53058

Ullrich-French, S., & Smith, A.L. (2006). Perceptions of relationships with parents and peers in youth sport: Independent and combined prediction of motivational outcomes. *Psychology of Sport and Exercise, 7,* 193-214.

Ullrich-French, S., & Smith, A.L. (2009). Social and motivational predictors of continued youth sport participation. *Psychology of Sport and Exercise, 10,* 87-95. doi:10.1016/j.psychsport.2008.06.007

Varca, P.E. (1980). An analysis of home and away game performance of male college basketball teams. *Journal of Sport Psychology, 2,* 245-257.

Vazou, S., Ntoumanis, N., & Duda, J.L. (2006). Predicting young athletes' motivational indices as a function of their perceptions of the coach- and peer-created climate. *Psychology of Sport and Exercise, 7,* 215-233. doi:10.1016/j.psychsport.2005.08.007

Vazou, S., Ntoumanis, N., & Duda, J.L. (2007). Perceptions of peer motivational climate in youth sport: Measurement development and implications for practice. In S. Jowett & D. Lavallee (Eds.), *Social Psychology of Sport* (pp. 145 – 156). Champaign, IL: Human Kinetics.

Weiss, M.R., McCullagh, P., Smith, A.L., & Berlant, A.R. (1998). Observational learning and the fearful child: Influence of peer models on swimming skill performance and psychological responses. *Research Quarterly for Exercise and Sport, 69,* 380-394. doi:10.1 080/02701367.1998.10607712

Weiss, M.R., & Smith, A.L. (1999). Quality of sport friendship: Measurement development and validation. *Journal of Sport and Exercise Psychology, 21,* 145-166.

Weiss, M.R., & Smith, A.L. (2002). Friendship quality in youth sport: Relationship to age, gender, and motivation. *Journal of Sport and Exercise Psychology, 24,* 420-437.

Weiss, M.R., Smith, A.L., & Theeboom, M. (1996). "That's what friends are for": Children's and teenagers' perceptions of peer relationships in the sport domain. *Journal of Sport and Exercise Psychology, 18,* 347-379.

Weiss, M.R., & Stuntz, C.P. (2004). A little friendly competition: Peer relationships and psychosocial development in youth sport and physical activity contexts. In M.R. Weiss (Ed.), *Developmental sport and exercise psychology: A lifespan perspective* (pp. 165-196). Morgantown, WV: Fitness Information Technology.

Wiese-Bjornstal, D.M., Smith, A.M., Shaffer, S.M., & Morrey, M.A. (1998). An integrated model of response to sport injury: Psychological and sociological dynamics. *Journal of Applied Sport Psychology, 10,* 46-69.

Williams, J.M., & Anderson, M.B. (1998). Psychosocial antecedents of sport injury: Review and critique of the stress and injury model. *Journal of Applied Sport Psychology, 10,* 5-25.

Wills, T.A., & Shinar, O. (2000). Measuring perceived and received social support. In S. Cohen, L.G. Underwood, & B.H. Gottlieb (Eds.), *Social support measurement and intervention: A guide for health and social scientists* (pp. 86-135). New York: Oxford University Press.

Yang, J., Peek-Asa, C., Lowe, J.B., Heiden, E., & Foster, D.T. (2010). Social support patterns of collegiate athletes before and after injury. *Journal of Athletic Training, 45*(4), 372-379.

Zajonc, R.B. (1965). Social facilitation. *Science, 149,* 269-274.

Chapter 15

Ardrey, R. (1966). *The territorial imperative.* New York: Atheneum.Bandura, A. (1965). Influence of models' reinforcement contingencies on the acquisition of imitative responses. *Journal of Personality and Social Psychology, 1,* 589-595.

Bandura, A. (1973). *Aggression: A social learning analysis.* Englewood Cliffs, NJ: Prentice Hall.

Bandura, A. (1986). *Social foundations of thought and action: A social cognitive theory.* Englewood Cliffs, NJ: Prentice Hall.

Bandura, A. (1991). A social cognitive theory of moral thought and action. In W.M. Kurtines & J.L. Gewirtz (Eds.), *Handbook of moral behavior and development: Theory, research and applications* (Vol. 1, pp. 45-103). Hillsdale, NJ: Erlbaum.

Bandura, A., Ross, D., & Ross, S.A. (1963a). Imitation of film mediated aggressive models. *Journal of Abnormal and Social Psychology, 66,* 3-11.

Bandura, A., Ross, D., & Ross, S.A. (1963b). Vicarious reinforcement and imitative learning. *Journal of Abnormal and Social Psychology, 67,* 601-607.

Baron, R.A., & Richardson, D.R. (1994). *Human aggression.* New York: Plenum Press.

Benson, P.L. (2006). *All kids are our kids: What communities must do to raise caring and responsible children and adolescents* (2nd ed.) San Francisco: Jossey-Bass.

Berkowitz, L. (1962). *Aggression: A social psychological analysis.* New York: McGraw-Hill.

Berkowitz, L. (1989). Frustration-aggression hypothesis: Examination and reformulation. *Psychological Bulletin, 106,* 59-73. doi:10.1037/0033-2909.106.1.59

Berkowitz, L. (1993). *Aggression: Its causes, consequences, and control.* Philadelphia: Temple University Press.

Berkowitz, L. (2008). On the consideration of automatic as well as controlled psychological processes in aggression. *Aggressive Behavior, 34,* 117-129. doi:10.1002/ab.20244

Blom, L.C., Judge, L., Whitley, M.A., Gerstein, L., Huffman, A., & Hillyer, S. (2015). Sport for development and peace: Experiences conducting U.S. and international programs. *Journal of Sport Psychology in Action, 6*(1), 1-16. doi:10.1080/21520704.2015.1006741

Boardley, I.D. (2014). Moral disengagement. In R.C. Eklund & G. Tenenbaum (Eds.), *Encyclopedia of sport and exercise psychology* (pp. 459-462). Thousand Oaks, CA: Sage.

Boardley, I.D., & Kavussanu, M. (2007). Development and validation of the moral disengagement in sport scale. *Journal of Sport and Exercise Psychology, 29,* 608-629. doi:10.1080/02640410902887283

Boardley, I.D., & Kavussanu, M. (2011). Moral disengagement in sport. *International Review of Sport and Exercise Psychology, 4,* 93-108. doi:10.1080/1750984X.2011.570361

Bredemeier, B.J., & Shields, D.L. (1986). Game reasoning and interactional morality. *Journal of Genetic Psychology, 147,* 257-275.

Bredemeier, B.J.L., & Shields, D.L.L. (1995). *Character development and physical activity.* Champaign, IL: Human Kinetics.

Bredemeier, B.L., & Shields, D.L. (2014). Moral reasoning. In R.C. Eklund & G. Tenenbaum (Eds.), *Encyclopedia of sport and exercise psychology* (pp. 465-469). Thousand Oaks, CA: Sage.

Bushman, B.J. (2002). Does venting anger feed or extinguish the flame? Catharsis, rumination, distraction, anger, and aggressive responding. *Personality and Social Psychology Bulletin, 28*(6), 724-731. doi:10.1177/0146167202289002

Bushman, B.J., & Anderson, C.A. (2001). Is it time to pull the plug on hostile versus instrumental aggression dichotomy? *Psychological Review, 108,* 273-279.

Bushman, B.J., & Huesmann, L.R. (2010). Aggression. In S.T. Fiske, D.T. Gilbert, & G. Lindzey (Eds.), *Handbook of social psychology* (5th ed., pp. 833-863). Hoboken, NJ: Wiley.

Bushman, B.J., Newman, K., Calvert, S.L., et al. (2016). Youth violence: What we know and what we need to know. *American Psychologist, 71*(1), 17-39. doi.org/10.1037/a0039687

Chinkov, A.E., & Holt, N.L. (2016). Implicit transfer of life skills through participation in Brazilian jiu-jitsu. *Journal of Applied Sport Psychology, 28*(2), 139-153. doi:10.1080/10413200.2015.1086447

Corrion, K., Long, T., Smith, A.L., & d'Arripe-Longueville, F. (2009). "It's not my fault; it's not serious": Athlete accounts of moral disengagement in competitive sport. *Sport Psychologist, 23,* 388-404.

Cote, J., Baker, J., & Abernethy, B. (2007). Practice and play in the development of sport expertise. In G. Tenenbaum & R. Eklund (Eds.), *Handbook of sport psychology* (3rd ed., pp. 184-202). Hoboken, NJ: Wiley.

Cote, J., Hancock, D.J., & Abernethy, B. (2014). Nurturing talent in youth sport. In A.G. Papaionnou & D. Hackfort (Eds.), *Routledge companion to sport and exercise psychology: Global perspectives and fundamental concepts* (pp. 22-33). London: Routledge.

d'Arripe-Longueville, F., Corrion, K., Scoffier, S., Roussel, P., & Chalabaev, A. (2010). Sociocognitive self-regulatory mechanisms governing judgments of the acceptability and likelihood of sport cheating. *Journal of Sport and Exercise Psychology, 32*, 595-618.

Dollard, J., Dobb, J., Miller, N., Mower, O., & Sears, R. (1939). *Frustration and aggression.* New Haven, CT: Yale University Press.

Duda, J.L., Olson, L.K., & Templin, T.J. (1991). The relationship of task and ego orientation to sportsmanship attitudes and perceived legitimacy of injurious acts. *Research Quarterly for Exercise and Sport, 62*, 79-87.

Dzewaltowski, D.A., & Rosenkranz, R.R. (2014). Youth development: An approach for physical activity behavioral science. *Kinesiology Review, 3*, 92-100. doi.org/10.1123/kr.2014-0042

Eime, R.M., Young, J.A., Harvey, J.T., Charity, M.J., & Payne, W.R. (2013). A systematic review of the psychological and social benefits of participation in sport for children and adolescents: Informing development of a conceptual model of health through sport. *International Journal of Behavioral Nutrition and Physical Activity, 10*, 98. doi:10.1186/1479-5868-10-98

Forneris, T., Whitley, M.A., & Barker, B. (2013). The reality of implementing community-based sport and physical activity programs to enhance the development of underserved youth: Challenges and potential strategies. *Quest, 65*(3), 313-331. http://doi.org/10.1080/00336297.2013.773527

Fry, M.D., & Gano-Overway, L.A. (2010). Exploring the contribution of the caring climate to the youth sport experience. *Journal of Applied Sport Psychology, 22*, 294-304. doi:10.1080/10413201003776352

Gano-Overway, L.A. (2013). Exploring the connections between caring and social behaviors in physical education. *Research Quarterly for Exercise and Sport, 84*, 104-114. doi: 10.1080/02701367.2013.762322

Gano-Overway, L.A., Newton, M., Magyar, T.M., Fry, M.D., Kim, M., & Guivernau, M. (2009). Influence of caring youth sport contexts on efficacy-related beliefs and social behaviors. *Developmental Psychology, 45*, 329-340. doi:10.1037/a0014067

Gee, C.J., & Potwarka, L.R. (2014). Controlling anger and aggression. In A.G. Papaionnou & D. Hackfort (Eds.), *Routledge companion to sport and exercise psychology: Global perspectives and fundamental concepts* (pp. 650-667). London: Routledge.

Gibbons, S.L., & Ebbeck, V. (1997). The effect of different teaching strategies on moral development of physical education students. *Journal of Teaching Physical Education, 17*, 85-98.

Gibbons, S.L., Ebbeck, V., & Weiss, M.R. (1995). Fair play for kids: Effects on the moral development of children in physical education. *Research Quarterly for Exercise and Sport, 66*, 247-255.

Gould, D., & Carson, S. (2008). Life skills development through sport: Current status and future directions. *International Review of Sport and Exercise Psychology, 1*, 58-78.

Gould, D., & Carson, S. (2011). Young athletes' perceptions of the relationship between coaching behaviors and developmental experiences. *International Journal of Coaching Science, 5*(2), 3-29.

Gould, D., Cowburn, I., & Shields, A. (2014). "Sports for All"—summary of the evidence of psychological and social outcomes of participation. *Elevate Health*: Research digest of the President's Council on Fitness, Sports & Nutrition. Series 15, No. 3, Special Issue 2014. Retrieved from www.fitness.gov/resource-center/elevate-health/

Gould, D., Flett, M.R., & Lauer, L. (2012). The relationship between psychosocial developmental and the sports climate experienced by underserved youth. *Psychology of Sport and Exercise, 13*(1), 80-87.

Haan, N. (1991). Moral development and action from a social constructivist perspective. In W.M. Kurtines & J.L. Gerwitz (Eds.), *Handbook of moral behavior and development: Vol. 1. Theory* (pp. 251-273). Hillsdale, NJ: Erlbaum.

Hansen, D.M., & Larson, R. (2007). Amplifiers of developmental and negative experiences in organized activities: Dosage, motivation, lead roles, and adult-youth ratios. *Journal of Applied Developmental Psychology, 28*, 360-374.

Hellison, D. (1983). Teaching self-responsibility (and more). *Journal of Physical Education, Recreation and Dance, 54*, 23, 28.

Hellison, D. (2011). *Teaching personal and social responsibility through physical activity* (3rd ed.). Champaign, IL: Human Kinetics.

Hellison, D., & Walsh, D. (2002). Responsibility-based youth programs evaluation: Investigating the investigations. *Quest, 54*, 292-307.

Hellison, D., & Wright, P. (2003). Retention in an urban extended day program: A process-based assessment. *Journal of Teaching in Physical Education, 22*, 369-381.

Hymel, S., & Swearer, S.M. (2015). Four decades of research on school bullying: An introduction.

American Psychologist, 70(4), 293-299. doi.org/10.1037/a0038928

Jacobs, J.J., & Wright, P.M. (2016). An alternative application of imagery in youth sport: Promoting the transfer of life skills to other contexts. *Journal of Sport Psychology in Action, 7*(1), 1-10.

Kavussanu, M. (2014). Moral behavior. In R.C. Eklund & G. Tenenbaum (Eds.), *Encyclopedia of sport and exercise psychology* (pp. 454-456). Thousand Oaks, CA: Sage.

Kavussanu, M., & Boardley, I.D. (2009). The Prosocial and Antisocial Behavior in Sport Scale. *Journal of Sport and Exercise Psychology, 31,* 97-117.

Kavussanu, M., Boardley, I.D., Sagar, S.S., & Ring, C. (2013). Bracketed morality revisited: How do athletes behave in two contexts? *Journal of Sport and Exercise Psychology, 35,* 449-463.

Kavussanu, M., & Ring, C. (2016). Moral thought and action in sport and student life: A study of bracketed morality. *Ethics and Behavior, 26*(4), 267-276. doi:10.1080/10508422.2015.1012764

Kavussanu, M., Stamp, R., Slade, G., & Ring, C. (2009). Observed prosocial and antisocial behaviors in male and female soccer players. *Journal of Applied Sport Psychology, 21,* S62-S76. doi:10.1080/10413200802624292

Kavussanu, M., Stanger, N., & Boardley, I.D. (2013). The Prosocial and Antisocial Behavior in Sport Scale: Further evidence for construct validity and reliability. *Journal of Sports Sciences, 31,* 1208-1221. doi:10.1080/0 2640414.2013.775473

Kavussanu, M., & Tenenbaum, G. (2014). Aggression. In R.C. Eklund & G. Tenenbaum (Eds.), *Encyclopedia of sport and exercise psychology* (pp. 24-27). Thousand Oaks, CA: Sage.

Kaye, M.P., & Hoar, S. (2015). Antisocial Sport Behaviors Survey: Instrument development and initial validation. *Journal of Sport and Exercise Psychology, 37,* 164-179. doi.org/10.1123/jsep.2014-0057

Kestila, L., Mäki-Opas, T., Kunst, A.E., Borodulin, K., Rahkonen, O., & Prättälä, R. (2015). Childhood adversities and socioeconomic position as predictors of leisure-time physical inactivity in early adulthood. *Journal of Physical Activity and Health, 12,* 193-199. http://dx.doi.org/10.1123/jpah.2013-0245

Kirker, B., Tenenbaum, G., & Mattson, J. (2000). An investigation of the dynamics of aggression: Direct observation in ice hockey and basketball. *Research Quarterly for Exercise and Sport, 71,* 373-386.

Larson, R. (2000). Toward a psychology of positive youth development. *American Psychologist, 55,* 170-183.

Larson, R.W., Hansen, D.M., & Moneta, G. (2006). Differing profiles of developmental experiences across types of organized youth activities. *Developmental Psychology, 42*(5), 849-863.

Lauer, L., & Paiement, C. (2009). The Playing Tough and Clean Hockey Program. *Sport Psychologist, 23*(4), 543-561.

Lerner, R.M., Almerigi, J.B., Theokas, C., & Lerner, J.V. (2005). Positive youth development: A view of the issues. *Journal of Early Adolescence, 25*(1), 10-16.

Lidor, R., & Blumenstein, G. (2011). Working with adolescent soccer and basketball players from conflicting cultures—a three-dimensional consultation approach. *Journal of Social Studies Issues, 35,* 229-245. doi:10.1177/0193723511416987

Long, T., Pantaléon, N., Bruant, G., & d'Arripe-Longueville, F. (2006). A qualitative study of moral reasoning of young elite athletes. *Sport Psychologist, 20,* 330-347.

Lorenz, K. (1966). *On aggression.* New York: Harcourt, Brace, & World.

Maro, C., Roberts, G.C., & Sorensen, M. (2009). Using sport to promote HIV/AIDS education for at-risk youths: An intervention using peer coaches in football. *Scandinavian Journal of Medicine and Science in Sports, 19,* 129-141.

Martinek, T., & Lee, O. (2012). From community gyms to classrooms: A framework for values transfer in schools. *Journal of Physical Education, Recreation and Dance, 83,* 33-51.

Martinek, T., Schilling, T.A., & Johnson, D. (2001). Transferring personal and social responsibility of underserved youth to the classroom. *Urban Review, 33*(1), 29-45.

Morra, N., & Smith, M.D. (1996). Interpersonal sources of violence in hockey: The influence of the media, parents, coaches, and game officials. In F.L. Smoll & R.E. Smith (Eds.), *Children and youth in sport: A biopsychosocial perspective* (pp. 142-155). Madison, WI: Brown & Benchmark.

Petitpas, A.J., Cornelius, A.E., Van Raalte, J.L., & Jones, T. (2005). A framework for planning youth sport programs that foster psychosocial development. *Sport Psychologist, 19,* 63-80.

Reifsteck, E.J., Gill, D.L., & Brooks, D.L. (2013). The relationship between athletic identity and physical activity among former college athletes. *Athletic Insight, 5*(3), 271-284.

Reifsteck, E.J., Gill, D.L., & Labban, J.D. (2016). "Athletes" and "Exercisers": Understanding identity, motivation, and physical activity participation in former college athletes. *Sport, Exercise, and Performance Psychology, 5,* 25-38. doi.org/10.1037/spy0000046

Ruiz, M.C., & Hanin, Y.L. (2011). Perceived impact of anger on performance of skilled karate athletes. *Psychology of Sport and Exercise, 12,* 242-249.

Ryan, E.D. (1970). The cathartic effect of vigorous motor activity on aggressive behavior. *Research Quarterly, 41,* 542-551.

Ryan, K.R., Williams, J.M., & Wimer, B. (1990). Athletic aggression: Perceived legitimacy and behavioral intentions in girls' high school basketball. *Journal of Sport and Exercise Psychology, 12,* 48-55.

Schilling, T., Martinek, T., & Carson, S. (2007). Developmental processes among youth leaders in an after-school, responsibility-based sport program: Antecedents and barriers to commitment. *Research Quarterly for Exercise and Sport, 78,* 48-60.

Schinke, R.J., Stambulova, N.R., Lidor, R., Papaioannou, A., & Ryba, T.V. (2016). ISSP position stand: Social missions through sport and exercise psychology. *International Journal of Sport and Exercise Psychology, 14*(1), 4-22. doi:10.1080/16121 97X.2014.999698

Shields, D.L., & Bredemeier, B.L. (2007). Advances in sport morality research. In G. Tenenbaum & R.C. Eklund (Eds.), *Handbook of sport psychology* (3rd ed., pp. 662-684). Hoboken, NJ: Wiley.

Shields, D.L., & Bredemeier, B.L. (2014). Promoting morality and character development. In A.G. Papaionnou & D. Hackfort (Eds.), *Routledge companion to sport and exercise psychology: Global perspectives and fundamental concepts* (pp. 636-649). London: Routledge.

Shields, D.L., Funk, C.D., & Bredemeier, B.L. (2015). Predictors of moral disengagement in sport. *Journal of Sport and Exercise Psychology, 37,* 646-658. http://dx.doi.org/10.1123/jsep.2015-0110

Smith, M.D. (1988). Interpersonal sources of violence in hockey: The influence of parents, coaches, and teammates. In F.L. Smoll, R.A. Magill, & M.J. Ash (Eds.), *Children in sport* (3rd ed., pp. 301-313). Champaign, IL: Human Kinetics.

Stambulova, N., & Wylleman, P. (2014). Athletes' career development and transitions. In A.G. Papaionnou & D. Hackfort (Eds.), *Routledge companion to sport and exercise psychology: Global perspectives and fundamental concepts* (pp. 605-620). London: Routledge.

Stanger, N., Kavussanu, M., McIntyre, D., & Ring, C. (2016). Empathy inhibits aggression in competition: The role of provocation, emotion, and gender. *Journal of Sport and Exercise Psychology, 38,* 4-14. doi.org/10.1123/jsep.2014-0332

Stephens, D.E. (2001). Predictors of aggressive tendencies in girls' basketball: An examination of beginning and advanced participants in a summer skills camp. *Research Quarterly for Exercise and Sport, 72,* 257-266.

Stephens, D.E. (2004). Moral atmosphere and aggression in collegiate intramural sport. *International Sports Journal, 8,* 66-75.

Stephens, D.E., & Kavanagh, B. (2003). Aggression in Canadian youth ice hockey: The role of moral atmosphere. *International Journal of Sport Psychology, 7,* 109-119.

Storr, A. (1968). *Human aggression.* New York: Atheneum.

Turnnidge, J., Cote, J., & Hancock, D.J. (2014). Positive youth development from sport to life: Explicit or implicit transfer? *Quest, 66*(2), 203-217. doi:10.1080/00336297.2013.867275

Walsh, D. (2008). Helping youth in underserved communities envision possible futures: An extension of the Teaching Personal and Social Responsibility model. *Research Quarterly for Exercise and Sport, 79,* 209-221.

Walsh, D.S., Ozaeta, J., & Wright, P.M. (2010). Transference of responsibility model goals to the school environment: Exploring the impact of a coaching club program. *Physical Education and Sport Pedagogy, 15,* 15-28.

Weiss, M.R. (2011). Teach the children well: A holistic approach to developing psychosocial and behavioral competencies through physical education. *Quest, 63*(1), 55-65.

Weiss, M.R., Stuntz, C.P., Bhalla, J.A., Bolter, N.D., & Price, M.S. (2013). "More than a game": Impact of The First Tee life skills programme on positive youth development: Project introduction and year 1 findings. *Qualitative Research in Sport, Exercise, and Health, 5,* 214-244.

Weiss, M.R., & Wiese-Bjornstal, D.M. (2009). Promoting positive youth development through physical activity. *President's Council on Physical Fitness and Sports Research Digest, 10*(3), 1-8.

Whitley, M.A., Forneris, T., & Barker, B. (2014). The reality of evaluating community-based sport and physical activity programs to enhance the development of underserved youth: Challenges and potential strategies. *Quest, 66,* 218-232.

Whitley, M.A., Forneris, T., & Barker, B. (2015). The reality of sustaining community-based sport and physical activity programs to enhance the development of underserved youth: Challenges and potential strategies, *Quest, 67*(4), 409-423. doi:10.1080/003 36297.2015.1084340

Wright, P.M., & Burton, S. (2008). Implementation and outcomes of a responsibility-based physical activity program integrated into an intact high school physical education class. *Journal of Teaching in Physical Education, 27*(2), 138-154.

Zillmann, D., Katcher, A.H., & Milavsky, B. (1972). Excitation transfer from physical exercise to subsequent aggressive behavior. *Journal of Experimental Social Psychology, 8,* 247-259.

Chapter 16

Bakeman, R., & Helmreich, R. (1975). Cohesiveness and performance: Covariation and causality in an undersea environment. *Journal of Experimental Social Psychology, 11,* 478-489.

Barrow, J.C. (1977). The variables of leadership: A review and conceptual framework. *Academy of Management Review, 74*, 231-251.

Bass, B.M. (1985). *Leadership and performance beyond expectations.* New York: Free Press.

Bass, B.M., & Riggio, R.E. (2006). *Transformational leadership* (2nd ed.). Mahwah, NJ: Erlbaum.

Beauchamp, M.R., Barling, J., Li, Z., Morton, K.L., Keith, S.E., & Zumbo, B.D. (2010). Development and psychometric properties of the transformational teaching questionnaire. *Journal of Health Psychology, 15*, 1123-1134.

Beauchamp, M.R., Barling, J., & Morton, K.L. (2011). Transformational teaching and adolescent self-determined motivation, self-efficacy, and intentions to engage in leisure time physical activity: A randomised controlled pilot trial. *Applied Psychology: Health and Well-Being, 3*(2), 127-150. doi:10.1111/j.1758-0854.2011.01048.x

Beauchamp, M.R., Bray, S.R., Eys, M.A., & Carron, A.V. (2002). Role ambiguity, role efficacy, and role performance: Multidimensional and mediational relationships within interdependent sport teams. *Group Dynamics: Theory, Research, and Practice, 6*, 229-242.

Beauchamp, M.R., Bray, S.R., Eys, M.A., & Carron, A.V. (2003). The effect of role ambiguity on competitive state anxiety. *Journal of Sport and Exercise Psychology, 25*, 77-92.

Beauchamp, M.R., & Morton, K.L. (2011). Transformational teaching and physical activity engagement among adolescents. *Exercise and Sport Sciences Reviews, 39*(3), 133-139.

Beauchamp, M.R., Welch, A.S., & Hulley, A.J. (2007). Transformational and transactional leadership and exercise-related self-efficacy: An exploratory study. *Journal of Health Psychology, 12*(1), 83-88. doi:10.1177/1359105307071742

Bosselut, G., McLaren, C.D., Eys, M.A., & Heuzé, J. (2012). Reciprocity of the relationship between role ambiguity and group cohesion in youth interdependent sport. *Psychology of Sport and Exercise, 13*(3), 341-348. doi:10.1016/j.psychsport.2011.09.002

Brawley, L.R., Carron, A.V., & Widmeyer, W.N. (1987). Assessing cohesion of teams: Validity of the Group Environment Questionnaire. *Journal of Sport Psychology, 9*, 275-294.

Brawley, L.R., & Paskevich, D.M. (1997). Conducting team building research in the context of sport and exercise. *Journal of Applied Sport Psychology, 9*, 11-40.

Bray, S.R., Millen, J.A., Eidsness, J., & Leuzinger, C. (2005). The effects of leadership style and exercise program choreography on enjoyment and intentions to exercise. *Psychology of Sport and Exercise, 6*, 415-425.

Bruner, M.W., Eys, M., Evans, M.B., & Wilson, K. (2015). Interdependence and social identity in youth sport teams. *Journal of Applied Sport Psychology, 27*(3), 351-358. doi:10.1080/10413200.2015.1010661

Bruner, M.W., Eys, M., Wilson, K.S., & Cote, J. (2014). Group cohesion and positive youth development in team sport athletes, *Sport, Exercise, and Performance Psychology, 3*(4), 219-227.

Burke, S.M., Carron, A.V., & Shapcott, K.M. (2008). Cohesion in exercise groups: An overview, *International Review of Sport and Exercise Psychology, 1*(2), 107-123. doi:10.1080/17509840802227065

Callow, N., Smith, M.J., Hardy, L., Arthur, C.A., & Hardy, J. (2009). Measurement of transformational leadership and its relationship with team cohesion and performance level. *Journal of Applied Sport Psychology, 21*(4), 395-412. doi:10.1080/10413200903204754

Carron, A.V. (1982). Cohesiveness in sport groups: Interpretations and considerations. *Journal of Sport Psychology, 4*, 123-138.

Carron, A.V., & Ball, J.R. (1977). Cause-effect characteristics of cohesiveness and participation motivation in intercollegiate hockey. *International Review of Sport Sociology, 12*, 49-60.

Carron, A.V., Brawley, L.R., & Widmeyer, W.N. (1998). The measurement of cohesiveness in sport groups. In J.L. Duda (Ed.), *Advancements in sport and exercise psychology measurement* (pp. 213-226). Morgantown, WV: Fitness Information Technology.

Carron, A.V., Brawley, L.R., & Widmeyer, W.N. (2002). *The Group Environment Questionnaire: Test manual.* Morgantown, WV: Fitness Information Technology.

Carron, A.V., Colman, M.M., Wheeler, J., & Stevens, D. (2002). Cohesion and performance in sport: A meta-analysis. *Journal of Sport and Exercise Psychology, 24*, 168-188.

Carron, A.V., & Eys, M.A. (2012). *Group dynamics in sport* (4th ed.). Morgantown, WV: Fitness Information Technology.

Carron, A.V., Hausenblas, H.A., & Mack, D. (1996). Social influence: A meta-analysis. *Journal of Sport and Exercise Psychology, 18*, 1-16.

Carron, A.V., & Spink, K.S. (1993). Team building in an exercise setting. *Sport Psychologist, 7*, 8-18.

Carron, A.V., Spink, K.S., & Prapavessis, H. (1997). Team building and cohesiveness in the sport and exercise setting: Use of indirect interventions. *Journal of Applied Sport Psychology, 9*, 61-72.

Carron, A.V., Widmeyer, W.N., & Brawley, L.R. (1985). The development of an instrument to assess cohesion in sport teams: The Group Environment Questionnaire. *Journal of Sport Psychology, 7*, 244-266.

Carron, A.V., Widmeyer, W.N., & Brawley, L.R. (1988). Group cohesion and individual adherence to physical activity. *Journal of Sport and Exercise Psychology, 10,* 119-126.

Charbonneau, D., Barling, J., & Kelloway, E.K. (2001). Transformational leadership and sports performance: The mediating role of intrinsic motivation. *Journal of Applied Social Psychology, 31,* 1521-1534.

Chase, M.A. (2010). Should coaches believe in innate ability? The importance of leadership mindset. *Quest, 62,* 296-307. doi.org/10.1080/00336297.2010.10483650

Chelladurai, P. (1984). Leadership in sports. In J.M. Silva & R.S. Weinberg (Eds.), *Psychological foundations of sport* (pp. 329-339). Champaign, IL: Human Kinetics.

Chelladurai, P. (1990). Leadership in sports: A review. *International Journal of Sport Psychology, 21*(4), 328-354.

Chelladurai, P. (2007). Leadership in sports. In G. Tenenbaum & R.C. Eklund (Eds.), *Handbook of sport psychology* (pp. 113-135). Hoboken, NJ: Wiley.

Chelladurai, P. (2014). Leadership in sport: Multidimensional model. In R.C. Eklund & G. Tenenbaum (Eds.), *Encyclopedia of sport and exercise psychology* (pp. 405-408). Thousand Oaks, CA: Sage.

Chelladurai, P., & Saleh, S.D. (1980). Dimensions of leader behavior in sports: Development of a leadership scale. *Journal of Sport Psychology, 2,* 34-45.

Chemers, M.M. (1997). *An integrative theory of leadership.* Mahwah, NJ: Erlbaum.

Chemers, M.M. (2001). Leadership effectiveness: An integrative review. In M.A. Hogg (Ed). *Blackwell handbook of social psychology: Group processes*; (pp. 376-399). Blackwell Publishers Ltd.: Oxford, UK.

Cope, C.J., Eys, M.A., Beauchamp, M.R., Schinke, R.J., & Bosselut, G. (2011). Informal roles on sport teams. *International Journal of Sport and Exercise Psychology, 9*(1), 19-30. doi:10.1080/1612197X.2011.563124

Crace, R.K., & Hardy, C.J. (1997). Individual values and the team building process. *Journal of Applied Sport Psychology, 9,* 41-60.

Dunlop, W.L., Falk, C.F., & Beauchamp, M.R. (2013). How dynamic are exercise group dynamics? Examining changes in cohesion within class-based exercise programs. *Health Psychology, 32*(12), 1240-1243.

Dunn, J.G.H., & Holt, N.L. (2004). A qualitative investigation of a personal-disclosure mutual-sharing team building activity. *Sport Psychologist, 18,* 363-380.

Dweck, C.S. (2006). *Mindset: The new psychology of success.* New York: Random House.

Estabrooks, P.A., & Carron, A.V. (2000). The Physical Activity Group Environment Questionnaire: An instrument for the assessment of cohesion in exercise classes. *Group Dynamics: Theory, Research, and Practice, 4,* 230-243.

Evans, M.B., & Eys, M.A. (2015). Collective goals and shared tasks: Interdependence structure and perceptions of individual sport team environments. *Scandinavian Journal of Medicine and Science in Sports, 25,* e139-e148. http://dx.doi.org/10.1111/sms.12235

Evans, M.B., Eys, M.A., & Bruner, M.W. (2012). Seeing the "we" in "me" sports: The need to consider individual sport team environments. *Canadian Psychology, 53,* 301-308. http://dx.doi.org/10.1037/a0030202

Eys, M.A., Burke, S.M., Dennis, P., & Evans, B. (2015). The sport team as an effective group. In J.M. Williams & V. Krane (Eds.), *Applied sport psychology* (7th ed., pp. 124-139). New York: McGraw-Hill.

Eys, M.A., Carron, A.V., Bray, S.R., & Beauchamp, M.R. (2003). Role ambiguity and athlete satisfaction. *Journal of Sports Sciences, 21,* 391-401.

Eys, M.A., Jewitt, E., Evans, M.B., Wolf, S., Bruner, M.W., & Loughead, T.M. (2013). Coach initiated motivational climate and cohesion in youth sport. *Research Quarterly for Exercise and Sport, 84,* 373-383. doi:10.1080/02701367.2013.814909

Eys, M.A., Loughead, T.M., Bray, S.R., & Carron, A.V. (2009). Development of a cohesion questionnaire for youth: The Youth Sport Environment Questionnaire. *Journal of Sport and Exercise Psychology, 31,* 390-408.

Festinger, L., Schachter, S., & Back, K. (1950). *Social pressures in informal groups.* New York: Harper & Row.

Fiedler, F.E. (1967). *A theory of leadership effectiveness.* New York: McGraw-Hill.

Fransen, K., Haslam, S.A., Steffens, N.K., Vanbeselaere, N., DeCuyper, B., & Boen, F. (2015). Believing in "us": Exploring leaders' capacity to enhance team confidence and performance by building a sense of shared social identity. *Journal of Experimental Psychology: Applied, 21,* 89-100. doi:10.1037/xap0000033

Fransen, K., Vanbeselaere, N., De Cuyper, B., Vande Broek, G., & Boen, F. (2014). The myth of the team captain as principal leader: Extending the athlete leadership classification within sport teams. *Journal of Sports Sciences, 32*(14), 1389-1397. doi:10.1080/02640414.2014.891291

Fransen, K., Van Puyenbroeck, S., Loughead, T.M., et al. (2015). Who takes the lead? Social network analysis as pioneering tool to investigate shared leadership within sports teams. *Social Networks, 43,* 28-38. doi:10.1016/j.socnet.2015.04.003

Gammage, K.L., Carron, A.V., & Estabrooks, P.A. (2001). Team cohesion and individual productivity: The influence of the norm for productivity and the identifiability of individual effort. *Small Group Research, 32,* 3-18. doi:10.1177/104649640103200101

Glenn, S.D., & Horn, T.S. (1993). Psychological and personal predictors of leadership behavior in female soccer athletes. *Journal of Applied Sport Psychology, 5,* 17-34.

Hackman, J.R., & Katz, N. (2010). Group behavior and performance. In S.T. Fiske, D.T. Gilbert, & G. Lindzey (Eds.), *Handbook of social psychology* (5th ed., pp. 1208-1251). Hoboken, NJ: Wiley.

Hardy, C.J., & Crace, R.K. (1997). Foundations of team building: Introduction to the team building primer. *Journal of Applied Sport Psychology, 9,* 1-10.

Hogg, M.A. (2010). Influence and leadership. In S.T. Fiske, D.T. Gilbert, & G. Lindzey (Eds.), *Handbook of social psychology* (5th ed., pp. 1166-1207). Hoboken, NJ: Wiley.

Holt, N.L., & Dunn, J.G.H. (2006). Guidelines for delivering personal-disclosure mutual sharing team building interventions. *Sport Psychologist, 20,* 348-367.

Horn, T.S. (2008). Coaching effectiveness in the sport domain. In T.S. Horn (Ed.), *Advances in sport psychology* (3rd ed., pp. 239-267). Champaign, IL: Human Kinetics.

Horn, T., Byrd, M., Martin, E., & Young, C. (2012). Perceived motivational climate and team cohesion in adolescent athletes. *Sport Science Review, 21,* 25-48.

Ingham, A.G., Levinger, G., Graves, J., & Peckham, V. (1974). The Ringelmann effect: Studies of group size and group performance. *Journal of Experimental Social Psychology, 10,* 371-384.

Jeffery-Tosoni, S.M., Eys, M.A., Schinke, R.J., & Lewko, J. (2011). Youth sport status and perceptions of satisfaction and cohesion. *Journal of Sport Behavior, 34,* 150-159.

Karau, S.J., & Williams, K.D. (1993). Social loafing: A meta-analytic review and theoretical integration. *Journal of Personality and Social Psychology, 65,* 681-706.

Karau, S.J., & Williams, K.D. (1995). Social loafing: Research findings, implications, and future directions. *Psychological Science, 4*(5), 134-139.

Kravitz, D.A., & Martin, B. (1986). Ringelmann rediscovered: The original article. *Journal of Personality and Social Psychology, 50,* 936-941.

Landers, D.M., Wilkinson, M.O., Hatfield, B.D., & Barber, H. (1982). Causality and the cohesion-performance relationship. *Journal of Sport Psychology, 4,* 170-183.

Latane, B., Williams, K.D., & Harkins, S.G. (1979). Many hands make light the work: The causes and consequences of social loafing. *Journal of Personality and Social Psychology, 37,* 823-832.

Loughhead, T.M., Hardy, J., & Eys, M.A. (2006). The nature of athlete leadership. *Journal of sport Behavior, 29,* 142-158.

Loughhead, T.M., Mawn, L., Hardy, J., & Munroe-Chandler, K.J. (2014). Athlete leadership. In A.G.

Papaionnou & D. Hackfort (Eds.), *Routledge companion to sport and exercise psychology: Global perspectives and fundamental concepts* (pp. 588-601). London: Routledge.

Martens, R., & Peterson, J.A. (1971). Group cohesiveness as a determinant of success and member satisfaction in team performance. *International Review of Sport Sociology, 6,* 49-61.

Martin, L.J., Carron, A.V., & Burke, S.M. (2009). Team building interventions in sport: A meta-analysis. *Sport and Exercise Psychology Review, 5*(2), 3-18.

Martin, L.J., Carron, A.V., Eys, M.A., & Loughhead, T.M. (2012). Development of a cohesion inventory for children's sport teams. *Group Dynamics: Theory, Research, and Practice, 16*(1), 68-79.

Martínez, R.N., & Tindale, R.S. (2015). Impact of organizational citizenship behavior on performance in women's sport teams. *Journal of Applied Sport Psychology, 27*(2), 200-215. doi:10.1080/10413200.2014.978045

McGrath, J.E. (1984). *Groups: Interaction and performance.* Englewood Cliffs, NJ: Prentice Hall.

McLaren, C.D., Eys, M.A., & Murray, R.A. (2015). A coach-initiated motivational climate intervention and athletes' perceptions of group cohesion in youth sport. *Sport, Exercise, and Performance Psychology, 4*(2), 113-126.

Moran, M.M., & Weiss, M.R. (2006). Peer leadership in sport: Links with friendship, peer acceptance, psychological characteristics, and athletic ability. *Journal of Applied Sport Psychology, 18*(2), 97-113. doi:10.1080/10413200600653501

Morton, K.L., Keith, S.E., & Beauchamp, M.R. (2010). Transformational teaching and physical activity: A new paradigm for adolescent health promotion? *Journal of Health Psychology, 15,* 248-257.

Morton, K.L., Sylvester, B.D., Wilson, A.J., Lonsdale, C., & Beauchamp, M.R. (2014). Transformational leadership. In A.G. Papaionnou & D. Hackfort (Eds.), *Routledge companion to sport and exercise psychology: Global perspectives and fundamental concepts* (pp. 571-587). London: Routledge.

Mullen, B., & Copper, C. (1994). The relation between group cohesiveness and performance: An integration. *Psychological Bulletin, 115,* 210-227.

Pain, M.A., & Harwood, C.G. (2009). Team building through mutual sharing and open discussion of team functioning. *Sport Psychologist, 23,* 523-542.

Peterson, J.A., & Martens, R. (1972). Success and residential affiliation as determinants of team cohesiveness. *Research Quarterly, 43,* 62-76.

Price, M.S., & Weiss, M.R. (2011). Peer leadership in sport: Relationships among personal characteristics, leader behaviors, and team outcomes. *Journal of Applied Sport Psychology, 23*(1), 49-64. doi:10.1080/10413200.2010.520300

Price, M.S., & Weiss, M.R. (2013). Relationships among coach leadership, peer leadership, and adolescent athletes' psychosocial and team outcomes: A test of transformational leadership theory. *Journal of Applied Sport Psychology, 25*(2), 265-279. doi:10.1080/10413200.2012.725703

Rowold, J. (2006). Transformational and transactional leadership in martial arts. *Journal of Applied Sport Psychology, 18*, 312-325.

Ruder, M.D., & Gill, D.L. (1982). Immediate effects of win-loss on perceptions of cohesion in intramural volleyball teams. *Journal of Sport Psychology, 4*, 227-234.

Smith, R.E. & Smoll, F.L. (2012). *Sport psychology for youth coaches: Developing champions in sports and life.* New York: Rowman & Littlefield Publishers.

Smoll, F.L., & Smith, R.E. (1989). Leadership behavior in sport: A theoretical model and research paradigm. *Journal of Applied Social Psychology, 19*, 1522-1551.

Spink, K.S., & Carron, A.V. (1992). Group cohesion and adherence in exercise classes. *Journal of Sport and Exercise Psychology, 14*, 78-86.

Spink, K.S., & Carron, A.V. (1993). The effects of team building on the adherence patterns of female exercise participants. *Journal of Sport and Exercise Psychology, 15*, 39-49.

Spink, K.S., & Carron, A.V. (1994). Group cohesion effects in exercise classes. *Small Group Research, 25*, 26-42.

Spink, K.S., Wilson, K.S., & Priebe, C.S. (2010). Groupness and adherence in structured exercise settings. *Group Dynamics: Theory, Research, and Practice, 14*, 163-173.

Steiner, I.D. (1972). *Group process and productivity.* New York: Academic Press.

Sterrett, J.D., & Janssen, J. (2015). Leadership in sports: The critical importance of coach and athlete leadership. In J.M. Williams & V. Krane (Eds.), *Applied sport psychology* (7th ed., pp. 101-123). New York: McGraw-Hill.

Swaab, R.I., Schaerer, M., Anicich, E.M., Ronay, R., & Galinsky, A.D. (2014). The too-much-talent effect: Team interdependence determines when more talent is too much or not enough. *Psychological Science, 25*, 1581-1591. doi:10.1177/0956797614537280

Tucker, S., Turner, N., Barling, J., & McEvoy, M. (2010). Transformational leadership and children's aggression in team settings: A short-term longitudinal study. *Leadership Quarterly, 21*, 389-399. doi:10.1016/j.leaqua.2010.03.004

Turner, E.E., Rejeski, W.J., & Brawley, L.R. (1997). Psychological benefits of physical activity are influenced by the social environment. *Journal of Sport and Exercise Psychology, 19*, 119-130.

Widmeyer, W.N., Brawley, L.R., & Carron, A.V. (1990). Group size in sport. *Journal of Sport and Exercise Psychology, 12*, 177-190.

Widmeyer, W.N., Brawley, L.R., & Carron, A.V. (2002). Group dynamics in sport. In T.S. Horn (Ed.), *Advances in sport psychology* (2nd ed., pp. 285-308). Champaign, IL: Human Kinetics.

Wiest, W.M., Porter, L.W., & Ghiselli, E.E. (1961). Relationships between individual proficiency and team performance and efficiency. *Journal of Applied Psychology, 45*, 435-440.

Williams, J.M., & Hacker, C.M. (1982). Causal relationships among cohesion, satisfaction and performance in women's intercollegiate field hockey teams. *Journal of Sport Psychology, 4*, 324-337.

Williams, K., Harkins, S., & Latane, B. (1981). Identifiability and social loafing: Two cheering experiments. *Journal of Personality and Social Psychology, 40*, 303-311.

Williams, K.D., Nida, S.A., Baca, L.D., & Latane, B. (1989). Social loafing and swimming: Effects of identifiability on individual and relay performance for intercollegiate swimmers. *Basic and Applied Sport Psychology, 10*, 73-81.

Williams, J.M., & Widmeyer, W.N. (1991). The cohesion-performance outcome relationship in a coacting sport. *Journal of Sport and Exercise Psychology, 13*, 364-371.

Yukelson, D. (1997). Principles of effective team building intervention in sport: A direct services approach at Penn State University. *Journal of Applied Sport Psychology, 9*, 73-96.

Chapter 17

Acosta, V.R., & Carpenter, L.J. (2014). Women in intercollegiate sport: A longitudinal, national study thirty-seven year update: 1977-2014. Retrieved from www.acostacarpenter.org

Adler, N.E., Boyce, T., Chesney, M.A., et al. (1994). Socioeconomic status and health: The challenge of the gradient. *American Psychologist, 49*, 15-24.

American Psychological Association (APA). (2003). Guidelines on multicultural education, training, research, practice and organizational change for psychologists. *American Psychologist, 58*, 377-402. Retrieved from www.apa.org/pi

Anderson, E. (2011). Masculinities and sexualities in sport and physical culture: Three decades of evolving research. *Journal of Homosexuality, 58*(5), 565-578.

Ashmore, R.D. (1990). Sex, gender, and the individual. In L.A. Pervin (Ed.), *Handbook of personality theory and research* (pp. 486-526). New York: Guilford.

Barber, H., & Krane, V. (2005). The elephant in the locker room: Opening the dialogue about sexual orientation on women's sport teams. In M.B. Anderson (Ed.), *Sport psychology in practice* (pp. 265-285). Champaign, IL: Human Kinetics.

Basow, S.A., & Rubin, L.R. (1999). Gender influences and adolescent development. In N.G. Johnson, M.C. Roberts, & J. Worell (Eds.), *Beyond appearance: A new look at adolescent girls* (pp. 25-52). Washington, DC: American Psychological Association.

Beilock, S.L., & McConnell, A.R. (2004). Stereotype threat and sport: Can athletic performance be threatened? *Journal of Sport and Exercise Psychology, 26,* 597-609.

Bem, S.L. (1978). Beyond androgyny: Some presumptuous prescriptions for a liberated sexual identity. In J. Sherman & F. Denmark (Eds.), *Psychology of women: Future directions for research* (pp. 1-23). New York: Psychological Dimensions.

Bem, S.L. (1993). *The lenses of gender.* New Haven, CT: Yale University Press.

Bernard, J. (1981). *The female world.* New York: Free Press.

Bernstein, D.A., & Borkovec, T.D. (1973). *Progressive relaxation: A manual for the helping professions.* Champaign, IL: Research Press.

Bethune, S. (2016, May). Discrimination linked to stress, poorer health. *Monitor on Psychology, 47*(5), 12-14.

Brackenridge, C. (2001). *Spoilsports: Understanding and preventing sexual exploitation in sport.* New York: Routledge.

Brackenridge, C.H., & Fasting, K. (Eds.). (2002). *Sexual harassment and abuse in sport: international research and policy perspectives.* London: Whiting and Birch.

Brooks, D., & Althouse, R. (2000). *Racism in college athletics: The African-American athlete's experience* (2nd ed.). Morgantown, WV: Fitness Information Technology.

Brownell, K.D. (2010). The humbling experience of treating obesity: Should we persist or desist? *Behavior Research and Therapy, 48,* 717-719.

Butryn, T.M. (2002). Critically examining white racial identity and privilege in sport psychology consulting. *Sport Psychologist, 16,* 316-336.

Carpenter, L.J., & Acosta, R.V. (2006). *Title IX.* Champaign, IL: Human Kinetics.

Caruso, C.M., & Gill, D.L. (1992). Strengthening physical self-perceptions through exercise. *Journal of Sports Medicine and Physical Fitness, 32,* 416-427.

Casper, J., Bocarro, J.N., Kanters, M.A., & Floyd, M.F. (2011). "Just let me play!" Understanding constraints that limit adolescent sport participation. *Journal of Physical Activity and Health, 8,* S32-S39.

Chalabaev, A., Sarrazin, P., & Fontayne, P. (2009). Stereotype endorsement and perceived ability as mediators of the girls' gender orientation-soccer performance relationship. *Psychology of Sport and Exercise, 10,* 297-299. doi.org/10.1016/j.psychsport.2008.08.002

Chalabaev, A., Sarrazin, P., Fontayne, P., Bioche, J., & Clément-Guillotin, C. (2013). The influence of sex stereotypes and gender roles on participation and performance in sport and exercise: Review and future directions. *Psychology of Sport and Exercise, 14,* 136-144. doi.org/10.1016/j.psychsport.2012.10.005

Chambliss, H.O., Finley, C.E., & Blair, S.N. (2004). Attitudes toward obese individuals among exercise science students. *Medicine and Science in Sports and Exercise, 36,* 468-474.

Conception, R.Y., & Ebbeck, V. (2005). Examining the physical activity experience of survivors of domestic violence in relation to self-views. *Journal of Sport and Exercise Psychology, 27,* 197-211.

Contrada, R.J., Ashmore, R.D., Gary, M.L., et al. (2000). Ethnicity-related sources of stress and their effects on well-being. *Current Directions in Psychological Science, 9,* 136-139.

Cooky, C., Messner, M.A., & Hextrum, R. (2013). Women play sports, but not on TV: A longitudinal study of televised news media. *Communication and Sport, 1,* 203-230.

Cooky, C., Messner, M.A., & Musto, M. (2015). "It's dude time!": A quarter century of excluding women's sports in televised news and highlight shows. *Communication and Sport, 3*(3), 261-287. doi:10.1177/2167479515588761

Corbett, D., & Johnson, W. (2000). The African-American female in collegiate sport: Sexism and racism. In D. Brooks & R. Althouse (Eds.), *Racism in college athletics: The African-American athlete's experience* (2nd ed., pp. 199-225). Morgantown, WV: Fitness Information Technology.

Craft, L.L., Pfeiffer, K.A., & Pivarnik, J.M. (2003). Predictors of physical competence in adolescent girls. *Journal of Youth and Adolescence, 32,* 431-438.

Crespo, C.J. (2005). Physical activity in minority populations: Overcoming a public health challenge. *President's Council on Physical Fitness and Sports Research Digest, 6*(2). Retrieved from http://fitness.foundation/research-digest.

Crespo, C.J., Ainsworth, B.E., Keteyian, S.J., Heath, G.W., & Smit, E. (1999). Prevalence of physical inactivity and its relations to social class in U.S. adults: Results from the Third National Health and Nutrition Examination Survey, 1988-1994. *Medicine and Science in Sports and Exercise, 31,* 1821-1827.

Cross, T., Bazron, B., Dennis, K., & Isaacs, M. (1999). *Towards a culturally competent system of care.* Washington, DC: National Institute of Mental Health, Child and Adolescent Service System Program Technical Assistance Center, Georgetown University Child Development Center.

DePauw, K.P. (1997). The (in)visibility of disability: Cultural context and "sporting bodies." *Quest, 49,* 416-430.

Devine, P.G., & Baker, S.M. (1991). Measurement of racial stereotype subtyping. *Personality and Social Psychology Bulletin, 17*(1), 44-50.

Donaghue, N., & Allen, M. (2016). "People don't care as much about their health as they do about their looks": Personal trainers as intermediaries between aesthetic and health-based discourses of exercise participation and weight management. *International Journal of Sport and Exercise Psychology, 14*(1), 42-56. doi:10.1080/1612197X.2015.1016086

Duda, J.L. (1986). A cross-cultural analysis of achievement motivation in sport and the classroom. In L. VanderVelden & J. Humphrey (Eds.), *Psychology and sociology in sport: Current selected research* (Vol. 1, pp. 115-134). New York: AMS Press.

Duda, J.L., & Allison, M.T. (1990). Cross-cultural analysis in exercise and sport psychology: A void in the field. *Journal of Sport and Exercise Psychology, 12,* 114-131.

Eccles, J.S. (1985). Sex differences in achievement patterns. In T. Sonderegger (Ed.), *Nebraska Symposium on Motivation, 1984: Psychology and gender* (pp. 97-132). Lincoln: University of Nebraska Press.

Eccles, J.S., Barber, B., Jozefowicz, D., Malenchuk, O., & Vida, M. (1999). Self-evaluation of competence, task values and self-esteem. In N.G. Johnson, M.C. Roberts, & J. Worell (Eds.), *Beyond appearance: A new look at adolescent girls* (pp. 53-84). Washington, DC: American Psychological Association.

Eccles, J.S., & Harrold, R.D. (1991). Gender differences in sport involvement: Applying the Eccles' expectancy-value model. *Journal of Applied Sport Psychology, 3,* 7-35.

Erkut, S., Fields, J.P., Sing, R., & Marx, F. (1996). Diversity in girls' experiences: Feeling good about who you are. In B.J. Ross-Leadbeater & N. Way (Eds.), *Urban girls: Resisting stereotypes, creating identities* (pp. 53-64). New York: New York University Press.

Faith, M.S., Leone, M.A., Ayers, T.S., Heo, M., & Pietrobelli, A. (2002). Weight criticism during physical activity, coping skills, and reported physical activity in children. *Pediatrics, 110*(2), e23.

Fasting, K. (2015). Assessing the sociology of sport: On sexual harassment research and policy. *International Review for the Sociology of Sport, 50*(4-5), 437-441.

Fasting, K., Brackenridge, C., & Sundgot-Borgen, J. (2004). Prevalence of sexual harassment among Norwegian female elite athletes in relation to sport type. *International Review for the Sociology of Sport, 39*(4), 373-386.

Fasting, K., Brackenridge, C., & Walseth, K. (2007). Women athletes' personal responses to sexual harassment in sport. *Journal of Applied Sport Psychology, 19*(4), 419-433.

Feltz, D.L., Schneider, R., Hwang, S., & Skogsberg, N.J. (2013). Predictors of collegiate student-athletes' susceptibility to stereotype threat. *Journal of College Student Development, 54,* 184-201. doi:10.1353/csd.2013.0014

Fisher, L.A., Butryn, T.M., & Roper, E.A. (2003). Diversifying (and politicizing) sport psychology through cultural studies: A promising perspective. *Sport Psychologist, 17,* 391-405.

Fontana, F., Furtado, O., Mazzararardo, O., Hong, D., & Campos, W. (2016). Anti-fat bias by professors teaching physical education majors. *European Physical Education Review.* Advance online publication. doi:10.1177/1356336X16643304

Fredericks, J.A., & Eccles, J.S. (2004). Parental influences on youth involvement in sports. In M.R. Weiss (Ed.), *Developmental sport and exercise psychology: A lifespan perspective* (pp. 145-164). Morgantown, WV: Fitness Information Technology.

Fredericks, J.A., & Eccles, J.S. (2005). Family socialization, gender and sport motivation and involvement. *Journal of Sport and Exercise Psychology, 27,* 3-31.

Galinsky, A.D., Hall, E.V., & Cuddy, A.J.C. (2013). Gendered races: Implications for interracial marriage, leadership selection, and athletic participation. *Psychological Science, 24,* 498-506. doi:10.1177/0956797612457783

Ghavami, N., & Peplau, L.A. (2013). An intersectional analysis of gender and ethnic stereotypes: testing three hypotheses. *Psychology of Women Quarterly, 37,* 113-127. doi:10.1177/0361684312464203

Gill, D.L., Morrow, R.G., Collins, K.E., Lucey, A.B., & Schultz, A.M. (2006). Attitudes and sexual prejudice in sport and physical activity. *Journal of Sport Management, 20,* 554-564.

Gill, D.L., Morrow, R.G., Collins, K.E., Lucey, A.B., & Schultz, A.M. (2010). Perceived climate in physical activity settings. *Journal of Homosexuality, 57,* 895-913.

GLSEN (Gay, Lesbian, Straight Education Network). (2013). The experiences of LGBT students in school athletics. Research brief. New York. Retrieved from www.glsen.org/binary-data/GLSEN_ATTACHMENTS/file/000/002/2140-1.pdf

Greenleaf, C., & Weiller, K. (2005). Perceptions of youth obesity among physical educators. *Social Psychology of Education, 8,* 407-423.

Griffin, P.S. (1998). *Strong women, deep closets: Lesbians and homophobia in sport.* Champaign, IL: Human Kinetics.

Guthrie, R.V. (2004). *Even the rat was white: A historical view of psychology* (Classic ed., 2nd ed.). Boston: Allyn & Bacon. (1st ed., 1976, New York: Harper & Row)

Hall, M.A. (1996). *Feminism and sporting bodies.* Champaign, IL: Human Kinetics.

Hall, R.L. (1998). Softly strong: African American women's use of exercise in therapy. In K.F. Hays (Ed.), *Integrating exercise, sports, movement and mind: Therapeutic unity* (pp. 81-100). Philadelphia: The Haworth Press.

Hall, R.L. (2001). Shaking the foundation: Women of color in sport. *Sport Psychologist, 15*, 386-400.

Hargie, O.D.W., Mitchell, D.H., & Somerville, I.J.A. (2015). "People have a knack of making you feel excluded if they catch on to your difference": Transgender experiences of exclusion in sport. *International Review for the Sociology of Sport,* 1-17. doi:10.1177/1012690215583283

Harris, O. (2000). African American predominance in sport. In D. Brooks & R. Althouse (Eds.), *Racism in college athletics: The African-American athlete's experience* (2nd ed., pp. 37-51). Morgantown, WV: Fitness Information Technology.

Harris, D.V., & Jennings, S.E. (1977). Self-perceptions of female distance runners. *Annals of the New York Academy of Sciences, 301*, 808-815.

Hausenblas, H.A., & Fallon, E A. (2006). Exercise and body image: A meta-analysis. *Psychology and Health, 21*, 33-47.

Heesch, K.C., Brown, D.R., & Blanton, C.J. (2000). Perceived barriers to exercise and stage of exercise adoption in older women of different racial/ethnic groups. *Women and Health, 30*, 61-76.

Heidrich, C., & Chiviacowsky, S. (2015). Stereotype threat affects learning of sport motor skills. *Psychology of Sport and Exercise, 18*, 42-46.

Henderson, K.A., & Bedini, L.A. (1995). "I have a soul that dances like Tina Turner, but my body can't": Physical activity and women with disability impairments. *Research Quarterly for Exercise and Sport, 66*, 151-161.

Herek, G.M. (2000). Psychology of sexual prejudice. *Current Directions in Psychological Science, 9*, 19-22.

Hoyt, C.L., Burnette, J.L., & Auster-Gussman, L. (2014). "Obesity is a disease": Examining the self-regulatory impact of this public-health message. *Psychological Science, 25*, 997-1002. doi:10.1177/0956797613516981

Human Rights Watch. (2001). Hatred in the hallways: Violence and discrimination against lesbian, gay, bisexual, and transgender students in U.S. schools. *American Journal of Health Education* [Online], *32*, 302-306. Retrieved from http://www.tandfonline.com/doi/abs/10.1080/19325037.2001.10603487.

Hyde, J.S. (2005). The gender similarities hypothesis. *American Psychologist, 60*, 581-592.

International Olympic Committee (IOC). (2007, February). IOC adopts consensus statement on "sexual harassment & abuse in sport." Retrieved from www.olympic.org/Documents/Reports/EN/en_report_1125.pdf.

Jamieson, K.M., Reel, J.J., & Gill, D.L. (2002). Beyond the racial binary: Stacking in women's collegiate softball. *Women's Sport and Physical Activity Journal, 11*, 89-106.

Jensen, C.D., & Steele, R.G. (2009). Body dissatisfaction, weight criticism, and self-reported physical activity in preadolescent children. *Journal of Pediatric Psychology, 34*, 822-826.

Johnson, D.L., Hallinan, C.J., & Westerfield, R.C. (1999). Picturing success: Photographs and stereotyping in men's collegiate basketball. *Journal of Sport Behavior, 22*, 45-53.

Kamphoff, C.S., Gill, D.L., Araki, K., & Hammond, C.C. (2010). A content analysis of cultural diversity in the Association for Applied Sport Psychology's conference programs. *Journal of Applied Sport Psychology, 22*, 231-245.

Kamphoff, C.S., & LaVoi, N. (2013). *Females in positions of power within U.S. high school sports.* Presentation at the American Alliance of Health, Physical Education, Recreation and Dance, Charlotte, NC.

Kane, M.J., & Parks, J.B. (1992). The social construction of gender difference and hierarchy in sport journalism—few new twists on very old themes. *Women in Sport and Physical Activity Journal, 1*, 49-83.

Kane, M.J., & Snyder, E. (1989). Sport "typing": The social "containment" of women. *Arena Review, 13*, 77-96.

Kanters, M.A., Bocarro, J.N., Edwards, M.B., Casper, J.M., & Floyd, M.F. (2013). School sport participation under two school sport policies: Comparisons by race/ethnicity, gender, and socioeconomic status. *Annals of Behavioral Medicine, 45*(Suppl. 1), S113-S121. doi:10.1007/s12160-012-9413-2

Kimm, S.Y., Glynn, N.W., Kriska, A.M., et al. (2002). Decline in physical activity in black girls and white girls during adolescence. *New England Journal of Medicine, 347*, 709-715.

Koca, C., & Asci, F.H. (2005). Gender role orientation in Turkish female athletes and non-athletes. *Women in Sport and Physical Activity Journal, 14*, 86-94.

Kosciw, J.G., Greytak, E.A., Bartkiewicz, M.J., Boesen, M.J., & Palmer, N.A. (2012). The 2013 National School Climate Survey: The experiences of lesbian, gay, bisexual and transgender youth in our nation's schools. New York: GLSEN. Retrieved from www.glsen.org/research

Koss, M.P. (1990). The women's mental health research agenda. *American Psychologist, 45*, 374-380.

Krane, V. (2001). One lesbian feminist epistemology: Integrating feminist standpoint, queer theory, and feminist cultural studies. *Sport Psychologist, 15*(4), 401-411.

Krane, V., & Barber, H. (2003). Lesbian experiences in sport: A social identity perspective. *Quest, 55*, 328-346.

Krane, V., & Mann, M. (2014). Heterosexism, homonegativism, and transprejudice. In R.C. Eklund & G.

Tenenbaum (Eds.), *Encyclopedia of sport and exercise psychology* (pp. 336-338). Thousand Oaks, CA: Sage.

Krane, V., & Symons, C. (2014). Gender and sexual orientation. In A. Papaionnou & D. Hackfort (Eds.), *Routledge companion to sport and exercise psychology* (pp. 119-135). New York: Routledge.

Krane, V., Waldron, J.J., Kauer, K.J., & Semerjian, T. (2010). Queering sport psychology. In T. Ryba, R. Schinke, & G. Tenenbaum (Eds.), *The cultural turn in sport and exercise psychology* (pp. 153-180). Morgantown, WV: Fitness Information Technology.

Krane, V., & Whaley, D.E. (2010). Quiet competence: Writing women into the history of U.S. sport and exercise psychology. *Sport Psychologist, 18*, 349-372.

Krueger, J. (1996). Personal beliefs and cultural stereotypes about racial characteristics. *Journal of Personality and Social Psychology, 71*, 536-548.

Lapchick, R. (2015). The 2015 Racial and Gender Report Card. Retrieved from www.tidesport.org./reports.html.

Lenskyj, H. (1992). Unsafe at home base: Women's experiences of sexual harassment in university sport and physical education. *Women in Sport and Physical Activity Journal, 1*, 19-33.

Lott, B. (2012). The social psychology of class and classism. *American Psychologist, 67*(8), 650-658. doi:10.1037/a0029369

Lox, C.L., Martin Ginis, K.A., & Petruzzello, S.J. (2014). *The psychology of exercise: Integrating theory and practice* (4th ed.). Scottsdale, AZ: Holcomb Hathaway.

Lucas-Carr, C.B., & Krane, V. (2011). What is the *T* in LGBT? Supporting transgender athletes through sport psychology. *Sport Psychologist, 25*(4), 532-548.

Luquis, R., Perez, M., & Young, K. (2006). Cultural competence development in health education professional preparation programs. *American Journal of Health Education, 37*(4), 233-240.

Maccoby, E., & Jacklin, C. (1974). *The psychology of sex differences*. Stanford, CA: Stanford University Press.

Mansfield, L., & Rich, E. (2013). Public health pedagogy, border crossings and physical activity at every size. *Critical Public Health, 23*(3), 356-370. doi.org/10.1080/09581596.2013.783685

Markus, H.R. (2008). Pride, prejudice, and ambivalence: Toward a unified theory of race and ethnicity. *American Psychologist, 63*(8), 651-670. http://doi.org/10.1037/0003-066X.63.8.651

Markus, H.R., Uchido, Y., Omoregie, H., Townsend, S.S.M., & Kitayama, S. (2006). Going for gold: Models of agency in Japanese and American context. *Psychological Science, 17*, 103-112.

Matthews, K.A., & Gallo, L.C. (2011). Psychological perspectives on pathways linking socioeconomic status and physical health. *Annual Review of Psychology, 62*, 501-530. http://doi.org/10.1146/annurev.psych.031809.130711

McIntosh, P. (1988). White privilege and male privilege: A personal account of coming to see correspondences through work in women's studies. Wellesley College, Center for Research on Women. Retrieved from http://www.collegeart.org/pdf/diversity/white-privilege-and-male-privilege.pdf.

Messner, M.A. (2002). *Taking the field: Women, men, and sports*. Minneapolis: University of Minnesota Press.

Messner, M.A. (2009). *It's all for the kids: Gender, families, and youth sports*. Berkeley: University of California Press.

Messner, M.A., Duncan, M.C., & Jensen, K. (1993). Separating the men from the girls: The gendered language of televised sports. In D.S. Eitzen (Ed.), *Sport in contemporary society: An anthology* (4th ed., pp. 219-233). New York: St. Martin's Press.

Metheny, E. (1965). Symbolic forms of movement: The feminine image in sports. In E. Metheny, *Connotations of movement in sport and dance* (pp. 43-56). Dubuque, IA: Brown.

Miller, K.E., Sabo, D.F., Farrell, M.P., Barnes, G.M., & Melnick, M.J. (1999). Sports, sexual behavior, contraceptive use, and pregnancy among female and male high school students: Testing cultural resource theory. *Sociology of Sport Journal, 16*, 366-387.

Mio, J.S., Barker-Hackett, L., & Tumambing, J. (2006). *Multicultural psychology: Understanding our diverse communities*. Boston: McGraw-Hill.

Morrow, R.G., & Gill, D.L. (2003). Perceptions of homophobia and heterosexism in physical education. *Research Quarterly for Exercise and Sport, 74*, 205-214.

National Amateur Athletic Federation, Women's Division. (1930). *Women and athletics. Compiled and edited by the Women's Division, National Amateur Athletic Federation*. New York: Barnes.

Norman, L. (2008). The UK coaching system is failing women coaches. *International Journal of Sports Science and Coaching, 3*(4), 447-467.

O'Brien, K.S., Hunter, J.A., & Banks, M. (2007). Implicit anti-fat bias in physical educators: Physical attributes, ideology and socialization. *International Journal of Obesity, 31*(2), 308-314.

Olkin, R., & Pledger, C. (2003). Can disability studies and psychology join hands? *American Psychologist, 58*, 296-304.

Pain, H., & Wiles, R. (2006). The experience of being disabled and obese. *Disability and Rehabilitation, 28*(19), 1211-1220.

Papaioannou, A.G., Machaira, E., & Theano, V. (2013). Fifteen years of publishing in English language journals of sport and exercise psychology: Authors' proficiency in English and editorial boards make a difference. *International Journal of Sport and Exercise Psychology, 11*(1), 1-10. doi:10.1080/1612197X.2013.753726

Parham, W.D. (2005). Raising the bar: Developing an understanding of athletes from racially, culturally, and ethnically diverse backgrounds. In M.B. Anderson (Ed.), *Sport psychology in practice* (pp. 201-215). Champaign, IL: Human Kinetics.

Parham, W.D. (2011). Research vs. me-search: Thinking more of thee and less of me when working within the context of culture. *Journal of Clinical Sport Psychology, 5,* 311-324.

Pate, R.R., Dowda, M., O'Neill, J.R., & Ward, D.S. (2007). Change in physical activity participation among adolescent girls from 8th to 12th grade. *Journal of Physical Activity and Health, 4,* 3-16.

Puhl, R., & Heuer, C.A. (2001). Obesity stigma: Important considerations for public health. *American Journal of Public Health, 100,* 1019-1028.

Puhl, R.M., & Wharton, C.M. (2007). Weight bias: A primer for the fitness industry. *ACSM's Health and Fitness Journal, 11*(3), 7-11.

Ram, N., Starek, J., & Johnson, J. (2004). Race, ethnicity, and sexual orientation: Still a void in sport and exercise psychology. *Journal of Sport and Exercise Psychology, 26,* 250-268.

Rankin, S.R. (2003). *Campus climate for gay, lesbian, bisexual, and transgender people: A national perspective.* New York: The Policy Institute of the National Gay and Lesbian Task Force. Retrieved from http://www.thetaskforce.org/static_html/downloads/reports/reports/CampusClimate.pdf.

Reis, H.T., & Carothers, B.J. (2014). Black and white or shades of gray: Are gender differences categorical or dimensional? *Current Directions in Psychological Science, 23,* 19-26. doi:10.1177/0963721413504105

Rimmer, J.H. (2005). The conspicuous absence of people with disabilities in public fitness and recreation facilities: Lack of interest or lack of access? *American Journal of Health Promotion, 19,* 327-329.

Robertson, N., & Vohora, R. (2008). Fitness vs. fatness: Implicit bias towards obesity among fitness professionals and regular exercisers. *Psychology of Sport and Exercise, 9,* 547-557.

Rodriguez, E.A., & Gill, D.L. (2011). Sexual harassment perceptions among Puerto Rican female former athletes. *International Journal of Sport and Exercise Psychology, 9,* 323-337.

Ryba, T.V., & Schinke, R.J. (2009). Methodology as a ritualized eurocentrism: Introduction to the special issue. *International Journal of Sport and Exercise Psychology, 7,* 263-274.

Ryba, T.V., Schinke, R.J., & Tenenbaum, G. (2010). *The cultural turn in sport psychology.* Morgantown, WV: Fitness Information Technology.

Ryba, T.V., Stambulova, N.B., Si, G., & Schinke, R.J. (2013). ISSP position stand: Culturally competent research and practice in sport and exercise psychology. *International Journal of Sport and Exercise*

Psychology, 11, 123-142. http://dx.doi.org/10.1080/1612197X.2013.779812

Ryba, T.V., & Wright, H.K. (2005). From mental game to cultural praxis: A cultural studies model's implications for the future of sport psychology. *Quest, 57,* 192-212.

Sabo, D., & Veliz, P. (2012). *Decade of decline: Gender equity in high school sports.* Ann Arbor, MI: SHARP Center for Women and Girls.

Sailes, G. (2000). The African American athlete: Social myths and stereotypes. In D. Brooks & R. Althouse (Eds.), *Racism in college athletics: The African-American athlete's experience* (2nd ed., pp. 53-63). Morgantown, WV: Fitness Information Technology.

Schinke, R., & Hanrahan, S. (2009). *Cultural sport psychology.* Champaign, IL: Human Kinetics.

Schinke, R., & Moore, Z.E. (2011). Culturally informed sport psychology: Introduction to the special issue. *Journal of Clinical Sport Psychology, 5,* 283-294.

Schinke, R.J., Papaioannou, A.G., & Schack, T. (2016). Sport psychology in emerging countries: An introduction. *International Journal of Sport and Exercise Psychology, 14*(2), 103-109. doi:10.1080/1612197X.2016.1155828

Semerjian, T.Z. (2010). Disability in sport and exercise psychology. In T.V. Ryba, R.J. Schinke, & G. Tenenbaum (Eds.), *The cultural turn in sport psychology* (pp. 259-285). Morgantown, WV: Fitness Information Technology.

Serra de Queiroz, F., Fogaça, J.L., Hanrahan, S.J., & Zizzi, S. (2016). Sport psychology in Brazil: Reflections on the past, present, and future of the field. *International Journal of Sport and Exercise Psychology, 14*(2), 168-185. doi:10.1080/1612197X.2016.1154090

Shang, Y-T., & Gill, D.L. (2012). Athletes' perceptions of the sport climate for athletes with non-gender-congruent expressions and non-heterosexual sexual orientations in Taiwan. *Journal for the Study of Sports and Athletes in Education, 6,* 67-82.

Shields, S.A. (2008). Gender: An intersectionality perspective. *Sex Roles, 59,* 301-311. doi:10.1007/s11199-008-9501-8

Smith, Y.R. (2000). Sociohistorical influences on African American elite sportswomen. In D. Brooks & R. Althouse (Eds.), *Racism in college athletics: The African-American athlete's experience* (2nd ed., 173-197). Morgantown, WV: Fitness Information Technology.

Smith, E., & Henderson, D. (2000). Stacking in the team sports of intercollegiate basketball. In D. Brooks & R. Althouse (Eds.), *Racism in college athletics: The African-American athlete's experience* (2nd ed., 65-83). Morgantown, WV: Fitness Information Technology.

Sorensen, M., Maro, C.N., & Roberts, G.C. (2016). Gender differences in HIV related psychological variables in a Tanzanian intervention using sport.

International Journal of Sport and Exercise Psychology, 14(2), 135-151. doi:10.1080/1612197X.2015.1121511

Spence, J.T., & Helmreich, R.L. (1978). *Masculinity and femininity: Their psychological dimensions, correlates, and antecedents.* Austin: University of Texas Press.

Staurowsky, E.J., DeSousa, M.J., Miller, K.E., et al. (2015). *Her life depends on it III: Sport, physical activity, and the health and well-being of American girls and women.* East Meadow, NY: Women's Sport Foundation.

Steele, C.M. (1997). A threat in the air: How stereotypes shape intellectual identity and performance. *American Psychologist, 52,* 613-629.

Steele, C.M., Spencer, S.J., & Aronson, J. (2002). Contending with group image: The psychology of stereotype and social identity threat. *Advances in experimental social psychology* (Vol. 34, pp. 379-440). New York: Academic Press.

Stone, J. (2002). Battling doubt by avoiding practice: The effects of stereotype threat on self-handicapping in White athletes. *Personality and Social Psychology Bulletin, 28,* 1667-1678.

Stone, J., Lynch, C.I., Sjomeling, M., & Darley, J.M. (1999). Stereotype threat effects on black and white athletic performance. *Journal of Personality and Social Psychology, 77,* 1213-1227.

Stone, J., Perry, Z.W., & Darley, J.M. (1997). White men can't jump: Evidence for the perceptual confirmation of racial stereotypes following a basketball game. *Basic and Applied Social Psychology, 19,* 291-306.

Storch, E.A., Milsom, V.A., DeBranganza, N., Lewis, A.B., Geffken, G.R., & Silverstein, J.H. (2007). Peer victimization, psychosocial adjustment, and physical activity in overweight and at-risk-for-overweight youth. *Journal of Pediatric Psychology, 32*(1), 80-89.

Sue, D.W. (2004). Whiteness and ethnocentric monoculturalism: Making the "invisible" visible. *American Psychologist, 59,* 761-769.

Sue, S. (2006). Cultural competency: From philosophy to research and practice. *Journal of Community Psychology, 34,* 237-245.

Sutin, A.R., Stephan, Y., & Terracciano, A. (2015). Weight discrimination and risk of mortality. *Psychological Science, 26,* 1803-1811. doi:10.1177/0956797 615601103

Thomas, S.L., Lewis, S., Hyde, J., Castle, D., & Komesaroff, P. (2010). "The solution needs to be complex." Obese adults' attitudes about the effectiveness of individual and population based interventions for obesity. *BMC Public Health, 10,* 420. Retrieved from www.biomedcentral.com/1471-2458/10/420

Tiggemann, M., & Williamson, S. (2000). The effect of exercise on body satisfaction and self-esteem as a function of gender and age. *Sex Roles, 43,* 119-127.

Tomiyama, A.J., Epel, E.S., McClatchey, T.M., et al. (2014). Associations of weight stigma with cortisol and oxidative stress independent of adiposity. *Health Psychology, 33*(8), 862-867.

Tshube, T., & Hanrahan, S.J. (2016). Sport psychology in Botswana: A prime breeding ground, *International Journal of Sport and Exercise Psychology, 14*(2), 126-134. doi:10.1080/1612197X.2016.1142462

Vartanian, L.R., & Novak, S.A. (2011). Internalized societal attitudes moderate the impact of weight stigma on avoidance of exercise. *Obesity, 19,* 757-762. doi:10.1038/oby.2010.234

Warner, L.R., & Shields, S.A. (2013). The intersections of sexuality, gender, and race: Identity research at the crossroads. *Sex Roles, 68,* 803-810. doi:10.1007/s11199-013-0281-4

West, C. (1993). *Race matters.* Boston: Beacon Press.

Whaley, D.E., & Krane, V. (2012). Resilient excellence: Challenges faced by trailblazing women in U.S. sport psychology. *Research Quarterly for Exercise and Sport, 83*(1), 65-76.

World Health Organization (WHO). (2014). Physical inactivity: A global public health problem. Retrieved from www.who.int/dietphysicalactivity/factsheet_inactivity/en

Yali, A.M., & Revenson, T.A. (2004). How changes in population demographics will impact health psychology: Incorporating a broader notion of cultural competence into the field. *Health Psychology, 23,* 147-155.

Zell, E., Krizan, Z., & Teeter, S.R. (2015). Evaluating gender similarities and differences using meta-synthesis. *American Psychologist, 70*(1), 10-20. doi.org/10.1037/a0038208

Index

Note: Page references followed by an italicized *f* or *t* indicate information contained in figures or tables, respectively.

A

AAHPER (American Association of Health, Physical Education and Recreation) 16-17
AASP (Association for Applied Sport Psychology) 10, 18, 19-20, 21, 263-264, 278
A-B-C model 101, 102-103
ability 127-129, 127*t*, 128*t*, 132
abstinence violation effect (AVE) 143
academic performance, physical activity and 179
achievement motivation
  about 126
  achievement goal theory 131-134, 133*f*
  Atkinson's theory of 131
  attributions and physical activity 126-130, 127*t*, 128*t*
  competence and 132-134, 133*t*
  motivational climate and 134-137
  Weiner's model of achievement attributions 127-129, 127*t*, 128*t*
ACSI (Athletic Coping Skills Inventory) 50-51
ACSM (American College of Sports Medicine) 18, 146
ACSM's Guidelines for Exercise Testing and Prescription 146
ACT (attentional control training) 65, 191
Active Living by Design 145
addiction 148, 174
adherence. *See* physical activity behavior participation
adherence, cohesion and 254
affect 5, 156
  affect grid 172
  circumplex model of 173-174, 173*f*
  Feeling Scale 172, 184
  models and measures of emotion and 172-173
  Positive and Negative Affect Schedule (PANAS) 172
  Profile of Mood States (POMS) 172-173
  Subjective Exercise Experiences Scale (SEES) 173
African American athletes 262-263, 273-274
aggression
  antecedents, in sport 228
  aversive stimulation theory 226
  consequences of 228
  defining 224-225
  frustration-aggression drive theory 226
  instinct theories of 225-226
  and moral behavior in sport 230-233
  and positive social development 233-238
  psychological skills to reduce 229-230
  social learning theories 226-227
  sport as catharsis for 227
agreeableness 41

AIMS (Athletic Identity Measurement Scale) 81
Alzheimer's disease 178
American Association of Health, Physical Education and Recreation (AAHPER) 16-17
American College of Sports Medicine (ACSM) 18, 146
American Psychological Association (APA) 5, 10, 26
AMI (Athletic Motivation Inventory) 43
amnesia, expertise-induced 61
analytic research 29
Anderson, W.G. 14
Antonelli, Ferruccio 16
anxiety
  anxiety-control techniques and performance 168
  anxiety patterns and performance 167-168
  anxiety-performance models 162-163
  and attention 62
  catastrophe model of anxiety 165-167, 166*f*
  Competitive State Anxiety Inventory-2 (CSAI-2) 162, 164-165
  focus on 157
  multidimensional anxiety and performance model 164-165
  physical activity and 176
  Sport Anxiety Scale (SAS) 48
  Sport Competition Anxiety Test (SCAT) 47-48
  state anxiety 48, 162
  State-Trait Anxiety Inventory (STAI) 162
  trait anxiety 38, 43, 48, 162
APA (American Psychological Association) 5, 10, 26
APA Division 47 10, 18, 21
application of sport and exercise physiology 32-33
approach goals 133-134
arousal 157, 162. *See also* emotion; stress; stress management
  drive theory 163
  Individualized Zone of Optimal Functioning (IZOF) 164
  inverted-U theory 163-164
  lowering levels of 186
Asian South Pacific Association of Sport Psychology (ASPASP) 10
association, dissociation, and performance 59
Association for Applied Sport Psychology (AASP) 10, 18, 19-20, 21, 263-264, 278
Association for Sport Psychology in Germany 17
Athletic Coping Skills Inventory (ACSI) 50-51
athletic identity 81-82
Athletic Identity Measurement Scale (AIMS) 81
Athletic Motivation Inventory (AMI) 43

About the Authors

Photo courtesy of the University of North Carolina at Greensboro.

Diane L. Gill, PhD, is a professor in the department of kinesiology at the University of North Carolina at Greensboro (UNCG). She held faculty positions at the University of Waterloo and the University of Iowa before moving to UNCG. At UNCG, she has served as associate dean of the School of Health and Human Performance, head of the department of exercise and sport science, and founding director of the Center for Women's Health and Wellness. She has more than 35 years of experience as a faculty member in sport and exercise psychology.

Dr. Gill has been engaged in research and scholarly activity in sport and exercise psychology throughout her career. She has more than 100 scholarly publications on sport and exercise psychology topics and has given many presentations at major national and international conferences. She serves on several editorial boards and is the former editor-in-chief of the *Journal of Sport and Exercise Psychology*. She is a fellow of several professional organizations, including the American Psychological Association (APA), the North American Society for the Psychology of Sport and Physical Activity (NASPSPA), and the Research Consortium of SHAPE – America as well as a former president of Division 47 (Exercise and Sport Psychology) of the APA.

In 2015, she received the Distinguished Contributions to Science and Research in Exercise and Sport Psychology Award. In 2014, Dr. Gill received the NASPSPA Distinguished Scholar award. Also, in 2010, UNCG named her the Linda Arnold Carlisle Distinguished Excellence Professor of Women's and Gender Studies. She received both her MS and PhD degrees from the University of Illinois and her undergraduate degree from the State University of New York at Cortland.

Photo courtesy of Guilford College.

Lavon Williams, PhD, is a professor of exercise and sport science at Guilford College. She held faculty positions at Western Illinois University, Northern Illinois University, and Purdue University before taking a position at Guilford College, where she is department chair and coordinator of the physical education teacher education program.

Actively involved in sport and exercise psychology research throughout her career, Dr. Williams has written more than 20 scholarly publications and has given more than 30 national and international presentations. She is the sport psychology academy chair-elect, chair, and past-chair of the National Association for Sport and Physical Education (NASPE) and secretary of the SHAPE – America Research Consortium.

Dr. Williams is a past member of the executive board and the former research and practice division head for the Association for Applied Sport Psychology (AASP). She is a member of the North American Society for the Psychology of Sport and Physical Activity (NASPSPA) and a fellow of the Research Consortium of SHAPE - America.

She is currently on the editorial board for *Research Quarterly for Exercise and Sport* (*RQES*) and *Measurement in Physical Education and Exercise Science.*

Dr. Williams served as an associate editor of the *AASP Newsletter,* a psychology section editor for *RQES,* an editorial board member for both *The Sport Psychologist* and *Women in Sport and Physical Activity Journal,* and a reviewer for the *Journal of Sport and Exercise Psychology, Journal of Applied Sport Psychology,* and *Psychology of Sport and Exercise.* She received her MS from the University of Oregon, her PhD from the University of North Carolina at Greensboro, and her bachelor's degree from Texas Christian University.

Photo courtesy of the University of North Carolina at Greensboro.

Erin J. Reifsteck, PhD, is an assistant professor in the department of kinesiology at the University of North Carolina at Greensboro (UNCG).

In 2015-2016, Dr. Reifsteck served as principal investigator for two National Collegiate Athletic Association-funded studies to develop and evaluate the *Moving On!* program, which is based on a theoretical framework that integrates sport and exercise psychology principles. She received the Association for Applied Sport Psychology (AASP) Young Researcher Award in 2015 and was named an American Kinesiology Writing Scholar in 2014.

Dr. Reifsteck's current research focuses on promoting lifetime physical activity and health through the translation of psychosocial theory into practice. Her scholarly interests also include gender issues in sport, and she currently serves on the Editorial Board for the *Women in Sport and Physical Activity Journal* (*WSPAJ*). She is a member of the North American Society for the Psychology of Sport and Physical Activity (NASP-SPA) and AASP where she also serves on the AASP research development committee.

Dr. Reifsteck received her PhD and MS in Kinesiology (Sport and Exercise Psychology concentration) with a doctoral minor in Educational Research Methodology from UNCG. She also received a graduate certificate in Women's and Gender Studies from UNCG and a health coach certificate through UNCG's Department of Public Health Education. She earned her BS in Psychology with a minor in Neuroscience from Saint Francis University (Pennsylvania) where she played field hockey and was a two-time Academic All-American and Northeast Conference Scholar Athlete of the Year.